CURRENT PROBLEMS IN RELIGION

CURRENT
PROBLEMS
IN
RELIGION

by Hermon F. Bell

PHILOSOPHICAL LIBRARY
New York

5367

Copyright, 1956, by
Philosophical Library, Inc.
15 East 40th Street, New York 16, N. Y.

Printed in the United States of America

INTRODUCTION

The various sections of this book may be taken up separately, because each section is on a separate topic. On the other hand, because the subject matters of the various sections are inter-related, reading and study of the various sections as part of one book is recommended.

Present day religion and theology are decidedly unsatisfying to the writer, mainly because they start with an erroneous premise, namely that religion, as a completed whole, has been divinely revealed. It is to be studied for better understanding, but such studies are for the purpose of gaining clearer insight and better knowledge of the divinely revealed religion, including the person of its founder and the meaning of its scriptures. The position of the writer is diametrically opposed to the foregoing. Belief in a complete and divinely revealed religion is deemed to be erroneous in itself, and also is a position under which dogmas and creeds necessarily take a front place and are road blocks to progress. The position of the writer is that freedom should be fundamental and is a necessary condition to studies and to progress. Religion, like law, government, medicine, and all the sciences and arts, progressively should become ever and ever fuller in content and meaning. It is no less, but more, a divine revelation that we have divinely given ability of research and of progress in religion with increasing experience. Needless to say no fixed, no final, creed is accepted; and tests or examinations as to agreement with official church decisions are completely out of order, both as respects members or communicants, and especially ministers or clergy.

V

The writer counts himself happy to be free, absolutely free, of such entanglements. This in the writer's opinion puts him in a unique and much preferred position.

The writer believes that open minded and free discussions in theology and in religion are absolutely necessary if organized religion is to be brought out of its present sorry state, where an educated or enlightened person can hardly be expected to really believe church teaching, and at best (or is it at worst) believes only under new interpretations or the reading into language of new meanings different from plain words. So it comes about, even as has been said, that the choice seems to be between imbecilities and Machiavellisms.

Christian Anthology, The Bible, is too restricted. There are not included therein many writings, before and since its time, that belong in any open and continuously inclusive book of religion or universal Bible.

In this volume, the writer, editor, or compiler, has intentionally made very wide use of quotations. This has been done whenever and wherever it has been deemed that such quotations express better than the writer could do in his own words. With respect to quotations it is to be understood that they do express the thoughts and beliefs of the editor. They are not masks behind which to hide. They are used on the basis of agreement therewith.

As respects the various sections of this volume, the editor wishes unqualifiedly to state that when a reader has completed a section, he should understand the editor to say wholeheartedly, This I believe, regardless of whether it is in his words, or wholly or in part in quotations from others, whether few or many, short or extended.

In the section captioned, Charles E. Garman, practically the entire section is from Letters, Lectures and Addresses of Charles Edward Garman, A Memorial Volume, prepared with the co-operation of the Class of 1884, Amherst College, by Eliza Miner

VI

Garman (his widow), and published by Houghton Mifflin Company, 1909 and 1911.

The present editor was first introduced to studies in philosophy by Professor Garman, in 1900-1901. He has ever since regarded Professor Garman with well nigh unspeakable respect and affection. The Memorial Volume contains pamphlets, letters and addresses of various dates. In the section of the present volume relating to Professor Garman and his teachings, this editor has tried to arrange material in natural progressive order. Professor Garman's words have been used throughout where feasible. Some rearrangements have been made in the direction of condensations, to try to avoid duplications, and to proceed logically, and according to course chronology. The editor first did this when asked, by one who had missed Professor Garman's course, for outline thereof for his own information.

The last section of the book is entitled, Religious Writings—An Anthology. That section, by reason of limitations of space and time, by no means contains all the writings that could well be included. The reader is also referred to an anthology compiled previously, and published in Religion Through The Ages, in 1948. The two anthologies are supplementary to each other. Even combined they are very far from exhausting the field.

Brief outline follows with respect to the writer.

Hermon F. Bell, residence 1821 Glenwood Road, Brooklyn 30, N. Y.

Born at Bristol, R. I., May 11, 1880; A.B. Amherst College; year of study in mathematics and engineering at Massachusetts Institute of Technology; three years at Yale Divinity School, B.D. in 1905.

Miscellaneous business and bookkeeping work, and study of accounting, 1905-1908; in employ of two firms of certified public accountants (no longer extant), 1908-1913; studies in philosophy and sociology at Columbia University under Frederick J.

E. Woodbridge, John Dewey, Felix Adler, Franklin H. Giddings, Walter B. Pitkin, and others; C.P.A. from University of the State of New York, July 6, 1911; also later certified public accountant in Pennsylvania, Illinois and Michigan; from 1913 to date with a nationally known outstanding firm of certified public accountants, first as staff member, then as partner from 1929.

Writer of numerous technical articles in the field of accounting; for eighteen years lecturer in Retail Accounting at Columbia University. Author of: An Introduction to Theology (1924); Retail Merchandise Accounting (1936); Religion Through The Ages, An Anthology, Assembled by Hermon F. Bell, Edited and Interpreted by Dr. Charles S. Macfarland (1948).

Life member Phi Beta Kappa Associates; President Phi Beta Kappa Alumni in New York for the year June 1, 1954-1955.

Member, American Institute of Accountants, New York State Society of Certified Public Accountants, National Association of Cost Accountants, American Accounting Association, Controllers' Congress of National Retail Dry Goods Association; member of Board of Governors, The Accountants Club of America, Inc.

TABLE OF CONTENTS

VI RELIGIOUS WRITINGS, or AN ANTHOLOGY

CURRENT PROBLEMS IN RELIGION

RELIGION

Over recent years and decades there have been tremendous developments and changes in science and arts, in education, means of communication, and methods and speeds of transportation, and in business organization and operation, and in social and political questions and problems. In some respects the world seems smaller, as what have been distant lands and peoples, little known to each other heretofore, have become neighbors and their actions, beliefs, and customs are now of daily moment. On the other hand our universe has vastly expanded as realms upon realms of the invisible world are opened up in science and its adventures. The ancient view of the universe has been enlarged almost beyond belief and the end is not yet.

What about religion and the creeds and beliefs and teachings thereof? Is religion correlated with our widened and widening life? Have there been commensurate changes in religion and theology or at least in the forms of expressing beliefs? Or is it perhaps true that religion differs from the sciences in that it received directly from heaven its full and complete and unchanging content? Is it true that religion calls for no expanding change but only further study and application of the faith once delivered to saints? Does religion differ from all else in that other fields of knowledge and life are developed by human research and study, and call for constant changes, amendments, developments, and new ideas, but that religion is not so subject to change but only to better understanding of the gospel once revealed? For the most part, it appears that organized churches or religious bodies are inclined to claim that they have the truth, the whole of

3

essential truth, and perhaps even nothing but the truth. As the ends of the earth are brought nearer together the fundamental beliefs of the followers or communicants of the different world religions, and of sects and religious groups, as respects other fields of human activities, become modified and become more and more alike through mutual actions and reactions. In religion have the sharp demarcations melted away or merged with greater likenesses in procedures? Men and nations in most activities come more and more to speak in similar or the same language; but not so in religion, the Christian remains Christian, the Mohammedan holds to his Mohammedanism, and similarly with other religions. Even institutions of higher learning which are positive enough in teaching science and its applications, seem to shy away from any positive religious and theological positions, and to imply that the students should have such subjects left to their own choices, without even guidance from the institutions of learning. On the other hand the more enlightened and liberal of the communicants of the various religions will admit that religions other than their own are not entirely bad but represent partial truths and imperfect strivings, but that after all they need to be replaced and fulfilled and completed by adoption of, or conversion to, the one true religion.

So it comes to pass that emphasis is placed on tolerance, but with the thought background that, as respects other religions than one's own, of course such other religions are not full and complete and are not to be valued as one values the one true and complete religion. Yet we should be courteous to those of the partial and imperfect religions or sects.

Possibly a few of those not strongly grounded in their own religion may be willing to take the position that, even as of old each country had its own gods, so different peoples or civilizations have their own religions. However it is the less positively religious, the less zealous in their own churches, who are willing to take these positions. And to most persons, to the extent that they feel at all on this subject, it seems that there must be one true

4

religion, their own, to which all other persons must sooner or later be brought.

The more positively one is a communicant of his own religion, the more strongly he will take the position that all ultimately should be brought to his own, the one divinely revealed religion.

The foregoing paragraphs are on what seems to be the common assumption, that religion, in contra distinction to other fields, is divinely revealed fully and completely. Whereas truths in physics or in chemistry or in mathematics, for example, are discovered by human endeavors, and these have at times included erroneous beliefs and assumptions, with subsequent corrections with increasing knowledge (the end is not yet), the truths of religion and its creeds are divinely revealed.

Perhaps the problems will be much clarified and simplified, if, after all, religion too is found to have been, and to be, developing, just as chemistry and physics, by human experience, including failures and mistakes. On this basis there will be no final and correct and fully revealed religion, but progress by human studies, trials and achievements, and experience. Of this alternative assumption (which is that of the writer) more in the pages that follow.

Where religion is accepted as divinely and fully revealed, acceptance of its beliefs is important; also that the divine religion be adequately and uniformly stated; also it is fundamental, as a test of membership of communicants and their acceptance into fellowship, and especially for the clergy, that the creedal beliefs be subscribed to and held (at least without outward question). Surely there was a time when the creedal beliefs were not fully and completely held in final form, that is while the religion was developing into its final form. But this is a question or problem for the adherent, not for this writer.

How may progress in religion be made? Presumably if religion is a complete divine gift directly from God, progress is not called for as religion is already complete and perfect. The only progress called for is better understanding of divinely revealed religion, such for example as through study of the religion's inspired books, say of The Bible,—"search the Scriptures," and study of the works and words of the divinely incarnated founder, and study of beliefs as formulated in the church creed.

On such basis study for ministry or for priesthood consists primarily in study of the Scriptures, and of the life and works and words of the divinely incarnated founder, and of the traditions of the church,—writings of church fathers, sacraments, creeds, etc.

The doctrine of the church, being divinely permanent, needs no special developments but only adaptation to changing conditions.

However why not briefly consider how greatly changed are the foregoing if religion, like chemistry is developed by human experience, discoveries and studies. Why should it be thought that religion, and religion only, has to be an exception? If religion comes to man as a divinely finished product, why should not physics and astronomy and law come to man as divine revelations also.

Man's science, and man's religion also, is as truly divine, if discovered by divinely implanted faculties in man as if fully revealed in finished and complete form once and for all. For religion, and for any science or art, as disclosed by studies and experience, and lives of men and women throughout history, this is in reality a far more exalted, as well as a truer conception, than as received in completed form in a divine revelation.

Our religion is not received completed but has developed through the needs and experiences of men and of women in all generations and in all climes and countries and is or should be developing and changing now, as science and art and experiences develop; and like them is never finished but subject to improvement forever and ever, just as human jurisprudence, and medical practice, and all the arts and sciences and all phases of human life.

6

To be ascribed to a divine and completed revelation, a religion or a book or a divine founder or prophet, has already to be accepted as divinely revealed; it cannot be proven, but has simply to be accepted as divine first of all.

An imperfect but developing religion, or an art progressively keeping pace with human experience, is in this respect like other phases of our lives; and it can look forward to possibility of a glorious future.

Such a religion has at no time a finished and completed creed. Instead of insistence upon uniformity it should promote research and study and progress, and constant changes onward and upward forever, still however restrained by widening experience.

There should be no closed membership based upon an accepted final creed, and its ministry should be free. The emphasis should be upon freedom rather than upon conformity; freedom restrained by human reason only and by accumulated experience. The divinity school curriculum would not be limited so largely to exegesis of a "divine" book, or apologia for a creed; the questions are,—what is true? rather than, what does it say? And the divinity student needs the widest possible outlook upon the widest circle of studies. Nothing human should be foreign to his theology and to his constantly widening creed. As religion comprehends all and touches all and is touched by all, its studies should be the broadest possible, lest it omit properly to evaluate any human interest or activity.

It is peculiarly unhappy that creedal limitation so limits membership and especially so limits studies for a participation in church ministry. The lay heretic can always be told that he has not sufficient professional knowledge or that he is not sufficiently informed as to the questions involved.

It will be a great day for religion when freedom is recognized to be its birthright, provided its freedom is not simply the result of general indifference.

Everyone ought to be interested in the great subjects of religion. I believe that many more are in reality deeply interested in such subjects than appear to be so concerned. But there is very little free discussion of such subjects, and little free and frank presentation of pertinent facts and considerations. One reason is that it is somewhat out of style frankly to discuss the deepest subjects of religion. To many it appears that discussions on such subjects simply promote dissension and disunity, all to no useful purpose. It seems to be widely accepted that religion is not a subject that should be discussed. It is felt that needless differences and quarrels are the only results, and that perhaps it is best to let each one keep his own beliefs, as he holds to them regardless of how he derived them, whether by tradition, or inheritance, or otherwise; and let there be polite and courteous tolerance, without reasonings or discussions. On the other hand, if creeds are concerned, the answers are pretty apt to be unsatisfactory except to those already convinced. Besides the enquirer comes to feel that the position is likely to be taken that he ought to believe thus and so; that if he does not, he needs conversion or a change in heart rather than argument.

And so it comes to pass that there appears widespread indifference. I am convinced that such indifference seems more widespread than it really is. The indifference may arise to a very large extent from the feeling that it is useless to enquire, because the answers are likely to be what some one feels he should believe rather than frank and direct and open answers.

And so it comes to pass that there is little frank and open discussion of religious subjects. And the earnest enquirer remains a seeker after the kingdom of heaven with little prospect of help from those who should be his guides and teachers.

And many who profess creedal beliefs are not adequately equipped to explain their reasons, except such as heritage or tradition. All too often they are unable intelligently (although of high intelligence otherwise) to give reasons for the articles of faith they profess to hold.

Perhaps it will not be amiss, therefore, to discuss a creed; and

8

give frankly the writer's answers or reactions to the various articles, and reasons therefore; and then, since it is not unlikely that there will at first seem little positive belief left in this creed, include outlines of his own beliefs as at present.

What about the following creed?

Articles of Creed	Writer's Notations as to his Belief, at Present
I believe in God, the Father Almighty, Maker of Heaven and Earth	Yes
And in Jesus Christ our Lord	No
Who was Conceived by the Holy Ghost	No (if the meaning is differently from other men)
Born of the Virgin Mary	No
Suffered under Pontius Pilate	Yes
Was Crucified	Yes
Dead	Yes
and Buried	Yes
The third day He Rose Again	No
Ascended into Heaven	No

9

Articles	Writer's Notations as to his Belief, at Present
And Sitteth on the Right Hand of God	No
Whence He shall come to Judge the Quick and the Dead	No

I believe in:

The Holy Ghost The Holy Catholic Church The Communion of Saints	} Yes,—if allowed to define and explain
The Resurrection of the Body and Life Everlasting	No Am not informed on this subject and so cannot answer

---

Take a Universalist Statement

We avow our faith in:

The Universal Fatherhood of God	Yes
The Spiritual Authority and Leadership of His Son, Jesus Christ	} Misleading in Present Form
The trustworthiness of the Bible as containing a Revelation from God	} Do

Articles of Creed	*Writer's Notations as to his Belief, at Present*
The certainty of just retribution for sin The final harmony of all souls with God	Probably; but not most directly vital articles of a creed

The following is expressive of the writer's beliefs:

I believe in God the Father Almighty, Maker of Heaven and Earth: in Whom, Truth and Goodness dwell absolutely, King of Kings, and Lord of Lords, from Whom all law derives its life and potency, Who has established for Himself a witness in every heart, and Who is eternal and all-conquering love.*

*See the following from Frederick Denison Maurice:

> Now supposing it were possible that truth and goodness are not abstractions, are not formulas, but are realities; and as the traces of them have been seen in the acts of persons, so that they dwell absolutely in a Person; supposing it were true that this Being is the King of kings and Lord of lords, from whom all law derives its life and potency; supposing this Being has established for Himself a witness in the heart of the poorest man in this world, and has decreed that there should be desires in that heart which any thing short of his own infinite perfection shall not satisfy; and has called this poor man to be a citizen of his kingdom, yea, a member incorporate thereof, and has said that he, as much as the richest man, is concerned in the order and organization of this kingdom, and may urge on the wheels in the midst of which the spirit of the living creature is moving; would it not then be true that the cravings of the philosopher, the necessities of the statesman, the hopes of the wayfarer, have all their highest interpretation in this worship which is said to be the idlest of all ceremonies? Are not the recorded deeds and desires of the world utterly unintelligible without

it? If this ceremony were abolished—if the idea of a perfect Being united to man, inspiring him with prayer, and hearing his prayers, were lost out of the universe,—would not the imperfect hope of the philosopher die too? would not the belief in Law become impossible? would not each man sink further and further into solitude and brutality, finding none able to raise him, none who was not assisting to deepen his degradation?

> (From "The Kingdom of Christ," see pages 302-303, Signs of Spiritual Society, D. Appleton & Company, N. Y., 1843)

I believe in the Brotherhood of Man
    based on the Fatherhood of God
I believe in the supreme worth of
    every Human Personality
What does the Lord require of you but to do justice, and to
    love kindness, and to walk humbly with your God?

(See Micah 6:8)

Or:—

> Love is the divine doctrine of this Church; the quest of truth is its sacrament and service is its prayer. To dwell together in peace; to seek knowledge in freedom, to serve mankind in fellowship; to the end that all souls shall grow into harmony with the Divine,—Thus do we covenant with each other and with God.
>
> So then we avow our faith in God as Eternal and All-conquering love; in the supreme worth of every human personality; in the authority of truth, known or to be known; in the power of goodwill and sacrificial spirit to overcome all evil and progressively to establish the kingdom of God.

(Church Covenant, All Souls Universalist Church, Bklyn.)

Why add more; why add, to the fatherhood of God and the brotherhood of man, a lot of other statements which divide and split universal religion into sects. At best about such matters we know little; and perhaps are not to know, as for example with respect to a future life.

One who holds to the fatherhood of God and the brotherhood of man, may not necessarily be a Christian in a technical or limited sense. Indeed, he should I believe reject such a limiting adjective. If a man is a chemist, he is a chemist. It only limits and restricts to call him some particular kind of chemist. If a man is a religious man it only detracts and limits to prefix an adjective such as Christian, Mohammedan, or Buddhist.

And the great evil of such qualifications is that it restricts freedom and is the beginning of closed sects, clerical creeds, and oligarchies in religion, while freedom is at the very foundation of present experience and of progress onward and upward. To us all, religion should be "transformed from a treasure timidly guarded and carefully concealed to a vital power which itself should guard the values of daily life." (Garman)

Years and years ago (in 1904 and 1905) I came before a Committee of the New Haven Association of Congregational Ministers for licensure. Truly I was on a spot. It was not strange that the Committee hardly felt like passing me; all the questions they asked called for negative answers. I did not believe in the Virgin Birth, or in the Resurrection. I did not believe in the deity of Jesus, or in the unique inspiration of the Bible.

I was especially surprised that the Committee asked so little about the fundamental question, belief in God. The Committee apparently did not want to go into that subject. At that era (and perhaps even now in some places) expressions such as "all we know of God we know through Jesus" were not uncommon. They were surprised in me as to the first plank or article; and to this day I believe they were not very much inclined to question or discussion thereof.

I finally came through with the request that they study my fitness for the ministry and decide on that basis. Under it I was finally accepted for licensure.

13

I had found some where an old New England test that read as follows: "If any who are given to change do rise up to unhinge the well established churches in this land, it will be the duty and interest of the churches to examine whether the men of this trespass are more prayerful, more watchful, more zealous, more patient, more heavenly, more universally conscientious, and harder students and better scholars and more willing to be informed and advised than those great and good men who left unto the churches what they now enjoy."

Truth and freedom, as fundamental in true religion, should be the heritage of the churches, of the persons entering into fellowship, that is the members, and especially of the clergy both for themselves and for others.

The four paragraphs that follow are from Charles Edward Garman:

> To be guided by the holy spirit of truth is to come into a larger apprehension of the divine character, and of the divine plan, and to be able to fit one's own life into that plan so that God may work through the individual both to will and to do His good pleasure.

> Nothing is clearer than the fact that the personality and sovereignty of God are not a large factor in the practical life and thought of our age.

> The Church must not merely affirm the personality of God—for to many this would be a mere formula—the church must help men realize the divine personality; it must force men to see that personality and sovereignty are the supreme facts of the universe.

> As it is the physical climate of a country which determines whether the date and palm shall grow in a given place, or the Norway evergreen, as it is a particular variation of climate which decides whether plants which are cultivated as exotics shall be dwarfed and stunted, or reach their most luxurious development; so it is the psychological climate of a man or an institution or a community which

14

decides whether truth and freedom shall grow at all, or in their stead superficiality and dogmatism; or, if they grow, it is the variety of the psychological climate which determines what the development shall be.

The following is from an eminent economist, namely from Walter Bagehot in Physics and Politics:

All the great movements of thought in ancient and modern times have been nearly connected in time with government by discussion. Athens, Rome, the Italian republics of the Middle Ages, the communes and states-general of feudal Europe, have all had a special and peculiar quickening influence, which they owed to their freedom, and which states without that freedom have never communicated. And it has been at the time of great epochs of thought—at the Peloponnesian war, at the fall of the Roman Republic, at the Reformation, at the French Revolution,—that such liberty of speaking and thinking have produced their full effect.

Three quotations from John Milton follow:

Many truths now of reverend esteem and credit had their birth and beginning once from singular and private thoughts.

Well knows he who uses to consider, that our faith and knowledge thrives by exercise, as well as our limbs and complexion. Truth is compar'd in Scripture to a streaming fountain; if her waters flow not in a perpetual progression, they sick'n into a muddy pool of conformity and tradition. A man may be a heretick in the truth; and if he believe things only because his Pastor sayes so, or the Assembly so determins, without knowing other reason, though his belief be true, yet the very truth he holds, becomes his heresie.

Give me the liberty to know, to utter, and to argue freely according to conscience, above all liberties.

How absurd it is to base fitness for the ministry, or in fact church membership, upon acceptance of a creed, may be seen

15

from the result of change in belief. A man may accept an article today, but not perhaps tomorrow, or vice versa. If by fuller knowledge a man grows into wider beliefs does he by so doing become ineligible for ministry or church membership?

There is a long and impressive line of persons who intended to train for the ministry but who found the creeds or church doctrines confining, with the result that their great work has been done outside, rather than within organized religion. Listen, for example, to Milton, Carlyle, and Emerson. How much greater would have been the influence of organized religion, if such men could have found therein the freedom they needed! And how greatly blessed would the churches and their members have been by such leadership!

The two paragraphs following are from Milton:

> In that day it shall no more be said as in scorne, this or that was never held so till this present Age, when men have better learnt that the times and seasons passe along under thy feet, to goe and come at thy bidding, and as thou didst dignifie our fathers dayes with many revelations above all the foregoing ages, since thou tookest the flesh; so thou canst vouchsafe to us (though unworthy) as large a portion of thy spirit as thou pleasest; for who shall prejudice thy all-governing will? seeing the power of thy grace is not past away with the primitive times, as fond and faithless men imagine, but thy Kingdom is now at hand, and thou standing at the dore.

> But were it the meanest underservice, if God by his Secretary conscience injoyn it, it were sad for me if I should draw back, for me especially, now when all men offer their aid to help ease and lighten the different labours of the Church, to whose service by the intentions of my parents and friends I was destin'd of a child, and in mine own resolutions, till coming to some maturity of years and perceaving what tyranny had invaded the Church, that he who

16

would take Orders must subscribe slave, and take an oath withall, which unlesse he took with a conscience that would retch, he must either strait perjure, or split his faith, I thought it better to preferre a blamelesse silence before the sacred office of speaking bought, and begun with servitude and forswearing.

Several paragraphs from Carlyle follow:

Observe that of man's whole terrestrial possessions and attainments, unspeakably the noblest are his Symbols, divine or divine-seeming; under which he marches and fights, with victorious assurance, in this life-battle; what we can call his Realized Ideals. Of which realized Ideals, omitting the rest, consider only these two: his Church, or Spiritual Guidance; his Kingship, or temporal one. The Church: what a word was there; richer than Golconda and the treasures of the world! In the heart of the remotest mountains rises the little Kirk.

Such virtue was in Belief; in these words well spoken; *I believe.* Well might men prize their *Credo,* and raise stateliest Temples for it, and reverend Hierarchies, and give it the tithe of their substance; it was worth living for and dying for.

But of these decadent ages in which no Ideal either grows or blossoms? When Belief and Loyalty have passed away, and only the cant and false echo of them remains; and all Solemnity has become Pageantry; and the Creed of persons in authority has become one of two things: an Imbecility or a Machiavelism?

In the way of being *worthy,* the first condition surely is that one *be.* Let Cant cease, at all risks and at all costs: till Cant cease, nothing else can begin. Of human Criminals, in these centuries, writes the Moralist, I find but one unforgiveable: the Quack. "Hateful to God," as divine Dante sings, "and to the Enemies of God."

But here enters the fatal circumstance of Idolatry, that, in the era of the Prophets, no man's mind *is* any longer honestly filled with his Idol or Symbol. Before the Prophet can arise who, seeing through it, knows it to be mere wood, many men must have begun dimly to doubt that it was little more. Condemnable Idolatry is *insincere* Idolatry. Doubt has eaten out the heart of it: a human soul is seen clinging spasmodically to an Ark of the Covenant, which it half feels now to have become a Phantasm. This is one of the balefulest sights. Souls are no longer *filled* with their Fetish; but only pretend to be filled, and would fain make themselves feel that they are filled. "You do not believe," said Coleridge; "you only believe that you believe." It is the final scene in all kinds of Worship and Symbolism; the sure symptom that death is now nigh. It is equivalent to what we call Formulism, and Worship of Formulas, in these days of ours. No more immoral act can be done by a human creature; for it is the beginning of all immorality, or rather it is the impossibility henceforth of any morality whatsoever: the innermost moral soul is paralyzed thereby, cast into fatal magnetic sleep! Men are no longer *sincere* men.

"The hungry young," he says, "looked up to their spiritual Nurses; and, for food, were bidden eat the east-wind. What vain jargon of controversial Metaphysic, Etymology, and mechanical Manipulation falsely named Science, was current there, I indeed learned, better perhaps than the most. Among eleven hundred Christian youths, there will not be wanting some eleven eager to learn. By collision with such, a certain warmth, a certain polish was communicated; by instinct and happy accident, I took less to rioting (*renommiren*), than to thinking and reading, which latter also I was free to do. Nay from the chaos of that Library, I succeeded in fishing up more books perhaps than had been known to the very keepers thereof."

Five paragraphs from Emerson follow:

To believe your own thought, to believe that what is true for you in your private heart is true for all men,—that is genius. Speak your latent conviction, and it shall be the universal sense; for the inmost in due time becomes the outmost,—and our first thought is rendered back to us by the trumpets of the Last Judgment. Familiar as the voice of the mind is to each, the highest merit we ascribe to Moses, Plato, and Milton is, that they set at naught books and traditions, and spoke not what men but what they thought.

Whoso would be a man must be a non-conformist. He who would gather immortal palms must not be hindered by the name of goodness, but must explore if it be goodness. Nothing is at last sacred but the integrity of your own mind. Absolve you to yourself, and you shall have the suffrage of the world.

Pythagoras was misunderstood, and Socrates, and Jesus, and Luther, and Copernicus, and Galileo, and Newton, and every pure and wise spirit that ever took flesh. To be great is to be misunderstood.

Christianity is rightly dear to the best of mankind; yet was there never a young philosopher whose breeding had fallen into the Christian Church, by whom the brave text of Paul's was not specially prized:— "Then shall also the Son be subject unto Him who put all things under him, that God may be all in all." Let the claims and virtue of persons be never so great and welcome, the instinct of man presses eagerly onward to the impersonal and illimitable, and gladly arms itself against the dogmatism of bigots with this generous word out of the book itself.

God offers to every mind its choice between truth and repose. Take which you please,—you can never have both. Between these, as a pendulum, man oscillates. He in whom the love of repose predominates will accept the first creed, the first philosophy, the first political party he meets,—most likely his father's. He gets rest, commodity, and reputation; but he shuts the door of truth. He in whom the love of truth predominates will keep himself aloof from all moorings, and afloat. He will abstain from dogmatism, and recognize all the opposite negations, between which, as walls, his being is swung. He submits to the inconvenience of suspense and imperfect opinion, but he is a candidate for truth, as the other is not, and respects the highest law of his being.

What is more absurd, and may not one say immoral, than to require acceptance of an iron bound creed, either for membership in a religious society, or, especially, as a creedal test for the clergy?

In the words of Coleridge:

Whatever is against right reason, that no faith can oblige us to believe.

Never be afraid to doubt, if only you have the disposition to believe, and doubt in order that you may end in believing the truth.

He who begins by loving Christianity better than truth, will proceed by loving his own sect better than Christianity, and end in loving himself better than all.

The foregoing section has dealt with the fundamental question, —Is religion given to us once and for all as a completed divine revelation, or is it a continuous growth grounded in experience and in freedom, and thus a continuous gift of God in whom we live and move and have our being?

Consideration of the content of religion grounded in freedom has necessarily been deferred to another section.

IF A MAN DIE, SHALL HE LIVE AGAIN?

My answer to the above question is, I do not know.

Moreover I do not believe that anyone else knows. So if any one gives you a definite answer, whether yes or no, you will do well to discount and doubt his answer, to enquire why he says as he does. Does he say yes, because of church creed, the Bible, or specifically Paul? In such case I believe the position is not well taken. He assumes knowledge where he has no knowledge. On the other hand if he dogmatically says no, he is presumptuous in assuming negative knowledge without basis therefor.

My own position is that we are given no knowledge on this point because we need none. The answer does not affect our vocation, which remains, regardless of what the correct answer is to the question,—If a man die, shall he live again? Since the answer is beyond us, a position on this question, whether yes or no, has no place in a creed.

Blessed be the hour in which I first resolved to inquire into myself and my vocation! All my doubts are solved, I know what I can know, and have no apprehensions regarding that which I cannot know. I am satisfied; perfect harmony and clearness reign in my soul, and a new and more glorious spiritual existence begins for me.

My entire complete vocation I cannot comprehend; what I shall be hereafter transcends all my thoughts. A part of that vocation is concealed from me; it is visible only to One, to the Father of Spirits, to whose care it is committed. I know only that it is sure, and that it is eternal and glorious like Himself. But that part of it which is confided to myself, I

21

know, and know it thoroughly, for it is the root of all my other knowledge. I know assuredly, in every moment of my life, what I ought to do; and this is my whole vocation in so far as it depends on me. From this point, since my knowledge does not reach beyond it, I shall not depart; I shall not desire to know aught beyond this; I shall take my stand upon this central point, and firmly root myself here. To this shall all my thoughts and endeavors, my whole powers be directed; my whole existence shall be interwoven with it.

(Fichte)

I have been minded to take up this subject,—"If a Man Die, Shall He Live Again?" out of order; at least to write on it before writing the far more important and fundamental section regarding belief in God, its nature and its content.

Certain practical considerations lead to discussion now under this chapter.

Moreover the importance of whether or not the resurrection of Jesus was to be accepted and believed loomed exceeding large to me in my divinity school years.

The following paragraphs on this subject are reproduced from *Religion Through The Ages* (Philosophical Library, Inc., 1948).

What a tragedy it would have been for me if I had not at the last minute gotten into Garman's course! How dreary and meaningless life would have been! Some would ask,— in view of all the anxiety Garman's course caused me— would I not have been better off without it? No, it was worth far more than it cost me in grief and in trouble. From that day on it has been my great ground of all that is best and most worth while. In Garman's class I had an entire new thought, a changed mental and spiritual outlook, too strong to follow anything else. Garman did not teach theology and I don't know just why I became so much concerned and interested in the theological implications of Garman's method. His course was largely concerned with methods— the ability to weigh evidence. He did not teach a system, whatever implications may have been inherent in his methods.

I have no reason to believe that Garman did not hold to the essentials of Christian theology. He always implied that it was a matter of studying the historical and other evidence. It always seemed to me that on the Incarnation, Virgin Birth, and Resurrection, he believed these doctrines would be supported by study of the evidence. My one explanation is that he was probably twenty-five years behind in their testimony. But when I came to look at the evidence, it seemed very weak or negative so I discarded it and rested upon the position I had from Garman and philosophy. After I had made this decision everything seemed clearer and better. I got the positive from Garman and the negative from Yale.

The student says he went to Yale expecting "to find there the historical evidences that would tie together both the Christian faith and the beliefs grounded in philosophy." He did not. "Trends were away from the metaphysical Christ." Liberal theology "seemed always taking away something."

"At the seminary the Christian element was becoming less and less. Somehow or other a great deal depended or seemed to depend upon the Resurrection. Spiritual resurrection appeared to me like a play upon words and could apply to others as well as to Jesus. I remember distinctly how after about two years at Yale, I definitely threw overboard belief in the Resurrection. I did so just as I was entering the dormitory from the courtyard. Clearing away that doctrine helped immeasurably."

That doctrine of the Resurrection has remained thrown overboard from 1904 to the present. The doctrine seems to me unworthy of acceptance or belief.

To digress, assuming that the Resurrection is unworthy of belief, it has to be granted that it was fundamental in the Christian theology of Paul. He says so definitely, for example:

23

I Corinthians 15:12-19

Now if Christ is preached that he hath been raised from the dead, how say some among you that there is no resurrection of the dead? But if there is no resurrection of the dead, neither hath Christ been raised: and if Christ hath not been raised, then is our preaching vain, and your faith also is vain. Yea, and we are found false witnesses of God; because we witnessed of God that he raised up Christ: whom he raised not up, if so be that the dead are not raised. For if the dead are not raised, neither hath Christ been raised: and if Christ has not been raised, your faith is vain; ye are yet in your sins. Then they that are fallen asleep in Christ have perished. If we have only hoped in Christ in this life, we are of all men most pitiable.

None the less I do not believe in the historic resurrection of Jesus.

Suppose Paul wrong about the resurrection. Without Paul it seems doubtful whether Christianity would have survived at all, much less become a world religion. Is the spread of Christianity based upon misbelief? I leave this question for others to consider and to study.

Paul was a great man, despite what he says regarding the resurrection. But why should any who disbelieve in the Resurrection—at Easter and at solemn funerals—repeat extracts from the New Testament as though they did believe in Paul's words?

Paul, a saint for the Church, a great man for humanity, represents that miracle, at once divine and human, conversion. It is he to whom the future has appeared. It leaves him haggard; and nothing can be more superb than this face, forever wondering, of the man conquered by the light. Paul, born a Pharisee, had been a weaver of camel's-hair for tents, and servant of one of the judges of Jesus Christ, Gamaliel; then the scribes, perceiving his fierce spirit, had educated him. He was a man of the past, he had guarded the clothes of the stone-throwers; he aspired, having studied with the priests, to become an executioner; he was on the road for this. All at once a wave of light emanates from the darkness and throws him down from his horse; and henceforth there will be in the history of the human race that wonderful thing,—the road to Damascus. That day of the metamorphosis of Saint Paul is a great day,—keep the date; it corresponds to the 25th of January in our Gregorian calendar. The road to Damascus is essential to the march of Progress. To fall into the truth and to rise a just man,—a transfiguring fall,—that is sublime. It is the history of Saint Paul; from his day it will be the history of humanity. The flash of light is something beyond the flash of lightning. Progress will be carried forward by a series of dazzling visions. As for Saint Paul, who has been thrown down by the force of new conviction, this harsh stroke from on high reveals to him his genius. Once more upon his feet, he goes forward; he will not pause again. "Forward!" is his cry. He is a cosmopolite. He loves the outsiders, whom Paganism calls Barbarians, and Christianity calls Gentiles; he devotes himself to them. He is the apostle of the outer world. He writes to the nations epistles in behalf of God. Listen to him speaking to the Galatians: "O foolish Galatians! how can ye go back to the yokes to which ye were tied? There are no longer either Jews, or Greeks, or slaves. Do not perform your grand ceremonies ordained by your laws. I declare unto you that all that is nothing. Love one another. It is all-important that man become a new creature. Ye are called to liberty." On Mars Hill at Athens there were steps hewn in rock, which may be seen to this day. Upon these steps sat the great judges before whom Orestes had appeared. There Socrates had been judged. Paul went there; and there, at night (the Areopagus sat only at night), he said to these austere men, "I come to declare unto you the unknown God." The Epistles of Paul to the Gentiles are simple and profound, with the subtlety so marked in its influence over savages. There are in these messages gleams of hallucination; Paul speaks of the celestial beings as if he distinctly saw them. Divided, like John, between life and eternity, it seems as though he had one part of his thought on the earth, and a part in the Unknown; and it would seem, at moments, that one of his verses answers to another from beyond the dark wall of the tomb. This half-possession of death gives him a personal certainty, often wholly apart from dogma, and stamps his individual convictions with an emphasis which makes him almost heretical. His humility, resting upon the mystery, is lofty. Peter says: "The words of Paul may be taken in a bad sense." Hilairius Diaconus and the Luciferians ascribe their schism to the epistles of Paul. Paul is at heart so anti-monarchical that King James I, very much encouraged by the orthodox University of Oxford, caused the Epistle to the Romans to be burned by the hand of the common hangman. It is true it was accompanied with a commentary by David Pareus. Many of Paul's works are rejected by the Church: they are the finest; and among them his Epistle to the Laodiceans, and above all his Apocalypse, cancelled by the Council of Rome under Gelasius. It would be curious to compare it with the Apocalypse of John. Over the opening that Paul had made to heaven the Church wrote, "No thoroughfare!" he is a saint none the less; that is his official consolation. Paul has the restlessness of the thinker; text and formulary are little for him; the letter does not suffice; the letter is mere body. Like all men of progress, he speaks with reserve of the written law; he prefers grace to the law, just as we prefer it to justice. What is grace? It is the inspiration from on high; it is the breath, *fiat ubi vult;* it is liberty. Grace is the spirit of law. This discovery of the spirit of the law belongs to Saint Paul, and what he calls "grace" from a heavenly point of view, we, from an earthly point of view, call "right." Such is Paul. The enlargement of a mind by the in-breaking of light, the beauty of the seizure of a soul by the truth, shines forth in his person. Herein, we insist, lies the virtue of the journey to Damascus. Whoever, henceforward, shall desire such growth as this, must follow the pointing finger of Saint Paul. All those to whom justice shall reveal itself, every blindness desirous of the day, all the cataracts looking to be healed; all searchers after conviction, all the great adventurers after virtue, all servants of the good in quest of the true, must follow this road. The light that they find there shall change nature, for the light is always relative to darkness; it shall increase in intensity; after having been revelation, it shall be rationalism; but it will ever be the light. . . . The road to Damascus shall be forever the route of great minds. It shall also be the route of nations. For nations, these vast individualisms, have, like each of us, their crisis and their hour.

(Victor Hugo)

We now digress briefly in that question of how and why error seems sometimes to be the vehicle necessary to use, or that was used, to attain the truth. When and why and how error should be such a vehicle in progress, I do not know; but that it is sometimes so seems scarcely to be doubted. I leave the philosophical studies relative to this topic to others and simply refer the reader to what others have said.

If you notice all the beneficent institutions of humanity when they first appeared on earth were disguised by what is now most repulsive to us. Religion in its earlier forms was a cruel superstition, offering human sacrifice. Government was a despotism such as you can at present hardly realize. Civilization itself took its first steps in progress in the form of war and slavery. Chemistry was alchemy, astronomy was astrology. Even so beneficent a science as medicine was disguised as magic. (Garman)

The great need of our students from a practical point of view is an ideal; the great danger is that they will become

27

visionary. Hence I cannot let them go until I hold out before them the ideals of a spiritual life, and then make such a practical application as will enable them to understand the evolution of religion, that is, how it was possible for a divine being to tolerate slavery, polygamy, etc., provided these are wrong. I show them that an ideal is like the north star which the colored slave would follow, not with the expectation of ever reaching the star, but under the hope that by following it he might better his condition. I bring in the laws of the unfolding of the life of the individual and of the community, until the men discover that the great question of human history is not so much "where we are as whither we are drifting," and that time is required for all progress.

(Garman)

The blessed work of helping the world forward, happily does not wait to be done by perfect men. (G. Eliot)

They believed in present miracles, in instantaneous conversions, in revelations by dreams and visions; they drew lots, and sought for Divine guidance by opening the Bible at hazard; having a literal way of interpreting the Scriptures, which is not at all sanctioned by approved commentators; and it is impossible for me to represent their diction as correct, or their instruction as liberal. Still—if I have read religious history aright—faith, hope, and charity have not always been found in a direct ratio with a sensibility to the three concords; and it is possible, thank Heaven! to have very erroneous theories and very sublime feelings. (G. Eliot)

Alas! we must re-climb a thousand times the peaks already scaled, and reconquer the points of view already won, —we must *fight the fight!* The human heart, like kings, signs mere truces under a pretence of perpetual peace. The eternal life is eternally to be re-won. (Amiel)

The old order changeth, yielding place to new,
And God fulfils himself in many ways. (Tennyson)

Our little systems have their day;
   They have their day and cease to be;
   They are but broken lights of thee,
And thou, O Lord, art more than they. (Tennyson)

Only the prism's obstruction shows aright
The secret of a sunbeam, breaks its light
Into the jewelled bow from blankest white;
   So may a glory from defect arise. (Browning)

God's gift was that man should conceive of truth
And yearn to gain it, catching at mistake,
As midway help till he reach fact indeed.
The statuary ere he mould a shape
Boasts a like gift, the shape's idea, and next
The aspiration to produce the same;
So taking clay, he calls his shape thereout,
Cries ever "Now I have the thing I see":
Yet all the while goes changing what was wrought,
From falsehood like the truth, to truth itself. (Browning)

But fresh and green from the rotting roots
Of primal forests the young growth shoots;
From the death of the old the new proceeds,
And the life of truth from the rot of creeds;
On the ladder of God, which upwards leads,
The steps of progress are human needs. (Whittier)

Naturally one who disbelieves in the resurrection of Jesus objects to affirmative creedal statement, or specifically to inclusion of, *the third day rose again, ascended into heaven, and sitteth on the right hand of God, whence He shall come to judge the quick and the dead.* To use by those who sincerely accept this literally, I do not see that objection can be taken, except that we believe they are mistaken. What particularly irks me is the solemn use of such statement by those who do not unequivocally and in

29

straight-forward manner hold such belief,—those for example who do not believe in the physical resurrection but who still claim to have a belief in a spiritual resurrection and who abound in nebulous phrases that have no plain and definite meaning to me.

At Easter time and at solemn funeral rites statements and phases are used that are particularly repulsive to me especially as used in such solemn occasions. It seems to me that those (and I believe there are many) who disbelieve in the physical resurrection of Jesus, are obligated in plain honesty to justify their use of obsolete and outgrown phraseology. Above all, religion in all of its expressions should be plainly honest and straight-forward, avoiding all subtle and double meaning language.

It is indeed a pertinent question what statements and expressions may be used, and not only so but what strong and positive statements not only may be used but are inherent in universal unfeigned religion.

Moreover one can never know how soon or how unexpectedly occasion may arise for appropriately expressed beliefs, either upon the passing of others, or at one's own decease.

When in a summer season, while a student at divinity school, I took my first churches, two churches eight miles apart, for summer season ministrations, this was forcibly brought to my notice. I had never conducted a funeral. On my arrival I found that the very first duty before me was to conduct the funeral service for a farmer, head of a family, who had died. Funeral rites awaited my arrival as the new minister. I was hustled off to conduct the funeral service, immediately upon my arrival.

If I should die, it would be particularly obnoxious to me in forward look; to realize that probably the greater part of the service would consist of Biblical selections in which I actually disbelieve, especially inappropriate would be extracts from the Epistles of Paul.

Accordingly it seems to me not inappropriate to list: (1) some of the Biblical selections that should not be used, which to me at least and I believe to many others also are outmoded and based

30

upon false premises; (2) some of the selections from the Bible which are believed to be highly appropriate; (3) selections from other sources, not only highly appropriate in themselves, but in some cases expressing the present deepest religious feelings of theism.

Let me just here anticipate our studies so far as to call attention to the possible extremes of view to be found in the history of human progress. The narrowest idea conceivable is that of fetichism, where each object is an entity by itself, and, in addition, all the more common attributes are personified into independent beings. The other extreme is theism (than which a broader, grander idea of the universe is impossible); it is this: God or Spirit is the only independent reality, and any other being or event is but a dependent "phase" or "state," or "product" of His activity. He is "the all in all." "In Him all things live and move and have their being." He is the Hebrew Jehovah, the "I AM," the self-existent and eternal One, who filleth immensity and inhabiteth eternity, The Ancient of Days, in terms of whose action Time itself is measured. Nature is related to God as "thought to the mind that thinks," as "music to the air that is in vibration," as "light to the ether." Nature is the "living garment of God," that is, the continued activity in which He manifests Himself.—Between these extremes would lie (1) The successive phases of Polytheism. These eventually lead to (2) Materialism, where science begins in its atomic form. The progress of science would make necessary at length (3) Dualism, or the doctrine that there are two independent entities, mind and matter; at this stage all the conflicts between science and religion arise. But this must, sooner or later, be resolved into the last and final position of philosophy, viz., (4) Theism as above explained.

(Garman)

Some of the Biblical Selections That Should Not Be Used

Romans 6:4-5

We were buried therefore with him through baptism unto death: that like as Christ was raised from the dead through the glory of the Father, so we also might walk in newness of life. For if we have become united with him in the likeness of his death, we shall be also in the likeness of his resurrection.

Romans 6:8-9

But if we died with Christ, we believe that we shall also live with him; knowing that Christ being raised from the dead dieth no more; death no more hath dominion over him.

Romans 10:9

If thou shalt confess with thy mouth Jesus as Lord, and shalt believe in thy heart that God raised him from the dead, thou shalt be saved.

1 Corinthians 15:3-8

For I delivered unto you first of all that which also I received: that Christ died for our sins according to the scriptures; and that he was buried; and that he hath been raised on the third day according to the scriptures; and that he appeared to Cephas; then to the twelve; then he appeared to above five hundred brethren at once, of whom the greater part remain until now, but some are fallen asleep; then he appeared to James; then to all the Apostles; and last of all, as to the child untimely born, he appeared to me also.

1 Corinthians 15:12-19

(Already quoted, in another connection, near the beginning of this section; hence not repeated here)

1 Corinthians 15:20-58

But now hath Christ been raised from the dead, the first-fruits of them that are asleep. For since by man came death, by man came also the resurrection of the dead. For as in

Adam all die, so also in Christ shall all be made alive. But each in his own order: Christ the first-fruits; then they that are Christ's, at his coming. Then cometh the end, when he shall deliver up the kingdom to God, even the Father; when he shall have abolished all rule and all authority and power. For he must reign, till he hath put all his enemies under his feet. The last enemy that shall be abolished is death. For, He put all things in subjection under his feet. But when he saith, All things are put in subjection, it is evident that he is excepted who did subject all things unto him. And when all things have been subjected unto him, then shall the Son also himself be subjected to him that did subject all things unto him, that God may be all in all.

Else what shall they do that are baptized for the dead? If the dead are not raised at all, why then are they baptized for them? why do we also stand in jeopardy every hour? I protest by that glorying in you brethren, which I have in Christ Jesus our Lord, I die daily. If after the manner of men I fought with beasts at Ephesus, what doth it profit me? If the dead are not raised, let us eat and drink, for to-morrow we die. Be not deceived: Evil companionships corrupt good morals. Awake to soberness righteously, and sin not; for some have no knowledge of God: I speak this to move you to shame.

But some one will say, How are the dead raised? and with what manner of body do they come? Thou foolish one, that which thou thyself sowest is not quickened except it die; and that which thou sowest, thou sowest not the body that shall be, but a bare grain, it may chance of wheat, or of some other kind; but God giveth it a body even as it pleased him, and to each seed a body of its own. All flesh is not the same flesh: but there is one flesh of men, and another flesh of beasts, and another flesh of birds, and another of fishes. There are also celestial bodies, and bodies terrestrial: but the glory of the celestial is one, and the glory of the terrestrial is another. There is one glory of the sun, and another glory of the moon, and another glory of the stars; for one star differeth from another star in glory. So also is the resurrection of the dead. It is sown in corruption; it is raised in incorruption: it is sown in dishonor; it is raised in glory: it is sown in weakness; it is raised in power: it is sown a natural body; it is raised a spiritual body. If there is a natural body, there is also a spiritual body. So also it is written, The first man Adam became a living soul. The last Adam became a life-giving spirit. Howbeit that is not first which is spiritual, but that which is natural; then that which is spiritual. The first man is of the earth, earthy: the second man is of heaven. As is the earthy, such are they also that are earthy: and as is the heavenly, such are they also that are heavenly. And as we have borne the image of the earthy, we shall also bear the image of the heavenly.

Now this I say, brethren, that flesh and blood cannot inherit the kingdom of God; neither doth corruption inherit incorruption. Behold, I tell you a mystery: We all shall not sleep, but we shall all be changed, in a moment, in the twinkling of an eye, at the last trump: for the trumpet shall sound, and the dead shall be raised incorruptible, and we shall be changed. For this corruptible must put on incorruption, and this mortal must put on immortality. But when this corruptible shall have put on incorruption, and this mortal shall have put on immortality, then shall come to pass the saying that is written. Death is swallowed up in victory. O Death, where is thy victory? O Death, where is thy sting? The sting of death is sin; and the power of sin is the law; but thanks be to God, who giveth us the victory through our Lord Jesus Christ. Wherefore, my beloved brethren, be ye stedfast, unmoveable, always abounding in the work of the Lord, for as much as ye know that your labor is not in vain in the Lord.

2 Corinthians 4:12-15

So then death worketh in us, but life in you. But having the same spirit of faith, according to that which is written, I believed, and therefore did I speak; we also believe, and therefore also we speak; knowing that he that raised up the Lord Jesus shall raise up us also with Jesus, and shall present us with you. For all things are for your sakes, that the grace, being multiplied through the many, may cause the thanksgiving to abound unto the glory of God.

1 Thessalonians 4:13-18

But we would not have you ignorant, brethren, concerning them that fall asleep; that ye sorrow not, even as the rest, who have no hope. For if we believe that Jesus died and rose again, even so them also that are fallen asleep in Jesus will God bring with him. For this we say unto you by the word of the Lord, that we that are alive, that are left unto the coming of the Lord, shall in no wise precede them that are fallen asleep. For the Lord himself shall descend from heaven, with a shout, with the voice of the archangel, and with the trump of God: and the dead in Christ shall rise first; then we that are alive, that are left, shall together with them be caught up in the clouds, to meet the Lord in the air: and so shall we ever be with the Lord. Wherefore comfort one another with these words.

1 Peter 1:3-5

Blessed be the God and Father of our Lord Jesus Christ, who according to his great mercy begat us again unto a living hope by the resurrection of Jesus Christ from the dead, unto an inheritance incorruptible, and undefiled, and that fadeth not away, reserved in heaven for you, who by the power of God are guarded through faith unto a salvation ready to be revealed in the last time.

1 Peter 1:18-21

Knowing that ye were redeemed, not with corruptible

things, with silver or gold, from your vain manner of life handed down from your fathers; but with precious blood, as of a lamb without blemish and without spot, even the blood of Christ: who was foreknown indeed before the foundation of the world, but was manifested at the end of the times for your sake, who through him are believers in God, that raised him from the dead, and gave him glory; so that your faith and hope might be in God.

Some of The Selections from the Bible Which Are Believed to Be Highly Appropriate

Many of the Psalms, including among others:

Psalm	8	O Lord, our Lord,
		How excellent is thy name in all the earth
"	19	The heavens declare the glory of God
"	23	The Lord is my shepherd
"	24	The earth is the Lord's
"	27	The Lord is my light and my salvation
"	33	Rejoice in the Lord, O ye righteous
"	34	I will bless the Lord at all times
"	42	As the hart panteth after the water brooks
"	46	God is our refuge and strength
"	48	Great is the Lord, and greatly to be praised
"	61	Hear my cry, O God
"	63	O God, thou art my God
"	67	God be merciful unto us, and bless us
"	71	In thee, O Lord, do I take refuge
"	72	Give the king, thy judgments, O God
"	84	How amiable are thy tabernacles
"	90	Lord, thou hast been our dwelling-place
"	91	He that dwelleth in the secret place of the Most High
"	92	It is a good thing to give thanks unto the Lord
"	97	The Lord reigneth; let the earth rejoice
"	98	Oh sing unto the Lord a new song
"	100	Make a joyful noise unto the Lord, all ye lands

36

Isaiah 40:1-31

Comfort ye, comfort ye my people, saith your God. Speak ye comfortably to Jerusalem; and cry unto her, that her warfare is accomplished, that her iniquity is pardoned, that she hath received of the Lord's hand double for all her sins.

The voice of one that crieth. Prepare ye in the wilderness the way of the Lord; make level in the desert a highway for our God. Every valley shall be exalted, and every mountain and hill shall be made low, and the uneven shall be made level, and the rough places a plain: and the glory of the Lord shall be revealed, and all flesh shall see it together; for the mouth of the Lord hath spoken it.

The voice of one saying, Cry. And one said, What shall I cry? All flesh is grass, and all the goodliness thereof is as the flower of the field: the grass withereth, the flower fadeth; but the word of our God shall stand forever.

O thou that tellest good tidings to Zion, get thee up on a high mountain; O thou that tellest good tidings to Jerusalem, lift up thy voice with strength; lift it up, be not afraid; say unto the cities of Judah, Behold your God! Behold, the Lord Jehovah will come as a mighty one, and his arm will rule for him: behold, his reward is with him, and his recompense before him. He will feed his flock like a shepherd, he will gather the lambs in his arm, and carry them in his bosom, and will gently lead those that have their young.

Who hath measured the waters in the hollow of his hand, and meted out heaven with the span, and comprehended the dust of the earth in a measure, and weighed the mountains in scales, and the hills in a balance? Who hath directed the Spirit of the Lord, or being his counsellor hath taught him? With whom took he counsel, and who instructed him, and taught him in the path of justice, and taught him knowledge, and showed to him the way of understanding? Behold, the nations are as a drop of a bucket, and are accounted as the small dust of the balance: behold, he taketh up the isles as a very little thing. And Lebanon is not sufficient to burn, nor the beasts thereof sufficient for a burnt-offering. All nations are as nothing before him; they are accounted by him as less than nothing, and vanity.

To whom then will ye liken God? or what likeness will ye compare unto him? The image, a workman hath cast it, and the goldsmith overlayeth it with gold, and casteth for it silver chains. He that is too impoverished for such an oblation chooseth a tree that will not rot; he seeketh unto him a skilful workman to set up a graven image, that shall not be moved. Have ye not known? have ye not heard? hath it not been told you from the beginning? have ye not understood from the foundations of the earth? It is he that sitteth above the circle of the earth, and the inhabitants thereof are as grasshoppers; that stretcheth out the heavens as a curtain, and spreadeth them out as a tent to dwell in; that bringeth princes to nothing; that maketh the judges of the earth as vanity. Yea, they have not been planted; yea, they have not been sown; yea, their stock hath not taken root in the earth; moreover he bloweth upon them, and they wither, and the whirlwind taketh them away as stubble. To whom then will ye liken me, that I should be equal to him? saith the Holy One. Lift up your eyes on high, and see who hath created these, that bringeth out their host by number; he calleth them all by name; by the greatness of his might, and for that he is strong in power, not one is lacking.

Why sayest thou, O Jacob, and speakest, O Israel. My way is hid from the Lord, and the justice due to me is passed away from my God? Hast thou not known? hast thou not heard? The everlasting God, the Lord, the Creator of the ends of the earth, fainteth not, neither is weary; there is no searching of his understanding. He giveth power to the faint; and to him that hath no might he increaseth strength. Even the youths shall faint and be weary, and the young men shall utterly fall: but they that wait for the Lord shall renew their strength; they shall mount up with wings as eagles; they shall run, and not be weary; they shall walk, and not faint.

Isaiah 41:8-20

But thou, Israel, my servant, Jacob whom I have chosen, the seed of Abraham my friend, thou whom I have taken hold of from the ends of the earth, and from the corners thereof, and said unto thee, Thou art my servant, I have chosen thee and not cast thee away; fear thou not, for I am with thee; be not dismayed, for I am thy God; I will strengthen thee; yea, I will help thee; yea I will uphold thee with the right hand of my righteousness. Behold, all they that are incensed against thee shall be put to shame and confounded: they that strive with thee shall be as nothing, and shall perish. Thou shalt seek them, and shalt not find them, even them that contend with thee: they that war against thee shall be as nothing, and as a thing of nought. For I the Lord thy God will hold thy right hand, saying unto thee, Fear not; I will help thee. Fear not, thou worm Jacob, and ye men of Israel; I will help thee, saith the Lord, and thy Redeemer is the Holy One of Israel. Behold, I have made thee to be a new sharp threshing instrument having teeth: thou shalt thresh the mountains, and beat them small, and shalt make the hills as chaff. Thou

39

shalt winnow them, and the wind shall carry them away, and the whirlwind shall scatter them; and thou shalt rejoice in the Lord, thou shalt glory in the Holy One of Israel.

The poor and needy seek water, and there is none, and their tongue faileth for thirst; I the Lord will answer them, **I the God of Israel will not forsake them.** I will open rivers on the bare heights, and fountains in the midst of the valleys; I will make the wilderness a pool of water, and the dry land springs of water. I will put in the wilderness the cedar, the acacia, and the myrtle, and the oil-tree; I will set in the desert the fir-tree, the pine, and the box-tree together: that they may see, and know, and consider, and understand together, that the hand of the Lord hath done this, and the Holy One of Israel hath created it.

Isaiah 42:1-12

Behold, my servant, whom I uphold; my chosen, in whom my soul delighteth: I have put my Spirit upon him; he will bring forth justice to the Gentiles. He will not cry, nor lift up his voice, nor cause it to be heard in the street. A bruised reed will he not break, and a dimly burning wick will he not quench: he will bring forth justice in truth. He will not fail nor be discouraged, till he hath set justice in the earth; and the isles shall wait for his law.

Thus saith God the Lord, he that created the heavens, and stretched them forth; he that spread abroad the earth and that which cometh out of it; he that giveth breath unto the people upon it, and spirit to them that walk therein: I the Lord have called thee in righteousness, and will hold thy hand, and will keep thee, and give thee for a covenant of the people, for a light of the Gentiles; to open the blind eyes, to bring out the prisoners from the dungeon, and them that sit in darkness out of the prison-house. I am the Lord, that is my name; and my glory will I not give to another, neither my praise unto graven images. Behold, the former

40

things are come to pass, and new things do I declare; before they spring forth I tell you of them.

Sing unto the Lord a new song, and his praise from the end of the earth; ye that go down to the sea, and all that is therein, the isles, and the inhabitants thereof. Let the wilderness and the cities thereof lift up their voice, the villages that Kedar doth inhabit; let the inhabitants of Sela sing, let them shout from the top of the mountains. Let them give glory unto the Lord, and declare his praise in the islands.

Isaiah 43:1-13

But now thus saith the Lord that created thee, O Jacob, and he that formed thee, O Israel: Fear not, for I have redeemed thee; I have called thee by thy name, thou art mine. When thou passest through the waters, I will be with thee; and through the rivers, they shall not overflow thee: where thou walkest through the fire, thou shalt not be burned; neither shall the flame kindle upon thee. For I am the Lord thy God, the Holy One of Israel, thy Saviour; I have given Egypt as thy ransom, Ethiopia and Seba in thy stead. Since thou hast been precious in my sight, and honorable, and I have loved thee; therefore will I give men in thy stead, and peoples instead of thy life. Fear not; for I am with thee: I will bring thy seed from the east, and gather thee from the west; I will say to the north, Give up; and to the south, Keep not back; bring my sons from far, and my daughters from the end of the earth; everyone that is called by my name, and whom I have created for my glory, whom I have formed, yea, whom I have made.

Bring forth the blind people that have eyes, and the deaf that have ears. Let all the nations be gathered together, and let the peoples be assembled: who among them can declare this, and show us former things? let them bring their witnesses, that they may be justified; or let them hear, and say, It is truth. Ye are my witnesses, saith the Lord, and my servant whom I have chosen; that ye may know and believe me, and understand that I am he: before me there was no God formed, neither shall there be after me. I, even I, am the Lord; and besides me there is no saviour. I have declared, and I have saved, and I have showed; and there was no strange god among you: therefore ye are my witnesses, saith the Lord, and I am God. Yea, since the day was I am he; and there is none that can deliver out of my hand: I will work, and who can hinder it?

Isaiah 53

Who hath believed our message? and to whom hath the arm of the Lord been revealed? For he grew up before him as a tender plant, and as a root out of dry ground: he hath no form nor comeliness; and when we see him, there is no beauty that we should desire him. He was despised, and rejected of men; a man of sorrow, and acquainted with grief: and as one from whom men hide their face he was despised; and we esteemed him not.

Surely he hath borne our griefs, and carried our sorrows; yet we did esteem him stricken, smitten of God, and afflicted. But he was wounded for our transgressions, he was bruised for our iniquities; the chastisement of our peace was upon him; and with his stripes we are healed. All we like sheep have gone astray; we have turned every one to his own way; and the Lord hath laid on him the iniquity of us all.

He was oppressed, yet when he was afflicted he opened not his mouth; as a lamb that is led to the slaughter, and as a sheep that before her shearers is dumb, so he opened not his mouth. By oppression and judgment he was taken away; and as for his generation, who among them considered that he was cut off out of the land of the living for the transgression of my people to whom the stroke was due? And they made his grave with the wicked, and with a rich man in his death; although he had done no violence, neither was there any deceit in his mouth.

Yet it pleased the Lord to bruise him; he hath put him to grief: when thou shalt make his soul an offering for sin, he shall see his seed, he shall prolong his days, and the pleasure of the Lord shall prosper in his hand. He shall see of the travail of his soul, and shall be satisfied: by the knowledge of himself shall my righteous servant justify many; and he shall bear their iniquities. Therefore will I divide him a portion with the great, and he shall divide the spoil with the strong; because he poured out his soul unto death, and was numbered with the transgressors; yet he bore the sin of many, and made intercession for the transgressors.

Isaiah 55

Ho, everyone that thirsteth, come ye to the waters, and he that hath no money; come ye, buy, and eat; yea, come, buy wine and milk without money and without price. Wherefore do ye spend money for that which is not bread? and your labor for that which satisfieth not? hearken diligently unto me, and eat ye that which is good, and let your soul delight itself in fatness. Incline your ear, and come unto me; hear, and your soul shall live: and I will make an everlasting covenant with you, even the sure mercies of David. Behold, I have given him for a witness to the peoples, a leader and commander to the peoples. Behold, thou shalt call a nation that thou knoweth not; and a nation that knew not thee shall run unto thee, because of the Lord thy God, and for the Holy One of Israel; for he hath glorified thee.

Seek ye the Lord while he may be found; call ye upon him while he is near: let the wicked forsake his way, and the unrighteous man his thoughts; and let him return unto the Lord, and he will have mercy upon him; and to our God, for he will abundantly pardon. For my thoughts are not your thoughts, neither are your ways my ways, saith the Lord. For as the heavens are higher than the earth, so are my ways higher than your ways, and my thoughts than your thoughts. For as the rain cometh down and the snow from heaven, and returneth not thither, but watereth the earth, and maketh it bring forth and bud, and giveth seed to the sower and bread to the eater; so shall my word be that goeth forth out of my mouth: it shall not return unto me void, but it shall accomplish that which I please, and it shall prosper in the thing whereto I sent it. For ye shall go out with joy, and be led forth with peace: the mountains and the hills shall break forth before you into singing, and all the trees of the field shall clap their hands. Instead of the thorn shall come up the fir-tree, and instead of the brier shall come up the myrtle tree: and it shall be to the Lord for a name, for an everlasting sign that shall not be cut off.

The following includable here, are not quoted but incorporated by reference:

Isaiah 60; Micah 6:8; Matthew 5:1-16; Matthew 6; Matthew 7:1-12; Luke 6:20-38; Luke 11:1-13; Luke 15; 1 Cor. 13.

Also, Revelation 21:1-7:

And I saw a new heaven and a new earth: for the first heaven and the first earth are passed away: and the sea is no more. And I saw the holy city, new Jerusalem, coming down out of heaven from God, made ready as a bride adorned for her husband. And I heard a great voice out of the throne saying, Behold, the tabernacle of God is with men, and he shall dwell with them, and they shall be his peoples, and God himself shall be with them, and be their God: and he shall wipe away every tear from their eyes; and death shall be no more; neither shall there be mourning, nor crying, nor pain, any more: the first things are passed away. And he that sitteth on the throne said, Behold, I make all things new. And he saith, Write: for these words are faithful and true. And he said unto me, They are come to pass I am the Alpha and the Omega, the beginning and the end. I will give unto him that is athirst of the fountain of the water of life freely. He that overcometh shall inherit these things; and I will be his God, and he shall be my son.

Some of The Selections from Writings Outside the Bible Which Are Believed To Be Highly Appropriate

Quotations that follow are made, as expressing the deep spirituality that should be the constant companion of thought upon this subject (If a Man Die, Shall He Live Again?).

I can be sure of my present relation to God. In Him only do I live and move and have my being. Faith calls for trust in Him from moment to moment,—Pray Thou in us, and pray Thou for us; Live Thou in us. Such should be our prayer.

Theoretical studies of the problem of evil, and as to things eschatological may be pursued for whatever light that may be derived therein. But statements upon these subjects are not in my creed. I don't believe they belong there. My primary concern is and should be with present relations and in being step by step with God as My Lord and as Source of all, *here* and *now.*

Now for some quotations.

The following are from words ascribed to Socrates and Plato:

A man who is good for anything ought not to calculate the chance of living or dying: he ought only to consider whether in doing anything he is doing right or wrong— acting the part of a good man or of a bad.

Let us reflect in another way, and see that there is great reason to hope that death is a good; for one of two things— **either death is a state of nothingness and utter unconscious-** ness, or as men say, there is a change and migration of the soul from this world to another. Now if you suppose that

45

there is no consciousness, but a sleep like the sleep of him who is undisturbed even by dreams, death will be an unspeakable gain. For if a person were to select the night in which his sleep was undisturbed even by dreams, and were to compare with this the other days and nights of his life, and then were to tell us how many days and nights he had passed in the course of his life better and more pleasantly than this one, I think that any man, I will not say a private man, but even the great king will not find many such days or nights, when compared with the others. Now if death be of such a nature, I say that to die is gain; for eternity is then only a single night. But if death is the journey to another place, and there, as men say, all the dead abide, what good, O my friends and judges, can be greater than this? If indeed when the pilgrim arrives in the world below, he is delivered from the professors of justice in this world, and finds the true judges who are said to give judgment there, Minos and Rhadamanthus and Aeneus and Triptolemus, and other sons of God who were righteous in their own life, that pilgrimage was worth making. What would not a man give if he might converse with Orpheus and Musaeus and Hesiod and Homer? Nay, if this be true, let me die again and again. I myself, too, shall have a wonderful interest in there meeting and conversing with Palamedes, and Ajax the son of Telamon, and any other ancient hero who has suffered death through an unjust judgment; and there will be no small pleasure, as I think, in comparing my own sufferings with theirs. Above all, I shall then be able to continue my search into true and false knowledge; as in this world, so also in the next; and I shall find out who is wise, and who pretends to be wise, and is not. What would not a man give, O judges, to be able to examine the leader of the great Trojan expedition; or Odysseus or Sisyphus, or numberless others, men and women too! What infinite delight would there be in conversing with them and asking them questions! In another world they do not put a man to death for asking questions: assuredly not. For besides being happier than we are, they will be immortal, if what is said is true.

Wherefore, O judges, be of good cheer about death, and know of a certainty, that no evil can befall a good man, either in life or after death.

Whereas I know but little of the world below, I do not suppose that I know: but I do know that injustice and disobedience to a better, whether God or man, is evil and dishonorable.

I had a singular feeling at being in his company. For I could hardly believe that I was present at the death of a friend, and therefore I did not pity him, Echecrates; he died so fearlessly, and his words and bearing were so noble and gracious, that to me he appeared blessed. I thought that in going to the other world he could not be without a divine call, and that he would be happy, if any man ever was, when he arrived there: and therefore I did not pity him as might have seemed natural at such an hour.

But then, O my friends, he said, if the soul is really immortal, what care should be taken of her, not only in respect of the portion of time which is called life, but of eternity!

A man of sense ought not to say, nor will I be very confident, that the description that I have given of the soul and her mansions is exactly true. But I do say that, inasmuch as the soul is shown to be immortal, he may venture to think, not improperly or unworthily, that something of the kind is true. The venture is a glorious one, and he ought to comfort himself with words like these, which is the reason why I lengthen out the tale. Wherefore, I say, let a man be of good cheer about his soul, who having cast away the pleasures and ornaments of the body as alien to him and working harm rather than good, has sought after the pleasures of knowledge, and has arrayed the soul, not in some foreign attire, but in her own proper jewels, temperance and justice, and courage, and nobility, and truth—in these adorned she is ready to go on her journey to the world below, when her hour comes.

The following are from Sir Thomas Browne, Religio Medici:

I remember that I am not alone, and therefore forget not to contemplate Him and His attributes Who is ever with me, especially those two mighty ones, His Wisdom and Eternity. With the one I recreate, with the other I confound, my understanding.

I know He is wise in all, wonderful in what we conceive, but far more in what we comprehend not.

One reason I tender so little Devotion unto Reliques, is, I think, the slender and doubtful respect I have always held unto Antiquities. For that indeed which I admire, is far before Antiquity, that is, Eternity; and that is, God Himself; Who, though He be styled *the Ancient of Days,* cannot receive the adjunct of Antiquity; Who was before the World, and shall be after it, yet is not older than it; for in His years there is no Climacter; His duration is Eternity, and far more venerable than Antiquity.

This I think charity, to love God for Himself, and our neighbour for God.

Bless me in this life with but peace of my Conscience, command of my affections, the love of Thyself and my dearest friends, and I shall be happy enough to pity Caesar. These are, O Lord, the humble desires of my most reasonable ambition, and all I dare call happiness on earth; wherein I set no rule or limit to Thy Hand of Providence. Dispose of me according to the wisdom of Thy pleasure: Thy will be done, though in my own undoing.

48

The following are from John Donne:

I have a sinne of feare, that when I have spunne
My last thread, I shall perish on the shore;
Swear by thy selfe, that at my death thy sonne
Shall shine as he shines now, and heretofore;
And having done that, Thou hast done,
        I feare no more.

We have a *Convenient Author*, who writ a *Discourse of Bells*, when he was prisoner in *Turkey*. How would hee have enlarged himselfe if he had beene my *fellow-prisoner* in this *sicke bed*, so neere to that *Steeple*, which never ceases, no more than the *harmony of the spheres*, but is more heard. When the *Turkes* took Constantinople, they melted the *Bells* into *Ordnance*; I have heard both *Bells* and *Ordnance*, but never been so much affected with those, as with these *Bells*. I have *lien* near a *Steeple*, in which there are said to be more than *thirty Bels*; And neere another, where there is one so bigge, as that the *Clapper* is said to weigh more than *six hundred pound*, yet never so affected as here. Here the *Bells* can scarse solemnise the funerall of any person, but that I knew him, or knew that he was my *Neighbour*: we dwelt in houses neere to one another before, but now hee has gone into that house, into which I must follow him. There is a way of correcting the *Children* of great persons; that other *Children* are corrected in their *behalfe*, and in their *names*, and this workes upon them, who indeed had more deserved it. And when these *Bells* tell me, that now one, and now another is buried, must not I acknowledge, that they have the *correction* due to me, and paid the *debt* that I owe? There is a story of a *Bell* in a *Monastery* which, when any of the house was sicke to death, rung alwaies *voluntarily*, and they knew the inevitablenesse of the danger by that. It rung once, when no man was sick; but the next day one of the house, fell from the *steeple*, and died, and the *Bell* held the reputation of a *Prophet* still. If these *Bells* that warne to a *Funerall* now, were appropriated to none, may not I, by the houre of the *Funerall,* supply? How many men that stand at an *execution,* if they would aske, for what dies that man, should heare their own faults condemned, and see themselves executed, by *Atturney?* We scarce heare of any man *preferred,* but wee thinke of our selves, that we might very well have beene that *Man,* why might not I have been that *Man,* that is carried to his *grave* now? Could I fit my selfe, to *stand,* or *sit* in any mans *place,* and not to lie in any mans *grave?* I may lacke much of the *good parts* of the meanest, but I lacke nothing of the *mortality* of the weakest; They may have acquired better *abilities* than I, but I was borne to as many *infirmities* as they. To be an *Incumbent* by lying down in a *grave,* to be a *Doctor* by teaching *Mortification* by *Example,* by *dying,* though I may have *seniors,* others may be *elder* than I, yet I have proceeded apace in a good *University,* and gone a great way in a little time, by the furtherance of a vehement *Fever;* and whomsoever these *Bells* bring to the ground to day, if hee and I had been compared yesterday, perchance I should have been thought likelier to come to this preferment, then, than he. *God* hath kept the power of *death* in his owne hands, leste any man should *bribe death.* If man knew the *gaine of death,* the *ease of death,* he would solicite, he would provoke *death* to assist him, by any hand, which he might use. But as when men see many of their owne professions preferd, it ministers a hope that that may light upon them; so when these hourely *Bells* tell me of so many *funeralls* of men like me, it presents, if not a desire that it may, yet a *comfort* whensoever mine shall come.

Perchance hee for whom this *Bell* tolls, may be so ill, as that he knowes not it tolls for him; And perchance I may thinke my selfe so much better than I am, as that they who are about mee, and see my state, may have caused it to toll for mee, and I know not that. The *Church* is *Catholike, universall,* so are all her *Actions; All* that she does, belongs to *all.* When she *baptizes a child,* that action concernes mee; for that child is thereby connected to that *Head* which is my *Head* too, and engraffed into that *body,* whereof I am a *member.* And when she *buries a Man,* that action concernes mee: All *mankinde* is of one *Author,* and is one *volume;* when one Man dies, one *Chapter* is not *torne* out of the *booke,* but *translated* into a better *language;* and every *Chapter* must be so *translated;* God emploies several *translators;* some pieces are translated by age, some by *sicknesse,* some by *warre,* some by *justice;* but God's hand is in every *translation;* and his hand shall binde up all our scattered leaves againe, for that *Librarie* where every *booke* shall lie open to one another: As therefore the *Bell* that rings to a *Sermon,* calls not upon the *Preacher* onely, but upon the *Congregation* to come; so this *Bell* calls us all: but how much more mee, who am brought so neere the *doore* by this *sicknesse.* There was a *contention* as far as a *suite,* (in which both *pietie* and *divinitie, religion,* and *estimation,* were mingled) which of the religious *Orders* should ring to *praiers* first in the *Morning;* and it was *determined,* that *they should ring first that rose earliest.* If we understand aright the *dignitie* of this *Belle* that tolls for our *evening prayer,* wee would bee glad to make it ours, by rising early, in that *application,* that it might bee ours, as wel as his, whose indeed it is. The *Bell* doth toll for him that *thinkes* it doth; and though it *intermit* againe, yet from that *minute,* that that occasion wrought upon him, hee is united to *God.* Who casts not up his *Eye* to the *Sunne* when it rises? but who takes off his *Eye* from a *Comet* when that breakes out? Who bends not his *eare* to any *bell,* which upon any occasion rings? but who can remove it from that *bell,* which is passing a *peece of himselfe* out of this *worlde?* No man is an *Iland,* intire of it selfe; every man is a peece of the

Continent, a part of the *maine; if a Clod* bee washed *away* by the *Sea, Europe* is the lesse, as well as if a Promontorie were, as well as if a *Mannor* of thy *friends* or of *thine owne* were; any mans *death* diminishes *me,* because I am involved in *Mankinde;* And therefore never send to know for whom the *bell* tolls; It tolls for *thee.* Neither can we call this a *begging* of *Miserie* or a *borrowing* of *Miserie,* as though we were not miserable enough of our selves, but must fetch in more from the next house, in taking upon us the *Miserie* of our *Neighbours.* Truly it were an excusable *covetousnesse* if wee did; for *affliction* is a *treasure,* and scarce any man hath *enough* of it. No man hath *affliction* enough that is not matured and ripened by it, and made fit for God by that *affliction.* If a man carry *treasure* in *bullion,* or in a *wedge* of *gold,* and have none coined into *current Monies,* his *treasure* will not defray him as he travells. *Tribulation* is *Treasure* in the *nature* of it, but it is not *current money* in the *use* of it, except wee get nearer and nearer our *home, Heaven,* by it. Another man may be sicke too, and sicke to *death,* and this *affliction* may lie in his *bowels,* as *gold* in a *Mine,* and be of no use to him; but this *bell,* that tells me of his *affliction,* digs out, and applies that *gold* to *mee:* if by this consideration of anothers danger, I take mine owne into contemplation, and so secure my selfe, by making my recourse to my *God,* who is our onely securitie.

The *Bell* rings out; the *pulse* thereof is changed; the *tolling* was a *faint,* and *intermitting pulse,* upon one side; this *stronger* and argues *more* and *better* life. His *soule* is gone out; and as a Man, who had a lease of 1000 *yeeres* after the expiration of a short one, or an inheritance after the *life* of a man in a *consumption,* he is now enterd into the possession of his *better estate.* His *soule* is gone; *whither?* Who saw it *come in,* or who saw it *go out. No body;* yet every body is sure, he *had one,* and *hath none.* If I will aske mere *Philosophers,* what the *soule* is, I shall finde amongst them, that will tell me, it is nothing, but the *temperament* and *harmony,* and *just and equall composition of the Elements in the body,* which produces all those *faculties* which we ascribe to the *soule;* and so, in it selfe is *nothing,* no *separable substance,* that overlives the *body.* They see the *soule* is nothing else in other *Creatures,* and they affect an *impious humilitie,* to think *as low* of *Man.* But if my *soule* were no more than the soul of a *beast,* I could not thinke so; that *soule* that can *reflect* upon it selfe, *consider* it selfe, is *more* than so. If I will aske, not meere *Philosophers,* but *mixt men, Philosophicall Divines, how* the *soule,* being a *separate substance,* enters into *Man,* I shall finde some that will tell me, that it is by *generation,* and *procreation* from *parents,* because they thinke it hard to charge the *soule* with the guiltiness of *originall sinne,* if the *soule* were infused into a *body,* in which it must necessarily grow *foule, and* contract *originall sinne,* whether it *will* or *no;* and I shall finde some that will tell mee, that it is by *immediate infusion from God,* because they think it hard, to *maintaine* an *immortality* in such a *soule,* as should be begotten, and derived with the *body* from *mortall parents.* If I will aske, not a *few men,* but almost *whole bodies, whole Churches,* what becomes of the *soules* of the *righteous* at the *departing* thereof from the *body,* I shall be told by some, *That they attend an expiation, a purification, in a place of torment;* By some, *that they attend the fruition of the sight of God, in a place of rest; but yet of expectation;* By some, *that they passe to an immediate possession of the presence of God.* S. *Augustine* studied the *nature* of the *soule,* as much as anything, but the *salvation of the soule;* and he sent an expresse *Messenger* to Saint *Hierome,* to consult of some things concerning the *soule:* But he satisfies himselfe with this: *Let the departure of my soule to salvation be evident to my faith, and I care the lesse, how darke the entrance of my soule, into my body, bee to my reason.*

53

It is the *going out* more than the *comming in*, that concernes us. This *soule*, this Bell tells me, is *gone out; Whither?* Who shall tell mee that? I know not *who it is;* much less *what he was:* The condition of the man, and the course of his life, which should tell mee *whither* hee is gone, I know not. I was not there in his *sicknesse*, nor at his *death; I* saw not his *way*, nor his *end*, nor can aske them, who did, thereby to *conclude*, or *argue*, whither he is gone. But yet I have one neerer mee than all these; mine owne *Charity; I* aske that; and that tels me, *He* is *gone to everlasting rest*, and *joy*, and *glory: I* owe him a good *opinion;* it is but *thankfull charity* in mee, because I received *benefit* and *instruction* from him when his *Bell* told: and I, being made the fitter to *pray*, by that disposition, wherein I was assisted by his occasion, did *pray* for him; and I *pray* not without *faith;* so I doe *charitably*, so I do *faithfully* believe, that that *soule* is gone to everlasting *rest*, and *joy*, and *glory*. But for the *body*, how poore a wretched thing is *that?* wee cannot expresse it *so fast*, as it grows *worse* and *worse*. That *body* which scarce three minutes since was such a *house*, as that that *soule*, which made but one step from thence to *Heaven*, was scarce thorowly content, to leave that for *Heaven:* that *body* hath lost the *name* of a *dwelling house*, because none dwells in it, and is making haste to lose the name of a *body*, and dissolve to *putrefaction*. Who would not be affected, to see a cleere and sweet *River* in the *Morning*, grow a *kennell* of muddy land water by *noone*, and condemned to the saltnesse of the *Sea* by *night?* And how lame a *picture*, how faint a *representation* is that, of the precipitation of mans body to *dissolution! Now* all the parts built up, and knit by a lovely *soule*, *now* but a *statue* of *clay*, and *now*, these limbs melted off, as if that *clay* were but *snow*, and now, the whole *house* is but a *handfull* of *sand*, so much *dust*, and but a *pecke* of *rubbidge*, so much *bone*. If *he*, who, as this *Bell* tells me, is gone now, were some *excellent Artificer*, who comes to him for a *clocke*, or for a *garment* now? or for *counsaile*, if hee were a *Lawyer*? If a *Magistrate*, for *Justice?* *Man*, before hee hath his *immortall soule*, hath a *soule* of *sense*, and a *soule* of *vegetation* before that: This *immortall soule* did not forbid other soules, to be in us before, but when this *soule* departs, it carries all with it; no more *vegetation*, no more *sense:* such a *Mother in law* is the *Earth*, in respect of our *naturall mother:* in her *wombe* we *grew:* and when she was delivered of us, wee were planted in some *place*, in some *calling* in the *world:* In the wombe of the *earth*, wee *diminish*, and when shee is *delivered* of us, our *grave opened* for another, wee were not *transplanted*, but *transported*, our *dust* blowne away with *prophane dust*, with every wind.

    When senses, which thy souldiers are,
Wee arme against thee, and they fight for sinne,
    When want, sent but to tame, doth warre
And worke despaire a breach to enter in,
      When plenty, Gods image, and scale
      Makes us Idolatrous,
And love it, not him, whome it should reveale,
    When we are mov'd to seem religious
Only to vent wit, Lord deliver us.

    In Churches, when th' infirmitie
Of him which speakes, diminishes the Word,
    When Magistrates doe mis-apply
To us, as we judge, lay or ghostly sword,
      When plague, which is thine Angell, raignes,
      Or wars, thy Champions, swaie,
When Heresie, thy second deluge, gaines;
    In th' houre of death, th' Eve of last judgement day,
Deliver us from the sinister way.

Heare us, O heare us Lord; to thee
A sinner is more musique, when he prayes,
Than spheares, or Angells praises bee,
In Panegyrique Allelujaes:
Heare us, for till thou heare us, Lord,
We know not what to say;
Thine eare to our sighs, teares, thoughts give voice and
word,
O Thou who Satan heard'st in Jobs sicke day,
Heare thy selfe now, for thou in us dost pray.

The following is from Boethius:

The common opinion, according to all men living, is that
God is eternal. Let us therefore consider what is eternity.
For eternity will, I think, make clear to us at the same time
the divine nature and knowledge.

Eternity is the simultaneous and complete possession of
infinite life. This will appear more clearly if we compare it
with temporal things. All that lives under the conditions of
time moves through the present from the past to the future;
there is nothing set in time which can at one moment grasp
the whole space of its lifetime. It cannot yet comprehend
tomorrow; yesterday it has already lost. And in this life of
to-day your life is no more than a changing, passing moment. And as Aristotle said of the universe, so it is of all
that is subject to time; though it never began to be, nor will
ever cease, and its life is co-extensive with the infinity of
time, yet it is not such as can be held to be eternal. For
though it apprehends and grasps a space of infinite lifetime,
it does not embrace the whole simultaneously; it has not
yet experienced the future. What we should rightly call
eternal is that which grasps and possesses wholly and simultaneously the fulness of unending life, which lacks naught
of the future, and has lost naught of the fleeting past; and

such an existence must be ever present in itself to control and aid itself, and also must keep present with itself the infinity of changing time. Therefore, people who hear that Plato thought that this universe had no beginning of time and will have no end, are not right in thinking that in this way the created world is co-eternal with its creator. For to pass through unending life, the attribute which Plato ascribes to the universe is one thing; but it is another thing to grasp simultaneously the whole of unending life in the present; this is plainly a peculiar property of the mind of God.

From Fichte:

The ground upon which I assume the existence of something beyond myself, does not lie out of myself, but within me, in the limitation of my own personality.

The world on which but now I gazed with wonder passes away from before us and sinks from my sight. With all the fulness of life, order, and increase which I beheld in it, it is yet but the curtain by which a world infinitely more perfect is concealed from me, and the germ from which the other will develop itself. My FAITH looks behind this veil, and cherishes and animates this germ. It sees nothing definite, but it expects more than it can conceive here below, more than it will ever be able to conceive in all time.

Thus do I live, thus am I, and thus am I unchangeable, firm, and completed for all Eternity;—for this is no existence assumed from without,—it is my own, true, essential Life and Being.

The ONE remains, the many change and pass;
Heaven's light forever shines; Earth's shadows fly;
Life, like a dome of many colored glass,
Stains the white radiance of Eternity,
Until Death tramples it to fragments.

The surest means of acquiring a conviction of a life after death, is so to act in this life that ye can venture to wish for another.

The following are from Emerson:

From within or from behind, a light shines through us upon things, and makes us aware that we are nothing, but the light is all.

Some thoughts always find us young, and keep us so. Such a thought is the love of the universal and eternal beauty. Every man parts from that contemplation with the feeling that it rather belongs to ages than to mortal life.

The following is from Coleridge:

In wonder all philosophy began; in wonder it ends; and admiration fills up the interspace. But the first wonder is the offspring of ignorance: the last is the parent of adoration

The first is the birth-throe of our knowledge: the last is its Euthanasy and *apotheosis*.

The following are from Schleiermacher:

To behold humanity within oneself, and never to lose sight of the vision when once found, is the only certain means of never straying from its sacred precincts. This vision is the intimate and necessary tie between conduct and the perception of truth.

In beholding himself, man triumphs over discouragement and weakness, for from the consciousness of inner freedom there blossoms eternal youth and joy. On these have I laid hold, nor shall I ever give them up, and so I can see with a smile my eyes growing dim, and my blond locks turning white. Nought can happen to affright my heart, and the pulse of my inner life will beat with vigor until death.

58

From Fenelon:

It does not follow necessarily that because we were yesterday, we should exist to-day; we might cease to be, we might relapse into the nothingness from whence we came, if the same all-powerful hand who called us from it did not still sustain us. We are nothing in ourselves; we are only what God has made us to be, and that only while it pleases him. He has only to withdraw the hand which supports us in order to replunge us into the abyss of our nothingness, as a stone which one holds in the air falls from its own weight as soon as the hand is unclosed which supported it. Thus do we hold existence only as the continual gift of God.

The following is from John Milton:

> To attaine
> The highth and depth of thy Eternal wayes
> All human thoughts come short, Supream of things;
> Thou in thyself art perfet, and in thee
> Is no deficiencie found.

The following is from Schiller:

Time and Eternity:—linked together by a single instant:—
Fearful key which lockes
behind me the prison-house of life, and opens
Before me the habitations of eternal night—tell me—
Oh, tell me—*Whither—Whither* wilt thou lead me!
Strange, unexplored land!—Humanity is unnerved at the *Fearful Thought*, the elasticity of our finite nature is paralyzed, and fancy, that wanton ape of the senses, juggles our credulity with appalling phantoms.—No! no! a man must be firm.—Be what thou wilt, thou *Undefined Futurity*, so I remain but true to *Myself*.—Be what thou wilt, so I but take this inward *Self* hence with me,—External forms are

59

but the trappings of the man.—My heaven or my hell is within.

From William Cullen Bryant:

To him who in the love of nature holds
Communion with her visible forms, she speaks
A various language; for his gayer hours
She has a voice of gladness, and a smile
And eloquence of beauty and she glides
Into his darker musings, with a mild
And healing sympathy, that steals away
Their sharpness, ere he is aware. When thoughts
Of the last bitter hour come like a blight
Over thy spirit, and sad images
Of the stern agony, and shroud, and pall,
And breathless darkness, and the narrow house,
Make thee to shudder, and grow sick at heart;—
Go forth, under the open sky, and list
To Nature's teachings, while from all around—
Earth and her waters, and the depths of air,—
Comes a still voice—Yet a few days, and thee
The all-beholding sun shall see no more
In all his course; nor yet in the cold ground,
Where thy pale form was laid, with many tears,
Nor in the embrace of ocean, shall exist
Thy image. Earth, that nourished thee, shall claim
Thy growth, to be resolved to earth again,
And, lost each human trace, surrendering up
Thine individual being, shalt thou go
To mix forever with the elements,
To be a brother to the insensible rock
And to the sluggish clod, which the rude swain
Turns with his share, and treads upon. The oak
Shall send his roots abroad, and pierce thy mould.

Yet not to thine eternal resting-place
Shalt thou retire alone—nor couldst thou wish
Couch more magnificent. Thou shalt lie down
With patriarchs of the infant world—with kings,
The powerful of the earth—the wise, the good,
Fair forms, and hoary seers of ages past,
All in one mighty sepulchre.—The hills
Rock-ribbed and ancient as the sun,—the vales
Stretching in pensive quietness between;
The venerable woods—rivers that move
In majesty, and the complaining brooks
That make the meadows green; and poured round all,
Old ocean's gray and melancholy waste,—
Are but the solemn decorations all
Of the great tomb of man. The golden sun,
The planets, all the infinite host of heaven,
Are shining on the sad abodes of death,
Through the still lapse of ages. All that tread
The globe are but a handful to the tribes
That slumber in its bosom—Take the wings
Of morning—and the Barcan desert pierce,
Or lose thyself in the continuous woods
Where rolls the Oregon, and hears no sound,
Save his own dashings—yet—the dead are there;
And millions in those solitudes, since first
The flight of years began, have laid them down
In their last sleep—the dead reign there alone.
So shalt thou rest—and what if thou withdraw
Unheeded by the living—and no friend
Take note of thy departure? All that breathe
Will share thy destiny. The gay will laugh
When thou art gone, the solemn brood of care
Plod on, and each one as before will chase
His favorite phantom; yet all these shall leave
Their mirth and their employments, and shall come,

61

And make their bed with thee. As the long train
Of ages glide away, the sons of men,
The youth in life's green spring, and he who goes
In the full strength of years, matron, and maid,
And the sweet babe, and the gray-headed man,—
Shall one by one be gathered to thy side,
By those, who in their turn shall follow them.
So live, that when thy summons comes to join
The innumerable caravan, that moves
To that mysterious realm, where each shall take
His chamber in the silent halls of death,
Thou go not, like the quarry-slave at night,
Scourged to his dungeon, but, sustained and soothed
By an unfaltering trust, approach thy grave,
Like one who wraps the drapery of his couch
About him, and lies down to pleasant dreams.

The following is from Charles E. Garman:

The idea that the universe in which we live is a whole—
the notion that mind and matter, history and revelation,
church and state, time and eternity, are not separate wholes,
but parts that somehow fit into each other, and can be understood only in relationship to the grand end they serve—
this is the idea both of philosophy and of religion, and is
coming to be the view of science itself.

The following are from Carlyle:

The sternest sum-total of all worldly misfortunes is Death;
nothing more *can* lie in the cup of human woe: yet many
men, in all ages, have triumphed over Death, and led it
captive; converting its physical victory into a moral victory
for themselves, into a seal and immortal consecration for
all that their past life had achieved. What has been done,
may be done again: nay, it is but the degree and not the

kind of such heroism that differs in different seasons; for without some portion of this spirit, not of boisterous daring, but of silent fearlessness, of Self-denial in all its forms, no good man, in any scene or time, has ever attained to be good.

The faith in an Invisible, Unnameable, Godlike, present everywhere in all that we see and suffer, is the essence of all faith whatsoever.

Or thinkest thou it were impossible, unimaginable? Is the past annihilated, then, or only past; is the Future non-extant, or only future? Those mystic faculties of thine, Memory and Hope, already answer: already through those mystic avenues, thou the Earth-blinded summonest both Past and Future, and communest with them, though as yet darkly, and with mute beckonings. The curtains of Yesterday drop down, the curtains of To-morrow roll up; but Yesterday and To-morrow both *are*. Pierce through the Time-element, glance into the Eternal. Believe what thou findest written in the sanctuaries of Man's Soul, even as all Thinkers, in all ages, have devoutly read it there: that Time and Space are not God, but creations of God; that with God as it is a universal HERE, so is it an everlasting NOW.

And seest thou therein any glimpses of IMMORTALITY? —O Heaven! Is the white Tomb of our Loved One, who died from our arms, and had to be left behind us there, which rises in the distance, like a pale, mournfully receding Milestone, to tell how many toilsome uncheered miles we have journeyed on alone,—but a pale spectral Illusion! Is the lost Friend still mysteriously Here, even as we are Here mysteriously, with God!—Know of a truth that only the Time-shadows have perished, or are perishable; that the real Being of whatever was, and whatever is, and whatever will be, *is* even now and forever. This, should it unhappily seem new, thou mayest ponder at thy leisure; for the next

63

twenty years, or the next twenty centuries: believe it thou must; understand it thou canst not.

That the Thought-forms, Space and Time, wherein, once for all, we are sent into this Earth to live, should condition and determine our whole Practical reasonings, conceptions, and imagings or imaginings, seems altogether fit, just, and unavoidable. But that they should, furthermore, usurp such sway over pure spiritual Meditation, and blind us to the wonder everywhere lying close on us, seems nowise so. Admit Space and Time to their due rank as Forms of Thought; nay, even, if thou wilt, to their quite undue rank of Realities: and consider, then, with thyself how their thin disguises hide from us the brightest God-effulgences! Thus, were it not miraculous, could I stretch forth my hand and clutch the Sun? Yet thou seest me daily stretch forth my hand and therewith clutch many a thing, and swing it hither and thither. Art thou a grown baby, then, to fancy that the Miracle lies in miles of distance, or in pounds avoirdupois of weight; and not to see that the true inexplicable God-revealing Miracle lies in this, that I can stretch forth my hand at all; that I have free Force to clutch aught therewith? Innumerable other of this sort are the deceptions, and wonder-hiding stupefactions, which Space practices on us.

Still worse is it with regard to Time. Your grand antimagician, and universal wonder-hider, is this same lying Time. Had we but the Time-annihilating Hat, to put on for once only, we should see ourselves in a World of Miracles, wherein all fabled and authentic Thaumaturgy, and feats of Magic, were outdone. But unhappily we have not such a Hat; and man, poor fool that he is, can seldom and scantily help himself without one.

Sweep away the Illusion of Time; glance, if thou have eyes, from the near moving-cause to its far-distant Mover: The stroke that came transmitted through a whole galaxy of elastic balls, was it less a stroke than if the last ball only had been struck, and sent flying? Oh, could I (with the Time-annihilating Hat) transport thee direct from the Beginnings to the Endings, how were thy eyesight unsealed, and thy heart set flaming in the Light-sea of celestial wonder! Then sawest thou that this fair Universe, were it in the meanest province thereof, is in very deed the star-domed City of God; that through every star, through every grass-blade, and most through every Living Soul, the glory of a present God still beams. But Nature, which is the Time-vesture of God, and reveals Him to the wise, hides Him from the foolish.

O Heaven, it is mysterious, it is awful to consider that we not only carry each a future Ghost within him; but are in very deed, Ghosts! These Limbs, whence had we them; this stormy Force; this lifeblood with its burning Passion? They are dust and shadow; a Shadow-system gathered round our ME; wherein, through some moments or years, the Divine Essence is to be revealed in the Flesh. That warrior on his strong war-horse, fire flashes through his eyes; force dwells in his arm and heart; but warrior and war-horse are a vision; a revealed Force, nothing more. Stately they tread the Earth, as if it were a firm substance: fool! the Earth is but a film; it cracks in twain, and warrior and war-horse sink beyond plummet's sounding. Plummets? Fantasy herself will not follow them. A little while ago, they were not; a little while, and they are not, their very ashes are not.

So has it been from the beginning, so will it be to the end. Generation after generation takes to itself the Form of a Body; and forth issuing from Cimmerian Night, on Heaven's mission Appears. What Force and Fire is in each he expends; one grinding in the mill of Industry; one hunter-like climbing the giddy Alpine heights of Science; one madly dashed in pieces on the rocks of Strife, in war

65

with his fellow:—and then the Heaven-sent is recalled; his earthly Vesture falls away, and soon even to Sense becomes a vanished Shadow. Thus, like some wild-flaming, wild-thundering train of Heaven's Artillery, does this mysterious Mankind thunder and flame, in long-drawn, quick-succeeding grandeur, through the unknown Deep. Thus, like a God-created, fire-breathing Spirit-host, we emerge from the Inane; haste stormfully across the astonished Earth; then plunge again into the Inane. Earth's mountains are levelled, and her seas filled up, in our passage; can the Earth, which is but dead and a vision, resist Spirits which have reality and are alive? On the hardest adamant some footprint of us is stamped-in; the last Rear of the host will read traces of the earliest Van. But whence?—O Heaven, whither? Sense knows not; Faith knows not; only that it is through Mystery to Mystery, from God to God.

From George Eliot:

O may I join the choir invisible
Of those immortal dead who live again
In minds made better by their presence: live
In pulses stirred to generosity,
In deeds of daring rectitude, in scorn
For miserable aims that end with self,
In thoughts sublime that pierce the night like stars,
And with their mild persistence urge men's search
To vaster issues.
      So to live is heaven:
To make undying music in the world,
Breathing a beauteous order that controls
With growing sway the growing life of man.
So we inherit that sweet purity
For which we struggled, failed, and agonized
With widening retrospect that bred despair.
Rebellious flesh that would not be subdued,

66

A vicious parent shaming still its child
Poor anxious penitence, is quick dissolved;
Its discords, quenched by meeting harmonies,
Die in the large and charitable air.
And all our rarer, better, truer self,
That sobbed religiously in yearning song,
That watched to ease the burden of the world,
Laboriously tracing what must be,
And what may yet be better—saw within
A worthier image for the sanctuary,
And shaped it forth before the multitude
Divinely human, raising worship so
To higher reverence more mixed with love—
That better self shall live till human Time
Shall fold its eyelids, and the human sky
Be gathered like a scroll within the tomb
Unread forever.
           This is life to come,
Which martyred men have made more glorious
For us who strive to follow. May I reach
That purest heaven, be to other souls
The cup of strength in some great agony,
Enkindle generous ardor, feed pure love,
Beget the smiles that have no cruelty—
Be the sweet presence of a good diffused,
And in diffusion ever more intense.
So may I join the choir invisible
Whose music is the gladness of the world.

It was probably a hard saying to the Pharisees, that
"there is more joy in heaven over one sinner that repenteth,
than over ninety and nine just persons that need no repentance." And certain ingenious philosophers of our own day
must surely take offence at a joy so entirely out of corre-
spondence with arithmetical proportion. But a heart that has

been taught by its own sore struggles to bleed for the woes of another—that has "learned pity through suffering"—is likely to find very imperfect satisfaction in the "balance of happiness," "doctrine of compensations," and other short and easy methods of obtaining thorough complacency in the presence of pain: and for such a heart that saying will not be altogether dark. The emotions, I have observed, are but slightly influenced by arithmetical considerations: the mother, when her sweet lisping little ones have all been taken from her one after another, and she is hanging over her last dead babe, finds small consolation in the fact that the tiny dimpled corpse is but one of a necessary average, and that a thousand other babes brought into the world at the same time are doing well, and are likely to live; and if you stood beside that mother—if you knew her pang and shared it—it is probable you would be equally unable to see a ground of complacency in statistics.

Doubtless a complacency resting on that basis is highly rational; but emotion, I fear, is obstinately irrational: it insists on caring for individuals; it absolutely refuses to adopt the quantitative view of human anguish, and to admit that thirteen happy lives are a set-off against twelve miserable lives, which leaves a clear balance on the side of satisfaction. This is the inherent imbecility of feeling, and one must be a great philosopher to have got quite clear of all that, and to have emerged into the serene air of pure intellect, in which it is evident that individuals really exist for no other purpose than that abstractions may be drawn from them— abstractions that may rise from heaps of ruined lives like the sweet savor of a sacrifice in the nostrils of philosophers, and of a philosophic Deity. And so it comes to pass that for the man who knows sympathy because he has known sorrow, that old, old saying about the joy of angels over the repentant sinner outweighing their joy over the ninety-nine just, has a meaning which does not jar with the language of

68

his own heart. It only tells him, that for angels too there is a transcendent value in human pain, which refuses to be settled by equations; that the eyes of angels too are turned away from the serene happiness of the righteous to bend with yearning pity on the poor erring soul wandering in the desert where no water is; that for angels too the misery of one casts so tremendous a shadow as to eclipse the bliss of ninety-nine.

When Death, the great Reconciler, has come, it is never our tenderness that we repent of, but our severity.

It's well we should feel as life's a reckoning we can't make twice over; there's no real making amends in this world, any more nor you can mend a wrong subtraction by doing your addition right.

The great river-courses which have shaped the lives of men have hardly changed; and those other streams, the life-currents that ebb and flow in human hearts, pulsate to the same great needs, the same great loves and terrors. As our thought follows close in the slow wake of the dawn, we are impressed with the broad sameness of the human lot, which never alters in the main headings of its history—hunger and labor, seed-time and harvest, love and death.

These things have not changed. The sunlight and shadows bring their old beauty and waken the old heart-strains at morning, noon, and even-tide; the little children are still the symbol of the eternal marriage between love and duty; and men still yearn for the reign of peace and righteousness —still own *that* life to be the highest which is a conscious voluntary sacrifice.

No radiant angel came across the gloom with a clear message for her. In those times, as now, there were human beings who never saw angels or heard perfectly clear messages. Such truth as came to them was brought confusedly in the voices and deeds of men not at all like the seraphs of unfailing wing and piercing vision—men who believed falsities as well as truths, and the wrong as well as the right. The helping hands stretched out to them were the hands of men who stumbled and often saw dimly, so that these beings unvisited by angels had no other choice than to grasp that stumbling guidance along the path of reliance and action which is the path of life, or else to pause in loneliness and disbelief, which is no path, but the arrest of inaction and death.

Deeds are the pulse of Time, his beating life,
And righteous or unrighteous, being done,
Must throb in after-throbs till Time itself
Be laid in darkness, and the universe
Quiver and breathe upon no mirror more.

In the chequered area of human experience the seasons are all mingled as in the golden age: fruit and blossom hang together; in the same moment the sickle is reaping and the seed is sprinkled; one tends the green cluster and another treads the wine-press. Nay, in each of our lives harvest and spring-time are continually one, until himself gathers us and sows us anew in his invisible fields.

The following are from Immanuel Kant:

There is in human nature a certain disingenuousness which, however, like everything that springs from nature, must contain a useful germ, namely a tendency to conceal one's own true sentiments, and to give expression to adopted opinions which are supposed to be good and creditable. There is no doubt that this tendency to conceal oneself and to assume a favourable appearance has helped towards the progress of civilization, nay, to a certain extent, of morality, because others, who could not see through the varnish of respectability, honesty, and correctness, were led to improve themselves by seeing everywhere these examples of goodness which they believed to be genuine. This tendency, however, to show oneself better than one really is, and to utter sentiments which one does not really share, can only serve provisionally to rescue men from a rude state, and to teach them to assume at least the appearance of what they know to be good. Afterwards, when genuine principles have once been developed and become part of our nature, that disingenuousness must be gradually conquered, because it will otherwise deprave the heart and not allow the good seeds of honest conviction to grow up among the tares of fair appearances.

I am sorry to observe the same disingenuousness, concealment, and hypocrisy even in the utterances of speculative thought, though there are here fewer hindrances in uttering our convictions openly and freely as we ought, and no advantage whatever in our not doing so. For what can be more mischievous to the advancement of knowledge than to communicate even our thoughts in a falsified form, to conceal doubts which we feel in our own assertions, and to impart an appearance of conclusiveness to arguments which we know ourselves to be inconclusive? So long as those tricks arise from personal vanity only (which is commonly the case with speculative arguments, as touching no particular interests, nor easily capable of apodictic certainty) they are mostly counteracted by the vanity of others, with the full approval of the public at large, and thus the result is generally the same as what would or might have been obtained sooner by means of pure ingenuousness and honesty. But where the public has once persuaded itself that certain subtle speculators aim at nothing less than to shake the very foundations of the common welfare of the people, it is supposed to be not only prudent, but even advisable and honourable, to come to the succour of what is called the good cause, by sophistries, rather than to allow to our supposed antagonists the satisfaction of having lowered our tone to that of a purely practical conviction, and having forced us to confess the absence of all speculative and apodictic certainty. I cannot believe this, nor can I admit that the intention of serving a good cause can ever be combined with trickery, misrepresentation and fraud. That in weighing the arguments of a speculative discussion we ought to be honest, seems the least that can be demanded; and if we could at least depend on this with perfect certainty, the conflict of speculative reason with regard to the important questions of God, the immortality of the soul, and freedom, would long ago have been decided, or would soon be brought to a conclusion. Thus it often happens that the purity of motives and sentiments stands on an inverse ratio to the goodness of the cause, and its supposed assailants are more honest and more straightforward than its defenders.

It is part of that freedom that we should be allowed openly to state our thoughts and our doubts which we cannot solve ourselves, without running the risk of being decried on that account as turbulent and dangerous citizens. This follows from the inherent rights of reason, which recognizes no other judge but universal human reason itself. Here everybody has a vote; and, as all improvements of which our state is capable must spring from thence, such rights are sacred and must never be minished. Nay, it would really be foolish to proclaim certain bold assertions, or reckless attacks upon assertions which enjoy the approval of the largest and best portion of the commonwealth, as dangerous; for that would be to impart to them an importance which they do not possess. Whenever I hear that some uncommon genius has demonstrated away the freedom of the human will, the hope of a future life, or the existence of

God, I am always desirous to read his book, for I expect that his talent will help me to improve my own insight into these problems.

Two things fill the mind with ever new and increasing admiration and awe, the oftener and the more steadily we reflect on them: *the starry heavens above and the moral law within*. I have not to search for them and conjecture them as though they were veiled in darkness or were in the transcendent region beyond my horizon; I see them before me and connect them directly with the consciousness of my existence. The former begins from the place I occupy in the external world of sense, and enlarges my connexion therein to an unbounded extent with worlds upon worlds and systems of systems, and moreover into limitless times of their periodic motion, its beginning and continuance. The second begins from my invisible self, my personality, and exhibits me in a world which has true infinity, but which is traceable only by the understanding, and with which I discern that I am not in a merely contingent but in a universal and necessary connexion, as I am also thereby with all those visible worlds. The former view of a countless multitude of worlds annihilates, as it were, my importance as an *animal creature*, which after it has been for a short time provided with vital power, one knows not how, must again give back the matter of which it was formed to the planet it inhabits (a mere speck in the universe). The second, on the contrary, infinitely elevates my worth as an *intelligence* by my personality, in which the moral law reveals to me a life independent on animality and even on the whole sensible world —at least so far as may be inferred from the destination assigned to my existence by this law, a destination not restricted to conditions and limits of this life, but reaching into the infinite.

From James Russell Lowell:

Just on the farther bound of sense,
Unproved by outward evidence,
But known by a deep influence
Which through our grosser clay doth shine
With light unwaning and divine,
Beyond where highest thought can fly
Stretcheth the world of Mystery—
And they not greatly overween
Who deem that nothing true hath been
Save the unspeakable Unseen.

One step beyond life's work-day things,
One more beat of the soul's broad wings,
One deeper sorrow sometimes brings
The spirit into that great Vast
Where neither future is nor past;
None knoweth how he entered there,
But, waking, finds his spirit where
He thought an angel could not soar,
And, what he called false dreams before,
The very air about his door.

These outward seemings are but shows
Whereby the body sees and knows;
Far down beneath, forever flows
A stream of subtlest sympathies
That make our spirits strangely wise
In awe, and fearful bodings dim
Which, from the sense's outer rim,
Stretch forth beyond our thought and sight,
Fine arteries of circling light,
Pulsed outward from the Infinite.

74

To let the new life in, we know,
    Desire must ope the portal;—
Perhaps the longing to be so
    Helps make the soul immortal.

From Amiel:

There is but one thing needful—to possess God. All our senses, all our powers of mind and soul, all our external resources, are so many ways of approaching the Divinity, so many modes of tasting and of adoring God. We must learn to detach ourselves from all that is capable of being lost, to bind ourselves absolutely only to what is absolute and eternal, and to enjoy the rest as a loan, a usufruct. . . . To adore, to understand, to receive, to feel, to give, to act: there is my law, my duty, my happiness, my heaven. Let come what come will—even death. Only be at peace with self, live in the presence of God, in communion with Him, and leave the guidance of existence to those universal powers against whom thou canst do nothing!—If death gives me time, so much the better. If its summons is near, so much the better still; if a half-death overtake me, still so much the better, for so the path of success is closed to me only that I may find opening before me the path of heroism, of moral greatness and resignation. Every life has its potentiality of greatness, and as it is impossible to be outside God, the best is consciously to dwell in Him.

The centre of life is neither in thought nor in feeling, nor in will, nor even in consciousness, so far as it thinks, feels, or wishes. For moral truth may have been penetrated and possessed in all these ways, and escape us still. Deeper even than consciousness there is our being itself, our very substance, our nature. Only those truths which have entered into this last region, which have become ourselves, become spontaneous and involuntary, instinctive and unconscious, are really our life—that is to say, something more than our

75

property. So long as we are able to distinguish any space whatever between the truth and us we remain outside it. The thought, the feeling, the desire, the consciousness of life, are not yet quite life. But peace and repose can nowhere be found except in life and in eternal life, and the eternal life is the divine life, is God. To become divine then is the aim of life: then only can truth be said to be ours beyond the possibility of loss, because it is no longer outside us, nor even in us, but we are it, and it is we; we ourselves are a truth, a will, a work of God. Liberty has become nature; the creature is one with its creator—one through love. It is what it ought to be; its education is finished, and its final happiness begins. The sun of time declines and the light of eternal blessedness arises.

The relegation of life to some distant future, and the separation of the holy man from the virtuous man, are the signs of a false religious conception. . . . The eternal life is not the future life; it is life in harmony with the true order of things,—life in God. We must learn to look upon time as a movement of eternity, as an undulation in the ocean of being. To live, so as to keep this consciousness of ours in perpetual relation with the eternal, is to be wise; to live, so as to personify and embody the eternal, is to be religious.

From Epictetus:

Men generally act as a traveller would do on his way to his own country, when he enters a good inn, and being pleased with it should remain there. Man, you have forgotten your purpose: you were not travelling to this inn, but you were passing through it.—But this is a pleasant inn.— And how many other inns are pleasant? and how many meadows are pleasant? yet only for passing through.

From Marcus Aurelius:

Whatsoever thou dost affect, whatsoever thou dost project, so do, and so project all, as one who, for aught thou knowest, may at this very present depart out of this life. And as for death, if there be any gods, it is no grievous thing to leave the society of men. The gods will do thee no hurt, thou mayest be sure. But if it be so that there be no gods, or that they take no care of the world, why should I desire to live in a world void of gods, and of all divine providence? But gods there be certainly, and they take care for the world; and as for those things which be truly evil, as vice and wickedness, such things they have put in a man's own power, that he might avoid them if he would: and had there been anything besides that had been truly bad and evil, they would have had a care of that also, that a man might have avoided it. But why should that be thought to hurt and prejudice a man's life in this world, which cannot any ways make man himself the better, or the worse in his own person?

If thou shouldst live three thousand, or as many as ten thousands of years, yet remember this, that man can part with no life properly, save with that little part of life, which he now lives: and that which he lives, is no other, than that which at every instant he parts with. That then which is longest of duration, and that which is shortest, come both to one effect. For although in regard of that which is already past there may be some inequality, yet that time which is now present and in being, is equal unto all men. And that being it which we part with whensoever we die, it doth manifestly appear, that it can be but a moment of time, that we then part with. For as for that which is either past or to come, a man cannot be said properly to part with it. For how should a man part with that which he hath not? These two things therefore thou must remember: First, that all things in the world from all eternity, by a perpetual revolution of the same times and things ever continued and renewed, are of one kind and nature; so that whether for a hundred or two hundred years only, or for an infinite space of time, a man see those things which are still the same, it **can be no matter of great moment.** And secondly, that that life which any the longest liver, or the shortest liver parts with, is for length and duration the very same, for that only which is present is that, which either of them can lose, as being that only which they have; for that which he hath not, no man can truly be said to lose.

The time of a man's life is as a point; the substance of it ever flowing, the sense obscure; and the whole composition of the body tending to corruption. His soul is restless, fortune uncertain, and fame doubtful; to be brief, as a stream so are all things belonging to the body; as a dream, or as a smoke, so are all that belong unto the soul. Our life is a warfare, and a mere pilgrimage.

From Wordsworth:

> One adequate support
> For the calamities of mortal life
> Exists—one only; an assured belief
> That the procession of our fate, howe'er
> Sad or disturbed, is ordered by a Being
> Of infinite benevolence and power;
> Whose everlasting purposes embrace
> All accidents, converting them to good.
> —The darts of anguish *fix* not where the seat
> Of suffering hath been thoroughly fortified
> By acquiescence in the Will supreme
> For time and for eternity; by faith,
> Faith absolute in God, including hope,
> And the defence that lies in boundless love
>
> Of his perfections; with habitual dread
> Of aught unworthily conceived, endured
> Impatiently, ill-done, or left undone,

To the dishonor of his holy name.
Soul of our Souls, and safeguard of the world!
Sustain, thou only canst, the sick of heart;
Restore their languid spirits, and recall
Their lost affections unto thee and thine!

There is
One great society alone on earth:
The noble Living and the noble Dead.

From Whittier:

No bird-song floated down the hill,
The tangled bank below was still;

No rustle from the birchen stem,
No ripple from the water's hem,

The dusk of twilight round us grew,
We felt the falling of the dew;

For, from us, ere the day was done,
The wooded hills shut out the sun.

But on the river's farther side
We saw the hill-tops glorified,—

A tender glow, exceeding fair,
A dream of day without its glare.

With us the damp, the chill, the gloom:
With them the sunset's rosy bloom;

While dark, through willowy vistas seen,
The river rolled in shade between.

From out the darkness where we trod,
We gazed upon those hills of God,

Whose light seemed not of moon or sun.
We spake not, but our thought was one.

We paused, as if from that bright shore
Beckoned our dear ones gone before;

And stilled our beating hearts to hear
The voices lost to mortal ear!

Sudden our pathway turned from night;
The hills swung open to the light;

Through their green gates the sunshine showed,
A long, slant splendor downward flowed.

Down glade and glen and bank it rolled;
It bridged the shaded stream with gold;

And, borne on piers of mist, allied
The shadowy with the sunlit side!

"So," prayed we, "when our feet draw near
The river dark, with mortal fear,

"And the night cometh chill with dew,
O Father! let Thy light break through!

"So let the hills of doubt divide,
So bridge with faith the sunless tide!

"So let the eyes that fail on earth
On Thy eternal hills look forth;

"And in Thy beckoning angels know
The dear ones whom we loved below!"

I am: how little more I know!
Whence came I? Whither do I go?
A centered self, which feels and is;
A cry between the silences;
A shadow-birth of clouds at strife
With sunshine on the hills of life;
A shaft from Nature's quiver cast

80

Into the Future from the Past;
Between the cradle and the shroud,
A meteor's flight from cloud to cloud.

Enough for me to feel and know
That He in whom the cause and end,
The past and future, meet and blend,—
Who, girt with his Immensities,
Our vast and star-hung system sees,
Small as the clustered Pleiades,
Moves not alone the heavenly quires,
But waves the spring-time's grassy spires,
Guards not archangel feet alone,
But deigns to guide and keep my own;
Speaks not alone the words of fate
Which worlds destroy, and worlds create,
But whispers in my spirit's ear,
In tones of love, or warning fear,
A language none beside may hear.

To Him, from wanderings long and wild,
I come, an over-wearied child,
In cool and shade His peace to find,
Like dew-fall settling on my mind.
Assured that all I know is best,
And humbly trusting for the rest,
I turn from Fancy's cloud-built scheme,
Dark creed, and mournful eastern dream
Of power, impersonal and cold,
Controlling all, itself controlled,
Maker and slave of iron laws,
Alike the subject and the cause;
From vain philosophies, that try
The sevenfold gates of mystery,
And, baffled ever, babble still,
Word-prodigal of fate and will;

From Nature, and her mockery, Art,
And book and speech of men apart,
To the still witness in my heart;
With reverence waiting to behold
His Avatár of love untold,
The Eternal Beauty new and old!

Thy mercy, O Eternal One!
    By means unmeasured yet
In joy or grief, in shade or sun,
    I never will forget.
I give the whole, and not a part,
    Of all Thou gavest me:
My goods, my life, my soul and heart,
    I yield them all to Thee!

We fast and plead, we weep and pray,
    From morning until even;
We feel to find the holy way,
    We knock at the gate of heaven!
And when in silent awe we wait,
And word and sign forbear,
The hinges of the golden gate
    Move, soundless, to our prayer!
Who hears the eternal harmonies
    Can heed no outward word;
Blind to all else is he who sees
    The vision of the Lord!

O soul, be patient, restrain thy tears,
    Have hope, and not despair;
As a tender mother heareth her child
    God hears the penitent prayer.
And not forever shall grief be thine;
    On the Heavenly Mother's breast,
Washed clean and white in waters of joy

Shall His seeking child find rest.
Console thyself with His word of grace
And cease thy wail of woe,
For His mercy never an equal hath,
    And His love no bounds can know,
Lean close unto Him in faith and hope;
    How many like thee have found
In Him a shelter and home of peace,
    By His mercy compassed round!
There, safe from sin and the sorrow it brings,
    They sing their grateful psalms,
And rest, at noon, by the wells of God,
    In the shade of His holy palms!

Scarcely Hope hath shaped for me
What the future life may be.
Other lips may well be bold;
Like the publican of old,
I can only urge the plea,
"Lord, be merciful to me!"
Nothing of desert I claim,
Unto me belongeth shame.
Not for me the crowns of gold,
Palms and harpings manifold;
Not for erring eye and feet
Jasper wall and golden street.
What thou wilt, O Father, give!
All is gain that I receive.
If my voice I may not raise
In the elders' song of praise,
If I may not, sin-defiled,
Claim my birthright as a child,
Suffer it that I to Thee
As an hired servant be;
Let the lowliest task be mine,

Grateful, so the work be Thine;
Let me find the humblest place
In the shadow of Thy grace:
Blest to me were any spot
Where temptation whispers not.
If there be some weaker one,
Give me strength to help him on;
If a blinder soul there be,
Let me guide him nearer Thee.
Make my mortal dreams come true
With the work I fain would do;
Clothe with Life the weak intent,
Let me be the thing I meant;
Let me find in Thy employ
Peace that dearer is than joy;
Out of self to love be led
And to heaven acclimated,
Until all things sweet and good
Seem my natural habitude.

From Dante:

Thenceforward, what I saw,
Was not for words to speak, nor memory's self
To stand against such outrage on her skill.
As one, who from a dream awaken'd, straight,
All he hath seen forgets; yet still retains
Impression of the feeling in his dream;
E'en such am I: for all the vision dies,
As 'twere, away; and yet the sense of sweet,
That sprang from it, still trickles in my heart.
Thus in the sun-thaw is the snow unseal'd;
Thus in the winds on flitting leaves was lost
The Sibyl's sentence. O eternal beam!
(Whose height what reach of mortal thought may soar?)
Yield me again some little particle

84

Of what thou then appearedst; give my tongue
Power, but to leave one sparkle of thy glory,
Unto the race to come, that shall not lose
Thy triumph wholly, if thou waken aught
Of memory in me, and endure to hear
The record sound in this unequal strain.

    Such keenness from the living ray I met,
That, if mine eyes had turn'd away, methinks,
I had been lost; but, so embolden'd, on
I pass'd, as I remember, till my view
Hover'd the brink of dread infinitude.

    O grace, unenvying of thy boon! that gavest
Boldness to fix so earnestly my ken
On the everlasting splendor, that I look'd,
While sight was unconsumed; and, in that depth,
Saw in one volume clasp'd of love, whate'er
The universe unfolds; all properties
Of substance and of accident, beheld,
Compounded, yet one individual light
The whole. And of such bond methinks I saw
The universal form; for that whene'er
I do but speak of it, my soul dilates
Beyond her proper self; and, till I speak,
One moment seems a longer lethargy,
Than five-and-twenty ages had appear'd
To that emprize, that first made Neptune wonder
At Argo's shadow darkening on his flood.

    With fixed heed, suspense and motionless,
Wondering I gazed; and admiration still
Was kindled as I gazed. It may not be,
That one, who looks upon that light, can turn
To other object, willingly, his view.
For all the good, that will may covet, there
Is summ'd; and all, elsewhere defective found,
Complete. My tongue shall utter now, no more

E'en what remembrance keeps, than could the babe's,
That yet is moisten'd at his mother's breast.
Not that the semblance of the living light
Was changed (that ever as at first remain'd)
But that my vision quickening, in that sole
Appearance, still new miracles descried,
And toil'd me with the change. In that abyss
Of radiance, clear and lofty, seem'd, methought,
Three orbs of triple hue, clipp'd in one bound:
And, from another, one reflected seem'd,
As rainbow is from rainbow: and the third
Seem'd fire, breathed equally from both. O speech!
How feeble and how faint art thou, to give
Conception birth. Yet this to what I saw
Is less than little. O eternal light!
Sole in thyself that dwell'st; and of thyself
Sole understood, past, present, or to come;
Thou smiledst, on that circling, which in thee
Seem'd as reflected splendor, while I mused;
For I therein, methought, in its own hue
Beheld our image painted: steadfastly
I therefore poured upon the view. As one,
Who versed in geometric lore, would fain
Measure the circle; and, though pondering long
And deeply, that beginning, which he needs,
Finds not: e'en such was I, intent to scan
The novel wonder, and trace out the form,
How to the circle fitted, and therein
How placed: but the flight was not for my wing;
Had not a flash darted athwart my mind,
And, in the spleen, unfolded what it sought.

    Here vigor fail'd the towering fantasy:
But yet the will roll'd onward, like a wheel
In even motion, by the love impell'd,
That moves the sun in heaven and all the stars.

From Victor Hugo:

The huge concentric waves of universal life are shoreless. The starry sky that we study is but a partial appearance. We grasp but a few meshes of the vast network of existence. The complication of the phenomenon, of which a glimpse can be caught beyond our senses only by contemplation and ecstasy, makes the mind giddy. The thinker who reaches so far is to other men only a visionary. The necessary interlacement of the perceptible with the non-perceptible strikes the philosopher with stupor. This plenitude is required by Thy omnipotence, which admits no gap. The interpenetration of universe with universe makes part of Thy infinitude. Here we extend the word "universe" to an order of facts that no astronomer can reach. In the Cosmos, invisible to fleshly eye, but revealed to vision, sphere blends with sphere without change of form, the creations being of diverse density; so that, to all appearance, with our world is inexplicably merged another, invisible to us as we to it.

From John Bunyan:

Now I saw in my dream that these two men went in at the gate: and lo, as they entered, they were transfigured, and they had raiment put on that shone like gold. There was also that met them with harps and crowns and gave to them—the harps to praise withal, and the crowns in token of honour. Then I heard in my dream that all the bells in the City rang again for joy, and it was said unto them, *"Enter ye Into the Joy of your Lord."* I also heard the men themselves that they sang with a loud voice, saying, *"Blessing and Honour and Glory, and Power, Be Unto Him That Sitteth Upon The Throne and Unto The Lamb, For Ever and Ever."*

Now just as the gates were opened to let in the men, I looked in after them, and, behold, the City shone like the sun; the streets also were paved with gold, and in them walked many men with crowns on their heads, palms in their hands, and golden harps to sing praises withal.

There were also of them that had wings, and they answered one another without intermission saying, "Holy, holy, holy is the Lord." And after that they shut up the gates; which, when I had seen, I wished myself among them.

After this it was noised abroad, that Mr. Valiant-for-truth was taken with a summons by the same post as the other; and had this for a token that the summons was true. "That his pitcher was broken at the fountain." When he understood it, he called for his friends, and told them of it. Then, said he, I am going to my Father's; and though with great difficulty I am got hither, yet now, do I not repent me of all the trouble I have been at to arrive where I am. My sword I give to him that shall succeed me in my pilgrimage, and my courage and skill to him that can get it. My marks and scars I carry with me, to be a witness for me, that I have fought his battles who will now be my rewarder. When the day that he must go hence was come, many accompanied him to the river side into which as he went he said, "Death, where is thy sting?" And as he went down deeper he said, "Grave, where is thy victory?" So he passed over, and all the trumpets sounded for him on the other side.

From Charles Edward Garman:

If you look over your past experience you will find those moments in your existence when you came the nearest to being your true self—when you were half conscious of a reserve power of manliness that made your ordinary life seem mean and narrow—were moments when you could look through the material as through a veil and be conscious that it was not all. It may have been at a time when some rank injustice made the blood boil in your veins. It may

88

have been when you were reading some deed of heroism in war. . . . When you look at such men as these, can you think for a moment that they were selfish? Does there not shine through their heroism "the light that never was, on sea or land"? In these moments of daring can you not realize something in your own heart that gives you a feeling of kinship? If not how could you admire their deed? Is not the true explanation of your admiration the words of Fichte?

> "the Eternal One
> Lives in my life, and sees in my beholding,
> Naught is but God, and God is naught but life."

From Robert Browning:

> 'Tis only when they spring to heaven that angels
> Reveal themselves to you; they sit all day
> Beside you, and lie down at night by you
> Who care not for their presence, muse or sleep,
> And all at once they leave you, and you know them!

> And I shall behold thee, face to face,
> O God, and in thy light retrace
> How in all I loved here, still was thou!
> Whom pressing to, then, as I fain would now,
> I shall find as able to satiate
> The love, thy gift, as my spirit's wonder
> Thou art able to quicken and sublimate,
> With this sky of thine, that I now walk under
> And glory in thee for, as I gaze
> Thus, thus! Oh, let men keep their ways
> Of seeking thee in a narrow shrine—
> Be this my way! And this is mine!

> I have looked to thee from the beginning,
> Straight up to thee through all the world
> Which, like an idle scroll, lay furled

89

To nothingness on either side:
And since the time thou wast descried,
Spite of the weak heart, so have I
Lived ever, and so fain would die.
Living and dying, thee before!
But if thou leavest me—

Well, it is gone at last, the palace of music I reared;
    Gone! and the good tears start, the praises that come too
        slow,
For one is assured at first, one scarce can say that he feared,
    That he even gave it a thought, the gone thing was to go.
Never to be again! But many more of the kind
    As good, nay, better perchance: is this your comfort to
        me?
To me, who must be saved because I cling with my mind
    To the same, same self, same love, same God: ay what
        was, shall be.

Therefore to whom turn I but to thee, the ineffable Name?
    Builder and maker, thou, of houses not made with hands!
What, have fear of change from thee who art ever the same?
    Doubt that thy power can fill the heart that thy power
        expands?
There shall never be one lost good! What was, shall live as
        before,
    The evil is null, is naught, is silence implying sound;
What was good shall be good, with, for evil, so much good
        more;
    On the earth the broken arcs; in the heaven a perfect
        round.

All we have willed or hoped or dreamed of good shall exist;
    Not its semblance, but itself; no beauty, nor good, nor
        power

Whose voice has gone forth, but each survives for the
  melodist
  When eternity affirms the conception of an hour.
The high that proved too high, the heroic for earth too hard,
  The passion that left the ground to lose itself in the sky,
Are music sent up to God by the lover and the bard;
  Enough that he heard it once: we shall hear it by and by.

And what is our failure here but a triumph's evidence
  For the fulness of the days? Have we withered or
    agonized?
Why else was the pause prolonged but that singing might
    issue thence?
  Why rushed the discords in, but that harmony should be
    prized?

Sorrow is hard to bear, and doubt is slow to clear,
  Each sufferer says his say, his scheme of the weal and woe:
But God has a few of us whom he whispers in the ear;
  The rest may reason and welcome: 'tis we musicians know.

For I say, this is death and the sole death,
When a man's loss comes to him from his gain,
Darkness from light, from knowledge ignorance,
And lack of love from love made manifest;
A lamp's death when, replete with oil, it chokes.

Fear death?—to feel the fog in my throat,
  The mist in my face,
When the snows begin, and the blasts denote
  I am nearing the place,
The power of the night, the press of the storm,
  The post of the foe;
Where he stands, the Arch Fear in a visible form,
  Yet the strong man must go:
For the journey is done and the summit attained,

And the barriers fall,
Though a battle's to fight ere the guerdon be gained,
The reward of it all.
I was ever a fighter, so—one fight more,
The best and the last!
I would hate that death bandaged my eyes, and forbore,
And bade me creep past.
No! let me taste the whole of it, fare like my peers
The heroes of old,
Bear the brunt, in a minute pay glad life's arrears
Of pain, darkness and cold.
For sudden the worst turns the best to the brave,
The black minute's at end,
And the elements' rage, the fiend-voices that rave,
Shall dwindle, shall blend,
Shall change, shall become first a peace out of pain,
Then a light, then thy breast;
O thou soul of my soul! I shall clasp thee again,
And with God be the rest!

All the more I know mankind,
The more I thank God, like my grandmother,
For making me a little lower than
The angels, honor-clothed and glory-crowned:
This is the honor,—that no thing I know,
Feel or conceive, but I can make my own
Somehow, by use of hand, or head or heart:
This is the glory,—that in all conceived,
Or felt or known, I recognize a mind
Not mine but like mine,—for the double joy,—
Making all things for me and me for Him.

O Thou, the one force in the whole variation
Of visible nature,—at work—do I doubt?—
From Thy first to our last, in perpetual creation—

A film hides us from Thee—'twixt inside and out,
A film, on this earth where Thou bringest about

New marvels, new forms of the glorious, the gracious,
    We bow to, we bless for: no star bursts heaven's dome
But Thy finger impels it, no weed peeps audacious
    Earth's clay floor from out, but Thy finger makes room
For one world's want the more in Thy Cosmos: presume

Shall Man, Microcosmos, to claim the conception
    Of grandeur, of beauty, in thought, word or deed?
I toiled, but Thy light on my dubiousest step shone:
    If I reach the glad goal, is it I who succeed
Who stumbled at starting tripped up by a reed,

Or Thou? Knowledge only and absolute, glory
    As utter be Thine who concedest a spark
Of Thy spheric perfection to earth's transitory
    Existences! Nothing that lives, but Thy mark
Gives law to—life's light: what is doomed to the dark?

From Tennyson:

    But we grow old. Ah! when shall all men's good
Be each man's rule, and universal Peace
Lie like a shaft of light across the land,
And like a lane of beams athwart the sea,
Thro' all the circle of the golden year?

Ah, folly! for it lies so far away,
Not in our time, nor in our children's time,
'Tis like the second world to us that live;
'Twere all as one to fix our hopes on heaven
As on this vision of the golden year.

      What stuff is this!
Old writers push'd the happy season back,—
The more fools they,—we forward; dreamers both—

You most, that, in an age when every hour
Must sweat her sixty minutes to the death,

Live on, God love us, as if the seedsman, rapt
Upon the teeming harvest, should not plunge
His hand into the bag; but well I know
That unto him who works, and feels he works,
This same grand year is ever at the doors.

Thine are these orbs of light and shade;
Thou madest Life in man and brute;
Thou madest Death; and lo, thy foot
Is on the skull which thou hast made.

Thou wilt not leave us in the dust:
Thou madest man, he knows not why,
He thinks he was not made to die;
And thou hast made him: thou art just.

Our little systems have their day;
    They have their day and cease to be;
    They are but broken lights of thee,
And thou, O Lord, art more than they.

We have but faith: we cannot know,
    For knowledge is of things we see;
    And yet we trust it comes from thee,
A beam in darkness: let it grow.

Let knowledge grow from more to more,
    But more of reverence in us dwell;
    That mind and soul, according well,
May make one music as before,
But vaster.

Hallowed be Thy name—Halleluiah!—
    Infinite Ideality!

94

Immeasurable Reality!
Infinite Personality!
Hallowed be Thy name—Halleluiah!

We feel we are nothing—for all is Thou and in Thee;
We feel we are something—*that* also has come from Thee;
We know we are nothing—But Thou wilt help us to be.
Hallowed be Thy name—Halleluiah!

Sunset and evening star,
  And one clear call for me!
And may there be no moaning of the bar,
  When I put out to sea,
But such a tide as moving seems asleep,
  Too full for sound and foam,
When that which drew from out the boundless deep
  Turns again home.

Twilight and evening bell,
  And after that the dark!
And may there be no sadness of farewell,
  When I embark;
For tho' from out our bourne of Time and Place
  The flood may bear me far,
I hope to see my Pilot face to face
  When I have crost the bar.

From Augustine:

Yet suffer me to speak unto Thy mercy, me, dust and
ashes. Yet, suffer me to speak, since I speak to Thy mercy,
and not to scornful man. Thou too perhaps dost laugh at
me, yet wilt Thou turn and have compassion upon me. For
what would I say, O Lord my God, but that I know not
whence I came into this dying life (shall I call it?) or living

death. Then immediately did the comforts of Thy compassion take me up, as I heard (for I remember it not) from the parents of my flesh, out of whose substance Thou didst sometime fashion me. Then the comforts of woman's milk entertained me. For neither my mother nor my nurses stored their own breasts for me; but Thou didst bestow the food of my infancy through them, according to Thine ordinance, whereby Thou distributest Thy riches through the hidden springs of all things. Thou also gavest me to desire no more than Thou gavest; and to my nurses willingly to give me what Thou gavest them. For they, with an heaven-taught affection, willingly gave me what they abounded with from Thee. For this my good from them, was good for them. For from Thee, O God, are all good things, and from my God is all my health. This I afterwards learned, when Thou, through these Thy benedictions, within me and without, proclaimedst Thyself unto me. For then I knew but to suck; to repose in what pleased, and cry at what offended my flesh; nothing more. Afterwards I began to smile; first in sleep, then waking, for so it was told me of myself, and I believed it; for we see the like in other infants, though of myself I remember it not. Thus, little by little, I began to find where I was; and to have a wish to express my wishes to those who could content them, and I could not; for the wishes were within me, and those persons without; nor could they by any sense of theirs enter within my soul. So I flung about at random limbs and voice, making the few signs I could, and such as I could, like, though in truth very little like, what I wished. And when I was not presently obeyed (my wishes being hurtful or unintelligible) then I was indignant with my elders for not submitting to me; with those owing me no service, for not serving me; and avenged myself on them by tears. Such have I learnt infants to be from observing them; and, that I was myself such, they, all unconscious, have shown me better than my nurses who knew it.

And lo! my infancy died long since, and I live. But Thou, Lord, who for ever livest, and in whom nothing dies; for before the foundation of the worlds, and before all that can be called "before," Thou art, and art God and Lord of all which Thou hast created: in Thee abide, fixed for ever, the first causes of all things abiding; and of all things changeable, the springs abide in Thee unchangeable: and in Thee live the eternal reasons of all things unreasoning and temporal. Say, Lord, to me, Thy suppliant; say, all-pitying, to me, Thy pitiable one; say, did my infancy succeed another age of mine that died before it? Was it that which I spent within my mother's womb? for of that I have heard somewhat, and have myself seen women with child. And what, again, was I before that life, O God my joy? Was I anywhere or anybody? For this have I none to tell me, neither father nor mother, nor experience of others, nor mine own memory. Dost Thou laugh at me for asking this and bid me praise Thee and acknowledge Thee, for that which I do know?

I acknowledge Thee, Lord of heaven and earth, and praise Thee for my first rudiments of being, and my infancy, whereof I remember nothing; for Thou hast appointed that man should from others guess much as to himself; and believe much on the authority of simple women. Even then I had a being and a life, and (at my infancy's close) I sought for signs, whereby to make myself known to others. Whence could such a being be, save from Thee, Lord? Shall any be his own artificer? or can there elsewhere be derived any vein, which may stream essence and life into us, save from Thee, O Lord, in whom essence and life are not several but one? for supremely to live is the very thing in itself which Thou art. For Thou art supreme, and art not changed, neither in Thee doth to-day come to a close; yet in Thee doth it come to a close; because all transitory things also are in Thee. For they had no way to pass away, unless Thou upheldest them. And since Thy years fail not, Thy years are one to-day.

How many of ours and our fathers' years have flowed away through Thy "to-day," and from it received the measure and the mould of a kind of being; and still others shall flow away, and so receive the mould of their kind of being. But Thou art still the same, and all things of to-morrow, and all beyond, and all of yesterday, and all behind it, Thou wilt do in this "to-day." What is it to me, though any comprehend not this? Let him rejoice even thus; and be content rather by not discovering to discover Thee, than by discovering not to discover Thee.

Thou, then, O Lord my God, who gavest life to this my infancy, furnishing thus with senses (we see) the frame Thou gavest, compacting its limbs, beautifying its proportions, and, for its general good and safety, implanting in it all vital functions. Thou commandest me to praise Thee in these things, to confess unto Thee, and sing unto Thy name, Thou most High. For Thou art God, Almighty and Good, even hadst Thou done naught but only this, which none could do but Thou: whose Unity is the mould of all things; who out of Thine own beauty makest all things fair; and orderest all things by Thy law.

O Lord, our God, under the shadow of Thy wings let us hope; protect us, and carry us. Thou wilt carry us both when little, and even to hoary hairs wilt Thou carry us; for our firmness, only when it is in Thee, is firmness; but when it is our own, it is infirmity. Our good ever lives with Thee; from which when we turn away, we are prevented. Let us then, O Lord, return that we may not be overturned; because with Thee good lives without any decay, for Thou art good; nor need we fear, lest there be no place whither to return, because we fell from it: for our mansion,—eternity, fell not when we left Thee.

Accept, O Lord, the sacrifice of my confessions, from the

ministry of my tongue, which Thou hast formed and stirred up to confess unto Thy name. Heal Thou all my bones, and let them say, O Lord who is like unto Thee? For he, who confesses unto Thee, doth not teach Thee what takes place within him; seeing a closed heart shuts not out Thy eye, nor can man's hardheartedness thrust back Thy hand: for Thou dissolvest it at Thy will in pity or in vengeance, and nothing can hide it from Thy heart. But let my soul praise Thee, that it may love Thee; and let it confess all Thy own mercies to Thee, that it may praise Thee. Thy whole creation ceaseth not, nor is silent in Thy praises; neither the spirit of man, with voice directed unto Thee, nor creation animate or inanimate, by the voice of those who meditate thereon: that so our souls may from their weariness arise towards Thee, leaning on those things which Thou hast created, and passing on to Thyself who madest them wonderfully; whereby cometh refreshment and true strength.

O Lord, I am Thy servant; I am Thy servant, and the son of Thine handmaid; Thou hast broken my bonds in sunder. I will offer to Thee the sacrifice of praise. Let my heart and my tongue praise Thee; yea, let all my bones say, "O Lord, who is like unto Thee?" Let them say, and answer Thou, and say unto my soul, "I am Thy salvation." Who am I, and what man am I? Rather what evil have I not been, either in deeds, or if not in my deeds, in my words, or if not in my words, in my will? But Thou, O Lord, art good and merciful, and Thy right hand had respect unto the depth of my death, and from the bottom of my heart emptied that abyss of corruption. And this Thy whole gift was, to nill what I willed, and to will what Thou willedst.

And all my hope is nowhere but in Thy exceeding great mercy. Give what Thou enjoinest, and enjoin what Thou wilt.

Blessed is the man that loveth Thee, and his friend in Thee, and his enemy for Thee. For he alone loses none dear to him, to whom all are dear in Him who cannot be lost. And who is this but our God, the God that made heaven and earth, and filleth them, because by filling them He created them? None loseth, but he who leaveth Thee. And who leaveth Thee, whither goeth or whither fleeth he, but from Thee pleased to Thee displeased? For doth he not find Thy law in his own punishment? And Thy law is truth, and truth is Thyself.

If a man die, shall he live again? I do not know nor do I need to know. Such knowledge is not necessary to my present life.

However suppose to the unborn child his life in this world could be laid out before him as it was, or is, or will be. Would not all seem as wonderful and as unbelievable as our efforts to look into the future or surmise with respect thereto?

We close repeating again words of Fenelon and of Fichte:

> We hold existence only as the continual gift of God.
> the Eternal One

> Lives in my life, and sees in my beholding,
> Naught is but God, and God is naught but life.

CONTENT OF BELIEF

It is indeed difficult to state clearly and concisely the *Content* of *Belief*.

Before attempting to make such statement, one can well say with Dante and with Milton:

> O grace, unenvying of thy boon! that gavest
> Boldness to fix so earnestly my ken
> On the everlasting splendour, that I look'd,
> While sight was unconsumed; and, in that depth,
> Saw in one volume clasp'd of love, whate'er
> The universe unfolds; all properties
> Of substance and of accident, beheld,
> Compounded, yet one individual light
> The whole.
>
> So much the rather thou Celestial light
> Shine inward, and the mind through all her powers
> Irradiate, there plant eyes, all mist from thence
> Purge and disperse, that I may see and tell
> Of things invisible to mortal sight.

To state briefly and concisely, or to attempt so to do,—we have a sense of infinite dependence on God, it is through Him alone that we live; literally in Him, we live and move and have our being. Our ability to know persons and things is because both they and we are grounded in the same All Sustaining God. Our theory of knowledge is inextricably bound up with our being in God. Science is possible to us only because of this relation; and likewise because of this relation we can communicate with our friends or with other persons. Because they and we are grounded in the same God, we can understand each other; we speak as it were the same language. We consequently believe in Idealism, in Personality, and in Sovereignty.

As members of one world we recognize that we are conditioned by people and things within our universe. Their gain is our gain; their loss is our loss.

Perfection of self is possible only through perfection of people and things, that is of objects. There is nothing absolutely good but good will. Our choice should be that our will should accord with the divine will.

In our contacts with persons and things we have to act. Our acts reflect our sovereignty, which partakes of the nature of the divine sovereignty, and depend upon the positions or conditions of those with whom we are in contact.

It was Charles E. Garman by whom I was brought to see and to accept the beliefs so sketchily outlined.

The beautiful text on the tomb of Johann Gottlieb Fichte would also be appropriate to Professor Garman,— "Thy teachers shall shine as the brightness of the firmament, and they that turn many to righteousness as the stars that shine for ever and ever."

I am extremely critical of the accepted creeds of the time, such as the Apostles Creed, the Nicaean Creed, or the Athanasian Creed. I am also critical with respect to my examination in 1904 and 1905 for licensure by the New Haven Association of Congregational Ministers. This is not only because of so many articles impossible of belief and so much excess baggage unrelated to the individual's present vital relation to God. My objection was and is not only to such articles as Virgin Birth, Resurrection, Deity of Jesus, etc., but to seemingly practical denial, by omission of emphasis, of the first article,—I believe in God. No one seemed to be concerned about that article or whether or not I had such belief or what its content was. I completely denied and dissented from the Ritschlian and related positions that all we know about God we learn from Jesus and from The Bible.

I had been taught and wholly accepted, and still do, that Theism is the solution of the problem of knowledge.

In summary my present creed or belief is based upon sense of dependence upon God, and love to Him. My relation to him is not a figure of speech, but one of absolute dependence. God is the ground and source of all science, all beauty, all justice, and all good. Based thereon is love to man. As for knowledge of God, it increases with our experience. The sacred canon of the Scriptures is not sixty-six books of the Old and New Testaments, but the world's entire literature as far as helpful in religion—here a little and there a little.

Also I repeat, Theism is the solution of the problem of knowledge.

Also I repeat and emphasize what was said in the Introduction, namely that intentionally and advisedly very wide use has been made of quotations, and that this has been done whenever and wherever it has been deemed that such quotations more adequately present what I believe and what I wish to say, than words of my own can do. One of the places where quotations seem especially called for is this section, Content of Belief, or I Believe. Many such follow.

From Schleiermacher:

> The common element in all howsoever diverse expressions of piety, by which these are conjointly distinguished from all other feelings, or, in other words, the self-identical essence of piety, is this: the consciousness of being absolutely dependent, or, which is the same thing, of being in relation with God.

> To behold humanity within oneself, and never to lose sight of the vision when once found, is the only certain means of never straying from its sacred precincts. This vis-

ion is the intimate and necessary tie between conduct and the perception of truth.

From Fichte:

It is an error to say that it is doubtful whether or not there is a God. It is not doubtful, but the most certain of all certainties,—nay, the foundation of all other certainties— the one absolutely valid objective truth,—that there is a moral order in the world; that to every rational being is assigned his particular place in that order, and the work which he has to do; that his destiny, in so far as it is not occasioned by his own conduct, is the result of this plan; that in no other way can even a hair fall from his head, nor a sparrow fall to the ground around him; that every true and good action prospers, and every bad action fails; and that all things must work together for good to those who truly love goodness. On the other hand, no one who reflects a moment, and honestly avows the result of his reflection, can remain in doubt that the conception of God as *a particular substance* is impossible and contradictory: and it is right candidly to say this, and to silence the babbling of the schools, in order that the true religion of cheerful virtue may be established in its room.

Two great poets have expressed this faith of good and thinking men with inimitable beauty. Such an one may adopt their language:—

Who dares to say,
"I believe in God"?
Who dares to name him
And to profess,
"I believe in him"?
Who can feel,
And yet affirm,

104

"I believe him not"?
The All-Embracer,
The All-Sustainer,
Does he not embrace, support,
Thee, me, himself?
Does not the vault of heaven arch o'er us there?
Does not the earth lie firmly here below?
And do not the eternal stars
Rise on us with their friendly beams?
Do I not see my image in thine eyes?
And does not the All
Press on thy head and heart,
And weave itself around thee, visibly and invisibly,
In eternal mystery?
Fill thy heart with it till it overflow;
And in the feeling, when thou'rt wholly blest,
Then call it what thou wilt,—
Happiness! Heart! Love! God!
I have no name for it:
Feeling is all; name is but sound and smoke,
Veiling the glow of heaven.

And the second sings—

And God is!—a holy Will that abides,
Though this human will may falter;
High over both Space and Time it rides,
The high thought that will never alter:
And while all things in change eternal roll,
It endures, through change, a motionless soul.

Man can will only what he loves; His love is the sole and
at the same time the infallible motive of his will and of all
his vital impulses and actions.

Further, he will perceive that, amid the various forms
which it received, not by chance, but according to a law

105

founded in God Himself, the spiritual life which alone really exists is one, the divine life itself, which exists and manifests itself only in living thought. He will thus learn to know and keep holy his own and every other spiritual life as an eternal link in the chain of the manifestations of the divine life. Only in immediate contact with God and in the direct emanation of his life from Him will he find life, light, and happiness, but in any separation from that immediate contact, death, darkness, and misery. In a word, this development will train him to religion; and this religion of the indwelling of our life in God shall indeed prevail and be carefully fostered in the new era. On the other hand, the religion of the past separated the spiritual life from the divine, and only by apostasy against the divine life could it procure for the spiritual life the absolute existence which it had ascribed to it. It used God as a means to introduce self-seeking into other worlds after the death of the mortal body, and through fear and hope of these other worlds to reinforce for the present world the self-seeking which would otherwise have remained weak. Such a religion, which was obviously a servant of selfishness, shall indeed be borne to the grave along with the past age. In the new era eternity does not dawn first on yon side of the grave, but comes into the midst of the present life; while self-seeking is dismissed from serving and from ruling, and departs, taking its servants with it.

Whatever is great and good in our own age is wholly due to this, that noble and strong men in the past have for the sake of ideas made sacrifice of all the enjoyments of life.

The ground upon which I assume the existence of something beyond myself, does not lie out of myself, but within me, in the limitation of my own personality.

The light is not out of, but in me, and I myself am the light.

This will unites me with himself; He also unites me with all finite beings like myself, and is the common mediator between us all. This is the great mystery of the invisible world, and its fundamental law, in so far as it is a world or system of many individual wills:—*the union, and direct reciprocal action, of many separate and independent wills;* a mystery which already lies clearly before every eye in the present life, without attracting the notice of any one, or being regarded as in any way wonderful. The voice of conscience, which imposes on each his particular duty, is the light-beam on which we come forth from the bosom of the Infinite, and assume our place as particular individual beings; it fixes the limits of our personality; it is thus the true original element of our nature, the foundation and material of all our life. The absolute freedom of the will, which we bring down with us from the Infinite into the world of Time, in the principle of this our life.

From Ralph Waldo Emerson:

There is one mind common to all individual men. Every man is an inlet to the same and to all of the same. He that is once admitted to the right of reason is made a freeman of the whole estate. What Plato has thought, he may think; what a saint has felt, he may feel; what at any time has befallen any man, he can understand. Who hath access to this universal mind is a party to all that is or can be done, for this is the only and sovereign agent.

I have no expectation that any man will read history aright, who thinks that what was done in a remote age, by men whose names have resounded far, has any deeper sense than what he is doing to-day.

To the poet, to the philosopher, to the saint, all things are friendly and sacred, all events profitable, all days holy, all men divine. For the eye is fastened on the life, and slights the circumstance.

I see that men of God have, from time to time, walked

107

among men and made their commission felt in the heart and soul of the commonest hearer.

In old Rome the public roads beginning at the Forum proceeded north, south, east, west, to the centre of every province of the empire, making each market-town of Persia, Spain, and Britain pervious to the soldiers of the capital: so out of the human heart go, as it were, highways to the heart of every object in nature, to reduce it under the dominion of man. A man is a bundle of relations, a knot of roots, whose flower and fruitage is the world.

In the light of these two facts, namely, that the mind is One, and that nature is its correlative, history is to be read and written.

In all conversations between two persons, tacit reference is made, as to a third party, to a common nature.

The experience of each new age requires a new confession and the world seems always waiting for its poet.

The possibility of interpretation lies in the identity of the observer with the observed. Each material thing has its celestial side, has its translation, through humanity, into the spiritual and necessary sphere, where it plays a part as indestructible as any other.

Life is girt all round with a zodiac of sciences, the contributions of men who have perished to add their point of light to our sky. Engineer, broker, jurist, physician, moralist, theologian, and every man, inasmuch as he has any science, is a definer and map-maker of the latitudes and longitudes of our condition. These road-makers on every hand enrich us. We must extend the area of life, and multiply our relations. We are as much gainers by finding a new property in the old earth, as by acquiring a new planet.

Men are helpful through the intellect and the affections. Other help, I find a false appearance. If you affect to give me bread and fire, I perceive that I pay for it the full price, and at last it leaves me as it found me, neither better nor worse: but all mental and moral force is a positive good.

With each new mind, a new secret of nature transpires; nor can the Bible be closed, until the last great man is born.

It is as real a loss that others should be low, as that we should be low; for we must have society.

Philosophy is the account which the human mind gives to itself of the constitution of the world. Two cardinal facts lie forever at the base; the one, and the two,—1. Unity, or Identity; and, 2. Variety. We unite all things, by perceiving the law which pervades them; by perceiving the superficial differences, and the profound resemblances. But every mental act,—this very perception of identity or oneness, recognizes the difference of things. Oneness and otherness. It is impossible to speak, or to think, without embracing both.

From Plato:

If there were not some community of feelings among mankind, however varying in different persons—I mean to say, if every man's feelings were peculiar to himself—and were not shared by the rest of his species—I do not see how we could ever communicate our impressions to one another.

From Schiller:

Three words of mighty moment I'll name,
    From mouth unto mouth they fly ever,
Yet the heart can alone their great value proclaim,
    For their source from without rises never.
No virtue, no merit, man's footsteps e'er guides,
When in those three words he no longer confides.

For *Liberty*, man is created,—*is* free,
    Though fetters around him chinking;
Let the cry of the mob never terrify thee,
    Not the scorn of the dolt and unthinking!
Fear not the bold slave when he breaks from his chains,
For the man who in freedom enduring remains!

And *Virtue* is more than an empty sound,
His practice thro' life man may make it;
And tho' oft, ere he yet the divine one has found,
He may stumble, he still may o'ertake it.
And that which the wise in his wisdom ne'er knew,
Can be done by the mind that is childlike and true.

And a *God,* too, there is, with a purpose sublime,
Tho' frail may be reason's dominion,
High over the regions of space and of time
The noblest of thoughts waves its pinion;
And tho' all things in ceaseless succession may roll,
Yet constant forever remains a calm soul.

Preserve, then, the three mighty words I have nam'd,
From mouth unto mouth spread them ever,
By thy heart will their infinite worth be proclaim'd,
Tho' their source from without rises never.
Forget not that virtue man's footsteps still guides,
While in those three words he with firmness confides.

What no ear could e'er hear, what no eye could e'er see,
Remains still the truthful, the glorious!
It is not without, for the fool seeks it there;
Within thee it flourishes, constant and fair.
What thou thinkest, belongs to all; what
Thou feel'st is thine only.
Would'st thou make him thine own, feel
Thou the God whom thou think'st!

Would'st thou know thyself, observe the actions of others,
Would'st thou other men know, look thou within thine own
heart.

From Coleridge:

For of all we see, hear, feel, and touch the substance is
and must be in ourselves; and therefore there is no alterna-

110

tive in reason between the dreary (and thank heaven! almost impossible) belief that everything around us is but a phantom, or that the life which is in us is in them likewise; and that to know is to resemble, when we speak of objects out of ourselves, even as within ourselves to learn is, according to Plato, only to recollect.

From hope and former faith to perfect love
Attracted and absorbed: and centred there
God only to behold, and know, and feel,
Till by exclusive consciousness of God
All self-annihilated it shall make
God its identity: God all in all!

       'Tis the sublime of man,
Our noonday majesty, to know ourselves.
Parts and proportions of one wondrous whole!
This fraternizes man, this constitutes
Our charities and bearings. But 'tis God
Diffused through all, that doth make us all one whole.

The Jews would not willingly tread upon the smallest piece of paper in their way, but took it up: for possibly, said they, the name of God may be on it. Though there was a little superstition in this, yet truly there is nothing but good religion in it, if we apply it to men. Trample not on any; there may be some work of grace there, that thou knowest not of. The name of God may be written upon that soul thou treadest on.

If you would have a good conscience, you must by all means have so much light, so much knowledge of the will of God, as may regulate you, and show you your way, may teach you how to do, and speak, and think, as in His presence.

It is the glory of the Gospel charter and the Christian

constitution, that its author and head is the Spirit of truth, essential reason as well as absolute and incomprehensible Will. Like a just monarch, he refers even his own causes to the judgment of his high courts.—He has his King's bench in the reason, his Court of Equity in the conscience; that the representative of his majesty and universal justice, this the nearest to the king's heart, and the dispenser of his particular decrees. He has likewise his Court of Common Pleas in the understanding, his Court of Exchequer in the prudence. The laws are his laws. And though by signs and miracles he has mercifully condescended to interline here and there with his own hand the great statute-book, which he has dictated to his *amanuensis*, Nature, yet has he been graciously pleased to forbid our receiving as the king's mandates aught that is not stamped with the Great Seal of the Conscience, and countersigned by the Reason.

What you have acquired by patient thought and cautious discrimination, demands a portion of the same effort in those who are to receive it from you.

From John Bunyan:

Let the Most Blessed be my guide,
    If't be his blessed will;
Unto his gate, into his fold,
    Up to his holy hill.

And let him never suffer me
    To swerve or turn aside
From his free grace, and holy ways,
    Whate'er shall me betide.

And let him gather them of mine,
    That I have left behind;
Lord, make them pray they may be thine,
    With all their heart and mind.

112

Bless'd be the day that I began
    A pilgrim for to be;
And blessed also be that man
    That thereto moved me.

'Tis true, 'twas long ere I began
    To seek to live forever;
But now I run fast as I can;
    'Tis better late than never.

Our tears to joy, our fears to faith,
    Are turned, as we see,
That our beginning, as one saith,
    Shows what our end will be.

This done and after these things had been somewhat di-
gested by Christiana and her company, the Interpreter takes
them apart again, and has them first into a room where was
a man that could look no way but downwards with a muck-
rake in his hand. There stood also one over his head with a
celestial crown in his hand, and proffered him that crown
for his muck-rake; but the man did neither look up, nor regard, but raked to himself the straws, the small sticks, and
dust of the floor.

And whereas thou seest him rather give heed to rake up
straws and sticks, and the dust of the floor, than to what He
says that calls to him from above with the celestial crown in
his hand, it is to show that heaven is but as a fable to some,
and that things here are counted the only things substantial.
Now, whereas it was also showed thee, that the man could
look no way but downwards it is to let thee know that earthly things when they are with power upon men's minds, quite
carry their hearts away from God.

From Tennyson:

I am part of all that I have met,
    Yet all experience is an arch wherethro'

Gleams that untravell'd world whose margin fades
Forever and forever when I move.

From Augustine:

Great art Thou, O Lord, and greatly to be praised; great
is Thy power, and Thy wisdom infinite. And Thee man
would praise; man, but a particle of Thy creation; man, that
bears about him his mortality, the witness of his sin, the
witness that Thou, O God, resistest the proud: yet would
man praise Thee; he, but a particle of Thy creation. Thou
awakest us to delight in Thy praise; for Thou madest us for
Thyself, and our heart is restless, until it repose in Thee.
Grant me, Lord, to know and understand which is first, to
call on Thee or to praise Thee, and again, to know Thee or
to call on Thee.

And, being thence admonished to return to myself, I entered even into my inward self, Thou being my Guide: and
I was able to do so because Thou wert become my Helper.
And I entered, and beheld with the eye of my soul (such as
it was), even above my soul, above my mind,—the Light
Unchangeable. Not this ordinary light, which all flesh may
look upon as it were a greater of the same kind, as though
the brightness of this should be manifold brighter, and with
its greatness take up all space. Not such was this light, but
different, far different from all these. Nor was it above my
soul, as oil is above water, nor yet as heaven above earth:
but above my soul, because it made me; and I was below It,
because I was made by It. He that knows the truth knows
what that Light is; and he that knows It, knows Eternity.
Love knoweth It.

O Truth Who art Eternity! and Love Who art Truth! and
Eternity Who art Love! Thou art my God,—to Thee do I
sigh night and day. When I first knew Thee, Thou liftedst
me up, that I might see there was somewhat for me to see,
and that I was not yet able to see. And Thou didst beat back

the weakness of my sight, streaming forth the beams of light upon me most strongly, and I trembled with love and awe; and I perceived myself to be far off from Thee, in the region of unlikeness, as if I heard this Thy voice from on high: "I am the food of grown men; grow, and thou shalt feed upon Me; nor shalt thou convert Me, like the food of thy flesh, into thee, but thou shalt be converted into Me." And I learned, that Thou for iniquity chastenest man, and Thou madest my soul to consume away like a spider. And I said, "Is Truth, therefore, nothing because it is not diffused through space finite or infinite?" And Thou criedst to me from afar; "Yea, verily, I Am That I Am." And I heard, as the heart heareth, nor had I room to doubt, and I should sooner doubt that I live, than that Truth is not, which is clearly seen, being understood by those things which are made.

And I beheld the other things below Thee, and I perceived that they neither altogether are, nor altogether are not; for they are, since they are from Thee, but are not, because they are not what Thou art. For that truly is which remains unchangeably. It is good then for me to hold fast unto God; for if I remain not in Him, I cannot in myself; but He remaining in Himself, reneweth all things. And Thou art the Lord my God, since Thou standest not in need of my goodness.

For it is one thing, from the mountain's shaggy top to see the land of peace, and to find no way thither, and in vain to strive towards it through paths impassable, opposed and beset by fugitives and deserters led by their captain the lion and the dragon; and quite another thing to keep on the way that leads thither, guarded by the hosts of the heavenly General, where those who have deserted the heavenly army spoil and rob not, for they avoid that army as very torment itself.

GOOD God! what takes place in man that he should more

rejoice at the salvation of a soul despaired of, and freed from greater peril, than if there had always been hope of him, or the danger had been less? For so Thou also, merciful Father, dost more rejoice over one penitent, than over ninety-nine just persons that need no repentance. And with much joyfulness do we hear, so often as we hear with what joy the sheep which has strayed is brought back upon the shepherd's shoulder, and the groat is restored to Thy treasury, the neighbors rejoicing with the woman who found it; and the joy of the solemn service of Thy house forceth to tears, when in Thy house it is read of Thy younger son, that he was dead and liveth again; had been lost and is found. For Thou rejoicest in us, and in Thy holy angels, holy through holy charity. For Thou art ever the same; for all things which abide not the same nor for ever, Thou for ever knowest in the same way. What then takes place in the soul, when it is more delighted at finding or recovering the things it loves, than if it had ever had them? yea, and other things witness hereunto; and all things are full of witnesses, crying out, "So is it."

The conquering commander triumpheth; yet had he not conquered unless he had fought; and the more peril there was in the battle, so much the more joy is there in the triumph. The storm tosses the sailors, threatens shipwreck; all wax pale at approaching death; sky and sea are calmed, and they are exceeding joyed, as having been exceeding afraid. A friend is sick, and his pulse threatens danger; all who long for his recovery are sick in mind with him. He is restored, though as yet he walks not with his former strength; yet there is such joy as was not when before he walked sound and strong.

Yea, the very pleasures of human life men acquire by difficulties, not only those which fall upon us unlooked for, and against our wills, but even by self-chosen, and pleasure-seeking trouble. Eating and drinking have no pleasure,

116

unless there precede the pinching of hunger and thirst. Men, given to drink, eat certain salt meats to procure a troublesome heat, which the drink allaying, causes pleasure. It is also ordered that the affianced bride should not at once be given, lest as a husband he should hold cheap her whom, as betrothed, he sighed not after.

This law holds in foul and accursed joy; in permitted and lawful joy; in the very purest perfection of friendship; in him who was dead, and lived again, had been lost and was found. Everywhere the greater joy is ushered in by the greater pain.

The following is also from Augustine. It seems to me that even if one were called upon to preach Sunday after Sunday, and in the same place, before the same congregation, we could do no better than to take this same text repeatedly. It is broad and deep enough to be the basis for a new sermon each week, especially the closing sentence:

But thy God is even unto thee Life of thy life.

Not with doubting, but with assured consciousness, do I love Thee, Lord. Thou hast smitten my heart with Thy word, and I loved Thee. Yea, also heaven, and earth, and all that therein is, behold on every side they bid me love Thee; nor cease to say so unto all, that they may be without excuse. But more deeply wilt Thou have mercy, and wilt have compassion on whom Thou hadst had compassion: else in deaf ears do the heaven and the earth speak Thy praises. But what do I love, when I love Thee? Not the beauty of bodies, nor the fair harmony of time, nor the brightness of the light so gladsome to our eyes, nor sweet melodies of varied songs, nor the fragrant smell of flowers and ointments and spices, not manna and honey, not limbs acceptable to the embracements of flesh. None of these do I love, when I love my God;

117

and yet I love a kind of light, a kind of melody, a kind of fragrance, a kind of meat, and a kind of embracement, when I love my God,—the light, the melody, the fragrance, the meat, the embracement of the inner man: where there shineth unto my soul, what space cannot contain, and there soundeth, what time beareth not away, and there smelleth, what breathing disperseth not, and there tasteth, what eating diminisheth not, and there clingeth, what satiety divorceth not. This is it which I love when I love my God.

And what is this? I asked the earth, and it answered me, "I am not He"; and whatsoever are in it confessed the same. I asked the sea and the deeps, and the living creeping things, and they answered, "We are not Thy God, seek above us." I asked the moving air; and the whole air with his inhabitants answered, "Anaximenes was deceived, I am not God." I asked the heavens, sun, moon, stars, "Nor (say they) are we the God whom thou seekest." And I replied unto all the things which encompass the door of my flesh: "Ye have told me of my God, that ye are not He; tell me something of Him." And they cried out with a loud voice, "He made us." My questioning them, was my thoughts in them: and their form of beauty gave the answer. And I turned myself unto myself, and said to myself, "Who art thou?" and I answered, "A man." And behold, in me there present themselves to me soul and body, one without, the other within.

By which of these ought I to seek my God? I had sought Him in the body from earth to heaven, so far as I could send messengers, the beams of mine eyes. But the better is the inner, for to it as presiding and judging, all the bodily messengers reported the answers of heaven and earth, and all things therein, who said, "We are not God, but He made us." These things did my inner man know by the ministry of the outer: I, the inner, knew them; I, the mind, through the senses of my body. I asked the whole frame of the world about my God; and it answered me, "I am not He, but He made me."

Now, O my soul (to thee I speak) thou art my better part: for thou quickenest the mass of my body, giving it life, which no body can give to a body: but thy God is even unto thee Life of thy life.

Following are quotations from a number of writers which the present compiler believes summarize, at least in part, the religious beliefs of the respective writers. The quotations as well as those already presented are given with approval; they represent beliefs of the present compiler. They are presented to readers for favorable consideration, critical review, acceptance, and active adoption.

From Francois Fenelon:

No human power can force the impenetrable intrenchments of liberty in the human heart. Force can never persuade men; it can only make them hypocrites. When kings interfere with religion, instead of protecting it, they enslave it. Grant to all religions a political toleration; not equally approving of all, as if you were indifferent, but patiently allowing all that God allows, and endeavoring to lead men by gentle persuasion.

How glorious is the spirit that is in man; it bears within itself what is far beyond its own comprehension. Its ideas are universal, eternal and immutable. They are universal, because when I say,—It is impossible to be and not to be; The whole is greater than a part; A perfectly circular line has no straight parts; Between two given points, the straightest line is the shortest; The center of a circle is equally distant from all the points in the circumference;—none of these truths can be controverted, there can be no line or circle that does not obey these laws. These truths are of all

119

time, or rather before all time, and will continue beyond it through an incomprehensible duration.

These fundamental ideas have no limits, and cannot be changed. It is impossible, whatever power we may exert over our minds, to make us seriously doubt anything that these ideas represent to us. The idea of infinity is within us in like manner. Change the ideas and you overthrow reason. Let us learn the greatness of our natures from this immutable idea of infinity, that is imprinted within us, and that can never be effaced. But, lest our real greatness should dazzle our eyes, and flatter us to our injury, let us hasten to contemplate our weakness.

The same mind that dwells upon the infinite, and through it sees the finite, is ignorant of all that surrounds it. It does not know itself. It gropes its way through an abyss of darkness. It knows not what it is itself. . . . It joins errors in opinion to a perverted will; and it is often reduced to groan and weep at the experience of its own corruption.

Two men who have never seen each other, who have never heard each other spoken of, and who have had no communication with any other man that could give them common notions, would speak, at the two extremities of the world, of certain truths in perfect unison. We know perfectly well beforehand in one hemisphere, what answer would be returned in the other, on certain truths. Men of all countries and of all times, whatever education they may have received, necessarily think and speak of some things in the same manner. It is the great Master that has taught us all, who thus bids us speak. Thus, when we think most of our own powers, of ourselves, that is, of our reason, this is what the least belongs to us, this is most truly a borrowed good.

We are every moment of our lives receiving a reason far superior to ourselves, just as we inhale the air from without, or as we see objects around us by the light of the sun that does not belong to our vision. It is this noble reason that reigns with an absolute dominion, to a certain point, over rational beings. It is this that makes a Canadian savage think many things that Greek and Roman philosophers have thought. It is this that led the Chinese geometricians to the discovery of the same truths that the Europeans, who knew nothing of them, have become acquainted with. It is this that makes men think upon various subjects, just as they thought a thousand years ago. It is this power that gives a uniformity to the opinions of men, the most opposed to each other in their natures. It is by this that men of all ages and countries are bound to an immovable centre to which they are held by certain invariable laws, which we call first principles; notwithstanding the infinite variety of opinions that are created by their passions, their distractions, their caprices upon all other less clear truths. It is this power that has kept men, depraved as they are, from daring to call virtue vice, and that has obliged them to put on the appearance, at least, of sincerity, moderation, and beneficence, when they would attract esteem.

They cannot esteem or despise anything according to their own arbitrary wills; they cannot force the eternal barriers of truth and justice. The law of the soul, which we call reason, reigns with an absolute sway; its reproaches are ever uttered and repeated at what is wrong; it sets bounds to the folly of the most audacious.

After vice has enjoyed so many ages of unrestrained sway, virtue is still called virtue; and it cannot be dispossessed of its name by its boldest and most brutal enemies. From thence it is that vice, although triumphant in the world, is still forced to disguise itself under the mask of hypocrisy, that it may secure a regard that it does not hope for when it is known as it is. Thus it renders in spite of itself, homage to virtue, by adorning itself with her charms, that it may receive the honors that are rendered to them. Men cavil, it is true, at the virtuous, and they are, in truth, always liable to censure, for they are still imperfect; but the most vicious men cannot succeed in effacing entirely the idea of virtue. No man has succeeded in persuading others, or himself, that it is more estimable to be deceitful, than to be sincere; to be violent and malignant, than to be gentle and do good. This inward and universal teacher declares the same truths, at all times and places. It is true that we often contradict it, and speak with a louder voice; but then we deceive ourselves, we go astray, we fear that we shall discover that we are wrong, and we shut our ears, lest we should be humbled by its corrections. Where is this wisdom, where is this oracle that ever speaks, and against which the prejudices of mankind can never prevail? Where is this noble reason that we are bound to consult, and which of itself inspires us with a desire to hear its voice? Where dwells this pure and gentle light, that not only enlightens eyes that are open to receive it, but uncloses those eyes that were shut, cures those that were diseased, gives vision to the blind; in short, inspires a desire for the light it can bestow, and makes itself beloved even by those who fear it?

Every eye has it; it would see nothing without it; it is by its pure rays alone that it can see anything. As the visible sun enlightens all material bodies, so the sun of intelligence illuminates all minds.

Universal Light! it is through thee alone that we see anything. Sun of the soul, who dost shine more brightly than the material sun! seeing nothing except through thee, we see not thee thyself. It is thou who givest all things, to the stars their light, to the fountains their waters and their courses, to the earth its plants, to the fruits their flavor, to all nature its riches and its beauty, to man health, reason, virtue, thou givest all, thou doest all, thou rulest over all; I see only thee, all other things vanish as a shadow before him who has once seen thee.

It is not to know thee, O God, to regard thee only as an

all-powerful being who gives laws to all nature, and who hast created everything which we see, it is only to know a part of thy being, it is not to know that which is most wonderful and most affecting to thy rational offspring. That which transports and melts my soul is to know that thou art the God of my heart. Thou doest there thy good pleasure.

There is a superior law that raises us above all this, and introduces us into the true liberty of the children of God. It is this; that we ever desire to do all that we can to please our Father in heaven, according to the excellent instruction of St. Augustin, Love God, and then do all you wish.

We never love our neighbor so truly, as when our love for him is prompted by the love of God.

The love of God never looks for perfection in created beings. It knows that it dwells with him alone. As it never expects perfection, it is never disappointed. It loves God and all his gifts to every living thing, according to their respective value. It loves less what is less excellent, and more what is nearer to perfection. It loves all, for there is no one that is not endowed with some good which is the gift of God, and it remembers that the vilest may become good, and receive that grace which they now want. He who loves God, loves all his works—all that he has commanded us to love. He loves more those whom God has pleased to render more dear to him. He sees in an earthly parent the love of his heavenly Father. In a relative, in a friend, he acknowledges those tender ties that God has ordained. The more strictly those bonds are in the order of his providence, the more the love of God sanctions them, and renders them strong and intimate.

Can we love God without loving those beings whom He has commanded us to love? It is He that inspires this love; it is his will that we should love them; shall we not obey Him?

This love can endure all things, suffer all things, hope all things, for our neighbor. It can conquer all difficulties; it flows from the heart, and sheds a charm upon the manners. It is melted at the sorrows of others, and thinks nothing of its own; it gives consolation where it is needed; it is gentle, it adapts itself to others; it weeps with those who weep; it rejoices with those who rejoice; it is all things to all men, not in a forced appearance and in cold demonstrations, but from a full and overflowing heart, in which the love of God is a living spring of the tenderest, the deepest, and the truest feeling. Nothing is so sterile, so cold, so senseless, as a heart that loves only itself in all things; while nothing can exceed the frankness, the tenderness, the gentle loveliness of a heart, filled and animated by the divine love.

From Immanuel Kant:

Nothing can possibly be conceived in the world, or even out of it, which can be called good without qualification, except a Good Will. Intelligence, wit, judgment, and the other *talents* of the mind, however they may be named, or courage, resolution, perseverance, as qualities of temperament, are undoubtedly good and desirable in many respects; but these gifts of nature may also become extremely bad and mischievous if the will which is to make use of them, and which, therefore, constitutes what is called *character*, is not good. It is the same with the *gifts of fortune*. Power, riches, honour, even health, and the general well-being and contentment with one's condition which is called *happiness*, inspire pride, and often presumption, if there is not a good will to correct the influence of these on the mind, and with this also to rectify the whole principle of acting, and adapt it to its end. The sight of a being who is not adorned with a single feature of a pure and good will, enjoying unbroken prosperity, can never give pleasure to an impartial rational spectator. Thus a good will appears to constitute the indispensable condition even of being worthy of happiness.

Nor could anything be more fatal to morality than that we should wish to derive it from examples. For every example of it that is set before me must be first itself tested by principles of morality, whether it is worthy to serve as an original example, *i.e.* as a pattern, but by no means can it authoritatively furnish the conception of morality. Even the Holy One of the Gospels must first be compared with our ideal of moral perfection before we can recognise Him as such; and so He says of Himself, "Why call ye ME (whom you see) good; none is good (the model of good) but God only (whom ye do not see)?" But whence have we the conception of God as the supreme good? Simply from the *idea* of moral perfection, which reason frames *à priori*, and connects inseparably with the notion of a free-will. Imitation finds no place at all in morality, and examples serve only for encouragement, *i.e.* they put beyond doubt the feasibility of what the law commands, they make visible that which the practical rule expresses more generally, but they can never authorise us to set aside the true original which lies in reason, and to guide ourselves by examples.

The imperative of duty may be expressed thus: *Act as if the maxim of thy action were to become by thy will a Universal Law of Nature.*

Man and generally any rational being *exists* as an end in himself, *not merely as a means* to be arbitrarily used by this or that will, but in all his actions, whether they concern himself or other rational beings, must be always regarded at the same time as an end. All objects of the inclinations have only a conditional worth, for if the inclinations and the wants founded on them did not exist, then their object would be without value. But the inclinations themselves being sources of want, are so far from having an absolute worth for which they should be desired, that on the contrary it must be the universal wish of every rational being to be wholly free from them. Thus the worth of any object which is to be *acquired* by our action is always conditional. Beings whose existence depends not on our will but on nature's, have nevertheless, if they are irrational beings, only a relative value as means, and are therefore called *things;* rational beings, on the contrary, are called persons, because their very nature points them out as ends in themselves, that is as something which must not be used merely as means, and so far therefore restricts freedom of action (and is an object of respect).

So act as to treat humanity, whether in thine own person or in that of any other, in every case as an end withal, never as means only.

The will of every rational being is a universally legislative will.

All rational beings come under the *law* that each of them must treat itself and all others *never merely as means,* but in every case *at the same time as ends in themselves.* Hence results a systematic union of rational beings by common objective laws, *i.e.,* a kingdom which may be called a kingdom of ends, since what these laws have in view is just the relation of these beings to one another as ends and means. It is certainly only an ideal.

A rational being belongs as a *member* to the kingdom of ends when, although giving universal laws in it, he is also himself subject to these laws. He belongs to it *as sovereign* when, while giving laws, he is not subject to the will of any other.

A rational being must always regard himself as giving laws either as member or as sovereign in a kingdom of ends which is rendered possible by the freedom of will. He cannot, however, maintain the latter position merely by the maxims of his will, but only in case he is a completely independent being without wants and with unrestricted power adequate to his will.

Morality consists then in the reference of all action to the legislation which alone can render a kingdom of ends possible. This legislation must be capable of existing in every rational being, and of emanating from his will, so that the principle of this will is, never to act on any maxim which could not without contradiction be also a universal law, and accordingly always so to act *that the will could at the same time regard itself as giving in its maxims universal laws.* If now the maxims of rational beings are not by their own nature coincident with this objective principle, then the necessity of acting on it is called practical necessitation, *i.e., duty.* Duty does not apply to the sovereign in the kingdom of ends, but it does to every member of it and to all in the same degree.

The practical necessity of acting on this principle, *i.e.,* duty, does not rest at all on feelings, impulses, or inclinations, but solely on the relation of rational beings to one another, a relation in which the will of a rational being must always be regarded as *legislative,* since otherwise it could not be conceived as *an end in itself.* Reason then refers every maxim of the will, regarding it as legislating universally, to every other will and also to every action towards oneself; and this not on account of any other practical motive or any future advantage, but from the idea of the *dignity* of a rational being, obeying no law but that which he himself also gives.

In the kingdom of ends everything has either Value or Dignity. Whatever has a value can be replaced by something else which is *equivalent;* whatever, on the other hand, is above value, and therefore admits of no equivalent, has a dignity.

Whatever has reference to the general inclinations and wants of mankind has a *market value;* whatever, without presupposing a want, corresponds to a certain taste, that is to a satisfaction in the mere purposeless play of our faculties, has a *fancy value;* but that which constitutes the condition under which alone anything can be an end in itself, this has not merely a relative worth, *i.e.,* value, but an intrinsic worth, that is *dignity.*

Now morality is the condition under which alone a rational being can be an end in himself, since by this alone it is possible that he should be a legislating member in the kingdom of ends. Thus morality, and humanity as capable of it, is that which alone has dignity. Skill and diligence in labour have a market value; wit, lively imagination, and humour, have fancy value; on the other hand, fidelity to promises, benevolence from principle (not from instinct), have an intrinsic worth. Neither nature nor art contains anything which in default of these it could put in their place, for their worth consists not in the effects which spring from them, not in the use and advantage which they secure, but in the disposition of mind, that is, the maxims of the will which are ready to manifest themselves in such actions, even though they should not have the desired effect. These actions also need no recommendation from any subjective taste or sentiment, that they may be looked on with immediate favour and satisfaction: they need no immediate propension or feeling for them; they exhibit the will that performs them as an object of an immediate respect, and nothing but reason is required to *impose* them on the will; not to *flatter* it into them, which, in the case of duties, would be a contradiction. This estimation therefore shows that the worth of such a disposition is dignity, and places it infinitely above all value, with which it cannot for a moment be brought into comparison or competition without as it were violating its sanctity.

What then is it which justifies virtue or the morally good disposition, in making such lofty claims? It is nothing less than the privilege it secures to the rational being of participating in the giving of universal laws, by which it qualifies him to be a member of a possible kingdom of ends, a privilege to which he was already destined by his own nature as being an end in himself, and on that account legislating in the kingdom of ends; free as regards all laws of physical nature, and obeying those only which he himself gives, and by which his maxims can belong to a system of universal law, to which at the same time he submits himself. For nothing has any worth except what the law assigns it. Now the legislation itself which assigns the worth of everything, must for that very reason possess dignity, that is an unconditional incomparable worth, and the word *respect* alone supplies a becoming expression for the esteem which a rational being must have for it. *Autonomy* then is the basis of human and of every rational nature.

Fontenelle says, "I bow before a great man, but my mind does not bow." I would add, before an humble plain man, in whom I perceive uprightness of character in a higher degree than I am conscious of in myself, *my mind bows* whether I choose it or not, and though I bear my head never so high that he may not forget my superior rank. Why is this? Because his example exhibits to me a law that humbles my self-conceit when I compare it with my conduct: a law, the *practicability* of obedience to which I see proved by fact before my eyes. Now, I may even be conscious of a like degree of uprightness, and yet the respect remains. For since in man all good is defective, the law made visible by an example still humbles my pride, my standard being furnished by a man whose imperfections, whatever they may be, are not known to me as my own are, and who therefore appears to me in a more favourable light. *Respect* is a *tribute* which we cannot refuse to merit, whether we will or not; we may indeed outwardly withhold it, but we cannot help feeling it inwardly.

There is something so singular in the unbounded esteem for the pure moral law, apart from all advantage, as it is

129

presented for our obedience by practical reason, the voice of which makes even the boldest sinner tremble, and compels him to hide himself from it, that we cannot wonder if we find this influence of a mere intellectual idea on the feelings quite incomprehensible to speculative reason, and have to be satisfied with seeing so much of this *à priori*, that such a feeling is inseparably connected with the conception of the moral law in every finite rational being.

Duty! Thou sublime and mighty name that dost embrace nothing charming or insinuating, but requirest submission, and yet seekest not to move the will by threatening aught that would arouse natural aversion or terror, but merely holdest forth a law which of itself finds entrance into the mind, and yet gains reluctant reverence (though not always obedience), a law before which all inclinations are dumb, even though they secretly counter-work it; what origin is there worthy of thee, and where is to be found the root of thy noble descent which proudly rejects all kindred with the inclinations; a root to be derived from which is the indispensable condition of the only worth which men can give themselves?

It can be nothing less than a power which elevates man above himself (as a part of the world of sense), a power which connects him with an order of things that only the understanding can conceive, with a world which at the same time commands the whole sensible world, and with it the empirically determinable existence of man in time, as well as the sum total of all ends (which totality alone suits such unconditional practical laws as the moral). This power is nothing but *personality*, that is, freedom and independence on the mechanism of nature, yet, regarded also as a faculty of a being which is subject to special laws, namely, pure practical laws given by its own reason; so that the person as belonging to the sensible world is subject to his own personality as belonging to the intelligible (supersensible) world.

It is then not to be wondered at that man, as belonging to both worlds, must regard his own nature in reference to its second and highest characteristic only with reverence and its laws with the highest respect.

On this origin are founded many expressions which designate the worth of objects according to moral ideas. The moral law is *holy* (inviolable). Man is indeed unholy enough, but he must regard *humanity* in his own person as holy. In all creation everything one chooses, and over which one has any power, may be used *merely as means;* man alone, and with him every rational creature, is an *end in himself.* By virtue of the autonomy of his freedom he is the subject of the moral law, which is holy. Just for this reason every will, even every person's own individual will, in relation to itself, is restricted to the condition of agreement with the *autonomy* of the rational being, that is to say, that it is not to be subject to any purpose which cannot accord with a law which might arise from the will of the passive subject himself; the latter is, therefore, never to be employed merely as means, but as itself also, concurrently, an end. We justly attribute this condition even to the Divine will, with regard to the rational beings in the world, which are His creatures, since it rests on their *personality,* by which alone they are ends in themselves.

From Dante:

His glory, by whose might all things are moved,
Pierces the universe, and in one part
Sheds more resplendence, elsewhere less.

Whate'er
Is in the church's keeping, all pertains
To such, as sue for heaven's sweet sake.

Keep
The choicest of thy love for God.

131

And, if I am a timid friend to truth,
I fear my life may perish among those,
To whom these days shall be of ancient date.

By that truth alone
Enlighten'd, beyond which no truth may roam,
Our mind can satisfy her thirst to know.

From Frederick Denison Maurice:

Above all, to reverence the facts of history, and to believe that the least perversion of them, for the sake of getting a moral from them, is at once a folly and a sin.

I learnt that beauty is neither an accidental nor an artificial thing, that it is to be sought out as something which is both in nature and in the mind of man, and which, by God's law, binds us to her.

Oftentimes, I doubt not, every man is tempted to repose in some little nook or dell of thought, where other men will not molest him, because he does not molest them; but those to whom any work is assigned are soon driven, by a power which they cannot resist, out of such retirement into the dusty highways of ordinary business and disputation.

A Church Universal, not built upon human inventions or human faith, but upon the very nature of God himself, and upon the union which He has formed with his creatures: a church revealed to man as a fixed and eternal reality by means which infinite wisdom had itself devised.

Assuredly the idea of an obedience in man, which has no ground to rest upon; which was foreseen by God, but not derived from Him; of something good, therefore, which cannot be traced ultimately to the Fountain of good; nay, which exists independently of it, that is to say, under what we are wont to consider the very condition of evil—is a most agonizing contradiction. And what need have we of it? Only do

132

not suppose the Being whom you worship to be a mere power; only acknowledge him to be that in reality which you say in words that He is, the essential truth and goodness; only suppose the absolute will to be a will to good, and how can we imagine that Happiness, Obedience, Freedom, have their origin any where but in Him; that misery, disobedience, slavery, mean any thing but revolt and separation from Him?

From Robert Browning:

Had the young David but sat first to dine on his cheeses with the Philistine, he had soon discovered an abundance of such common sympathies. He of Gath, it is recorded, was born of a father and mother, had brothers and sisters like another man,—they, no more than the sons of Jesse, were used to eat each other. But, for the sake of one broad antipathy that had existed from the beginning, David slung the stone, cut off the giant's head, made a spoil of it, and after ate his cheeses alone, with the better appetite, for all I can learn. My friend, as you, with a quickened eyesight, go on discovering much good on the worse side, remember that the same process should proportionably magnify and demonstrate to you the much more good on the better side! And when I profess no sympathy for the Goliaths of our time, and you object that a large nature should sympathize with every form of intelligence, and see the good in it, however limited,—I answer, "So I do; but preserve the proportions of my sympathy, however finelier or widelier I may extend its action." I desire to be able, with a quickened eyesight, to descry beauty in corruption where others see foulness only; but I hope I shall also continue to see a redoubled beauty in the higher forms of matter, where already everybody sees no foulness at all. I must retain, too, my old power of selection, and choice of appropriation, to apply to

133

such new gifts; else they only dazzle instead of enlightening
me. God has his archangels and consorts with them: though
he made too, and intimately sees what is good in, the worm.

After how many modes, this Christmas-Eve,
Does the self-same weary thing take place?
The same endeavor to make you believe,
And with much the same effect, no more:
Each method abundantly convincing,
As I say, to those convinced before,
But scarce to be swallowed without wincing
By the not-as-yet-convinced. For me,
I have my own church equally:
And in this church my faith sprang first!
(I said, as I reached the rising ground,
And the wind began again, with a burst
Of rain in my face, and a glad rebound
From the heart beneath, as if, God speeding me,
I entered his church-door, nature leading me)
—In youth I looked to these very skies,
And probing their immensities,
I found God there, his visible power;
Yet felt in my heart, amid all its sense
Of the power, an equal evidence
That his love, there too, was the nobler dower.

God who registers the cup
Of mere cold water, for his sake
To a disciple rendered,
Disdains not his own thirst to slake
At the poorest love was ever offered:
And beause my heart I proffered,
With true love trembling at the brim,
He suffers me to follow him
Forever, my own way,—dispensed

From seeking to be influenced
By all the less immediate ways
That earth, in worships manifold,
Adopts to reach, by prayer and praise,
The garment's hem, which, lo, I hold!

Needs must there be one way, our chief
Best way of worship: let me strive
To find it, and when found, contrive
My fellows also take their share!
This constitutes my earthly care:
God's is above it and distinct,
For I, a man, with men am linked
And not a brute with brutes; no gain
That I experience, must remain
Unshared: but should my best endeavor
To share it, fail—subsisteth ever
God's care above, and I exult
That God, by God's own ways occult,
May—doth, I will believe—bring back
All wanderers to a single track.
Meantime, I can but testify
God's care for me—no more, can I—
It is but for myself I know.

The common problem, yours, mine, every one's,
Is—not to fancy what were fair in life
Provided it could be,—but, finding first
What may be, then find how to make it fair
Up to our means: a very different thing!

My business is not to remake myself,
But make the absolute best of what God made.

I have not chanted verse like Homer, no—
Nor swept string like Terpander, no—nor carved
And painted men like Phidias and his friend:

I am not great as they are, point by point.
But I have entered into sympathy
With these four, running these into one soul,
Who, separate, ignored each other's art.
Say, is it nothing that I know them all?
The wild flower was the larger; I have dashed
Rose-blood upon its petals, pricked its cup's
Honey with wine, and driven its seed to fruit,
And show a better flower if not so large;

From Jonathan Edwards:

Whatever controversies and variety of opinions there are
about the nature of virtue, yet all (excepting some skeptics,
who deny any real difference between virtue and vice) mean
by it, something *beautiful*, or rather some kind of *beauty*,
or excellency. It is not *all* beauty, that is called virtue; for
instance, not the beauty of a building, of a flower, or of the
rainbow: But some beauty belonging to Beings that have
perception and *will*. It is not all beauty of *mankind* that is
called virtue; for instance, not the external beauty of the
countenance, or shape, gracefulness of motion, or harmony
of voice: But it is a beauty that has its original seat in the
mind. But yet perhaps not *every* thing that may be called a
beauty of mind is properly called virtue. There is a beauty
of understanding and speculation. There is something in
the ideas and conceptions of great philosophers and statesmen that may be called beautiful; which is a different thing
from what is commonly meant by virtue. But virtue is the
beauty of those qualities and acts of the mind, that are of a
moral nature, i.e., such as are attended with desert or worth-
iness of *praise*, or *blame*. Things of this sort, it is generally
agreed, so far as I know, are not anything belonging merely
to speculation; but to the *disposition* and *will*, or (to use a
general word, I suppose, commonly well understood) the

heart. Therefore I suppose, I shall not depart from the common opinion, when I say, that virtue is the beauty of the qualities and exercises of the heart, or those actions which proceed from them.

Those *schemes* of religion or moral philosophy, which, however well in some respects, they may treat of benevolence to *mankind,* and other virtues depending on it, yet have not a supreme regard to God, and love to him, laid in the *foundation,* and all other virtues handled in a *connexion* with this, and in a *subordination* to this, are not true schemes of philosophy, but are fundamentally and essentially defective. And whatever other benevolence or generosity towards mankind, and other virtues, or moral qualifications which go by that name, any are possessed of, that are not attended with a *love to God* which is altogether above them, and to which they are subordinate, and on which they are dependent, there is nothing of the nature of true virtue or religion in them. And it may be asserted in general that nothing is of the nature of true virtue in which God is not the *first* and the *last;* or which with regard to their exercises in general, have not their first foundation and source in apprehensions of God's supreme dignity and glory, and in answerable esteem and love of him, and have not respect to God as the supreme end.

There is a twofold understanding or knowledge of good that God has made the mind of man capable of. The first, that which is merely speculative and notional; as when a person only speculatively judges that anything is, which, by the agreement of mankind, is called good or excellent, viz. that which is most to general advantage, and between which and a reward there is a suitableness, and the like. And the other is, that which consists in the sense of the heart: As when there is a sense of the beauty, amiableness, or sweetness of a thing; so that the heart is sensible of pleasure and delight in the presence of the idea of it. In the former is exercised merely the speculative faculty, or the understanding, strictly so called, or as spoken of in distinction from the will or disposition of the soul. In the latter, the will, or inclination, or heart is mainly concerned.

Thus there is a difference between having an opinion, that God is holy and gracious, and having a sense of the loveliness and beauty of that holiness and grace. There is a difference between having a rational judgment that honey is sweet, and having a sense of its sweetness. A man may have the former, that knows not how honey tastes; but a man cannot have the latter unless he has an idea of the taste of honey in his mind. So there is a difference between believing that a person is beautiful, and having a sense of his beauty. The former may be obtained by hearsay, but the latter only by seeing the countenance. There is a wide difference between mere speculative rational judging any thing to be excellent, and having a sense of its sweetness and beauty. The former rests only in the head, speculation only is concerned in it; but the heart is concerned in the latter. When the heart is sensible of the beauty and amiableness of a thing, it necessarily feels pleasure in the apprehension. It is implied in a person's being heartily sensible of the loveliness of a thing, that the idea of it is sweet and pleasant to the soul; which is a far different thing from having a rational opinion that it is excellent.

Although to true religion there must indeed be something else besides affection; yet true religion consists so much in the affections, that there can be no true religion without them. He who has no religious affection is in a state of spiritual death, and is wholly destitute of the powerful quickening, saving influences of the Spirit of God upon his heart. As there is no true religion where there is nothing but affection, so there is no true religion where there is no religious affection. As on the one hand there must be light in the understanding, as well as an affected fervent heat; or where there is heat without light, there can be nothing divine or heavenly in that heart: so, on the other hand, where there is a kind of light without heat, a head stored with notions and speculations with a cold and unaffected heart, there can be nothing divine in that light; that knowledge is no true spiritual knowledge of divine things.

If the great things of religion are rightly understood they will affect the heart. The reason men are not affected by such infinitely great, important, glorious, and wonderful things, as they often hear and read of in the word of God, is, undoubtedly, because they are blind; if they were not so, it would be impossible, and utterly inconsistent with human nature that their hearts should be otherwise than strongly impressed, and greatly moved by such things.

From Elizabeth Barrett Browning:

> For the truth itself,
> That's neither man's nor woman's, but just God's;
> None else has reason to be proud of truth;
> Himself will see it sifted, disinthralled,
> And kept upon the height and in the light,
> As far as and no farther than 'tis truth:
> For now he has left off calling firmaments
> And strata, flowers and creatures, very good,
> He says it still of truth, which is his own.

> "There's nothing great
> Nor small," has said a poet of our day,
> Whose voice will ring beyond the curfew of eve,
> And not be thrown out by the matin's bell:
> And truly, I reiterate, Nothing's small!

> No lily-muffled hum of a summer-bee,
> But finds some coupling with the spinning stars;
> No pebble at your foot, but proves a sphere;
> No chaffinch, but implies the cherubim;

And (glancing on my own thin, veined wrist)
In such a little tremor of the blood
The whole strong clamor of a vehement soul
Doth utter itself distinct. Earth's crammed with heaven,
And every common bush afire with God;
But only he who sees takes off his shoes,
The rest sit round it and pluck blackberries,
And daub their natural faces unaware
More and more from the first similitude.

How sure it is,
That, if we say a true word, instantly
We feel, 'tis God's, not ours, and pass it on,
Like bread at sacrament we taste and pass,
Nor handle for a moment, as indeed
We dared to set up any claim to such!

What height we know not, but the way we know,
And how, by mounting ever, we attain,
And so climb on. It is the hour for souls,
That bodies, leavened by the will and love,
Be lightened to redemption. The world's old;
But the old world waits the time to be renewed,
Toward which new hearts in individual growth
Must quicken, and increase to multitude
In new dynasties of the race of men,
Developed whence shall grow spontaneously
New churches, new economies, new laws
Admitting freedom, new societies
Excluding falsehood: HE shall make all new.

From Amiel:

To be misunderstood even by those whom one loves is
the cross and bitterness of life. It is the secret of that sad
and melancholy smile on the lips of great men which so few

140

understand; it is the cruelest trial reserved for self-devotion; . . . if God could suffer, it would be the wound we should be forever inflicting upon Him. He also—He above all—is the great misunderstood, the least comprehended. Alas! alas! Never to tire, never to grow cold; to be patient, sympathetic, tender; to look for the budding flower and the opening heart; to hope always, like God; to love always,—this is duty.

Each man enters into God so much as God enters into him, or as Angelus, I think, said 'the eye by which I see God is the same eye by which He sees me.'

The cardinal question is that of sin. The question of immanence or of dualism is secondary. The Trinity, the life to come, paradise and hell, may cease to be dogmas and spiritual realities, the form and the letter may vanish away, —the question of humanity remains: What is it which saves? How can man be led to be truly man? Is the ultimate root of his being responsibility,—yes or no? And is doing or knowing the right, acting or thinking, his ultimate end? If science does not produce love it is insufficient. Now, all that science gives is the *amor intellectualis* of Spinoza, light without warmth, a resignation which is contemplative and grandiose, but inhuman, because it is scarcely transmissible and remains a privilege, one of the rarest of all. Moral love places the centre of the individual in the centre of being. It has at least salvation in principle, the germ of eternal life. *To love is virtually to know; to know is not virtually to love;* there you have the relation of these two modes of man. The redemption wrought by science or by intellectual love is then inferior to the redemption wrought by will or by moral love. The first may free a man from himself, it may enfranchise him from egotism. The second drives the *ego* out of itself, makes it active and fruitful. The one is critical, purifying, negative; and the other is vivifying, fertilising, positive. Science, however spiritual and substantial it may

141

be in itself, is still formal relatively to love. Moral force is then the vital point.

And this force is only produced by moral force. Like alone acts upon like. Therefore do not amend by reasoning, but by example; approach feeling by feeling; do not hope to excite love except by love. Be what you wish others to become. Let yourself and not your words preach for you.

Science is the power of man, and love his strength; man *becomes* man only by the intelligence, but he *is* man only by the heart. Knowledge, love, power,—there is the complete life.

Every life is a profession of faith, and exercises an inevitable and silent propaganda. As far as lies in its power, it tends to transform the universe and humanity into its own image. Thus we have all a cure of souls. Every man is a centre of perpetual radiation like a luminous body; he is, as it were, a beacon which entices a ship upon the rocks if it does guide it into port. Every man is a priest, even involuntarily: his conduct is an unspoken sermon, which is for ever preaching to others;—but there are priests of Baal, of Moloch, and of all the false gods. Such is the high importance of example. Thence comes the terrible responsibility which weighs upon us all. An evil example is a spiritual poison; it is the proclamation of a sacrilegious faith, of an impure God. Sin would be only an evil for him who commits it, were it not a crime towards the weak brethren, whom it corrupts. Therefore it has been said: 'It were better for a man not to have been born than to offend one of these little ones.'

Every despotism has a specially keen and hostile instinct for whatever keeps up human dignity and independence. And it is curious to see scientific and realist teaching used everywhere as a means of stifling all freedom of investigation as addressed to moral questions, under a dead weight of facts. Materialism is the auxiliary doctrine of every tyranny, whether of one or of the masses. To crush what is spiritual, moral, human—so to speak—in man, by specialising him; to form mere wheels of the great social machine, instead of perfect individuals; to make society and not conscience the centre of life, to enslave the soul to things, to de-personalise man,—this is the dominant drift of our epoch. Everywhere you may see a tendency to substitute the laws of dead matter (number, mass) for the laws of the moral nature (persuasion, adhesion, faith); equality, the principle of mediocrity, becoming a dogma; unity aimed at through uniformity; numbers doing duty for argument; negative liberty, which has no law *in itself*, and recognises no limit except in force, everywhere taking the place of positive liberty, which means action guided by an inner law and curbed by a moral authority.

What is threatened to-day is moral liberty, conscience, respect for the soul, the very nobility of man. To defend the soul, its interests, its rights, its dignity, is the most pressing duty for whoever sees the danger. What the writer, the teacher, the pastor, the philosopher, has to do, is to defend humanity in man. Man! the true man, the ideal man! Such should be their motto, their rallying cry. War to all that debases, diminishes, hinders, and degrades him; protection for all that fortifies, ennobles, and raises him. The test of every religious, political, or educational system, is the man which it forms. If a system injures the intelligence it is bad. If it injures the character it is vicious. If it injures the conscience it is criminal.

Love at its highest point,—love sublime, unique, invincible,—leads us straight to the brink of the great abyss, for it speaks to us directly of the infinite and of eternity. It is eminently religious: it may even become religion.—When all around a man is wavering and changing,—when everything is growing dark and featureless to him in the far distance of an unknown future,—when the world seems but a

143

fiction or a fairy tale, and the universe a chimera,—when the whole edifice of ideas vanishes in smoke, and all realities are penetrated with doubt,—what is the fixed point which may still be his? ... Who knows if love and its beatitude, clear manifestation as it is of the universal harmony of things, is not the best demonstration of a fatherly and understanding God, just as it is the shortest road by which to reach Him? Love is a faith, and one faith leads to another. And this faith is happiness, light, and force. Only by it does a man enter into the series of the living, the awakened, the happy, the redeemed,—of those true men who know the value of existence and who labour for the glory of God and of the Truth.

Truth above all, even when it upsets and overwhelms us! But what I believe is that the highest idea we can conceive of the principle of things will be the truest, and that the truest truth is that which makes man the most wholly good, wisest, greatest, and happiest.

My creed is in transition. Yet I still believe in God, and the immortality of the soul. I believe in holiness, truth, beauty; I believe in the redemption of the soul by faith in forgiveness. I believe in love, devotion, honour. I believe in duty and the moral conscience. I believe even in prayer. I believe in the fundamental intuitions of the human race, and in the great affirmations of the inspired of all ages. I believe that our higher nature is our true nature.

Wisdom never grows old, for she is the expression of order itself,—that is of the Eternal. Only the wise man draws from life, and from every stage of it, its true savour, because only he feels the beauty, the dignity, and the value of life. The flowers of youth may fade, but the summer, the autumn, and even the winter of human existence, have their majestic grandeur, which the wise man recognises and glorifies. To see all things in God, to make of one's own life a journey towards the ideal; to live with gratitude, with devoutness, with gentleness and courage;—this was the splendid aim of Marcus Aurelius. And if you add to it the humility which kneels, and the charity which gives, you have the whole wisdom of the children of God.

From Epictetus:

With respect to gods, there are some who say that a divine being does not exist; others say that it exists, but is inactive and careless, and takes no forethought about anything; a third class say that such a being exists and exercises forethought, but only about great things and heavenly things, and about nothing on the earth; a fourth class say that a divine being exercises forethought both about things on the earth and heavenly things, but in a general way only, and not about things severally. There is a fifth class to whom Ulysses and Socrates belong, who say: "I move not without thy knowledge."

For he knew that no man is an orphan; but it is the father who takes care of all men always and continuously. For it was not as mere report that he had heard that Zeus is the father of men, for he thought that Zeus was his own father, and he called him so, and to him he looked when he was doing what he did. Therefore he was enabled to live happily in all places.

From Marcus Aurelius:

If any man is able to convince me and show me that I do not think or act right, I will gladly change; for I seek the truth, by which no man was ever injured. But he is injured who abides in his error and ignorance.

To them that ask thee, Where hast thou seen the Gods, or how knowest thou certainly that there be Gods, that thou art so devout in their worship? I answer first of all, that even to the very eye, they are in some manner visible and apparent. Secondly, neither have I ever seen mine own soul, and yet I respect and honour it. So then for the Gods, by the daily experience that I have of their power and providence towards myself and others, I know certainly that they are, and therefore worship them.

From Cleanthes:

All-glorious Eternal of many a name, almighty for aye;
God, Lord of Nature, whose laws all worlds in the universe
    sway,
All hail!—it is fitting that mortals uplift their voices to thee,
For thine offspring we are; alone in thine image created
    are we,
What mortals soever be living and moving the wide earth
    o'er.

O God all-giver, O Rider on dark cloud, Levin-lord,
From the drear dank mist of our ignorance lift us heaven-
    ward!
O Father, dispel from our souls this darkness! To Wisdom's
    school
Guide us, for thou in her strength with justice the worlds
    dost rule;
That the honour vouchsafed us of thee we may with worship
    requite,
Unceasingly hymning thy mighty works, as is meet and
    right.
No greater glory for mortals nor yet for immortals can be
Than to chant the Law universal on justice founded of thee.

From John Greenleaf Whittier:

O Golden Age, whose light is of the dawn,
And not of sunset, forward, not behind,
Flood the new heavens and earth, and with thee bring
All the old virtues, whatsoever things

146

Are pure and honest and of good repute,
But add thereto whatever bard has sung
Or seer has told of when in trance and dream
They saw the Happy Isles of prophecy!
Let Justice hold her scale, and Truth divide
Between the right and wrong; but give the heart
The freedom of its fair inheritance;
Let the poor prisoner, cramped and starved so long,
At nature's table feast his ear and eye
With joy and wonder; let all the harmonies
Of sound, form, color, motion, wait upon
The princely guest, whether in soft attire
Of leisure clad, or the coarse frock of toil.

Let common need, the brotherhood of prayer,
The heirship of an unknown destiny,
The unsolved mystery round about us, make
A man more precious than the gold of Ophir.
Sacred, inviolate, unto whom all things
Should minister, as outward types and signs
Of the eternal beauty which fulfils
The one great purpose of creation, Love,
The sole necessity of Earth and Heaven!

　　　Truth is one;
And in all lands beneath the sun,
Whoso hath eyes to see may see
The tokens of its unity.
No scroll of creed its fulness wraps,
We trace it not by school-boy maps,
Free as the sun and air it is
Of latitudes and boundaries.
In Vedic verse, in dull Koran,
Are messages of good to man;
The angels to our Aryan sires
Talked by the earliest household fires;

147

The prophets of the elder day,
The slant-eyed sages of Cathay,
Read not the riddle all amiss
Of higher life evolved from this.
The path of life we walk to-day
    Is strange as that the Hebrews trod:
We need the shadowing rock, as they,—
    We need, like them, the guides of God.

God send His angels, Cloud and Fire,
    To lead us o'er the desert sand!
God give our hearts their long desire,
    His shadow in a weary land!

Enough for me to feel and know
That He in whom the cause and end,
The past, and future, meet and blend,—
Who, girt with his Immensities,
Our vast and star-hung system sees,
Small as the clustered Pleiades,—
Moves not alone the heavenly quires,
But waves the spring-time's grassy spires,
Guards not archangel feet alone,
But deigns to guide and keep my own;
Speaks not alone the words of fate
Which worlds destroy and worlds create,
But whispers in my spirit's ear,
In tones of love or warning fear,
A language none beside may hear.

To Him from wanderings long and wild,
I come, an over-wearied child,
In cool and shade His peace to find,
Like dew-fall settling on my mind.
Assured that all I know is best,
And humbly trusting for the rest,
I turn from Fancy's cloud-built scheme,

Dark creed, and mournful eastern dream
Of power, impersonal and cold,
Controlling all, itself controlled,
Maker and slave of iron laws,
Alike the subject and the cause;
From vain philosophies, that try
The sevenfold gates of mystery,
And, baffled ever, babble still,
Word-prodigal of fate and will;
From Nature and her mockery, Art,
And book and speech of men apart,
To the still witness in my heart;
With reverence waiting to behold
His Avatar of love untold,
The Eternal Beauty new and old!

I too am weak, and faith is small,
And blindness happeneth unto all.

Yet sometimes glimpses on my sight,
Through present wrong, the eternal right;
And, step by step, since time began,
I see the steady gain of man;

That all of good that past hath had
Remains to make our time glad,
Our common daily life divine,
And every land a Palestine.

Thou weariest of thy present state;
What gain to thee time's holiest date?
The doubter now perchance had been
As High Priest or as Pilate then!

O friend! we need nor rock nor sand,
Nor storied stream of Morning-Land;
The heavens are glassed in Merrimac,—
What more could Jordan render back?

We lack but open eye and ear
To find the Orient's marvels here;
The still small voice in autumn's hush,
Yon maple wood the burning bush.

For still the new transcends the old,
In signs and tokens manifold;
Slaves rise up men; the olive waves,
With roots deep set in battle graves!

Through the harsh noises of our day
A low, sweet prelude finds its way;
Through clouds of doubt and creeds of fear,
A light is breaking, calm and clear.

That song of Love, now low and far,
Erelong shall swell from star to star!
That light the breaking day, which tips
The golden-spired Apocalypse!

From George Eliot:

No man must begin to mould himself on a faith or an idea
without rising to a higher order of experience: a principle
of subordination, of self-mastery, has been introduced into
his nature; he is no longer a mere bundle of impressions,
desires, and impulses.

Yet surely, surely the only true knowledge of our fellow-
man is that which enables us to feel with him—which gives
us a fine ear for the heart-pulses that are beating under the
mere clothes of circumstance and opinion. Our subtlest
analysis of schools and sects must miss the essential truth,
unless it be lit up by the love that sees in all forms of human
thought and work the life and death struggles of separate
human beings.

Do not philosophic doctors tell us that we are unable to
discern so much as a tree, except by an unconscious cun-

ning, which combines many past and separate sensations; that no one sense is independent of another, so that in the dark we can hardly taste a fricassee, or tell whether our pipe is alight or not, and the most intelligent boy, if accommodated with claws or hoofs instead of fingers, would be likely to remain on the lowest form? If so, it is easy to understand that our discernment of men's motives must depend on the completeness of the elements we can bring from our own susceptibility and our own experience. See to it, friend, before you pronounce a too hasty judgment, that your own moral sensibilities are not of a hoofed or clawed character. The keenest eye will not serve, unless you have the delicate fingers, with their subtle nerve-filaments, which elude scientific lenses, and lose themselves in the invisible world of human sensations.

It would be a poor result of all our anguish and our wrestling, if we won nothing but our old selves at the end of it—if we could return to the same blind loves, the same self-confident blame, the same light thoughts of human suffering, the same frivolous gossip over blighted human lives, the same feeble sense of that Unknown towards which we have sent forth irrepressible cries in our loneliness. Let us be thankful rather that our sorrow lives in us as an indestructible force, only changing its forms, and passing from pain into sympathy—the one poor word which includes all our best insight and our best love.

Rough men and weary-hearted women drank in a faith which was a rudimentary culture, which linked their thoughts with the past, lifted their imagination above the sordid details of their own narrow lives, and suffused their souls with the sense of a pitying, loving, Presence, sweet as summer to the houseless needy.

An eminent philosopher among my friends, who can dignify even your ugly furniture by lifting it into the serene light of science, has shown me this pregnant little fact. Your

151

pier-glass or extensive surface of polished steel made to be rubbed by a house-maid, will be minutely and multitudinously scratched in all directions; but now place against it a lighted candle as a centre of illumination, and lo! the scratches will seem to arrange themselves in a fine series of concentric circles round that little sun. It is demonstrable that the scratches are going everywhere impartially, and it is only your candle which produces the flattering illusion of a concentric arrangement, its light falling with an exclusive optical selection. These things are a parable. The scratches are events, and the candle is the egoism of any person now absent.

Religion can only change when the emotions which fill it are changed; and the religion of personal fear remains nearly at the level of the savage.

I have a belief of my own, and it comforts me.

What is that?

That by desiring what is perfectly good, even when we don't quite know what it is and cannot do what we would, we are part of the divine power against evil—widening the skirt of light and making the struggle with darkness narrower.

That is a beautiful mysticism—it is a—

Please not to call it by any name. You will say it is Persian, or something else geographical. It is my life. I have found it out, and cannot part with it. I have always been finding out my religion.

None of our theories are quite large enough for all the disclosures of time, and to the end of men's struggles a penalty will remain for those who sink from the ranks of the heroes into the crowd for whom the heroes fight and die.

The mind of man is as a country which was once open to squatters, who have bred and multiplied and become masters of the land. But then happeneth a time when new and hungry comers dispute the land; and there is trial of strength, and the stronger wins. Nevertheless the first squatters be they who have prepared the ground, and the crops to the end will be sequent (though chiefly on the nature of the soil, as of light sand, mixed loam or heavy clay, yet) somewhat on the primal labor and sowing.

What we call illusions are often in truth a wider vision of past and present realities—a willing movement of a man's soul with the larger sweep of the world's forces—a movement toward a more assured end than the chances of a single life. We see human heroism broken into units and say this unit did little—might as well have not been. But in this way we might break up a great army into units; in this way we might break the sunlight into fragments, and think that this and the other might be cheaply parted with. Let us rather raise a monument to the soldiers whose brave hearts only kept the ranks unbroken, and met death—a monument to the faithful who were not famous, and who are precious as the continuity of the sunbeam is precious, though some of them fall unseen and on barrenness.

No man believes that many-textured knowledge and skill —as a just idea of the solar system, or the power of painting flesh, or of reading written harmonies—can come late and of a sudden; yet many will not stick at believing that happiness can come at any day and hour solely by a new disposition of events; though there is naught less capable of a magical production than a mortal's happiness, which is mainly a complex of habitual relations and dispositions not to be wrought by news from foreign parts, or any whirling of fortune's wheel for one on whose brow Time has written legibly.

Our guides, we pretend, must be sinless: as if those were not often the best teachers who only yesterday got corrected for their mistakes.

I said, let my body dwell in poverty, and my hands be as

the hands of the toiler; but let my soul be as a temple of remembrance where the treasures of knowledge enter and the inner sanctuary is hope.

Error and folly have had their hecatombs of martyrs. Reduce the grandest type of man hitherto known to an abstract statement of his qualities and efforts, and he appears in dangerous company; say that, like Copernicus and Galileo, he was immovably convinced in the face of hissing incredulity; but so is the contriver of perpetual motion. We cannot fairly try the spirits by this sort of test. If we want to avoid giving the dose of hemlock or the sentence of banishment in the wrong case, nothing will do but a capacity to understand the subject-matter on which the immovable man is convinced, and fellowship with human travail, both near and afar, to hinder us from scanning any deep experience lightly. Shall we say, "Let the ages try the spirits, and see what they are worth?" Why, we are at the beginning of the ages, which can only be just by virtue of just judgments in separate human breasts—separate yet combined. Even steam-engines could not have got made without that condition, but must have stayed in the mind of James Watt.

The chief elements of greatness; a mind consciously, energetically moving with the larger march of human destinies, but not the less full of conscience and tender heart for the footsteps that tread near and need a leaning-place; capable of conceiving and choosing a life's task with far-off issues, yet capable of the unapplauded heroism which turns off the road of achievement at the call of the nearer duty whose effect lies within the beatings of the hearts that are close to us, as the hunger of the unfledged bird to the breast of its parent.

In complete unity a part possesses the whole as the whole possesses every part: and in this way human life is tending towards the image of the Supreme Unity: for as our life becomes more spiritual by capacity of thought, and joy therein, possession tends to become more universal, being independent of gross material contact; so that in a brief day the soul of a man may know in fuller volume the good which has been and is, nay is to come, than all he could possess in a whole life where he had to follow the creeping paths of the senses.

The grief and the glory are mingled as the smoke and the flame. It is because we children have inherited the good that we feel the evil.

All things are bound together in that Omnipresence which is the place and habitation of the world, and events are of a glass wherethrough our eyes see some of the pathways. And if it seems that the erring and unloving wills of men have helped to prepare you, as Moses was prepared, to serve your people the better, that depends on another order than the law which must guide our foot-steps. For the evil will of man makes not a people's good except by stirring the righteous will of man; and beneath all the clouds with which our thought encompasses the Eternal, this is clear—that a people can be blessed only by having counsellors and a multitude whose will moves in obedience to the laws of justice and love.

From James Russell Lowell:

We all are tall enough to reach God's hand.

How great it is to breathe with human breath,
To be but poor foot-soldiers in the ranks
Of our old exiled king, Humanity;
Encamping after every hard-won field
Nearer and nearer Heaven's happy plains.

The true sceptre of all power is love
And humbleness the palace-gate of truth.

155

In every thing that lovely is
He loves and hath His home.

Our fathers fought for Liberty,
  They struggled long and well,
  History of their deeds can tell—
But *ourselves* must set us free.

Why mourn we for the golden prime
When our young souls *were* kingly, strong, and true?
  The soul is greater than all time,
It changes not, but yet is ever new.

But that the soul *is* noble, we
Could never know what nobleness had been;
  Be what ye dream! and earth shall see
A greater greatness than she e'er hath seen.

  The flower pines not to be fair,
It never asketh to be sweet and dear,
  But gives itself to sun and air,
And so is fresh and full from year to year.

For many are by whom all truth,
That speaks not in their mother-tongue,
Is stoned to death with hands unruth,
Or hath its patient spirit wrung
Cold words and colder looks among.

Yet fear not! for skies are fair
To all whose souls are fair within.

Thou doest not a worthy deed the less
Because the world may not its greatness see.
We should love all things better, if we knew
What claims the meanest have upon our hearts.

  Save in Act, thy Love is all in vain.

A gentleness that grows of steady faith;
A joy that sheds its sunshine everywhere;
A humble strength and readiness to bear
Those burdens which strict duty ever lay'th
Upon our souls;—which unto sorrow saith,
"Here is no soil for thee to strike thy roots,

Here only grow those sweet and precious fruits;
Which ripen for the soul that well obey'th;"
A patience which the world can neither give
Nor take away; a courage strong and high,
That dares in a simple usefulness to live,
And without one sad look behind to die
When that day comes;—these tell me that our love
Is building for itself a home above.

For, whom the heart of man shuts out,
    Sometimes the heart of God takes in,
And fences them all about
    With silence mid the world's loud din.

All thoughts that mould the age begin
Deep down within the primitive soul,
And from the many slowly upward win
To one who grasps the whole.

Nor is he far astray who deems
That every hope, which rises and grows broad
In the world's heart, by ordered impulse streams
From the great heart of God.

Believe it, 't is the mass of men He loves;
And, where there is most sorrow and most want,
Where the high heart of man is trodden down
The most, 't is not because He hides his face
From them in wrath, as purblind teachers prate:
Not so: there most is He, for there is He
Most needed.

Get but the truth once uttered, and 't is like
A star new-born, that drops into its place,
And which, once circling in its placid round,
Not all the tumult of the earth can shake.

If the chosen soul could never be alone
In deep mid-silence, open-doored to God,
No greatness ever had been dreamed or done;
Among dull hearts a prophet never grew;
The nurse of full-grown souls is solitude.

Children are God's apostles, day by day
Sent forth to preach of love, and hope, and peace.

Looking within myself, I note how thin
   A plank of station, chance, or prosperous fate,
Doth fence me from the clutching waves of sin;—
    In my own heart I find the worst man's mate,
    And see not dimly the smooth-hinged gate
      That opens to those abysses
Where ye grope darkly,—ye who never knew
On your young hearts love's consecrating dew,
    Or felt a mother's kisses,
   Or home's restraining tendrils round you curled.
   Ah, side by side with heart's-ease in this world
The fatal night-shade grows and bitter rue!

We owe allegiance to the State; but deeper, truer, more,
To the sympathies that God hath set within our spirit's
       core:—
Our country claims our fealty; we grant it so, but then
Before Man made us citizens, great Nature made us men.

He's true to God who's true to man; wherever wrong is done,
To the humblest and the weakest, neath the all-beholding
       sun,
That wrong is also done to us; and they are slaves most
       base,

Whose love of right is for themselves, and not for all their
    race.

God works for all. Ye cannot hem the hope of being free
With parallels of latitude, with mountain-range or sea.
Put golden padlocks on Truth's lips, be callous as ye will,
From soul to soul o'er all the world, leaps one electric thrill.

Slow are the steps of Freedom, but her feet
    Turn never backward: hers no bloody glare;
Her light is calm, and innocent, and sweet,
    And where it enters there is no despair.

Be noble! and the nobleness that lies
In other men, sleeping, but never dead,
Will rise in majesty to meet thine own:
Then wilt thou see it gleam in many eyes,
Then will pure light around thy path be shed,
And thou wilt never more be sad and lone.

Great Truths are portions of the soul of man;
Great souls are portions of Eternity;
Each drop of blood that e'er through true heart ran
With lofty message, ran for thee and me;
For God's law, since the starry song began,
Hath been, and still for evermore must be,
That every deed which shall outlast Time's span
Must goad the soul to be erect and free;
Slave is no word of deathless lineage sprung,—
Too many noble souls have thought and died,
Too many mighty poets have lived and sung,
And our good Saxon, from lips purified
With martyr-fire, throughout the world hath rung
Too long to have God's holy cause denied.

Where is the true man's fatherland?
    Is it where he by chance is born?
    Doth not the yearning spirit scorn

159

In such scant borders to be spanned?
O, yes! his fatherland must be
As the blue heaven wide and free!

Is it alone where freedom is,
 Where God is God and man is man?
 Doth he not claim a broader span
For the soul's love of home than this?
O, yes! his fatherland must be
As the blue heaven wide and free!

Where'er a human heart doth wear
 Joy's myrtle-wreath or sorrow's gyves,
 Where'er a human spirit strives
After a life more true and fair,
There is the true man's birthplace grand,
His is a world-wide fatherland!

Where'er a single slave doth pine,
 Where'er one man may help another,—
 Thank God for such a birthright, brother,
That spot of earth is thine and mine!
There is the true man's birthplace grand,
His is a world-wide fatherland!

Not only around our infancy
Doth heaven with all its splendors lie,
Daily, with souls that cringe and plot,
We Sinais climb and know it not.

He gives nothing but worthless gold
 Who gives from a sense of duty;
But he who gives a slender mite,
And gives to that which is out of sight,
 That thread of the all-sustaining Beauty
Which runs through all and doth all unite,—
The hand cannot clasp the whole of his alms,

The heart outstretches its eager palms,
For a god goes with it and makes it store
To the soul that was starving in darkness before.

Bowing thyself in dust before a Book,
And thinking the great God is thine alone,
O rash iconoclast, though wilt not brook
What Gods the heathen carves in wood and stone,
As if the Shepherd who from outer cold
Leads all his shivering lambs to one sure fold
Were careful for the fashion of his crook.

There is no broken reed so poor and base,
No rush, the bending tilt of swamp-fly blue,
But he therewith the ravening wolf can chase,
And guide his flock to springs and pastures new;
Through ways unlooked for, and through many lands,
Far from the rich folds built with human hands,
The gracious footprints of his love I trace.

Thou hear'st not well the mountain organ-tones
By prophet ears from Hor and Sinai caught,
Thinking the cisterns of those Hebrew brains
Drew dry the springs of the All-knower's thought,
Nor shall thy lips be touched with living fire,
Who blow'st old altar-coals with sole desire
To weld anew the spirit's broken chains.

God is not dumb, that he should speak no more;
If thou hast wanderings in the wilderness
And find'st not Sinai, 't is thy soul is poor;
There towers the mountain of the Voice no less,
Which whoso seeks shall find, but he who bends,
Intent on manna still and mortal ends,
Sees it not, neither hears its thundered lore.

Slowly the Bible of the race is writ,
And not on paper leaves nor leaves of stone;

Each age, each kindred adds a verse to it,
Texts of despair or hope, of joy or moan.
While swings the sea, while mists the mountains shroud,
While thunder's surges burst on cliffs of cloud,
Still at the prophets' feet the nations sit.

We see but half the causes of our deeds,
Seeking them wholly in the outer life,
And heedless of the encircling spirit-world,
Which though unseen, is felt, and sows in us
All germs of pure and world-wide purposes.
From one stage of our being to the next
We pass unconscious o'er a slender bridge,
The momentary work of unseen hands,
Which crumbles down behind us; looking back,
We see the other shore, the gulf between,
And, marvelling how we won to where we stand,
Content ourselves to call the builder Chance.
We trace the wisdom to the apple's fall,
Not to the birth-throes of a mighty Truth
Which, for long ages in blank Chaos dumb,
Yet yearned to be incarnate, and had found
At last a spirit meet to be the womb
From which it might be born to bless mankind,—
Not to the soul of Newton, ripe with all
The hoarded thoughtfulness of earnest years,
And waiting but one ray of sunlight more
To blossom fully.

                    But whence came that ray?
We call our sorrows Destiny, but ought
Rather to name our high successes so.
Only the instincts of great souls are Fate,
And have predestined sway: all other things,
Except by leave of us, could never be.
For Destiny is but the breath of God

Still moving in us, the last fragment left
Of our unfallen nature, waking oft
Within our thought, to beckon us beyond
The narrow circle of the seen and known,
And always tending to a noble end.

From Victor Hugo:

The beautiful is as useful as the useful. Perhaps more so.

Oh, Thou who art!

Ecclesiastes names Thee the Almighty; Maccabees names Thee Creator; the Epistle to the Ephesians names Thee Liberty; Baruch names Thee Immensity; the Psalms name Thee Wisdom and Truth; John names Thee Light; the Book of Kings names Thee Lord; Exodus calls Thee Providence; Leviticus, Holiness; Esdras, Justice; Creation calls Thee God; man names Thee Father; but Solomon names Thee Compassion, and that is the most beautiful of all Thy names.

His rich penitents and the pious women of D had often contributed the money for a beautiful new altar for monseigneur's oratory; but he had always taken the money and given it to the poor. "The most beautiful of altars," said he, "is the soul of an unhappy man who is comforted and thanks God."

One day he saw some country folks very busy pulling up nettles; he looked at the heap of plants, uprooted, and already wilted and said: "This is dead; but it would be well if we knew how to put it to some use. When the nettle is young the leaves make excellent greens; when it grows old it has filaments and fibres like hemp and flax. Cloth made from the nettle is worth as much as that made from hemp. Chopped up, the nettle is good for poultry; pounded, it is good for horned cattle. The seed of the nettle mixed with the fodder of animals gives a luster to their skin; the root

163

mixed with salt produces a beautiful yellow dye. It makes, moreover, excellent hay, as it can be cut twice in a season. And what does the nettle need? Very little soil, no culture, except that the seeds fall as fast as they ripen, and it is difficult to gather them; that is all. If we would take a little pains the nettle would be useful; we neglect it and it becomes harmful. Then we kill it. How much men are like the nettle!" After a short silence, he added: "My friends, remember this, that there are no bad herbs and no bad men; there are only bad cultivators."

They pray.
To whom?
To God.
Pray to God? What is meant by that?
Is there an infinite outside of us? Is this infinite one, inherent, permanent; necessarily substantial, because it is infinite, and because if matter were wanting to it it would in that respect be limited; necessarily intelligent, because it is infinite, and because, if it lacked intelligence, it would be to that extent finite? Does this infinite awaken in us the idea of essence, while we are able to attribute to ourselves the idea of existence only? In other words, is it not the absolute of which we are the relative?

At the same time, while there is an infinite outside of us, is there not an infinite within us? These two infinites (fearful plural!)—do they not rest super-posed on one another? Does not the second infinite underlie the first, so to speak? Is it not the mirror, the reflection, the echo of the first, an abyss concentric with another abyss? Is this second infinite intelligent also? Does it think? Does it love? Does it will? If the two infinites be intelligent, each one of them has a will principle, and there is a "me" in the infinite above as there is a "me" in the infinite below. The "me" below is the soul; the "me" above is God.

To place, by process of thought, the infinite below in contact with the infinite above, is called "prayer."

Let us not take anything away from the human mind; suppression is evil. We must reform and transform. Certain faculties of man are directed toward the unknown; thought, meditation, prayer. The unknown is an ocean. What is conscience? It is the compass of the unknown. Thought, meditation, prayer—these are the great, mysterious pointings of the needle. Let us respect them. Whither tend these majestic irradiations of the soul? Into the shadow—that is toward the light.

The grandeur of democracy is that it denies nothing and denounces nothing of humanity. Close by the rights of man, side by side with them, at least, are the rights of the soul.

To crush out fanaticisms and revere the infinite, such is the law. Let us not confine ourselves to falling prostrate beneath the tree of creation and contemplating its vast ramification full of stars. We have a duty to perform, to cultivate the human soul, to defend mystery against miracle, to adore the incomprehensible and reject the absurd; to admit nothing that is inexplicable excepting what is necessary, to purify faith and obliterate superstition from the face of religion, to remove the vermin from the garden of God.

Man lives by affirmation even more than he does by bread.

We do not comprehend either man as a starting-point, or progress as the goal, without these two forces which are the two great motors, faith and love.

Progress is the name, the ideal is the model.

What is the ideal? It is God.

Ideal, absolute, perfection, the infinite—these are identical words.

History and philosophy have eternal duties, which are at the same time simple duties—to oppose Caiaphas as bishop,

Draco as judge, Trimalcion as legislator and Tiberius as emperor.

This conflict of the right and the fact endures from the origin of society. To bring the duel to an end, to amalgamate the pure ideal with the human reality, to make the right peacefully interpenetrate the fact, and the fact right, this is the work of the wise.

The world lets everything fall and die which is nothing but selfishness, everything which does not represent a virtue or an idea for the human race.

No man is a good historian of the open, visible, signal and public life of the nations, if he is not, at the same time, to a certain extent, the historian of their deeper and hidden life; and no man is a good historian of the interior if he knows not how to be, whenever there is need, the historian of the exterior. The history of morals and ideas interpenetrates the history of events, and vice versa. They are two orders of different facts which answer to each other, which are always linked with and often produce each other.

Man is not a circle with a single center; he is an ellipse with two foci. Facts are one, ideas are the other.

Are you what is called a fortunate man? Well, you are sad every day. Each day has its great grief or its little care. Yesterday you were trembling for the health of one who is dear to you, to-day you fear for your own; to-morrow it will be an anxiety about money, the next day the slanders of a calumniator, the day after the misfortune of a friend; then the weather, then something broken or lost, then a pleasure for which you are reproached by your conscience or your vertebral column reproaches you; another time, the course of public affairs. Without counting heart troubles. And so on. One cloud is dissipated, another gathers. Hardly one day in a hundred of unbroken joy and unbroken sunshine. And you are of that small number who are fortunate! As to other men, stagnant night is upon them.

Reflecting minds make little use of this expression; the happy and the unhappy. In this world, the vestibule of another evidently, there is none happy.

The true division of humanity is this: the luminous and the dark.

To diminish the number of the dark, to increase the number of the luminous, behold the aim. This is why we cry: education, knowledge! to learn to read is to kindle a fire; every syllable spelled sparkles.

But he who says light does not necessarily say joy. There is suffering in the light; in excess it burns. Flame is hostile to the wing. To burn and yet to fly, this is the miracle of genius.

When you know and when you love you shall suffer still. The day dawns in tears. The luminous weep, were it only over the dark.

Intellectual and moral growth is not less indispensable than material amelioration. Knowledge is a viaticum, thought is of primary necessity, truth is nourishment as well as wheat. A reason, by fasting from knowledge and wisdom, becomes puny. Let us lament as over stomachs, over minds which do not eat. If there is anything more poignant than a body agonizing for want of bread it is a soul which is dying of hunger for light.

All progress is tending toward the solution. Some day we shall be astounded. The human race rising, the lower strata will quite naturally come out from the zone of distress. The abolition of misery will be brought about by a simple elevation of level.

This blessed solution we should do wrong to distrust.

The past, it is true, is very strong at the present hour.

It is reviving. This revivification of a corpse is surprising. Here it is walking and advancing. It seems victorious; this dead man is a conqueror. He comes with his legion, the superstitious, with his sword, despotism; with his banner, ignorance; within a little time he has won ten battles. He advances, he threatens, he laughs, he is at our doors. As for ourselves we shall not despair. Let us sell the field whereon Hannibal is camped.

We who believe, what can we fear?

There is no backward flow of ideas more than of rivers.

But let those who desire not the future think of it. In saying no to progress it is not the future which they condemn, but themselves. They give themselves a melancholy disease; they inoculate themselves with the past. There is but one way of refusing tomorrow, that is to die.

Now, no death, that of the body as late as possible, that of the soul, never, is what we desire.

Love has no middle term; either it destroys or it saves. All human destiny is this dilemma. This dilemma, destruction or salvation, no fatality proposes more inexorably than love. Love is life, if it be not death. Cradle, coffin also. The same sentiment says yes and no in the human heart. Of all the things which God has made, the human heart is that which sheds most light, and, alas! most night.

We are never done with conscience. Choose your course by it, Brutus: choose your course by it, Cato. It is bottomless, being God. We cast into this pit the labor of our whole life, we cast in our fortune, we cast in our riches, we cast in our success, we cast in our liberty or our country, we cast in our well-being, we cast in our repose, we cast in our happiness. More! more! more! Empty the vase! turn out the urn! We must at last cast in our heart.

By the word GOD—let us fix the sense of this word also—we mean the Living Infinite.

The latent EGO of the visible Infinite, that is God.

God is the invisible made evident.

The world concentrated, is God. God expanded, is the world.

168

We, who are speaking, believe in nothing out of God.

That being said, let us proceed. God creates Art by man, having for a tool the human intellect. The great Workman has made this tool for himself; he has no other.

What has the human race been since the beginning of time? A reader. For a long time he has spelled; he spells yet: soon he will read.

This child, six thousand years old, has been at school from the first. Where? In Nature. At the beginning, having no other book, he spelled the universe. He has had his primary instructions from the clouds, from the firmament, from meteors, flowers, animals, forests, seasons, phenomena. The Ionian fisherman studies the wave; the Chaldean shepherd spells the star. Then came the first books,—a sublime advance. The book is vaster yet than that grand scene, the world; for to the fact it adds the idea. If anything is greater than God seen in the sun, it is God seen in Homer.

The universe without the book, is science becoming rudely outlined; the universe with the book, is the ideal making its appearance. Thence an immediate modification in human affairs; where there had been only force, power is revealed. The application of the ideal to actual facts produces civilization. Poetry written and sung begins its work, —a gloriously effective deduction from the poetry only seen. It is startling to perceive that where science was dreaming, poetry acts. With a touch of the lyre, the thinker dispels ferocity.

We shall return, later on, to this power of the book; we do not insist on it at present; it is clear as light. Many writers then, few readers: such has the world been up to this day. But a change is at hand. Compulsory education is a recruitment of souls for the light. Henceforth all human advancement will be accomplished by swelling the legions of those who read. The diameter of the moral and ideal

169

good corresponds always to the calibre of men's minds. In proportion to the worth of the brain is the worth of the heart.

The book is the tool of this transformation. What humanity requires, is to be fed with light; such nourishment is found in reading. Thence the importance of the school, everywhere adequate to civilization. The human race is at last on the point of spreading the book wide open. The immense human Bible, composed of all the prophets, of all the poets, of all the philosophers, is about to shine and blaze under the focus of that enormous luminous lens,—compulsory education.

Humanity reading is humanity knowing.

What nonsense, then, it is to cry, "Poetry is passing away!" We might say, on the contrary, poetry is coming. For who says poetry, says philosophy and light.

On all sides the deep layers of effects and causes, heaped one behind the other, wrap you with mist. The man who meditates not, lives in blindness; the man who meditates, lives in darkness. The choice between darkness and darkness,—that is all we have. In that darkness, which thus far is nearly all our science, experience gropes, observation lies in wait, supposition wanders about. If you gaze into it very often, you become the *vates*. Protracted religious meditation takes possession of you.

Every man has within him his Patmos. He is free to go, or not to go, out upon that frightful promontory of thought from which one perceives the shadow. If he goes not, he remains in the common life, with the common conscience, with the common virtue, with the common faith, or with the common doubt; and it is well. For inward peace it is evidently the best. If he goes out upon those heights, he is taken captive. The profound waves of the marvellous have appeared to him. No one views with impunity that ocean. Henceforth he will be the thinker, dilated, enlarged, but

170

floating; that is to say, the dreamer. He will partake of the poet and of the prophet. Henceforth a certain portion of him belongs to the shadow. An element of the boundless enters into his life, into his conscience, into his virtue, into his philosophy. Having a different measure from other men, he becomes extraordinary in their eyes. He has duties which they have not. He lives in a sort of diffused prayer, and, strange indeed, attaches himself to an indeterminate certainty which he calls God. He distinguishes in that twilight enough of the anterior life and enough of the ulterior life to seize these two ends of the dark thread, and with them to bind his soul to life. Who has drunk will drink, who has dreamed will dream. He will not give up the alluring abyss, that sounding of the fathomless, that indifference for the world and for this life, that entrance into the forbidden, that effort to handle the impalpable and to see the invisible: he returns to it, he leans and bends over it, he takes one step forward, then two; and thus it is that one penetrates into the impenetrable, and thus it is that one finds the boundless release of infinite meditation.

He who descends there is a Kant; he who falls there is a Swedenborg.

To preserve the freedom of the will in that expansion, is to be great. But, however great one may be, the problems cannot be so solved. One may ply the fathomless with questions: nothing more. As for the answers, they are there, but veiled by the shadow. The colossal lineaments of truth seem at times to appear for a moment; then they fade away, and are lost in the absolute. Of all these questions, that among them all which besets the intellect, that among them all which weighs upon the heart, is the question of the soul.

The huge concentric waves of universal life are shoreless. The starry sky that we study is but a partial appearance. We grasp but a few meshes of the vast network of existence. The complication of the phenomenon, of which a glimpse can be caught beyond our senses only by contemplation and ecstasy, makes the mind giddy. The thinker who reaches so far is to other men only a visionary. The necessary interlacement of the perceptible with the non-perceptible strikes the philosopher with stupor. This plenitude is required by Thy omnipotence, which admits no gap. The interpenetration of universe with universe makes part of Thy infinitude. Here we extend the word "universe" to an order of facts that no astronomer can reach. In the Cosmos, invisible to fleshly eye, but revealed to vision, sphere blends with sphere without change of form, the creations being of diverse density; so that, to all appearance, with our world is inexplicably merged another, invisible to us as we to it.

For it is beautiful on this sombre earth, during this dark life, brief passage to something beyond,—it is beautiful that Force should have Right for a master, that Progress should have Courage as a leader, that Intelligence should have Honor as a sovereign, that Conscience should have Duty as a despot, that Civilization should have Liberty as a queen, and that the servant of Ignorance should be the Light.

It is important, at the present time, to bear in mind that the human soul has still greater need of the ideal than of the real.

It is by the real that we exist; it is by the ideal that we live.

Literature secretes civilization, poetry secretes the ideal. That is why literature is one of the wants of societies; that is why poetry is a hunger of the soul.

That is why poets are the first instructors of the people.

That is why Shakespeare must be translated in France.

That is why Molière must be translated in England.

That is why all the poets, all the philosophers, all the thinkers, all the producers of nobility of soul must be translated, commented on, published, printed, reprinted, stereotyped, distributed, hawked about, explained, recited, spread

172

abroad, given to all, given cheaply, given at cost price, given for nothing.

To enjoy a full stomach, a satisfied digestion, a satiated belly, is doubtless something, for it is the enjoyment of the brute. However, one may set one's ambition higher.

Certainly, a good salary is a fine thing. To have beneath one's feet the firm ground of good wages, is pleasant. The wise man likes to want nothing. To assure his own position is the characteristic of an intelligent man. An official chair, with ten thousand sesterces a year, is a graceful and convenient seat; liberal emoluments give a fresh complexion and good health; one lives to an old age in pleasant well-paid sinecures; the high financial world, abounding in profits, is a place agreeable to live in; to be on a good footing at court settles a family well and brings a fortune. As for myself, I prefer to all these solid comforts the old leaky vessel in which Bishop Quodvultdeus embarks with a smile.

The great problem is to restore to the human mind something of the ideal. Whence shall we draw the ideal? Wherever it is to be found. The poets, the philosophers, the thinkers are its urns. The ideal is in Æschylus, in Isaiah, in Juvenal, in Alighieri, in Shakespeare. Throw Æschylus, throw Isaiah, throw Juvenal, throw Dante, throw Shakespeare into the deep soul of the human race.

Pour Job, Solomon, Pindar, Ezekiel, Sophocles, Euripides, Herodotus, Theocritus, Plautus, Lucretius, Virgil, Terence, Horace, Catullus, Tacitus, Saint Paul, Saint Augustine, Tertullian, Petrarch, Pascal, Milton, Descartes, Corneille, La Fontaine, Montesquieu, Diderot, Rousseau, Beaumarchais, Sedaine, André Chénier, Kant, Byron, Schiller,—pour all these souls into man.

Pour in all the wits from Æsop up to Molière, all the intellects from Plato up to Newton, all the encyclopaedists from Aristotle up to Voltaire.

By this means you will cure the present malady and establish forever the health of the human mind.

You will cure the middle-class, and found the people.

As already indicated, after the destruction which has delivered the world, you will construct the home for the permanent life of the race.

What an aim—to construct the people! Principles combined with science, all possible quantity of the absolute introduced by degrees into the fact, Utopia treated successively by every mode of realization,—by political economy, by philosophy, by physics, by chemistry, by dynamics, by logic, by art; union gradually replacing antagonism, and unity replacing union; for religion God, for priest the father, for prayer virtue, for field the whole earth, for language the word, for law the right, for motive-power duty, for hygiene labor, for economy universal peace, for canvas the very life, for the goal progress, for authority freedom, for people the man. Such is the simplification.

And at the summit the ideal.

From Plato:

If there were not some community of feeling among mankind, however varying in different persons—I mean to say, if every man's feelings were peculiar to himself—and were not shared by the rest of his species—I do not see how we could ever communicate our impressions to one another.

From Carlyle:

How true, that there is nothing dead in this Universe; that what we call dead is only changed, its forces working in inverse order! "The leaf that lies rotting in moist winds," says one, "has still force; else how could it *rot*?" Our whole Universe is but an infinite Complex of Forces; thousand-fold, from Gravitation up to Thought and Will; man's Freedom environed with Necessity of Nature: in all which nothing at any moment slumbers, but all is forever awake and busy. The thing that lies isolated inactive thou shalt nowhere discover; seek everywhere, from the granite mountain, slow-mouldering since Creation, to the passing cloud-vapor, to the living man; to the action, to the spoken word of man. The word that is spoken, as we know, flies irrevocable: not less, but more, the action that is done. "The gods themselves," sings Pindar, "cannot annihilate the action that is done." No: this once done, is done always; cast forth into endless Time; and, long conspicuous or soon hidden, must verily work and grow forever there, an indestructible new element in the Infinite of Things. Or, indeed, what is this Infinite of Things itself, which men name Universe, but an Action, a sum-total of Actions and Activities? The living ready-made sum-total of these three,—which Calculation cannot add, cannot bring on its tablets; yet the sum we say, is written visible: All that has been done, All that is doing, All that will be done! Understand it well, the Thing thou beholdest, that Thing is an Action, the product and expression of exerted Force: the All of Things is an infinite conjugation of the verb *to do*. Shoreless Fountain-Ocean of Force, of power to *do*; wherein Force rolls and circles, billowing, many-streamed, harmonious; wide as Immensity, deep as Eternity; beautiful and terrible, not to be comprehended: this is what man names Existence and Universe; this thousand-tinted Flame-image, at once veil and revelation, reflex such as he, in his poor brain and heart, can paint of One Unnameable, dwelling in inaccessible light! From beyond the star-galaxies, from before the Beginnings of Days, it billows and rolls,—round *thee*, nay thyself art of it, in this point of Space where thou now standest, in this moment which thy clock measures.

Or, apart from all Transcendentalism, is it not a plain truth of sense, which the duller mind can even consider as

a truism, that human things wholly are in continual movement, and action and reaction; working continually forward,
phasis after phasis, by unalterable laws, towards prescribed
issues? How often must we say, and yet not rightly lay to
heart: the seed that is sown, it will spring! Given the summer's blossoming, then there is also given the autumnal
withering: so is it ordered not with seed-fields only, but with
transactions, arrangements, philosophies, societies, French
Revolutions, whatsoever man works with in this lower world.
The Beginning holds in it the End, and all that leads thereto; as the acorn does the oak and its fortunes. Solemn
enough, did we think of it,—which unhappily, and also
happily, we do not very much! Thou there canst begin; the
Beginning is for thee, and there: but where, and of what
sort, and for whom will the End be? All grows, and seeks
and endures its destinies: consider likewise how much
grows, as the trees do, whether *we* think of it or not. So that
when your Epimenides, your somnolent Peter Klaus, since
named Rip Van Winkle, awakens again, he finds it a
changed world. In that seven-years' sleep of his, so much
has changed! All that is without us will change while we
think not of it; much even that is within us. The truth that
was yesterday a restless Problem, has to-day grown a Belief
burning to be uttered: on the morrow, contradiction has exasperated it into mad Fanaticism; obstruction has dulled it
into sick Inertness; it is sinking towards silence, of satisfaction or of resignation. Today is not Yesterday, for man or
for thing. Yesterday there was the oath of Love; to-day has
come the curse of Hate. Not willingly: ah, no; but it could
not help coming. The golden radiance of youth, would it
willingly have tarnished itself into the dimness of old age?
—Fearful: how we stand enveloped, deep-sunk, in that
Mystery of Time; and are Sons of Time; fashioned and
woven out of Time; and on us and on all that we have, or

see, or do, is written: Rest not, Continue not, Forward to thy doom!

The frightfulest Births of Time are never the loud-speaking ones, for these soon die; they are the silent ones, which can live from century to century! Anarchy, hateful as Death, is abhorrent to the whole nature of man; and so must itself soon die.

Wherefore let all men know what of depth and of height is still revealed in man; and with fear and wonder, with just sympathy and just antipathy, with clear eye and open heart, contemplate it and appropriate it; and draw innumerable inferences from it.

Hast thou considered how Thought is stronger than Artillery-parks, and (were it fifty years after death and martyrdom, or were it two thousand years) writes and unwrites Acts of Parliament, removes mountains; models the World like soft clay? Also how the beginning of all Thought, worth the name, is Love; and the wise head never yet was, without first the generous heart?

Meanwhile we will hate Anarchy as Death, which it is; and the things worse than Anarchy shall be hated *more*. Surely Peace alone is fruitful. Anarchy is destruction; a burning up, say, of Shams and Insupportabilities; but which leaves Vacancy behind. Know this also that out of a world of Unwise nothing but an Unwisdom can be made.

If all wars, civil and other, are misunderstandings, what a thing must right-understanding be!

Universal History, the history of what man has accomplished in this world, is at bottom the History of the Great Men who have worked here. They were the leaders of men, these great ones; the modellers, the patterns, and in a wide sense creators, of whatsoever the general mass of men contrived to do or to attain; all things that we see standing accomplished in the world are properly the outer material re-

177

sult, the practical realization and embodiment, of Thoughts that dwelt in the Great Men sent into the world: the soul of the whole world's history, it may justly be considered, were the history of these.

Great Men, taken up in any way, are profitable company. We cannot look, however imperfectly, upon a great man, without gaining something by him. He is the living light-fountain, which it is good and pleasant to be near. The light which enlightens, which has enlightened the darkness of the world; and this not as a kindled lamp only, but rather as a natural luminary shining by the gift of Heaven; a flowing light-fountain . . . of native original insight, of manhood and heroic nobleness;—in whose radiance all souls feel that it is well with them.

It is well said, in every sense, that a man's religion is the chief fact with regard to him. A man's, or a nation of men's. By religion I do not mean here the church-creed which he professes, the articles of faith which he will sign and, in words or otherwise, assert; not this wholly, in many cases not this at all. We see men of all kinds of professed creeds attain to almost all degrees of worth or worthlessness under each or any of them. This is not what I call religion, this profession and assertion; which is often only a profession and assertion from the outworks of the man, from the mere argumentative region of him, if even so deep as that. But the thing a man does practically believe (and this is often enough *without* asserting it even to himself, much less to others); the thing a man does practically lay to heart, and know for certain, concerning his vital relations to this mysterious Universe, and his duty and destiny there, that is in all cases the primary thing for him, and creatively determines all the rest. That is his *religion;* or it may be, his mere scepticism and *no-religion;* the manner it is in which he feels himself to be spiritually related to the Unseen World or No-World; and I say, if you tell me what that is, you tell me to a very great extent what the man is, what the kind of things he will do is.

That men should have worshipped their poor fellow-man as a God, and not him only, but stocks and stones, and all manner of animate and inanimate objects; and fashioned for themselves such a distracted chaos of hallucinations by way of Theory of the Universe: all this looks like an incredible fable. Nevertheless it is a clear fact that they did it. Such hideous inextricable jungle of misworships, misbeliefs, men, made as we are, did actually hold by, and live at home in. This is strange. Yes, we may pause in sorrow and silence over the depths of darkness that are in man; if we rejoice in the heights of purer vision he has attained to. Such things were and are in man; in all men: in us too.

Some speculators have a short way of accounting for the Pagan religion: mere quackery, priestcraft, and dupery, say they; no sane man ever did believe it,—merely contrived to persuade other men, not worthy of the name of sane, to believe it! It will be often our duty to protest against this sort of hypothesis about men's doings and history; and I here, on the very threshold, protest against it in reference to Paganism, and to all other *isms* by which man has ever for a length of time striven to walk in this world. They have all had a truth in them, or men would not have taken them up. Quackery and dupery do abound; in religions, above all in the more advanced decaying stages of religions, they have fearfully abounded; but quackery was never the originating influence in such things, but their disease, the sure precursor of their being about to die! Let us never forget this. It seems to me a most mournful hypothesis, that of quackery giving birth to any faith even in savage men. Quackery gives birth to nothing; gives death to all things. We shall not see into the true heart of anything, if we look merely at the quackeries of it; if we do not reject the quackeries altogether; as mere diseases, corruptions, with which our and

179

all men's sole duty is to have done with them, to sweep them out of our thoughts as out of our practice. Man everywhere is the born enemy of lies.

Another theory, somewhat more respectable, attributes such things to Allegory. It was a play of poetic minds, say these theorists; a shadowing forth, in allegorical fable, in personification and visual form, of what such poetic minds had known and felt of this Universe. Which agrees, add they, with a primary law of human nature, still everywhere observably at work, though in less important things, That what a man feels intensely, he struggles to speak out of him, to see represented before him in visual shape, and as if with a kind of life and historical reality in it. Now doubtless there is such a law, and it is one of the deepest in human nature; neither need we doubt that it did operate fundamentally in this business. The hypothesis which ascribes Paganism wholly or mostly to this agency, I call a little more respectable; but I cannot yet call it the true hypothesis. Think, would *we* believe, and take with us as our life-guidance, an allegory, a poetic sport? Not sport but earnest is what we should require. It is a most earnest thing to be alive in this world; to die is not sport for a man. Man's life never was a sport to him; it was a stern reality, altogether a serious matter to be alive!

Now if all things whatsoever that we look upon are emblems to us of the Highest God, I add that more so than any of them is man such an emblem. You have heard of St. Chrysostom's celebrated saying in reference to the Shekinah, or Ark of Testimony, visible Revelation of God, among the Hebrews: "The true Shekinah is Man!" Yes, it is even so: this is no vain phrase; it is veritably so. The essence of our being, the mystery in us that calls itself "I,"—ah, what words have we for such things?—is a breath of Heaven; the Highest Being reveals himself in man. This body, these faculties, this life of ours, is it not all as a vesture for that

Unnamed? "There is but one Temple in the Universe," says the devout Novalis, "and that is the Body of Man. Nothing is holier than that high form. Bending before men is a reverence done to this Revelation in the Flesh. We touch Heaven when we lay our hand on a human body!" This sounds much like a mere flourish of rhetoric; but it is not so. If well meditated, it will turn out to be a scientific fact; the expression, in such words as can be had, of the actual truth of the thing. We are the miracle of miracles,—the great inscrutable mystery of God. We cannot understand it, we know not how to speak of it; but we may feel and know, if we like, that it is verily so.

It is an everlasting duty, valid in our day as in that, the duty of being brave: *Valor* is still *value*. The first duty for a man is still that of subduing *Fear*. We must get rid of Fear; we can not act at all till then. A man's acts are slavish, not true but specious; his very thoughts are false, he thinks too as a slave and coward till he have got Fear under his feet . . . A man shall and must be valiant: he must march forward and quit himself like a man,—trusting imperturbably in the appointment and choice of the upper Powers; and, on the whole, not fear at all. Now and always, the completeness of his victory over Fear will determine how much of a man he is.

Valor is the fountain of Pity too;—of Truth, and all that is great and good in man.

In the history of the world there will not again be any man, never so great, whom his fellowmen will take for a god. Nay we might rationally ask, Did any set of human beings ever really think the man they saw there standing beside them a god, the maker of this world? Perhaps not: it was usually some man they remembered, or had seen. But neither can this any more be. The Great Man is not recognized henceforth as a god any more.

It was a rude gross error, that of counting the Great Man

181

a god. Yet let us say that it is at all times difficult to know what he is, or how to account of him and receive him! The most significant feature in the history of an epoch is the manner it has of welcoming a Great Man. Ever, to the true instincts of men, there will be something godlike in him. Whether they shall take him to be a god, to be a prophet, or what they shall take him to be? that is ever a grand question; by their way of answering that, we shall see, as through a little window, into the very heart of these men's spiritual condition.

A Hero has this first distinction, the Alpha and Omega of his whole Heroism, That he looks through the show of things into *things*. Use and wont, respectable hearsay, respectable formula: all these are good, or are not good. There is something behind and beyond all these, which all these must correspond with, be the image of, or they are *Idolatries* . . . Though all men walk by them, what good is it? The great Reality stands glaring there upon *him*. He there has to answer it, or perish miserably. Now, even now, or else through all Eternity never!

All death is but of the body, not of the essence or soul; all destruction, by violent revolution or howsoever it be, is but new creation on a wider scale. Odinism was *Valor;* Christianity was *Humility* a nobler kind of Valor. No thought that ever dwelt honestly as true in the heart of man but *was* an honest insight into God's truth on man's part, and *has* an essential truth in it which endures through all changes, an everlasting possession for us all. And, on the other hand, what a melancholy notion is that, which has to represent all men, in all countries and times except our own, as having spent their life in blind condemnable error, mere lost Pagans, Scandinavians, Mahometans, only that we might have the true ultimate knowledge! All generations of men were lost and wrong, only that this present little section of a generation might be saved and right. They all marched forward there, all generations since the beginning of the world, like the Russian soldiers into the ditch of Schweidnitz Fort, only to fill up the ditch with their dead bodies, that we might march over and take the place!

It is an important fact in the nature of man, that he tends to reckon his own insight as final, and goes upon it as such. He will always do it, I suppose, in one or the other way; but it must be in some wider, wiser way than this. Are not all true men that live, or that ever lived, soldiers of the same army, enlisted, under Heaven's captaincy, to do battle against the same enemy, the empire of Darkness and Wrong? Why should we misknow one another, fight not against the enemy but against ourselves, from mere difference of uniform? All uniforms shall be good, so they hold in them true valiant men. All fashions of arms, the Arab turban and swift scimitar, Thor's strong hammer smiting down Jötuns shall be welcome. Luther's battle-voice, Dante's march-melody, all genuine things are with us, not against us. We are all under one Captain, soldiers of the same host.

Idol is *Eidolon,* a thing seen, a symbol. It is not God, but a symbol of God; and perhaps one may question whether any the most benighted mortal ever took it for more than a Symbol. I fancy, he did not think that the poor image his own hands had made *was* God; but that God was emblemed by it, that God was in it some way or other. And now in this sense, one may ask, Is not all worship whatsoever a worship by Symbols, by *eidola,* or things seen? Whether seen, rendered visible as an image or picture to the bodily eye; or visible only to the inward eye, to the imagination, to the intellect: this makes a superficial, but no substantial difference. It is still a Thing seen, significant of Godhead; an Idol. The most rigorous Puritan has his Confession of Faith and intellectual Representation of Divine things, and worships thereby; thereby is worship first made possible for him. All creeds, liturgies, religious forms, conceptions that

183

fitly invest religious feelings, are in this sense *eidola*, things seen. All worship whatsoever must proceed by Symbols, by Idols:—we may say all Idolatry is comparative, and the worst Idolatry is only more idolatrous.

Where, then, lies the evil of it? Some fatal evil must lie in it, or earnest prophetic men would not on all hands so reprobate it. Why is Idolatry so hateful to Prophets? It seems to me as if, in the worship of these poor wooden symbols, the thing that had chiefly provoked the Prophet, and filled his inmost soul with indignation and aversion, was not exactly what suggested itself to his own thought, and came out of him in words to others, as the thing. The rudest heathen that worshipped Canopus or the Caabah Black-Stone, he was superior to the horse that worshipped nothing at all! Nay there was a kind of lasting merit in that poor act of his; analogous to what is still meritorious in Poets; recognition of a certain endless *divine* beauty and significance in stars and all natural objects whatsoever. Why should the Prophet so mercilessly condemn him? The poorest mortal worshipping his Fetish . . . let his heart be honestly full of it, the whole space of his dark narrow mind illuminated thereby; in one word, let him entirely *believe* in his Fetish,—it will then be, if not well with him, yet as well as it can readily be made to be.

Note: A paragraph at this point is omitted, because included in Section captioned Religion. See page 18, paragraph commencing, "But here enters the fatal circumstance of Idolatry" and ending, "Men are no longer *sincere* men."

It is the property of every Hero, in every time, in every place and situation, that he come back to reality; that he stand upon things, and not shows of things. According as he loves, and venerates, articulately or with deep speechless thought, the awful realities of things, so will the hollow shows of things, however regular, decorous, accredited by

Koreishes or Conclaves, be intolerable and detestable to him. Protestantism, too, is the work of a Prophet: the prophet-work of that sixteenth century. The first stroke of honest demolition to an ancient thing grown false and idolatrous; preparatory afar off to a new thing, which shall be true, and authentically divine!

No iron chain, or outward force of any kind, could ever compel the soul of a man to believe or to disbelieve: it is his own indefeasible light, that judgment of his; he will reign, and believe there, by the grace of God alone!

The exercise of private judgment, faithfully gone about, does by no means necessarily end in selfish independence, isolation; but rather ends necessarily in the opposite of that. It is not honest inquiry that makes anarchy; but it is error, insincerity, half-belief and untruth that make it. A man protesting against error is on the way towards uniting himself with all men that believe in truth. There is no communion possible among men who believe only in hearsays. The heart of each is lying dead; has no power of sympathy even with *things*,—or he would believe *them* and not hearsays. No sympathy even with things; how much less with his fellow-men! He cannot unite with men; he is an anarchic man. Only in a world of sincere men is unity possible;— and there, in the long-run, it is as good as *certain*.

It is not necessary a man should himself have *discovered* the truth he is to believe in, and never so *sincerely* to believe in . . . The merit of *originality* is not novelty; it is sincerity. The believing man is the original man; whatsoever he believes, he believes it for himself, not for another.

And what, then, had these men . . . ? Two things both which, it seems to us, are indispensable for such men. They had a true, religious principle of morals; and a single, not a double aim in their activity. They were not self-seekers and self-worshippers; but seekers and worshippers of something far better than Self. Not personal enjoyment was their

185

object; but a high heroic idea of Religion, of Patriotism, of heavenly Wisdom, in one or the other form, ever hovered before them; in which cause they neither shrank from suffering, nor called on the earth to witness it as something wonderful; but patiently endured, counting it blessedness enough so to spend and be spent. Thus the "golden-calf of Self-love," however curiously carved, was not their Deity; but the Invisible Goodness, which alone is man's reasonable service. This feeling was as a celestial fountain, whose streams refreshed into gladness and beauty all the provinces of their otherwise too desolate existence. In a word, they willed one thing, to which all other things were subordinated and made subservient; and therefore they accomplished it. The wedge will rend rocks; but its edge must be sharp and single: if it be double, the wedge is bruised in pieces and will rend nothing.

Men's hearts ought not to be set against one another; but set with one another, and all against the Evil thing only. Men's souls ought to be left to see clearly; not jaundiced, blinded, twisted all awry, by revenge, mutual abhorrence, and the like.

The faith in an Invisible, Unnameable, Godlike, present everywhere in all that we see and suffer, is the essence of all faith whatsoever.

The Maker's Laws, whether they are promulgated in Sinai Thunder, to the ear or imagination, or quite otherwise promulgated, are the Laws of God; transcendent, everlasting, imperatively demanding obedience from all men. This, without any thunder, or with never so much thunder, thou, if there be any soul left in thee, canst know of a truth. The Universe is made by Law; the great Soul of the World is just and not unjust. Look thou, if thou have eyes or soul left, into this great shoreless Incomprehensible: in the heart of its tumultuous Appearances, Embroilments and mad Time-vortexes, is there not, silent, eternal, an All-just, and

All-beautiful sole Reality and ultimate controlling Power of the whole? This is not a figure of speech; this is a fact. The fact of Gravitation known to all animals, is not surer than this inner Fact, which may be known to all men. He who knows this, it will sink silent, awful, unspeakable, into his heart. He will say with Faust: "Who *dare* name Him?" Most rituals or "namings" he will fall in with at present, are like to be "namings"—which shall be nameless! In silence, in the Eternal Temple, let him worship, if there be no fit word. Such knowledge, the crown of his whole spiritual being, the life of his life, let him keep and sacredly walk by. He has a religion. Hourly and daily, for himself, and for the whole world, a faithful, unspoken, but not ineffectual prayer rises, "Thy will be done." His whole work on Earth is an emblematic spoken or acted prayer, Be the will of God done on Earth,—not the Devil's will, or any of the Devil's servants' wills! He has a religion, this man; an everlasting Loadstar that beams the brighter in the Heavens, the darker here on Earth grows the night around him. Thou, if thou know not this, what are all rituals, liturgies, mythologies, mass-chantings, turnings of rotary calabash? They are as nothing; in a good many respects they are as *less*. Divorced from this, getting half-divorced from this, they are a thing to fill one with a kind of horror; with a sacred inexpressible pity and fear. The most tragical thing a human eye can look on. It was said to the prophet, "Behold, I will show thee worse things than these: women weeping to Thammuz." That was the acme of the Prophet's vision,—then as now.

Men believe in Bibles, and disbelieve in them: but of all Bibles the frightfulest to disbelieve in is this "Bible of Universal History." This is the Eternal Bible and God's-Book, "which every born man," till once the soul and eyesight are extinguished in him, "can and must, with his own eyes, see the God's-Finger writing!" To discredit this, is an *infidelity* like no other. Such infidelity you would punish, if not by fire

187

and fagot, which are difficult to manage in our times, yet by the most peremptory order, To hold its peace till it got something wiser to say. Why should the blessed silence be broken into noises, to communicate only the like of this? If the Past have no God's-Reason in it, nothing but Devil's-Unreason, let the Past be eternally forgotten: mention it no more;—we whose ancestors were all hanged, why should we talk of ropes!

It is not true that men ever lived by Delirium, Hypocrisy, Injustice, or any form of Unreason, since they came to inhabit this Planet. It is not true that they never did, or ever will, live except by the reverse of these. Men will be again taught this. Their acted History will then again be a Heroism; their written History, what it once was, an Epic. Nay, forever it is either such, or else it virtually is—Nothing. Were it written in a thousand volumes, the Unheroic of such volumes hastens incessantly to be forgotten; the net content of an Alexandrian Library of Unheroics is, and will ultimately show itself to be, *zero*. What man is interested to remember it; have not all men, at all times, the liveliest interest to forget it?—"Revelations," if not celestial, then infernal, will teach us that God is; we shall then, if needful, discern without difficulty that He has always been!

It is written, "Many shall run to and fro, and knowledge shall be increased." Surely the plain rule is, Let each considerate person have his way, and see what it will lead to. For not this man and that man, but all men make up mankind, and their united tasks the task of mankind. How often have we seen some such adventurous, and perhaps much-censured wanderer light on some outlying, neglected, yet vitally momentous province; the hidden treasure of which he first discovered, and kept proclaiming till the general eye and effort were directed thither, and the conquest was completed;—thereby, in these his seemingly so aimless rambles, planting new standards, founding new habitable

188

colonies, in the immeasurable circumambient realm of Nothingness and Night! Wise man was he who counseled that Speculation should have free course, and look fearlessly towards all the thirty-two points of the compass, whithersoever and howsoever it listed.

Man is emphatically a proselytizing creature.

If new-got gold is said to burn the pockets till it be cast forth into circulation, much more may new truth.

In our historical and critical capacity, we hope we are strangers to all the world; have feud or favor with no one,—save indeed the Devil, with whom, as with the Prince of Lies and Darkness, we do at all times wage internecine war.

"To the eye of vulgar Logic," says he, "what is man? An omnivorous Biped that wears Breeches. To the eye of Pure Reason what is he? A Soul, A Spirit, and divine Apparition. Round his mysterious ME, there lies, under all those woolrags, a Garment of Flesh (or of Senses), contextured in the Loom of Heaven; whereby he is revealed to his like, and dwells with them in UNION and DIVISION; and sees and fashions for himself a Universe, with azure Starry Spaces, and long Thousands of years. Deep-hidden is he under that strange Garment; amid Sounds and Colors and Forms, as it were, swathed in, and inextricably over-shrouded: yet it is sky-woven, and worthy of a God. Stands he not thereby in the center of Immensities, in the conflux of Eternities? He feels; power has been given him to know, to believe; nay does not the spirit of Love, free in its celestial primeval brightness, even here, though but for moments, look through? Well said Saint Chrysostom, with his lips of gold, 'the true SHEKINAH is Man:' where else is the GOD'S—PRESENCE manifested not to our eyes only, but to our hearts, as in our fellow-man?"

Well sang the Hebrew Psalmist: "If I take the wings of the morning and dwell in the uttermost parts of the universe, God is there." Thou thyself, O cultivated reader, who

189

too probably art no Psalmist, but a Prosaist, knowing GOD only by tradition, knowest thou any corner of the world where at least FORCE is not? The drop which thou shakest from thy wet hand, rests not where it falls, but to-morrow thou findest it swept away; already on the wings of the North-wind, it is nearing the Tropic of Cancer. How came it to evaporate, and not lie motionless; without Force, and utterly dead?

As I rode through the Schwarzwald, I said to myself: That little fire which glows star-like across the dark-growing (nachtende) moor, where the sooty smith bends over his anvil, and thou hopest to replace thy lost horse-shoe,—is it a detached, separated speck, cut off from the whole Universe; or indissolubly joined to the whole. Thou fool, that smithy-fire was (primarily) kindled at the Sun; is fed by air that circulates from before Noah's Deluge, from beyond the Dogstar; therein, with Iron Force, and Coal Force, and the far stranger Force of Man, are cunning affinities and battles and victories of Force brought about; it is a little ganglion, or nervous center, in the great vital system of Immensity. Call it, if thou wilt, an unconscious Altar, kindled on the bosom of the All; whose iron sacrifice, whose iron smoke and influence reach quite through the All; whose dingy Priest, not by word, yet by brain and sinew, preaches forth the mystery of Force; nay preaches forth (exoterically enough) one little textlet from the Gospel of Freedom, the Gospel of Man's Force, commanding, and one day to be all-commanding.

Thy true Beginning and Father is in Heaven, whom with the bodily eye thou shalt never behold, but only with the Spiritual.

Any road, this simple Entepfuhl road, will lead you to the end of the World!

Nevertheless, I were but a vain dreamer to say, that even then my felicity was perfect. I had, once for all, come down from Heaven into the Earth. Among the rainbow colors that glowed on my horizon, lay even in childhood a dark ring of Care, as yet no thicker than a thread, and often quite overshone; yet always it reappeared, nay ever waxing broader and broader; till in after-years it almost overshadowed my whole canopy, and threatened to ingulf me in final night. It was the ring of Necessity whereby we are all begirt; happy he for whom a kind heavenly Sun brightens it into a ring of Duty, and plays round it with beautiful prismatic diffractions; yet ever, as basis and as bourn for our whole being, it is there.

How indestructibly the Good grows, and propagates itself, even among the weedy entanglements of Evil! The highest whom I knew on Earth I here saw bowed down, with awe unspeakable, before a Higher in Heaven: such things, especially in infancy, reach inwards to the very core of your being; mysteriously does a Holy of Holies build itself into visibility in the mysterious deeps; and Reverence, the divinest in man, springs forth undying from its mean envelopment of Fear.

A certain groundplan of Human Nature and Life began to fashion itself in me; wondrous enough, now when I look back on it; for my whole Universe, physical and spiritual, was as yet a Machine! However, such a conscious, recognized groundplan, the truest I had, *was* beginning to be there, and by additional experiments might be corrected and indefinitely extended.

Thus from poverty does the strong educe nobler wealth; thus in the destitution of the wild desert does our young Ishmael acquire for himself the highest of all possessions, that of Self-help. Nevertheless a desert this was, waste, and howling with savage monsters. Teufelsdröckh gives us long details of his "fever-paroxysms of Doubt"; his Inquiries concerning Miracles and the Evidences of religious Faith; and how "in the silent night-watches, still darker in his heart than over sky and earth, he has cast himself before the All-seeing, and with audible prayers cried vehemently for Light, for deliverance from Death and the Grave. Not till after long years, and unspeakable agonies, did the believing heart surrender; sink into spell-bound sleep, under the nightmare, Unbelief; and, in this hag-ridden dream, mistake God's fair living world for a pallid, vacant Hades and extinct Pandemonium. "But through such Purgatory pain," continues he, "it is appointed us to pass; first must the dead Letter of Religion own itself dead, and drop piecemeal into dust, if the living Spirit of Religion, freed from this its charnel-house, is to arise on us, new-born of Heaven, and with new healing under its wings."

"Not what I Have," continues he, "but what I Do is my Kingdom. To each is given a certain inward Talent, a certain outward Environment of Fortune; to each, by wisest combination of these two, certain maximum of Capability. But the hardest problem were ever this first: To find by study of yourself, and of the ground you stand on, what your combined inward and outward Capability specially is. For, alas, our young soul is all budding with Capabilities, and we see not yet which is the main and true one. Always too the new man is in a new time, under new conditions: his course can be the *fac-simile* of no prior one, but is by its nature original. And then how seldom will the outward Capability fit the inward: though talented enough, we are poor, unfriended, dyspeptical, bashful; nay what is worse than all, we are foolish. Thus, in a whole imbroglio of Capabilities, we go stupidly groping about, to grope which is ours, and often clutch the wrong one: in this mad work must several years of our small term be spent, till the purblind Youth, by practice, acquire notions of distance, and become a seeing Man. Nay, many so spend their whole term, and in ever-new expectation, ever-new disappointment, shift from enterprise to enterprise, and from side to side:

till at length, as exasperated striplings of threescore-and-ten, they shift into their last enterprise, that of getting buried.

"Such, since the most of us are too ophthalmic, would be the general fate; were it not that one thing saves us: our Hunger. For on this ground, as the prompt nature of Hunger is well known, must a prompt choice be made: hence have we, with wise foresight, Indentures and Apprenticeships for our irrational young, whereby, in due season the vague universality of a Man shall find himself ready-moulded into a specific Craftsman; and so thenceforth work, with much or with little waste of Capability as it may be; yet not with the worst waste, that of time. Nay even in matters spiritual, since the spiritual artist too is born blind, and does not, like certain other creatures, receive sight in nine days, but far later, sometimes never,—is it not well that there should be what we call Professions, or Bread-studies (*Brodzwecke*), preappointed us? Here, circling like the gin-horse, for whom partial or total blindness is no evil, the Bread-artist can travel contentedly round and round, still fancying that it is forward and forward; and realize much: for himself victual; for the world an additional horse's power in the grand corn-mill and hemp-mill or Economic Society. For me too had such a leading-string been provided; only that it proved a neck-halter, and had nigh throttled me, till I broke it off."

Like a very young person, I imagined it was with Work alone, and not also with Folly and Sin, in myself and others, that I had been appointed to struggle.

"The Universe," he says, "was as a mighty Sphinx-riddle, which I knew so little of, yet must rede, or be devoured. In red streaks of unspeakable grandeur, yet also in the blackness of darkness, was Life, to my too unfurnished Thought, unfolding itself. A strange contradiction lay in me; and I as yet knew not the solution of it; knew not that spiritual

193

music can spring only from discords set in harmony; that but for Evil there were no Good, as victory is only possible by battle."

For man's well-being, Faith is properly the one thing needful; how, with it, Martyrs, otherwise weak, can cheerfully endure the shame and the cross; and without it, Worldlings puke up their sick existence, by suicide, in the midst of luxury.

The Professor says, he here first got eye on the Knot that had been strangling him, and straightway could unfasten it, and was free. "A vain interminable controversy," writes he, "touching what is at present called Origin of Evil, or some such thing, arises in every soul, since the beginning of the world; and in every soul, that would pass from idle Suffering into actual Endeavoring, must first be put an end to. The most, in our time, have to go content with a simple, incomplete enough Suppression of this controversy; to a few some Solution of it is indispensable. In every new Era, too, such Solution comes out in different terms; and ever the Solution of the last era has become obsolete, and is found unserviceable. For it is man's nature to change his Dialect from century to century; he cannot help it though he would. The authentic *Church-Catechism* of our present century has not yet fallen into my hands; meanwhile, for my own private behoof, I attempt to elucidate the matter so. Man's Unhappiness, as I construe, comes of his Greatness; it is because there is an Infinite in him, which with all his cunning he cannot quite bury under the Finite. Will the whole Finance Ministers and Upholsterers and Confectioners of modern Europe undertake, in joint-stock company, to make one Shoeblack Happy? They cannot accomplish it, above an hour or two: for the Shoeblack also has a Soul quite other than his Stomach; and would require, if you consider it, for his permanent satisfaction and saturation, simply this allotment, no more and no less; *God's infinite Universe al-*

together to himself, therein to enjoy infinitely, and fill every wish as fast as it rose. Oceans of Hochheimer, a Throat like that of Ophiuchus: speak not of them; to the infinite Shoeblack they are as nothing. No sooner is your ocean filled, than he grumbles that it might have been of better vintage. Try him with half of a Universe, of an Omnipotence, he sets to quarrelling with the proprietor of the other half, and declares himself the most maltreated of men.—Always there is a black-spot in our sunshine, it is even, as I said, the *Shadow of Ourselves.*"

"*Es leuchtet mir ein,* I see a glimpse of it!" cries he elsewhere: "there is in man a Higher than Love of Happiness: he can do without Happiness, and instead thereof find Blessedness! Was it not to preach forth this same Higher that sages and martyrs, the Poet and the Priest, in all times, have spoken and suffered; bearing testimony, through life and through death, of the Godlike that is in Man, and how in the God-like only has he Strength and Freedom? Which God-inspired Doctrine art thou also honored to be taught; O Heavens! and broken with manifold Afflictions, even till thou become contrite, and learn it! O, thank thy Destiny for these; thankfully bear what yet remain: thou hadst need of them; the Self in thee needed to be annihilated. By benignant fever-paroxysms is Life rooting out the deep-seated chronic Disease, and triumphs over Death. On the roaring billows of Time, thou art not engulfed, but borne aloft into the azure of Eternity. Love not Pleasure; love God. This is the Everlasting Yea, wherein all contradiction is solved: wherein whoso walks and works, it is well with him."

"Cease, my much-respected Herr von Voltaire," thus apostrophizes the Professor: "shut thy sweet voice; for the task appointed thee seems finished. Sufficiently hast thou demonstrated this proposition, considerable or otherwise; That the Mythus of the Christian Religion looks not in the eighteenth century as it did in the eighth. Alas, were thy six-and-thirty quartos, and the six-and-thirty thousand other quartos and folios, and flying sheets or reams, printed before and since on the same subject, all needed to convince us of so little! But what next? Wilt thou help us to embody the divine Spirit of that Religion in a new Mythus, in a new vehicle and vesture, that our Souls, otherwise too like perishing, may live? What! thou hast no faculty in that kind? Only a torch for burning, no hammer for building? Take our thanks, then, and—thyself away.

"Meanwhile what are antiquated Mythuses to me? Or is the God present, felt in my own heart, a thing which Herr von Voltaire will dispute out of me; or dispute into me? To the *'Worship of Sorrow'* ascribe what origin and genesis thou pleasest, *has* not that Worship originated, and been generated; is it not *here?* Feel it in thy heart, and then say whether it is of God! This is Belief; all else is Opinion,— for which latter whoso will, let him worry and be worried."

"Neither," observes he elsewhere, "shall ye tear out one another's eyes, struggling over 'Plenary Inspiration,' and such-like: try rather to get a little even Partial Inspiration, each of you for himself. One Bible I know, of whose Plenary Inspiration doubt is not so much as possible; nay with my own eyes I saw the God's-Hand writing it: thereof all other Bibles are but Leaves,—say, in Picture-Writing to assist the weaker faculty."

"But indeed Conviction, were it never so excellent, is worthless till it convert itself into Conduct. Nay properly Conviction is not possible till then; inasmuch as all Speculation is by nature endless, formless, a vortex amid vortices: only by a felt indubitable certainty of Experience does it find any center to revolve round, and so fashion itself into a system. Most true is it, as a wise man teaches us, that 'Doubt of any sort cannot be removed except by Action.' On which ground, too, let him who gropes painfully in darkness or uncertain light, and prays vehemently that the dawn may ripen into day, lay this other precept well to heart, which to me was of invaluable service: '*Do the Duty Which lies nearest thee*,' which thou knowest to be a Duty! Thy second Duty will already have become clearer."

May we not say, however, that the hour of Spiritual Enfranchisement is even this: When your Ideal World, wherein the whole man has been dimly struggling and inexpressibly languishing to work, becomes revealed, and thrown open; and you discover, with amazement enough, like the Lothario in *Wilhelm Meister*, that your 'America is here or nowhere'? The Situation that has not its Duty, its Ideal, was never yet occupied by man. Yes, here, in this poor, miserable, hampered, despicable Actual, wherein thou even now standest, here or nowhere is thy Ideal: work it out therefrom; and working, believe, live, be free. Fool! the Ideal is in thyself, the impediment too is in thyself: thy Condition is but the stuff thou are to shape that same Ideal out of: what matters whether such stuff be of this sort or that, so the Form thou give it be heroic, be poetic? O thou that pinest in the imprisonment of the Actual, and criest bitterly to the gods for a kingdom wherein to rule and create, know this of a truth: the thing thou seekest is already with thee, "here or nowhere," couldst thou only see!

But it is with man's Soul as it was with Nature: the beginning of Creation is—Light. Till the eye have vision, the whole members are in bonds. Divine moment, when over the tempest-tost Soul, as once over the wild-weltering Chaos, it is spoken: Let there be Light! Ever to the greatest that has felt such moment, is it not miraculous and God-announcing; even as, under simpler Figures, to the simplest and least. The mad primeval Discord is hushed; the rudely-jumbled conflicting elements bind themselves into separate Firmaments: deep silent rock-foundations are built beneath;

197

and the skyey vault with its everlasting Luminaries above: instead of a dark Wasteful Chaos, we have a blooming, fertile heaven-encompassed World.

I too could now say to myself: Be no longer a Chaos, but a World, or even Worldkin. Produce! Produce! Were it but the pitifullest infinitesimal fraction of a Product, produce it, in God's name! Up, up! Whatsoever thy hand findeth to do, do it with thy whole might. Work while it is called To-day; for the Night cometh, wherein no man can work.

Outward Religion originates by Society, Society becomes possible by Religion. Nay, perhaps, every conceivable Society, past and present, may well be figured as properly and wholly a Church, in one or other of these three predicaments: an audibly preaching and prophesying Church, which is the best; second, a Church that struggles to preach and prophesy, but cannot as yet, till its Pentecost come; and third and worst, a Church gone dumb with old age, or which only mumbles delirium prior to dissolution. "Whoso fancies that by Church is here meant Chapterhouses and Cathedrals, or by preaching and prophesying mere speech and chanting, let him," says the oracular Professor, "read on, light of heart (getrosten Muthes)."

For if Government is, so to speak, the outward SKIN of the Body Politic, holding the whole together and protecting it; and all your Craft-Guilds, and Associations for Industry, of hand or of head, are the Fleshly Clothes, the muscular and osseous Tissues (lying *under* such SKIN), whereby Society stands and works;—then is Religion the inmost Pericardial and Nervous Tissue, which ministers Life and warm Circulation to the whole. Without which Pericardial Tissue the Bones and Muscles (of Industry) were inert, or animated only by a Galvanic vitality; the SKIN would become shriveled pelt, or fast-rotting rawhide; and Society itself a dead carcass,—deserving to be buried.

198

Men were no longer Social, but Gregarious; which latter state also could not continue, but must gradually issue in universal selfish discord, hatred, savage isolation, and dispersion;—whereby, as we might continue to say, the very dust and dead body of Society would have evaporated and become abolished. Such, and so all-important, all-sustaining, are the Church-Clothes to civilized or even to rational men.

Meanwhile, in our era of the World, those same Church-Clothes have gone sorrowfully out-at-elbows: nay, far worse, many of them have become mere hollow Shapes, or Masks, under which no living Figure or Spirit any longer dwells; but only spiders and unclean beetles, in horrid accumulation, drive their trade; and the mask still glares on you with its glass eyes, in ghastly affectation of Life,—some generation-and-half after Religion has quite withdrawn from it, and in unnoticed nooks is weaving for herself new Vestures, wherewith to reappear, and bless us, or our sons or grandsons.

It is not because of his toils that I lament for the poor; we must all toil, or steal (howsoever we name our stealing), which is worse; no faithful workman finds his task a pastime. The poor is hungry and athirst; but for him also there is food and drink: he is heavy-laden and weary; but for him also the Heavens send Sleep, and of the deepest; in his smoky cribs, a clear dewey heaven of Rest envelops him and fitful glitterings of cloud-skirted Dreams. But what I do mourn over is, that the lamp of his soul should go out; that no ray of heavenly, or even of earthly knowledge, should visit him; but only, in the haggard darkness, like two spectres, Fear and Indignation bear him company. Alas, while the Body stands so broad and brawny, must the soul lie blinded, dwarfed, stupefied, almost annihilated! Alas, was this too a Breath of God; bestowed in Heaven, but on earth never to be unfolded!—That there should one Man die ignorant who had capacity for Knowledge, this I call a tragedy, were it to happen more than twenty times in the minute, as by some computations it does. The miserable fraction of Science which our united Mankind, in a wide Universe of Nescience, has acquired, why is not this, with all diligence imparted to all?

The golden age, which a blind tradition has hitherto placed in the Past, is before us.

Yes, truly, if Nature is one, and a living indivisible whole, much more is Mankind, the Image that reflects and creates Nature, without which Nature were not. As palpable life-streams in that wondrous Individual Mankind, among so many life-streams that are not palpable, flow on those main currents of what we call Opinion; as preserved in Institutions, Politics, Churches, above all in Books. Beautiful it is to understand and know that a Thought did never yet die; that as thou, the originator thereof, hast gathered it and created it from the whole Past, so thou wilt transmit it to the whole Future. It is thus that the heroic heart, the seeing eye of the first times, still feels and sees in us of the latest; that the Wise Man stands ever encompassed, and spiritually embraced, by a cloud of witnesses and brothers; and there is a living literal *Communion of Saints*, wide as the World itself, and as the History of the World.

There is no Church, sayest thou? The voice of Prophecy has gone dumb? This is even what I dispute: but in any case, hast thou not still Preaching enough? A Preaching Friar settles himself in every village; and builds a pulpit, which he calls Newspaper. Therefrom he preaches what most momentous doctrine is in him, for man's salvation; and dost not thou listen, and believe? Look well, thou seest everywhere a new Clergy of the Mendicant Orders, some barefooted, some almost bare-backed, fashion itself into shape, and teach and preach, zealously enough, for copper alms and the love of God. These break in pieces the ancient idols; and, though themselves too often reprobate, as idol-breakers are wont to be, mark out the sites of new Churches, where the true God-ordained, that are to follow, may find audience, and minister. Said I not, Before the old skin was shed, the new had formed itself beneath it?

"But there is no Religion," reiterates the Professor. Fool! I tell thee, there is. Hast thou well considered all that lies in this immeasurable froth-ocean we name LITERA-TURE? Fragments of a genuine Church-Homiletic lie scattered there, which Time will assort: nay, fractions even of a Liturgy could I point out. And knowest thou no Prophet, even in the vesture, environment, and dialect of this age? None to whom the Godlike had revealed itself, through all meanest and highest forms of the Common; and by him been again prophetically revealed: in whose inspired melody, even in these rag-gathering and rag-burning days, Man's Life again begins, were it but afar off, to be divine? Knowest thou none such?

But thou as yet standest in no Temple; joinest in no Psalm-worship; feelest well that, where there is no ministering Priest, the people perish? Be of comfort! Thou art not alone, if thou have Faith. Spake we not of a Communion of Saints, unseen, yet not unreal, accompanying and brotherlike embracing thee, so thou be worthy? Their heroic Sufferings rise up melodiously together to Heaven, out of all lands, and out of all times, as a sacred *Miserere;* their heroic Actions also, as a boundless everlasting Psalm of Triumph. Neither say that thou hast now no Symbol of the Godlike. Is not God's Universe a Symbol of the Godlike; is not Immensity a Temple; is not Man's History, and Men's History, a perpetual Evangel? Listen, and for organ music thou wilt ever, as of old, hear the Morning Stars sing together.

How true is that of Novalis: 'It is certain, my Belief gains quite *infinitely* the moment I can convince another mind thereof?' Gaze thou in the face of thy Brother, in those eyes where plays the lambent fire of Kindness, or in those where rages the lurid conflagration of Anger; feel how thy own so quiet Soul is straightway involuntarily kindled with the like, and ye blaze and reverberate on each other, till it is all one limitless confluent flame (of embracing Love, or of deadly-grappling Hate); and then say what miraculous virtue goes out of man into man. But if so, through all the thick-plied hulls of our Earthly Life; how much more when it is of the Divine Life we speak, and inmost ME is, as it were, brought into contact with inmost ME!

CHARLES EDWARD GARMAN

"The educational process has not yet begun and it never will begin for most men, without guidance and methods of instruction which excite the student's intellectual curiosity, develop his intellectual self-reliance, and inspire in him faith in the truth and his ability to find it. It is the introduction of these spiritual and intellectual ferments into the educational process which marks the difference between intellectual sterility and the beginning of that moral and intellectual growth which is the first essential of all true education. And whenever that has occurred, from the time of Socrates to the days of Garman or of some of the teachers you and I knew in professional school, there you will find more than books and courses and curricula. You will find a man whose students rise to call him blessed because his was the God-given gift of the teacher." (Chief Justice Harlan Fiske Stone at the Fiftieth Reunion of his class in 1944—see *Amherst Alumni Council News*, July, 1944.)

"The determining note in Professor Garman's teaching of philosophy was his conception of philosophy. It was not for him primarily a subject to be studied for its own sake. One might say it was not studied as a subject at all. He believed that every man who thinks at all must sooner or later face the alternatives which are represented in general by a spiritual or a materialistic view of the world and of human action. He conceived it his task to aid young men in facing the problem squarely, and with a method for its solution. For this purpose he selected his material, planned the order of subjects, and developed the technique of his instruction."*

"Theism was for him the solution of the problem of knowledge; the biblical history was a revelation of an unfolding divine plan; the New Testament doctrine "not to be ministered unto but to minister" was his central ethical principle; the conception of a change of heart was primary in his theory of social reform; the principles of divine sovereignty and atonement afforded in his judgment the true basis of human political society; the teaching of philosophy was an opportunity to show men the eternal and to aid in shaping their lives."*

*From Letters, Lectures and Addresses of Charles E. Garman (Houghton Mifflin Co.),—see Introduction, pages 31, and 37-38.

From Charles E. Garman:

Everybody philosophizes; this is only saying that everybody has some idea of the world in which he lives. Even the child or the savage has his ultimate premises from which he reasons to the particular facts about him. Aristotle used to say that we must philosophize, and if one saith that he may not philosophize (of course the statement would mean nothing unless he gave some reason to support it, and a reason would imply certain premises in the light of which his statement was a conclusion), therefore in that very statement he doth philosophize and must.

Scientific philosophizing is solely a matter of evidence. The investigator does not ask what is the universe, or what may it be, or why could it not be so; his whole inquiry is,

What does evidence reveal concerning the actual world in which we live? Having found that appearances are deceitful and having discovered that the senses give us simply effects, he considers that any attempt to appeal ultimately to sense perception as the basis for knowledge of things as they really are is so ridiculous that every honest man can have no respect for those who deliberately make the attempt. He can see no difference between these people and the heathen who set up graven images made by their own hands for their gods, and then fall down and worship them as their creators.

Here, then, is the line of cleavage which runs through humanity. All start in ignorance in childhood and all attempt to get some conception of the world they live in, and all make blunders. But some fall back simply on the imagination, and postulate a world dogmatically which is gained through abstraction from their own experience. Others attempt a scientific analysis of their experience and insist on weighing evidence, and then they take this great step, namely, they affirm that concerning the things for which we have not a vestige of evidence we must speak and act in exactly the same way as we do concerning the things that do not exist.

If this world is governed by law, law is by its very nature universal. There can be no exceptions, given the conditions. Therefore whenever a man claims the privilege of being an exception, and adopts modes of thought and of life that he would not approve if every one else did exactly the same under the same conditions, he confesses himself to be unscientific, lawless, criminal. He stands self-condemned, and when he condemns himself he cannot wonder that others join in the condemnation.

The choice is between living up to the light you have or doing something infinitely worse. It is not between living up to the light you have or being guided by an infallible instinct that acts blindly and always turns you in the right direction, just as the needle points to the pole. Matter can act that way, but mind cannot. Matter never errs; it always obeys the laws of nature without varying a hair's-breadth. But the mind cannot do right without intelligence to guide it. . . . That is the penalty man pays for his exaltation. He has got to be something better than matter or he will be infinitely worse. The scientist realizes it, accepts the issue, and determines to work out his own salvation. But the dogmatist shuts his eyes to this fact and does what he can for his own destruction. The fact that he sometimes does not get destroyed is due not to himself but to the influence of the environment upon him, provided he is so fortunate as to live in an age when the traditions that he imitates have been produced by a prior science and therefore not wholly in the wrong direction.

There are any number of people who have absolutely no faith at all in the ability of the human mind to come out anywhere if it once begins to think about serious things. It seems to me worth everything to young men if they can see once for themselves that there is something more to truth than the superficial glimpses and side issues with which ordinary thought is occupied. It creates a spirit of candor and inquiry and faith in human effort, and at the same time a depth of humility and carefulness as they realize how often mistakes are made.

Man as a thinking being is largely a spectator in the universe, discovering and formulating knowledge of what already exists. But man as an ethical being is a creator of social and political relations and institutions whose perfection cannot be attained save through a long struggle on the part of the individual and the race towards an ideal. Correct ideals are shown to be as essential to the ethical life of the individual and the community as are correct architectural drawings and calculations in architecture and civil engineering.

205

It is our conviction that in the churches at the present day there is a subtle agnosticism that is sapping the very vitals of life, and that men cannot experience the inspiration of apostolic days without the deep convictions and realizations of the divine presence and of man's responsibility to God which the Apostles had.

Analyze external nature as you will and not a single attribute can you find there that is not mental so far as it goes. You have projected it out there or you could never have found it there. You remember the words of Coleridge:

> "we receive but what we give,
> And in our life alone does nature live;
> Ours is her wedding-garment, ours her shroud."

It is common to look at life in an economic way and to consider each deed on its own merits. From that point of view it is affirmed that a man can reform from evil practices as easily as he can turn his hand over. But if we clearly realize what a decision means we shall see that the change of a very simple act may be possible only on condition that a very profound governing purpose can be removed, which would be harder to accomplish than to move a mountain into the sea.

It is this act of sovereignty of the supreme choice which gives unity to our life. This is only another form of saying that all intelligence works backward; that a man must have an end in view in every intelligent action, and the end must sooner or later imply an ultimate end. The doctrine of the Scripture is that "Ye must be born again." That is, if the man's supreme choice is bad he cannot be changed by halves. There is no change that is radical that does not change the supreme choice.

To be personal is to be sovereign. When circumstances conspire to bring a matter in the sphere of our knowledge, then we have to interfere, either in the line of aiding and abetting or in that of resisting. This is the only sovereignty that can exist consistently with personality. The question of how we shall aid or how we shall resist is wholly a question of means. We may do it in an organized form and then we have government, or we do so without a form of organization and we have simply society, but in both cases we have sovereignty.

Sovereignty, we may say, then, is the interference of one individual with the affairs of another individual, either in the line of resisting or in that of assisting. You will see that it does not depend upon any compact any more than the attraction of the earth by the sun depends upon compact. You see that it is only a form of that relationship of cause and effect by virtue of which personal life is possible. Sovereignty simply postulates that the mind is a cause in the universe as truly as matter, the only difference being, matter can work automatically without intelligence, mind can work only when it is intelligent. Matter can work only one way, that is, it is fated. Mind can work either rightly or wrongly if you have free will. But when man does wrong he interferes with his fellow-man and exercises sovereignty as truly as when he does right, unless you please to define sovereignty as right interference, and tyranny as wrong interference. It seems to be better, however, to speak of sovereignty as interference. Human sovereignty has limits, but they are simply limits of knowledge and ability. Our ability is much more limited than our knowledge. Many things which we know about we have not strength enough to remedy; hence we aid and abet them unwillingly. Other things we are not skillful enough to remedy, but should do greater evil if we attempted it. The ordinary man is not skillful enough to perform an operation upon appendicitis, and if, on a hunting tour, he is with his friend who is taken ill in this way, he would have to allow him to die a natural death rather than to torture him to death by a bungling operation. These are simply the limitations of finiteness. They do not exist with God, who is the ideal sovereign, and who cannot know human deeds without interfering either in the line of aiding or in that of resisting them.

Business is the action and reaction on the state under conditions of equality. The law is that each person engaged in the transaction must be both means and end. This occurs only when the service rendered is an equivalent for the service received. This is justice, and only this can be allowed by the organism. Observe that such a transaction under the conditions is as truly a *"labor of love,"* that is, as truly conforms to the requirements of the organic unity, as charity and martyrdom under different conditions.

Charity is the action and reaction that takes place in the state under conditions of relative inequality on the part of those engaged. It is a condition of a diseased organism. The law of charity is that, for the time being, the strong shall help the weak without recompense, i.e., shall be means, not end, until the condition of health is restored. If the hand is diseased the body must heal it, and, in the mean time, give it rest. This may be a severer test, but is no more a labor of love than is business. Charity under conditions of relative equality is as truly a crime as dishonesty.

It is freely granted that the truths of a scientific sociology will not regenerate humanity in a day, that forces of evil in human nature are deep-seated; but the more you say about their strength and persistence, the more you emphasize the need of ideals for society. For there are no other human agencies to antagonize these powers of evil except the spiritual impulses that can be awakened only by a knowledge of ideals, and whose strength and efficiency are proportioned to the clearness with which those ideals are realized.

It is sometimes claimed that mystery is essential to religion, and that if the mysteries could be removed it would be taking away our reverence; that a God understood would be no God at all. But I beg leave to ask you to what are you looking forward in your future life? To a period of greater mystery, or, with the Apostle Paul, do you say, "Then shall I know even as I am known?" Will the sanctity, the love, and the adoration of worshipers in the New Jerusalem be diminished by this increase of knowledge? Must not the law of life which holds in heaven hold on earth? Therefore in proportion as we can reach out towards that larger knowledge of God, is not the light of that other world breaking upon the hilltops of this life with its morning splendor? This is the aim of philosophy, and I feel that to this end the preacher must strive if the Spirit speaks through him to the church.

The public at large are beginning to feel that there is no dividing line between time and eternity, the here and the hereafter; that a man's character will be governed by exactly the same laws, no matter how changed his environment may be. From a scientific point of view, then, men determine the value of religion by its influence upon the present life. If not essential for the life that now is, they ask what evidence do we have that it will be of any avail hereafter? On the other hand, if you can show us that it is the mainspring of existence here, we will trust it now, and we will trust it for the future also.

Whatever may be true of men's creed, nothing is clearer than the fact that the personality and the sovereignty of God are not a large factor in the practical life and thought of our age.

The church must not merely affirm the personality of God —for to many this would be a mere formula—the church must help men realize the divine personality; it must force men to see that personality and sovereignty are the supreme facts of the universe. But this cannot be done unless you philosophize.

Some time ago a student expressed his estimate of German philosophy in these words: "Bricks without straw, but plenty of mud, though," and this is about the estimate that any one will have who gives to philosophical writers only a superficial attention. . . . But if one were not making a campaign of criticism, if one were really in earnest in his search for truth, he would find this so-called mud very different stuff from what it first appeared to be. He would find it composed of ingredients quite as marvelous as those Ruskin found in the mud of a manufacturing village. You remember Ruskin's description of these chemical elements, which at first had so repelled him. He says: "Beginning with the clay. Leave it still quiet to follow its own instinct of unity, and it becomes not only white, but clear, not only clear, but hard, not only clear and hard, but so set that it can deal with the light in a wonderful way and gather out of it the loveliest blue rays, refusing the rest. We call it then a sapphire."

Then he takes the sand and, under similar conditions, finds it arranging itself in such a form that it has the power to reflect not merely the blue rays, but blue, green, purple, and red in the greatest beauty in which they can be seen through any hard material whatsoever. We call it then an opal.

Encouraged by these discoveries, Ruskin sets himself to examine what appears to be the filthy soot. It cannot make itself white at first, but, instead of being discouraged, tries harder and harder and comes out at last the hardest thing in the world; in exchange for the blackness that it had, it obtains the power of reflecting all the rays of the sun at once, in the vividest blaze that any solid thing can shoot. We call it then a diamond. The ounce of slime which we despised has, under favorable conditions, become three of the most precious jewels—a sapphire, an opal, and a diamond.

In a similar manner those difficult and confusing philo-

210

sophical treatises, with their repulsive terminology, that seemed so absurd on their first reading, will, if time and thought are given to them by a candid mind, crystallize into the most precious truths that have ever rewarded the search of a finite human being. It is just these truths, in their crystallized form, that preachers need to make accessible to their congregation in this age of criticism and reconstruction.

Among the great truths thus brought within our reach are these three:

First, Idealism; or the conception of the universe, material as truly as moral, as dependent of God for its continued existence from moment to moment, as truly as the rainbow on the continued shining of the sun. Philosophy takes literally Christ's words, that not a sparrow falls to the ground "without your Father." So also the words of the Apostle Paul: "For in Him we live, and move, and have our being."

Secondly, the conception of Personality is the ultimate fact of the universe. From which it follows that all nature as truly as all human history has not merely a scientific, but also an ethical and a religious, import, and is progressing towards the realization of divine ideals. This is the foundation for all true optimism.

The great doctrine of Sovereignty is the third of the jewels that crystallize out of philosophical discussions. This is something infinitely more than mere cause and effect. It is the ultimate principle of all personal relationship, not merely between God and man, but quite as much between man and his fellows. Philosophy shows that human government and divine government stand or fall together. We cannot hold to the former and deny the latter.

Either human beings cannot think at all, or the conceptions they apply to men must be the standards by which they judge of God. Our mental processes are exactly the same whether we think about divine things or about human affairs. It follows that if personality, intelligence, consciousness is a transitional stage with men, it cannot be attributed to God. He must be perfect, therefore He must have advanced beyond this stage of existence.

A true philosophy lays the axe at the root of this tree. It recognizes clearly that spiritual impulses are not blind, but can act only through intelligence. Then perfection of life will consist in perfection of knowledge and personality; then it will be impossible to think of the Divine Being as other than omniscient, the tender, loving Father. Impersonal law will give place to the liberty of the sons of God. This is the only true view. Take Longfellow's Evangeline. The impulse to follow her lover through all those years of wandering is indeed the mainspring of her action, but can this impulse, acting blindly, find him? Is there a more pathetic scene in literature than when, floating down the Ohio River, her party lands on an island for rest, in the middle of the day, at the very time when her lover is rowing by on the other side? The animal impulse to rest can execute itself without intelligence. When Evangeline was tired she could drop to sleep without understanding the processes involved in slumber; she could take a reclining position without knowing the physiological principles which required it, for these animal impulses are as blind and automatic as magnetism which turns the needle to the pole. Had her spiritual impulse of devotion to her lover been of this type she would have moved towards him as unconsciously as a stone falls towards the earth. But because the spiritual impulses could only be guided by intelligence, and she knew not what was going on about her, she embarks again, and every hour carries her farther and farther in the direction opposite to that taken by her lover.

What is true here is true in the religious life, if we do not add to our faith knowledge in the services of God. We need a philosophy of the divine life to fit our own actions into the course of events and make our lives count in our generation.

Students think of intellect and forms and leave out of account will power; but just as the most powerful engine is helpless without fuel, so the most brilliantly equipped mind is weakness itself without a strong will. But will is not an accident; it depends on inspiration, and inspiration is impossible without motive.

All history teaches that the deepest, truest, most efficient motives come only from ethical and religious convictions.

It is my conviction that a young man can obtain inspiration, enthusiasm, absence of self-consciousness only by the steady contemplation of great truths; that if he is wholly absorbed in imitation he is like a person whose whole work is that of a proofreader; if he is successful he is taken as a matter of course, and he gets no credit; if he is unsuccessful and makes mistakes he is awkward; he is ridiculed beyond endurance; he soon realizes that the most promising rewards for the most careful efforts are negative, and he soon becomes indifferent and is simply goaded on from fear of the consequences of failure. But the young man who philosophizes, who really understands himself and appreciates the truth, is no longer a slave of form, but is filled with admiration that is genuine and lasting.

When the idea fairly dawns upon them that true scholarship consists, not in some mystical quality of genius which ordinary men do not possess, but in simple honesty to one's self in following out the Cartesian Golden Rule, then they experience a new birth, they are no longer boys or slaves, but men. If they attain citizenship in the kingdom of truth, they perceive that the difference between the greatest and the smallest consists only in the quickness and comprehensiveness and thoroughness and humility of their work. Truth to one man is truth to all if they can get exactly the

213

same data and exactly the same standards. Henceforth they call no man master or lord, for all are brethren.

But if you can get the man so far along as to make him have confidence in the power of weighing evidence, to realize how much civilization owes to it; how every department of life can be progressive only through scientific thinking, and then make it a moral question, and show that intellectual honesty and supreme choice of truth for truth's sake, and determination to follow evidence to the best of one's ability, is the great line of cleavage between the saints and the sinners,—if you can force the issue here and win, then the class are entirely different afterwards. I do not believe without this moral battle, without considering the ethical phases of the question, it would be possible to get the best intellectual results.

It is so easy for them to feel that our knowledge of the material world is simple, and our knowledge of moral obligation and of spiritual life a mere matter of opinion, that I cannot content myself with leaving the class until they realize just the reverse.

Our standards of thinking are spiritual. Unless we can use these standards in judging others, and in interpreting nature, and in interpreting human life and human destiny, we are guilty of the worst form of anthropomorphism, an anthropomorphism for which there is not the slightest justification. But with the application of these standards moral obligations are authoritative, and society cannot dispense with them.

The student who has taken philosophy realizes how the part is to be estimated in the light of the whole; he realizes this more completely than he could from any other study. He also realizes the dignity which a part may secure from the grandeur of the whole to which it belongs, and the little things in life have a depth of meaning for him which they could not have if he had not this point of view.

Some time ago a child from the country was taken by its parents to the seaside, and under the care of its mother one day walked out on a long low, rocky ledge jutting out into the surf. It was a trying position for any landsman as a first experience, and the child soon cried lustily because the rock was floating out to sea and they would soon be beyond reach of help.

We can laugh at this childishness, but do we never make a mistake equally foolish? The child knew better and his mother assured him that the rocks could not float, but his senses affirmed in the most positive manner just the reverse; his childishness consisted in rejecting the testimony of judgment concerning what was really true, and in accepting merely the appearances instead. This is the line of cleavage which runs through all society. Its beginnings are low down in the animal world. Its endings are the Day of Judgment in the separation of the sheep and the goats. We may distinguish cleavage by different phraseology such as childishness or intelligence, wisdom or folly, barbarism or civilization, superstition or science, saint or sinner. In every case the discrimination is between appearances in the one case and reality in the other, and in each case a severe test of character is involved when dealing with a new problem. Indeed, it makes little odds how simple the question is, the supreme choice between truth for truth's sake, and personal convenience in following the inclination of the moment, is clearly involved.

There came a time when men distrusted appearances, and though the dreams were none the less real, and though indeed they became more and more frequent, yet they no longer were conceded to be true.

Now this is simply saying that men had taken the first step in that long journey whose highest expression is in the language of the Apostle, "We walk by faith, and not by sight." It is judgment substantiated by evidence as opposed

215

to sense reality. Thousands of years have passed since that
first step was taken. . . . The progress from fetichism, when
the world was governed by caprice, up to the nineteenth
century with its reign of physical law has been a battle in
which each foot of the ground has been contested in the
most stubborn manner. . . . Theism claims to furnish evidence of the most conclusive type, that the whole common
sense perception of the world is only appearance, as ridiculously unreal as the old Ptolemaic astronomy or savage
witchcraft. It claims to show that if thousands of valuable
lives were sacrificed to the superstitions of the Indian
medicine-man, or at a later time to the oracles of the astrologer, at the present time every life is being marred by faith
in the reality of the show world of common sense and that
the foundations of our social order are being undermined
by the logical conclusions which are drawn from these show
premises.

Theism claims to furnish evidence so clear that the way-
faringman, though a fool, may not err therein. It does not,
however, claim to be able to dissolve the appearances. The
Copernican system of astronomy with all its evidence has
not succeeded in enabling Professor Huxley to free himself
from seeing the sun set instead of the horizon lift. The sky
is still to us a vault and the earth a plane. The stars are all
at equal distance over our heads and we cannot for a
moment realize their actual magnitude. Though we are no
longer deceived by appearances, the oar is still bent to our
eyes in the water; and there are just as many stars in the
pond at night to us as to our savage ancestors. But a person
would be considered insane who should for a moment be
the slave of these appearances.

Human nature is a country like Holland; it is below the
sea level of superstition. The tidal wave of fanaticism has
rolled over human history again and again, wrecking all that
was fair and promising and leaving behind only death and

216

moral pestilence. Against this terrible disaster there is only one protection. We must build dikes around human nature, and the only dikes that will stand will be those constructed on evidence. Then men may live in peace and safety. He who destroys those dikes is the arch traitor of the race. He is attempting to again flood humanity with passion and credulity. Look back through history and see what a sad record it is. Mothers offering their own children in sacrifice to imaginary deities; hecatombs of human victims slain to avert pestilence; men made in the image of God languishing for years in foul caves till they became as insane as one possessed of the devil, hoping thereby to atone for crimes that had no existence; the whole human race absolutely blind to the beauty of nature, ignorant of the infinite wealth of the soil and the mines, living in a universe governed by law and finding there only caprice and fraud; not men sitting in darkness but blind men walking in great light, all because they were hypnotized by fanaticism and persecuted evidence. Living the life of tradition and imitation, a life of brain paths worthy only of the ape, they refused to exercise the God-given power of weighing evidence that would transform their world from chaos into cosmos, lifting them out of their slavery and giving them the liberty of the sons of God. See what a fight it has been to win what little progress in science we have already gained and then tell me if the man who adopts as his mode of life those processes which, if adopted universally, would stop all progress, annihilate all the achievements of science, and once more enthrone superstition,—tell me if he is not the arch traitor of humanity, the enemy of civilization, the incarnation of a fiend himself.

Men differ in wealth, in health, in knowledge, in power, in wit, in wisdom, but none of these constitute a line of cleavage that is fundamental. The wisest man does not know very much compared with all that is to be known. The most stupid man could learn a good deal if he only kept at it through all eternity. The witty man is simply one who emphasizes unusual likenesses and differences between things not too farfetched, at the same time not too true. . . . He surely would be the last to claim that he differed from others essentially. It is all a mere question of knack or skill. All differences in quantity are insignificant when you have eternity in view. The fundamental problem is not "where we are, but whither we are drifting." If you only give a man time enough, if he is going in the right direction he will make no mean progress. But if he is going in the wrong direction, the more time he has the more hopeless his case. And now what is the right direction? The reply is, weighing evidence and attempting to find the truth. To such a being, no matter how stupid, how ignorant, how weak, truth can be gradually revealed. For him the Divine Being can mark out an infinite future of progress. But a man who refuses to shape his life by evidence, who will weigh evidence only when it favors some pet scheme or plan, or when he can discomfort his enemy, but immediately drops it when it demands personal sacrifice for himself,—he is the man to whom you cannot appeal through the truth.

In social life we are ashamed to make the stranger the enemy as they did in old times. We are courteous to newcomers and give them a fair chance to show themselves worthy of our confidence before we pass judgment on them, but not so with new ideas. But the good time will come when progress shall be made here. The Bible tells us, "Be not forgetful to entertain strangers: for thereby some have entertained angels unawares." The truly inductive mind is not forgetful to entertain new ideas, new hypotheses, for some have thereby entertained the truth itself unawares.

If man is made only in the image of the animals and that is all there is to him, he is a contemptible being, for he surely pretends to be more. If he is made in the image of God, so that just as truly as we do it unto one of the least of these human beings, we do it unto God Himself, then our whole sense of values will be changed all along the line of social action.

We begin with the doctrine of the State and show that actual life is impossible apart from relationships. Then we go on to show that man has no dual personality; he is not endowed with two minds, the one to be used in the sphere of religion and the other in the sphere of government and society; that man is always and everywhere himself; that he has but one set of principles by which to guide his conduct; that love to God and love to man are, from the point of view of the finite, exactly the same process. From this point of view it is impossible to take up the study of objective ethics at all without covering the sphere of the State and of society. We make, therefore, the study of political obligations the very basis of our work. We attempt to show that as gravitation acts according to the same law, whether in the case of a planet or in the case of a pendulum, so man has exactly the same standard of obligation and the same principles of ethical judgment in dealing with human affairs that he has in dealing with God. If the powers that be are all ordained by God, then the law which governs these must be divine. We throw our whole weight on the doctrine that there is no such thing as political ethics apart from divine ethics, and any attempt so to consider human life is an abandonment of ethics altogether to mere calculations of expediency.

If all thought is a function of the brain, there is no such thing as "science" and no such thing as "truth" *for us.*

If we have the power to weigh evidence and get science, there is some thought whose action squares not with the line of least resistance in the brain, but with the truth, and oftentimes that action will be for the brain the line of greatest resistance.

Here we have it then: Either absolutely no trace of knowledge, no science, no physics of the brain, or "personality" is something more than a brain function.

No finite being is self-existent, but dependent on his creator. He will live just so long as his creator perpetuates him. It would be necessary for us to consider why man exists at all, why anything finite exists at all, if we are to ask the question how long we are to exist.

Theism is the only metaphysical position that has any consistent answer to the problem of life. It affirms that there is one law of being for the entire universe, God and man, namely, that "consciousness of subject is possible only through consciousness of object." We cannot think without thinking about something. If God is to continue his consciousness of self, He must maintain a universe of objects. But unity of self-consciousness is possible only through unity of objects.

If man can weigh evidence and get real truths, he has "qualitatively" a power as good as God's, for He—with all His omniscience—cannot do better than get exact truth. He has all truth, man only a little, but that is a difference in quantity, a difference unimportant from the point of view of eternity. The process is exactly the same, no higher can exist.

It is not a solution of the problem of evil, of the great mysteries of life and suffering and death, but only a star shining through the clouds that has been a help to at least one mariner in steering when the storm was fiercest and the rocks were very near. I have been greatly helped in getting my bearings by the theistic point of view.

Just as one must enlarge his physical universe so as to include more than the earth or he cannot calculate or explain the tides or the seasons, just as one must have an astronomy or he cannot have navigation or commerce outside of the coast, so we must enlarge the material world and admit that it is only part of a spiritual universe, or there could never exist chemistry, or physics, or physiology, or the science of evolution. Physical nature never studies science. The stars have studded the heavens for thousands of years, but they never studied astronomy. That, and all science, is the work of consciousness.

To recur to Kant's illustration. We know that no effort at flight can ever take the bird beyond the atmosphere of the earth, because when we know *what* it is to fly we see that it is merely to receive support from the air. So when we investigate what it is "to think," "to judge," "to get science," we see that it is to weigh accurately the evidence concerning the data in consciousness, and to do it according to the *constitution of consciousness* (laws of thought). So all our science is merely a knowledge of the world of consciousness.

If the material world is "a whole by itself" and consciousness is "another world apart," we have no physics, no chemistry, no physiology, nothing but various departments of psychology. But if theism is true there is only one world: "In Him we live, and move, and have our being." There is no outside to God. The universe is his mental creation as truly as our dreams are the products of our thoughts, as truly as Shakespeare's Hamlet was the incarnation of the author. If this is true, then we must distinguish between "consciousness' and "my consciousness." By weighing evidence concerning data in "my consciousness," I do discover the truth concerning the constitutional processes of "consciousness," provided that I am subjective to God; just as a triangle, if conscious of self, might discover truths concerning the *space* in which it exists. No line can be drawn between where God ends and man begins, any more than you can say where the ocean ends and the wave of the ocean begins. The finite does not limit the infinite. The infinite includes (not excludes) the finite. Then the material world is indeed external to me, but

221

not to God's consciousness; that is, the material world is only *a part* of the spiritual universe, as much so as heaven. Physical law is merely a statement of the way God's mind works when it does a certain kind of work, just as "logical laws" are a formulation of the way the human mind works when it does "judicial tasks." Only on this basis can a finite mind, "by weighing evidence concerning its own data," i.e., by *studying itself,* discover "physical laws." Take any problem in physics: is it soluble, or not? If not, why spend time on it? Why build a laboratory to investigate it? Data are worthless if they cannot aid in a solution. What, then, do we postulate when we *investigate nature?* The answer is perfectly clear when we realize what we are doing. Unless nature is "rational" through and through—that is, is *spiritual*—no solution can be hoped for. The laws of thought can *be known* as good only *for thought and its products.* If there be a world outside of and apart from consciousness, it were as absurd to affirm that the laws of our thought (that is, the true constitutional nature of our consciousness) rule there as it were to affirm that the constitutional nature of space must also govern time. A law is nothing but a statement of how a thing acts under certain conditions. But how a thing acts or exists under these conditions is determined by its constitution. Therefore a law can hold only *of things having the same constitution.*

All knowledge is vicarious. I learn of nature not by study of nature first hand, for I can never get it first hand; I learn of nature only *mediately,* i.e., through study of self, and of my mental pictures gained by aid of senses. These pictures are simply effects in consciousness, *"impressions."* I study them to learn how the laws of consciousness require them to have been made. Vicarious knowledge is absurd if the things are really distinct, but the easiest attainment in the world if things are all modes of activity of the same infinite mind. We "judge," "feel," and "will" for nature and our fellow-men vicariously, and must. It is absurd to make ourselves the standard for others and for nature, if we are distinct beings who may have entirely different constitutions.

The question begins to be vital as to what this "constitution," identical in every man and everything, and revealed so clearly in our own consciousness, is striving to realize in this world of objects. Either the question is insoluble, absolutely so, or the answer must come as do all others, *viz.*, vicariously, by the study of self. Either God is not revealed at all and can never be, or He can be known through the workings of our own inner life. Theism proves that we are partakers of the divine nature, made in His image; so in knowing the deepest truths of our own being, we discover the laws that hold of Him. We are more sure of our knowledge of God than of our knowledge of nature or of men, for if these truths concerning ourselves do not hold of Him, how can we know them to hold of things and beings outside of and apart from us? e.g., we are more sure of the truths of space than we are of the planets, for how know them if geometry is false?

Self-realization is the ultimate impulse of self; not merely to exist, but to exist in the fullness of one's power, in the completeness of life which is the perfection of (1) self-consciousness, (2) self-direction and control, and (3) self-appreciation or valuation. This alone is personality. The self is ever striving for true personal existence.

How is self-realization for God and men possible? "Consciousness of self or subject is possible only through consciousness of objects. A worldless God is as impossible as a Godless world."

If perfection of self is possible only through perfection of objects, then the universe must be perfect or God is not. This is the problem of evil.

If we know God, if we really understand the impulse that dominates Him, we can walk in the battle of life by faith

223

that "He doeth all things well," though man may not. We can believe that when the facts are known in the other life we can find nothing to criticise *in Him*, though much to blame in *our fellow men and our ancestors*. We can have perfect confidence in His justice and love while we most deeply regret the sad results of man's crime. So the more confidence we have in our knowledge of a personal God, the easier to have faith in any crisis.

As science advances, our faith increases. That it is in the power of the race so to use every material thing as to derive from it only help, that in a perfect civilization there should be "nothing to harm," is the wonderful prediction of the book of Revelation.

How can the limits of knowledge be determined? Since the days of Kant this question has been answered by an illustration. A child who sees a dove flying in a storm and buffeted by the wind hastily concludes that if only it could get above the atmosphere it would be unhindered, and might easily leave this earth and soar to heaven. But when the child learns how the dove flies at all, when he understands that only through the resistance of the air is the bird borne up and able to move on the wing, then he discovers the limits of its highest flight. Never again can he think of its getting beyond the atmosphere of earth. So when we accurately determine the processes of attaining knowledge we shall realize that all subjects that cannot be brought within these processes are forever beyond our ken. Here, then, is our problem: "What are the true and only processes by which knowledge is gained?"

If the laws of thought are not known to be the laws of things, how can we ever know things? And can the laws of thought be known to be the laws of things—mark the word, I do not say the laws of thought be the laws of things, but *be known* to be the laws of things—unless we first know that both thought and things are products of exactly the same larger self, whom we may call God? Here is my problem. Must we not take this view of our limitations or be absolutely agnostic concerning everything that transcends the smaller self? If the world is made up of separate independent entities, and if I were only one of them, they may or they may not be like me but could I ever know whether they were or not?

From the physical contact of our friends, i.e., words uttered, expressions of countenance, gestures (what Hume would call superficial properties), we must infer the secret hidden character and motives, distinguish between jest and earnest, knowledge and ignorance, frankness and reserve. This is a scientific problem. Beginning in childhood, and making at first the most embarrassing mistakes, we carefully repeat the inductive process till we get hypotheses that stand criticism, and in time gain confidence that our work is correct. This is our study of human nature. What is its basis? Simply this. If we had done these deeds, uttered these words, hesitated, become excited, then gone off abruptly, we should have had definite embarrassment and no little anger, therefore our friend felt the same. Here is (a) vicarious knowledge of his mind following on vicarious knowledge of his external physical deeds. If all beings are separate and independent realities, we ought to have an agnosticism raised (lowered, possibly, would be more accurate) to the second power concerning the mental life of friends. But this is just one thing we are most confident of. That and only that makes life worth living. Did an agnostic ever live who really doubted this knowledge? Why do agnostics publish books to prove their doctrine? Why do they answer up so sharply when criticised? How know that others meant by those words what they interpret them to mean? No, men are not agnostic on this subject. Not that we know all about others, but that we do know something of their thought and of the intent of their hearts. The phrases mother, father, mean this or they are mere mockeries. To be really agnostic on this question would be out and out insanity. So long as a spark of life glows in us we shall hold to our faith in our ability to read the thoughts of other members of the human race when we have adequate data. Some are quicker and keener than we in this work, but even a woman's intuitions are no miraculous power. The process so far as it may be carried is always and everywhere inductive, or when this has been completed and we simply apply its results, deductive. There is only one possible ground on which it can rest, viz., that we know human nature as truly as physical nature to be uniform with our own conscious processes. Given this cognition and the path is so plain that the wayfaring man even, though a pluralist, need not err therein; but without this cognition the greatest genius is helpless. Indeed, the clearer his mental vision the quicker will he realize his isolation from every one else.

If a man is honestly searching for the truth, the whole truth, and nothing but the truth, can he logically be confident about the objective existence and purposes of his friends but agnostic concerning God, the true self on whom all are dependent? Logically, are we not more sure of the existence of this Being and of some, not all, of the processes and laws that govern His actions, than we are of the existence of a physical world and of our ability to communicate with our companions. Until we are sure of this Being and of the dependence of all things upon Him, can we be sure that our inferences really take us beyond the subjective? Some hesitate to rest on these conclusions. There is no flaw in the logic, but they are afraid of anthropomorphism. If God were an absentee deity, living off somewhere in the distance from us, we should be anthropomorphic in ascribing to Him laws that govern us. We should not have a vestige of evidence to base such predicates upon. But if we are His workmanship more truly than the swinging of the pendulum is the work of gravity, the case is different. Our inner life is a laboratory where His processes are revealed. Uniformity under the same conditions is tautology. We are not predicating human attributes of God, but divine attributes of man, simply affirming that man partakes of the divine nature, is made in the image of God. This is not anthropomorphism, but theomorphism. This is scientific. How else can you have vicarious knowledge?

Only as men believe in God can they believe in humanity.

In affirming the dependence of nature on God we do not deny the reality of the material world nor limit physical science. Just the reverse. Science aims at discovering the laws of nature. Theism believes that nature is God in action, a mode of operation of the infinite. But this does not tell us how God acts or what He accomplishes. This we must and can learn by observation and experiment, and such knowledge is of infinite value. Science is thinking God's thoughts after Him just as truly as when we read the scripture. Nature is the word of God—"He spake, and it was done"; science is the commentary on this revelation. The scientist is the seer or prophet who reveals to us divine laws written, some of them on tables of stone, others in letters of light, others so obscurely that without his aid we could never have known them. It is simply habit that makes nature seem less real when we think of it as dependent. The Indian considers light as a substance and the rainbow as a real arch of something solid. Tell him that all is a mere mode of motion of ether and you seem to take away the reality. Mere motion, what is that? Yet it is true all the same, and when you get used to this truth rainbows are as beautiful as ever and a thousand times more significant. So also of music. It is real in spite of the fact that science has demolished the old doctrines on this subject. Passion and love are subjective, yet they are realities, terribly serious ones, too, in human history.

227

There is absolutely no objective science, either physical or mental, unless from one, namely, the self, we can learn all.

If a man's life is to fit into the lives of others and become a part of one social order, so that his appointments are understood and followed by his friends, if history can have any significance to him, it will be because all others date and locate themselves and their plans in the same objective science which he has made the basis of his own personal identity. How could they work in the same way in which he works, get the same results that he gets, write history that he can read, literature that fills him with inspiration, enact laws that bind his conscience, unless they were dependent on the same source for their existence that nature and his own mind find working in themselves?

If we are to have a form of society which grants liberty, equality, and fraternity, it will be only on the basis of discussion. The ultimate appeal will be, not to force, but to evidence. This postulates that what is evidence to one mind is evidence to every mind when seen in connection with exactly the same data. How could you ever use the "therefore" in a syllogism unless, whether men willed it or not, they were obliged to assent to the conclusion when they had exactly your premises? They may be hasty, they may shut their eyes and refuse to see the matter at all, they may even persecute and ridicule, but you have an invincible ally in their own bosoms and they know it. They dare not allow themselves to think, for their whole nature will befriend you if you are right. When Darwin wrote "The Origin of Species" it was greeted by a storm of derision. But what cared he? His appeal was not to some outside power that might force men to believe (which faith he despised); no, he appealed from Philip drunk to Philip sober, from the thoughtless public to the thoughtful public; and when they had time to think they were simply so many Darwins themselves. They found him within their own inner life, awaiting a chance to speak out and make himself heard. That is discussion, and if it is not that, it is nothing. When you discuss with a man it is simply because you yourself are within that man's inner life. You speak to his ear and he does not hear, but you speak to his heart from within and he cannot be deaf. Discussion is simply finding yourself in another, and that is the reason why you are courteous and respectful to others, when you respect yourself.

There are two parts to our nature, brain paths and weighing evidence. The brain paths work along the lines of least resistance, and here force is the determining factor. But here man is only an animal. The human part of man is the power that can work in the lines of greatest resistance and square solely with evidence, and here man is in the image of God. Now whenever you substitute for evidence any form of force (and bribery is a form of force), you attempt murder, not of the body, but of the mind. You are doing what you can to do away with the spiritual and make man in the image of the beasts and birds and creeping things.

Let me just here anticipate our studies so far as to call attention to the possible extremes of view to be found in the history of human progress. The narrowest idea conceivable is that of fetichism, when each object is an entity by itself, and in addition, all the more common attributes are personified into independent beings. The other extreme is theism (than which a broader, grander idea of the universe is impossible); it is this: God or Spirit is the only independent reality, and any other being or event is but a dependent "phase" or "state," or "product" of this activity. He is "the all in all." "In Him all things live and move and have their being." He is the Hebrew Jehovah, the "I AM," the self-existent and eternal One, who filleth immensity and inhabiteth eternity. The Ancient of Days, in terms of whose action Time itself is measured. Nature is related to God as

229

"thought to the mind that thinks," as "music to the air that is in vibration," as "light to the ether." Nature is the "living garment of God," that is, the continued activity in which He manifests Himself.—Between these extremes would lie (1) The successive phases of Polytheism. These eventually lead to (2) Materialism, where science begins in its atomic form. The progress of science would make necessary at length (3) Dualism, or the doctrine that there are two independent entities, mind and matter; at this stage all the conflicts between science and religion arise. But this must, sooner or later, be resolved into the last and final position of philosophy, viz.; (4) Theism as above explained.

As the mathematician studies the very nature of space in the laboratory of his own room, and, having determined its geometry, says, these are the laws of space among the fixed stars, since space is one and the same there as here; so we may study the nature of spirit within the laboratory of our own consciousness and, having thus learned its noumenal laws, find that we have discovered the laws of action of the external world, since there can be but one and the same spirit there also. It is in this way we know *noumenally* that the laws (not habits) of thought are also the laws of things. *Both thought and things must be phases of one and the same Universal Spirit.*

Could the preacher hold up beside the higher criticism the philosophic view which makes all nature and human history the word of God, and show that revelation is a commentary on those great truths of the moral life which God has written, not on tables of stone, but on the fleshy tables of our hearts, then the congregation would discover that the fundamental truths of religion are unchanged by all the changes that are taking place about us, and that the foundations of God stand sure.

If we look back over the history of human thinking, we find these stages clearly marked. The first great era was oc-

230

cupied with the problem, "What is nature?" In prehistoric times men were afraid of nature; it was their enemy, the hiding-place of ghosts and hobgoblins and malicious spirits who were bent on doing men harm. The first era of philosophic thought worked out the mechanical conception of nature and taught man that it was neither friend nor foe, but simply his tool, to be used with skill instead of ignorance. The modern atomic theory was originated by Democritus; the theory of evolution was crudely formulated by Empedocles, and most of our modern scientific conceptions had some prototype in this early stage of Greek reflection. This was a wonderful step in progress and the world has never been quite the same as it was before. You know how it is with the century plant. It lives and grows, but generations come and go before it blossoms. Science is not a century plant, but a plant of millenniums. It took root in this earliest day of Greek thinking, but two thousand years passed before it blossomed. We today see the beauty of the flower.

The next great problem was, "What is man?" Before this question was asked, he was a nobody. The state was everything, the individual nothing. But under the influence of the sophists, of Socrates, Plato, and Aristotle, the work of man as an individual began to be revealed. Even Meno's slave was found to possess a divine nature that made him a peer of those who had despised him. The worth of man as man, his power to know truth that had before seemed only the prerogative of the gods to know, arrested attention. There was no longer "Greek nor Jew, Barbarian, Scythian, bond nor free," but mind was all in all. In the breaking up of Greek political life, in the loss of their material splendor, when their national sun had set, the stars of the spiritual firmament began to shine and all the wise men wondered.

The next great question was, "What is God?" And as the more advanced and candid thought on this question, they gradually gave up their polytheism and their pluralism and came out squarely on the monistic basis. Stoicism was through and through monistic. It was just at this time that Christ came and taught the Fatherhood of God and the doctrine of the atonement. This great truth swept the Roman Empire, and in three centuries seated a follower of the Nazarene on the throne of the Caesars.

The fourth great question was, "The problem of evil." Here we have the great Augustinian controversies. It was a period of decay; the corruption of the Roman Empire was everywhere revolting. The beginning of the night of the Middle Ages brought a return from the monistic conception back again to pluralism. First, because on this basis it seemed so much easier to explain evil; and secondly, because the barbarians could more easily understand pluralism, whereas monism was hard to grasp.

The fifth great question was, "How can sinful man be just with God?" This was the time of the Protestant Reformation, and it brought out the problem of justification by faith, the forgiveness of sins through repentance. It formulated the doctrine of the atonement as vicarious punishment.

The sixth great question was, "How shall man be just with his sinful fellow-man?" . . . You remember one scene in Christ's life where He went up into the mountain and, while there, was transfigured; His disciples saw Him no longer a man of sorrows acquainted with grief, but in His divine grandeur, and with Him Moses, who represented the law that He fulfilled, and Elias, who represented the prophecies which He had brought to pass. It seems to me that philosophy is the mount of transfiguration of human nature, and that if we study it rightly we no longer see only that which is base and mean and selfish and slavish, which actual life makes so much of, but we have revealed to us the divine spirit which is working out through it all. Then we discover that this side of human life alone gives meaning to science, which stands for law in modern times, and to society, which has ever looked forward to a future beyond the power of mere man to realize. Industrial life, which has been so often condemned as having nothing but selfishness in it, is seen to be a reincarnation of the divine in human character; for it is nothing but sovereignty on its positive side, where the strong make the service given an equivalent for the service received in business, and in charity the strong help the weak to become strong and thus help themselves. . . . And man will adopt the same schemes for resisting the sins of his fellow-man that God has adopted for resisting the sin of the world. Then man will not merely think God's thought after Him in physical science, but will live God's life after Him in his social existence.

The idea that the universe in which we live is a whole—the notion that mind and matter, history and revelation, church and state, time and eternity, are not separate wholes, but parts that somehow fit into each other, and can be understood only in relationship to the grand end they serve —this is the idea both of philosophy and of religion, and is coming to be the view of science itself.

There are some who affirm that as a true knowledge of the material heavens was a revelation to men of that very earth with which they supposed themselves so familiar, and transformed their ideas of its size, its importance, and its laws, taking all the flatness out of it, and revealing it to us as one of the stars, so a true knowledge of the spiritual firmament would alter our whole estimate of life; would make many things that now seem of undue importance appear trivial, and the things that are now trivial of prime importance; would for the first time reveal the true dignity and grandeur of human nature, and would make the heavy afflictions of the present seem light because we should discover that in reality they are working out for us an exceeding and eternal weight of glory. All this it is claimed we could discover if we would only look, not at the things that are seen with the physical eye, for these are temporal and fragmentary and not the true whole; but at the things which are not seen, that is, at the eternal plan in accordance with which the universe is working itself out. To do this is the attempt of philosophy.

If a steel needle is something so grand, so wonderful, that the most thorough scientific study has not yet begun to conceive aright its real nature, if there is such a hidden depth of meaning and miracle in its motions, can you blame the philosopher for pausing, with reverence and awe, in his study of a finite human mind, even though it be that of a mere child?

Truth shines the brightest in just such a time as the present. Philosophy is something like astronomy, in that night is a peculiarly favorable time to make observations. Had the sun always been above the horizon, we should have had no astronomy, and Columbus would never have learned to pilot his way across unknown seas to America. For stars there would have been none, and without these we never could have divined the mysteries of the heavens or the revelation of the earth. "A dome of blue lighted by a single torch; an irregular plain of sand and water" would ever have remained our universe. Astronomy was born of superstition (astrology) and cradled in the dark.

Philosophy had a similar birth. It did not originate in the immediate light of revelation. Had men always dwelt in the dread mysterious presence of oracles and miracles, had there been no ominous silence, no moral darkness that might be felt; men had never dreamed of that firmament of thought wherein arise and shine the truths of the eternal. They would still be looking for God in the heavens above, or in the earth beneath; they would not easily find Him in the still small voice, in that holy of holies in our hearts.

So long as the nations of the world are selfish they must

devour the weaker races. There must be wars and rumors of wars. It is only by the regeneration of mankind—it is only when the state, and institutions, as truly as individuals, are born again, and the reign of righteousness and love, that is, self-sacrifice, shall be established, that the age of universal peace will dawn upon us.

Truth and Freedom; Truth coming from whatever direction, Freedom knowing no bounds but those that Truth has set.

I think it is conceded that one is so far justified in believing in natural law in the spiritual world as to affirm that what holds of gravitation holds of our moral life. As our physical weight depends upon the size of the planet on which we live, as a man who weighs one hundred and fifty pounds on the earth would weigh more than a ton if transported to a body as large as the sun, so it is with our mental weight. It depends upon the size of the world in which we consciously live. The man who takes a superficial view of the great problems of human life, and the great truths of religion, narrows himself as much as he does his world; he becomes frivolous, insincere, cynical, the prey to all sorts of temptations and moral degradation. For this there is no other remedy than a more profound apprehension of the truth. You can make him pharisaical by natural means, but you can make him religious only by the truth.

Reason inspired by love of truth is the only eye with which man can see the spiritual heavens above us.

The reception accorded to a humble man by others is determined, not by his merit, but by the largeness of their hearts and the genuineness of their manhood.

We are not different from those who have gone before. Every one of the prophets of the Old Testament and all the apostles were men like ourselves with the single exception that they had fewer advantages than we have. Nearly every one of them, in recalling his past life, found scenes upon

235

which he could look only with tears; but there came a time when they differed from us; to them the power of the Lord was revealed.

When Elijah was waiting with impatience for the Divine Presence in the wilderness, he found that God was not clothed in the whirlwind or in the earthquake, but that He was in the still small voice of duty.

What the electric wire from the dynamo is to the arc light or the electric car, duty is to the one who is seeking God's presence. Connect with duty, and the light shall shine in your lives, the power shall course through your limbs and tongue which shall make you like Peter on the day of Pentecost.

Christ's discourses were in Aramaic and have come down to us only in translations, some of which are bungling and full of errors, but when he sent his disciples forth as living words on the day of Pentecost he sent a message that did not have to be translated. Parthians and Medes, and Elamites and the dwellers in Mesopotamia, and Cappadocia, in Pontus, and Asia, strangers of Rome, Jews and proselytes, could all understand lives of heroism and self-denying service, for character is the mother tongue of every nation. Those who have long forgotten this native speech are touched when they hear of heroism and devotion as though they listened to the tender accents of home at their mother's knee.

It is the general law of all mental life that consciousness of self is possible only through consciousness of object. A similar law holds in moral life and the social order. We may state this in the formula, A determines himself never directly, but always through B, i.e., a man determines his character and personality by the attitude and relations he assumes towards his world of nature and persons.

If A determines himself through B, then there are only four possible spheres of life for A, due to the four possible

236

conditions of B, since A's life will be limited to the change in B:

1. B may be strong and do right.
2. B may be strong and do wrong.
3. B may be weak and do right.
4. B may be weak and do wrong.

Every phase of life comes in here.

(1) is the sphere of business, where action and reaction should be equal; (2) is the sphere of punishment, where the action must take the form of resistance to the wrongdoer; (3) is the sphere of charity where the strong must help the weak; (4) is the sphere for the atonement where the strong must resist by assistance.

The common view makes the individual first and the relationships secondary. Of course, this is so. How could there be a relationship unless there were some things to be related? No relationship is necessary; surely not that involved in sovereignty. If you hold these premises, only one motive can influence the individual, and that is expediency. Liberty, equality, fraternity are simply forms of courtesy; they mean nothing. When it comes to the test, self-preference is the ultimate motive. . . . Might makes right. There is, therefore, no mean between anarchy and tyranny. The successful man is the tyrant, the under dog in the fight is the anarchist. This is the last word on all governmental and social problems the moment you tell truth. It is not expedient to do so always. Might includes trick and diplomacy and shrewdness, yes, and lying too, quite as much as physical power.

The theistic view is a startling paradox. It affirms that the relationship is first and that the individual is its product. This is all of the subject the common man will care to know. Such a view is moonshine, a mere theory. Wit is a discoverer of incongruities of a certain type and nothing is more incongruous with the common view than this doctrine. From the days of Plato to the present time it has been a fair target for ridicule. But let us look at the facts. If man is a dependent being, his relationship to God is that which gives him existence. Can a wave continue to be if it leaves the water? Can a thought exist apart from the person who thinks it? Secondly, if all other things are dependent on God, they necessarily determine each other.

Take our physical life. Does a man first exist and then come into certain relationships? Take those of the physical world, e.g., that of gravitation. Does a man at a definite time in his life conclude to submit himself to this particular law, or must gravitation be first, in order for the man to exist at all? Suspend gravitation for a moment and what would happen to him? Not a particle of atmosphere would enter his lungs, all the finer blood-vessels would instantly burst when the pressure was removed, and the rotation of the earth would whirl him off in a tangent into empty space at the rate of a thousand miles an hour. Take those relationships that are expressed by chemical affinity. Suspend these and what would become of nutrition, and how long would a man exist if there were no chemical action at all in his physical frame? Suspend the law of cause and effect and what could man do for himself? When he put out his foot to walk the ground would offer no resistance. When he sat down the chair would give him no support. When he turned his eyes towards the sun it would give him no sensations of sight. Neither could he have hearing, touch, taste, or smell. When we say that these relationships are first we mean logically rather than chronologically. Chronologically they are simultaneous, as cause and effect always are. If a cause ceased to exist before the effect came into being, then this would be an effect without a cause.

Let us discuss mental relations. Most people think that personality is a unity, just like gold; that one is passively

238

personal, therefore one could act as a personal being even if everything else in the world were annihilated. But this is superficial. Personality is always an achievement, not gained once for all, but requiring infinite repetition. A personal being is simply a conscious being whose consciousness has reached the grade in which it knows itself. But power reveals itself only in work done. If the self did nothing, it could not be self-conscious. The grade of self-consciousness is determined, then, by the amount the self does, not once for all, way back in the past, but continually. Hence our personality is fluctuating with our activity.

It is the contact of mind with mind that is the only condition of a human life. This is only saying that the perfection of the subject depends upon the perfection of its objects. Our social relations, including family relations, are first, and sanity is the product. We consider it a personal loss when our friends die; it takes away just so much of our personality. Here, then, is the great fact concerning our existence. In no instance can we free ourselves from the law that the relationship is first and we are the product, and our life continues only so long as the relationship continues. This is the formula: A determines B and B determines A; that is, A never determines himself directly, but only through B.

Society is not composed of individuals; society is a relationship by virtue of which individuals come into existence and without which they would have no being as personal.

We now have a sixth theory for punishment. Why do we punish the criminal? The reply is, We never punish the deed, but only the doer. We punish only when we cannot help acting, when we are obliged to assist or resist the criminal. Punishment is the resistance of the wrongdoer. Assistance to the right doer is the reward. Now why do we punish? Not for the sake of vengeance, or reformation, or retribution, or prevention, in the historic meaning of that word, but simply for our own sake. If we are in such circumstances that we must act, we will act rightly, whether others do or not.

The converse is true also. Why do we reward good conduct?

All noble-minded people feel that they degrade themselves when they do not render "honor to whom honor is due."

The person who has no respect for himself cannot be relied upon to be courteous towards others.

Sovereignty is a very much broader term than government. Government is only a very particular administration of sovereignty under certain conditions.

There are only two fountains from which men can ever attempt to drink. If one seeks satisfaction in quantity, water from that well will not prevent him from thirsting again. But, if he drink of the divine fountain of quality, these waters become in him "a well of water springing up into everlasting life," and each individual becomes a fountain which makes an oasis in the desert. In Eden, man fell by eating of the fruit of the tree of knowledge. He went simply so far as to find what was good for food and suited to make one wise. The remedy for human evils is to eat of the tree of life, which yields the knowledge, not of our selfish interests, but of our spiritual obligations, of our true dignity and grandeur.

This section, *Content of Belief*, or *I Believe*, sets forth what I at present believe. It states the content of my belief today.

HOW CAN THE OLD AND THE NEW IN THEOLOGY
LIVE TOGETHER?

It will at once be evident that Changing Religion or New Theology will produce many and difficult practical problems. Probably much of modern tolerance is due to the lack of decided views one way or another. The innovator in theology or in religion, or the progressive, can scarcely overlook that he may become a stumbling block and tend to upset many sincere and true believers. Besides, ordinarily the Church stands for, or is supposed to stand for, light and leading in civic matters and in promotion of good character. One who criticises the church or who leaves it by reason of unbelief in its creed may likely seem to be out of step with the best forces and moral and ethical aims of the community. Also in the past, and even in the present, quarrels and hatreds have been so blamed upon religious differences that even fair and open discussions are avoided lest there be renewal of religious strife. Almost everyone seems to have decided religion and theology to be personal matters—to be accepted as they are. Indifference to many seems better than quarrels. Discussion it is felt may degenerate into wrangling from which we all want to be delivered. So even if the view is true, is there not widespread disinclination even to hear about it? Is it not likely to be said all over,—"a plague on both your houses."

In this section, as in all the other sections of this volume, a large part of it is not in my words, but in words quoted from many, sometimes at considerable length. This is done, it is repeated, because my thoughts are in this way expressed for me better than I could do myself.

241

I am primarily concerned with understandable presentation of my beliefs. I want the best possible presentation to be made. I believe that in many places others have made better presentations than I could do. So in such cases I am glad to quote writings of others, long or short. In my search for truth I have found it in many places. I am glad to present it as found. Even so the innovator is pretty apt to be looked upon as an atheist, or destroyer of religious beliefs; so Socrates; so Jesus; so many a reformer; and many other forward looking men.

The two following paragraphs are from John Wesley:

The work of God does not, cannot need the work of the devil to forward it. And a calm, even spirit goes through rough work far better than a furious one. Although, therefore, God did use, at the time of the Reformation, some sour, overbearing, passionate men, yet He did not use them because they were such, but notwithstanding they were so. And there is no doubt, He would have used them much more, had they been of an humbler and milder spirit.

How delicate a thing it is to reprove! To do it well requires more than human wisdom.

From Walter Bagehot (Physics and Politics):

In old times a few ideas got possession of men and communities, but this is happily now possible no longer. We see how incomplete these old ideas were; how almost by chance one seized on one nation, and another on another; how often one set of men have persecuted another set for opinions on subjects of which neither, we now perceive, knew anything. It might be well if a greater number of effectual demonstrations existed among mankind; but while no such demonstrations exist, and while the evidence which completely convinces one man seems to another trifling and insufficient, let us recognize the plain position of inevitable doubt. Let us not be bigots with a doubt, and persecutors without a creed. We are beginning to see this, and we are railed at for so beginning. But it is a great benefit, and it is to the incessant prevalence of detective discussion that our doubts are due.

Tolerance too is learned in discussion, and, as history shows, is only so learned. In all customary societies bigotry is the ruling principle. In rude places to this day anyone who says anything new is looked on with suspicion, and is persecuted by opinion if not injured by penalty. One of the greatest pains to human nature is the pain of a new idea. It is, as common people say, so "upsetting"; it makes you think that, after all, your favorite notions may be wrong, your firmest beliefs illfounded; it is certain that till now there was no place allotted in your mind to the new and startling inhabitant, and now that it has conquered an entrance, you do not at once see which of your old ideas it will or will not turn out, with which of them it can be reconciled, and with which it is at essential enmity. Naturally, therefore, common men hate a new idea, and are disposed more or less to ill-treat the original man who brings it. Even nations with long habits of discussion are intolerant enough.

So rare is great originality among mankind, and so great are its fruits, that this one benefit of free government probably outweighs what are in many cases its accessory evils. Of itself it justifies or goes far to justify our saying with Montesquieu, "Whatever be the cost of this glorious liberty, we must be content to pay it to heaven."

Every sort of philosophy has been systematized, and yet as these philosophies utterly contradict one another, most of them cannot be true. Unproved abstract principles without number have been eagerly caught up by sanguine men, and then carefully spun out into books and theories, which were to explain the whole world. But the world goes clear against these abstractions, and it must do so, as they require it to go in antagonistic directions. The mass of a system attracts the young and impresses the unwary; but cultivated people are very dubious about it. They are ready to receive hints and suggestions, and the smallest real truth is ever welcome. But a large book of deductive philosophy is much to be suspected. No doubt the deductions may be right; in most writers they are so; but where did the premises come from? Who is sure that they are the whole truth, and nothing but the truth, of the matter in hand? Who is not almost sure beforehand that they will contain a strange mixture of truth and error, and, therefore, that it will not be worth while to spend life in reasoning over their consequences? In a word, the superfluous energy of mankind has flowed over into philosophy, and has worked into big systems what should have been left as little suggestions.

And if the old systems of thought are not true as systems, neither is the new revolt from them to be trusted in its whole vigor. There is the same original vice in that also. There is an excessive energy in revolutions if there is such energy anywhere. The passion for action is quite as ready to pull down as to build up; probably it is more ready, for the task is easier:

> "Old things need not be therefore true,
> O brother men, not yet the new;
> Ah, still awhile the old thought retain,
> And yet consider it again."

From Jonathan Edwards:

Spiritual pride commonly occasions a certain stiffness and inflexibility in persons, in their own judgment and their own ways; whereas the eminently humble person, though he be inflexible in his duty, and in those things wherein God's honor is concerned; and with regard to temptation to those

244

things he apprehends to be sinful, though in never so small a degree, he is not at all of a yieldable spirit, but is like a brazen wall; yet in other things he is of a pliable disposition, not disposed to set up his own opinion or his own will; he is ready to pay deference to others' opinions, and loves to comply with their inclinations, and has a heart that is tender and flexible like a little child.

From Sir Thomas Browne:

Persecution is a bad and indirect way to plant Religion.

I cannot fall out or contemn a man for an errour, or conceive why a difference in Opinion should divide an affection; for Controversies, Disputes, and Argumentations, both in Philosophy and in Divinity, if they meet with discreet and peaceable natures, do not infringe the Laws of Charity. In all disputes, so much as there is of passion, so much there is of nothing to the purpose.

From Emerson:

Everywhere I am hindered of meeting God in my brother, because he has shut his own temple doors, and recites fables merely of his brother's or his brother's brother's God.

From Lessing:

One of those enthusiasts who dream
They know, they only, the true way to God.

And feel themselves compelled
To lead all others who have missed the way
Back to the same—and scarcely can do other—
For be it true this way alone can be
The way of safety, can they be content
To see their friends upon another road,
Which leads to loss, to everlasting loss?

Thus is it possible, for the self-same people,
And at the self-same time, to love and hate.

You get on so well with good people. But when will you
learn how to put up with bad ones? For they are people too.
And often not nearly so bad as they seem.

The superstition in which we grew up,
Doth not, because we see it as it is,
Lose, therefore, all its power upon our souls.
They are not all free men who mock their chains.

How light I feel me now
Since there is nothing further in the world
I have to hide! and even as in Thy sight
Can walk in man's sight too, who judge a man,
Must judge, by deeds alone.

From Alexander Pope:

In words, as fashions, the same rule will hold;
Alike fantastic, if too new, or old:
Be not the first by whom the new are tried,
Nor yet the last to lay the old aside.

Some foreign writers, some our own despise;
The ancients only, or the moderns prize.
Thus wit, like faith, by each man is applied
To one small sect, and all are damned beside.
Meanly they seek the blessing to confine,
And force that sun but on a part to shine,
Which not alone the southern wit sublimes,
But ripens spirits in cold northern climes;
Which from the first has shone on ages past,
Enlights the present, and shall warm the last;
Though each may feel increases and decays,
And see now clearer and now darker days:

Regard not then if wit be old or new,
But blame the false, and value still the true.

Be thou the first true merit to befriend,
His praise is lost, who stays, till all commend.

'Tis not enough, your counsel still be true;
Blunt truth more mischief than nice falsehoods do;
Men must be taught as if you taught them not,
And things unknown proposed as things forgot.

For modes of faith let graceless zealots fight;
His can't be wrong whose life is in the right;
In Faith and Hope the world will disagree,
But all mankind's concern is Charity:
All must be false that thwart this one great end;
And all of God, that bless mankind or mend.

To Thee, whose temple is all space,
    Whose altar, earth, sea, skies,
One chorus let all being raise;
    All nature's incense rise!

From Fichte:

In all ages and among all peoples true greatness has remained the same in this respect, that it was not vain; just as,
on the other hand, whatever displayed vanity has always
been beyond a doubt base and petty. True greatness, resting
on itself, finds no pleasure in monuments erected by contemporaries, or in being called "The Great," or in the
shrieking applauses and praises of the mob; rather it rejects
these things with fitting contempt, and awaits first the verdict on itself from its own indwelling judge, and then the
public verdict from the judgment of posterity. True greatness has always had this further characteristic: it is filled
with awe and reverence in the face of dark and mysterious
fate, it is mindful of the ever-rolling wheel of destiny, and

never allows itself to be counted great or happy before its end.

Let our standard be the old one: that alone is great which is capable of receiving the ideas which always bring nothing but salvation upon the peoples, and which is inspired by those ideas.

Whoever believes in spirituality and in the freedom of this spirituality, and who wills the eternal development of this spirituality by freedom, wherever he may have been born, and whatever language he speaks, is of our blood; he is one of us, and will come over to our side.

From Robert Browning:

> Hear the truth, and bear the truth,
> And bring the truth to bear on all you are
> And do, assured that only good comes thence
> Whate'er the shape good take!

> Do the best with the least change possible:
> Carry the incompleteness on, a stage,
> Make what was crooked straight, and roughness smooth,
> And weakness strong.

From Schleiermacher:

When friends extend to each other the hand of fellowship, the bond should issue in something greater than each could achieve independently; each ought to grant the other full play to follow the promptings of his spirit, offering assistance only where the other feels a lack, and not insinuating his own ideas in place of his friend's. In this wise each would find life and strength in the other, and the potentialities within him would be fully realized.

Culture will develop out of barbarism, and life will spring even from the sleep of death! The elements of a better life are already present. Their superior potency will not remain forever in dormant hiding; sooner or later the spirit dwelling in man will arouse them into activity. As the cultivation of the earth for man's benefit is now superior to that crude dominion over nature, wherein men fled timidly before every manifestation of her powers, so the blessed time when a true and spiritual society shall arise cannot be remote from this present childhood of humanity.

Yet of our present, much vaunted enlightenment developed out of a wretched barbarism, in which the germs of progress are scarcely discernible even now to a vision trained by the subsequent course of events, why should not our chaotic philistinism, amid which the eye already discerns through sinking mists the rudiments of a better world, **give place at last to the sublime rule of moral and spiritual** cultivation? It is coming! Why should I with faint heart count the hours which must still transpire or the generations that must pass away ere then? Why let the time of its coming trouble me, since time does not comprehend my inner life?

Wherever I do see a spark of the hidden fire that must sooner or later consume the outworn and recreate the world, I am drawn toward it with love and true hope as to a welcome sign of my distant home. And close at hand the sacred flame has appeared shedding its unearthly light, a sign, to the knowing, that the spirit is there. All who like myself belong to the future are drawing toward each other in love and hope, and each in his every word and act cements and extends a spiritual bond by which we are pledged to better times.

No one can live simply and in the way of beauty save he who hates lifeless formulas, seeks after genuine self-cultivation, and so belongs to a world that is yet to be.

Amid all the diversities of the world's motley spectacle I learned to discount appearances and to recognize the same reality whatever its garb, and I also learned to translate the many tongues that it acquires in various circles.

What a galaxy of individuals I see close at hand, men so different from myself yet all of them engaged in perfecting the humanity that is in them! What an amazing number of learned men are about me, who out of pride or hospitality offer me the golden fruit of their lives in handsome jars, and the plants of distant times and places too, transplanted to the fatherland by their faithful toil!

From Schiller:

The way of ancient ordinance, though it winds,
Is yet no devious path. Straight forward goes
The lightning's path, and straight the fearful path
Of the cannon ball. Direct it flies, and rapid;
Shattering what it *may* reach, and shattering what it reaches.
My son! the road the human being travels,
That, on which BLESSING comes and goes, doth follow
The river's course, the valley's playful windings,
Curves round the corn-field and the hill of vines,
Honouring the holy bounds of property!
And thus secure, though late, leads to its end.

      'Tis not merely
The human being's Pride that peoples space
With life and mystical predominance;
Since likewise for the stricken heart of Love
This visible nature, and this common world,
Is all too narrow; yea, a deeper import
Lurks in the legend told my infant years
Than lies upon that truth, we live to learn.
For fable is Love's world, his home, his birth-place;
Delightedly dwells he 'mong fays and talismans,
And spirits; and delightedly believes
Divinities, being himself divine.
The intelligible forms of ancient poets,

The fair humanities of old religion,
The Power, the Beauty, and the Majesty,
That had her haunts in dale, or piny mountain,
Or forest by slow stream, or pebbly spring,
Or chasms, and wat'ry depths; all these have vanish'd.
They live no longer in the faith of reason!
But still the heart doth need a language, still
Doth the old instinct bring back the old names,
And to yon starry world they now are gone,
Spirits or gods, that used to share this earth
With man as with their friend; and to the lover
Yonder they move, from yonder visible sky
Shoot influence down: and even at this day
'Tis Jupiter who brings whate'er is great,
And Venus who brings everything that's fair.

For of the wholly common is man made,
And custom is his nurse! Woe then to them,
Who lay irreverent hands upon his old
House furniture, the dear inheritance
From his forefathers! For time consecrates;
And what is grey with age becomes religion.

The doing evil to avoid an evil
Cannot be good!

Which religion do I acknowledge? None that thou namest.
"None that I name? And why so?"—
Why, for religion's own sake!

See how we hate, how we quarrel, how thought and how
        feeling divide us!
But thy locks, friend, like mine, meanwhile
        are bleachening fast.

   How lovely a thing it is when brethren dwell together in
unity; as the dew drops of heaven that fall upon the mountains of Zion.—Learn to deserve that happiness, young man,

and the angels of heaven will sun themselves in thy glory.
Let thy wisdom be the wisdom of gray hairs, but let thy
heart be the heart of innocent childhood.

Yet have I ever heard it said, that those
Who watch men's looks, and carry tales about,
Have done more mischief in this world of ours,
Than the assassin's knife, or poison'd bowl.

From John Milton:

While yet we live, scarce one short hour perhaps,
Between us two let there be peace.

He who thinks we are to pitch our tent here, and have
attain'd the utmost prospect of reformation, that the mortall
glasse wherein we contemplate, can shew us, till we come to
beatific vision, that man by this very opinion declares, that
he is yet farre short of truth.

We boast our light; but if we look not wisely on the Sun
it self, it smites us into darknes. Who can discern those
planets that are oft *Combust,* and those stars of brightest
magnitude that rise and set with the Sun, untill the opposite motion of their orbs bring them to such a place in the
firmament, where they may be seen evning or morning. The
light that we have gain'd, was given us, not to be ever staring on, but by it to discover onward things more remote
from our knowledge.

They are the troublers, they are the dividers of unity, who
neglect and permit not others to unite those dissever'd
peeces which are yet wanting to the body of Truth. To be
still searching what we know not, by what we know, still
closing up truth to truth as we find it (for all her body is
homogeneal, and proportionall) this is the golden rule in
Theology as well as in *Arithmetick,* and makes up the best
harmony in a Church; not the forc't and outward union of
cold, and neutrall, and inwardly divided minds.

252

What great purchase is this Christian liberty which Paul so often boasts of. His doctrine is, that he who eats or eats not, regards a day, or regards it not, may doe either to the Lord. How many other things might be tolerated in peace; and left to conscience had we but charity, and were it not the chief stronghold of our hypocrisie to be ever judging one another?

From Coleridge:

Never yet did there exist a full faith in the Divine Word (by whom light, as well as immortality, was brought into the world), which did not expand the intellect, while it purified the heart;—which did not multiply the aims and objects of the understanding, while it fixed and simplified those of the desires and passions.

Among the various undertakings of men, can there be mentioned any more important, can there be conceived any more sublime, than an intention to form the human mind anew after the Divine Image? The very intention, if it be sincere, is a ray of its dawning.

In general, morality may be compared to the consonant; prudence to the vowel. The former cannot be uttered (reduced to practice) but by means of the latter.

We are in the silent school of reflection, in the secret confessional of thought. Should we *lie for God,* and that to our own thoughts? . . . They, indeed, who dare do the one, will soon be able to do the other.

There have been too many commentators who are content not to understand a text themselves, if only they can make the reader believe they do.

When, after variances, men are brought to an agreement, they are much subject to this, rather to cover their remaining malices with superficial verbal forgiveness than to dislodge them and free the heart of them. This is a poor self-deceit. As the philosopher said to him, who being ashamed

253

that he was espied by him in a tavern in the outer room, withdrew himself to the inner, "That is not the way out; the more you go that way, you will be the farther in:"—so when hatreds are upon admonition not thrown out, but retire inward to hide themselves, they grow deeper and stronger than before; and those constrained semblances of reconcilement are but a false healing, do but skin the wound over, and therefore it usually breaks forth worse again.

Where there is a great deal of smoke and no clear flame, it argues much moisture in the matter, yet it witnesseth certainly that there is fire there; and therefore dubious questioning is a much better evidence, than that senseless deadness which most take for believing. Men that know nothing in science, have no doubts. He never truly believed, who was not made first sensible and convinced of unbelief.

Never be afraid to doubt, if only you have the disposition to believe, and doubt in order that you may end in believing the truth.

Much of our common union of minds, I fear, proceeds from no other than the aforementioned causes, want of knowledge, and want of affection in religion. You that boast you live comformably to the appointments of the Church, and that no one hears of your noise, we may thank the ignorance of your minds for that kind of quietness.

Seek much after this, to speak nothing with God, nor men, but what is the sense of a single unfeigned heart. O sweet truth! excellent but rare sincerity! He that *loves that truth within*, and who is Himself at once *The Truth* and *The Life*, He alone can work it there! Seek it of him.

In conversation seek not so much either to vent thy knowledge, or to increase it, as to know more spiritually and effectually what thou dost know. And in this way those mean despised truths, that every one thinks he is sufficiently seen in, will have a new sweetness and use in them, which thou

254

didst not so well perceive before—(for these flowers cannot be sucked dry); and in this humble sincere way thou shalt *grow in grace and in knowledge too.*

Truth needs not the service of passion; yea, nothing so disserves it, as passion when set to serve it. The *Spirit of Truth* is withal the *Spirit of Meekness.*

The boasted peaceableness about questions of faith too often proceeds from a superficial temper, and not seldom from a supercilious disdain of whatever has no marketable use or value, and from indifference to religion itself. Toleration is a herb of spontaneous growth in the soil of indifference; but the weed has none of the virtue of the medicinal plant, reared by humility in the garden of zeal. Those, who regard religions as matters of taste, may consistently include all religious differences in the old adage, *De Gustibus non est disputandum.* And many there be among those of Gallio's temper, who *care for none of these things,* and who account all questions in religion, as he did, but matters of words and names. And by this all religions may agree together. But that were not a natural union produced by the active heat of the spirit, but a confusion rather, arising from the want of it; not a knitting together, but a freezing together, as cold congregates all bodies how heterogeneous soever, sticks, stones, and water,—but heat makes first a separation of different things, and then unites those that are of the same nature.

Imprudence makes some kind of Christians lose much of their labour in speaking for religion, and drive those further off, whom they would draw into it.

The confidence that attends a Christian's belief makes the believer not fear men, to whom he answers, but still he fears his God, for whom he answers, and whose interest is chief in those things he speaks of. The soul that hath the deepest sense of spiritual things, and the truest knowledge

255

of God, is most afraid to miscarry in speaking of Him, most tender and wary how to acquit itself when engaged to speak of and for God.

If you would have a good conscience, you must by all means have so much light, so much knowledge of the will of God, as may regulate you, and show you your way, may teach you how to do, and speak, and think, as in His presence.

The origin of Evil, meanwhile, is a question interesting only to the metaphysician, and in a system of moral and religious philosophy. The man of sober mind who seeks for truths that possess a moral and practical interest, is content to be certain, first, that evil must have had a beginning, since otherwise it must either be God, or a co-eternal and co-equal rival of God; both impious notions, and the latter foolish to boot:—secondly that it could not originate in God; for if so, it would be at once evil and not evil, or God would be at once God, that is, infinite goodness, and not God—both alike impossible positions. Instead, therefore, of troubling himself with this barren controversy, he more profitably turns his inquiries to the evil which most concerns himself, and of which he may find the origin.

Whatever is against right reason, that no faith can oblige us to believe. For though reason is not the positive and affirmative measure of our faith, and our faith ought to be larger than (speculative) reason, and take something into her heart, that reason can never take into her eye; yet in all our creed there can be nothing against reason. If reason justly contradicts an article, it is not of the household of faith.

He that speaks against his own reason, speaks against his own conscience: and therefore it is certain, no man serves God with a good conscience, who serves him against his reason.

256

This Section is closed with the following quotations from Amiel:

We shut our eyes to the beginnings of evil because they are small, and in this weakness is contained the germ of our defeat.

Heaven and earth may pass away, but good *ought* to be, and injustice ought *not* to be. Such is the creed of the human race. Nature will be conquered by spirit: the eternal will triumph over time.

If liberty is to be saved, it will not be by the doubters, the men of science, or the materialists; it will be by religious conviction, by the faith of individuals, who believe that God wills man to be free but also pure; it will be by the seekers after holiness.

There is no curing a sick man who believes himself in health.

Material results are but the tardy sign of invisible activities. The bullet has started long before the noise of the report has reached us. The decisive events of the world take place in the intellect.

To renounce happiness and think only of duty, to put conscience in the place of feeling;—this voluntary martyrdom has its nobility. The natural man in us flinches, but the better self submits. To hope for justice in the world is a sign of sickly sensibility; we must be able to do without it. True manliness consists in such independence. Let the world think what it will of us, it is its own affair. If it will not give us the place which is lawfully ours until after our death, or perhaps not at all, it is but acting within its right. It is our business to behave as though our country were grateful, as though the world were equitable, as though opinion were clear-sighted, as though life were just, as though men were good.

The germs of all things are in every heart, and the greatest criminals as well as the greatest heroes are but different modes of ourselves. Only evil grows of itself, while for goodness we want effort and courage.

For the sake of satisfying a thinking and instructed public, is it wise to sacrifice the influence of religion over the multitude? Answer. A pious fiction is still a fiction. Truth has the highest claim. It is for the world to accommodate itself to truth, and not *vice versa*. Copernicus upset the astronomy of the Middle Ages,—so much the worse for it! The Eternal Gospel revolutionises modern churches— what matter! When symbols become transparent, they have no further binding force. We see in them a poem, an allegory, a metaphor; but we believe in them no longer.

It is not to the clever folk, or even to the scientific folk, that the empire over souls belongs, but to those who impress us as having conquered nature by grace, as having passed through the burning bush, and as speaking, not the language of human wisdom, but that of the divine will. In religious matters it is holiness which gives authority; it is love, or the power of devotion and sacrifice, which goes to the heart, which moves and persuades.

What all religious, poetical, pure, and tender souls are least able to pardon is the diminution or degradation of their ideal. We must never rouse an ideal against us; our business is to point men to another ideal, purer, higher, more spiritual than the old, and so to raise behind a lofty summit one more lofty still. In this way no one is despoiled; we gain men's confidence while at the same time forcing them to think, and enabling those minds which are already tending towards change to perceive new objects and goals for thought. Only that which is replaced is destroyed, and an ideal is only replaced by satisfying the conditions of the old with some advantages over.

PROFESSOR CHARLES E. GARMAN

of

AMHERST COLLEGE

It was Professor Charles E. Garman, who in the fall of 1900 introduced me to the study of philosophy and from whom in the ensuing year I received belief in theism. In short from him I received the foundation of all the positive in religious beliefs, as held from that day to the present, with increasing fervor, regardless of increasing scepticism and disbelief as to many positions associated with orthodox theology.

Professor Garman died in February, 1907.

OBITUARY*
Prof. Garman of Amherst

Prof. Charles E. Garman, one of the most prominent members of the faculty of Amherst College, died at his home in Amherst to-day after an illness of about three weeks from bronchitis, which developed into a malignant throat disease. He was Professor of Moral Philosophy and Metaphysics and had been connected with the college since 1880. He was 57 years old and is survived by a widow.

Charles E. Garman was born in Limington, Me., and was graduated from Amherst in 1872. He was Principal of the Ware High School for four years, then studied at the Yale Divinity School until 1879. The following year he came to Amherst as instructor in mathematics, and in 1881 was made instructor in philosophy. From 1882 to 1889 he served as associate Professor of Moral Philosophy and in 1892 was made Professor of Moral Philosophy and Metaphysics, retaining this position for the remainder of his life. Amherst College conferred the degree of Doctor of Divinity upon Prof. Garman in 1896. At the last Amherst Commencement 13 of Prof. Garman's former pupils who are now college Presidents and professors presented to him a book on philosophy, which they had prepared. Prof. Garman was a trustee of Mount Holyoke College.

*Newspaper Clipping.

Professor Garman had concentrated on teaching; he seldom preached or lectured outside of his classroom, published no books and left but scanty records of his work other than in its potent influence on the minds of his pupils.

Aside from the memories and notes of his students, the source book to which reference should be made is:

LETTERS

LECTURES and ADDRESSES

of

CHARLES EDWARD GARMAN

A Memorial Volume

Prepared with the Cooperation of
The Class of 1884, Amherst College

by
Eliza Miner Garman

Houghton Mifflin Company
1909 and 1911.

260

Generally speaking most Amherst students took Garman, which was an elective course. Here and there a few did not elect the course for one reason or another. Such failure to take Garman was by option of the student. Occasionally there would be students to whom the benefits of Garman's course were unavailable because of his extended illness or leave on Sabbatical year or otherwise. Some of the students who missed Garman's course have had an undefined but strong sense of the unavoidable, unwilling loss that was probably theirs. The uncertainty and indefiniteness of their loss sometimes makes it at times loom very large. And many like myself who had the course, by their exceeding enthusiasm and devotion, add still further to the sense of loss.

To one student of long ago who unwillingly missed Garman's course, I wrote a long, long letter in 1952, upon the subject, including an attempted summary of Professor Garman's course about as I had it in 1900-1901. My attempted summary stuck close to the text of the Memorial Volume for the sake of accuracy. I attempted arrangement of the subjects in logical sequence rather than by order of chapters in the Memorial Volume.

It has seemed advisable, hoping it may be helpful to some, to include herein the outline that I prepared for my correspondent.

Comparative Outline, With References by Topics, as in Letter to Correspondent, and as in Memorial Volume, Regarding Professor Garman and His Course.

(Page references are to Letter to Correspondent, and to Memorial Volume. References to Letter to Correspondent have been retained although not pertinent herein.)

Outline Herein	Pages	Memorial Volume	Pages
Introductory and Tributes }	1-7	Introduction } Letter to President Hall Appendix	53 57-71 555-611
Moral Earnestness	8-17	Moral Earnestness }	Various & Scattered
Esoteric or Mysterious Aspects of Course }	17-23	Esoteric or Mysterious Aspects of Course }	Do
Terminology	23-25	Terminology	Scattered
General Law of All Mental Life }	25-27	General Formula of All Mental and Spiritual Life }	322
An Outline of Course	28-46	A General Survey of Course }	129-150
Automatism	46-69	Automatism	151-178
Hume	70-83	Hume	179-191
Communicating With Friends }	83-101	Communicating With Friends }	208-227

262

Before embarking on the main part of this Section, I wish once again to express my appreciation of Professor Garman and his course and to acknowledge once again my tremendous indebtedness to him.

After the lapse of a year (at Massachusetts Institute of Technology), subsequent to leaving Amherst, I decided to enter Yale Divinity School. I had no intention of such a course of study, before entering Garman's course at Amherst.

Of personal interest to me is letter from Mrs. Garman, dated September 23, 1902. Copy of Mrs. Garman's letter referred to follows. How I wish I could then have contributed towards books and pamphlets, an opportunity gone, it seems, forever.

As I read Mrs. Garman's letter it is:

Amherst, September 23, 1902

My dear Mr. Bell:—

Mr. Garman has been sick with bronchitis so he asked me to write to you for him of your decision to go to Yale. Professor Sanders wrote to him yesterday making some inquiries and he has just dictated a letter for me to send him commending you to their kind care and telling them how much you were esteemed at Amherst. So I hope you will receive your fall notice of your acceptance to all the privileges you ask for and that you will have a most delightful year there. Mr. Garman hopes to be able to meet his classes by Thursday. Talking sets him to coughing so he will have to gain a good deal in the next two days to be in shape to meet a new class of about seventy-five Juniors, and I do not know how many Seniors the hour before that. He needs a whole year of rest and I hope he will be able to take it before long. A summer vacation is not quite long enough to recuperate after so hard a year's work as last, six days in a week with one hundred and forty students to look after in a study like Psychology and all the outside work he does with the men in evening. If you ever hear of any wealthy people who are wondering where a few hundred dollars will do the most good I wish you would remind them of the need of duplicate copies of books for the psychological department. I think those who have taken the course in philosophy must fully appreciate the value of the books thus loaned. Mr. Garman sends his very kindest remembrances.

Yours sincerely
(Signed) Eliza M. Garman

To my correspondent with respect to outline of Professor Garman's course I wrote as follows:

October 29, 1952

Dear —— — :

I have assumed that you have a copy of the Memorial Volume,—Letters, Lectures and Addresses of Charles Edward Garman, published by Houghton, Mifflin Co., 1909 and 1911. I have quoted from it throughout in the outline.

If you do not have a copy, one should if possible be obtained for you.

Very truly yours,
Hermon F. Bell.

October 29, 1952

Dear —— — :

When we were both at Amherst in early June of 1952, you reiterated to me that when in college your class had missed Garman's course because of his illness or absence for other reason during your senior year. I have elsewhere borne testimony to my belief that my having taken Garman during my last year at Amherst 1900-1901 was for me an event of primary importance, one for which I cannot be too grateful, and thankfulness for which I cannot even begin to adequately express. Consequently I do have a keen sense of the loss your class suffered through circumstances beyond your control.

You have expressed surprise that Garman's course was not continued after his untimely death in February 1907 and that no complete record has been made with respect to his course and his teaching. To an extent I sympathize with your questions. But perhaps the answers are not too far off.

In his tribute at the Memorial Service, February 12, 1907, Professor John M. Tyler said,—

> Do you remember in Pilgrim's Progress how Mr. Valiant-for-Truth went over the river and "all the trumpets sounded for him on the other side"? His last words were: "My sword I give to him that shall succeed me in my pilgrimage, and my courage and skill to him that can get it. My marks and scars I carry with me, to be a witness for me, that I have fought His battles, who will now be my rewarder."

At the same time Edmund B. Delabarre of the Class of 1886 wrote to The Amherst Student:

> It is no exaggeration to say that Professor Garman was one of the greatest of men. It is not alone in politics and war, in leadership and organization, in industry and wealth, that greatness manifests itself. Not alone those who make themselves worthily prominent in the eyes of their fellow-men are great. He who with earnest labor and clear vision seeks for truth, and who with untiring zeal and effective method helps others to grasp it and make it a living force, may be among the first in directing the steps of our race in its slow upward progress; and in doing that alone lies true greatness. Professor Garman's service in this respect was of the highest order.

———————

The Amherst of today is more than all else the Amherst of Garman. And it will probably never have another Garman. His successors must work out their own individualities, pursue other methods, seek to know and to teach the ideals of knowledge and of conduct in their own personal ways. But Garman himself will truly remain. His work is not done. His genius and his nobility of character will live to bless the generations of Amherst students yet to come.

266

It is I believe to be regretted that Professor Garman did not live to publish. In this connection, everyone should read Professor Garman's letter to President G. Stanley Hall, as found on pages 57 to 71 inclusive of Letters, Lectures and Addresses of Charles Edward Garman, A Memorial Volume, published by Houghton Mifflin Company, 1909 and 1911. Said letter is therein reprinted from the American Journal of Psychology, volume ix, 1898.

I gained the impression when at College that Professor Garman did hope sometime to publish, but that he did not wish to do so at the expense of letting down in the high standards he had set for himself in his class teaching. Also in the state of his health publication would entail added burdens. But still I felt Professor Garman did hope to publish some time. He was however keenly aware of the great amount of work involved in presenting his course adequately and in such a manner as not to subject it to factious or unwarranted criticism.

Upon the death of Professor Garman in 1907 President G. Stanley Hall wrote in The Amherst Student:

> As a teacher of philosophical subjects, I believe Professor Garman should rank in our day as Mark Hopkins did in his. Both were uniquely effective and masterly as teachers, and both mutually yearned for the mental and spiritual welfare of their students, and both sought to lay solid and deep foundations upon which not only any, however great, intellectual superstructure could be safely reared, but also desired to make philosophy indeed the guide of life and the basis of good character and citizenship. The age in which Professor Garman wrought was far more advanced, the problems more difficult, and his own scholarship was vastly larger. I cannot think of any one in the country who could fill his place. Next to personal grief and profound regret for the loss that higher education has suffered by his death, my greatest solicitude is that the world be given, and that speedily, the benefit of the publication of his system. His remarkable pedagogic instinct made him feel profoundly the

267

difference between the philosophy needed by college men and the development of a finished system which should appeal to experts. I always felt that his reluctance to make known his methods was based upon the conviction I believe, alas, only too true, that most of his fellow-teachers in his field would not do justice to this discrimination. I profoundly hope that neither the condition of his notes, most of which I understand were already printed, nor any expression left by him, will prevent their being speedily placed in the hands of some judicious, sympathetic and able professor of philosophy, who should also be a student of his, and that they will soon be printed.

In 1904, Professor Garman wrote to an alumnus,—

There is nothing I desire more than to publish my work if only I can get it in such form that it will really express to the readers my deepest convictions. With quite a large portion of the material at hand this is not difficult. But the part I am most interested in has not yet been reduced to such a form that I dare to send it out into the world "alone." In the class room my first presentation generally means little or nothing to the students. It has to be drilled in, reviewed, applied, tested, and then I must begin all over anew the next term, and take each step as carefully as before. This is not a logical age. Evidence has very little influence on most men, even when well-educated. A man will follow conscientiously my argument and at the close forget the beginning and the middle. Nowadays people care for results, not processes. They see things as a whole, not part by part; that which is too large to be taken in at a glance they leave for scientists to examine.

But these are just the people I most want to reach, and I firmly believe it can be done. Each year I get new light on how to do it. But each new class makes me very humble, because they convince me that I have not got along quite so far as I had hoped.

268

Reference has already been made to Letters, Lectures and Addresses of Charles Edward Garman, A Memorial Volume, published by Houghton, Mifflin Co., 1909 and 1911. In the pages that follow and those preceding, I have used this volume freely without specific credit references. In that volume various topics are taken up, for a considerable part however with some repetition and without logical or topical organization and presentation.

It was an oft repeated admonition of Professor Garman that a dwarf standing on a giant's shoulders could see farther than that giant. In what follows I shall endeavor to present Professor Garman's course without any modifications due to my own views or thinking.

I was as you know among the later but not the very last classes that Professor Garman taught. As you know the course was not a course where formal lectures were delivered for note taking, neither was one, or a few, textbook used. While it may be that emphasis of the course varied from year to year I am inclined to the opinion that substantially the same course was given year after year but that the component materials, especially the books referred to, did vary from time to time. Parts of a few books were intensively studied in connection with certain specific subjects. Then references for presentations of specific topics were made to numerous volumes. In some cases such extracts were printed in pamphlet form by Professor Garman. Such pamphlets were loaned to the class but promptly recalled when they had served their specific purposes. There were other pamphlets, written by Professor Garman. These were similarly loaned but always promptly recalled. Pamphlets were not allowed to be kept by class members. In some cases they presented questions, or answers, or one side of a question under discussion. Professor Garman considered his use of pamphlets as of great value, a particularly happy invention of his. They were very costly to him in time and in money. But they did allow a presentation of one aspect to be made. In a book questions and answers and discussions might all appear. The pamphlets promoted independent consideration of specific problems. Professor Garman, rightly I believe, considered the invention of pamphlets as great an invention in its way as the invention of movable type.

Of the earlier pamphlets several were outlines or explanations of Hickok's texts; several were designed to aid in the study of the classics—Descartes, Berkeley, Hume, and Kant; a third class consisted of selections or arrangements of passages from authors —a favorite in this class was "The Revelation of the Universal," based on Emerson. None from these three classes of pamphlets are reproduced in the Memorial Volume, except two on Hume and Kant which represent a somewhat intermediate stage. The first pamphlets used on Hume and Kant were more nearly a series of questions. It is further to be noted that in the later years Professor Garman was accustomed to buy many duplicate copies of books or periodicals to be loaned to his classes, besides reprinting extracts in pamphlet form. Thus with the class of 1907, up to the middle of the Senior year he had employed forty-four pamphlets and thirty-seven books or periodicals.

What Professor Garman wrote in 1893 of the whole series of pamphlets is still more true of any selection: "These pamphlets are very fragmentary and are devoted to elucidating or amplifying some of the topics of the text-book, and it would be impossible for a person to judge them except in connection with the oral lectures and criticisms which I am accustomed to add in the class room. They in no sense present the syllabus of a course."

Hereinafter I plan to outline the course quoting freely from the book referred to. In this connection it is interesting to note the interest that Professor Garman showed as respects outline. He would frequently come back to outline of the course. And it was an almost sure question in any examination or test. The student could be practically sure that he would be asked to give a rather complete outline of the course. This is evidence to me at least of the unity and sequence of the course, never haphazard, but always purposeful and progressing logically throughout.

Before attempting to give either in outline or in detail the sub-

270

stance of the course I wish to express my hesitancy in doing so, but I believe I should try to do my best. Still if Professor Garman hesitated to publish for fear of possible inadequacy of presentation, how much greater should be my hesitancy unless I am one of those whom Alexander Pope had in mind when he wrote,— fools rush in where angels fear to tread.

Before outline or presentation of the subject matter of the course there are two topics which are worthy of attention. First, everyone attributes great moral earnestness to Professor Garman. His primary interest was in the intellectual and spiritual well-being of his students. Consequently some presentation is attempted of Professor Garman's purpose and aims in presenting the course. Second, the course in my day had somewhat of a secret and esoteric nature. The course was surrounded with an atmosphere of mystery. The fact that Professor Garman was in my day (1900-1901) a semi-invalid heightened this impression. Students except of his own classes seldom saw him. He was never at chapel or seen walking around the campus. From his home up beyond Deke house he was driven to class by Mrs. Garman in an ancient buggy drawn by an ancient horse. Mrs. Garman waited for him and after class drove him home. His own students even saw him practically never except in his class room or at home. Besides he lacked bodily or physical warmth or heat so that it sometimes happened that even in warm weather he might be bundled up in a great coat. It was not at all unusual for him to wear a heavy overcoat in class. And room temperature at his home was kept high.

Strangers were not welcome in his class. And at times he would request the class members not to discuss the subjects of the course with outsiders. The reasons for this attitude will later be discussed. Suffice to say at this point that from a single class session and a single question one might get a very erroneous conception of what was being taught or of the course itself. So the course had an atmosphere of deep mystery at times. This phase of the course will be further elaborated at the proper time and place.

Professor Garman from his boyhood had a marvelous familiarity with the Bible which made its imagery the symbol and its phrase the language in which Professor Garman spontaneously embodied or illustrated nearly every thought. And he was always giving a deep spiritual meaning as for example, referring to Pentecost and the speaking with tongues,—

> Christ's discourses were in Aramaic and have come down to us only in translations, some of which are bungling and full of errors, but when he sent his disciples forth as living words on the day of Pentecost he sent a message that did not have to be translated. Parthians, and Medes, and Elamites, and the dwellers in Mesopotamia, and Cappadocia, in Pontus, and Asia, strangers of Rome, Jews and proselytes, could all understand lives of heroism and self-denying service, for character is the mother tongue of every nation. Those who have long forgotten this native speech are touched when they hear of heroism and devotion as though they listened to the tender accents of home at their mother's knee.

or referring to The Transfiguration,—

> You remember one scene in Christ's life where He went up into the mountain and, while there, was transfigured; His disciples saw Him then no longer a man of sorrows acquainted with grief, but in His divine grandeur, and with Him Moses, who represented the law that He fulfilled, and Elias, who represented the prophecies that He had brought to pass. It seems to me that philosophy is the mount of transfiguration of human nature, and that if we study it rightly we no longer see only that which is base and mean and selfish and slavish, which actual life makes so much of, but we have revealed to us the divine spirit which is working out through it all. Then we discover that this side of human life alone gives meaning to science, which stands for law in modern

272

times, and to society, which has ever looked forward to a future beyond the power of man to realize. Industrial life, which has been so often condemned as having nothing but selfishness in it, is seen to be a reincarnation of the divine in human character; for it is nothing but sovereignty on its positive side, where the strong make the service given an equivalent for the service received in business, and in charity the strong help the weak to become strong and thus help themselves.

Professor Garman wrote:—

The moral excellence, the personal loveliness of the pupil is the true crown of glory to a teacher. As well instruct a brute as a child, if the beauty of manhood or womanhood does not unfold, if no ambition, no aspiration after a noble life is awakened, if there are no bright dreams of the future. It has long been known that certain plastic substances brought in contact with mother-of-pearl and allowed time to harden will take on its own variegated splendor. To impress one's self thus on an immortal being—an impression time can never efface—may well excite the envy of angels in heaven. It is immortality.

and again

With a teacher *vacation* is like the moments when an artist lays down his brush and *steps back* to look upon his finished painting. Some of the colors are pale at first but deepen with age, some of your work does not appear at all now. Some instruction is like invisible ink, it's all there but it takes a chemical process to bring it out. It will take the chemistry of years and of the experience of life before the true results of your influence on the students will show. You can see only the outlines of your picture now. There's more to it, infinitely more, than you have ever dared to dream. The beauty of future manhood and womanhood are your work. There is a halo of fame around the memory of Phidias

273

and Raphael, but ages and ages after their works have all crumbled to dust this shall endure in its eternal freshness, for the material is immortal. This is the only true art, for it shall decorate the 'Heavenly City.' I am a regular Socrates in my estimation of a successful teacher.

In the words of Professor John E. Russell of Williams College,—

Garman was, I think, always a teacher in reality. His interest in truth was that of a teacher even when he was a student. He seemed to play the double role of student and teacher—he compelled himself to see every truth, every problem, from those two points of view. Garman's ambition was to be more than a scholar: his scholarship he would make the medium of his personality. Truth had always in his estimation a service beyond itself: he was always seeing through every truth he gained to its possible uses in some ministry to his fellow men.

The determining note in Professor Garman's teaching of philosophy was his conception of philosophy. It was not for him primarily a subject to be studied for its own sake. One might say it was not studied as a subject at all. He believed that every man who thinks at all must sooner or later face the alternatives which are represented in general by a spiritual or a materialistic view of the world and of human action. He conceived it his task to aid young men in facing the problem squarely, and with a method for its solution. For this purpose he selected his material, planned his order of subjects, and developed the technique of his instruction.

We note that though the centre of emphasis changed there was always a fundamental religious element in the course which corresponded to Garman's deeply religious nature and to his religious conception of philosophy. The constant use of biblical imagery was a symbol of the fact that for him to think of any subject philosophically meant toinvest it with all the emotion as

274

well as with all the significance that belongs to a part when viewed in the light of the whole. Theism was for him the solution of the problem of knowledge; the biblical history was a revelation of an unfolding divine plan; the New Testament doctrine "not to be ministered unto but to minister" was his central ethical principle; the conception of a change of heart was primary in his theory of social reform; the principles of divine sovereignty and the atonement afforded in his judgment the true basis of human political society; the teaching of philosophy was an opportunity to show men the eternal and to aid in shaping their lives.

Nothing in his course was more difficult for some of the students to adjust themselves to than this interpenetration of philosophy, religion, and practical life. Those to whom religion had been cut off by watertight bulkheads, whether they cherished it as too sacred for scrutiny, or treated it with indifference as sentimental and "not for them," found Garman's attitude disturbing to old habits. But by the end of the course few of the latter class failed to gain a respect for religion as Garman interpreted it, and many in the former class found religion transformed from a treasure timidly guarded and carefully concealed to a vital power which itself should guard the values of daily life. To adopt in slightly different form one of his own metaphors, they were no longer the anxious disciples concerned for a dead body taken away, but bold apostles who had seen the vision of a risen Master, and believed him not a body to be protected, but a power that would itself protect and inspire.

Along with all the gifts and methods which combined to give charm and compelling form to the classroom was a characteristic which both enabled him to aim his instruction directly at the mark, and contributed strongly to the permanence of his hold upon his students in after life. To say that this was a profound and abiding interest in the intellectual and spiritual life of each student might not at first convey all that is meant. Many teachers

275

cultivate such an interest as part of their vocation. But with Garman it seemed to be a "first intention." Like the bent of a Newton or a Darwin for investigation it had no need of external stimulation and was eager to seize and hold fast any clue.

We might go on to add this or that which contributed to Professor Garman's success,—but after all, if these qualities that we have named and others that might be named had not been the genuine expressions of a great mind and heart, seeking and finding its life by a certain inward necessity in the Socratic Eros, they would have become mechanical and failed. It was because there was first of all this great personality, with a genuine interest in every student, that Professor Garman has achieved the immortality which Plato tells us every great soul craves, the living on in ideals, aspirations, and enthusiasms that it has begotten in other souls.

Professor Garman on the occasion of the presentation of the Commemorative Volume at Commencement 1906, said among other things,—

I have been fortunate in working in an age when the profoundest questions have occupied human thought. During the early classes, the religious life of young men was undergoing the most serious ferment that had been experienced in the history of the institution. The transition from extreme Calvinism to a scientific point of view that should find a place for evolution and higher criticism, was no small shock for a student to experience during the short four years of college life. Those who suffered most were those who had been most carefully sheltered from the new ideas before entering college. With many of these, the tares and the wheat were rooted up together; but in every age philosophy has been to a few young men what it was to Augustine and Neander, a star of Bethlehem, leading their steps from out the far country of skepticism, by a long and circuitous route, to be sure, but ultimately to the manger, where they worshipped. It has been my privilege to point out this star to our students, and to follow with them along that road.

Why is this (readjusting of their views) necessary, i.e., what is it meant to accomplish? The earlier life of the students has been one of imitation and obedience to authority; it corresponds to traditionalism in tribal or national existence . . . The earlier education of the student must be wholly by imitation . . . But there comes a time when the young man must assume responsibility for what he does; there must be self-possession and self-direction instead of dependence on authority, and this is a new experience to him, an experience which many shrink from even in very little things. . . . There is no hope for a young man at this time if he does not meet the obligations of life with the spirit of self-reliance, but to do this he must have some confidence in his own judgment and the standards by which he judges. This is the spirit of philosophy. . . .

It is my conviction that a young man can obtain inspiration, enthusiasm, absence of self-consciousness only by the steady contemplation of great truths; that if he is wholly absorbed in imitation he is like a person whose whole work is that of a proof-reader; if he is successful he is taken as a matter of course, and he gets no credit; if he is unsuccessful and makes mistakes, he is awkward; he is ridiculed beyond endurance; he soon realizes that the most promising rewards for the most careful efforts are negative, and he soon becomes indifferent, and is simply goaded on from fear of the consequences of failure. But the young man who philosophizes, who really understands himself and appreciates the truth, is no longer a slave of form, but is filled with admiration that is genuine and lasting.

Why should philosophy, psychology and ethics be the studies **which most favor self-reliance, rather than mathematics or the sciences?**

It seems to me that mathematics fails to meet the demand for two reasons; first there is no difference of opinion on all these subjects; . . . secondly, he oftentimes knows pretty nearly what the answer will be; . . . he is not a Columbus sailing over unknown seas with everything before him untried.

With regard to physical sciences, there is some difference of opinion here . . . but he accepts a great many positions in science without really testing them; . . . but when he comes to philosophy it is a new world. . . . He is obliged, therefore, to weigh evidence and to let himself down with all his weight upon his own feet. . . . They are greatly surprised to find the extent to which they have blindly followed authority,—they are almost as frightened as some horses are when the blinders are taken off. But when the idea fairly dawns upon them that true scholarship consists, not in some mystical quality of genius that ordinary men do not possess, but in simple honesty to one's self in following out the Cartesian Golden Rule, then they experience a new birth, they are no longer boys or slaves, but men. If they attain citizenship in the kingdom of truth, they perceive that the difference between the greatest and the smallest consists only in the quickness and comprehensiveness and thoroughness and humility of their work. Truth to one man is truth to all if they can get exactly the same standards. Henceforth they call no man master or lord, for all are brethren.

I do feel that the teaching of philosophy is an opportunity which no other study offers. I feel that the student who has been through these doubts and worked them out for himself has learned the strength and at the same time the limitations of the finite, and that he will have a degree of courage and patience in adversity, a degree of self-reliance and humility which others can secure only by those peculiar experiences which occasionally occur in actual business or politics or the professional life. The student who has taken philosophy realizes how the part is to be estimated in the light of the whole; he realizes this more completely than he could from any other study. He also realizes the dignity which a part may secure from the grandeur of the whole to which it belongs, and the little things of life have a depth of

278

meaning for him which they could not have if he had not this point of view.

To bring his students to an intellectual plane where they were in possession of an ineradicable conviction that the processes of thought, if rightly used, could be made to yield them the truth, was, I believe, one of Professor Garman's most cherished ambitions. To teach a student how to weigh evidence and to arouse in him the conviction that he could do his own independent weighing and that truth's ultimate appeal lay in his own mind,— these were the constant endeavors of the class room and the private conversation.

He guided the thinking of his students toward what he believed to be sound conclusions. . . . Some of them did not reach his conclusions; more of them forgot the conclusions which they did reach; but practically all of them were inspired by the spirit of free inquiry, and with the conviction that free inquiry conducted with reverence for the truth can be trusted eventually to reach trustworthy conclusions.

Re: Esoteric or Mysterious Aspects of Course

There was a fundamental difference between President Seelye's and Professor Garman's methods of presenting the subject. "Give them the light first," was President Seelye's maxim, and he had achieved great results with the earlier generations of Amherst students. Garman became more and more convinced that the light of reason was not and could not be appreciated by the students of his day unless they were first awakened to feel their need of it. It was necessary, Garman believed, to show that darkness was dangerous, and that life might be shipwrecked if its master did not learn to take observations of the fixed stars. The logical results of typical attitudes were shown, and the futility of blinking or evading the issues were forced home, until a large proportion of the class were anxious to investigate and willing to work hard for their results. This preliminary process was naturally to a considerable degree negative. The old complaints made against Socrates were occasionally heard. Partly for this reason, Professor Garman was at one time accustomed to ask his students not to discuss their work with others until they had reached the constructive portions—a caution which to those that did not understand the whole situation seemed to give a sort of esoteric character to the course.

Dr. Charles H. Parkhurst once amused a New York alumni gathering by telling of a boy in his own congregation back from college for his Christmas vacation. Interrogating him as to how he liked Garman's course, this reply was received: "Well, Garman has taken a good part of the fall term to state the argument for agnosticism, but next term he says he is going to refute it. But what is bothering me just now is what will become of me if I should die, not having had next term's course."

One did need the whole year with Garman to grasp his viewpoint and to understand his methods. There was now and then a man also who, coming to college with a traditional but never reasoned out system of belief, revolted at first from some things he heard in the class room. . . . But there were other men who were thrilled and fascinated by Garman's fair, candid, generous presentations of all the sides of a great question, and they were patient enough to wait until the outlines of the fair temple of truth began to appear.

A distinctive feature of Professor Garman's teaching was his extraordinarily facile use of illustration. No one of his students will ever forget the brilliancy and aptness of his figures. . . . The vigor and vividness of presentation that resulted from the use of this method produced remarkable results in the minds of most of his hearers.

Visitors to Professor Garman's classes were extremely few. The outsider, curious to get a glimpse of the ways of this man who could so wield philosophy as to stir the student soul to its very depths, was not made welcome. In Professor Garman's opinion, a stranger tended to introduce a disturbing element into the atmosphere, and his presence tended to make it seem that philosophy and its methods were on exhibition, a situation that Professor Garman abhorred as subversive of the aim that he was attempting to accomplish. If sometimes this attitude, together with some of the devices which were integral parts of Professor Garman's method, seemed too esoteric to comport well with the modern teaching of philosophy sufficient justification was felt to exist in the fact that thereby the student was made to feel that he was on sacred ground, at the very portals of the inner shrine of truth.

In the words of Professor Garman,—

Our course is psychology is often criticized as involving two parts: first, the negative work which is understood to be an undermining of the student's faith, and a familiarizing him with various objections of a more or less philosophical and scientific type which leads strongly towards materialism. The view is strengthened by the fact that the students do become more or less unsettled in their views at a certain stage in our work. The second part of our course is supposed to be positive in its nature; it is supposed that, taking the students with their foundations all undermined, we then proceed to do what we can towards giving them positive conceptions concerning God, and duty, and nature. Many friends of the college, and indeed some of the students themselves, would feel that an illustration of our work might be drawn from the fate of Chicago, which had to be destroyed by fire in order to be rebuilt on a much broader scale. No doubt that to the city as a whole the fire was a blessing, but to individuals it was enormously expensive. My answer to this criticism is that while unjust, there is just shadow enough of truth in it to make an explanation needed.

No teacher has a right to ignore entirely the age in which he lives, and the point of view that is prevalent in the department in which he teaches. The new psychology has broken absolutely with philosophy, and claims to be a science; it goes farther than this, and claims to be a psychology without a soul. . . .

Take the following quotation from Professor James: "It is indeed true that psychological science has come to the conclusion cited (that our inner life is a function of that famous material, the so-called 'gray matter' of our cerebral convolutions), and we must confess that in so doing she has only carried out a little farther the common belief of mankind. Every one knows that arrests of brain development occasion imbecility, that blows on the head abolish memory or consciousness, and that brain stimulants and poisons change the quality of our ideas. The anatomists, physiologists, and pathologists have only shown this generally admitted fact of a dependence to be detailed. What the laboratories and hospitals have lately been teaching us is not only that thought in general is one of the brain's functions, but that the various special forms of thinking are functions of special portions of the brain."

For the purpose of my argument now, I wish to adopt this general doctrine as if it were established absolutely, with no possible restriction. During this hour I wish you to accept it as a postulate; whether you think it incontrovertibly established or not, so I beg you to agree with me today in subscribing to the great psycho-physical formula: *Thought is a function of the brain.*

Man has a physical nature and it is important that the students should understand their nervous system and learn how to make their brain "their ally instead of their enemy"; learn the terrible consequences of disobeying these positions, as well as the great blessings that may be gained through obedience.

So long as the students do not know accurately the limitations of the physical side of our being, they cannot be persuaded that the brain is not able to account for all that takes place. A careful study, therefore, of philosophy and of the limitations which are obvious is the best possible preparation to make them candid, and prepare for a study of spiritual truths.

Therefore, though we take up these problems, and though the effect is to some extent unsettling, yet we feel that our work here is not negative but positive. It is unsettling only in that it is incomplete in the early stages of the course. The subject is so large that it cannot be covered in a single sitting, or in a single term. Therefore in the meantime the students do undoubtedly use their imagination in judging as to where we may possibly come out. But it is positive work, just as the study of the temperature sense and the muscle and joint sense is real, positive acquisition of knowledge, though it can be proved that through these senses we do not gain either sight or hearing. These senses are a part, and as such as worthy of study as the latter and more exalted senses. So brain conditions are real; the facts are beyond dispute, and a study of these is as truly constructive work, as truly positive, as anything that comes in our course. It is only when the students fear that this may turn out to be all there is to man that it is unsettling to their religious faith. But this is absolutely unavoidable if the men are to be inspired with the right spirit when they come to the study of the more difficult problems which require more careful analysis, and which cannot be demonstrated by physical instruments.

Terminology

To the newcomer in Professor Garman's course, or to the students electing it, some of the phraseology in common use was impressive and strange. They found Professor Garman using names or phrases or expressions that they were unaccustomed to. Yet Professor Garman used them as if everyone was equally conversant therewith. Generally speaking they were not introduced as new terms or so defined. Neither do we now attempt definitions.

283

In the class they soon came to have full, even if not complete, content.

It may be in order at least to mention some of these terms, phrases or expressions so that the reader in due time, as the course is outlined and discussed, may consider them and come to understanding thereof.

One of these expressions has already been used,—Thought is a function of the brain. Is thinking according to habit and does it all follow the lines of least resistance? Or is there action with effort, following the lines not of least resistance but of greatest resistance? Other terms were association of ideas, ideo-motor action, function of the will, apperception mass.

Darwinian evolution and moral evolution were contrasted. Kidd's expression, cake of custom, was used. And of course monism and monists as well as pluralism and pluralists were new terms to most of us, but now found to be in constant use.

Garman seemed always to be talking of vicarious thinking (science), vicarious willing (theory of the state, which was used as a much wider term than government), and vicarious judgment (and theories of punishment).

Sovereignty was a word much used. A striking contrast was set up between selfishness and altruism, as illustrated by Nietzsche and Tolstoy. Particularly striking was Professor Garman's criticism of altruism. He regarded it as highly immoral. As opposed to selfishness on the one hand and to altruism on the other hand, Garman emphasized *selfness*.

Communication with friends was made the basis for an important discussion and presentation.

Governing motives was an important subject, including the function of the will.

Liberty, equality and fraternity were discussed, including the question whether these were possible.

The laws of mind and the laws of things were basic subjects.

Idealism, personality and sovereignty were basic concepts. So

284

were action and reaction; and related conduct, and supreme choice.

Professor Garman's concept of sovereignty was wonderful, and fundamental; his concept was that we must act and that the way we must act is determined by and conditioned upon the person or thing to which we must react or upon which we must act. We never determine ourselves directly but indirectly through other persons or things. A determines himself never directly but only indirectly through B. This introduces Garman's great original and fundamental "General Formula of All Mental and Spiritual Life." This I consider an original and basic concept, the importance of which cannot be sufficiently stressed, a distinctive and permeating feature of Professor Garman's philosophy.

It is the general law of all mental life that consciousness of self is possible only through consciousness of objects. A similar law holds in moral life and the social order. We may state this in the formula, A determines himself never directly, but always through B, i.e., a man determines his character and personality by the attitude and relations he assumes towards his world of nature and persons.

If A determines himself through B, then there are only four possible spheres of life for A, due to the four possible conditions of B, since A's life will be limited to the change in B:

1. B may be strong and do right.
2. B may be strong and do wrong.
3. B may be weak and do right.
4. B may be weak and do wrong.
Every phase of life comes in here.

(1) is the sphere of business, where action and reaction should be equal; (2) is the sphere of punishment, where the action must take the form of *resistance* to the wrongdoer; (3) is the sphere of charity, where the strong must

285

help the weak; (4) is the sphere for the atonement, where the strong must resist by assistance. Under these four heads come nearly all the questions of the later part of the course. Incidentally, Professor Garman frequently wrote atonement as at-one-ment.

Before beginning an attempt at outline of Professor Garman's course, specific mention should be made of items (2) and (4) above. We have stated that we believe the General Formula of All Mental and Spiritual Life, as related to Professor Garman's concept of sovereignty, to be distinctive; so perhaps most original therein is the concept of authority and punishment. There is some evidence that Professor Garman considered these as among the most original and important of his contributions.

Your nature demands sovereignty. You feel the need of it; you cannot do without it. Modern religion does not offer sovereignty, and see its weakness. Christianity asserts it. . . .

Atonement means justice. What is justice? Not the prevention of evil. That is impossible unless you prevent the good also, since man must be free to do either if he is to be a man. But justice is aiding the right and resisting the wrong every time.

Then what, finally, is authority? It is the realization of the state. And what is the state? The state is the condition of action and reaction between all parts of the universe, which is due because they are *creatures*, i.e., dependent entities. How does it realize itself? Through ethics; that is the process, the *how*. If every person does wrong, that is no reason why I should do wrong. If they do right and I do right, that is rewarding. If they do wrong and I do right, that is in the line of punishment.

AN OUTLINE OF THE COURSE

I was a week or ten days, at least, late in entering Professor Garman's course. So I cannot state just how the first hour of the

286

course started. I believe we were studying William James when I arrived.

Take the following quotation from Professor Titchener:

> The question: Is there anything behind the mental process, any permanent mind? If there is, what is its nature?—is a question that has often been asked, and which it is well worth while to try to answer. But it is not a question which can be raised by psychology. Psychology sees in mind nothing more than the whole sum of mental processes experienced in a single lifetime.
>
> It will be seen that to psychology the term "mind" means no more than the word "tune" in music, which is used to denote the sum of the notes that form a continuous relationship with each other.

Professor James then goes on to speak of the work of Professor Flechsig, who carries brain localization still farther, and accounts thereby for the complexion of our emotional life, and eventually decides whether one shall be a callous brute or a criminal, an unbalanced sentimentalist or a character accessible to feeling and yet well poised.

He then goes on to say, "Such special opinions may have to be corrected; yet so firmly established are the main positions worked out by the anatomists, physiologists and pathologists, that the youth of our medical schools are everywhere taught unhesitatingly to believe them. The assurance that observation will go on and establish them more and more minutely is the inspirer of all contemporary research. Almost any of our young psychologists will tell you that only a few belated scholastics, or possibly some crack-brain theosophist or psychical researcher, can be found holding back, and still talking as if mental phenomena might exist as independent variables in the world."

Habit.

Our work begins with the law of association as explained in

287

terms of brain action. This involves a study of habit as resting upon a physiological basis.

Ideo-Motor Action.

We next take up physical action or what might be called volition. We find that a nerve current coming in through the senses invariably finds its way out in the muscles through action, if it is strong enough to overcome the resistance of inertia. This is the doctrine of ideo-motor action, that an idea cannot exist in the mind without producing motor effects, at least incipiently. These motor effects may be inhibited by motor power or contrary ideas, but no act of will intervenes between the thought and the action. The function of the will is effort at attention; its sphere is to resist the impulses which would turn our thoughts contrary to its decision, and hold the ideas of its choice before the mind until they completely dominate consciousness.

The old view of thought might be compared to the old form of fire alarm. When the alarm was received at the central office, a telegraph operator was needed to read it, and then to ring the general summons. Or we perhaps compare thought to the clock aboard a locomotive which has no power except to indicate time. The whole to be compared to the engineer, without whose services the throttle could not be opened and the engine started. Ideo-motor action claims that the engineer has no other function than that of regulating the clock, for the clock is so fixed that automatically, at the proper time through electrical connections, it pulls the throttle and regulates the speed of the train. Perhaps a more accurate illustration would be that of a modern thermostat for regulating our furnaces. Formerly intelligence would be compared to the thermometer which informed us of the temperature of the room. But the furnace would be ineffectual until the fireman should intervene and open or close the dampers. But the modern thermostat is ideo-motor action, and the fireman has no function aside from feeding the coal and supervising the setting of the thermometer.

288

We then proceed to point out the enormous importance of this changed point of view. Under the old view man might think of evil, so long as he did not will it, without being a criminal. But under this view as a man thinketh in his heart so is he. The thought is the deed incipiently. The student should realize that one could not take fire into his bosom without being burned, and that he needed no farther consent to degradation than simply the willingness to see.

Hypnotism.

We next take up the subject of hypnotism and show that the larger part of hypnotic phenomena is simply ideo-motor action freed from inhibitions of conflicting ideas. The mere suggestion of the idea under such circumstances sets the mental machinery at work and lets the brakes off. Hypnotism thus shows a tendency of ideas. In ordinary life these tendencies may be restrained in a large measure by conflicting ideas.

Illusions and Hallucinations.

This, then, leads to the study of illusions and hallucinations which are found to be based on sensations centrally excited. It is affirmed that in all probability an impression coming from the senses stimulates exactly the same tracts in the brain that are excited in imagination and memory, the only difference being in the intensity. It is then shown that under favorable conditions this difference can be eliminated, and the centrally excited sensations which we call imagination may have all the vividness and reality of objective experience. These conditions are carefully determined, and a study of these problems is found to lie at the basis of accurate weighing of testimony of eye-witnesses in court, and in history.

Sense Perception.

We then take up the subject of sense perception in general, and find that there are always two factors in adult life: the sensations given by the senses, and the apperception mass or associations of our past experience; and the perception is neither one nor the other of these but a resultant according to certain laws; and that centrally excited sensations appear in the larger part of our perceptions. Notice the mistakes made in proofreading; notice the fact that the blind spot in the eye is always unnoticed, the field of vision being filled in with sensations centrally excited; that the peripheral portions of the eye are colorblind, and yet the sky and landscape are not mutilated in their appearance.

Sensation.

We then take up a more particular study of sensation and we notice that the senses are connected with the different centres of the brain, and that these are differently developed in different people. The background of one's mental life, that is, the power to imagine will differ in different people; some will be eye-minded, others ear-minded, others motor-minded, etc.

We notice that when these brain centres are destroyed, for instance, the centre of sight, one not merely loses the use of that particular sense but also the power of imagining color in visual form; he is as though he had been born blind.

We notice that the association of one sense with another, and thus the fusion of sensation into ideas, is due to certain paths connecting these brain centres, and we see that if these paths are injured by tumor then this association becomes impossible; a person is blind and idiotic. Here we study the facts of aphasia and ataxia, and other pathological cases.

We then proceed to enumerate the different kinds of sensation; how many are furnished by the eye, by the ear, etc., and explain the mental tests by which these questions can be answered with precision. This involves laboratory work.

Berkeley.

Before going farther we interrupt our psychology to ask

exactly how much knowledge is gained through sensation, and here we take up Berkeley and also the Sophists and show that their demonstration remains still unoverthrown; that through sensation we gain only effects of the external world but not a knowledge of that world; that sensation is a resultant of the stimulus and the receiving agency, but is neither one nor the other, any more than the music of the piano, which is the resultant of the tension of a cord and blow of a hammer, could by any possibility be considered as like or identical with the cord or hammer. We then ask: "May we not through the effect infer the cause?" and this Berkeley attempts to do with the following form of reasoning. It is axiomatic that unlikes cannot act upon each other. Now it is universally agreed that matter and mind, if they are distinct agencies, must be unlike each other. It is impossible to define matter as a distinct agency from mind in any other way than by indicating all the attributes of mind. From this he concludes that matter cannot be the cause of our sensations, and therefore the causes of our sensations must be common, either our own or some other mind, either finite or infinite.

Huxley.

We then turn to Professor Huxley in his criticism of Berkeley; he affirms that Berkeley's reasoning is irrefragable; that if he were forced to choose between idealism and materialism he would not hesitate to take Berkeley. But this he refuses to do. We conclude that when a man says the reasoning is irrefragable, but does not accept the conclusion, he must attack the premise. There is but one possible ground of objection to Berkeley's premise, and that is that axioms are simply inherited convictions, as Darwin would say that he hesitates to trust the convictions of a mind derived from a monkey. This implies that all our knowledge is limited to sensations and the association of sensations, either our own or those derived from inheritance; consequently an axiom would be good for experience but worthless when used outside of experience. For instance, the pronunciation of vowels

291

and consonants is learned by experience, and the rustic becomes so familiar with this method of pronunciation that it does not seem to him that any other is possible, but we at once recognise the absurdity of his applying the laws of English to the pronunciation of French and German. Why, then, should we tolerate the application of axioms to the objective world if axioms are simply laws of thought dependent on our experience.

Can The Laws of Thought Be Proved To Be The Law of Things?

If not, Huxley's position is sound and agnosticism is the only true view. Here, then, are two positions brought before us: the one that famous position of Berkeley which accepts axioms without investigating them and makes them apply universally as true without any limitations; on which basis we should be obliged to deny the reality of the material cause for our sensations—but this is to deny the reality of the material world as material. On the other hand, the position of Huxley which would make axioms and all that hangs upon them purely relative, true to us within our limited experience but quite likely as ridiculous to beings differently endowed from ourselves as the college student's pronunciation of French and German would be to a foreigner.

Is The Question of Practical Importance?

But is this really a question of any practical importance? None of you questions the reality of experience. What odds does it make whether we can come to any knowledge of these cases? Take electricity, for instance. We know what its effects are, though scientists are far from knowing what electricity itself is. Do we need to know? Can we not press the button and illuminate our buildings just as well if we do not decide between different conflicting theories?

Without attempting a satisfactory answer to the above question with regard to the value of experience itself, which would take us over into the study of Kant at this stage, we notice that there are certain important ethical considerations at stake here.

292

If all knowledge is relative, if the human mind can know only effects, then the highest ethical consideration possible for a human being would be, as stated by the Sophist, nothing more than individual utilitarianism, the individual man becomes the measure of all things.

This would make government and law impossible; one man's meat would become another man's poison. The effects would not be the same except by accident. Our jury system would be ridiculous, for how could twelve strangers know the malice-aforethought of the accused when they could simply know how certain provocations would have affected them? We are thus led to a form of nihilism and individualism which is extreme.

Not at all that we attempt to judge of the truth of the position by its effects, but in this way we seek to determine whether the question is important enough to warrant the exact study which a careful investigation demands.

Herbert Spencer.

We then turn from the Sophists to Herbert Spencer and take up in his *Data of Ethics* his statement of the doctrine that the ultimate motive of human action must be happiness, and his attempt to show that this is postulated by all those schools of thought who suppose themselves maintaining a different view. Having gotten before the students the fact that to question the value of our [moral standards(?)], to refer them to sensations and associations of sensations for their originating, is to make some form of utility necessary, we then raise the question as to what stability human society and progress can have on this basis.

Kidd's Social Evolution.

We take up here certain chapters from Benjamin Kidd's *Social Evolution* which show that so far as the laws of evolution apply to human life, and there is a struggle for existence with the survival of only the fittest, the interests of the masses must be opposed to such a kind of progress; that the animal world living unaware of such a fact would allow the evolution to go on; that mankind, when they have reached that stage of intelligence which leads them to take their bearings and realize their interests, would discover that such a competition with such results, however much it might benefit the species, is sacrificing the majority of the individuals to the welfare of the future ages. Other factors indeed may come in, and do come in, but assuming that men know only effects and the consequences that may be anticipated from them, and therefore have no higher motive than their own selfishness, must not the masses attempt to suspend this law of competition through some form of socialism, regardless of its consequences to the race? For the greatest good to the greatest number must mean, not greatest good to the greatest number of those now living, but greatest good to all those who shall live in the future; whereas those who are now living, and are by hypothesis interested only in themselves, have no motive furnished by evolution to make the sacrifice which it demands if evolution alone is to work out the regeneration of the race. There is only one alternative, and that is that a man may find happiness in sacrificing himself for others. The highest ethical illustration of this is parental altruism. But this has been evolved, if it is to be accounted for solely by evolution, through countless generations, starting in with the life of the animal. All parental altruism shrinks and shrivels the moment the age is reached when men begin to calculate their own interests, as in France and Greece, and Rome. What are the probabilities, then, of an abstract altruism, which leads one to sacrifice for those who are not yet born? What are the probabilities of such an altruism being evolved, starting in the hotbed of utilitarianism and calculation of prudence, in two or three generations? Are we not moving in exactly the opposite direction so far as the struggle for existence is concerned? We show that Kidd's reasoning is beyond criticism, if we are to limit human life as Huxley and Spencer postulate we do limit it. Therefore, without some other sanction of self-sacrifice than utilitarianism progress could not

294

continue. Now must this higher sanction be ultra rational? Surely it must, and Mr. Kidd is right if intelligence is simply sensations and association of sensations.

Impulse, the Source of Conduct.

But may not intelligence be something more? Is not our true course to study more carefully the whole subject of association and determine whether axioms are so derived? To see if there are not other mental processes which give us true knowledge, true standards of judgment, instead of mere effects and their groupings? The question becomes all the more important when we notice what is the mainspring of human life. Many writers are now agreed that human action is impulsive, that impulse is the source of conduct. But two views are possible. The one, that impulse is like instinct in that it acts blindly and yet may be hindered by intelligence. This seems to be Mr. Kidd's view. The other view is that impulses are of different kinds and that those that are distinctly human as distinguished from those of the animal cannot be awakened to action save through the proper cognition; that we do not have an impulse to go to the rescue of our friends until we know of the shipwreck and of their presence on the boat, and that if we could be persuaded that they were not on the boat, and that the boat was not wrecked, there would be no impulse to inspire action. From this point of view religious impulses can never be awakened save through a cognition of God, of our relationship and obligations to Him. And anything which awakens these cognitions would disturb the mainspring of our religious life. A good illustration would be found in Darwin, who was originally orthodox, but as he gradually lost his convictions as to the trustworthiness of a mind derived from a monkey, he gradually lost his religious inspiration and with it admiration and enjoyment for our higher literature and the spiritual achievements of men, though he still retained the keenest interest in literature that dealt with practical affairs, even though outside of science.

Settling the question, then, as to whether man can know God and duty is determining the life or death of those spiritual impulses which have done most to ennoble the race and inspire human history with justice and self-sacrifice. Of course one can have his convictions without investigating, but that is not true of an age. The spirit of science is abroad in the land; it has already begun its investigations, and it makes a world of difference to the public whether science shall persuade the world that man can know or that he cannot know. When people believed in witchcraft and astrology they ordered their lives accordingly. Science convinced the world, or the larger part of it, that it had no such knowledge, and there the faith disappeared, and with it the impulse and the conduct. We do not believe that science will ever convince the world that it can have no knowledge of divine and spiritual things, but if it can prove that all our knowledge is limited to sensations and associations of sensation it will, in time, find such conviction an easy task; and it has already convinced some of our bright young men with all the results that we have here predicted. There is, at the present day, among our young men a spirit of epicurean utilitarianism and ridicule for a serious conviction, a lack of sincere patriotism, and a tendency to make merchandise of their country's highest welfare—a spirit which is ashamed of but one crime, and that is the sin of being found out. It is by no means affirmed that the mere conviction of the absolute truth of man's highest cognitions would change the character of these young men; but it is affirmed that no human being can have these convictions and allow himself to think of them without stirring the deepest impulses that human nature can experience in antagonism to such a career and that when a community is persuaded of these things it bestows no honor upon the transgressor. It is our conviction that in the churches at the present day there is a subtle agnosticism that is sapping the very vitals of life, and that men cannot experience the inspiration of apostolic days without the deep convictions and realizations of

296

the divine presence and of man's responsibility to God which the Apostles had.

Supreme Choice.

We take up here a more careful study of human impulse in different grades, and also the general subject of investment of choice, showing that all our deliberate actions must have a motive, which motive is either ultimate or is subordinate to some ultimate purpose. There are two supreme choices conceivable; selfishness and righteousness. All those who deny the possibility of man's knowing right and justice are obliged to reduce human character to retaining a form of self-interest.

Association.

Having brought before the students the real import of our problem, we turn to the subject of association, and ask, Is it not possible to derive intuitions or axioms in that way? This involves, first, the study of the nervous system, of reflex action, with the special functions of the hemispheres of the brain which is extremely interesting and startling in its results. It involves more or less anthropological study, where we trace the influences that have shadowed human evolution and which have dominated the minds of earlier peoples. Tremendous pressure has thus been brought to fix certain ideas and have them inherited from generation to generation.

We then come to the particular question, and as a test we select this axiom which has an advantage over all others—the uniformity of nature under the same conditions. How does the human mind come to get this conviction? for without it, if we believed that nature was not uniform, or had any doubts about it, we could not even have experience ordered with regard to the future. Assume that the laws of nature will change tomorrow at twelve o'clock, and then see how difficult it would be for you to make plans for tomorrow afternoon. Here is a cognition, then,

297

which in order to be valuable relatively must be valuable absolutely. Now, how does the human mind get it?

We take up the discussion of this problem as given in Hume and carried on by John Stuart Mill and Herbert Spencer. Then we show the consequences of making axioms simply dependent on association, with regard to the practical and social problems of life. When we have finished this subject the students feel they have the outline of the most that could possibly be done through association, and then they ask, Does the human mind accomplish something more?

This we take up in the form of a particular topic. Association is a brain function; the brain is governed by physical law; all matter is absolutely obedient, so far as it is matter, to the great law of physics, namely, that of acting along the line of least resistance according to the parallelogram of forces. Now, if all thought is a function of the brain in the sense of being determined by brain paths, would it be possible for thought to weigh evidence? It is shown that you can construct a machine so that it would produce the most accurate results, and the brain might be constructed so that its thinking would be perfect, if it can think at all. But then the reason why a machine gives these results is not because they are true, but simply because its mechanism makes such products easy,—the line of least resistance,— while all others are impossible. Change the number of cogs and the machine will just as readily give you some other answer. If then, brain paths determine my thinking, the reason I say: All men are mortal, Socrates is a man and therefore "mortal," is not at all because truth requires it, but simply because such a conclusion is the line of least resistance in my brain. But my brain might easily be so ordered that some other conclusion could just as well be affirmed from these premises.

To state the same problem more broadly: all physical action has nothing to do with truth or falsehood. Physical action is simply an event; it neither affirms nor denies any other event. The snow piles up in a drift which may or may not be like the

298

drift of last year, but surely not for the sake of becoming a muddle of what has been or what will be, and if human thinking was brain action it would be neither true nor false; it would be like the ravings of delirium, simply a succession of mental states; just as the squeaking of the rusty hinges of an iron gate is a succession of noises, and that is all. But if that is all, then the human mind has no science even of the brain, even of association, even of evolution; these words simply indicate so many mental states which have no more truth or falsehood in them than has neuralgia or hysterical ataxia.

The whole question then becomes transformed into this: Do we have any kind of science or not? Do we have physiology or theosophy, or do we have any kind of science? If so, the human mind has the power to weigh evidence—to conclude not along the lines of least resistance, but along the lines of greatest resistance, if need be, for its action is determined not by habit and association, but by evidence. It can therefore work independently of brain laws—this is not saying independently of brain conditions. It is affirming, however, that its action is not controlled by those conditions. The mind is therefore an agency in the universe outside of and beyond the physical and the physiological. Now if this is so, if the "therefore" in a syllogism means glorious emancipation from the line of least resistance, and ability to square our decision solely according to truth, regardless of the amount of effort that it costs, then these acts of mind must be studied by themselves and their own laws determined, and to insist in studying them in terms of physics is the height of inconsistency. No physical analogy can be appealed to to settle a mental problem; there is no natural law governing here and in the spiritual world. They may be analogies, but nothing more. Here is the Magna Charta of the spiritual life. The physiological psychology is modern Pharisaism, when made to include the whole of human life. To try to subject human thought to physiological laws is suicidal, it is to deny the possibility of the science of physiology itself, or any other science. Darwin hesitated to accept the conclusions of a mind derived from a monkey because the stream could not rise higher than the fountain, but he mistook altogether stream and fountain. For how did he, Darwin, know the facts of evolution? How trust his mind when it drew the sweeping conclusion that it was derived from a monkey? He supposed that he was talking about the stream of evolution, of animal life; but he was not; he was talking about the stream of science, of *knowledge* of evolution, and the fountain of that stream was the power of Darwin's mind to weigh evidence; the value of his science can never rise higher than that particular fountain. Take in earnest his denial of the conviction of the human mind and you find that he has denied the trustworthiness of his doctrine of evolution. But if evolution is not true, if man did not evolve from a monkey, then what becomes of his problem? Here is a possibility absolutely unstable; no stream can ever have more value than is credited to the power of the mind to weigh evidence, no objection would ever have more force. The one indisputable fact postulated and reaffirmed by every school of thought, consciously or unconsciously, must be the primacy of human thinking over all material and mechanical law. Then we ask, why attempt to study the mind in terms of physical and mechanical law? The best that would be claimed for the brain would be that it was an indispensable condition; that without it the mind was not able to work, but that with it the mind works as an independent variable.

We should then in our physiological psychology be contributing enormously to the knowledge of the most favorable conditions of the mind to accomplish its mission; we should learn how to take care to keep these conditions from being disturbed, and learn many practical truths that will be worth everything to a young man, for it would help him make his physical system "his ally instead of his enemy." But that is all. We shall not have entered the great temple of human life, we shall not have come into the august presence of mental processes themselves.

W. T. Harris says that Saul, the son of Kish, went out to find asses, and he found not them, but a kingdom. He then goes on to say that very many other people have gone out to find a kingdom but have found only asses; and he concludes that physiological psychology has shared the latter fate. Asses are very useful beasts of burden and not to be despised. In a Santiago campaign they are indispensable, but they are not all, and this judgment is in no way a detraction from physiological psychology, except in so far as it becomes dogmatic and denies the existence of any other.

At this stage of our work the students perceive that we have been perfectly fair to all that can be offered for brain functions, and yet have demonstrated the right to study the mind in terms of itself. Either at this stage or at a later time upon the review would come the study of Kant and the history of philosophical speculations as far as Lotze.

The question at issue is, What must be our conception which would make it possible for the mind, by weighing evidence, to discover the truth that should hold for experience beyond the present and past? This involves a discussion of the question of theism, of the universe as dependent upon Deity, and of the personality of God. We take up such writers as Paulsen and his *Introduction to Philosophy*, Royce's *Religious Aspects of Philosophy*, John Fiske's *Idea of God*, with lectures on Lotze, and various other references. From the point of view of theism we examine the foundations of physical science, of art, of religion, and of ethics.

The great problem in the student's mind at this stage is the fact of evil. How can there be such a thing as sin in God's universe. The problem becomes so overwhelming that it cannot be avoided. There is absolutely no way to treat this subject without taking up the whole question of what is meant by government; for sin cannot be merely a physical imperfection, it must be a moral one; therefore, God's relationship to sin cannot be that of a Creator, but that of a governor, and this introduces us to the whole problem of the State. Without this question theism becomes a flat contradiction, and the students will be either pessimists or fatalists.

AUTOMATISM
I. ITS POSTULATES

1. Automatism postulates that thought is not a cause producing either (a) mental effects or (b) physical results. To illustrate:

(a) The choice of a profession is supposed to fix a man's attention on a particular line of work, to shape his subsequent plans, to fill his mind with anxiety, and create an interest in investigations that will contribute to his success. All this is mythological, worthy of an age when it was supposed that the position of the stars in the skies determined riots and revolutions, political earthquakes, as well as the private career, the failure or fortune of mortals.

In the struggle against temptation it has been supposed that effort at attention could be added to weak ideals until they were strong enough to down evil thoughts, and thus make them more than a match for the strongest propensity. But this is just as absurd as to suppose that in archery when the arrow has left the bow and is being deflected from its course by the wind, the archer can bring it back into line by the writhing and twisting of his own body in the opposite direction, as we often see him attempt to do.

When we weigh evidence, as we suppose, the common view is that a candid man's premises actually determine his conclusions, and that in the syllogism "therefore" marks a real causal relationship in the mental world which is as real as cause and effect in the physical nature. This is a very widespread conviction, e.g., it is considered a severe criticism on a speaker to affirm that there is no connection in his discourse, that on analysis it becomes a mere jumble of sentences. Now if you will carefully consider the automatism theory you will see how absurd is this view. Thought is merely an epiphenomenon related to brain

302

action something as the shadow is to the moving train. One thought follows another, not because of the evidence which demands it, but because two successive brain discharges happen to cast their shadows thus. Take the moving pictures that are thrown on the screen by the vitascope. One man is seen to strike another and to knock him down; his victim's fall seems to be caused by the blow, but if you go to the instrument you will find that each event is the shadow of a separate picture. By a slight change in mechanism the blow delivered by the ruffian would be followed by the Madonna and her child and would have every appearance of producing that effect. There is absolutely no causal relation between the events that appear on the screen. Appearances are wholly an illusion. The same must be true of the sequence of our thoughts in the mental world; each one of them is simply the molecular action of the brain seen from the inside. Consciousness is a continuous panorama, but each part is distinct from every other, the only causal connection being the material sequence in the brain. Psychology is thus only physics wrong side out.

(b) Neither can thought nor will cause or control brain action. To illustrate: A plan in no way guides a man's conduct. Malice aforethought had nothing whatever to do with the murder the criminal committed. That was a physical deed, therefore determined only by physical agencies. The purpose to do it had no more influence on the act than the intention of astronomers to observe a total eclipse of the sun last summer actually scattered the clouds and made the day suitable for such observations. The world would raise a loud laugh over a person who actually took seriously the oft-repeated remark about the power of the weather clerk. Will not the time come when the public will laugh as loudly over the twelve jurymen, poor deluded persons, who suppose that malice aforethought, mere ideas and intentions, in any way could have found expression through the deed of the prisoner at the bar? Will not future ages look upon our court-houses and legislative halls, which by that time will be unused and

303

falling to ruins, as we now regard what is left of the old Greek temples—monuments each one of them of a wonderful superstition, slaughter-houses withal, since many a victim owed his death to their existence?

2. The automatism theory is obliged to make thought an original attribute of the atom. We must now add to the spatial, temporal, and dynamic attributes of matter one more property, viz., a hidden psychical endowment. This consciousness must be indescribably simple, but it is really mind, and the raw material out of which all the wealth of human life is composed. If we allowed consciousness to influence physical action in the brain, we should have to grant this power all the way to the simplest inorganic elements. Then chemical composition would be determined in part by the likes and dislikes of ultimate material particles. But this would be repeating on a grander scale the superstitions of our ancestors who supposed that every natural object had its spirit or genius that acted through it. It is claimed that we have no choice, either be fetich worshippers and done with it, either out-heathen the heathen in our devotion to this creed, or everywhere and always deny that thought has the slightest influence upon the physical world. Just the same results would follow if we allowed brain action to create thought. Consciousness must, therefore, be an original property of the atom. The mental states and the physical changes may be parallel, but as Clifford says, each series goes along by itself; the one can have no effect on the other.

Having stated the relations between thought and brain action which are required by the automaton theory, let us now state the evidence for and against the theory itself.

II. ARGUMENTS FOR THE THEORY

1. Evolution points out the continuity between animal and human life. It makes it extremely probable that one law governs the whole. Nowhere can you say, here the animal ends and the

304

divine begins. But the simplest forms of animal life are equally difficult to distinguish from the vegetable world. Some species seem to be vegetable during a part of their existence and animal at a later period. The protoplasm of the cell of the animal is essentially like that of the vegetable, and surely the latter must have in it potentially all that is in the animal, because from this as food he derives his support and strength. Where can we stop? Must we not say with Tyndall:

> We break a magnet and find two poles in each of its fragments. We continue the process of breaking; but, however small the parts, each carries with it, though enfeebled, the polarity of the whole. And when we can break no longer, we prolong the individual vision to the polar molecules. Are we not urged to do something similar in the case of life? . . . By an intellectual necessity I cross the boundary of the experimental evidence, and discern in that Matter which we, in our ignorance of its latent powers, and notwithstanding our professed reverence for its Creator, have hitherto covered with opprobrium, the promise and potency of all terrestrial life.

2. Inconceivability, even if it is a matter of brain paths, is relied upon by the advocates of the automaton theory to prove their case. They affirm that it is entirely unintelligible to speak of the conversion of physical energy into consciousness. Consciousness is wholly outside the physical universe. Such conversion would mean annihilation of physical energy to every one except the being whose conscious powers were increased thereby. It would mean more than that. It would be quite as ridiculous as converting space into time. Take the following quotation from Tyndall:

> But the passage from the physics of the brain to the corresponding facts of consciousness is unthinkable. Granted that a definite thought, and a definite molecular action in the brain, occur simultaneously, we do not possess the intellectual organ, nor apparently any rudiment of the

organ, which would enable us to pass, by a process of reasoning, from the one to the other. They appear together, but we do not know why. Were our minds and senses so expanded, strengthened, and illuminated, as to enable us to see and feel the very molecules of the brain, were we capable of following all their motions, all their groupings, all their electric discharges, if such there be; and were we intimately acquainted with the corresponding states of thought and feeling, we should be as far as ever from the solution of the problem, 'How are these physical processes connected with the facts of consciousness?' The chasm between the two classes of phenomena would still remain intellectually impassable. Let the consciousness of *love*, for example be associated with a right-handed spiral motion of the molecules of the brain, and the consciousness of *hate* with a left-handed spiral motion. We should then know, when we love, that the motion is in one direction, and, when we hate, that the motion is in the other; but the 'Why?' would remain as unanswerable as before.

Clifford, quoted by James, says:

It will be found excellent practice in the mental operations required by this doctrine to imagine a train, the fore part of which is an engine and three carriages linked with iron couplings, and the hind part three other carriages linked with iron couplings; the bond between the two parts being made up out of the sentiments of amity subsisting between the stoker and the guard.

3. Considerable is made of another argument. If thought is not exactly parallel to brain action, if, when physical conduct is of a given type, thought can be now this and now that under exactly the same physical conditions, how could we ever guess the mind of our nearest friend? We can know only physical action. All the rest is inference, but can we infer that which is wholly a matter of chance? If at one time when our friend laughs he is joyous; if at another time when there is the same merry

ring to his laughter he is on the verge of despair; if, again, when we can detect no difference in the physical manifestations he is angry or insane or absolutely indifferent, should we ever know how to take him? Could literature express the mind of the author, or words have any meaning?

4. If thought is exactly parallel to brain action, then we have "X rays" by which to examine the brain more delicately than any yet devised. Thought is the shadow of brain action. A physician then, by conversing with his patient can determine very accurately, through inference, the condition of the brain, e.g., when it is overworking and needs rest, when it is dangerously near to brain disease and must stop altogether or it will be too late. He can also determine what kind of associations are most economical for a given make-up; and in what particular profession there may be hope of greatest achievement.

5. Conscience and moral character seem often to be wholly functions of the brain. A drug will completely change for the time being one's whole system of moral values; a good night's rest will transform a coward into a hero. A tumor in a certain part of the brain involves loss of moral honor, and absolute indifference to shame and disgrace; and that, too, in a man who has been the very soul of manliness. Now if a diseased brain is the devil himself, why may not the sound brain be all there is to the saint? This is a point that comes home with tremendous force to the physician when he sees his patient who has been a conspicuous public character, always identified with the right, slowly change into an idiot with hardly a trace of moral sense about him.

6. Professor Tyndall asks: If we consider the body as the instrument of the soul, like the telegraph instrument used by the operator, why should a single blow on the head make the mind unconscious? When the operator's lines are down, he cannot communicate with the outside world, to be sure; but after the wires are restored, he can tell you all about the way he employed his time during his enforced leisure. He was conscious, his char-

acter did not change, he simply could not talk with the outsiders, an inconvenience, indeed, but not a loss of existence. But the mind becomes absolutely unconscious when the brain is sufficiently injured. In the act of giving a command in full, officers have been hit by a shell which fractured the skull. Hours passed before the surgeon could attend to them. In the meantime they were totally unconscious., When the operation was performed and the pressure of the bone lifted from the brain, consciousness returned like an electric light when you connect the circuit. The interesting fact is that they picked up their threads just where they dropped them; they had not the slightest consciousness of intervening time. The first word they uttered was the one that would have come next in the command they were giving when wounded. If the mind were different from the brain, what was it about all this time and why should it act so like a phonograph which after being stopped for a period begins when started at exactly the same place where it stopped? Does not all this seem to be the work of a machine instead of a person? Does not the analogy of operator and instrument absolutely break down? When death comes, what may we reasonably anticipate? Do you wonder that such a writer as Haeckel feels positively sure that immortality is wholly an illusion and that this life is the beginning and end of it all? Huxley in his letter to Morley says:

It is a curious thing that I find my dislike to the thought of extinction increasing as I get older and nearer the goal. It flashes across me at all sorts of times with a sort of horror that in 1900 I shall probably know no more of what is going on than I did in 1800. I had sooner be in hell a good deal—at any rate in one of the upper circles, where the climate and company are not too trying.

7. But the main argument of the automaton theory is conservation of energy. This means that whenever energy disappears in the physical world an exact equivalent reappears in some other form of physical energy, actual or potential. In running a steam engine a certain amount of heat is used up, but it has not

308

been annihilated; it is simply transformed into motion or electricity, and the equivalence is so exact that we can determine it with mathematical precision. It is like the bank that will convert the nickels and dimes of the trolley company into bills of larger and smaller denominations without charging any commission.

Now if the will moves the arm, it causes the physical part of our being to do something that it would not have done if we had not willed. Therefore a certain amount of energy must be created by the will, since the brain is a physical agent and its action can be changed only by physical energy. To affirm, as some have done, that the will can control the arm without creating physical energy is to affirm that the brain under exactly the same physical conditions does not always act in exactly the same way, which would mean that an event had taken place without a cause. Whenever in the physical world a change in action takes place, that must be a change in the resultant of physical forces at that point, either by the addition or subtraction of physical energy. If the will, therefore, causes my arm to move, it must either create or annihilate a certain amount of physical energy, or you introduce the doctrine that events happen by chance.

But those who hold the automaton theory sometimes lapse into phraseology that implies that a sensation or state of consciousness can be created by brain actions. Huxley says, "If a man does not believe this doctrine, let him stick a pin into himself and see whether it is true or not." Clearly the automaton theory will allow no such explanation of our experience. If sensation is caused by brain action, a certain amount of physical energy must disappear from the physical world and reappear in the mental. Huxley uses the illustration of the steam whistle to explain the relation of thought to brain action. "The sound is produced by the locomotive, but does not in turn control the movements of the engine." We reply, that whatever steam is employed for blowing the whistle is taken away from the pistons, and thus diminishes the speed of the train on an up grade. In the early days of steam power there was on the Mississippi river

309

a boat with a very small boiler and a very large whistle. Whenever they blew the whistle the engine stopped. Evidently Huxley's position is wholly illogical. Either the theory of the conservation of energy holds—in which case a state of consciousness is neither produced by brain action nor can it cause brain action —or we are obliged to take the opposite view clear through. To concede that sensations are produced by sticking a pin into yourself is to affirm that conservation of energy is broken, and that, therefore, thought determines some brain action.

III. ARGUMENTS AGAINST THE AUTOMATON THEORY

1. Consciousness is, according to Clifford, wholly subjective, known only to itself directly. It is exclusive, a little universe by itself, and can never be an object to any other. Others may infer its existence, but they have absolutely no means of perceiving any other consciousness than their own. The physical world is objective, inclusive, common to all, and the same to all. This is a matter of infinite importance in discussing the automaton theory. And the importance is not emphasized merely by the antagonists of this position: It is the cornerstone of all those who hold that doctrine. It is their main reason for holding that physical energy cannot be converted into thought. Such a statement, they say, would be equivalent to believing in the annihilation of physical energy to every one except the man whose consciousness was enriched thereby.

2. The automaton theory necessitates the mind-stuff theory— the two must stand or fall together. The mind-stuff theory affirms that consciousness is made up of units infinitely simple. Thus fourteen vibrations a second may perhaps be distinguished as fourteen separate vibrations, but if we increase the number they fuse, and we perceive only a tone. With some ears forty thousand vibrations a second fuse to form a musical note that seems perfectly simple. Must we not conclude that all consciousness is very complex? Can we believe that any conscious state known to man

310

is simple? If thought is simply the shadow of brain action, and if the brain is composed of atoms each of which has its own psychical attribute, must not every thought that we have be composed of as many psychical units as there are atoms directly concerned in that particular part of brain action of which this thought is the shadow? Is not this view necessitated by the doctrine that the ultimate unit of all material bodies is the atom?

No other conclusion could for a moment be considered, for atoms never fuse, not even in the brain. Each retains its own identity and individuality in all chemical compositions. Brain is a name for a certain number of these atoms, arranged in certain ways, just as "Senior class" is a name for a certain number of students related to each other and acting in harmony with each other. Take away all the atoms from the brain, and there is no brain left. There must, therefore, be just as many units in consciousness as there are atoms concerned in the particular brain activity with which the consciousness has to do.

James shows that there can be no such thing as fusion, and therefore the mind-stuff theory is out and out a contradiction. From which it follows the automaton theory is inconceivable.

Proof.

The atom cannot give up its own conscious attribute to form a common stock of consciousness or resultant for two reasons. (a) If it did, the atom would then change and be without the attribute it once possessed. Nature could not then be uniform. Uniformity requires a changeless atom. (b) Consciousness is by its very nature exclusive, exists directly only to itself. Others may infer it; they can never have it. Others may have a like consciousness, but it will never be that identical consciousness. The consciousness of one atom can never fuse with the consciousness of any other atom, but will ever be a distinct and separate existence. Fusion is in every instance not a reality but an effect on some third party. Oxygen and hydrogen do not really fuse to

311

form water; they are simply so arranged as to seem to the eye to fuse. The vibrations of music in a tone do not really fuse and lose their identity; if so, the tone would not be made up of separate vibrations; they simply seem to the ear to fuse. The question has been asked, May not attributes fuse even if atoms remain distinct? The case cited is that of several men separated by some distance yet standing so that their shadows fuse. We reply: Are shadows attributes? If so, a man may lose an attribute through no change whatever on his part, but simply through extinction of a light, be it ever so distant. The truth is, the illustration is misleading. Opacity is the attribute and shadow is its effect on something else. The opacities of different persons never fuse, but they may cooperate to produce a single effect. This is James' doctrine, that nowhere "can entities (call them as you like, material particles, forces, or mental elements) sum themselves together." Each retains its identity. "The sum exists only for the bystander" or "in the shape of some other effect on an entity external" to the one in question.

It follows, therefore, if the states of consciousness of the several atoms are to constitute a complex consciousness, they must still retain their individuality and identity, but seem to fuse to some third party, to some agent like the soul, who might be there as a spectator—just as the soldiers in a regiment seem to fuse together into a mass or wave to some looker-on who sees the battle from a distance. But according to the automaton theory there is no soul. To get an exact illustration, we should have the vibrations which make up a musical note remain absolutely distinct and yet each vibration be a spectator or hearer to perceive all the other vibrations and make them seem to fuse. Could you ever get a tune in this way? How is some one vibration, which exists at this second, to perceive vibrations that passed out of existence some time before, and other vibrations that are to come into existence some time hence? But the illustration of a tune is a very poor one. That belongs to the physical world, where objects are objective and the same to all. We should have

312

to ask: How can the consciousness of a particular atom be wholly subjective and exclusive, known only to itself, and at the same time not be subjective and exclusive, but be known to the consciousness of every other atom and in its own turn perceive their psychical states and make them seem to fuse together? Dr. Ward says, "Paradox is too mild a word for it. Even contradictions will hardly suffice." You remember the illustration given by the author of the paper presented to the class on this subject. Suppose three men to have absolutely no communication, that is, to be deaf, dumb, and blind. Let one man eat sugar; he has the consciousness of sweetness. Let another man drink water; his thirst is slated. Let the third man suck a lemon; his sensation is that of a particularly acid taste. Please tell us how under these circumstances there is to arise in this little company of strangers the taste of lemonade.

The automaton theory logically leads us to the conclusion that the most complex brain cannot be possessed of a consciousness one whit richer than that of the individual atoms that compose it. If America is composed of seventy million people, each of whom is possessed of a small sum of money in his pocket, and if each is so constituted that it is absolutely impossible for him ever to part with this money, i.e., if not a single one of the seventy million can ever pay a cent of taxes, please tell us how much the treasurer of the United States has in his possession. Could he have a penny more than was his by original endowment? Now a theory which makes the consciousness of the complex brain as primitive as that of the original atom contradicts the one fact that we know more about than any other. No one can deny that he is immediately conscious of his own states of consciousness. He knows what they are, he knows their wealth as he knows nothing else in the universe. Whatever else he gives up, he cannot give up this knowledge. All other knowledge is gained by inference from this.

3. Is memory possible on this basis? Can any physical object remember? The clock strikes twelve this noon; it did so yester-

day, it did so last year. Could this noon stroke be called a recollection of former ones, or is it an entirely new event? A music box repeats tonight the tune it played at Christmas when it was first received. Is this a recollection of Christmas or simply a new performance? A phonograph is very patient and will say the same thing over and over, but does it remember that it has said it before? Here is the peculiarity of memory. It is a present picture. We always remember in the present. We say we recall the past. This is only rhetoric. We do not actually turn back the wheels of time and live over again the original event, otherwise old people who forget all but the scenes of their childhood could actually recall their youth. No. The past has gone forever, and when we remember we simply make a present picture in consciousness. It may or may not be like some former state of consciousness. But however close the remembrance, it can never be identically the same. It is a new state like the new stroke of the clock, or the repetition of the tune. But memory is more than this. It is a present state that claims to know that it is a copy of some previous experience. How can it without comparing itself with that experience? But that can never be done, since the experience is forever passed. If there were any causal relationship between the different states of consciousness, a possibility for verifying the present would be revealed. But there is no causal relationship whatever. If one is as distinct from another as are the several notes in the tune, how can the present mental picture vouch for the past? Is it not simply a new experience without reference to anything gone before? God may know the resemblance, but can the state itself know it? If you affirm that this is possible, then why limit memory to the events in a simple person's life? Why not be able to make present pictures that can vouch for the accuracy of their resemblance to states of consciousness experienced by Caesar or Cicero, Paul or Nero; or for that matter why limit the possibility to this planet; why not be omniscient and done with it? If a present mental picture can know its resemblance to something in no way related to it by

314

cause and effect, what difference does it make how remote that "something" may be?

4. Could there be any personal identity upon this basis? By this phrase we mean not the actual identity of an individual, but his knowledge that he is the same now as at former times. In dreams and in insanity there is loss of identity. If our life is made up of a series of states of consciousness not causally connected but really as disconnected as the different views in a biograph, of a series which could seem to be fused only to a third party like God, could any one of these states have any knowledge of the whole series? Could any one note in a tune know the whole tune?

5. Could there be on the automaton theory any weighing of evidence? If the reason why one thought follows another is the same as that which explains why one note in the music box follows another, namely, on account of certain mechanical constructions of the instrument, then the question whether the right thought or the wrong thought follows from the premises is not a matter of evidence, but solely an accident due to the lines of least resistance in the brain. These lines have been made extremely complex agencies and not by an intelligent maker. We have inherited the superstitious tendencies of our fathers. We have given way to the passions and follies of childhood when the brain was extremely plastic, and permanent habits have been thus formed. We have been subject to the influences of an environment in no way concerned with the higher moral life. Our lines of least resistance are thus peculiar to each one. No two persons can be just alike. How, then, could the jury of twelve men, perhaps of different nationalities, be expected by thinking to get the same verdict? If men ever do have the same habits of thought, is it because they are wholly passive while the environment plows out the paths in each as a glacier cuts parallel grooves in the rocks? Or is it because by weighing evidence each gets the truth and then forces himself to follow it by acting along the lines of greatest resistance.

If you say that a machine may be the ideal of accuracy, I reply, (a) the more complex and delicate the machine, the more likely it is to get out of order and become inaccurate. The Hipp chronoscope is made with great care and is intended to measure time down to one thousandth part of a second. It is affected by slight changes in temperature and wear. When we use it in the laboratory for accurate work it has to be tested every hour and corrections made for its errors. It is said that at Baden-Baden a shrewd mechanic watched the roulette table for weeks, since he knew that no machine could run accurately for any length of time. It would begin to wear in one place more than another. Once begun, the error would increase, until it would become visible. So he watched until he succeeded in discovering the defect which gave a special advantage to a certain color. He then began to bet on that color and broke the bank.

(b) My second answer is, Could any machine recognize its own error and make allowance therefor? Man can do it for the machine, but can the machine do it for itself? The answer is No; the machine does not care. It would as soon go wrong as right. It follows only one law, namely, the law of least resistance. You may have the compensating pendulum, but accuracy is not the motive of the pendulum. Its action depends wholly upon the way it is set by the clock-maker. It would expand and contract just as easily when such a change would make an error as when it corrects one. It is said that in the Bank of England there is an arrangement for detecting counterfeit coins and those short in weight. Each coin must drop through a particular slot; if it is too large it will not go through. Those that go through fall into the pan of delicate scales. If they are underweight that arm goes up, and they slide out into the jaws of a machine which stamps them as mutilated. They then go to the mint and there are tested to see whether they are genuine or counterfeit, and are worth only their bullion value. If they are the right weight, the arm of the scale tips down, and the coin slides out into deposit boxes. Meantime you can have an automatic arrangement for counting

316

them. This is marvelous, indeed, yet this machine is not intelligence. If dust should accumulate in the opposite arm of the balance the accuracy would be impaired and genuine coins might begin to go up and fall into the mutilated pile. The scales would never care, and if they should become worn the error might be very considerable, but they would never find it out. The scales would never remove their own dust or repair their wear. We have remarkable pieces of mechanism able to do extremely accurate work when made by intelligence and kept in order by skill. But the more delicate these instruments are the more they need supervision. If the brain is to respond to the slightest change of stimulus it must be so unstable that it would be very easy for it to get out of order. The agency which has made the lines of least resistance according to evolution is not intelligence, but the superstitions of savage ancestors, and the passions and appetites of a long line of animal progenitors. Can such an instrument know when its results are right? Is none of its work wrong? Who or what then is to distinguish and say this product is scientific, that is erroneous.

To Weigh Evidence Is To Have One's Conclusions Influenced Only By The Truth.

Take a syllogism. All men are mortal; Socrates was a man; therefore let us have a banquet. If a child was purely mechanical, just following lines of least resistance, this or any other absurdity would go well enough. But the moment he becomes a man and is critical, he insists that the conclusion shall square with the premises, not only in this case, but wherever truth is sought, even though it mean an unusual and disagreeable effort on his part. There is no scholarship that does not involve at times action along the lines of greatest resistance. *Truth is the same the universe through, therefore the same to all men.* Lines of least resistance vary with the individual and his inheritance. If all can possibly get truth, then all can by effort agree. But not without effort, for truth with many must be along the lines of greatest resistance. Such thought as has scientific value cannot be wholly a function of the brain; rather must some brain action be a function of this thought. Wherever this power was introduced in the history of evolution a new agency appeared on earth. Wundt calls it *psychical causality*. It would be as ridiculous to determine the laws of psychical causality by a study of the brain as it would be to get laws for electricity by studying only gravitation or geometry. Each agency must be studied in terms of itself, for some things are peculiar to it, and these peculiar attributes are vital.

This, then, is our claim: Human society must be organized in accordance with human nature or there will be trouble. If the main agency in man is psychical causality, to disregard it entirely or attempt to construct social life on an animal basis would be the supreme mistake of the age. It would be like trying to make birds live under water because their remote ancestors were fishes and could live in no other way. There is something wrong somewhere in our social institutions or there would not be so much friction or failure. Haeckel says, "To our great regret we must endorse the words of Alfred Wallace: 'Compared with our astounding progress in physical science and its practical application, our system of government, of administrative justice, and of national education, and our entire social and moral organization remain in the state of barbarism.'"

6. If you accept the doctrine of evolution, would it be possible to account for the development of consciousness on the automaton theory? James brings out the idea that there is nothing sentimental about evolution. It tends to drop everything that is not an advantage in the struggle for existence. If consciousness never does anything in the line of controlling the organism, why has evolution preserved and developed it? Again, how does it happen that unpleasant things are disagreeable and beneficial things pleasant, unless pleasure and pain are sentinels to warn the organism of approaching danger and point out the way of escape. There is nothing intrinsically objectionable to the conception

318

that pleasure and pain should have no relationship whatever to the physical welfare of our being. As the electric light seems perfectly agreeable to the moth, and intoxication to the drunkard, so pestilential odors of the sewer and filthy surroundings might cause ecstasy of delight to human beings, as these seem to do to vermin, were it not for the fact that evolution quickly weeds out all those who like harmful things. But surely nature would never take that trouble if pleasure and pain did not exercise a real influence on conduct, i.e., violate the law of conservation of energy.

James carries the point farther. The brains of the lower animals are fairly stable in their chemical composition. But such an organ would be of little service to man. He needs to note very exact discriminations. The very delicate appreciation involved in wit and humor, in scientific observation and the higher forms of thought, especially in artistic creations, requires that the genius should have a brain of extremely unstable equilibrium. Would such a brain be safe if it were not controlled by a power not of itself? Does it not need a governor to restrain it and is not intelligence and moral purpose admirably suited for just that task? This is the question at issue. Could nature herself have developed the wild crab-apple into the golden pippin, or brought out the modern race-horse with only grass to feed him on? Must not natural selection be supplemented by intelligent selection to secure the most wonderful products? Must not intelligence to some extent make "brain the function of thought," form the right kind of habits by acting along the lines of greatest resistance, and thus create its own instruments as a mechanic makes his tools? Otherwise could humanity have ever come upon the stage of action? Otherwise would not the beginnings of the human brain have produced a character so unstable as to have led to its own destruction, just as a high-strung horse when he gets away from his master takes fright and often kills himself? The very qualities which make the horse excellent make him also a slave for his own sake as well as for his owner's use. He

319

must have a master or he can't live the complex life and do the right thing which he actually accomplishes. Is it not so with the brain, especially that of the human species? What has been the fate of genius where there has been a lack of moral control?

Again when certain parts of the brain have been injured permanently by accident, temporary derangement is experienced, but in time the work is taken up by other regions, and when these are thoroughly trained much of the mental embarrassment is removed. James asks if this is the working of mere mechanism. "A machine in working order acts fatally in one way. Take out a valve, throw a wheel out of gear, or bend a pivot, and it becomes a different machine, acting just as fatally in another way which we call wrong. But the machine knows nothing of wrong or right; matter has no ideals to pursue. A locomotive will carry its train through an open drawbridge as cheerfully as to any other destruction." "So a brain with a part scooped out is virtually a new machine," and its acts at first are abnormal. Why does it often right itself? Does it not look as though it were not left entirely to itself?

7. There are only two ways of attempting to get science: (a) that of the schoolmen who shut themselves up in cloisters and spun their theories about the universe from their own inner consciousness just as a spider spins his web from his own bowels; (b) the scientific method of induction which demands observation and experiment. But what are these? We observe through the senses, that is, we get mental pictures which are wholly subjective, and from these reason to that which caused or produced them. We do this so often and so frequently that the process becomes wholly unconscious, and we seem to be passive witnesses of what is going on in nature. This is not true, for we learned in James that perception is never a mere sensation, but sensation interpreted by our whole apperception mass. Just here comes in the difficulty. Cause and effect is the principal constituent of that apperception mass. If these sensations were not caused by any object in the physical world, not even by brain

320

action (and this is the view of the automaton theory), then how can we perceive correctly? How can the subjective mental picture ever help us to any knowledge or observation of the external world? All physical facts go along by themselves and all mental facts go along by themselves, and how can a state of consciousness say whether the two series are parallel or just the reverse.

One step farther. Berkeley affirms that there is not the slightest evidence for the existence of any material world. How do we know but that the whole series of physical facts which Clifford speaks of is simply the figment of the imagination, and that Berkeley is right when he affirms that what we call physics is simply a department of psychology? This is his argument: (a) What are the mountains, hills, seas, plains, that you are talking about in physics? You reply, things we see. (b) What do you see, of what are you immediately conscious? The reply is mental pictures and nothing else. We are immediately conscious of states of consciousness, phenomena not noumena; everything else is inference. (c) It is absurd to suppose that there could be a state of consciousness outside consciousness or that the dead material world outside the mind could in any way resemble what is inside the living mind. Hence, he concludes, the physical world we observe is as subjective in our waking moments as in the dream landscape when we sleep. If you want to accept this view you must mean by mountains, hills, seas, and plains not the things you see but the external agents which cause your sensation. This is the common meaning of the scientist. He does not say the grass is green, but the grass looks green, that is, produces that effect in me; not that iron is heavy, but that it feels heavy, i.e., causes that perception in me. Matter is that which produces these phenomena. Very well, says Berkeley, you shall have it so. By your hypothesis (the automaton theory) the physical world and the brain could not possibly produce a sensation, therefore they are not the cause of your perceptions. What, then, is their cause? What is that matter that you infer? With what world are you dealing when you observe? It must belong to the mental series, it must be a function of mind if it is to cause sensation. Does not Berkeley seem to have the best of this argument if you accept Clifford's postulate?

It seems to me that there is no way in which a finite being can reason to that which lies beyond his own mental states except through the causal relation; that is the only bridge over which thought can travel. If there is no causal relation it would be the miracle of miracles for a man by knowledge of the sensation to know something entirely disconnected from it, which occurred not in the mental series, but in the material world—say, for instance, the fact that Darwinian evolution has really taken place and is the explanation of the present form of society. If a man could know one thing thus absolutely disconnected from his data in consciousness, please tell me which one thing it would be in the universe, and why this one thing and not some other. Why could he not just as well be omniscient and know all things as to know this one? No; we should have to give them all up and content ourselves with Berkeley, and make physical science a part of mental science, just as we do logic and grammar.

Again, science involves experiment, and experiment means determining or controlling the conditions under which physical events take place. It is not true that in every instance this postulates that thought or will can determine brain action and thus guide the hands of the experimenter, yet if you will go back to childhood and learn how the infant's perceptions were made objective you will realize that causal efficiency of the mind, whereby he actually controlled his hands and feet, his playthings and other objects in nature, was the only condition under which he came to distinguish those mental pictures that had an objective cause from those originated by himself. No child says, I dreamed. At first every vivid picture is real. Gradually he learns that he has a self, and for some things he alone is responsible. Then comes a period in every child's life when he will be responsible for everything, and generally he does not completely get over this period until he receives a few lessons at the hands of sophomores in his freshman year. Scientific personality is the correlate of accurate scientific experiment. Only as consciousness is a cause and actually changes conditions in nature does it correctly distinguish between subjective and objective, and perceive things as they are. We are just beginning to emphasize this truth in child study. The practical side of this postulate gives proper attention to muscular activity. Formerly this was supposed to be mere physical skill, but it is now realized to be the prime condition of general education and development. If deprived of all muscular control a child would grow up an idiot.

To sum up:—Science is wholly the work of mind. Atoms never write chemistries, the stars know nothing of astronomy, physical forces are entirely ignorant of the laws in accordance with which they act, science does not get itself, nature never studies herself. All science is the work of mind. If the automaton theory is true, mind can never observe nature or experiment upon it. Mind is shut up like the schoolman, in its own little cloister so narrow that the scholastic monastery was an infinite expanse in comparison. In this little cloister, if it is not omniscient it can only study a physical world that is as subjective in its waking moments as is the dream world when it is asleep, and Berkeley's idealism must be accepted as the ultimate philosophy. That Tyndall actually feels the difficulty may be inferred from the following quotation:

> Do states of consciousness enter as links into the chain of antecedence and sequence, which give rise to bodily actions, and to other states of consciousness; or are they merely by-products, which are not essential to the physical processes going on in the brain? Speaking for myself, it is certain that I have no power of imagining states of consciousness, interposed between the molecules of the brain, and influencing the transference of motion among the molecules. The thought 'eludes all mental presentation'; and hence the logic seems of iron strength which claims for

the brain an automatic action, uninfluenced by states of consciousness. But it is, I believe, admitted by those who hold the automaton theory, that states of consciousness are produced by the marshaling of the molecules of the brain; and this production of consciousness by molecular motion is to me quite as unthinkable as the production of molecular motion by consciousness. If, therefore, unthinkability be the proper test, I must equally reject both classes of phenomena. I, however, reject neither, and thus stand in the presence of two incomprehensibles, instead of one incomprehensible. While accepting fearlessly the facts of materialism dwelt upon in these pages, I bow my head in the dust before that mystery of mind which has hitherto defied its own penetrative power, and which may ultimately resolve itself into a demonstrable impossibility of self-penetration.

HUME ON THE LIMITS OF KNOWLEDGE

Problem. To determine the limits of knowledge, i.e., not those we have already reached, for this would be a mere matter of inventory, but the limits beyond which no amount of effort will enable us to pass.

Note. In law all questions so serious as to have to do with the life or liberty of a citizen must first be passed upon by a grand jury, who determine whether the evidence is sufficient to warrant a trial. This is one of the safeguards of our republic; it prevents, on the one hand, waste of time and money on the part of the court, and, on the other, the hardship of individuals being forced to carry on an unnecessary suit. It is evident that philosophy renders a similar service. It prevents the individual from wasting time and strength on problems that are insoluble; at the same time it secures the public from being perpetually harassed by calls to investigate "—isms" for which there cannot be sufficient evidence. If we are not "blown about by every wind of doctrine," it is because of the protection furnished by this grand jury of the intellect.

Postulate. All our *knowledge* is from experience, [more than this, the mind is incapable even of conceiving of any *fiction* that is not also derived from experience. Hence the formula should be: "All our ideas, true or false, are derived from impressions."]

Proposition 1. Knowledge is either (a) our individual experience itself, or (b) that which is derived from this experience.

Proposition 2. The limitations of personal experience are clear enough. New instruments may be invented whereby sight and hearing shall be rendered more acute and comprehensive than at present, but no devices will ever enable the senses to get beyond the bounds of the material world.

Proposition 3. The limits of knowledge derived from experience are not so apparent. A majority of writers prior to Hume held that from the things that are seen we can *infer* the great truths of the "unseen," the spiritual world. Let us deal with this question with greatest caution. We will make an exhaustive classification of this knowledge and ascertain the limits of each kind.

Proposition 4. Knowledge derived from our experience can all be included in two divisions, (a) that given in memory, (b) that outside our individual senses and memory.

Proposition 5. The limitations of memory clearly are those of our senses. It is a mere record of what we have experienced.

Proposition 6. The great question is concerning knowledge outside our senses and memory. We can determine its limits only by asking *how* it is obtained.

Note. At first sight it seems as if a bird were hindered by the air, and that, could it get above the atmosphere, it might fly any distance without fatigue. But the moment we ascertain *how* it is able to leave the solid ground and fly at all, we know the limits beyond which wings can never carry it.

Proposition 7. There seem at first sight to be two methods of obtaining knowledge not given in sense and memory, viz., (a) by *a priori* reasoning, that is, by demonstration; (b) by empirical reasoning, or reasoning on matters of fact. This is often known as *moral*, not in the ethical sense but as giving *"moral"* as opposed to *"mathematical"* certainty.

Note. The first (a) is a very inviting process, for it seems to have no limits. So pleased with it were the schoolmen of the Middle Ages (and also the majority of modern theologians) that they discarded the other altogether. Shutting themselves in their cloisters, they spun systems of theology and even of physics merely from their own brains as a spider spins a web from his own bowels. But Hume finds that this *a priori* demonstration has to do only with the "relationship of ideas," and it is *analytic*. It gives no new facts. Therefore the schoolmen made no real discoveries in this way. As some one has said, they thought they were marching, while in reality they were only marking time. To recur to our former illustration: To attempt to attain new knowledge through "relationship of ideas" would be like a bird's attempting to fly above the atmosphere. We therefore turn to the second method. (b) We surely do attain some knowledge beyond our own senses and memory. Now how do we do it? The "how" will determine the "what," and once knowing the "limits" we shall turn aside from all subjects, no matter how important and inviting, that lie beyond.

Answer. We can attain knowledge of *matters of fact* beyond sense and memory only by *cause and effect*. That is, we must start with some fact in sense or memory and by the causal relation determine the fact outside.

Illustration. The operator in a switch tower knows that the switch miles away has been moved, but how? We answer only as some change takes place within the tower, between which and the change without he knows there is a causal relation, viz., an electric current; sever this connection and his knowledge cannot go beyond the tower.

Note. This raises the question, "How do we know cause and effect?"

326

There are limits to this relation, otherwise it carries us too far. Beginning with an object in our hand we should infer its cause or maker; then the same reasoning would inform us of this maker's cause, and so on till we come to the Creator, who also would need a cause to account for his existence. Cause and effect proves too much unless we can ascertain its true limits. How then do we know cause and effect?

Answer. We gain cause and effect, (a) never *a priori*, (b) but always by experience.

Note. Every one admits that in chemistry this is true. Every laboratory is a monument to this conviction. But the theological writers think that in the sphere of natural theology, where we can have no experience to guide us, it is legitimate to reason from effect to cause *a priori*. So they establish the argument from design to prove the existence of an intelligent First Cause. Go into the woods and find a watch, say they, and you are justified in affirming a maker whom you have never seen. And if the watch is accurately made and keeps perfect time, you are also justified in asserting the intelligence and skill of its author. How much more, then, may we be certain of the wisdom and power of the Creator!

But if cause and effect is a valid basis for reasoning *only when derived from experience*, the argument from design falls to pieces. It is fair to reason from the watch to its maker because *experience* has taught us how machinery is made; but what experience has ever revealed to us the creation of matter? Who, then, can tell us how it was produced and what cause was needed therefor? Must we not here "bow our heads in the dust" and "refuse to speculate concerning this great mystery?" Surely this is the only honest course if cause and effect cannot be used *a priori*. So important is this question that Hume stops to give proof of this position.

Proof 1. Cause and effect can never be gained *a priori*, since the *cause is entirely different from the effect;* therefore examine either one as carefully as you please and you will never discover it in the other, *simply because it is not there*. Medicine is the cause, the health of the patient is the effect. Can one who knows nothing experimentally of drugs or diseases tell in advance by looking at the medicine what its effect will be? Why not? Can a person then discover God by studying matter? Are not the two entirely distinct?

Proof 2. Supposing by accident we perceive the true effect of a given cause, can we be sure that it is the effect rather than an event occurring by mere coincidence? We by all our examination can never discover the force or power that binds the effect to its cause, and makes just this and no other of the millions conceivable necessary. Can we then be sure that at any future time this cause will be followed by a like event?

Note. If cause and effect comes only through experience, it becomes important to ask "How?" Our individual experience is historic; how is it ever able to teach us anything more than past history?

Answer. Individual experience can become scientific experience, which alone is the basis for reasoning from cause and effect, only on the ground that we know "nature to be uniform under the same conditions"; if this be true, then from a single instance where the conditions are accurately determined we can learn all events, past, present, and future, happening under similar circumstances.

Note. This brings us to our ultimate inquiry. All questions as to "how" we gain knowledge outside senses and memory become translated into the question, "How do we know nature to be uniform?" All the knowledge of matters of fact—(other than our own history)—can never have more validity than this one cognition. Hume answers the question first negatively, then positively.

A. Negatively

Knowledge of the uniformity of nature does not come through any form of reasoning.

328

Proof. He divides all kinds of reasoning into two classes, (a) demonstrative, (b) moral (empirical), and shows that it cannot come from either.

(a) It cannot come from demonstration, since this can be used only when the opposite of a proposition involves a contradiction. But no contradiction is involved in the opposite of the doctrine that nature is uniform. Indeed, the fact that the doctrine of miracles has been maintained proves that the supporters of this doctrine could find no contradiction in denying the uniformity of nature.

(b) It cannot come from moral reasoning, since we can never reason in that way at all till we know the uniformity of nature. That is, science can never by experiment prove uniformity, for there can be no scientific experiment, nothing but history, till we know that nature is uniform.

Take Tyndall's prayer gauge. He would scientifically prove that God answers (i.e., does now and will in the future) prayer. Now answer to prayer is a miracle. Suppose his experiment successful twenty times, that twenty miracles are performed, does that give us science or history? And have we not history already, e.g., the Old and New Testaments? Why then do we want more? "If they hear not Moses and the prophets, neither will they be (scientifically) persuaded through one rose from the dead."

(c) We may add that knowledge of uniformity does not come from reasoning, for, if so, children and animals could not attain it; yet surely they act on that basis.

B. Positively

If uniformity of nature is not given in our own historic senses and memory, nor on the other hand does it come from any form of reasoning, then surely we do not "*know*" it at all: we simply have a "*conviction*" thereof, and we only need to explain how we come by this. In the sections we have taken in Hume he makes three points: 1. This conviction can come from custom. 2.

It cannot be derived from any other source. 3. Knowing "how" we derive the conviction, we can easily determine its value, i.e., can give a true definition of the causal relation.

1. *The conviction of the causal relation can come from custom.*

(1) Save in questions concerning relationship of ideas, the difference between fact and fiction is not in intellect but in the susceptibility.

(2) It is a general law of mind that feelings can be transferred from objects that excite them to those with which they have no legitimate connection, provided there be no resistance.

Illustrations. (a) *Anger* is often manifested toward those who have done nothing to offend us. In Eastern countries it is not safe for even the most faithful friends of a tyrant to inform him of bad news. His wrath at the misfortune easily transfers itself to those who announce it, and often they are put to death. An animal wounded by a hunter vents his rage on the bushes or whatever may come in his way.

(b) *Fear.* An engineer who has once been through an accident is likely to lose nerve. His hand is always on the air-brake, and at the slightest suspicion he slows up. Some of the most daring men have in this way lost the power of running their trains on time and have been discharged from the service.

If an inhabitant of Siam who had never heard of ice should visit our northern country in the fall, and see a pond, one day nothing but water, the next completely frozen over, could he bring himself to walk thereon? He might see others heavier than himself supported with safety. His reason might show him the folly of hesitation, but could it bring the conviction of safety? Would not the fear of water be transferred to ice? Read Matt. XIV, 22-33.

(c) *Surprise.* If a friend who has always been in perfect health, one with whom we have been very intimate, whom we left only a few hours ago, suddenly dies, can we realize it? Does not the feeling of reality of life transfer itself from the past to the present moment?

(d) *Apparent Inconsistency.* Are those who earnestly profess a new departure in their religion, or business, or politics, and yet continually belie their profession by their deeds—are they hypocrites?

Dr. Storrs recently related an experience that occurred in the days of slavery to this effect: There were many people then who asserted that it was a religious, a Christian duty, to return a fugitive slave to his master. In support of this position they cited the example of Paul, who sent Onesimus back to his owner, and they claimed that as the "powers that be are ordained of God," persons were resisting a divine sovereign when they refused to carry out the laws of the United States requiring this action. Among these people was one, I think a clergyman, who had often been somewhat severe in his criticism of Dr. Storrs for holding the opposite view. But one evening in a severe storm, Dr. Storrs's doorbell rang, and on going to the door, whom should he find but this same gentleman with a fugitive slave under his protection. By mistake the runaway had applied to him for help, and he, instead of carrying out his doctrine, took the stranger over to Dr. Storrs to find out the best method of sending him on the so-called underground railway to Canada. Dr. Storrs gave directions and then begged to relieve his friend of the burden, lest the deed might be one that he could not conscientiously perform, but not even the eloquence of the Brooklyn preacher could persuade the pro-slavery champion to give up his charge. Was this act inconsistency in the sense of hypocrisy or had the feeling of compassion and regard for the rights of man acquired such a momentum by life in the North among a free people that it transferred itself, in spite of creed and party, from white man to the unfortunate black?

Do we not need a similar explanation to account for the conduct of honest, candid, conscientious men who, when a disreputable candidate is nominated by their party, threaten to

331

bolt, but as election draws near find their affection for the party transfer itself to the man who stands upon the platform, and so swing into line and vote the straight ticket?

When a skeptic, who in early life reverenced his mother's faith, comes to a great crisis and in his danger prays, or when a heathen converted to Christianity reverts temporarily to the superstition of his fathers in times of sore temptation, is it really a change of character, or the momentum of his former convictions?

(3) Applying this general law to the particular feeling of conviction, we affirm that belief can be transferred from the ideas to which it belongs to those that are entirely fictitious, if only the resistance thereto can be removed. Hence belief is no indication of the truth of an idea. Only in this way can we account for the numerous false creeds of superstition.

(4) *Explanation.* (a) Feelings cannot act without acquiring momentum. (b) The momentum takes them along the line of least resistance. (c) Custom will form a line of least resistance, and even remove all resistance.

Note. Bend a paper once, and it bends easier there a second time. You may bend it so often that it requires no effort at all to fold it. Our proposition is this: If we have been accustomed to experience a certain sequence of events, then, according to the laws of association, when one is perceived by the senses, the momentum of thought compels us to think of its consequent. Now the mind is so constituted that sense-perception arouses conviction. This is the way the feeling is originated. But its momentum takes it along the line of custom, i.e., least resistance, and fastens it in full force to the idea of the consequent. This may be so intense as to produce subjective sensation to the extent of our seeing the event before it actually happens. The author proves his position by arguments from analogy. The laws of association, viz., *Resemblance, Contiguity, Cause* and *Effect,* are lines of least resistance. It can be shown that under each

332

of them the feeling of reality transfers itself from an object present to the senses to the idea of the unseen object "associated" with it.

2. *The conviction of the uniformity of nature can arise in no other way, for:—*

(1) All our ideas come from impressions.

(2) From no single event can the impression of power be experienced, since the senses never perceive force. Therefore, if it were necessary to derive it directly from sense, it could not be originated at all.

(3) But custom does produce an inseparable association of antecedent and consequent in our minds. We come to be unable to think of one without the other. Thus arises the feeling or conviction of their sequence.

(4) It is a law of the mind that limitations of thought are projected out by "extradition of consciousness' into things, and then the mind forgets that these are wholly subjective, just as the earth projects its motion into the heavens, and then seems to be at rest while they revolve.

(5) Therefore the only experience out of which the idea of necessary connection in nature could arise is the experience of inseparable association of those ideas in our own mind projected outwards.

3. *Knowing how we derive the conviction, we can easily determine its value.*

It is purely subjective—like all the habits formed in response to the environment, it is of great practical use, but no more a part of nature than is the horizon of the actual landscape. Hence we define cause as, "An object followed by another, whose appearance *always conveys the thought* to that other." That is:—

> When we say that one object is connected with another, we mean *only that they have acquired a connection in our thoughts.*

Conclusion. Hume's position is now generally accepted by the scientific school of writers, of whom Spencer, Huxley, Tyndall are representatives. There is, however, a single amendment that they insist upon with great emphasis. It is clearly seen that if each individual had to begin life *de novo,* his earlier experience would not be uniform enough to originate customary conviction so rapidly as he actually attains it. A child does not have to be burned often in order to dread the fire. But if we take into account the fact of heredity, all this difficulty vanishes. *Customs are inherited.* Convictions, therefore, are the result of our own customary experience, plus the experience of ancestors back for thousands of generations. What they claim for the conviction of the uniformity of nature they also assert is true of all our ultimate moral and religious ideas and axioms. None of these do they affirm to be absolutely true, all knowledge (conviction) is relative. They occupy their works with the examination of the several ideas we consider most sacred, attempting to study the customs of primitive man and show just what external circumstances these originated from, tracing ideas to their origin and showing their transformation, as the philologist traces English words to Greek roots. This is where this school of thought undermines the very foundation of ethics and religion, and forces every candid man to follow in Kant's footsteps in examining the premises, when he sees that, admit the premises, the conclusion must follow; therefore we must ask, is it true that all our knowledge comes from (sense) experience?

To me many of the doubts and difficulties that have been discussed seem wonderfully to clear up in studying pamphlet entitled, What is Implied in Communicating With Friends (see pages 208-227, that is Chapter IX of Memorial Volume). Therefore I particularly commend this chapter to careful consideration. Practically I rest strongly upon it.   H. F. Bell.

334

WHAT IS IMPLIED
IN COMMUNICATING WITH FRIENDS?

Either all our knowledge comes from experience—more than that, all our ideas are either true or false, i.e., our wildest superstitions as truly as science itself, come from experience—or the mind is able to obtain knowledge and ideas outside of and beyond experience.

If we assume that the latter is true, we may call these ideas and cognitions *a priori*. *A priori* knowledge must be obtained in a particular way. If this is denied one must fall back on mysticism and say we simply possess it, or that it is a divine gift, a miraculous inheritance, or that the mind in some way creates it out of nothing. If there is a particular way in which we obtain such cognitions it would be proper to inquire just what are the steps that the mind takes. What process does it go through with in order to attain such marvelous results? Until this question is answered, would it be possible to have absolute confidence that these ideas were not mere convictions, possibly necessary and unavoidable, just as the horizon is to physical vision, nevertheless, not actual knowledge of things as they are? On the other hand, if the mind simply possesses these convictions and can give no account of them, would the mere fact that we value them highly preclude an honest searcher for truth from raising the question whether they had any validity? Might not a mind be so constituted as to have just the opposite *a priori* ideas and value them just as much? Do these questions seem absurd or would you encourage a student to push them as far as possible?

If all our knowledge comes from experience, it seems fair to inquire what are its limits. Men wasted much valuable time and many private fortunes trying to discover perpetual motion. All this might have been saved if only they had understood the limits of mechanical possibilities as expressed in "conservation of energy." Might we not save many useless discussions and avoid widespread superstitions by determining the exact limits of knowledge, and then excluding all topics or policies that fall outside these? Is not strict agnosticism concerning everything beyond these limits not merely our duty, but also our own safety?

How can the limits of knowledge be determined? Since the days of Kant this question has been answered by an illustration. A child who sees a dove flying in a storm and buffeted by the wind hastily concludes that if only it could get above the atmosphere it would be unhindered, and might easily leave this earth and soar to heaven. But when the child learns how the dove flies at all, when he understands that only through the resistance of the air is the bird borne up and able to move on the wing, then he discovers the limits of its highest flight. Never again can he think of its getting beyond the atmosphere of earth. So when we accurately determine the processes of attaining knowledge we shall realize that all subjects that cannot be brought within these processes are forever beyond our ken. Here then is our problem: "What are the true and only processes by which knowledge is gained?"

1. Let us answer this question by investigating a particular case, viz., just what must one do in order to communicate with his friends, i.e., know the very thoughts, motives, and purposes of his most intimate companion at a given time. Surely he must begin with what his senses give. This, we have demonstrated, is merely phenomena, not noumena; merely states of consciousness or mental pictures—color, sound, form, touch, every sensation is merely the effect upon the consciousness of some external cause, and may be as unlike that cause as music is unlike the piano that provides it. Press your eye, and the whole room with all the people it contains will visibly be displaced. Is it the real room or the mental image that moves? When a man is intoxicated the whole street is unsteady and the largest buildings reel. Has there been an earthquake or are his objects all as subjective as a dream world? When one approaches Walker Hall it grows in size; when

he moves backward it becomes sensibly smaller. He has the testimony of his own eyes to the fact; can he doubt it? Surely not, but he may ask what the fact really is. Is he dealing with the objective building or with its effects on his consciousness? Is there anything more wonderful here than that these effects vary when he changes, even though the external object remains the same?

Everything we see, hear, touch, taste, or smell is immediately known only as a state of consciousness as truly subjective as any creation of imagination. All are merely ideas. The difference consists simply in this: (a) Generally ideas produced by imagination are faint while those produced by sense are vivid. This is not always true. In dreams, in illusions, and in illness (hallucinations), pictures of imagination are as vivid as those of sense and often quite indistinguishable from them. (b) Works of imagination are generally subject to our control; and we can vary them by effort, while sense pictures are little influenced by our acts. What I see when I open my eyes is not a matter of my choice. Be it ever so unwelcome, I can avoid it only by turning away. I cannot change the picture itself. We conclude that the cause of the former is the self, but the cause of the latter, we infer to be an outside agent. But is that agent outside the true mind, the universal mind, or merely outside the finite consciousness? Note that memory resembles sense pictures more nearly than those of imagination, viz., it has a vividness or reality that belongs to the former, and it refuses to change at our command. Mr. Gough told Amherst students that he would give his right arm if he could blot out certain memories. But are memories therefore the product of some external non-mental agent?

2. This brings us to the next step or process in communicating with our friends. We must use these mental pictures as data and from them infer their cause. This process is similar to the telegraph clerk's work. She receives from her instrument merely clicks. Upon these she fits the code of the office and then spells out a message. But suppose her code is not the one used by the

337

sender of the message? When I was at college my classmate was startled by a telegram ordering him to get a hearse and meet his father at the station at a certain train. Often the task more nearly resembles translating a cipher dispatch; things appear so different from what they really are, and our phenomena are so mixed up as often to exactly reverse the order of events in nature. Thus the earth seems to be flat and immovable, while the sun rises and sets. Huxley says, "I have often stood at close of day with my face towards the west and tried to see the horizon rise and veil the sun, but in spite of all I can do, it simply stays there while the sun slowly drops below it. Yet I know the reverse is the fact, and my faith in modern astronomy is not shaken by the testimony of my senses." Take a simpler case. I am in the fields in autumn; a bird drops dead at my feet, then I hear an explosion and looking up see smoke around the muzzle of a rifle. Did the senses tell the truth here? Could a bird by falling produce a sound so loud, and did this jar the rifle and cause it to discharge, or must I rearrange these events, and if so according to what code? I never see the four sides of Walker Hall simultaneously but in succession. The same is generally true of the inside of different rooms in this building. Can I trust the senses and see that really they do not exist side by side, but instead that here is a panorama in which one follows another? I see in the same field of view two objects in the heavens above; surely these coexist, who can doubt that? But one is a flash of lightning, the other the north star so remote that it takes forty-nine years for its light to reach my eye; therefore if it were annihilated tonight I should continue to see it for forty-nine years to come, if I lived so long. Can I then be sure that because these two objects are affirmed by the senses to coexist they do so objectively, or have I simply evidence through vision that the north star was there about a half century ago tonight? Many people are not afraid of lightning but they are of thunder. Some years ago cattle were killed in Shutesbury during a shower; the reporter of the *Springfield Republican* went

338

to the owner to get the facts. Among other questions was this: "Did you see the flash of lightning that killed them?" To which the farmer replied, "It wa'n't the lightning at all, 'twas a 'tunk of thunder' that did the business." Did he not have the evidence of his senses? therefore why not trust them?

Everywhere we are correcting and rearranging sense phenomena according to our code. What does not square with this we call illusion, such as the bending of the oar blade when it is put under water, the meeting of earth and sky on the horizon, the existence of a whole room inside a mirror, or a firmament of stars in a pond at night, the increase and decrease in size of a building as we approach or recede, or the movement of the landscape when we ride swiftly in the train. Then, again, as to the order of phenomena. Just keep a "day-book" and record your mental pictures exactly as experienced and note the inextricable confusion. Here is a sample: Sitting in my study during a summer evening I am startled by a brilliant flash of lightning; item No. 1. Someone cries out in fear; Item No. 2. Doorbell rings. A book agent enters and insists on showing me a new atlas. Just as I am looking at the chart giving the ocean currents I hear a heavy clap of thunder; items 3, 4, and 5. Next the rain falls in torrents. My telephone rings and I talk with my friends who tell me that their home was struck. The railroad train whistles. Then comes a gust of wind that is a veritable hurricane. Conversation follows about the storm. Book agent presses his claims for further examination of maps and I am soon in China studying the position of Russia. Storm subsides—other flashes of lightning—telephone again rings—more thunder—other callers come. I retire and dream of China. Here are numerous items badly confused. In the morning I go to my classes. In the afternoon I take a drive and find a bridge up and a tree shattered. Here are a few phenomena, but there are a multitude that I have not recorded. No two days is there the same sequence, yet somehow all this confusion causes me no trouble, for from the "day-book" I post a ledger and connect events not as they appeared but as they really occurred. Then I make the lightning the antecedent, not of the coming of the book agent, but of the thunder and the river tree. The loss of the bridge was the sequence, not of my drive, but of the storm of the night before. Not in the day-book of sense, but in the ledger of common sense or judgment is there order. Sometimes the ledger cannot be posted as in the case of the raw recruit in battle, or the rustic in the business part of the city, or where one is recovering from illness, or in climbing a mast on a ship in a storm; then the head swims and the person becomes impersonal. Panic seizes the soldiers, the sailor falls into the water, the rustic is dazed or crazed. What would life be if the messages of sense were not corrected, the defective parts (and there are many) supplied, and the order rearranged by our code? Is it not important to ask where we get this code, and is it the right one, and does our ledger really represent the facts in nature, or are we simply writing mythology instead of history or science?

The code we use is one expressing the laws of thought, the one stating how the mind itself would have worked if it had created or imagined these sense pictures. No other code is possible for us. But what right have we to assume that the material world outside works like mind, i.e., that this code will fit there? If it does not, what is the value of the message we infer by this process? You reply, we cannot be sure, of course, but we make the hypothesis, and if it fits and explains these phenomena that is certainly enough for us. I reply that here you beg the whole question. (a) You assume that external nature is a cosmos, not chaos, simply because your mind must so work or you are insane, therefore whatever reduces phenomena to order you call objective. (b) Again, you assume consistency in nature, you give no weight to a hypothesis that contradicts itself. Such a hypothesis you say is not worth spending any time over. But what does this imply? If matter and mind are distinct realities, why should nature be such that it would seem consistent when

340

judged by mind? We know how ridiculous it would be for a rustic who has heard only English to attempt to pass judgment upon the pronunciation of students who claim to speak good French. Of course he would praise the one who pronounces the foreign tongue most nearly like English, and ridicule the others; therein consists his error. Are we not constantly making a similar mistake? We can have no knowledge of nature except through induction. This process begins with a hypothesis, and the hypothesis, you say, must be a reasonable one. But what is it "to stand to reason?" Reason is simply a thought process. To conform to it is to make your ideas square simply with the laws of mind. But why should a thought process have anything in common with a physical process? Why should not the most unreasonable hypothesis be just as likely, yes, even more likely, to square with the events in nature than a reasonable one?

Suppose space to be given the power of reasoning, that is, to become personal. Its laws of thought would be the truths concerning its own nature, viz., "extension in three dimensions." To affirm that a round square would be a contradiction would mean, not that the subject contradicted the predicate, but that the very nature of space was opposed to this figure and so made it impossible. The relation of circumference to diameter of a circle is fixed, not arbitrarily, but by the nature of space. This ratio was as true before the first mathematician existed as it is today. Annihilate every circle in the universe but leave space still in existence and the ratio would be as true as ever. If at any time a circle should actually be drawn it would merely conform to, not create, this truth. If then space could reason, it would discover all the truths of geometry, and could pass judgment on the forms proposed for architecture and works of art, i.e., upon all schemes that concerned extension, for nothing could ever exist in space that did not conform perfectly to its own laws. But could space reason about time? The one cannot change, the other cannot rest; all parts of space must coexist, no two points

341

in time could coexist. Their very constitutions are different; how then could either by reasoning (that is, making its ideas conform to its own nature) know anything about the other?

With us, too, reasonable is wholly a relative term. It simply means, in harmony with our mental nature or our mental processes. Of course everything that is subjective to mind must be reasonable, but why should the objective world, if wholly outside mind and independent of it be reasonable too? Many people who intend to be very humble are unwilling to admit these limitations of thought. With them reason is the power to get truth. What is truth? Why, just truth, they say. If every thing or being were annihilated in the universe, even God Himself, they suppose truth would still be true, and if any other beings ever did exist they would have to conform to these truths. This conception is a bare abstraction personified into an independent entity. No; Plato long ago taught the world that all truth is concrete. It holds only of particular things; destroy these things and with them go those truths too. Eternal truth holds only of an eternal being. Could there be not this but some other eternal being, just the opposite truths might be valid. Let us recur again to our illustration taken from geometry. This science is a series of truths concerning space. All geometrical axioms are true wherever this particular three-dimensional space exists, and they are just as eternal as this space and no more so. Could space be annihilated, not a wreck of geometry would be left behind. Could some other space be substituted for ours, we could no more guess as to what its geometry would be than we can imagine what a tenth sense might reveal. It is clear, then, that everything that exists in our space must be geometrical. This is self-evident. But why should that which does not exist in space, that which is not spatial, why should such a reality as time, or virtue, or love, or God, be made to square with geometry? True, if our supposedly personal space is to think of these things at all it must do so solely in terms of itself, but is that any justification for predicating its own attribute of them? Would it not be vastly

342

more consistent for space to simply decline to think of that which is not subjective? Would not absolute agnosticism on all such topics be the only course of honesty?

Can we not take the same position concerning mind? If we think at all concerning a world outside of our true selves, must we not do so in terms of, or according to, the laws of mind and is not this ridiculous? An hypothesis concerning that world might be more thinkable if it were reasonable, but will it come any nearer to expressing the actual facts that transpire there than the most unreasonable guess we could formulate? Would not its very reasonableness be the one thing that should excite our suspicion of it? The law of all inference from the sense phenomena is that of cause and effect. Is this wholly mental, you ask. Do we not know that causality holds in nature? The evidence here is absolutely conclusive. If all our knowledge comes from experience, we can have no experience of anything save of what is in the mind. As well might a man born blind get the knowledge of color, or the man born deaf get the idea of sound, as for us to get the idea of cause and effect in any other way than by the experience of mental or psychical causality. Causality is, we know, true of our mental processes. This much can be vouched for by direct introspection without the aid of inference. For any one to deny that the mind can really know its own states as they really are is to affirm that very fact in the act of making the denial, since unless your mind in the present instance is sure and accurate in its knowledge of the fact *that it denies the possibility of such knowledge* there is no real denial, and the whole question is left untouched. Unless consciousness is accurate in the distinctions it draws for itself, denial and affirmation are exactly the same thing, doubt and conviction in no way differ, truth and untruth are not opposites. It is simply impossible to doubt the power of the mind to know accurately its own processes and its own subjective states. James goes so far as to affirm that this knowledge is always with equal clearness. What we call an indefinite vague idea differs from a clear idea, not in your certitude of it, but simply in its own make-up. In a picture of a hazy October afternoon the view of the mountains makes the haze a part of the picture, and such a picture is just as really and completely in your own gallery when you hang it up as is one of a Colorado landscape where all the outlines startle you with their boldness. The eye sees one picture as it is just as clearly as the other, the difference being in the pictures, not in clearness of vision. So of mental states.

If you are willing to admit that these are the logical consequences of affirming that all our knowledge is derived from experience, will you find very much difficulty in settling the limits of our knowledge? Could we ever imagine, I will not say know, but ever imagine anything that is not a mental act or state? Could we ever dream of any law or axiom that was not simply a formula of our own mental processes or mental perspectives? Would there be the slightest reason for supposing that any of these ideas or axioms or laws hold of any other being or thing than our own mind? Do you suppose that your joy or your sorrow could be experienced by something outside of yourself and not endowed with consciousness? Why, then, should you think that the laws which govern your thought should hold of something outside the self which has no power of thought, that is, of dead matter? Would that not be affirming and denying thought out there all at the same time? Would you feel disposed to make the truths of your subjective three-dimension space apply to that which did not come within the sphere of your mental perspective? Would not such a procedure be the same thing as saying that it did, and at the same time that it did not, come into that sphere? How, then, do we come to have an idea of dead matter at all? We answer, clearly it is merely an abstraction. We fix our attention on some attributes of a state of consciousness and forget all others,—forget that it is merely a state of consciousness,—then we consider this abstraction as an independent reality, just as the Greeks did Minerva, and this is our physical universe. Dream landscapes are not real existences outside the mind, yet for all the world they seem so. But analyze external nature as you will and not a single attribute can you find there that is not mental so far as it goes. You have projected it out there or you could never have found it there.

You remember the words of Coleridge:

> we receive but what we give,
> And in our life alone does nature live;
> Ours is her wedding garment, ours her shroud.

Have I overdrawn the case, or is this a plain, honest inventory of just what experience is and just what thinking and reasoning really are, and therefore of their limits? Must I not, then, when I talk about the outside world, mean, not really that which is outside of self, but distinguish between two selves, the immediate present thinking, calculating, choosing, refusing, loving, hating, careless, careful, finite, dependent self which often is a mere caricature, a misrepresentation of the real self because so partial and incomplete as compared with that truer, larger, nobler self that seeks to find expression in all we do or say? Must I not distinguish between this present self and the larger independent self? Suppose the true self to be doing a great many things outside of the narrow limits of a state of consciousness which we call ours, then I would mean by the external world not that which is external to his mind in its largest sense, but external to the narrower self, the present mental states. For me to infer the cause of my sensations would be to fit the laws of the present self to these data in order to determine how the larger self produced these data, just as in memory I take present pictures and by making them stand to reason verify my recollection of what I did at a period of time before this present. Observation is a process, then, [in which we go outside] of a narrower state of consciousness, but not outside of the universal self. We do so by inference from present sensations, thus learning what the larger self is doing. Memory is a similar process, learning what the smaller self did in the past.

Put the question in a different way. If the laws of thought are not known to be the laws of things, how can we ever know things? And can the laws of thought be known to be the laws of things—mark the word, I do not say the laws of thought be the laws of things, but *be known* to be the laws of things—unless we first know that both thought and things are products of exactly the same larger self, whom we may call God? Here is my problem. Must we not take this view of our limitations or be absolutely agnostic concerning everything that transcends the smaller self? If the world is made up of separate independent entities, and if I were only one of them, they may or they may not be like me, but could I ever know whether they were or not? Should I have any right to guess at them by studying myself? Would not that be begging the whole question, and affirming that the laws of my thought really did apply to them? Put the question stronger than that. Could there be the slightest probability, if probability means a guess supported by *evidence?* There may be credulity of any possible grade, but not probability. I cannot see why one credulity is not just as good as another if you have no evidence to base your selection on.

3. The third step in the process of communicating with our friends comes after we persuade ourselves that we have gained accurate knowledge of the external physical world through the senses. From the physical contact of our friends, i.e., words uttered, expressions of countenance, gestures (what Hume would call superficial properties), we must infer the secret hidden character and motives, distinguish between jest and earnest, knowledge and ignorance, frankness and reserve. This is a scientific problem. Beginning in childhood, and making at first the most embarrassing mistakes, we carefully repeat the inductive process till we get hypotheses that stand criticism, and in time gain confidence that our work is correct. This is our study of human nature. What is its basis? Simply this: If we had done these deeds, uttered these words, hesitated, become excited, then gone off abruptly, we should have had definite em-

barrassment and no little anger, therefore our friend felt the same. Here is (a) vicarious knowledge of his mind following on vicarious knowledge of his external physical deeds. If all beings are separate and independent realities, we ought to have an agnosticism raised (lowered, possibly would be more accurate) to the second power concerning the mental life of friends. But this is just the one thing we are most confident of. That and only that makes life worth living. Did an agnostic ever live who really doubted this knowledge? Why do agnostics publish books to prove their doctrine? Why do they answer up so sharply when criticised? How know that others meant by those words what they interpret them to mean? No, men are not agnostic on this subject. Not that we know all about others, but that we do know something of their thought and of the intent of their hearts. The phrases mother, father, mean this or they are mere mockeries. To be really agnostic on this question would be out and out insanity. So long as a spark of life glows in us we shall hold to our faith in our ability to read the thoughts of other members of the human race when we have adequate data. Some are quicker and keener than we in this work, but even a woman's intuitions are no miraculous power. The process as far as it may be carried is always and everywhere inductive, or when this has been completed and we simply apply its results, deductive. There is only one possible ground on which it can rest, viz., that we know human nature as truly as physical nature to be uniform with our own conscious processes. Given this cognition and the path is so plain that the wayfaring man, even though a pluralist, need not err therein; but without this cognition the greatest genius is helpless. Indeed, the clearer his mental vision the quicker will he realize his isolation from every one else.

But here is the old question. How is the pluralist going to know that other human beings are uniform with himself? Must he not logically believe in monism and refuse to consider the world as made up of separate independent entities? Is there any other possible ground for the conviction that our true thought processes, and therefore our laws of thought, are universal? On any other basis could we give preference, in considering the external world, to a reasonable hypothesis over one that was absurd (which means simply unreasonable)?

I cannot sympathize with many who publish extremely attractive books in which the view is taken that we need not bother ourselves with any such problems, but may just simply go right ahead and assume that the world is just what it appears to be, and never raise the question, "What are the limits of our knowledge." I am perfectly willing to concede that appearances seem real, but I am obliged to do the same for my dreams. Dream friendships, dream classrooms, dream students are just as real and vivid, so long as they last subjectively, as any mental pictures that my waking moments ever give, and for the moment I generally give myself up to the illusion. Sometimes I suspect at the time that it is all a dream, and then things grow shadowy and fail to inspire, even though they may not disappear. It would take away a great deal of inspiration in my life to really believe that the whole drama was all one vast dream, and that I should wake up in the Beyond to find that my joys and sorrows, hopes and fears have been wholly concerned with a phantom universe of my own creating. I still cling to the conviction that my friends are really what I suppose them to be, and I can hold that view only on the monistic basis. This is so because surely my immediate acquaintance with the material world, and with my friends in it, is not with that world at all, but only with the mental phenomena subjective to my consciousness. Press your eye, and what seems to be the whole room swims. Go towards what seems to be your friend and he grows larger, go away from him and he grows smaller. You cannot believe that the real objective friend changes through your act, surely not; simply that the mental picture which you make of him varies because of some things you have done. If you became dizzy the landscape would swim, if you were ill darkness would fall upon the world at noonday. Is it the real world that you are so intimately

348

concerned with, or simply the subjective phenomenal world through which you gain your knowledge of the external nou- menon? If so, then there is room for the horrid question, "do you have that knowledge?" and if so "how do you get it?" Can you get it if monism be not true? Is there not a dim conscious- ness of monism in every mind which asserts itself the moment one becomes in earnest. We know the laws of thought are the laws of things. And is not this the reason why we are so con- fident in our judgment of others, and is not this the explanation of sovereignty and of courts of justice? If science did not appeal to this consciousness, should we have any faith in science? Those who do not believe in discussing this question, but simply in trusting appearances, do not believe in trusting all appearances. . . . When it suits their purpose they are the sharpest kind of critics, but the moment a man in serious earnestness questions pluralism and wonders whether there is not some better premise upon which to discuss sociological questions, then they pounce upon him and reproach him for being a metaphysician. Pluralism is just as much metaphysics as monism. Metaphysics is nothing under the sun but a discussion of the premises with which all conclusions are ultimately concerned. What they object to is really a scientific method in metaphysics. They want just enough dogmatic metaphysics to enable them to enter into their particular department of physical science, but no more. They will take a part, but not the whole, since then they would have conclusions that are inconvenient.

When Descartes discovered that his own conscious existence was involved in his doubt, he found not appearance but reality. Consciousness is real. The only question, then, will be, How far can a study of consciousness carry us? This is evidently our real world. Or to approach the problem in another way, the possibility of science, as well as of such practical cooperation as is involved in a jury trial, implies a common universe; man and nature, man and his fellow, must belong to one world. This is the doctrine of "monism," and if this one universe is regarded as a spiritual universe the monism is called theism.

Ideas play a part in deciding our purposes, and our purposes or "investments" affect our feeling and emotion. Education must develop these rational sentiments and not rely on natural "interest." A man may not plead that his affections are wholly outside his control.

In considering the motives and standards of the moral life two alternatives present themselves: either pleasure is the only motive or there is a spiritual nature and with it spiritual impulses; either expediency is the only standard or this spiritual nature and its constitution which involves justice and right is the ultimate measure of value.

THE LINE OF CLEAVAGE

Some time ago a child from the country was taken by its parents to the seaside, and under the care of its mother one day walked out on a long, low, rocky ledge jutting out into the surf. It was a trying position for any landsman as a first experience, and the child soon cried lustily because the rock was floating out to sea and they would soon be beyond reach of help.

We can laugh at this childishness, but do we never make a mistake equally foolish? The child knew better, and his mother assured him that the rocks could not float, but his senses affirmed in the most positive manner just the reverse; his childishness consisted in rejecting the testimony of judgment concerning what was really true, and in accepting merely the appearances instead. This is the line of cleavage which runs through all society. Its beginnings are low down even in the animal world. Its endings are the Day of Judgment in the separation of the sheep and the goats. We may distinguish cleavage by different phraseology, such as childishness or intelligence, wisdom or folly, barbarism or civilization, superstition or science, saint or sinner. In every

350

case the discrimination is between appearances in the one case and reality in the other, and in each case a severe test of character is involved when dealing with a new problem. Indeed, it makes little odds how simple the question is, the supreme choice between truth for truth's sake, and personal convenience in following the inclination of the moment, is clearly involved. The delicate chemical tests are the most valuable, and in the twenty-fifth chapter of Matthew, Christ selects those where the individual at the time of the deed was unconscious that it was a test.

Accepting the doctrine of evolution as provisionally true, it is clear that the human race has gained each step in its progress only by freeing itself from the bondage of appearances, that is, from the world as seen through the senses. To the savage man, the universe seems not merely spatial, temporal, and material, but also capricious. A savage never says, "I dreamed," neither does a child until he has been taught. Dreams are real sense perceptions; to distrust them would be, for him, to give up all standards of certainty. It must be conceded that savages are not so likely to dream as civilized peoples, as their physical health and animal existence cause a minimum expenditure of nerve energy. It is rather in times of illness or when injured that sleep is troubled and then they see their enemy or some wild animal torturing them. This is the origin of witchcraft. All savages believe that objects have a visible and invisible existence. The water that is now dew on the grass is gone, but no one thinks of it as annihilated; a cloud appears in the clear sky, no one thinks of it as created; at night-time there is a whole vault of stars in every pond of water, but by day they are there no longer. Things are constantly taking on the invisible form of existence, and when the savage sleeps in his hut and dreams of the chase, he accounts for the paradox, not by saying it is a dream, but by saying that his invisible or double went hunting. Therefore when he suffers pain and at night sees his enemy torturing him, the mystery of pain is all explained. It is the invisible presence of his enemy that accounts for all the ills of life. Hence the remedy for sickness among savages is not medicine but the pow-wow that shall frighten away the invisible foe. Chinese firecrackers are exploded every night at sundown on Chinese ships simply to frighten away enemies. Grant the savage man's premises and his conclusions are strictly logical. Herbert Spencer has shown that the whole practice of medicine originated in these premises. This is the whence to which our noblest medical schools owe their existence. How do we account for the change? It is simply this: There came a time when men distrusted appearances, and though the dreams were none the less real, and though indeed they became more and more frequent, yet they no longer were conceded to be true.

Now this is simply saying that men had taken the first step in that long journey whose highest expression is in the language of the Apostle, "We walk by faith, and not by sight." It is judgment, substantiated evidence, as opposed to sense reality. Thousands of years have passed away since that first step was taken, and even to this day some of our educated people believe in dreams when unusually vivid and uncanny. The progress from fetichism, when the world was governed by caprice, up to the nineteenth century with its reign of physical law has been a battle in which each foot of the ground has been contested in the most stubborn manner. In vain might Galileo prove that the earth turned on its axis instead of the sun's rising and setting; appearances were against him, and the whole force of the Church was brought to bear to force him to recant. In vain did Newton affirm the gravitation of the planets; astrology was too old a superstition to be pulled up by the roots with a single effort, and some of the greatest intellects of the day declined to yield to his evidence. In our own time Darwin suffered no small persecution when he affirmed the variation of species, for it appeared ridiculous to trace man's descent back to the lower forms of animal life; but slowly the victory has been won; first in one position and then in another until now the very centre of the citadel is besieged. Theism claims to furnish evidence of the most conclusive type, that the whole common sense perception of the world is only appearance, as ridiculously unreal as the old Ptolemaic astronomy or savage witchcraft. It claims to show that if thousands of valuable lives were sacrificed to the superstitions of the Indian medicine-man, or at a later time to the oracles of the astrologer, at the present time every life is being marred by faith in the reality of the show world of common sense, and that the foundations of our social order are being undermined by the logical conclusions which are drawn from these show premises.

Theism claims to furnish evidence so clear that the wayfaring man, though a fool, may not err therein. It does not, however, claim to be able to dissolve the appearances. The Copernican system of astronomy with all its evidence has not succeeded in enabling Professor Huxley to free himself from seeing the sun set instead of the horizon lift. The sky is still to us a vault and the earth a plane. The stars are all at equal distance over our heads and we cannot for a moment realize their actual magnitude. Though we are no longer deceived by appearances, the oar is still bent to our eyes in the water; and there are just as many stars in the pond at night to us as to our savage ancestors. But a person would be considered insane who should for a moment be the slave of these appearances. The reason for their strength and persistence Mr. Balfour explains by the law of natural selection. The life of the savage was wholly a response to environment. It was a life of violence and constant risk requiring instantaneous action on the spur of the moment. To hesitate often meant death. It is clear that those individuals who yielded most to the senses would be quickest in their action. Deliberation requires time, the weighing of evidence. This meant hesitation in an emergency, often indecision. The odds in the lower animals were therefore all against the thinker. Those only were safe who would flee on the slightest provocation, and those who wait to determine whether there has not been a false alarm will often never have a chance to wait again. It is thus seen that natural selection preserved the slaves of the senses and destroyed the children of reason. That is, those who ate of the fruit of the tree of knowledge suffered the penalty of instant death. It will take generations of heredity slowly accumulated to give our spiritual nature, our rational cognitions and ethical impulses, a tithe of the strength or sense of reality which appearance and passion possess. Mr. Balfour concludes that we ought therefore not to be disturbed in any way by the difficulty of making spiritual things seem real. On the other hand, that we ought the rather to suspect our natural inclinations and tendencies all the more because of their vividness.

The drunkard and the debauchee find a reality in their passions that makes the still small voice seem like a ghost, and they cannot understand how any one believes in eternal righteousness. They see nothing but sensuality to life. But the virtuous man is undisturbed by the earthquake and whirlwind of passion, and in the still small voice he finds truth itself, for which he is ready to sacrifice his life. The question you have before you is, on which side of this line of cleavage you will stand. Because of your education and the assistance of others, you can laugh at the superstitions of the savage and the frank crudeness of the rustic. You can despise the slavery of the sensualist, that is, these are not test questions with you. But are you sure that if you had existed in these bygone ages you would have been among the first to withstand the whole current of your age, and accept the evidence against witchcraft, astrology, and caprice in nature? This question you can answer easily by a simple test. Take the subject with which philosophy has to deal and see whether you can hold yourself absolutely true to evidence and care naught for appearances and the decision of the multitude. To some in the class this is not an easy thing to do. Are you sure that if you insist on denying theism and holding on to the show world of sense in spite of all the evidence which epistemology presents,— are you sure that with only the data of an earlier age you would have escaped its error and folly?

354

But why do I lay so much stress on distinguishing between appearance and reality. Granted that the appearances are illusions, one rowing can steer by stars in a pond which do not exist, and why not follow these appearances since they are so good for a practical life? That is just my point. It narrows your whole existence down to what you call practical life; it destroys your manly existence and makes you merely a social animal. It determines the question of your psychological climate.

If you look over your past experience you will find those moments in your existence when you came the nearest to being your true self—when you were half conscious of a reserve power of manliness that made your ordinary life seem mean and narrow—were moments when you could look through the material as through a veil and be conscious that it was not all. It may have been at a time when some rank injustice made the blood boil in your veins. It may have been when you were reading some deed of heroism in war like that stated by Mr. Forbes which he calls the bravest deed he ever saw, or like that of Cushing in blowing up the Albemarle, or that of Graham in his lone and single-handed capture of the rebel guerrilla. When you look at such men as these, can you think for a moment that they were selfish? Does there not shine through their heroism "the light that never was, on sea or land"? In these moments of daring can you not realize something in your own heart that gives you a feeling of kinship? If not how could you admire their deed? Is not the true explanation of your admiration the words of Fichte?

the Eternal One
Lives in my life, and sees in my beholding,
Naught is but God, and God is naught but life.

1. Everybody philosophizes; this is only saying that everybody has some idea of the world in which he lives. Even the child or the savage has his ultimate premises from which he reasons to the particular facts about him. Aristotle used to say that we must

355

philosophize, and if one saith that he may not philosophize (of course the statement would mean nothing unless he gave some reason to support it, and a reason would imply certain premises in the light of which his statement was a conclusion), therefore in that very statement he doth philosophize and must.

2. There are two methods of philosophizing; we call these the literary and the scientific. The literary discards all evidence; it creates a universe, say, for instance, fairyland, and cares for only two things: (a) that it shall be an attractive universe; (b) that it shall be fairly consistent. It will be noticed that this is not real creation. As the man born blind cannot originate the idea of color, so the author and the dreamer find every factor of their imaginary world in their own experience. Fairyland has three dimensions to its space, so has ordinary experience. In fairyland the genius is visible and then invisible, so is the dew on the grass or the moisture in the air. In fairyland they talk and sing, and touch and taste, but there is no trace of any more sense perceptions than we have in everyday life. The creations of the imagination differ from those of experience in two particulars only. First, the elements derived from experience are combined differently, and secondly, while the known factors are added the particular ones of daily experience may be left out. It would be very easy to assume that a certain messenger of the gods was not subject to the law of gravitation. In all other particulars he might be a human being, but this very attribute in his case might be entirely omitted. We might find a witch who could live without food, or who could pass through fire without being burned, or who could take the most deadly poison and suffer no harm, but in every other respect be like ordinary mortals. Such a person would be human with the exception of these three attributes: anabolism and katabolism of the nervous system, chemical changes effected by heat, and chemical changes caused by particular drugs. You see it is simply a case of abstraction. Now all such philosophizing as this is pure fiction. It is simply a romance, or a tragedy, or a comedy; and those

who accept such philosophy are simply dogmatics, as much as the schoolmen in the Middle Ages. They are simply fossils who have not yet found their way to a museum, or relics of a primitive civilization where the struggle for existence was not quite severe enough to cause all the unfittest to perish.

Scientific philosophizing is solely a matter of evidence. The investigator does not ask what is the universe, or what may it be, or why could it not be so; his whole inquiry is, What does the evidence reveal concerning the actual world in which we live? Having found that appearances are deceitful and having discovered that the senses give us simply effects, he considers that any attempt to appeal ultimately to sense perception as the basis for knowledge of things as they really are is so ridiculous that every honest man can have no respect for those who deliberately make the attempt. He can see no difference between these people and the heathen who set up graven images made by their own hands for their gods, and then fall down and worship them as their creators.

Here, then, is the line of cleavage which runs through humanity. All start in ignorance in childhood and all attempt to get some conception of the world they live in, and all make blunders. But some fall back simply on the imagination, and postulate a world dogmatically which is gained through abstraction from their own experience. Others attempt a scientific analysis of their experience and insist on weighing evidence, and then they take this great step, namely, they affirm that concerning the things for which we have not a vestige of evidence we must speak and act in exactly the same way as we do concerning the things that do not exist. There may be witches, there may be a fourth dimension space, there may be other universes besides our own in which the whole range of mythology is true; but we are humble finite beings, and the only way we can distinguish between superstition and fact is to limit ourselves to evidence, and until we have evidence of witches, a fourth dimension space, and mythological deities, we cannot let these things enter as a factor

357

into our thinking or into our lives. Human nature is a country like Holland; it is below the sea level of superstition. The tidal wave of fanaticism has rolled over human history again and again, wrecking all that was fair and promising and leaving behind only death and moral pestilence. Against this terrible disaster there is only one protection. We must build dikes around human nature, and the only dikes that will stand will be those constructed on evidence. Then men may live in peace and safety. He who destroys these dikes is the arch traitor of the race. He is attempting to again flood humanity with passion and credulity. Look back through history and see what a sad record it is. Mothers offering their own children in sacrifice to imaginary deities; hecatombs of human victims slain to avert pestilence; men made in the image of God languishing for years in foul caves till they became as insane as one possessed of the devil, hoping thereby to atone for crimes that had no existence; the whole human race absolutely blind to the beauty of nature, ignorant of the infinite wealth of the soil and the mines, living in a universe governed by law and finding there only caprice and fraud; not men sitting in darkness but blind men walking in great light, all because they were hypnotized by fanaticism and persecuted evidence. Living the life of tradition and imitation, a life of brain paths worthy only of the ape, they refused to exercise the God-given power of weighing evidence that could transfer their world from chaos into cosmos, lifting them out of their slavery and giving them the liberty of the sons of God. See what a fight it has been to win what little progress in science we have already gained, and then tell me if the man who adopts as his mode of life those processes which, if adopted universally, would stop all progress, annihilate all the achievements of science, and once more enthrone superstition,—tell me if he is not the arch traitor of humanity, the enemy of civilization, the incarnation of a fiend himself.

If this world is governed by law, law is by its very nature universal. There can be no exceptions, given the conditions. Therefore whenever a man claims the privilege of being an exception and adopts modes of thought and of life that he would not approve if every one else did exactly the same under the same conditions, he confesses himself to be unscientific, lawless, criminal. He stands self-condemned, and when he condemns himself he cannot wonder that others join in the condemnation.

Here we have the issue before us. Shall a man walk in the light or shall he close his eyes and walk in darkness where there is great light? I freely grant that any finite being who attempts to weigh evidence will necessarily make mistakes; that is the penalty of being finite. But will he escape mistakes by refusing to weigh evidence, or will he make greater ones? If a man lives up to the light he has, he oftentimes will be like the man whose eyes Christ opened, and who saw things not as they were, but distorted, for he saw men as trees walking. How ridiculous! But was it not better to see as much as that rather than not see at all? Was that not a great miracle of healing? Was not that period only transient? And did he not soon see clearly and accurately? Would you make that an argument against all sight, and affirm, therefore, that it was the duty of every man to put his eyes out and become totally blind? Yet this is exactly the way a great many reason. Because there have been mistakes made in philosophy, honest mistakes, mistakes that were extremely helpful in climbing to a higher point of view, any number of people would condemn scientific philosophy completely and insist upon falling back on dogmatism.

The choice is between living up to the light you have or doing something infinitely worse. It is not between living up to the light you have or being guided by an infallible instinct that acts blindly and always turns you in the right direction, just as the needle points to the pole. Matter can act that way, but mind cannot. Matter never errs; it always obeys the laws of nature without varying a hair's breadth. But the mind cannot do right without intelligence to guide it. The compass will point to the pole in a fog, but the ship captain unaided by it cannot do it;

359

until he can take observations on the stars and reckon his position he is simply hopeless. That is the penalty man pays for his exaltation. He has got to be something better than matter or he will be infinitely worse. The scientist realizes it, accepts the issue and determines to work out his own salvation. But the dogmatist shuts his eyes to this fact and does what he can for his own destruction. The fact that he sometimes does not get destroyed is due not to himself but to the influence of the environment upon him, provided he is so fortunate as to live in an age when the traditions that he imitates have been produced by a prior science and therefore not wholly in the wrong direction.

Men differ in wealth, in health, in knowledge, in power, in wit, in wisdom, but none of these constitute a line of cleavage that is fundamental. The wisest man does not know very much compared with all that is to be known. The most stupid man could learn a great deal if he only kept at it through all eternity. The witty man is simply one who emphasizes unusual likenesses and differences between things not too farfetched, at the same time not too true. His jokes will not bear many repetitions. The moment he becomes serious he may become eloquent, but he is no longer witty. He is related to the truth just about as a tailor is to the statesman. He cuts the garments and makes them fit, but he is only a hand doing his task, or following his profession, earning his living by his trade. He surely would be the last to claim that he differed from others essentially. It is all a mere question of knack or skill. All differences in quantity are insignificant when you have eternity in view. The fundamental problem is not "where we are, but whither we are drifting." If you only give a man time enough, if he is going in the right direction he will make no mean progress. But if he is going in the wrong direction, the more time he has the more hopeless his case. And now what is the right direction? The reply is, weighing evidence and attempting to find the truth. To such a being, no matter how stupid, how ignorant, how weak, truth can be gradually revealed. For him the Divine Being can mark out an infinite future of progress. But a man who refuses to shape his life by evidence, who will weigh evidence only when it favors some pet scheme or plan, or when he can discomfort his enemy, but immediately drops it when it demands personal sacrifice for himself,—he is the man to whom you cannot appeal through the truth. To do so would be like focusing the sunlight on a man who closed his eyes; it would not make him open them, but close them all the tighter. If a man wants to do wrong, are you going to change him by convincing him that he is doing wrong, or will that confirm him in his career? Take the coward who is running away from the battle to a place of safety. Would you make him a hero by arguing with him and proving to him that he was getting away from the enemy out beyond the reach of their bullets into a place where he could accomplish nothing in resisting them? Or would that make him all the more persistent in following that path? You might use force on him. Then you would be acting and using him as an agent. It would not be his virtue; it would be yours. But we are talking about a man's character itself. If he refuses to weigh evidence and shape his life accordingly, could an infinite God, I will not say do anything with him, but do anything for him? If he persists in that course all through eternity, will not his case be constantly growing worse instead of better? Has not such a man blasphemed against the Holy Spirit, that is, the spirit of truth, and would not a scientific judge discover in him a total difference as compared with those who have sworn allegiance to the truth? Is not this then blasphemy against the Holy Ghost which neither God nor man can forgive?

Philosophy means literally love of the truth; not love in the sense of like, as a child likes molasses, for everybody must like the truth provided it is favorable to himself. But love in the sense of service, allegiance in the pursuit of the truth, is the real meaning of the term philosophy. It does not mean that a man is wise, but simply that he is striving to know what is true in order that he may do what is right. It does not mean that he can investigate every problem for himself. When he is sick he will have to call the doctor, when he is traveling he will have to trust a guide; but whose authority will he take? The reply is, he will follow only the leader who has himself allegiance to the truth and who has sought and found it. Now when you condemn such a man, and when you sing the praises of one who sneers at the truth, exactly what are you doing, against whom are you blaspheming? If it be true that without Him we cannot so much as think a good thought, since everything that is good and true holds only of Himself and of us as we partake of His nature, would not Christ say, "Inasmuch as ye do unto one of the least of these, ye do it unto me"?

————————

You are not indifferent, you are not neutral; you are either assisting or resisting the service of the truth in those about you.

SCIENCE AND THEISM

If a man is honestly searching for the truth, the whole truth, and nothing but the truth, can he logically be confident about the objective existence and purposes of his friends but agnostic concerning God, the true self on whom all are dependent? Logically, are we not more sure of the existence of this Being and of some, not all, of the processes and laws that govern His actions, than we are of the existence of a physical world and of our ability to communicate with our companions? Until we are sure of this Being and of the dependence of all things upon Him, can we be sure that our inferences really take us beyond the subjective? Some hesitate to rest on these conclusions. There is no flaw in the logic, but they are afraid of anthropomorphism. If God were an absentee deity, living off somewhere in the distance from us, we should be anthropomorphic in ascribing to Him laws that govern us. We should not have a vestige of evidence to base such predicates upon. But if we are His workmanship more truly than the swinging of the pendulum is the work of

362

gravity, the case is different. Our inner life is a laboratory where His processes are revealed. Uniformity under the same conditions is tautology. We are not predicating human attributes of God, but divine attributes of man, simply affirming that man partakes of the divine nature, is made in the image of God. This is not anthropomorphism, but theomorphism. This is scientific. How else can you have vicarious knowledge?

Just a word as to the sociological bearing of this view. You may give up the automaton theory but still believe that thought is only a function of the brain (as it surely is in some instances, in insanity—for example). This leaves you with an estimate of man, as made not in the image of God but in the image of animals. Look at the loss of faith in humanity so common today. Almost every one is accused of having his price. The moment a workingman is old or ill or injured a dozen are ready to take his place, and he simply drops out of sight with less ado than would be made over a race-horse. The "sweating system" makes impossible the decencies of life simply because money is worth more than manhood. Look at municipal government in our large cities. How can public sentiment be changed here? We reply, only as it is seen that evolution states only a part of the truth, not the whole truth, concerning man. He is an animal and as such comes under the laws of the animal world; his life is a struggle for existence, with survival of the fittest. But he is more. If monism is true, he is partaker of the divine nature. "Inasmuch as ye do it unto one of the least of these, ye do it unto God Himself." Only as men believe in God can they believe in humanity. "Ye believe in God, believe also in me." Man is a wonderful being. Tyndall is wrong in his quotation. "What is man that thou art mindful of him," etc. This is a mistranslation; the true idea is, "How glorious a being is man that thou art mindful of him, and the son of man, that thou visitest him. Thou hast made him only a little lower than the angels and hast crowned him with glory and honor." Man has a reserve power never yet exhausted. James taught us that in times of temptation ideals alone are weak

363

and propensities strong, but that effort added to ideal is more than a match for the strongest propensity; and that the amount of effort increases with the resistance. Can we be quite sure that it is not infinite? We never reach a point where we feel that we could not put forth a little more of the heroic. Is this what Paul meant when he said, "I can do all things through Christ which strengtheneth me?" Dare you mark out your future and say, thus far and no farther? Or are you conscious of latent possibilities, of a depth to your spiritual nature that no plummet has yet sounded? Power reveals itself only in work done. Provide the right conditions and the measure of your imagination will not reach the limit of your future attainment. This is true, not merely of the individual, but of the nation. Did our fathers anticipate the present magnitude and grandeur of America? Did Washington dream just how much was potential in free institutions? Can you forecast what the middle of the twentieth century will reveal? If you believe in monism you have some basis for optimism. There is the prophecy, "We shall be changed into the same image from glory to glory." "We shall be like him, for we shall see him as he is." "Be ye therefore perfect (in process not product), even as your Father which is in heaven is perfect." This is the doctrine that monism declares, "As we have borne the image of the earthy, so shall we also bear the image of the heavenly."

In affirming the dependence of nature on God we do not deny the reality of the material world nor limit physical science. Just the reverse. Science aims at discovering the laws of nature. Theism believes that nature is God in action, a mode of operation of the infinite. But this does not tell us how God acts or what He accomplishes. This we must and can learn by observation and experiment, and such knowledge is of infinite value. Science is thinking God's thoughts after Him just as truly as when we read the scripture. Nature is the word of God—"He spake, and it was done;" science is the commentary on this revelation. The scientist is the seer or prophet who reveals to us divine laws written, some of them on tables of stone, others in letters of light, others so obscurely that without his aid we could never have known them. It is simply habit that makes nature seem less real when we think of it as dependent. The Indian considers light as a substance and the rainbow as a real arch of something solid. Tell him that all is a mere mode of motion of ether and you seem to take away the reality. Mere motion, what is that? Yet it is true all the same, and when you get used to this truth rainbows are as beautiful as ever and a thousand times more significant. So also of music. It is real in spite of the fact that science has demolished the old doctrines on this subject. Passion and love are subjective, yet they are realities, terribly serious ones, too, in human history. Imprison a burglar, sentenced to death, in your strongest dungeon, does he fear the massive masonry and iron barred windows? No, for if left to himself he would find a way of cutting through these. His great danger is the purpose of the guard. An incorruptible purpose in the jailor is to him the reality that will not yield to his art. Here is something more solid than adamant, yet it is only a mode of mental working. Does he think spiritual things are mere shadows, dim ghosts of reality? Take a jilted lover. What is it that discourages him? Not time, nor distance, nor frost, nor burning sun, for he would go to the ends of the earth if thereby he could win. It is only a fixed idea in the lady's mind, but 'twere easier to move a mountain than to overcome that prejudice. The power of money that in our age is able to overcome almost all physical obstacles and transform the whole face of nature is simply the power of human desire. Gold is not a power. In the mines it did none of these things, in the bank vault, it is wholly passive. Not gold, but man's desire for it is the motor force of the age. It is a mental not a physical agency that the new century worships. Does it seem any the less real on that account? Why, then, should the whole of nature seem less real because we believe it to be a mode of God's activity?

Possibly one reason why a nature dependent on God seems unreal is because we consider mental action as merely capricious,

365

i.e., we ourselves are not yet quite personal. Note that there are at least two types everywhere recognized. A friend is approached on a certain matter. The answer often is, "If it is an affair of business we must arrange it thus; but if it is merely personal we can manage it between ourselves differently." Business and society are two different processes, yet both are mental. So also are official conduct and private life. The difference is in the conditions. A general is very careful to insist on organization in his army and on rules that often demand great personal sacrifice of his own comfort, yet in his family he leaves red tape at the door. It sometimes happens that the personal friend of a bank president will ask for a loan. Sometimes he gets the reply, "As an officer of the bank I cannot do it; it is against the rules, but as a friend I will let you have the money out of my own private funds." Everywhere we note these two processes, and often we are puzzled to determine whether the conditions require one or the other. Even in colleges we have our system of administration where teachers themselves have no authority to suspend certain regulations, as for example the "cut system." But this does not exclude the possibility of social relations with the students outside the classroom without any such restrictions. If nature is dependent on God, His action there is formal, legal, official; otherwise we should never know what to anticipate. In this way nature is both reasonable and yet law-abiding. To illustrate: You do not doubt that the Constitution of the United States is relatively fixed; that it should be a very formal thing for the American nation to amend it; and yet this does not for a moment make you hesitate to ascribe its continuance from generation to generation, from week to week, to exactly the same public sentiment that in other and simpler matters, for instance, style of dress and forms of amusements, changes its mode of action radically several times a season. If you can have constitutional law on the basis of a democracy of finite beings, is it impossible to have faith in physical law on the basis of theism?

There is really a fourth step involved in communicating with

366

friends. It begins with one's own identity; where this is lost, people cannot understand or be understood. Maintaining consciousness of identity involves a very definite thought process. We must remember our past life and connect with that recollection our present experience in such a way as to view the part in the light of the whole; we must, in short, know "where we are at." In dual personality people have been most seriously embarrassed by waking into their primary consciousness but being entirely unable to locate themselves. They found themselves perhaps in a strange place; they were in a swiftly moving railroad car, but whither were they going? In what part of the world were they? There was no luggage in the seat with them. Was there on the train a trunk of theirs with necessary clothing for the night; if so, where would it be put off? Had they any money in their pockets, or any to their credit in any bank? How long had they been unconscious? How did they get where they were? Were they going through a new form of Rip Van Winkle experience? Were any of their friends still alive? If so, of course they were anxious about them. The thought of a possible explanation on the basis of dual personality may have occurred to them; if so, they might ask, Had they been guilty of crime or immoral character and was their reputation blasted? It will be seen that a thousand questions would come into a person's mind under such conditions, and one might be easily driven to the very verge of insanity when he found that many vital ones could not be answered.

Why are we not troubled in this way every morning when we awake? There is one answer, and only one. Consciousness of subject comes through consciousness of object; identity of subject only as we are able to identify our objects; unity of subject, only as we discover a unity in the world about us and our place therein. We can reckon time, we can remember the order of our own past states of consciousness, only as we make these states of consciousness parts of the great series of events taking place in the objective world. If you sleep soundly during the night you would be conscious of no lapse of time; indeed some persons have been absolutely sure they did not sleep at all. Generally we reckon these periods in terms of the physical changes that take place in our own body. We feel rested upon waking up. But these tests are very unreliable, and we correct them by identifying the objects about us and noting the changes that have taken place there. It was dark when we retired, and now the gray dawn is seen through the windows. Time is absolutely invisible. If it were a great chain with visible links all numbered, and each event hung in its proper place, we could tell by looking just what time it is. But time is not such a visible reality! We therefore have to reckon in terms of objective nature, and this brings up again the whole problem of vicarious knowledge. Under what conditions can we have physical science? Either some science or insanity. To pick up the threads of consciousness when we wake from sleep, we must first note the order of changes that take place in nature, the whole series, and the order in which the separate phases follow. We must then find out what particular phase of the process is now present and locate this properly in the whole order that has occurred, e.g., if the sun moves from east to west in a continuous orbit, then its position at any given time enables us to determine how long since it rose. But if there were no path of the sun, if it were like a flash of lightning in a thunderstorm which appeared now in this quarter of the sky, now in that, you could not determine what the previous positions had been by determining its present location, that is, you could not reckon time by it. The same of a clock. If the hands must move clear around the circle only in one direction, by locating them you can determine what has been. But if the hands were taken off and put on arbitrarily their present position would indicate nothing definite. Here, then, is the great truth. Unless we are able to go outside of our present states of consciousness and note the order of nature as it has actually occurred (or be thoroughly convinced that we do), we cannot connect our present life with our past, we cannot tell how long we have slept, we should very

368

soon get confused as to the order of our past experience, we could not distinguish illusions from realities, imaginations from sense perceptions; in short we could not remain sane. More than this. If you are to live in civilization others must reckon their lives as parts of exactly the same objective nature in terms of which you have wrought out your own personal identity. When we have an appointed hour for recitation, if one man's reckoning of time did not square with the time reckoning of others, one calling the day Sunday, others Friday, etc., one March, another July, how could we keep the appointment?

To sum up our question. If all calculation is simply fitting together data gained through the senses, namely, mental phenomena, in such a way that they are made to square with our thought processes and thus conform to the laws of mind, how would it be possible by this process (a) to get any knowledge at all of the external world, if it were not known to be the working of exactly the same infinite mind who is working through us, and therefore governed by the same laws? (b) How could we know the thought and intention of our friends unless they, too, were dependent on the same source and governed by the same laws? All this is saying that if we ever get outside of our present state of consciousness, that knowledge will be vicarious knowledge, and further that vicarious knowledge is an absurdity unless that which is outside is known to be uniform with that which is inside. There is absolutely no objective science, either physical or mental, unless from one, namely, the self, we can learn all. But if all are different in identity, distinct existences, there is no problem about it. It is simply impossible to have that knowledge, and there the matter ends. (c) And the same question comes up with regard to one's own personal identity, that is, his ability to connect his present experience with his past experience or to have a unity to his life. This can never be done by a dead lift of memory, but only through consciousness of objects and through our ability to determine the changes through which they pass and the place into which our life fits. This takes

369

us right back to the possibility of objective science again. (d) If a man's life is to fit into the life of others and become a part of one social order, so that his appointments are understood and followed by his friends, if history can have any significance to him, it will be because all others date and locate themselves and their plans in the same objective science which he has made the basis of his own personal identity. How could they work in the same way in which he works, get the same results that he gets, write history that he can read, literature that fills him with inspiration, enact laws that bind his conscience, unless they were dependent on the same sources for their existence that nature and his own mind find working in themselves?

(e) If we are to have a form of society which grants liberty, equality, and fraternity, it will be only on the basis of discussion. The ultimate appeal will be, not to force, but to evidence. This postulates that what is evidence to one mind is evidence to every mind when seen in connection with exactly the same data. How could you ever use the "therefore" in a syllogism unless, whether men willed it or not, they were obliged to assent to the conclusion when they had exactly your premises? They may be hasty, they may shut their eyes and refuse to see the matter at all, they may even persecute and ridicule, but you have an invincible ally in their own bosoms and they know it. They dare not allow themselves to think, for their whole nature will befriend you if you are right. When Darwin wrote "The Origin of Species," it was greeted by a storm of derision. But what cared he? His appeal was not to some outside power that might force men to believe (which faith he despised); no, he appealed from Philip drunk to Philip sober, from the thoughtless public to the thoughtful public; and when they had time to think they were simply so many Darwins themselves. They found him within their own inner life, awaiting a chance to speak out and make himself heard. That is discussion, and if it is not that, it is nothing. When you discuss with a man it is simply because you yourself are within that man's inner life. You speak to the ear

370

and he does not hear, but you speak to the heart from within and he cannot be deaf. Discussion is simply finding yourself in another, and that is the reason why you are courteous and respectful to others when you respect yourself. Now let us suppose that this was not true, that the same infinite self was not in all, that when men worked out their salvation it was not the same God who worked in every man. It would be absolutely inconceivable that the fourteen million separate voters who cast their ballot in the last presidential election in the United States could all think alike if they were separate and independent existences. The law of chances determined by mathematical science is wholly against it. Huxley somewhere says, "If I throw dice and they come down double sixes once, it is fortunate; if they come down double sixes twice, I am lucky; if they come down double sixes three times, it is a marvel; if they come down double sixes four times, there is no marvel about it." The dice were loaded, the whole thing was fixed from the beginning, and the problem is solved. Dice have only six faces, six possible things to do. Human life is infinitely complicated; and here is this government representing almost every nationality under the sun. How could fourteen million separate individual voters discuss for three months the extremely complicated problems of imperialism and finance with any hope whatever of any approach toward an agreement? Would not the three months' discussion simply reveal the hopelessness of such an outcome? Why, then, should the decision of the majority be accepted by the minority? Why should not each follow his own judgment and thus have anarchy? Only one answer can be given. Evidence would play no part in the matter; it would be simply a question of might. The majority would have might enough possibly to restrain the minority. But this would be a state of war instead of peace. Power always appeals to artifice and fraud and strategy for eluding it, as the Boers have done in South Africa so successfully for months. No, if you are to have republican institutions you must have faith in discussion; you must believe that however the presidential elec-

371

tion is decided the question is not closed so but that it will be reopened the moment the new administration begins. It will be reviewed in the press and in Congress and in the club, and if the majority have made a mistake that mistake will be pointed out, and if they are in the right the truth will be more clear. The minority can submit when they know the justice of their cause is to be reviewed by the people, when they are convinced that the deepest, truest voice of the people is the voice of God Himself. This is arbitration not war. This is liberty, equality, fraternity, not tyranny. This is monism, not pluralism. (f) What do we mean by freedom of the press? Not freedom to lie or to slander and misrepresent, but freedom to weigh evidence on the basis that when this is carefully done it will express the only verdict of each individual man who thinks the problem through and obtains the necessary data. The press, then, becomes the mouth-piece of every honest citizen; to muzzle it is to muzzle himself, for his deepest, truest self is really attempting to speak through the editor. If this is the spirit of the press, they may make blunders, they may be even carried away by passion, but these blunders will be reviewed and corrected; these passions will be rebuked and be a source of shame, and make the editors more careful next time. Then the only danger to the republic will be the secrecy with which error is promulgated. When once it has been made public, and openly proclaimed, if the press shall weigh the evidence, the absurdity will be exposed. Poisonous germs can thrive only in filthy, dark, ill-ventilated rooms. Sunlight is the most powerful germicide there is. Suppression of freedom of the press will develop your secret organizations. We know not the damage they may do. But remove the censorship, bring everything to the open, weigh the evidence, and you are absolutely safe.

It is simply because men have no faith in reason, no love for the truth, that they question on the one hand the value of free discussions, and on the other hand become superstitious and servile imitators of society, asking not whether a thing is true, but whether it is good form, whether Mrs. Grundy approves. When these are the ideals of society, yellow journalism will thrive like a plague in India. There is a lack of moral sanitation, an absence of faith in humanity, when men cease to care for the truth supremely. Pluralism could have no other result, for then there could be no universal truth. Nothing would be possible for men except to imitate and become slaves. But monism clears the atmosphere of shame and reproach, falsehood and error, and gives all the dignity of God Himself to the truth. Do we not need a little monism in the public thought at the present time? Christ came to bear witness to the truth, but the coward Pilate sneered at the truth and sold himself as a slave to the bidding of the Pharisees. Which was the monist and which was the pluralist? (g) Freedom of our universities is a matter of considerable concern. It is often asked, "Has not a man a right to do what he will with his own money? If he believes in a certain creed, and is willing to give a million dollars or ten million dollars to establish an institution to teach that creed, has he not a right to do it? If he pays for it, is it not his to do with as he pleases? Have we not a right then, to establish sectarian institutions?" On the basis of pluralism, most surely, but on the basis of monism, never. Look at it a moment. Has a man a right to form his own opinion arbitrarily, or only by the weighing of evidence? Well, then, if that is his duty, if his own conclusions must be shaped so as to square with the evidence, has he a right to do anything that would lead others to form their conclusions in a different way, to prevent them from weighing evidence, and make them borrow their results like a phonograph, that is, de-personalize them and take away the divine likeness with which God has endowed them? What would you think of a man giving a sum of money to establish a court of justice where the jury were to be fixed so that they would always give a decision in favor of the particular party or particular creed that the donor believed? Would it not come fearfully near bribery, and what penalty would suggest itself as appropriate for such an attempt? There are two facts to our nature, brain paths and weighing evidence. The brain paths work along the lines of least resistance, and here force is the determining factor. But here man is only an animal. The human part of man is the power that can work in the lines of greatest resistance and square solely with evidence, and here man is in the image of God. Now whenever you substitute for evidence any form of force (and bribery is a form of force), you attempt murder, not of the body, but of the mind. You are doing what you can to do away with the spiritual and make man in the image of the beasts and birds and creeping things. Could monism justify this?

Let me just here anticipate our studies so far as to call attention to the possible extremes of view to be found in the history of human progress. The narrowest idea conceivable is that of fetichism, where each object is an entity by itself, and, in addition, all the more common attributes are personified into independent beings. The other extreme is theism (than which a broader, grander idea of universe is impossible); it is this: God or Spirit is the only independent reality, and any other being or event is but a dependent "phase" or "state," or "product" of His activity. He is "the all in all." "In Him all things live and move and have their being." He is the Hebrew Jehovah, the "I AM," the self-existent and eternal One, who filleth immensity and inhabiteth eternity. The Ancient of Days, in terms of whose action Time itself is measured. Nature is related to God as "thought to the mind that thinks," as "music to the air that is in vibration," as "light to the ether." Nature is the "living garment of God," that is, the continued activity in which He manifests Himself. Between these extremes would be (1) The successive phases of Polytheism. These eventually lead to (2) Materialism, where science begins in its atomic form. The progress of science would make necessary at length (3) Dualism, or the doctrine that there are two independent entities, mind and matter; at this stage all the conflicts between science and religion arise. But this must, sooner or later, be resolved into the last and final position of philosophy, viz., (4) Theism as above explained.

The only attempt to get beyond theism that is possible would be to deny the existence of all independent beings, and leave nothing but "phases" or "states." The absurdity of such an attempt is so apparent that we hardly need ask what then could be meant by "dependent realities."

1. A body can act only where it is. Before it comes into being it can do nothing. After it passes out of being it can do nothing.

2. While a body exists, it can act only where it is, since the action is merely a phase or state or condition in which it exists, that is, an attribute of it.

3. Two atoms separated by a distance, therefore, cannot act and react on each other, since each is not *where* the other is.

4. Two atoms in spatial contact are still separated by a mathematical plane, i.e., each still preserves its identity, therefore the action of one is entirely uninfluenced by the other.

5. The same is true could the atoms occupy the same space at the same time if they still preserve their identity. To illustrate: Were time and space each conscious, the fact that time pervades all space would not enable its consciousness to be communicated to the latter, any more than God can communicate His omniscience to man.

6. It is, therefore, true that the atom cannot be an independent entity: but all atoms must be phases or states of some one self-existent, independent being. For the phases or states of one substance must mutually determine each other, and *this is the only condition conceivable on which there can be action and reaction.* For example, if we have but one ocean, then a wave here must produce a depression elsewhere and thus affect all other waves, but not if the oceans are entirely distinct. If we have *one* equation in algebra, to change its value of "x" will be to

375

affect the value of all the other terms, which would not be true if they belonged to entirely distinct equations.

7. It is, therefore, a contradiction to speak of more than one substance in *one* UNI-*verse*. The unity of the universe is the unity of the series of states and phases (actions) that mutually determine each other. Therefore, when we say the sun attracts the earth, we mean no more than when we say in grammar that *the subject of a sentence governs the predicate*. If words are separate independent entities they have no relation to each other at all. But words are expressions of thought, and thoughts are states of the consciousness of *one* mind, and so mutually determine each other. Therefore the above rule in grammar must not mean that the "subject word" governs the "predicate word," but that the mind that expresses itself thus in the subject is required by consistency to modify its utterance accordingly in the predicate. By the sun we understand that particular constant exercise of power by the universal substance. We say that it attracts the earth, meaning that this exertion of power requires a corresponding expression of energy through the entire series of actions of the same substance, the earth being simply one of them.

8. Now, what is this substance of which all atoms are phases? If we appeal to our sense-inferences we should affirm that it was material force. The senses give no evidence of the existence of anything else. But what is material force? Is it subject to the limitations of space as are our phenomena? Does it take time for the sun to attract the earth as it does for light to come to us from the north star? Can you limit force as you do phenomena, so that no two forces can occupy the same place at the same time?—When the disciples were in the upper room for the fear of the Jews, the door being shut and made fast, Christ was in their midst. How did He get in? But when we are in this room with all the doors and windows closed, is not Gravitation in our midst? And could we bury ourselves in the centre of the earth, should we escape it there? Has not this so-called "material force" very many of the essential attributes of *spirit*? Cannot we say of

Gravitation as the Hebrew Psalmist says of God: "Whither shall I flee from thy presence? If I ascend up into heaven, thou art there; if I make my bed in hell, behold, thou art there. If I take the wings of the morning, and dwell in the uttermost parts of the sea; even there shall thy hand lead me, and thy right hand shall hold me.

"If I say, Surely the darkness shall cover me; even the night shall be light about me. Yea, the darkness hideth not from thee; but the night shineth as the day; the darkness and the light are both alike to thee."

When the President preached his sermon from the text, "Are not two sparrows sold for a farthing? and one of them shall not fall on the ground without your Father," he began by saying, "Christ does not contradict science, but supplements it." Science says, "Not a sparrow falleth without Gravitation." Christ replies, "Quite true, O Science, but what do you understand by Gravitation? Now since you are silent and evidently do not know, I will tell you. *It is your Father.*" Spirit is the only substance in the universe, and material force is one mode of its manifestation and constant activity.

9. How can we know more of this spirit? We answer, that since the entire universe is dependent upon it, we who are a part of the universe, like it, live and move and have our being in it (Him). If we try to study its (His) mode of action outside ourselves we can only use the senses and obtain *phenomena*. But if we look within, we have the real noumenal spirit revealed in our own consciousness. And as the mathematician studies the very nature of space in the laboratory of his own room, and, having determined its geometry, says, these are the laws of space among the fixed stars, since space is one and the same there as here; so we may study the nature of spirit within the laboratory of our own consciousness and, having thus learned its noumenal laws, find that we have discovered the laws of action of the external world, since there can be but one and the same spirit there also. It is in this way we know *noumenally*

that the laws (not habits) of thought are also the laws of things. *Both thought and things must be phases of one and the same Universal Spirit.*

THE WILL AND THE SENTIMENTS

When we have once made up our mind to a certain course of life, the decision does not have to be continually emphasized by attention. A student does not affirm every morning as he begins the day that he has decided to pursue a liberal course of study and therefore must attend recitation; that he is going to be an attorney at law, therefore such lectures cannot be missed. Neither on a journey do we continually remind ourselves every time the train stops that we are going to New York and therefore must not get off at intermediate places. In some way the great decision of will sinks into unconsciousness, but it may be there as potent in controlling our life as though it were the object of our immediate thought.

Take so simple an act as reading the newspapers. Notice that each man selects those items which fall in with his choice of profession. The soldier in the regular army somehow catches the little paragraphs concerning the death or transference of even subordinate officers; the businessman finds the most conspicuous thing on the page is the market quotations; the student of literature is not aware that the paper contains any information about either of these facts, but is quick to notice the reviews of new books or magazine articles; while the politician will busy himself in reports of campaign oratory, never once thinking that he is at all different in his tastes from his neighbor the poet or the soldier. As the sun and the moon, when they are below the horizon, are potent to create the spring tides, so is a decision when it is below the threshold of consciousness.

All choices are not equally comprehensive; some require more, others fewer actions to realize them. We shall find a sort of military system of rank and authority in these apparently separate choices; let us examine them one by one.

First, governing purposes. What does a purpose govern? Clearly the means which are necessary for its fulfillment so far as the individual can control them. When a man has formed a purpose to take a foreign trip the matter does not end there, any more than did Caesar's crossing the Rubicon. In a small way the event is as truly an epoch-making one as that historic deed. The decision governs, governs with absolute necessity even the smallest affairs in its line.

It is common to look at life in an economic way and to consider each deed on its own merits. From that point of view it is affirmed that a man can reform from evil practices as easily as he can turn his hand over. But if we clearly realize what a decision means we shall see that the change of a very simple act may be possible only on condition that a very profound governing purpose can be removed, which would be harder to accomplish than to move a mountain into the sea.

It will be noticed that as the subordinate act is controlled by a governing purpose, this purpose itself has a superior military commander to whom or which it is so responsible that no freedom whatever can be processed by it.

It will be found that there are only two commanders-in-chief and that all our thoughtful actions report to one of these through whatever course of governing purposes. It will be perceived that these supreme choices cannot both govern action; if there is freedom it is here alone, it is solely in the decision whether righteousness or selfishness shall be our supreme aim in existence.

This is the doctrine of a new birth in Scripture. The claim is that no man ever does a deed without a motive. In a given instance the obvious motive is either itself a supreme motive and thus we have discovered the ultimate aim, or it is a secondary purpose, subordinate to some other choice which in turn is subordinate to a third, and so on till it comes to the ultimate. It is this act of sovereignty of the supreme choice which gives unity to our life. This is only another way of saying that all intelligence works backward; that a man must have an end in view in every intelligent action, and the end must sooner or later imply an ultimate end. The doctrine of the Scripture is that "Ye must be born again." That is, if the man's supreme choice is bad he cannot be changed by halves. There is no change that is radical that does not change the supreme choice.

Now let us notice some of the methods of reform. Let us take a dishonest man whose sole aim is money and let us put him into a community where he can do nothing unless he wins the confidence of the people, and let us suppose that the people give their confidence most readily to a religious man. In short, this is his only certainty of not being found out in his defalcations. Is this man truly religious because he joins the church and leads the Sunday school? Do you not need to go a little deeper and change his supreme choice? That is the doctrine of the Scripture when it says, "Ye must be born again." Christ puts it in another phrase when he says, "The tree is known by its fruits; men do not gather grapes of thorns, or figs of thistles." That is, make the tree good and the fruit will be good of itself; make the tree evil and the fruit will necessarily be evil. We interpret it to mean just the reverse, that a tree is made, not known, by its fruits. Therefore, we think if we can only get by change of environment certain external deeds that are wise, then we have reformed the individual. This method of reform is undoubtedly a negative change which prevents certain progress of evil habits, but does it make a person good? Is it possible by holding out punishment as an inducement to make a selfish man unselfish in heart? Is not his external deed, his external obedience, simply the surest way of realizing his selfishness? At Christmas time we are wont to relapse into the mythological age. We take a tree of any convenient form into our parlors out of the cold, and then proceed to wire on various adornments and fruits, and, thereby, to a child's fancy, transform its character into whatever we please.

It seems to me there is a great deal of Christmas-tree Christianity at the present time. We take men whose hearts are unchanged, and by external agencies we wire on a certain amount of reform, a certain number of prayer-meetings per week, a certain amount of courtesy, a certain amount of honesty, and then we publish statistics of the wonderful achievements which we have secured. Is this Christianity, or is it Pharisaism which polished the exterior of the sepulchre like to a palace, but within it was a sepulchre all the same?

When a decision has actually been made, when the Rubicon has been crossed, the world is not quite as it was before and we are different. Not merely in the fact that we have an end in view, but that certain feelings arise, certain estimates of value are put on things which could not otherwise have existed. These feelings or estimates are called in popular language sentiments. Our proposition is that a sentiment has strength in proportion to the importance of the choice. Let us illustrate: When a man has purchased a piece of ground, has invested in it his property, the knowledge that what happens to it affects him, produces a feeling of ownership which means, not merely that he owns it, but also that it owns him; he is no longer free as he was before. The plan of the city government for laying out new streets was a matter that he could pass by without any anxiety; now its action is not indifferent to him. If his influence, if his conduct of affairs, can change the direction of these streets, he finds it impossible to let the course of events go on without meddling, whereas a few months before he could easily have washed his hands of the whole matter and gone off on a vacation. Our property owns us, and we might just as well acknowledge our master. Such a knowledge produces the feeling called *sentiment*.

Now we can formulate our proposition. *An act of decision is an investment in the object or end chosen.* Henceforth life and welfare are bound up in it; we are not our own, but its. This produces the feeling of ownership in proportion to the amount of investment. Consciousness of ownership in turn is a bias of attention, and so controls our thinking that under the law of ideo-motor action our entire physical being will be different from what it would have been had the choice not been made.

Notice how, as time goes on, the countenance of the lawyer or physician differs from that of the day laborer or sailor, and yet these men, playmates in youth, then looked so nearly alike that strangers could hardly tell them apart.

We understand now the meaning of Scripture when it says, "Lay not up for yourselves treasures upon earth, where moth and rust doth corrupt, and where thieves break through and steal." This is the ordinary way of quoting this passage, and we are led to infer that the reason for avoiding earthly treasures is because they are liable to take wing and fly away. Therefore, for prudence' sake we should not risk too much. But such was not the meaning of Christ. He adds, "For where your treasure is, there your heart (your sentiment, your thought) will be also." The treasure is the end or object of our choice. If we live for earthly things, then these thoughts drive out all others and ideo-motor action makes us of the earth, earthy. But if we choose heavenly things, the divine ideal of manliness and honor, we become conscious of ownership by such a master, our endeavors are identified with such a cause, and thoughts on such subjects so fill our minds as to drive out everything base and mean and earthy; ideo-motor action stamps such a likeness upon our countenance. Therefore wherever and whatever your treasure (end) is, you yourself will be, and it is simply a choice of which world you will live in now.

Religion is a matter of character, of apperceptive mass, which is to the mind what physical health is to the body—only infinitely more, for this apperceptive mass determines what our known world shall be.

Sentiment, if sufficiently comprehensive, is called the heart. In the moral as opposed to the popular point of view a heartless individual is not necessarily an unsympathetic person. Nero was naturally so sympathetic that when he was first called upon as

382

emperor to sign a death warrant, he regretted that he had ever learned to write, since now by the stroke of his pen a human being would lose his life.

Sentiments can be changed, but never directly, only by changing our investment. It often happens that selfish individuals are greatly embarrassed by their strong bias and passion, and they would be willing to pay a large price for deliverance from these unpleasant consequences. That is, they want to retain their investment in self, but they would like to be free from the strength of sentiment, from the manners and habits which this produces. This is just as impossible as it is to have a line curved on the inside and straight on the outside. Sentiment and investment are inseparably connected.

The element of time introduces what seems to be a contradiction. The investment may reach its full strength at once, the sentiment is a gradual growth; it involves a realization of all that is implied in the investment, and this cannot be attained except by time. The result is that a man often approaches a paradoxical condition. Suppose that he has been narrow and selfish for forty years and then passes through a crisis in his life, barely escapes committing murder through accident, so that it is no credit to him. He becomes so alarmed that he determines to change, and really, squarely, makes a new supreme choice. The question is, Will he be free himself at once from the old sentiment and habits? May we not illustrate his condition by the railroad train? Call the choice the throttle valve and the sentiment the momentum of the train. In the case of a selfish man it will be momentum on the down grade. When the engineer reverses the throttle, does the train stop instantly, or reverse its momentum? No, a power has been introduced that will arrest the downward motion and will even get up a fair measure of speed in the opposite direction, but it will require sufficient time and be at the cost of a terrible struggle, a prodigious effort. Read the last verses of the seventh chapter of the Romans and see if this is not exactly the biography of Paul.

383

We maintained some time ago that freedom of will could be only in the supreme choice, that the different governing purposes are subordinate to this and to each other, analogous to the military commanders in an army. This leads to the question, Is it possible for us always to determine in advance the grade which a subordinate choice shall occupy? Can a man feel concerning the comrades whom he selects or the business to which he devotes himself that it will always have the relative importance that he now attributes to it, or is it a matter which depends upon the environment? This is a matter of great importance to many a man as he starts out in life; it is the turning-point of tragedy in many a character in literature. Let me illustrate my meaning. In the recent expeditions to Cuba old steamboats have been purchased and very valuable cargoes of arms and explosives have been shipped stealthily. The steamboat was worth comparatively little; the cargo, according to a Cuban's value of it was worth everything. Such is the ratio of the investment. But now suppose that a hurricane comes up and the ship begins to leak, and it is apparent that it cannot endure the weather; if the ship goes down the cargo is surely lost, and human life in addition. If the cargo can be thrown overboard life may be saved for another and more successful attempt and so the relative importance of ship and cargo have suddenly changed places; the latter is given up to save the ship.

Righteousness can never change. If a leader has allied himself with righteousness, there will never come a time when honor can be saved by going back on him. Therefore such relationships are constant; but if selfishness is the supreme choice, it is beyond the control of any individual to decide whether he will or not play traitor at some time in the future.

Our supreme choices determine our sentiments; our likes and dislikes, our constitutional feelings, may be akin, but if the sentiments differ these will be more or less inhibited and we shall drift apart. The old phrases, "A man is known by the company he keeps," and "Birds of a feather flock together," have for

384

their foundation this psychological principle—that ideas are intolerant of each other. Each idea demands our entire personality; or if some antagonistic thought presents itself to our mind it is resisted by every agency at our command, for we know that to listen to this thought is to drive out all others that are hostile to it. It is an act of self-preservation, for ideas have to struggle for existence just as truly as animals do, but our likes and dislikes determine the ideas. It follows, then, that when two persons with opposite sentiments associate together one of two things will take place: either the character of the one will be moulded to that of the other or they will find that they have nothing in common and so drift apart. What the one likes the other hates. Out of the abundance of the heart the mouth speaketh; the conversation of the one exasperates the other. How can they walk together? It will be seen that the strongest conflicts that have ever occurred have been due to the antagonism of ideas and feelings. Now we take one step in advance and say those whose supreme choice is selfishness are dependent solely on the environment. At any moment a high governing purpose may be subordinated to a lower, when the environment requires it. Therefore no permanent friendship is possible on this basis.

The point I want to emphasize is that in deciding the supreme choice we decide a thousand other things that have not yet been thought of; that we cannot depend on the future, for the environment will change; we can depend, therefore, solely on the right. He who builds on anything else builds his house upon the sand.

PLEASURE OR RIGHTEOUSNESS

In considering the motives and standards of the moral life two alternatives present themselves: either pleasure is the only motive or there is a spiritual nature and with it spiritual impulses; either expediency is the only standard or this spiritual nature and its constitution which involves justice and right is the ultimate measure of value.

Let us test Mr. Spencer's criticism of Carlyle's doctrine of blessedness by using the same argument on another subject. Suppose a being from the spirit world, one who had never lived a mortal life, should visit the earth on a tour of inspection. During his stay he comes to Amherst when the students are preparing for the fall athletic meet. He is as ignorant of athletics as some people are of the facts concerning the spiritual life. The peculiar conduct of the few in training soon arrests his attention. "What are they doing?" "Why do they move about in such queer ways?" he asks a bystander. "Practicing for the prize," is the reply. A week later he puts a similar question to another stranger and receives as answer, "They are working for the honor of the college." Time passes but no results appear to justify such an interpretation. At length he ventures to ask again, "What are these fellows doing?" "Trying to break a record," is the rejoinder.

Puzzled more than ever, he starts a series of reflections. "Running for a prize," but where and what is it? And why should a prize be given in an educational institution merely for running? "Breaking a record," none of them can run half as fast as a hound or a horse, or for that matter as certain Indians I saw two months ago. When express trains go ninety miles an hour and every one in a hurry travels by rail, what odds does it make whether one fellow can jog along a little faster or a little slower than his mate? Most people do not run at all; they are ashamed to, at least in public. By and by our celestial visitor concludes that he has been "gulled" by his informants. Remembering that on each occasion the athletes were scantily clothed, while the wind was cold and raw, he concludes that this whole performance is simply an effort to keep warm. He reasons thus: There are only three possible effects of running: either it must make the runner colder, or leave his temperature unchanged, or make him warmer. In every instance I have noticed that exercise has simply one effect: it creates heat in proportion to its severity and duration. Here, then, is the solution of the whole matter, for this is the only result the poor fellows always and everywhere attain.

Simply because happiness is clearly a result of all conduct called blessed by Carlyle, does it follow that it is the end in the sense of motive or object in view, or is it merely an accidental by-product, like perspiration in running for a prize? In short, does Spencer prove that blessedness is happiness, and thus that selfishness is the only end of action? Has he done more than to show that possibly happiness may incidentally be always caused by blessedness? Friction and wear are inevitably produced wherever machinery is used, yet what should we think of a scientist who, having demonstrated the necessity of this, should then claim to have proved that all machinery, even that in the most costly manufacturing plant, was constructed by men for that end and for no other?

Do not misunderstand me. I simply claim that Spencer, though he professes to have refuted Carlyle, yet really leaves the whole question just where he found it. This surely is not scholarly. The burden of proof is on him, since the other view is the prevailing one among the masses, and has been held by some of our ablest thinkers. It has ingrained itself into literature and life and cannot be extirpated without evidence sufficient to prove it false.

To get the exact problem before us, take the case of the Good Samaritan. Why has he, and not the priest and the Levite who passed by on the other side, been the theme of art and admiration for nearly two thousand years?

If you accept the happiness theory of Spencer, must you not admit that the Good Samaritan had a similar motive, and was not one bit unselfish? In relieving the man who had been robbed, he saved himself considerable annoyance and possibly several nights' sleep by getting the thought of the sufferer out of mind. Are you satisfied with this explanation? If so, ought you to admire the Samaritan rather than the priest and the Levite, who were less sentimental? This time he helped the right man, to be sure, but would he always?

387

But what is the motive that actuates Spencer's hero? By hypothesis it is not his own happiness. What, then, is it? You reply, "The happiness of others." Well, what is that to him? Why should he suffer that they may not suffer? No sane man acts without a motive; what motive do you give him for making the sacrifice? If it were nothing to him, if he were perfectly indifferent to their welfare, of course he would not go out of his way to help them.

I can find only two answers possible here. (1) The thought of others' enjoyment may be a source of greater pleasure to him than those pleasures which he has sacrificed; that is, his own highest happiness is not direct enjoyment, but induced through consciousness of the welfare of others; just as in a Ruhmkorff coil the direct current cannot be compared in intensity with the indirect. But this is the view, that he experiences a surplus of pleasure over pain, and therefore contradicts the facts admitted by Spencer. Such altruism would be no altruism at all, only shrewd selfishness. (2) That there is some other standard of conduct than pleasure. Christ, for instance, did not consider what He was to gain or lose by His career any more than an auditor of a bank, when he follows the multiplication table, is looking for a reward. He figures "five times five are twenty-five," not because that number will give him more happiness than either a higher or a lower one, but simply because it is the truth. Why may not truth (justice) be as ultimate for the will as for the intellect? If so, process not product would be our standard in ethics as truly as in mathematics.

But, you ask, is not a third position possible, viz., unselfishness, or the welfare of others? May not one bear a surplus of suffering just for the sake of benefiting the race, i.e., for the greatest good to the greatest number? Since so many advocate this view, it surely must be conceivable. Why, then, do you affirm that the above two motives are all that are possible?

We reply that if it is admitted that all our knowledge comes from experience, that a man born blind can know nothing of the artist's delight in color and a man born deaf can have no conception of the inspiration of music, then one is obliged to go a step farther and admit that all experience is originally subjective; therefore all knowledge of others is vicarious. I know and can know nothing concerning the life of my dearest friend save in terms of my own inner life, and what is true of man is true of my knowledge of God. "With the pure thou wilt show thyself pure, and with the froward thou wilt show thyself froward." "Blessed are the pure in heart, for they shall see God." It follows, then, that what is right for self must be judged the ideal life for all others under the same conditions. If my life would be debased if devoted supremely to my own highest happiness, how can I strive to bring about that result in my neighbors? Would I degrade them to a level I myself avoid? Either I must abstain from all judgment concerning others or I must believe that the processes that make me unworthy cannot ennoble them. This is the supreme point; we may not like this limitation, but, fret about it as much as we will, how can we escape it? To recur to Kant's illustration, "As the dove can never fly beyond the atmosphere which alone makes flight at all possible," so a finite being who is not creative, but in the highest flights of his imagination can only recombine data gained by experience, can never know or guess of another life as governed by different laws than his own. Wherever we seem to accomplish such a result we have simply been the slaves of abstraction. In fairy stories we take certain attributes from our own experience, and, neglecting all others, get queer products. But make your thought concrete, remove the abstraction and incompleteness of your fairyland, and its contradictions and absurdities become apparent. Actual life is always concrete, and speaking of that alone our proposition holds, viz., there can be no such thing as altruism in the sense that one obliterates himself solely for the happiness of others, or that he is willing to be damned (not merely to suffer unjustly but to be damned justly) for the glory of God. If it is noble to obliterate self, then it is noble to do what we can

389

to help others to obliterate, not to magnify, themselves and their happiness. If we ought to do that which can justly be damned, we must have the same ideal for God, and must strive not for His glory but for His damnation. Either this conclusion or you must prove that all our knowledge is not vicarious. Either there is no science at all, either we are absolutely agnostic concerning God and man, or what is right for one is right for all given the same conditions.

When Spencer concedes that an individual is justified in choosing a surplus of suffering under certain conditions, he concedes that happiness is not an end, but a by-product, i.e., gives up his whole case. *Falsus in uno, falsus in omnibus* is the scientific standard of inductive reasoning. To this position there is a possible objection, viz., it is not happiness itself, but the striving for one's own happiness, that is, selfishness, that debases a man. Therefore, in working for another's welfare it is not that other's enjoyment, but your own disinterested spirit of self-sacrifice, that gives nobility to your character. Consequently by making another happy you are not degrading him, since you are not compelling him to strive for his own happiness, that is be selfish. All the while he may be inspired with the same altruism that animates you.

To this objection we reply, that it abandons the whole principle of altruism, for it makes self and not another the centre of one's horizon. The real ultimate end of action, on this basis, is one's own character. The fact that this character happens to cause happiness to others is a mere accident. Happiness is a by-product instead of the motive power. Indeed, there is not a trace of evidence to show that such character will always produce such a result. If self-sacrifice brings pain to yourself, why may it not likewise bring pain to your friends? Did the self-sacrifice of Christ bring joy to His disciples or to His mother? If the whole matter had ended as human lives must end under like conditions, would it ever have brought joy to the world?

This is a commercial age, and mere quantity is everything to some minds. "Greatest good to the greatest number" implies to them that mere numbers introduce some new factor into the problem of conduct. What answer can be made to these persons? —There can be no doubt of their sincerity. It is true that in some spheres difference in degree or mere magnitude makes a difference of kind in results attained. For instance: under fourteen vibrations a second the ear detects only separate noises, but above that number we may get a musical note. At a given temperature plants grow and blossom; diminish the heat sufficiently and they are killed by frost. It is one thing to talk with an individual acquaintance, but quite another to address a large audience. A chemist is satisfied with a small bottle of sea water for analysis, since he thereby determines the composition of the ocean itself. But if the whole of Neptune's kingdom were put into bottles, and the Wandering Jew should live long enough to examine each one singly, he would have seen no ocean, no ebb and flow of tides, no dashing of breakers, no earthquake waves. Mere quantity is a vital matter. This is especially true in monetary affairs, and it is not strange that a commercial age jumps to the conclusion that it is everything in ethics. But if you look not at results, but at processes, the case is different. Tyndall tells us that "where law is concerned there is no great and no small. The force that moulds the tear rounds the planet." Gravity can be tested as truly by the pendulum as by a whole heaven full of stars. In ethics we are concerned with processes.

How, then, can mere numbers figure in determining the right process of moral conduct? Law simply states how a thing acts; the cause of its action is in its own constitution: till this is changed the law cannot vary. Numbers in society do change the conditions under which we act, and give us a wider opportunity; they do not change the constitution of the actor. The man who lives in the city may have a higher grade of development than one who lives in the country, but this simply makes actual what was potential in his nature all the time. Looking not at products but at processes, good to one is good to and for all; the greatest

391

good to one is the greatest good, the only ultimate good, to every one, not simply to the majority.

It is a mistake to affirm that the happiness of the community is so much greater than that of individuals, that they should, therefore, be sacrificed for the good of the whole. There is no such thing as happiness of the community. The happiness of one person does not fuse with that of ten thousand others to make an aggregate, any more than their personalities fuse to constitute a *Zeitgeist*. Springs of water may mingle their overflow and make a brook, brooks may empty into each other and produce a river, then all rivers flow into the ocean and become part of one vast aggregate of waters; but this never happens in the personal life of individuals. The community, as the term is here used, is composed of individuals in relationship, therefore the happiness of the whole can never be greater in degree than the happiness of the most favored individual therein.

Now that we are on the subject of altruism, I must say a word as to its essential immorality (when taken in the sense of making one's self "merely a means" to others' happiness). The term surprises you, but it is not a whit too strong. If it is possible to put self and its welfare completely out of sight in order to labor solely for others, it will be equally possible to put out of sight self and its responsibilities and obligations. Unless self is the centre of one's horizon and is degraded by wrong doing and ennobled by right doing, there is nothing to tie to, nothing to bind the person to the path of duty. Life becomes impersonal, *merely a means to an end, and never an end in itself;* hence a mere thing to be used or abused by others. Now this is exactly the principal of bossism.

You know what this self-abnegation has meant in religious history. Freedom of scientific thought, right of private interpretation of Scripture, conscience, friendships the most sacred, all have been offered up at the command of the Church.

Further, it is not commonly supposed that altruism is practically absurd; but a moment's thought will make this appear.

Just test the principle by making it universal. Nothing in science is a law unless it holds in all cases under the same conditions. Therefore, suppose the altruistic millennium to have actually been reached, and that every one in the world is striving for the complete abnegation of self in the attempt to work for others. Each is then striving to bestow on his neighbor just what that neighbor is most unwilling to receive.

Here, then, is our problem clearly before us. Altruism in the ordinary meaning of the term is a mere abstraction as mythological as fairyland. Only two supreme choices are conceivable when we think concretely. Either one must be supremely selfish, make his own happiness the end of his existence and sacrifice temporary advantages for others' welfare only as a way of getting greater pleasure or of avoiding something unpleasant, or he must drop out happiness altogether as an end, not merely his own, but that of others and even of the race. It may be a means, a by-product, just as truly as health or wealth; therefore it may be even a duty to strive for it when conditions make it an effective means. Happiness means anabolism of nerve tissue. . . . It behooves a young man to do his best to store up nerve energy as a capitalist lays up cash. But it must always be valued at its true worth, and one cannot be too careful to avoid the mistake of the miser who makes the means the end.

Which of these two ends is the right one, that is, the one that squares with our spiritual nature? If man were merely a creature of brain paths, all would concede the proposition we affirmed in the Fall term. But since there is some thought not a function of the brain, what is true for this sphere? We may get strong though not conclusive evidence on this problem if we note the standard of criticism in literature and history. What does admiration for great men mean? Why has the world honored Christ, Socrates, Paul, Luther, Lincoln? Is it because they were shrewder than others and made investments that returned larger dividends in personal happiness than, for instance, did Judas or Nero? Is a man great in proportion to what he gets out of life? If Benedict

Arnold had won, would the world have admired him and have execrated the name of Washington? Or does history judge a man, as art estimates a statue, on his own merit? The standard is not the amount of fun he enjoys, but the kind of character he is, i.e., whether his life squares with the laws of his spiritual being. When you criticise a person who lived so long ago that you can eliminate the personal equation, is not your one question simply this: Was he true to his truest self, to the divine nature of which he was a partaker, or did he prostitute this gift to action along the lines of least resistance? If this is the standard by which you judge others, it is surely the ideal of your own life, for you know nothing about others save in terms of yourself. No man can have two sets of values, one for self, the other for historic characters, if he is thinking of processes instead of products. Does the world in its sober moments ever admire anything that will not stand the test of truth? Men are dazzled by success. But take the cases of honor bestowed on the boss, on the tyrant like Napoleon, on the train robber like Jesse James: Is it the evil deed that is worshipped, or the courage, persistence, self-control, patience, endurance, will power, independence, or brilliant intellectual ability revealed in the deed under such dangerous conditions, that inspires enthusiasm? Are not these in themselves all noble qualities, just what every man ought to aspire to? Men worship power because it is divine. Even when wrongly used it is still a divine gift that has been debased.

The main thing in life is the right impulsive action, the agreeableness is a by-product. Wherever this order is reversed, disappointment must follow. Happiness is not to be gained by seeking it. He that will have his life, i.e., make it an end, shall lose it, but he that will lose his life rightly shall find it, and with it the by-product in question. Very early in the development of the animal kingdom pleasure and its opposite had a reflex influence on the impulse, either intensifying or inhibiting it. Then in time individuals who liked injurious experiences destroyed themselves. Evolution thus began a weeding-out process, and secured that to a considerable extent pleasure should be identified with anabolism of the nervous system, and unpleasantness with katabolism. Affections then became more and more a *means* of self-preservation. Now by following their likes and dislikes the higher animals, which have no science and which would miserably perish at once if they had to rely on cognition, live for a longer or shorter period a very complex life.

Bear in mind that this is not because there is any virtue in pleasure *per se*. It does not teach us that if we follow our own highest happiness we shall come out all right; rather, probably, just the reverse. The standard of evolution is not the greatest good to the greatest number, but only to the few fittest. A race can preserve its position only by the same processes by which it evolved; suspend these and there will be speedy reversion to a lower level. The struggle for existence must be sharp enough to secure that those who have advantageous qualities shall continually forge ahead, while the masses are forced to fall behind. Were there no spiritual nature to man, he would necessarily make his own happiness his end, and by this agency evolution would secure—if he happened to belong to the elect, for whom accidental variation had done so much—that he would work out his own perfection, and through heredity the progress of the species. But if, as would be most likely in any given case, he belonged to the great majority, he would in this way shorten his life and thus help purify the race of characteristics that ought not to be perpetuated. For the unfortunate there would be no hope: "The soul that sinneth, it shall die." No regeneration of the individual is possible. To evolution, expediency means not the expediency of the average individual, nor of the masses, but of the few fittest and of the future race.

But man has a spiritual nature and with it spiritual impulses. These are original and ultimate. They require certain cognitions as the condition essential to their activity, as truly as the vital force in plants must have rain and sunlight and soil in order to

395

produce growth and a harvest. But, given the essential condition, the spiritual impulses are self-active and self-directed. There is no "why" or "because" that can explain them, since they are constitutional. They are self-directed towards the realization of all that is potential in that spiritual nature. Since truth or justice to us are simply that which squares with this spiritual constitution, we shorten up the phraseology and say: The end of these impulses is "right for right's sake." Undoubtedly such action will often produce happiness, but this is a by-product, not a motive. It then becomes possible for science to supplant evolution in perfecting the race. It is no longer necessary to have the masses perish in order that the few fittest may survive, because the individual may be regenerated. If his likes and dislikes are wrong, he may resist them and restrain himself. Not selfishness, but service, becomes the process of the moral life. The law, "A can determine himself only through B," brings the social order into a condition of peace and interdependence instead of war and independence. Utilitarianism is the order of Darwinian evolution; justice and mercy are the order of moral evolution. Brain paths are on the side of the former. Of course it is not easy to change a point of view when the whole stress of physical heredity is against the spiritual life. But man is made in the image of God as truly as in the image of the animals, and he thus inherits the divine nature with all its possibilities. It is for him to decide which set of impulses shall control his career.

It is the general law of all mental and spiritual life that the subject does not determine himself directly but only through his objects; in practical life a man becomes great, not by remaining shut up in himself, but by doing a great work. If we apply this to the universe it would seem to require that God can be perfect only if the universe is so. The position that this is a spiritual universe encounters the difficulty of the existence of evil. Hence it is necessary to consider what is involved in the nature of moral agents and what are the conditions of an evolution of religion and of a spiritual development. This leads to a study of the general principles of sovereignty and its treatment of wrong doing.

AUTHORITY AND PUNISHMENT

(Professor Garman it is believed considered his treatment of these topics as among his most important contributions.)

In studying punishment we are studying the principle of authority, just as Newton studied the apple and found the laws of science.

Our first proposition is that all pain is not punishment. If the proper authority should inflict punishment on the righteous man, it would not be punishment; it would be injustice. Suffering is a means and not an end.

Coming now to the theories of punishment, we have a phrase that a person "paid the debt," or that he "ought to have suffered." Taken literally what does it mean? If you pay the debt, there has been an exchange. Some of the consequences may be undone, and some may not. But if the idea is to right a wrong which has been committed, it is useless, because the wrong, considered as a moral deed, cannot be undone. So (1) punishment is not to right a wrong. Two wrongs can never make a right. Why should this individual be made to suffer because he has made others suffer?

(2) Is punishment to reform? Then the criminal by his crime would put the state under obligation to do the best for his health, and this might be to send him to Europe and give him an education. A poor man who hadn't had an education might commit a crime and make the state educate him.

(3) Is punishment to prevent a man from doing a deed again? We kill a man for committing a murder; then why didn't we kill him before he committed the murder? Cannot you go down into the slums of New York and pick out the men who would commit murder if they had the chance? . . . Now who is there in the whole crowd that, under temptation enough, wouldn't be a

dangerous person to have around? When the woman taken in adultery was brought to Jesus, He said, "He that is without sin among you, let him first cast a stone at her." And then they began to think that if they were enough tempted they wouldn't be quite safe, and they skulked out, from the greatest to the least. And yet we hear over and over again that punishment is to protect the state. That may be an effect of it, as the growing of the grass is an effect of the shining of the sun. We are after the *nature* of punishment now.

(4) May not punishment be to prevent *others* from committing crime? We will make an example of the criminal. Once in English history a judge sentenced a man for stealing sheep. The judge said: "You are not punished because *you* steal sheep, but in order that sheep may not be stolen." The reply was, "What's that to me, sir?" Gentlemen, where you make one suffer for the wrong of another, do you call that punishment or martyrdom? Is that justice or injustice? The criminal may say: If others were not so frail and so weak, I should not have to suffer. It may be *expedient*. So stealing works admirably sometimes. In this case there is no ethics to it. But *then* you are really claiming that this whole system of government is wrong through and through; that might makes right. And when you come to the question of might, you can see that the individual has powers that society has not, e.g., the individual can hide himself, society cannot.

You say you have got to have punishment, or the state will go to smash. But is it *right?* If we hold that might is right, then we are Nihilists. Similarly, God's authority has generally been taken on the principle that might makes right, but, if it does with God, it does with us. If we are Nihilists, let us say so right out.

What, then, is authority? Stating it first in the most general form, we say authority is nothing more nor less than the constitutional reaction on the individual by the universe. The action of nature is always to reward when we live in harmony with it, and to punish us when we do not. The motion of my hand when I bring it down on the table is a deed which is a resultant of my own action on the one side and all the forces in the universe on the other. This is constitutional. But if you and I exist in the universe, we are parts of the universe, and it is not "We ought to act on the universe," but "We do act on the universe." Leave out the question of divine sovereignty now, and consider your own. My proposition is that we belong to the same universe; not that we ought to, but that we do.

But, you object, action and reaction are merely constitutional not ethical. I reply: Our action on the universe doesn't take place without knowledge. Our physical bodies act without knowledge. But you do not reply to me without knowing something. The physical reacts automatically and immediately, but the mental requires time; there must be thought. The physical action is always "right"—in a physical sense of the term.

But human action is liable to mistake. There is in mere physical reaction no ethical foundation for the state, no ethical basis for authority. There is no ethics in my mere existence. The ethics begins with the problem as to *how* I shall act. The question of how you shall use this authority is a question of ethics. Our proposition is that an individual shall do nothing that is not a deed of spiritual health and life. And secondly, every individual must do a deed when any one else does a deed. See how this holds.

Take a policeman. Suppose I am injuring you. He sees me, but will not do anything. But he then lets me do it and becomes an accomplice. If he says, "I am not going to meddle with that fight," by that very statement he allows it to go on. It is impossible for him to avoid doing something, but the question is, What shall he do. So we see there is always reaction. When I do a deed, the entire universe reacts. Punishment is reaction in the line of resistance. Rewarding is in the line of assistance.

But if the Universe reacts in the line of resistance, what becomes of the independent entity? If he should actually resist us through and through where should we be? James says in the lesson assigned for today that there is no hell like living in the world and being unrecognized; that is, being in the universe and not being reacted upon. If we couldn't appropriate anything in the universe, where should we be? Thus "the wages of sin is death." The logical outcome is instant annihilation. Resistance ends in annihilation. That means annihilation of the spirit. But do not introduce the question of future punishment here.

Can transgressions be forgiven? There are various interpretations of forgiveness. The empirical effect is the same,—the penalty is not inflected. So, is it possible for the Divine Being to react in the line of resistance and yet do so without inflicting the punishment? It is not a question of avoiding the reaction. If the reaction is in the line of resistance and at the same time brings misfortune on the sinner, he does not have any more chance.

If forgiveness is possible, then God is just while He justifies. "Just" means that He reacts in the line of full resistance and yet remits the penalty. If this is possible, there may be forgiveness of sins; if not, there can be none. There must be resistance. The whole question is whether or not it is possible to resist the sinner without killing him. If not, there is no chance for his salvation, because the element of time does not enter into Divine Justice as it does into human. When the Divine Being reacts, it is an event in history. Historically considered the above is the atonement.

Atonement means (a) sovereignty of God, e.g., since He is omniscient He must assist the right and resist the wrong, or aid and abet.

(b) Herein we discover the power of Christianity. Stoicism holds out a high ideal, but what does it accomplish? Why toil? Ask yourself. If a lesson is assigned to the class, but they are informed that there will be no recitation, no approval if they are faithful, no disapproval if they neglect it, I ask you whether it is as easy to do scholarly work as when your work is sure to be reviewed and judged? Why have intercollegiate debates? You might work up the subject of labor unions by yourself and thoroughly master it. If you did you would get the discipline.

How many students in college are likely to do it? The same of commencement orations. Your nature demands sovereignty. You feel the need of it; you cannot do without it. Modern religion does not offer sovereignty and see its weakness. Christianity asserts it. See its power even in the decaying civilization of Rome. See the steadfastness of the early Christians under fire. What is it due to?

(c) Atonement means justice. What is justice? Not the prevention of evil. That is impossible unless you prevent the good also, since man must be free to do either if he is to be man. But justice is aiding the right and resisting the wrong, every time.

Then, what, finally is authority? It is the realization of the state. And what is the state? The state is the condition of action and reaction between all parts of the universe, which is due because they are *creatures*, i.e., dependent entities. How does it realize itself? Through ethics; that is the process, the *how*. If every person does wrong, there is no reason why I should do wrong. If they do right and I do right, that is rewarding. If they do wrong and I do right, that is in the line of punishment.

Do we need authority? The only condition on which I can become moral is that my fellow-man be moral.

No man can know for me; no man can feel for me. I must know for myself. Otherwise, what marvelous students we should have here in college, for the faculty are certainly as interested and faithful as possible in the class room. Now, could God create an individual with a completely developed intelligence and character? If He did, that character would not be the man's own. So development is absolutely necessary to character. Then for the fulfillment of the divine plan we certainly need authority. Suppose the parent lets the child do just as it pleases; then the peace of that household is very much disturbed. And if different individuals are left to do as they please in the universe, so will the peace of this universal household be disturbed.

Spirit *must* act in harmony with the nature of the Universal. The only question is whether it acts in harmony, considering all the questions or only a part. Emerson says, "The entire aim of the sinful man is abstraction." As in the case of the licentious man, he doesn't think of his deeds in relation to the whole universe. "What God hath joined together, let no man put asunder." All sin is an attempt to divorce. Animals cannot sin because they have no self-consciousness. But while having self-consciousness, if we recognize only our animal nature, we sin, we abstract.

We recognize this in our social relations. If we deal with a man simply as a laborer, we treat him as a part, we abstract. This is largely the trouble with our social questions,—we deal with men only on business relations. But they are something more than business men. So we abstract, and become antagonized by the rest of nature.

A General Formula of All Mental and Spiritual Life

It is a general law of all mental life that consciousness of self is possible only through consciousness of objects. A similar law holds in moral life and the social order. We may state this in the formula, A determines himself never directly, but always through B, i.e., a man determines his character and personality by the attitude and relations he assumes towards his world of nature and persons.

If A determines himself through B, then there are only four possible spheres of life for A, due to the four possible conditions of B, since A's life will be limited to the change in B:

1. B may be strong and do right.
2. B may be strong and do wrong.
3. B may be weak and do right.
4. B may be weak and do wrong.

Every phase of life comes in here.

(1) is the sphere of business, where action and reaction should be equal; (2) is the sphere of punishment, where the action must take the form of *resistance* to the wrongdoer; (3) is the sphere of charity, where the strong must help the weak; (4) is the sphere for the atonement, where the strong must resist by

402

assistance. Under these four heads come nearly all the questions of the later part of the course.

SOVEREIGNTY FROM THE STANDPOINT OF THEISM

The common view makes the individual first and relationship secondary. Of course this is so. How could there be a relationship unless there were some things to be related? No relationship is necessary; surely not that involved in sovereignty. If you hold these premises, only one motive can influence the individual, and that is expediency. Liberty, equality, fraternity are simply forms of courtesy; they mean nothing. When it comes to the test, self-preference is the ultimate motive. If two men are on a spar drowning, one will push the other off, and that one will be the stronger. Might makes right. There is, therefore, no mean between anarchy and tyranny. The successful man is the tyrant, the underdog in the fight is the anarchist. This is the last word on all governmental and social problems the moment you tell the truth. It is not expedient to do so always. Might includes trick and diplomacy and shrewdness, yes, and lying too, quite as much as physical power.

The theistic view is a startling paradox. It affirms that the relationship is first and that the individual is its product. This is all of the subject the common man will care to know. Such a view is moonshine, a mere theory. Wit is a discoverer of incongruities of a certain type, and nothing is more incongruous with the common view than this doctrine. From the days of Plato to the present time it has been a fair target for ridicule. But let us look at the facts. If man is a dependent being, his relationship to God is that which gives him existence. Can a wave continue if it leaves the water? Can a thought exist apart from the person who thinks it? Secondly, if all other things are dependent on God, they necessarily determine each other. What the Divine Being already has done conditions Him in His next act. Illustrate by a republican government. If the people have

403

formed a constitution, they are limited by it. If they have elected a republican President, that determines the administration for the next four years. If they give judicial power to the Supreme Court, they cannot at the same time bestow it on Congress and the President. Then the court would mean nothing. The veto power of the President is determined by the form of government. Destroy the republic, and substitute despotism on the one hand or anarchy on the other, and where is the veto power? The several parts of government do not first exist and then come together to make a whole called democracy, but the conception of the whole is in the minds of the people first, and their attempt to realize it creates subordinate parts. If God is a person, His intelligence works backwards as truly as ours. He has a plan for the whole, a design, and the particular individuals He creates are called into being by the demands of that plan. They will exist only so long as they are necessary to that plan, and when they serve it no longer they will cease to be. This is the universal law of intelligence. You hire a janitor, or a porter, or a cook, or a guide only when and so long as these are required for you to carry out your schemes, and when they have done their work their function ceases. But this is only saying that the relationship is first and the office that a person holds is its product. Now let us test the case and see if facts do not verify this illustration. Take our physical life. Does a man first exist and then come into certain relationships? Take those of the physical world, e.g., that of gravitation. Does a man at a definite time in his life conclude to submit himself to this particular law, or must gravitation be first, in order for the man to exist at all? Suspend gravitation for a moment and what would happen to him? Not a particle of atmosphere would enter his lungs, all the finer blood-vessels would instantly burst when the pressure was removed, and the rotation of the earth would whirl him off in a tangent into empty space at the rate of a thousand miles an hour. Take those relationships that are expressed by chemical affinity. Suspend these and what would become of nutrition, and how long would a man exist if there were no chemical action at all in his physical frame? Suspend the law of cause and effect and what could man do for himself? When he put out his foot to walk the ground would offer no resistance. When he sat down the chair would give him no support. When he turned his eyes towards the sun it would give him no sensations of sight. Neither could he have hearing, touch, taste, or smell. When we say that these relationships are first we mean logically rather than chronologically. Chronologically they are simultaneous, as cause and effect always are. If a cause ceased to exist before the effect came into being, then this would be an event without a cause.

Let us discuss mental relations. Most people think that personality is a unity, just like gold; that one is passively personal, therefore one could act as a personal being even if everything else in the world were annihilated. But this is superficial. Personality is always an achievement, not gained once for all, but requiring infinite repetition. A personal being is simply a conscious being whose consciousness has reached the grade in what it knows itself. But power reveals itself only in work done. If the self did nothing, it could not be self-conscious. The grade of self-consciousness is determined, then, by the amount the self does, not once for all, way back in the past, but continually. Hence our personality is fluctuating with our activity. When an orator outdoes himself he rises to a very high level of personality; when he fails, he sinks pretty low in his own estimation. Now there are only three kinds of activity possible: knowing or thinking, feeling, and willing. Let us take thinking, since we cannot very well will or feel until we know. You cannot think without thinking about something, either objects about you or ideas that you originate. If you have no objects either in nature or in imagination, then you have no thought, no personality. This is what is meant by the statement, "Consciousness of subject is possible only through consciousness of object." One step more. Imagination is not really creative. A blind man cannot create color; a man born deaf cannot create sound. Unless in childhood nature actually existed and related herself to us in a causal way, producing sensations in us as our earliest objects, we never could have begun the personal life. Here we are, then. Relationship is logically first and personality is its product. A child born deaf, dumb, and blind, without taste, smell, or touch, would never become personal.

But you must go farther than this. So far we have touched only the animal existence. If a child is not instructed by his parents and those about him, if he were left alone on an island and by some accident succeeded in maintaining a physical life, he would become insane, not personal. Shepherds who are alone with their flocks for an indefinite period suffer degeneration. It is the contact of mind with mind that is the only condition of a human life. This is only saying that the perfection of the subject depends upon the perfection of its objects. Our social relations, including family relations, are first, and sanity is the product. We consider it a personal loss when our friends die; it takes away just so much of our personality. Here, then, is the great fact concerning our existence. In no instance can we free ourselves from the law that the relationship is first and we are the product, and our life continues only so long as the relationship continues. This is the formula: A determines B and B determines A; that is, A never determines himself directly, but only through B. If you walk, you act upon the ground, it reacts, giving you support, and you move forward. If you row, you act upon the water, and only when it reacts does your boat move. When you think, mind must act upon the brain, and only when the brain reacts upon the mind is there a continuation of consciousness. That is the reason we are here in college. We cannot educate ourselves. We are inspired and lifted up by our contact with each other. It will be seen, then, that the whole is very different from an aggregation of parts. The civil compact theory affirms that because one man has no prerogative over another, society can have no prerogative over the individual, because society is made up of individuals and the whole cannot be greater than the sum of the parts. Nothing is more ridiculous than this system. The workmen who handled every brick at the brickyard which went into the structure of the new laboratory have had nothing whatever to do with the laboratory itself. The laboratory is not a pile of bricks, but those bricks in a particular relationship; you may take out every brick and substitute an entirely different individual, and if you preserve just this relationship you have exactly the same laboratory. There is not a student here in college who was here ten years ago, and not all of the faculty are the same, yet it is the same college. There is not a man alive now who existed when the Constitution of the United States was first adopted, and yet this is the same nation. Society is not composed of individuals; society is a relationship by virtue of which individuals come into existence and without which they would have no being as personal.

We may now ask: What is this relationship which constitutes sovereignty, and how is it that on our new premises sovereignty does not de-personalize the individual? Sovereignty is a particular relationship which is not created by man and which he cannot divest himself of. By virtue of this relationship only does he become personal. Let us see if we can find this particular relationship. Suppose an ocean liner trying to break its record. When passing the Newfoundland banks it discovers a shipwrecked sailor afloat on a spar half a mile off. All eyes see him and bring him to the notice of the captain. What of it? An interesting sight, no doubt, gives them something to talk about and breaks up the tedium of the voyage. That sailor is a foreigner. What do people on that steamer care for him or his life? And yet their knowledge of his situation makes it impossible for them to go on their way and leave him there without becoming murderers. Here is the simple law. Man is so constituted that there is a peculiar relationship between his intellect and his will, and when he knows, he is obliged to act. *How* he acts is decided by the will if it is free, but the will cannot decide whether it will act or not under such conditions as are now present. That ship captain has got to stop his vessel, lose his record, and save that sailor or be a murderer. He may care as little as he pleases for the sailor, but if he cares for his own moral character he will stop that ship. This is not a matter of his choosing. He abominates the whole predicament. But there he is, and he has only one question before him, How will he act? Take another case. A policeman standing on the corner of a street in a rough part of a city sees a scoundrel assault a woman who makes desperate resistance. The moment the policeman knows what is going on, he, too, must act. If he stands there and renders no assistance, he is an accomplice of the criminal, aiding and abetting him in his crime, that is, he too, becomes criminal. He may regret extremely the necessity that is upon him, but he cannot escape by doing nothing. In some way he must act, and the only question is, How. If the ship captain or the policeman had not known what was going on, the dilemma would not have arisen, but the moment knowledge comes, sovereignty begins. We may see this more clearly in the case of the assassination of Lincoln. When Booth had made his escape any man who recognized him and failed to report him was considered as his accomplice, aiding and abetting Booth and resisting the government. Such an accomplice was liable to the extreme penalty of the law. See how embarrassing was the position. If a person had not recognized him, had not known anything about the crime, there would have been no occasion for action. But when circumstances placed the individual where he had the knowledge, then he entered into a new life; either he became a criminal himself or he became an avenger of the martyred President. No longer could he be inactive. This is the penalty he pays for being personal. To be personal is to be sovereign. When circumstances conspire to bring a matter in the sphere of our knowledge, then we have to interfere, either in the line of aiding and abetting or in that of resisting. This is the only sovereignty that can exist consistently with personality. The question of how we shall aid or how we shall resist is wholly a question of means. We may do it in an

408

organized form and then we shall have government, or we may do so without a form of organization and then we have simply society, but in both cases we have sovereignty.

Sovereignty, we may say, then, is the interference of one individual with the affairs of another individual, either in the line of resisting or in that of assisting. You will see that it does not depend upon any compact any more than the attraction of the earth by the sun depends upon compact. You see that it is only a form of that relationship of cause and effect by virtue of which personal life is possible. Sovereignty simply postulates that the mind is a cause in the universe as truly as matter, the only difference being, matter can work automatically, without intelligence, mind can work only when it is intelligent. Matter can act only one way, that is, it is fated. Mind can work either rightly or wrongly if you have free will. But when man does wrong he interferes with his fellow-man and exercises sovereignty as truly as when he does right, unless you please to define sovereignty as right interference, and tyranny as wrong interference. It seems to be better, however, to speak of sovereignty as interference. Human sovereignty has limits, but they are simply limits of knowledge and ability. Our ability is much more limited than our knowledge. Many things which we know about we have not strength enough to remedy; hence we aid and abet them unwillingly. Other things we are not skillful enough to remedy, but should do greater evil if we attempted it. The ordinary man is not skillful enough to perform an operation upon appendicitis; and if, on a hunting tour, he is with his friend who is taken ill in this way, he would have to allow him to die a natural death rather than to torture him to death by a bungling operation. These are simply the limitations of finiteness. They do not exist with God, who is the ideal sovereign, and who cannot know human deeds without interfering either in the line of aiding or in that of resisting them.

We have now a sixth theory for punishment. Why do we punish the criminal? The reply is, We never punish the deed but only the doer. We punish only when we cannot help acting, when we are obliged to assist or resist the criminal. Punishment is the resistance of the wrongdoer. Assistance to the right doer is the reward. Now why do we punish? Not for the sake of vengeance, or reformation, or retribution, or prevention in the historic meaning of that word, but simply for our own sake. If we are in such circumstances that we must act, we will act rightly, whether others do or not. Suppose a woman is assaulted by a tramp; why would she resist him? Why—because she must either resist or assist. He is strong and she is weak; her resistance may not be effectual as far as the crime is concerned, but it will be so far as her character is concerned. President Seelye was quite fond of a quotation from Goethe, "Man may treat woman shamefully, but he can never make her ashamed." That is the secret of all punishment. If others do wrong there is no reason why we should when we are forced to act. The Spartans at Thermopylae won the admiration of history, not because their defense was successful, but because they died game. They would do nothing to aid the invaders of their own land. Now the deepest insight of human nature recognizes the truth of this position. When a person is insulted by another without resenting the insult, we have no respect for him whatever; if he consents to that insult he then insults himself too. How he is to resent it is not the proper question, but he must resent it in some way or aid and abet and thus insult himself; this everyone sees. Here is the dignity and grandeur of life, and man can never be placed in any circumstances where he cannot be manly to the full measure of his intelligence. Even the newsboy has no respect for his mates when they fail to insist upon their honor by resenting degrading treatment from another. This is punishment; because when you are forced to act, if you act rightly while the person on whom you act is acting wrongly, there will be a collision, and pain inflicted as a result of sovereignty. But you see that it is not vicarious. Others indeed may take warning and not collide with us. But that is a by-product. If there was only one transgressor in the universe and we were so situated that we could not avoid assisting or resisting him, we should be under just as much obligation to resist as though every one were an evil doer. Our sole motive, if righteous, would be, not to cause him to suffer but to prevent becoming criminal ourselves. The converse is true, also. Why do we reward good conduct? Why did the whole world honor Queen Victoria at her death? Not because it did her any good, but because the knowledge of that event required some action on their part, and reverence and respect as opposed to indifference and insult was the only manly conduct. Self-respect was the true explanation. All noble-minded people feel that they degrade themselves when they do not render "honor to whom honor is due." The question, then, What kind of treatment shall we receive from different classes of society? is easily answered. Frederick Douglass affirms that Lincoln was the only man who treated him in such a way as to make him forget he was colored. A mob would not do this, and you can easily see the reason. The person who has no respect for himself cannot be relied upon to be courteous towards others. It is seen, therefore, that sovereignty is a very much broader term than government. Government is only a very particular administration of sovereignty under certain conditions.

THE MEMBERS OF THE STATE

Proposition 1. In all cases the first consideration must be the needs of the State. There are two conditions in which it may be: (a) *"Health,"* i.e., where all the members of the organization are relatively equal (not that they have the same abilities, but that in its own sphere the lowest is as well able to perform its particular kind of work as the most exalted to achieve its more important and therefore more honorable task); (b) *"Disease,"* where from ignorance or vice, or through misfortune, some parts of the organism are incapacitated for service.

Proposition 2. In the condition of health of the entire organ-

411

ism we ascertain the kind and amount of service due from the individual by considering primarily his *ability*, and after that his opportunities.

Since the organism has been created according to a perfect plan, any difference of endowments or of functions in its parts is not an accident, but has been determined by the needs of the whole. In 1 Cor. 12:18, we read, "But now hath God set the members each one of them in the body, even as it pleased Him." If the diversities of gifts have a divine origin, as the Apostle affirms, a man is not to despise any honest profession in life for which he is supremely fitted. He has no right to look on the ministry as a sacred calling and on all others as profane, but rather must he consider every occupation, from that of day laborer to that of sovereign on his throne, as a position for rendering service to the state. The powers that be are (all) ordained of God. To spoil an excellent business man or scientist or inventor to make a poor preacher is as much of an injury to the Kingdom of God as it would be to a physical body for the hand to refuse to do manual labor that might callous the fingers, and insist on doing by sense of touch the work of the eye. In case of blindness nothing could be more desirable, but in a perfectly sound body what could be more ridiculous? This is not merely a duty to the state but also to one's self, for nowhere can one attain spiritual life so absolutely as where he can be most successful. Every man must make a success of what he undertakes or the result is disastrous to his own manhood.

Proposition 3. *Opportunities*. It is to be observed that these constitute a factor in the problem of determining the service a man owes to the state. I owe no service to the inhabitants of the planets, simply because I can render none. Professor Harris says that this is the true explanation of Christ's command, Love thy neighbor as and including thyself. "Who is my neighbor?" This Christ answered, in the parable of the Good Samaritan, as being any person in need, even of a different nationality, who comes within our reach.

412

Proposition 4. Where opportunities and needs are equal, service is most efficient to our nearest neighbor; then here lies our first duty.

Under these conditions, since a man is his own nearest neighbor, his first duties are to himself and the members of his family. 1 Tim. 5:8, "But if any provide not for his own, and specially for those of his own house, he hath denied the faith, and is worse than an infidel."

It is commonly supposed that anything done for self is not a labor of love for the state, that we ought to deny self. A soldier in the front ranks who should follow out this idea would refuse to ask for ammunition for himself, or to defend his own post, for fear that he might be acting under self-interest. The truth is he is not his own, but a member of the army; he asks for cartridges, not as a personal favor, but as a means to serve the army. To fail to do this is to be a traitor and to be worse than an enemy. He risks the whole in risking himself.

Proposition 5. Where the organism is in a condition of disease, i.e., where the needs of all are not relatively equal, the former order must be reversed, and the individual consider first the *opportunities* for serving the needs of others, and secondly his ability. Illustrate by the hands doing the work of the eye in case of blindness. From this point of view, explain 1 Cor. 12:14-20.

Proposition 6. Business is the action and reaction that takes place in the state under conditions of equality. The law is that each person engaged in the transaction must be both means and end. This occurs only when the service rendered is an equivalent for the service received. This is justice, and only this can be allowed by the organism. Observe that such a transaction under the conditions is as truly a *"labor of love,"* that is, as truly conforms to the requirements of the organic unity, as charity and martyrdom under different conditions.

Proposition 7. Charity is the action and reaction that takes place in the state under conditions of relative inequality on the part of those engaged. It is a condition of a diseased organism.

413

The law of charity is that, for the time being, the strong shall help the weak without recompense, i.e., shall be means, not end, until the condition of health is restored. If the hand is diseased the body must heal it, and, in the meantime, give it rest. This may be a severer test, but is no more a labor of love than is business. Charity under conditions of relative equality is as truly a crime as dishonesty. 2 Thess. 3:10: "For even when we were with you, this we commanded you, that if any would not work neither should he eat."

THE RIGHT OF PROPERTY

The right of property is exactly the doctrine of the state. It is the right of the dependent entity to the independent on which it depends. That surely touches the question of individual ownership. My ownership in my body is necessarily individual, cannot be anything else. We find that there are other parts of the universe which the individual cannot control without the help of others, e.g., a home. I have no home alone, none except another shall be associated with me. It is very clear that the home belongs not to the individual, but to the partnership. On the other hand, it is clear that there is some property which is essentially individual. The orange I have for dinner can belong only to me, not to the copartnership. But the streets which I walk cannot be mine alone. You have now reached your extremes. On the one hand, there are parts which we necessarily appropriate alone; others which we cannot without the help of others.

Now the question of whether land is the former or the latter is the question of our appropriating it. Can you appropriate land alone? Some of it you must. The place on which you stand, you alone can stand on. But there is a difference between appropriating and owning. Suppose that I bought up the whole world. But can I use it myself? Is it possible for me thus to appropriate the universe to any great extent alone, or must I not get help?

In the matter of our sanitary conditions we are necessarily

partners: we must have the help of others. It is called taxation when the state makes us work together, because we can do nothing otherwise. Or to protect the country against foreign invasion, military service is required. Taxation in money is only one kind of service. Military service is another, nursing in the hospital is another. If you don't tax children for money, it is because the children haven't the money to give. If you don't tax women for military service, it is because they are not fit to give it.

How much may the state tax? All that it needs. On the other hand, when I am in need and in danger, how much money may I tax the state? All that I need. I can call upon the entire state to help me. You cannot hold onto the basis of demanding an equivalent for what you give in taxing. For the fact is that the more the state taxes, as in time of war, the less you get in return.

Christ had the true idea,—that of stewardship. Each individual has a right to serve the state in his full capacity and so act right to the reaction of the state. But if the state cannot react, then you do not get an equivalent.

If all property is a mode in which the state—the system of social relationships—becomes realized, then the question of individual control and state (not government) control vanishes. All property must be under state control; it is only a question of how the state shall control it. One bank may be under government control and the other not, but you cannot say one is under state control and the other is not. Haven't you seen places where the banks have been infinitely better controlled by the State than the post office has been? When the State brings in government to help control, it still cannot take away individual control. The post office is in the hands of individuals, and so would the railroads be if they were put under the government. The whole question, thus, is whether you can control this property better without the aid of government or not. The whole drift and tendency is towards the state without government. For government is more or less a mediate agency, and so there is more or less of friction. My body is under my control. Generally the state can

415

get better control of it without the aid of government, but in time of war, with government. If I am very selfish and very ugly, the state has to control me by the aid of government. . . .

The larger part of our great enterprises have been undertaken by individuals. Bellamy makes a great mistake here. He says these things should be put under the control, not of the state, but of the government, and the people would be inspired to do much better work. But our savage ancestor was much averse to work, was lazy. So Bellamy must change human nature in order to have his scheme work. The idea of the honorableness of labor is something yet new in the world, and has not reached some parts of Europe. How is Bellamy going to overcome all these influences of heredity inside of a few centuries?

In spiritual things there is no conflict in appropriating the entire universe. Others are not excluded. The artist who paints a picture makes something which all may admire. All through spiritual things, the more others appropriate them, the more we can appropriate them. Some say this doesn't hold in material things. But if you appropriate for *service,* then others can appropriate the things you do when you serve them. It is only in regard to immediate wants, as the supply of food, that there is this contradiction, and it is only apparent. These immediate wants seem to contradict. The orange has got to be individual. The question is, To whom does it belong? The reply is, To him who appropriates it. We appropriate the universe by service. Now, if we have appropriated nature, it is ours, and another person can have a claim to it only by appropriating, i.e., serving us. Here comes in our relation of buying and selling, or partnership.

How about the quantity of property? How much may I have? All I can appropriate. But it is injustice to try to own what I cannot appropriate. That is the root of all our labor troubles. What is it to appropriate? If I appropriate food, I make it a part of myself. To appropriate the cane in my hand, I make it a part of myself by extradition of consciousness. But I am a part of the state. My aim is to serve the state. The more I have, the more

416

I serve the state; so I don't rob the state. On this basis, there can be no labor troubles. Are the students jealous of the college when the college increases its power of serving them? Not at all. And the same of the poor and the rich.

When a man tries to own that which he cannot use, he is preventing others from its use. If I own one thousand acres of land and can use only one, then there are nine hundred and ninety-nine which are taken away from others. It must be the highest service. To appropriate it means not to use it for my own benefit, but to make it a part of myself and so serve the state.

If I have a hundred servants to attend to my special wants, take care of my wardrobe, and do things which I have leisure for and could just as well do for myself, you see they are not copartners with, but are withdrawn from, the service of the community. This much has to be said against the methods of using our wealth. It means not that the money is destroyed, for that is not the more serious trouble, but that service is lost. So it may be said of keeping standing armies. It may be necessary to keep them if there is danger of attack. But that is due to the iniquity of human nature. It is only a negative service. But suppose that there was no such iniquity, and that France, Germany, and Austria kept their millions of soldiers. They would be withdrawn from necessary service, and so humanity would be going backward there and forward in America.

Service and furnishing employment are two different things. Suppose I should arrange pieces of paper on this desk,—a million of them, perhaps after the fashion of the Sibyls. And suppose I should leave the windows open so the papers should blow all over, and then make you put them in order every morning. Would that be employment or service?

Some employment may keep people from a state of suffering, and may keep idle hands busy. But why should not all employment be in the line of service, of public improvements instead of useless work for some rich man?

The positions that man has freedom in the power to weigh

evidence and to affect conduct by ideals, and further that he belongs to a spiritual universe in which he gains full life only through his relationships to Nature and other persons, have important consequences for social reform. On the basis of a mechanical "pluralism" or individualism the natural law might seem to be each for himself. But if each individual reaches full life only through fulfilling his function in a moral world, then a law of service is indicated. Business no less than government and charity affords this opportunity and must, if morally conducted, conform to this law.

SCIENTIFIC IDEALS AND SOCIAL PRACTICE

It is easy for students to misunderstand an attempt to study society by scientific methods. It seems to them all theory, a theory that never can be actually realized in practical life.

When a new man-of-war is put into commission, newspapers give a detailed account of the ship, in which they include the "indicated horsepower." This is figured out according to scientific methods; but most readers do not believe that in actual daily usage such energy could even be developed. They think it infinitely better to know the number of horsepower available in a crisis than to have so much stress laid in scientific figures. So students are quite anxious to know the actual facts concerning society, the world in which they have got to live; but the scientific sociology which presents the ideals of social life seems to them extremely visionary.

This point of view is a great mistake, one of the most serious a young man can make. In the account of the man-of-war above referred to, the problem is entirely different from that with which we are confronted in the study of sociology. A warship is a huge fighting machine to be used to the best advantage, and that is all. It is practically a changeless thing, if we except the slight wear due to use. But society is not a means to an end, but an end in itself. Neither is it mechanical; it is organic and never any two

418

years the same. What it is and in what directions it changes depend very largely upon the ideals that possess the community. Change those ideals, as Luther did at the time of the Reformation, as Christ did at the time when Pharisaism was fossilizing the Jewish nation, and the whole course of social development is different.

When the negro slave, before the Civil War, left his master's plantation, and, hiding in the swamps by day, traveled night after night with his eye fixed on the North Star, he did not expect ever to reach that star; but by going in that direction he did hope to get out of the "house of bondage" into the land of freedom, where manhood was not determined by the color of one's skin. Was the North Star, because it was out of his reach, therefore of no practical importance to him? Was some candle that he could actually take hold of and carry with him, one that would light up the swamp at his feet better for his purpose? Is there no analogy between this and the ideals of a constantly growing civilization? Is our aim in sociology to know simply just what society is now? or do we aspire to find the path of progress? not merely to explore the social swamp, but rather to find the way out? History is full of the wreckage of social life; both nations and individuals have found it terribly hard both to make progress and to retain the little that they have made. It is said that when a fugitive gets lost he naturally travels in a circle, and when he thinks he has put miles between himself and his pursuer, he finds that, after hours and hours of travel, he is back at just the place he started from. Is there no natural tendency in the moral life of the individual, or the social life of the times, to move thus in a circle, and lose all the advantage that has been gained?

Let us beg the students not to underestimate the ideal in sociology because they do properly discount it in machinery. In the latter, the ideal is simply descriptive, but in society the ideal is creative.

Physical impulses are automatic and take care of themselves. Therefore a student jumps to a conclusion that a man's moral life will take care of itself in the same way, that spiritual life is a matter of temperament, that, if the community has the right blood in it, it will work out its salvation under the guidance of blind instinct, and we need have no more thought or worry as to the future of such a nation as the United States than we have of the progress of the seasons. There may be bad weather in May, and snowflakes in the air, but no one fears that we are going back to March and February. June is as sure to come as the sun is to rise on the morrow, and everybody knows that the twentieth century is to be the June of that civilization which the nineteenth has so well established. I am not a pessimist, I have no doubt at all of the glory of the twentieth century, but my confidence is founded on something infinitely better than the miserable superstition described above. Look at the doctrine that blood will tell, that all is a matter of temperament, and you find that you have simply the old heathen doctrine of Fate with changed names. Science teaches that there are two factors in our nature: brain paths on the one hand, and power to weigh evidence on the other. It teaches that brain paths alone are automatic and take care of themselves, and it teaches that wherever a civilization has been left to brain paths it invariably fossilizes or runs backward and destroys itself. Boast as you will of the Teuton race, there is no organizing power in it, says Burgess, for those tribes made no progress from the days of Tacitus till Christian missions quickened their life. It teaches that the only point that can successfully overcome these tendencies are those spiritual impulses that can be stimulated to activity only by the discussion and clear realization of the eternal principles of human obligation and relationship. The spiritual impulses are not automatic, they will not take care of themselves, they cannot be kept active a moment except under the inspiration of ideals. Cloud the ideals of a community, persuade men that high moral obligations are wholly theory and of no practical importance, and that therefore they would better turn their thoughts to the real world about them, and what in a short time would the real world

420

become? Everywhere propensities would rule supreme and moral life expire. Christ came to bear witness to the truth: "If ye know the truth, the truth shall make you free." He who was the Truth said, "I, if I be lifted up, will draw all men unto Me." A person cannot be a Christian without following the example of his Master. The only hope of civilization is in those spiritual impulses that can be stimulated to action only through the truth made conspicuous by those who aspire to be workers together with Him.

We do not expect a millennium in the twentieth century. We are pretty well satisfied with the nineteenth as it is. Many are not much disturbed by social evils; this age is good enough for them. But what is the secret of this age? Is it not the scientific spirit and the search for truth that has awakened the consciences of men? Would the curse of slavery ever have been lifted from our country if high ideals of human life and obligations had not been held up before us by such prophets as Phillips, Sumner, and Lincoln? Was it not the same that successfully overcame the spirit of the anarchists in their attempt on our institutions in the Chicago riot? Can anything else enable us to hold our own in the presence of that increasing crowd of immigrants gathered out of every nation and kindred and tribe? See the reign of terror that the Italian secret society established in New Orleans. Realize how serious a thing it is for the lower classes, who in their foreign homes have been governed wholly by force and tradition to find themselves in America without their traditions and without the tyranny which they have been accustomed to identify with government and religion. How can they help giving themselves over to license and becoming an explosive element in our slums?

The difficulty is not confined to foreigners. For ages the ancestors of the American people have been inspired and quickened by their religious faith. They believed in verbal inspiration of the Scriptures. The church laid the greatest possible stress on this life as a preparation for the future, with its awful rewards

421

and punishments of heaven and hell. We can hardly imagine the strength of these motives. What a check they were to wrongdoing. As an illustration of their power, take the Puritan observance of the Sabbath day. Jonathan Edwards preached his sermon in Northampton on future punishment with such unction that his audience felt the Judgment Day had come; evil doers seemed to themselves to be falling downwards into the pit, and they actually laid hold of the seats, as a drowning man grasps at a rope to save him. All this has changed now. Whether rightly or wrongly, the higher criticism is working havoc with the doctrine of inspiration in the popular mind. Sunday is fast losing its sanctity. The holy day is now a holiday. The doctrine of evolution has taken the place occupied by Calvinistic theology, and our preachers now rarely mention the subject of future punishment which formerly found such a large place in their sermons. President Walker in his Phi Beta Kappa address at Harvard a few years ago declared that men nowadays think ninety-nine times as to how they are going to live, to once as to how they are going to die.

It is clear that the public have not the old motives for action that shaped the early history of our country. Now, what new motives are you going to put in the place of the old, if not the power of the spiritual impulses awakened by the knowledge of the truth? Take the municipal corruption in our cities; the power of the "boss" in politics, . . . and realize that you have got a struggle to the death. These forces will either conquer or be conquered, and what agencies have you got arrayed against them? Herbert Spencer felt that issue very keenly; he realized that evolution had destroyed the old motives that used to influence the masses, and that, unless new motives of the strongest type were put in their place, serious consequences would follow. He therefore stopped his work on the synthetic philosophy as he had planned it, and jumped over several volumes which the logical order would have required him to write, in order that he might present to the public the first instalment of his discussion on ethics, fearing that the accident of death might prevent this work from appearing, and that without it his previous work in behalf of evolution might sap the moral life of many whose previous faith had been destroyed thereby.

It is freely granted that the truths of a scientific sociology will not regenerate humanity in a day, that forces of evil in human nature are deep-seated; but the more you say about their strength and persistence, the more you emphasize the need of ideals for society. For there are no other human agencies to antagonize these powers of evil except the spiritual impulses that can be awakened only by a knowledge of ideals, and whose strength and efficiency are proportioned to the clearness with which those ideals are realized.

What is true for society is true for the individual. You cannot overcome your passions and downward tendencies by dead effort of will. You must have help. You must have the working of counter-impulses; and you can get this help, you can stimulate these impulses, only in one way. You must know the truth concerning the spiritual life and your relationship to your fellowmen. You must not merely know it, you must "think on these things." Your effort of attention must be directed towards holding these ideals before the mind till they shall take possession of your thought, and color all your estimates of duty.

Spiritual impulses seem to us very weak; is it because they are weak or because they have never been stimulated? Only a few years ago electricity was supposed to be only a very insignificant agent manifested only in amber, and making lint adhere to your clothes, and the like, but how mistaken that judgment? What a tremendous power it has become at the close of the nineteenth century! Are you sure that spiritual impulses are weak instead of being undeveloped? If the ideals of man's spiritual life could be made as real to the community as the truths of physical science, are you sure that righteous impulses would be impotent? Was that force that wrought out the Reformation contemptible for its weakness? Was the conscience

423

of the country on the matter of slavery in the darkest hours of the Civil War a power to be sneered at? Is not the energy there, and has it not shown itself the most tremendous power in history on those rare occasions when it has been stimulated to act?

Grant that the age is mean, that men are selfish and corrupt, and that, preach ideals as you will, by an effort of the will, they will refuse to follow them; does that mean that the scientific study of sociology will be impotent? Does it not rather mean that, if scientific ideals are proclaimed and made real to the public, the strongest impulses of human nature will be stimulated to resist the meanness and selfishness of the age, and that base men who will not reform will experience the maximum of opposition to their evil career, both in their own consciences and the consciences of the community? Is the achievement of such a result as this insignificant? .... Christ lost in his struggle with the Jews, but did they not pay too heavily for the victory? Would not a similar defeat of ideals in modern society be followed by a resurrection that would make them omnipotent? Would not such a fate be the surest path to ultimate victory?

THE COMING REFORM

In all the schemes that are proposed by politicians, labor agitators, statesmen, and scholars, we are able by careful study to discover that there are only two distinct trends. Antagonistic as these writers are to each other in details, there is only one comprehensive antagonism. We can overlook particular differences and give our attention to the fundamental distinction that sharply outlines the position of all writers as belonging to either one party or the other. The first party, including by far the larger number, is devoted to the great effort of bringing about the millennium through a variety of contrivances, all of which reduce to attempts of a purely quantitative character. Just as in music you get harmony or discord, treble or bass, by a quantitative increase or decrease in the number of vibrations, so that the whole

424

scheme of music can be worked out in terms of mathematics; so there are writers and critics who aim by simply quantitative devices for distributing wealth, or suffrage, or wages, to change the great national discord to be found in each country to a grand anthem of contentment and prosperity.

The other great party, while not undervaluing the efforts for quantitative justice, yet feel that the labor problems, the political evils, the corruption of municipal politics, are but symptoms of deep-seated disease in human nature for which there is no remedy of a superficial character that is seriously worth experimenting with. We must go to the very source of the whole trouble and seek a change in the quality of human life. There must be truer conceptions of human nature and less selfishness. These thinkers are never tired of reëchoing the words of Christ to Nicodemus as the great hope for the evils of our time, "YE MUST BE BORN AGAIN." This is true not merely of individuals, but of institutions and society itself. The time has come when business and social organizations must be regenerated; when the aim of life shall no longer be simply to get, but to be heroic and noble, and to achieve great things.

It is our aim at the present time to contrast these two schools of thought and discover what results can be expected from each. We begin with the school demanding quantitative justice.

I

In a general way we may divide people whose whole life is devoted to simply quantitative gain into two classes: first, those who seek the largest amount of satisfaction in the present, and to this end are willing to discount the future; and secondly, those who seek the largest amount of welfare in the long run, and have the courage and heroism to discount the present for the future. The same individual at different periods of his life may belong now to one class and now to the other, but sooner or later he will cease this changing allegiance and become permanently

425

allied with those who live for the present or with those who live for the future.

First, those who live for the present. We are so familiar with the people of these characteristics that no description is needed. We find them everywhere in business. They are quick to take present gains and spend as they go, rather than lay up money for a rainy day when it can be done only at the expense of saying No, to some strong appeal to appetite or passion. And what is true of money is also true of health, which is sacrificed freely when some immediate gain can be reached by late hours or undue exposure.

Such men in college will remind you that they are young only once and ought to have a good time now, as otherwise they can never have it; they urge, therefore, that even though they neglect studies and discipline, and thus may seriously embarrass their professional career, they will yet be sure to have a happy memory of college days. Such people are often extremely agreeable, ready to respond to any excitement, and very entertaining in their companionship.

The other class are the shrewd, long-headed fellows who know how to work, to endure present suffering for the greater gain which is to come in time. They are not disturbed by the pity or the criticism which is so freely given them, for they have their eye on a prize which, when it is won, never fails to excite the admiration and the worship of those who despised them in the days of their privation.

What are the relations which in time must necessarily come to exist between these two classes? We reply there is but one relation conceivable: that of the master and the slave, that of the lion and the lamb. Long-headed men unimpeded by conscience and inspired only by shrewdness cannot fail to discover the enormous opportunity for gain which is afforded by offering some present profit to their short-sighted but passionate brethren. Sooner or later Jacob, by fair means or by foul, will have gotten

426

the birthright from his brother Esau. The prize is too great and the conditions altogether too favorable for any other result. The problem of purely governmental reform is to devise some means of making the lion lie down with the lamb. (There never has been any success in this undertaking until the lamb has first been stored away within the lion.) The lion is by his very nature a carnivorous animal; he cannot live except it be on the lamb; to ask him to give up his prize is to ask him to starve to death, and he is too full of resources to do this. Hence all our governmental restrictions will succeed simply in changing the method by which the results will be reached, but can neither hasten nor delay the result. That is, slavery of the short-sighted to the long-sighted has always existed and always will exist so long as quantity is the aim of each. The only question that can possibly be discussed is, what form of slavery shall prevail at a given time?

First, we affirm this proposition: the progress of physical science makes it absolutely necessary that all changes in the relationship between these two classes shall be such as increase the power and appetite of the lion, and diminish the ability of the lamb to resist. We will attempt to prove by particular cases each part of the proposition.

1. Inventions increase the power of long-headed men. . . . New machines are continually invented to do the work which formerly has been done by hand. From such inventions skilled labor is reduced to unskilled. . . .

2. The progress of science not merely increases the power of the lion over the lamb; it increases also the ferocity of his nature. The more he has the more he wants. The Greek meaning of the word covetousness is not a desire for little, not a desire for much, but a desire for more. Weber's law shows that "more" means a perceptible increase, and the gain necessary for a perceptible increase depends upon the amount which one already possesses. To a man who gets a dollar a day an addition of

427

twenty-five cents is a very perceptible increase. But to a man who gets a thousand dollars a day an addition of twenty-five cents is a laughing stock.

3. Additional stimulus to the long-headed man to exploit the weak comes from the fact that the progress of inventions is continually destroying property by making the plant of an establishment out of date and requiring better machinery for successful competition with rivals.

A large army under a poor general is easily whipped by a few soldiers under a Napoleon. A dollar in the hands of a shrewd, long-headed man is more potent than many dollars in the hands of a short-sighted fellow. But when we come to reverse the relationship and give Napoleon the large army and the poor general only a few soldiers, then what hope has the latter of surviving?

Bellamy thinks these consequences can be avoided by a governmental change, so that the desire of the long-headed fellow for property and the desire of the short-sighted fellow for immediate happiness can be restricted. In other words, that by means of the industrial army, man will take the same delight in working without pay that soldiers do in fighting purely from the sense of honor. But Bellamy forgets that the military qualities of our race come from untold generations of heredity; whereas antagonism to work is the inheritance from savage ancestors who thought that to fight and to rob were manly, but to do work was to be a squaw. Can you by any governmental legislation eliminate heredity?

It is clear that the progress of scientific inventions increases the power of the long-headed, selfish man, that these inventions also increase his ferociousness, and at the same time sting him by the occasional cruel losses which they inflict on any particular investment. How can he hope to make good these losses and satisfy his larger appetite for gain unless he uses this increased power for the more extensive destruction of the lamb? Let us now turn to the other side of the conflict.

428

4. It is easy to see that the advance of civilization renders the lamb more helpless to resist or elude the lion. Present gratification is enormously increased by the discoveries of science, and therefore the temptations to discount the future in terms of the present are infinitely more powerful now than formerly.

If this matter is to be fought out simply between the long-headed and the short-sighted men, can there be any doubt that sooner or later the conflict will cease altogether and the lamb will lie down inside the lion?

II

What remedy have we to propose for this state of affairs? The answer is very simple. The Christian doctrine is that the lion can lie down with the lamb, only by having his nature changed so that he can eat straw like the ox; in other words, he must cease being a carnivorous animal and become herbivorous, and then he has no motive for destruction. On the other hand, the lamb must also be regenerated and be no longer a mutton-head, but learn to sacrifice the present for the future, and thus be transformed from an animal to a person.

This scheme is not a mere ideal; it is the only practical scheme of living. This will be seen from the following considerations.

1. Whenever we make our ultimate appeal to quality instead of quantity, all men become persons and are peers with God. There is no longer Greek nor Jew, Barbarian, Scythian, bond nor free; but Christ is all and in all. No caste system.

2. The law of personal service between equals is that the service rendered shall be practically equivalent to the service received. Between unequals the law is, the strong shall serve the weak and make them strong before expecting compensation.

3. This point of view insures, first, justice as opposed to a sentimental charity that feeds the tramp; and, secondly, true charity which does away with all jealousy towards the more fortunate members of society. For instance, in a steamboat dis-

aster the women and children are not jealous of the life-saving crew who risk their lives to save them. . . . Increased ability means increased responsibility, and, instead of the struggle for existence and the survival of the fittest, we find the struggle for the existence of others, in which the truest and the noblest fill the most difficult places, and spend and are spent for the elevation of those who are trying to help themselves.

Critics have noticed three stages in the development of human civilization. First: the let alone policy; every man to look out for number one. This is the age of selfishness. Second: the opposite pole of thinking; every man to do somebody else's work for him. This is the dry rot of sentimentality that feeds tramps and enacts poor laws such as excite the indignation of Herbert Spencer. But the third stage is represented by our formula: every man must render and receive the best conceivable service, except in the case of inequality, and there the strong must help the weak to help themselves; only on this condition is help given. This is the true interpretation of the life of Christ. On the first basis he would have remained in heaven and let the earth take care of itself. On the second basis He would have come to earth with His hands full of gold and silver treasures, satisfying every want that unfortunate humanity could have devised. But on the third basis He comes to earth in the form of a servant who is at the same time a master, commanding His disciples to take up their cross and follow Him; it is sovereignty through service as opposed to slavery through service. He refuses to make the world wealthy, but He offers to help them make themselves wealthy with true riches which shall be a hundred fold more, even in this life, than that which was offered them by any former system.

This is the only true conception of business; the only idea of wealth and power; just as every true government devotes its own strength for benefiting its citizens, and they, in turn, when they become strong, strengthen the resources of the government.

4. Every corporation like a railroad or a factory renders a

thousand times more service to its individual employees than they can individually render it.

There is no labor problem in the savage world. No matter how despicable the condition of a man, he will rest contentedly until the ideals of manliness and freedom have dawned upon his mind, for we know the imperfect only in the light of the perfect. When we have seen the ideal we become dissatisfied. Christianity is largely responsible for the labor trouble. Christ came not to send peace on the earth, but a sword, and we are beginning to realize the truth of His words. How shall this great unrest, how shall these many wants, be met?

There are only two fountains from which men can ever attempt to drink. If one seeks satisfaction in quantity, water from that well will not prevent him from thirsting again. But, if he drink of the divine fountain of quality, these waters become in him "a well of water springing up into everlasting life," and each individual becomes a fountain which makes an oasis in the desert. In Eden, man fell by eating of the fruit of the tree of knowledge. He went simply so far as to find what was good for food and suited to make one wise. The remedy for human evils is to eat of the tree of life, which yields the knowledge, not of our selfish interests, but of our spiritual obligations, of our true dignity and grandeur. When the laborers seek by merely increasing their wages to remove their difficulties they are increasing the evils of the times. When the laborers seek not to get, but to give, better service, and demand the same of their masters, and ask that manhood shall depend not on wealth, but on merit, then a new star, which is the star of Bethlehem, has begun to shine in their sky.

The most satisfied men in history are not those who have received the largest pay, but those who have rendered the greatest service to their age, often entirely without pay. What is the financial compensation which Christ received? and we may ask the same question as to Socrates, Washington, Phillips, Sumner,

431

Gladstone, Van Moltke. How much compensation do our ablest scientific authors receive for their contributions to human welfare?

Whatever you may say of the laborer, he is a man, and will never be satisfied until he lives the life of a man. All attempts to deal with the labor problem on the maxim that you must deal with men as they are, and not as they ought to be—all these attempts are doomed to failure, for the laborers at present are not their true selves, and the system which just fits them now cannot give satisfaction, since they cannot now be satisfied with their present selves. Those who call themselves practical, and look on men as mean and tricky and subject to the motives of bribery—these people are visionary and dreamy and impracticable leaders. For, whatever a man may say about himself, he is infinitely more than all these, and his reserve powers have got to be reckoned with. You may carry a certain explosive as you would any other weight, and test it by the balance of scales, and say that is all there is to it. Judging by appearances, this is the estimate explosives have of themselves. But the man who allows himself to be deceived and to deal with them in that way is simply a fool. Their chemical composition is unstable and without warning their true nature asserts itself. Human nature has often done the same. The French Revolution, the American Revolution, the War of the Rebellion were great surprises to the practical politicians, and to the diplomatists, who sneered at man's spiritual nature. The true reformer . . . will discover in men the image of God, and he will establish institutions that will stand the test of divine standards.

If we now take a brief review of the past we shall see that the progress of civilization will so increase the power of machinery that in time all mechanical work will be performed by machines. The workman will no longer be a hand, but a head. In olden times men-of-war were propelled by slaves, whose oars were arranged in one, two, or three banks. Just as the steam engine has driven out the slave and made the engineer who runs it a regular

432

officer of the line, ranking with the captain, so will machines drive out slave labor in our mills and make the work, that was once so degrading, a task of skill stimulating the brain to its most careful exercise. Until this day comes, man will not be enthroned as master of nature, but when it does arrive, and machines in all their tedious details are automatic, then humanity will be made conscious of its sovereign dignity.

This means that in the struggle for existence, humanity must evolve out of the region of the animal into the intelligence of the human sphere, and those who will not so progress, and who will not attain the skill and manly ability to take charge of these complicated machines, shall be completely driven out of work and driven to the wall.

In Homer's day, greatness consisted in mere size or in mere numbers of warriors, but you will notice everywhere through Homer that the victory is given not to the Cyclops but to the crafty Ulysses; not even to the mighty Achilles, who for ten years waged war around Troy without accomplishing visible results, but to the strategy employed in the wooden horse. Homer is the great epic which sings the contrast between brain and brawn at its very beginning, at a time when people had no more faith in mere shrewdness than many people now have for the success of Sunday-school virtue in business and politics. But the time will come when it will be hard for the world to understand the point of view of Homer's age. A time will come when brain shall be almost everything, and machinery will do the rest.

The advent of this day will bring many changes. It will first bring very much leisure.

A second step in progress will be to greatly multiply human wants. Just as the invention of sewing machines, instead of driving out of existence poor needlewomen, multiplies the work to be done a thousand fold, and makes it possible for the humblest member of society to purchase, ready made, a style of garment requiring so much work that fifty years ago it would have been extravagant even for a wealthy person,—so the invention of ma-

433

chinery will multiply products and reduce their price to such an extent that the same expenditure will give many times the present returns. As, according to Weber's law, increased desires demand an increase of products for their satisfaction, which soon becomes almost infinite, so the ultimate outcome of these inventions will be so to increase the wants and the comforts of society that there shall be infinitely more employment than at present.

Thirdly, the gradual standard of manliness and social recognition will require companionship and culture as well as skill. The great truth of Scripture will begin to be wrought out in our whole life that man cannot live by bread alone. He is not born into this world simply to spend his time in keeping body and soul together or in administering to his physical body. The age will come when the moral and spiritual life will be recognized to be as much superior to the purely material as, in Homer's Iliad, craft and strategy are superior to brute force. A certain amount of leisure, therefore, will be demanded by all classes for their spiritual improvement, for their culture, for art, and for literature, and thus the hours of work will be greatly reduced. As man will be master of the machine, so the manly and spiritual will master, instead of being mastered by, man's material nature.

THE TWENTIETH CENTURY

Macaulay paints only the dark outlines to the picture. He has left out the main factor, namely, the spiritual nature of man, which never can be quite obliterated, even in the blackest criminal. It has been the aim of our course to study the evidence in favor of the existence of this nature and to determine the laws according to which it operates. We have gone far enough to discover that "brain paths" and pursuit of happiness are not all there is to life, even in the lowliest; that true manhood, the spiritual nature, can be developed, not merely in the palace and the counting-room, but in the workshop and among the rank and

434

file of the industrial army; and it is quite possible that the mission of America in the history of the world is to accomplish just this task. We have laid great stress in the past on wealth and social position, but we are coming to a time in our history when all cannot hope to be wealthy in the new sense of that term; when there will be an impassable barrier between the great fortunes and the common people. Now, the result may be the formation of classes in society with antagonistic interests. If this occurs there will be some chance of realizing the prophecy of Macaulay. But we hope for better things; the ethical conception of human life must be pushed to the front. Then service, not wealth, will be the standard of honor. If the great fortunes are used for the service of the community, if machines are made to do mechanical work and laborers are no longer hands but heads, if their whole time is not spent in barely winning a livelihood, but through education and religion fair emphasis is given to the moral, social, and intellectual nature, Macaulay's prophecy will seem short-sighted and narrow.

If we look back over the history of human thinking, we find these stages clearly marked. The first great era was occupied with the problem, "What is nature?" In prehistoric times men were afraid of nature; it was their enemy, the hiding-place of ghosts and hobgoblins and malicious spirits who were bent on doing men harm. The first era of philosophic thought worked out the mechanical conception of nature and taught man that it was neither friend nor foe, but simply his tool, to be used with skill instead of ignorance. The modern atomic theory was originated by Democritus; the theory of evolution was crudely formulated by Empedocles, and most of our modern scientific conceptions had some prototype in this early stage of Greek reflection. This was a wonderful step in progress, and the world has never been quite the same as it was before. You know how it is with the century plant. It lives and grows, but generations come and go before it blossoms. Science is not a century plant, but a plant of millenniums. It took root in the earliest day of Greek thinking,

435

but two thousand years passed away before it blossomed. We today see the beauty of the flower.

The next great problem was, "What is man?" Before this question was asked he was a nobody. The state was everything, the individual nothing. But under the influence of the sophists, of Socrates, Plato, and Aristotle, the work of man as an individual began to be revealed. Even Meno's slave was found to possess a divine nature that made him a peer of those who had despised him. The worth of man as man, his power to know truth that had before seemed only the prerogative of the gods to know, arrested attention. There was no longer "Greek nor Jew, Barbarian, Scythian, bond nor free," but mind was all and in all. In the breaking up of Greek political life, in the loss of their material splendor, when their national sun had set, the stars of the spiritual firmament began to shine and all the wise men wondered.

The next great question was, "What is God?" And as the more advanced and candid thought on this question they gradually gave up their polytheism and their pluralism and came out squarely on the monistic basis. Stoicism was through and through monistic. It was just at this time that Christ came and taught the Fatherhood of God and the doctrine of the atonement. This great truth swept the Roman Empire, and in three centuries seated a follower of the Nazarene on the throne of the Caesars.

The fourth great question was, "The problem of evil." Here we have the great Augustinian controversies. It was a period of decay; the corruption of the Roman Empire was everywhere revolting. The beginning of the night of the Middle Ages brought a return from the monistic conception back to pluralism. First, because on this basis it seemed so much easier to explain evil; and secondly, because the barbarians could more easily understand pluralism, whereas monism was hard to grasp.

The fifth great question was, "How can sinful man be just with God?" This was the time of the Protestant Reformation, and it brought out the problem of justification by faith, the forgiveness of sins through repentance. It formulated the doctrine

436

of the atonement as vicarious-vicarious punishment. "Thou hast laid upon him the iniquities of us all, and by his stripes we are healed."

The sixth great question was, "How shall man be just with his sinful fellow-man?" It will be noticed that the other questions are old-world questions, and it will be seen that during all those ages, while they were being wrought out and thought out, America was shrouded in eternal night. But just at the time when the Reformation began, America was revealed; and just when men began to realize, as President Seelye said, that they were sons of God, therefore brethren, children of a common father, and not divided up into privileged castes,—when they discovered that they were sons of God, they reasoned that they could not be the slaves of man,—then America was opened up and became an asylum for civil and religious liberty. The contest whereby the power of church and despots was broken was wholly negative. Political liberty was not real liberty, but simply an opportunity. In this America had little part. The positive side of that question is social and industrial freedom, and here America is the battle-ground. If God makes atonement for the sins of man, then man ought to make atonement for the sins of his fellow-man. In Christ's first coming in Judea we have the crisis of the divine atonement. In his second coming, when he incarnates himself, not in human form, but in human relationships, in human institutions, i.e., in a Christian civilization, may we not find the crisis in human atonement in America?

You remember one scene in Christ's life where He went up into the mountain and, while there, was transfigured; His disciples saw Him no longer a man of sorrows acquainted with grief, but in His divine grandeur, and with Him Moses, who represented the law that He fulfilled, and Elias, who represented the prophecies which He had brought to pass. It seems to me that philosophy is the mount of transfiguration of human nature, and that if we study it rightly we no longer see only that which is base and mean and selfish and slavish, which actual life makes so much of, but we have revealed to us the divine spirit which is working out through it all. Then we discover that this side of human life alone gives meaning to science, which stands for law in modern times, and to society, which has ever looked forward to a future beyond the power of mere man to realize. Industrial life, which has been so often condemned as having nothing but selfishness in it, is seen to be a reincarnation of the divine in human character; for it is nothing but sovereignty on its positive side, where the strong make the service given an equivalent for the service received in business, and in charity the strong help the weak to become strong and thus help themselves. This, then, is the particular problem of America. In regenerating business and charity, in purging them of all that is selfish and merely traditional, and placing them squarely on the basis of service, we have a second coming of Christ, the realization of the Kingdom of God on earth. And man will adopt the same schemes for resisting the sins of his fellow-man that God has adopted for resisting the sin of the world. Then man will not merely think God's thought after Him in physical science, but he will live God's life after Him in his social existence. Then the same mind will exist in us that existed in Christ Jesus our Lord.

Now for the solution of these questions, America has peculiarly favorable conditions. In the first place our population is made up of composite stock. It was said that God sifted three nations to get the seed wherewith to plant New England civilization in the time of the Puritans. Since that time we have been receiving, not the worn-out and effete remains of a decadent race, but the vigorous, hardy elements from all the races of the world. When Corinth was sacked by the Romans, as the temples burned, the statues of the gods made of gold and silver and bronze melted and fused together into a common alloy which was known as Corinthian bronze, and had such peculiarly delicate qualities that its value was priceless. As a result of the tribulations, wars, and persecutions in Europe the best and bravest of many stocks have come together and fused in America, and formed a race

438

superior to any in the world. Here, free from the old traditions, and from the old caste systems, we have a new rich territory in which to work out our destiny. Let me recall here the lines written by Edward Everett Hale, and ask if there is not a deep truth in their meaning.

> Give me white paper!
> This which you use is black and rough with smears
> Of sweat and grime and fraud and blood and tears,
> Crossed with the story of men's sins and fears,
> Of battle and of famine all these years.
> > When all God's children had forgot their birth,
> > And drudged and fought and died like beasts of earth.
>
> Give me white paper!
> One storm-trained seaman listened to the word;
> What no man saw he saw; he heard what no man heard.
> > In answer he compelled the sea
> > To eager men to tell
> > The secret she had kept so well!
> Left blood and guilt and tyranny behind,—
> Sailing still West the hidden shore to find;
> > For all mankind that unstained scroll unfurled,
> > Where God might write anew the story of the World.

I believe that early in the twentieth century events will have progressed so far that America will begin to realize her mission and address herself mainly to this particular task. We have been dazzled by wealth, we have been envious, and we have wanted our share. Men have been selfish and greedy, but I feel that they will soon wake up, and their better nature will find expression, at least in the better classes in the community. It is your privilege to be on the scene of action at such a time in the world's history. As the twelve disciples were given the privilege of laying the foundations of the early church, young men of this age are given the opportunity of instructing the people in the true foundations of a Christian civilization. It is your opportunity to do something.

This is a new way of looking at things, and it requires something besides thinking to take this view. No one can follow truth without being an actual hero, for the multitude do not go that way; they follow custom. Remember the experience of Columbus when he dared to live up to the evidence which proved to him that the world was round. Derided by his contemporaries, he steered his ships towards the west with nothing to guide him except the great truths which science had revealed. Was the courage of that man a small achievement? To be a hero in battle is merely to follow the footsteps of a great company of patriots who fairly blaze with glory. But to be alone on an unknown sea, where the very laws of nature seem to be changing and the most trusted friends call you crazy, and then to dare every peril, inspired by the faith in the unseen country, is sublime. Let this be a prophecy for your life. The old country from which you set sail on your voyage of life is the material shore. It is the kingdom of brain paths, where selfishness is not sovereign, but tyrant. It is the prevailing view of the citizens of this country that there is no other land. We have given evidence to show that there is a Western hemisphere, a spiritual America, the home of freedom, a commonwealth whose inhabitants are citizens of the kingdom of Truth, whose achievements constitute all that is grand and heroic in human life. I beg you to follow Columbus. You will be ridiculed for your faith as he was for his. But refuse to deal with men simply as selfish beings. If your efforts seem to come to naught, and even those who are your helpers beg you to give up the voyage and turn back, push boldly on towards the other shore. If your heart does not fail, there will come a time when you shall have passed the fogs of doubt, weathered the storms of ridicule, and at last made a harbor in the spiritual life of humanity; then you will be men of power.

CHAPTER 1

PLATO

Plato was born about 427 B.C. and died eighty years later, 347
B.C. His real name was Aristocles and he was a member of one of
the oldest and noblest families of Athenian aristocracy. This man
whose influence has been so deep and lasting is known to posterity
by his nickname which means "The Broad."

There are five distinct periods in Plato's life.

1. 427-407 B.C. Plato received an excellent education. He was im-
pressed by the Peloponnesian War (431-404), which ruined the
Athenian Empire.

2. 407-399 B.C. A pupil of Socrates, Plato learned the Socratic
method, the dialectic, the irony, the doctrine that knowledge is vir-
tue and virtue is happiness. Plato was present at the trial, but not at
the death of Socrates.

3. 399-387 B.C. This was a period of study and travel. In
389 B.C. Plato made his first journey to Sicily. Stories are told of
his capture by pirates and his ransom on his return from Sicily. In
388 he purchased the Academy at Athens, a public park or grove,
equipped as a gymnasium, and founded his school of philosophy
there.

4. 387-367 B.C. This was a period of constructive activity. Plato
developed the Academy and engaged in his most brilliant literary
activity. In 367 B.C. he undertook his second journey to Sicily.

5. 367-347 B.C. This may be termed the dialectical period. In 367
B.C. Plato's greatest pupil, Aristotle, entered the Academy. Aristotle
said of his teacher, "Plato is my friend, but truth is a greater friend."
Plato made his third visit to Sicily, 362-360 B.C.

Plato was active until his death. Every work published by Plato

*is written in the form of a dialogue. Most of them are full of dra-
matic life. Some are gay comedies. Speech has been given to both
historical and fictitious persons but hardly ever to the author himself who attributed most of his own thoughts to his teacher Socrates.*

But of the many falsehoods told by them, there was one that
quite amazed me;—I mean when they said that you should be on
your guard and not allow yourselves to be deceived by the force
of my eloquence. To say this, when they were certain to be de-
tected as soon as I opened my lips and proved myself to be anything but a great speaker, did indeed appear to me most shameless—unless by the force of eloquence they mean the force of
truth; for if such is their meaning, I admit that I am eloquent.(1)

I know only too well how many are the enmities which I have
incurred, and this is what will be my destruction if I am
destroyed;—not Meletus, nor yet Anytus, but the envy and
detraction of the world, which has been the death of many good
men, and will probably be the death of many more; there is no
danger of my being the last of them. (2)

A man who is good for anything ought not to calculate the
chance of living or dying; he ought only to consider whether in
doing anything he is doing right or wrong—acting the part of a
good man or of a bad. (3)

For wherever a man's place is, whether the place which he has
chosen or that in which he has been placed by a commander,
there he ought to remain in the hour of danger; he should not
think of death or of anything but disgrace. And this, O men of
Athens, is a true saying. (4)

Strange, indeed, would be my conduct, O men of Athens, if I
who, when I was ordered by the generals whom you chose to
command me at Potidaea and Amphipolis and Delium, remained
where they placed me, like any other man, facing death—if now,
when, as I conceive and imagine, God orders me to fulfil the
philosopher's mission of searching into myself and other men, I
were to desert my post through fear of death, or any other fear;

442

that would indeed be strange, and I might justly be arraigned in court for denying the existence of the gods, if I disobeyed the oracle because I was afraid of death, fancying that I was wise when I was not wise. For the fear of death is indeed the pretence of wisdom, and not real wisdom, being a pretence of knowing the unknown; and no one knows whether death, which men in their fear apprehend to be the greatest evil, may not be the greatest good. (5)

Whereas I know but little of the world below, I do not suppose that I know: but I do know that injustice and disobedience to a better, whether God or man, is evil and dishonourable, and I will never fear or avoid a possible good rather than a certain evil. (6)

If you say to me, Socrates, this time we will not mind Anytus, and you shall be let off, but upon one condition, that you are not to enquire and speculate in this way any more, and that if you are caught doing so again you shall die;—if this was the condition on which you let me go, I should reply: Men of Athens, I honour and love you; but I shall obey God rather than you, and while I have life and strength I shall never cease from the practice and teaching of philosophy, exhorting anyone whom I meet and saying to him after my manner: You, my friend,—a citizen of the great and mighty and wise city of Athens,—are you not ashamed of heaping up the greatest amount of money and honour and reputation, and caring so little about wisdom and truth and the greatest improvement of the soul, which you never regard or heed at all? And if the person with whom I am arguing, says: Yes, but I do care; then I do not leave him or let him go at once: but I proceed to interrogate and examine and cross-examine him, and if I think that he has no virtue in him, but only says that he has, I reproach him with undervaluing the greater, and overvaluing the less. And I shall repeat the same words to everyone whom I meet, young and old, citizens and alien, but especially to the citizens, inasmuch as they are my brethren. For know that this is the command of God; and I believe that no greater good has ever happened in the state than my service to the God. For I do nothing but go about persuading you all, old and young alike, not to take thought for your persons or your properties, but first and chiefly to care about the greatest improvement of the soul. I tell you that virtue is not given by money, but that from virtue comes money and every other good of man, public as well as private. (7)

I would have you know, that if you kill such an one as I am, you will injure yourselves more than you will injure me. Nothing will injure me, not Meletus nor yet Anytus—they cannot, for a bad man is not permitted to injure a better than himself. I do not deny that Anytus may, perhaps, kill him, or drive him into exile, or deprive him of civil rights; and he may imagine, and others may imagine, that he is inflicting a great injury upon him: but there I do not agree. For the evil of doing as he is doing— the evil of unjustly taking away the life of another—is greater far. (8)

For neither in war nor yet at law ought I or any man to use every way of escaping death. Often in battle there can be no doubt that if a man will throw away his arms, and fall upon his knees before his pursuers, he may escape death; and in other dangers there are other ways of escaping death, if a man is willing to say and do anything. The difficulty, my friends, is not to avoid death, but to avoid unrighteousness; for that runs faster than death. I am old and move slowly, and the slower runner has overtaken me, and my accusers are keen and quick, and the faster runner, who is unrighteousness, has overtaken them. And now I depart hence condemned by you to suffer the penalty of death,—they too go their ways condemned by the truth to suffer the penalty of villainy and wrong; and I must abide by my award —let them abide by theirs. I suppose that these things may be regarded as fated,—and I think that they are well. (9)

If you think that by killing men you can prevent some one from censuring your evil lives, you are mistaken; that is not a way of escape which is either possible or honourable; the easiest and the noblest way is not to be disabling others, but to be improving yourselves. (10)

Let us reflect in another way, and we shall see that there is great reason to hope that death is a good; for one of two things —either death is a state of nothingness and utter unconsciousness, or, as men say, there is a change and migration of the soul from this world to another. Now if you suppose that there is no consciousness, but a sleep like the sleep of him who is undisturbed even by dreams, death will be an unspeakable gain. For if a person were to select the night in which his sleep was undisturbed even by dreams, and were to compare with this the other days and nights of his life, and then were to tell us how many days and nights he had passed in the course of his life better and more pleasantly than this one, I think that any man, I will not say a private man, but even the great king will not find many such days or nights, when compared with the others. Now if death be of such a nature, I say that to die is gain; for eternity is then only a single night. But if death is the journey to another place, and there, as men say, all the dead abide, what good, O my friends and judges, can be greater than this? If indeed when the pilgrim arrives in the world below, he is delivered from the professors of justice in this world, and finds the true judges who are said to give judgment there, Minos and Rhadamanthus and Aeacus and Triptolemus, and other sons of God who were righteous in their own life, that pilgrimage would be worth making. What would not a man give if he might converse with Orpheus and Musaeus and Hesiod and Homer? Nay, if this be true, let me die again and again. I myself, too, shall have a wonderful interest in there meeting and conversing with Palamedes, and Ajax the son of Telamon, and any other ancient hero who has suffered death through an unjust judgment; and there will be no small pleasure, as I think, in comparing my own sufferings with theirs. Above all, I shall then be able to continue my search into true and false knowledge; as in this world, so also in the next;

445

and I shall find out who is wise, and who pretends to be wise, and is not. What would not a man give, O judges, to be able to examine the leader of the great Trojan expedition; or Odysseus or Sisyphus, or numberless others, men and women too! What infinite delight would there be in conversing with them and asking them questions! In another world they do not put a man to death for asking questions: assuredly not. For besides being happier than we are, they will be immortal, if what is said is true. (11)

Wherefore, O judges, be of good cheer about death, and know of a certainty, that no evil can happen to a good man, either in life or after death. (12)

The hour of departure has arrived, and we go our ways—I to die, and you to live. Which is better God only knows. (13)

No man should bring children into the world who is unwilling to persevere to the end in their nurture and education. (14)

Dear Crito, your zeal is invaluable, if a right one; but if wrong, the greater the zeal the greater the danger; and therefore we ought to consider whether I shall or shall not do as you say. For I am and always have been one of those natures who must be guided by reason, whatever the reason may be which upon reflection appears to me to be the best. (15)

Not life, but a good life, is to be chiefly valued. (16)

Nor when injured injure in return, as the many imagine, for we must injure no one at all. (17)

This, dear Crito, is the voice which I seem to hear murmuring in my ears, like the sound of the flute in the ears of the mystic; that voice, I say, is humming in my ears, and prevents me from hearing any other. And I know that anything more which you may say will be vain. Yet speak, if you have anything to say.

I have nothing to say, Socrates.

Leave me then, Crito, to fulfil the will of God, and to follow whither he leads. (18)

I had a singular feeling at being in his company. For I could hardly believe that I was present at the death of a friend, and therefore I did not pity him, Echecrates; he died so fearlessly, and his words and bearing were so noble and gracious, that to me he appeared blessed. I thought that in going to the other world he could not be without a divine call, and that he would be happy, if any man ever was, when he arrived there; and therefore I did not pity him as might have seemed natural at such an hour. (19)

But then, O my friends, he said, if the soul is really immortal, what care should be taken of her, not only in respect of the portion of time which is called life, but of eternity! (20)

A man of sense ought not to say, nor will I be very confident, that the description that I have given of the soul and her mansions is exactly true. But I do say that, inasmuch as the soul is shown to be immortal, he may venture to think, not improperly or unworthily, that something of the kind is true. The venture is a glorious one, and he ought to comfort himself with words like these, which is the reason why I lengthen out the tale. Wherefore, I say, let a man be of good cheer about his soul, who having cast away the pleasures and ornaments of the body as alien to him and working harm rather than good, has sought after the pleasures of knowledge, and has arrayed the soul, not in some foreign attire, but in her own proper jewels, temperance and justice, and courage, and nobility, and truth—in these adorned she is ready to go on her journey to the world below, when her hour comes. (21)

There is far greater peril in buying knowledge than in buying meat and drink: the one you purchase of the wholesale or retail dealer, and carry them away in other vessels, and before you receive them into the body as food, you may deposit them at home and call in any experienced friend who knows what is good to be eaten or drunken, and what not, and how much, and when; and then the danger of purchasing them is not so great. But you cannot buy the wares of knowledge and carry them away in another vessel; when you have paid for them you must receive them into your soul and go your way, either greatly harmed or greatly benefited. (22)

That we shall be better and braver and less helpless if we think that we ought to enquire, than we should have been if we indulged in the idle fancy that there was no knowing and no use in seeking to know what we do not know,—that is a theme upon which I am ready to fight, in word and deed, to the utmost of my power. (23)

If there were not some community of feelings among mankind, however varying in different persons—I mean to say, if every man's feelings were peculiar to himself—and were not shared by the rest of his species—I do not see how we could ever communicate our impressions to one another. (24)

I would rather that my lyre should be inharmonious, and that there should be no music in the chorus which I provided; aye, or that the whole world should be at odds with me, and oppose me, rather than that I myself should be at odds with myself, and contradict myself. (25)

There should be no secret corner of illiberality; nothing can be more antagonistic than meanness to a soul which is ever longing after the whole of things both divine and human. (26)

The true lover of knowledge is always striving after being— that is his nature; he will not rest in the multiplicity of individuals which is an appearance only, but will go on—the keen edge will not be blunted, nor the force of his desire abate until he have attained the knowledge of the true nature of every essence by a sympathetic and kindred power in the soul, and by that power drawing near and mingling and becoming incorporate with very being, having begotten mind and truth, he will have knowledge and will live and grow truly, and then, and not till then, will he cease from his travail. (27)

There is an absolute beauty and an absolute good. (28)

The soul is like the eye: when resting upon that on which truth and being shine, the soul perceives and understands, and is radiant with intelligence; but when turned toward the twilight of becoming and perishing, then she has opinion only, and goes

448

blinking about, and is first of one opinion and then of another, and seems to have no intelligence. (29)

That which imparts truth to the known and the power of knowing to the knower is what I would have you term the idea of good, and this you will deem to be the cause of science, and of truth in so far as the latter becomes the subject of knowledge; beautiful too, as are both truth and knowledge, you will be right in esteeming this other nature as more beautiful than either; and as in the previous instance, light and sight may be truly said to be like the sun, and yet not to be the sun, so in this other sphere, science and truth may be deemed to be like the good, but not the good; the good has a place of honour yet higher. (30)

What a wonder of beauty that must be which is the author of science and truth, and yet surpasses them in beauty. (31)

The good may be said to be not only the author of knowledge to all things known, but of their being and essence, and yet the good is not essence, but far exceeds essence in dignity and power. (32)

My opinion is that in the world of knowledge the idea of good appears last of all, and is seen only with an effort; and, when seen, is also inferred to be the universal author of all things beautiful and right, parent of light and of the lord of light in this visible world, and the immediate source of reason and truth in the intellectual; and that this is the power upon which he who would act rationally either in public or private life must have his eye fixed. (33)

When a person starts on the discovery of the absolute by the light of reason only, and without any assistance of sense, and perseveres until by pure intelligence he arrives at the perception of the absolute good, he at last finds himself at the end of the intellectual world, as in the case of sight at the end of the visible. (34)

The time has now arrived at which they must raise the eye of the soul to the universal light which lightens all things, and behold the absolute good. (35)

449

Wherefore my counsel is, that we hold fast ever to the heavenly way and follow after justice and virtue always, considering that the soul is immortal and able to endure every sort of good and every sort of evil. (36)

When the father and creator saw the creature which he had made moving and living, the created image of the eternal gods, he rejoiced, and in his joy determined to make the copy still more like the original; and as this was eternal, he sought to make the universe eternal, so far as might be. Now the nature of the ideal being was everlasting, but to bestow this attribute in its fulness upon a creature was impossible. Wherefore he resolved to have a moving image of eternity, and when he set in order the heaven, he made this image eternal but moving according to number, while eternity itself rests in unity; and this image we call time. For there were no days and nights and months and years before the heaven was created, but when he constructed the heaven he created them also. They are all parts of time, and the past and future are created species of time, which we unconsciously but wrongly transfer to the eternal essence; for we say that he 'was,' he 'is,' he 'will be,' but the truth is that 'is' alone is properly attributed to him, and that 'was' and 'will be' are only to be spoken of becoming in time, for they are motions, but that which is immovably the same cannot become older or younger by time, nor ever did or has become, or hereafter will be, older or younger, nor is subject at all to any of those states which affect moving and sensible things and of which generation is the cause. These are the forms of time, which imitates eternity and resolves according to a law of number. (37)

450

CHAPTER II

SOPHOCLES

Sophocles was born in 496 or 495 B.C. and lived for ninety years until 405 B.C. He was thus born some thirty years or so after Aeschylus, and from ten ot fifteen years before Euripides, whom he survived a short time.

Sophocles' family was wealthy. While he never forsook Athens he repeatedly went on embassies to other Greek states. In the Samian War of 440 B.C. he was general, jointly with Pericles.

In 468 when he was twenty-eight years old, in the Athenian competition he won first place over Aeschylus. Not only in time but as respects his outlook upon life and the characteristics of his dramatic productions, he is between Aeschylus and Euripides, resembling each in certain ways, much more than they themselves resemble one another.

Although Sophocles is believed to have written perhaps as many as 125 plays only seven are extant. The quotations that follow in this chapter are from Oedipus the King *and from* Antigone. *The other extant plays are*: Oedipus at Colonnus, Electra, Philoctetes, Ajax, Maidens of Trachis. *He never fell below second place in competition. He was defeated by Euripides for first place in 441 B.C.*

When a man shrinks not from a deed, neither is he scared by a word. (1)

Man's noblest task is to help others by his best means and powers. (2)

It is not right to adjudge bad men good at random, or good men bad. I count it a like thing for a man to cast off a true friend as to cast away the life in his own bosom, which most he loves.

Nay, thou wilt learn these things with sureness in time, for time alone shows a just man; but thou couldst discern a knave even in one day. (3)

Alas, ye generations of men, how mere a shadow do I count your life! Where, where is the mortal who wins more of happiness than just the seeming, and, after the semblance, a falling away? (4)

Those griefs smart most which are seen to be of our own choice. (5)

'Tis unmeet to name what 'tis unmeet to do. (6)

Therefore, while our eyes wait to see the destined final day, we must call no one happy who is of mortal race, until he hath crossed life's border, free from pain. (7)

Remembering this, that our country is the ship that bears us safe, and that only while she prospers in our voyage can we make true friends. (8)

Dread news makes one pause long. (9)

It is not well to love gain from every source. For thou wilt find that illgotten pelf brings more men to ruin than to weal. (10)

Cunning beyond fancy's dream is the fertile skill which brings him, now to evil, now to good. When he honours the laws of the land, and that justice which he hath sworn by the gods to uphold, proudly stands his city: no city hath he who, for his rashness, dwells with sin. Never may he share my hearth, never think my thoughts, who doth these things! (11)

Not such are the laws set among men by the Justice who dwells with the gods below; nor deemed I that thy decrees were of such force, that a mortal could override the unwritten and unfailing statutes of heaven. For their life is not of today, or yesterday, but from all time, and no man knows when they were first put forth. (12)

So oft, before the deed, the mind stands self-convicted in its treason, when folks are plotting mischief in the dark. But verily this, too, is hateful,—when one who hath been caught in wickedness then seeks to make the crime a glory. (13)

452

'Tis not my nature to join in hating, but in loving. (14)

One world approved thy wisdom; another mine. (15)

For if any man thinks that he alone is wise—that in speech, or in mind, he hath no peer,—such a soul, when laid open, is ever found empty. (16)

Though a man be wise, 'tis no shame for him to learn many things, and to bend in season. Seest thou, beside the wintry torrent's course, how the trees that yield to it save every twig, while the stiff-necked perish root and branch? And even thus he who keeps the sheet of his sail taut, and never slackens it, upsets his boat, and finishes his voyage with keel uppermost. (17)

All men are liable to err; but when an error hath been made, that man is no longer witless or unblest who heals the ill into which he hath fallen, and remains not stubborn. (18)

Truth is ever best. (19)

He hath witnessed to mankind that, of all curses which cleave to man, ill counsel is the sovereign curse. (20)

Excess of silence, too, may have a perilous meaning. (21)

Wisdom is the supreme part of happiness; and reverence towards the gods must be inviolate. Great words of prideful men are ever punished with great blows, and, in old age, teach the chastened to be wise. (22)

CHAPTER III

MONTESQUIEU

Montesquieu, Charles Louis Secondat de la Brède, was born at the Chateau de la Brède, near Bordeaux in 1689. He died in 1755 at the age of 66 years. Montesquieu was a wine grower, but it is for his writings that he is known and remembered.

Montesquieu was a high judge in France but he was critical of the regime that he served. In his youth he had been a member of the "First Floor Club" in Paris, a secret society strongly opposed to absolutism and clerical orthodoxy. He remained faithful to the club's principles but became rather moderate in his judgment of the advantages of other political systems.

His Persian Letters *(1721), a thinly veiled satirical criticism of French life made a great sensation. His* Reflections on the Causes of the Greatness and the Decadence of the Romans *(1734) is considered one of the most important monuments of modern historical literature. Montesquieu's principal work is* The Spirit of Laws *(1748). It was the result of fourteen years of strenuous study into political history and comparative legislation, of reading sources and observing life by traveling through many countries of Europe, and above all, of a stay in England.*

The principle of separation of powers, or of checks and balances, which is characteristic of the Constitution of the United States, was formulated in such a striking manner by Montesquieu that Jefferson, Hamilton, Adams, and Madison, and others, were deeply impressed by it, and held it more or less clearly in mind when they gave the Constitution its shape.

Next to Locke, Montesquieu was probably the most influential champion of liberalism in the 18th century.

God is related to the universe, as Creator and Preserver; the laws by which He created all things are those by which He preserves them. He acts according to these rules, because He knows them; He knows them, because He made them; and He made them, because they are in relation of His Wisdom and power.(1)

Particular intelligent beings may have laws of their own making, but they have some likewise which they never made. Before there were intelligent beings, they were possible; they had therefore possible relations, and consequently possible laws. Before laws were made, there were relations of possible justice. To say that there is nothing just or unjust but what is commanded or forbidden by positive laws, is the same as saying that before the describing of a circle all the radii were not equal.

We must therefore acknowledge relations of justice antecedent to the positive law by which they are established. (2)

Law in general is human reason, inasmuch as it governs all the inhabitants of the earth: the political and civil laws of each nation ought to be only the particular cases in which human reason is applied. (3)

To form a moderate government, it is necessary to combine the several powers; to regulate, temper, and set them in motion; to give, as it were, ballast to one, in order to enable it to counterpoise the other. This is a masterpiece of legislation, rarely produced by hazard, and seldom attained by prudence. On the contrary, a despotic government offers itself, as it were, at first sight; it is uniform throughout; and as passions only are requisite to establish it, this is what every capacity may reach. (4)

Political liberty does not consist in an unlimited freedom. In governments, that is, in societies directed by laws, liberty can consist only in the power of doing what we ought to will, and in not being constrained to do what we ought not to will. (5)

Human laws, made to direct the will, ought to give precepts, and not counsels; religion, made to influence the heart, should give many counsels, and few precepts. (6)

Men who are knaves by retail are extremely honest in the gross; they love morality. (7)

455

CHAPTER IV

LESSING

Gotthold Ephraim Lessing was born in 1729 in Kamenz, a small town in Saxony, where his father was chief pastor. He died at the comparatively early age of 52.

Poet, dramatist, critic of art and literature, archeologist, historian and theologian, Lessing was the first man of letters in Germany who dared to earn his living as a free-lance writer. Living among people who recoiled from activities involving personal responsibility, Lessing valued independent thinking and feeling, criticism and knowledge as the highest energies of life and mind; he endeavored to awaken the spirit of responsibility among the German people. He also tried to establish standards of judgment and principles of poetic and artistic creation. This latter he did in his Hamburgische Drama- turgie *and* Laokoön *(1766-1767).*

The latter part of the life of Lessing was devoted to freeing and broadening the conception of religion and defending the application of criticism to Christianity. In this cause he published Zur Geschichte und Litteratur *(1774-1778). In the well-known drama* Nathan der Weise *(1779) Lessing pointed out the unity of aim in Mohammedan- ism, Judaism and Christianity, and in his great work* Die Erziehung des Menschengeschechts *(1780 [The Education of the Human Race], he portrayed life as the education of man through successive Divine revelations. These works have had a marked influence in promoting religious breadth and tolerance.*

Lessing proclaimed that he put striving for truth above possession of truth.

Unquestionably the laws must not usurp power over the sci- ences, for the ultimate purpose of the sciences is truth. Truth is

a necessity of the soul; and it is nothing but tyranny to offer her
the slightest violence in satisfying this essential need. (1)

    Chief miracle it is
That the true miracles become to us
So commonplace, so everyday. Without
This universal miracle could it be
That thinking men should use the word like children,
Who only gape and stare upon what's strange,
And think what's newest is most wonderful. (2)

    But come! I need not teach you what you know!
How easier far is dreaming pious dreams
    Than acting bravely; how a worthless creature
Will dream fine dreams, in order to escape—
(Though oft his object's hidden from himself)—
    Some serviceable labour. (3)

The will, the will
Makes givers, not the gift. (4)

Hold to the best,
Only the best, and praise the Lord who knows
    Best how to reconcile them. (5)

    The superstition in which we grew up,
Doth not, because we see it as it is,
Lose, therefore, all its power upon our souls.
They are not all free men who mock their chains. (6)

How light I feel me now
Since there is nothing further in the world
I have to hide! and even as in Thy sight
Can walk in man's sight too, who judge a man,
Must judge, by deeds alone. (7)

One of those enthusiasts who dream
They know, they only, the true way to God. (8)

And feel themselves compelled
To lead all others who have missed the way
Back to the same—and scarcely can do other—
For be it true this way alone can be
The way of safety, can they be content
To see their friends upon another road,
Which leads to loss, to everlasting loss?
Thus is it possible, for the self-same people,
And at the self-same time, to love and hate. (9)

He who presumes upon a good deed done,
Takes it all back. (10)

Don't trust the heart too much. It is too ready to say what you
want it to say. If the mouth were to speak as the heart does, the
fashion of wearing padlocks on the lips would have come in long
ago. (11)

People don't talk about the virtues they have, but rather of
those they haven't. (12)

Friend or foe alike admit he is the bravest man in the world.
But who ever heard him talk of courage? He has the most upright
heart, yet honesty and nobility are words he never uses. (13)

You get on so well with good people. But when will you learn
how to put up with bad ones? For they are people too. And often
not nearly so bad as they seem. (14)

Saladin:
I desire
Instruction of you in another field,
Quite other; and to use your wisdom there.
Since you are wise, tell me as to a friend,
What faith, what law, have satisfied you best.

458

Nathan:
Sultan, I am a Jew.—
Saladin:
A Muslim I.
The Christian stands between us. Of these three
Religions only one can be the true one.
A man like you will not consent to stay
Where'er the accident of birth has cast him;
Or if he stays, 'twill be of's own election
As insight, reason, choice of best things, prompt him.
Come, then, impart to me your insight: let me hear
The moving reasons: since for this high quest
Time was not granted me. Tell me the choice,
Tell me the grounds—of course, in confidence—
Which fixed the choice, that I may make it mine.

——————————

Nathan:
There lived a man in a far Eastern clime
In hoar antiquity, who had from the hand
Of his most dear beloved received a ring
Of priceless estimate. An opal 'twas
Which split a hundred lovely radiances
And had a magic power, that whoso wore it,
Trusting therein, found grace with God and man.
What wonder therefore that this man o' the East
Let it not from his finger, and took pains
To keep it to his household for all time.
Thus he bequeathed the jewel to the son
Of all his sons he loved best, and provided
That he in turn bequeath it to the son
Who was to him the dearest; evermore
The best-beloved, without respect of birth,
By right o' the ring alone should be the head,
The house's prince.

459

———————————

Well this ring,
From son to son descending, came at last
Unto a father of three sons, who all
To him, all three, were dutiful alike,
And whom, all three, in natural consequence,
He loved alike. Only from time to time
Now this; now that one; now the third, as each
Might be alone with him, the other twain
Not sharing his o'erflowing heart, appeared
Worthiest the ring: and then, piously weak,
He promised it to each. And so things went
Long as they could. But dying hour drawn near
Brought the good father to perplexity.
It pained him, the two sons, trusting his word,
Should thus be wounded. What was he to do?
Quickly he sends for an artificer,
To make him on the model of his ring
Two others, bidding spare nor cost nor pains
To make them in all points identical;
And this the artist did. When they were brought
Even the father scarcely can distinguish
His pattern-ring. So full of joy, he calls
His sons, and each to him separately;
And gives to each son separately his blessing,
Gives each his ring; and dies.

———————————

The tale is finished.
For what still follows, any man may guess.
Scarce was the father dead, but each one comes
And shows his ring, and each one claims to be
True prince o' the house. Vainly they search, strive, argue,
The true ring was not proved or provable.—

460

Almost as hard to prove as to us now
What the true creed is.

— — — — — — —

Saladin:
The rings! You play with me! It was my thought
That the religions I have named to you
Were plainly, easily distinguishable,
Down even to clothing, down to meat and drink!
Nathan:
Only not so in questions of foundation—
For base not all their creeds on history,
Written or handed down? And history
Must be received in faith implicitly.
Is't not so? Then on whom rest we this faith
Implicit, doubting not? Surely on our own?
Them from whose blood we spring? Surely on them
Who from our childhood gave us proofs of love?
Who never have deceived us, saving when
'Twere happier, safer so to be deceived?
How, then, shall I my fathers less believe
Than you your own? or in the other case,
Can I demand that you should give the lie
To your forefathers, that mine be not gainsaid?
And, yet again, the same holds of the Christians.
Is't not so?

— — — — — — —

Nathan:
Then let us come again
Back to our rings. As we have said—the sons
Appealed to law, and swore before the Judge
Out of the father's hand, immediately,
To have received the ring—and this was true—
After for long he had the promise sure
One day to enjoy the privilege of the ring—

461

And this no less was true. Each cried the father
Could not be false towards him, and ere he might
Let such suspicion stain him, must believe,
Glad as he were to think the best of them,
His brothers played him false, and he should soon
Expose the traitors, justify himself.

Saladin:

And now, the Judge? I'm waiting, fain to hear
What you will make him say. What was his verdict?

Nathan:

Thus spake the Judge: Bring me the father here
To witness; I will hear him; and if not
Leave then my judgment seat. Think you this chair
Is set for reading of riddles? Do you wait,
Expecting the true ring to open mouth?
Yet halt! I hear, the genuine ring possesses
The magic power to bring its wearer love
And grace with God and man. That must decide;
For never can the false rings have this virtue.
Well, then; say whom do two of you love best!
Come, speak! What! silent! Is the ring's effect
But backward and not outward? Is it so
That each one loves himself most? Then I judge
All three of you are traitors and betrayed!
Your rings all three are false. The genuine ring
Perchance the father lost, and to replace it
And hide the loss, had three rings made for one.

— — — — — — —

So, went on the Judge,
You may not seek my counsel, but my verdict;
But go! My counsel is, you take the thing
Exactly as it lies. If each of you
Received his ring from his good father's hand,
Then each of you believe his ring the true one—

462

'Tis possible the father would not suffer
Longer the one ring tyrannise in's house,
Certain, he loved all three, and equal loved,
And would not injure two to favour one.
Well, then, let each one strive most zealously
To show a love untainted by self-care,
Each with his might vie with the rest to bring
Into the day the virtue of the jewel
His finger wears, and help this virtue forth
By gentleness, by spirit tractable,
By kind deeds and true piety towards God;
And when in days to come the magic powers
Of these fair rings among your children's children
Brighten the world, I call you once again,
After a thousand thousand years are lapsed,
Before this seat of judgment. On that day
A wiser man shall sit on it and speak. (15)

CHAPTER V

ALEXANDER POPE

Alexander Pope was born in Lombard Street, London, in May 1688. His father was a linen draper who had accumulated a considerable fortune for that time. The family was Roman Catholic. Moreover, Alexander was born just when the Stuarts were being finally supplanted, and the country was violently anti-catholic. The boy's education seems as far as school attendance is concerned to have been somewhat irregular. But for a considerable period he had a most excellent tutor, beginning when he was only eight years old to read English and Latin verse and then Greek.

Pope was small and slight, with a spinal ailment, but he led an active life. Pope was precocious; in fact as early as 1704 he had Pastorals *in manuscript form. His literary life can well be grouped into three periods, namely:*

1. Up to about 1715 or a year or two later. To this period, in addition to Pastorals *(1704 in manuscript, finally published in 1709), belong* An Essay on Criticism *(1711),* The Rape of the Lock *(1712, revised in 1714), which greatly enhanced his fame,* Elegy to the Memory of an Unfortunate Lady, *and* Eloisa to Abelard *in 1717, also in this period, earlier,* Temple of Fame *and* Windsor Forest. *At an early age Pope became a close friend of several prominent literary and political figures, in particular Jonathan Swift and Viscount Bolingbroke, as well as other Tory writers and statesmen.*

2. Translation of the Iliad *(1715-20), and the* Odyssey *(1725-6). From the Iliad he derived not only fame but substantial reward, buying his villa at Twickenham about this time.*

464

3. The Duncaid (*1728, revised 1743*); An Essay on Man *and*
Moral Essays, *as well as satires, epistles, etc.*

*Alexander Pope died at the age of 56, May 30, 1744, at Twicken-
ham, Middlesex.*

*It is remarkable how many common expressions, or phrases often
quoted come from Pope. A few illustrative examples follow:*

> *"The feast of reason and the flow of soul."*
> *"Man never is but always to be blest."*
> *"To err is human; to forgive divine."*
> *"Fools rush in where angels fear to tread."*
> *"An honest man's the noblest work of God."*
> *"Who looks through nature up to Nature's God."*
> *"A little learning is a dangerous thing."*
> *"Hope springs eternal in the human breast."*
> *"The proper study of mankind is man."*
> *"He can't be wrong whose life is in the right."*
> *"Order is heaven's first law."*
> *"Whatever is, is right."*
> *"Who shall decide, when doctors disagree."*
> *"Just as the twig is bent the tree's inclined."*
> *"Honour and shame from no condition rise."*
> *"The glory, jest, and riddle of the world!"*

Of all the causes which conspire to blind
Man's erring judgment, and misguide the mind,
What the weak head with strongest bias rules,
Is pride, the never-failing voice of fools.
Whatever nature has in worth denied,
She gives in large recruits of needful pride;
For as in bodies, thus in souls, we find
What wants in blood and spirits, swelled with wind:
Pride, where wit fails, steps in to our defence,
And fills up all the mighty void of sense.
If once right reason drives that cloud away,
Truth breaks upon us with resistless day.
Trust not yourself; but your defects to know,

Make use of ev'ry friend—and ev'ry foe.
  A little learning is a dang'rous thing;
Drink deep, or taste not the Pierian spring. (1)

True wit is nature to advantage dressed,
What oft was thought, but ne'er so well expressed;
Something, whose truth convinced at sight we find,
That gives us back the image of our mind. (2)

Words are like leaves; and where they most abound,
Much fruit of sense beneath is rarely found. (3)

In words, as fashions, the same rule will hold;
Alike fantastic, if too new, or old:
Be not the first by whom the new are tried,
Nor yet the last to lay the old aside. (4)

  Some foreign writers, some our own despise;
The ancients only, or the moderns prize.
Thus wit, like faith, by each man is applied
To one small sect, and all are damned beside.
Meanly they seek the blessing to confine,
And force that sun but on a part to shine,
Which not alone the southern wit sublimes,
But ripens spirits in cold northern climes;
Which from the first has shone on ages past,
Enlights the present, and shall warm the last;
Though each may feel increases and decays,
And see now clearer and now darker days:
Regard not then if wit be old or new,
But blame the false, and value still the true. (5)

  Be thou the first true merit to befriend,
His praise is lost, who stays, till all commend. (6)

466

To err is human, to forgive, divine. (7)

'Tis not enough, your counsel still be true;
Blunt truth more mischief than nice falsehoods do;
Men must be taught as if you taught them not,
And things unknown proposed as things forgot. (8)

What future bliss, He gives not thee to know,
But gives that hope to be thy blessing now.
Hope springs eternal in the human breast:
Man never Is, but always To be blest:
The soul, uneasy and confined from home,
Rests and expatiates in a life to come. (9)

All nature is but art, unknown to thee;
All chance, direction, which thou canst not see;
All discord, harmony not understood;
All partial evil, universal good:
And, spite of pride, in erring reason's spite,
One truth is clear, Whatever is, is right. (10)

Know then thyself, presume not God to scan:
The proper study of mankind is man.
Placed on this isthmus of a middle state,
A being darkly wise, and rudely great:
With too much knowledge for the sceptic side,
With too much weakness for the stoic's pride,
He hangs between; in doubt to act, or rest;
In doubt to deem himself a god, or beast;
In doubt his mind or body to prefer;
Born but to die, and reasoning but to err;
Alike in ignorance, his reason such,
Whether he thinks too little, or too much:
Chaos of thought and passion, all confused;
Still by himself abused, or disabused;

Created half to rise, and half to fall;
Great lord of all things, yet a prey to all;
Sole judge of truth, in endless error hurled:
The glory, jest, and riddle of the world. (11)

For modes of faith let graceless zealots fight;
His can't be wrong whose life is in the right;
In Faith and Hope the world will disagree,
But all mankind's concern is Charity:
All must be false that thwart this one great end;
And all of God, that bless mankind or mend. (12)

   Honour and shame from no condition rise;
Act well your part, there all the honour lies. (13)

'Tis phrase absurd to call a villain great:
Who wickedly is wise, or madly brave,
Is but the more a fool, the more a knave.
Who noble ends by noble means obtains,
Or failing, smiles in exile or in chains,
Like good Aurelius let him reign or bleed
Like Socrates, that man is great indeed. (14)

   An honest man's the noblest work of God. (15)

   See the sole bliss Heav'n could on all bestow!
Which who but feels could taste, but thinks can know:
Yet poor with fortune, and with learning blind,
The bad must miss; the good, untaught, will find;
Slave to no sect, who takes no private road,
But looks through nature up to nature's God;
Pursues that chain which links the immense design,
Joins heav'n and earth, and mortal and divine;
Sees, that no being any bliss can know,
But touches some above, and some below:

468

Learns, from this union of the rising whole,
The first, last purpose of the human soul;
And knows, where faith, law, morals, all began,
All end, in love of God, and love of man. (16)

Father of all! in ev'ry age,
   In ev'ry clime adored,
By saint, by savage, and by sage,
   Jehovah, Jove, or Lord!

Thou Great First Cause, least understood:
   Who all my sense confined
To know but this, that Thou art good,
   And that myself am blind;

Yet gave me, in this dark estate,
   To see the good from ill;
And binding Nature fast in Fate,
   Left free the human will.

What conscience dictates to be done,
   Or warns me not to do,
This, teach me more than hell to shun,
   That, more than heav'n pursue.

What blessings Thy free bounty gives,
   Let me not cast away;
For God is paid when man receives:
   To enjoy is to obey.

Yet not to earth's contracted span
   Thy goodness let me bound,
Or think Thee Lord alone of man,
   When thousand worlds are round.

469

Let not this weak unknowing hand
    Presume thy bolts to throw,
And deal damnation round the land,
    On each I judge Thy foe.

If I am right, Thy grace impart,
    Still in the right to stay;
If I am wrong, oh, teach my heart
    To find that better way.

Save me alike from foolish pride,
    Or impious discontent,
At aught Thy wisdom has denied,
    Or aught Thy goodness lent.

Teach me to feel another's woe,
    To hide the fault I see;
That mercy I to others show,
    That mercy show to me.

Mean though I am, not wholly so,
    Since quickened by thy breath;
Oh, lead me whereso'er I go,
    Through this day's life or death.

This day, be bread and peace my lot:
    All else beneath the sun,
Thou know'st if best bestowed or not;
    And let Thy will be done.

To Thee, whose temple is all space,
    Whose altar, earth, sea, skies,
One chorus let all being raise;
    All nature's incense rise! (17)

470

CHAPTER VI

JOHN MILTON

John Milton was born in London in 1608. He died in 1674. As is well known the sixty-six year period of his life was a tumultuous one in England and especially in London. The years of the Commonwealth and of Oliver Cromwell as Lord Protector were in Milton's middle life.

Milton was educated at St. Paul's School and Christ's College, Cambridge, receiving B.A. degree in 1629 and M.A. in 1632. Milton devoted the early years of his maturity to private study and to the writing of verse, both English and Latin, in a variety of Renaissance traditions. In this period of his life, 1638-1639, he spent fifteen months in travel in Europe. "There it was," in Florence, "that I found and visited the famous Galileo grown old, a prisoner to the Inquisition, for thinking in Astronomy other than the Franciscan and Dominican licencers thought."

Among Milton's relatively early poems are On the Morning of Christ's Nativity, *composed in 1629, and the famed* L'Allegro *and* Il Penseroso, *1632.*

Starting as an Anglican of moderate Puritan leanings, Milton became successively Presbyterian and Independent. From 1641 to 1660 Milton was active in public affairs, serving as Secretary to the Council of State. During this period he produced a notable series of pamphlets on ecclesiastical, sociological and political subjects. Famed Areopagitica, A Speech for the Liberty of Unlicenc'd Printing, *dates from 1644.*

During his later years, spent in blindness and enforced retirement, Milton wrote his major epic, Paradise Lost (1667), *a shorter epic,* Paradise Regained (1671) *and a drama,* Samson Agonistes (1671), *as well as a considerable body of prose.*

471

When I consider how my light is spent,
    E're half my days, in this dark world and wide,
    And that one talent which is death to hide,
    Lodg'd with me useless, though my Soul more bent
To serve therewith my Maker, and present
    My true account, least he returning chide,
    Doth God exact day-labour, light deny'd,
    I fondly ask; But patience to prevent
That murmur, soon replies, God doth not need
    Either man's work or his own gifts, who best
    Bear his milde yoak, they serve him best, his State
Is Kingly. Thousands at his bidding speed
    And post o're Land and Ocean without rest:
    They also serve who only stand and waite. (1)

    Peace hath her Victories no less than those of War. (2)

And chiefly Thou O Spirit, that dost prefer
Before all Temples th' upright heart and pure,
Instruct me, for Thou know'st; Thou from the first
Wast present, and with mighty wings outspread
Dove-like satst brooding on the vast Abyss
And mad'st it pregnant: What in me is dark
Illumin, what is low raise and support,
That to the highth of this great Argument
I may assert Eternal Providence,
And justifie the wayes of God to men. (3)

The mind is its own place, and in itself
Can make a Heav'n of Hell, a Hell of Heav'n. (4)

Who overcomes
By force, hath overcome but half his foe. (5)

472

O shame to men! Devil with Devil damn'd
Firm concord holds, men onely disagree
Of Creatures rational, though under hope
Of heavenly Grace; and God proclaiming peace,
Yet live in hatred, enmitie, and strife
Among themselves, and levie cruel warres,
Wasting the Earth, each other to destroy:
As if (which might induce us to accord)
Man had not hellish foes anow besides,
That day and night for his destruction waite. (6)

So much the rather thou Celestial light
Shine inward, and the mind through all her powers
Irradiate, there plant eyes, all mist from thence
Purge and disperse, that I may see and tell
Of things invisible to mortal sight. (7)

For neither Man nor Angel can discern
Hypocrisie, the only evil that walks
Invisible, except to God alone,
By his permissive will, through Heav'n and Earth:
And oft though wisdom wake, suspicion sleeps
At wisdoms Gate, and to simplicitie
Resigns her charge, while goodness thinks no ill
Where no ill seems. (8)

For within him Hell
He brings, and round about him, nor from Hell
One step no more then from himself can fly
By change of place. (9)

Which way I flie is Hell; myself am Hell;
And in the lowest deep a lower deep
Still threatening to devour me opens wide,
To which the Hell I suffer seems a Heav'n. (10)

    To recount Almightie works
What words or tongue of Seraph can suffice,
Or heart of man suffice to comprehend? (11)

And Earth be chang'd to Heav'n, and Heav'n to Earth,
One Kingdom, Joy and Union without end. (12)

Immediate are the Acts of God, more swift
Then time or motion. (13)

Great are thy works, *Jehovah*, infinite
Thy power; what thought can measure thee or tongue
Relate thee. (14)

Who seekes
To lessen thee, against his purpose serves
To manifest the more thy might; his evil
Thou usest, and from thence creat'st more good. (15)

But apte the Mind or Fancie is to roave
Uncheckt, and of her roaving is no end;
Till warn'd, or by experience taught, she learne,
That not to know at large of things remote
From use, obscure and suttle, but to know
That which before us lies in daily life,
Is the prime Wisdom. (16)

Among unequals what societie
Can sort, what harmonie or true delight?
Which must be mutual, in proportion due
Giv'n and received. (17)

To attaine
The highth and depth of thy Eternal wayes
All human thoughts come short, Supream of things;
Thou in thyself art perfet, and in thee
Is no deficience found. (18)

474

While yet we live, scarce one short hour perhaps,
Between us two let there be peace. (19)

But rise, let us no more contend, nor blame
Each other, blam'd enough elsewhere, but strive
In offices of Love, how we may light'n
Each others burden in our share of woe. (20)

Thus they in lowliest plight repentant stood
Praying, for from the Mercie-seat above
Prevenient Grace descending had remov'd
The stonie from their hearts, and made new flesh
Regenerate grow instead, that sighs now breath'd
Unutterable, which the Spirit of prayer
Inspir'd, and wing'd for Heav'n with speedier flight
Then loudest Oratorie. (21)

This most afflicts me, that departing hence,
As from his face I shall be hid, depriv'd
His blessed count'nance; here I could frequent,
With worship, place by place where he voutsaf'd
Presence Divine, and to my Sons Relate;
On this Mount he appeerd, under this Tree
Stood visible, among these Pines his voice
I heard, here with him at this Fountain talk'd:
So many grateful Altars I would reare
Of grassie Terfe, and pile up every Stone
Of lustre from the brook, in memorie,
Or monument to Ages, and thereon
Offer sweet smelling Gumms and Fruits and Flours:
In yonder nether World where shall I seek
His bright appearances, or footsteps trace?
For though I fled him angrie, yet recall'd
To life prolongd and promisd Race, I now
Gladly behold though but his utmost skirts
Of glory, and farr off his steps adore. (22)

Adam, thou know'st Heav'n his, and all the Earth,
Not this Rock onely; his Omnipresence fills
Land, Sea, and Aire, and every kinde that lives,
Fomented by his virtual power and warmd:
All the Earth he gave thee to possess and rule,
No despicable gift; surmise not then
His presence to these narrow bounds confin'd
Of Paradise or *Eden:* this had been
Perhaps thy Capital Seate, from whence had spred
All generations, and had hither come
From all the ends of th' Earth, to celebrate
And reverence thee thir great Progenitor.
But this preeminence thou hast lost, brought down
To dwell on eeven ground now with thy Sons:
Yet doubt not but in Vallie and in plaine
God is as here, and will be found alike
Present, and of his presence many a signe
Still following thee, still compassing thee round
With goodness and paternal Love, his Face
Express, and of his steps the track Divine. (23)

Nor love thy Life, nor hate; but what thou livst
Live well, how long or short permit to Heav'n. (24)

Judg not what is best
By pleasure, though to Nature seeming meet,
Created, as thou art, to nobler end
Holie and pure, conformitie divine. (25)

But what more oft in Nations grown corrupt,
And by their vices brought to servitude,
Then to love Bondage more than Liberty,
Bondage with ease then strenuous liberty. (26)

    In that day it shall no more bee said as in scorne, this or that
was never held so till this present Age, when men have better

learnt that the times and seasons passe along under thy feet, to goe and come at thy bidding, and as thou didst dignifie our fathers dayes with many revelations above all the fore-going ages, since thou tookst the flesh; so thou canst vouchsafe to us (though unworthy) as large a portion of thy spirit as thou pleasest; for who shall prejudice thy all-governing will? seeing the power of thy grace is not past away with the primitive times, as fond and faithless men imagine, but thy Kingdom is now at hand, and thou standing at the dore. (27)

But were it the meanest underservice, if God by his Secretary conscience injoyn it, it were sad for me if I should draw back, for me especially, now when all men offer their aid to help ease and lighten the difficult labours of the Church, to whose service by the intentions of my parents and friends I was destin'd of a child, and in mine own resolutions, till coming to some maturity of years and perceaving what tyranny had invaded the Church, that he who would take Orders must subscribe slave, and take an oath withall, which unlesse he took with a conscience that would retch, he must either strait perjure, or split his faith, I thought it better to preferre a blamelesse silence before the sacred office of speaking bought, and begun with servitude and forswearing. (28)

It was thought of old in Philosophy, that shame or to call it better, the reverence of our elders, our brethren, and friends was the greatest incitement to vertuous deeds and the greatest dis-suasion from unworthy attempts that might be. Hence we may read in the Iliad where *Hector* being wisht to retire from the battel, many of his forces being routed, makes answer that he durst not for shame, lest the Trojan Knights and Dames should think he did ignobly. And certain it is that whereas Terror is thought such a great stickler in a Commonwealth, honourable shame is a farre greater, and has more reason. For where shame is there is fear, but where fear is there is not presently shame. And if any thing may be done to inbreed in us this generous and Christianly reverence one of another, the very Nurs and Guardian of piety and vertue, it can not sooner be then by such a discipline in the Church, as may use us to have in aw the assemblies of the faithful, and to count it a thing most grievous, next to the grieving of Gods Spirit, to offend those whom he hath put in autority, as a healing superintendence over our lives and behaviours, both in our own happiness and that we may not give offence to good men, who without amends by us made, dare not against Gods command hold communion with us in holy things. And this will be accompanied with a religious dred of being outcast, from the company of Saints, and from the fatherly protection of God in his Church, to consort with the devil and his angels. But there is yet a more ingenuous and noble degree of honest shame, or call it if you will an esteem, whereby men bear an inward reverence toward their own persons. And if the love of God as a fire sent from Heaven to be ever kept alive upon the altar of our hearts, be the first principle of all godly and vertuous actions in men, this pious and just honouring of ourselves is the second, and may be thought as the radical moisture and fountain head, whence every laudable and worthy enterprize issues forth. (29)

Something I confesse it is to be asham'd of evil doing in the presence of any, and to reverence the opinion and the countenance of a good man rather then a bad, fearing most in his sight to offend, goes so farre as almost to be vertuous; yet this is but still the feare of infamy, and many such, when they find themselves alone, saving their reputation will compound with other scruples, and come to a close treaty with their dearer vices in secret. But he that holds himself in reverence and due esteem, both for the dignity of Gods image upon him, and for the price of his redemption, which he thinks is visibly markt upon his forehead, accounts himselfe both a fit person to do the noblest and godliest deeds, and much better worth then to deject and defile, with such a debasement and such a pollution as sin is, himselfe so highly ransom'd and enobl'd to a new friendship and filiall relation with God. Nor can he fear so much the offence and reproach of others, as he dreads and would blush at the reflection

478

of his own severe and modest eye upon himselfe, if it should see him doing or imagining that which is sinfull though in the deepest secrecy. How shall a man know to do himselfe this right, how to performe this honourable duty of estimation and respect towards his own soul and body? which way will leade him beste to this hill top of sanctity and goodnesse above which there is no higher ascent but to the love of God which from this self-pious regard cannot be assunder? no better way doubtlesse then to let him duly understand that as he is call'd by the high calling of God to be holy and pure, so is he by the same appointment ordain'd, and by the Churches call admitted to such offices of discipline in the Church to which his owne spirituall gifts by the example of Apostolick institution have autoriz'd him. (30)

I shall alwayes be of this opinion, that obedience to the spirit of God, rather then to the faire seeming pretences of men, is the best and most dutifull order that a Christian can observe. (31)

Truth is as impossible to be soil'd by any outward touch, as the Sun beam. (32)

Honest liberty is the greatest foe to dishonest licence. (33)

Let not other men thinke their conscience bound to search continually after truth, to pray for enlightning from above, to publish what they think they have so obtain'd, and debar me from conceiving myself ty'd by the same duties. (34)

Mark then, Judges and Lawgivers, and ye whose office it is to be our teachers, for I will utter now a doctrine, if every any other, though neglected or not understood, yet of great and powerfull importance to the governing of mankind. He who wisely would restrain the reasonable Soul of man within due bounds, must first himself know perfectly, how far the territory and dominion extends of just and honest liberty. As little must he offer to bind that which God hath loos'n'd, as to loos'n that which he hath bound. The ignorance and mistake of this high point, hath heapt up one huge half of all the misery that hath bin since Adam. In the Gospel we shall read a supercilious crew of masters, whose holinesse, or rather whose evil eye, grieving that God should be so facil to man, was to set straiter limits to obedience, then God had set; to inslave the dignity of man, to put a garrison upon his neck of empty and overdignifi'd precepts: And we shall read our Saviour never more greev'd and troubl'd, then to meet with such a peevish madnesse among men against their own freedome. (35)

The greatest burden in the world is superstition; not only of ceremonies in the Church, but of imaginary and scarcrow sins at home. What greater weakning, what more suttle stratagem against our Christian warfare, when besides the grosse body of real transgressions to encounter; wee shall be terrifi'd by a vain and shadowy menacing of faults that are not: When things indifferent shall be set to overfront us, under the banners of sin, what wonder if wee be routed, and by this art of our Adversary, fall into the subjection of worst and deadliest offences. (36)

No place in Heav'n or Earth, except Hell, where charity may not enter. (37)

Let the statutes of God be turn'd over, be scann'd a new, and consider'd; not altogether by the narrow intellectuals of quotationists and common placers, but (as was the ancient right of Counsels) by men of what liberall profession soever, of eminent spirit and breeding joyn'd with a diffuse and various knowledge of divine and human things; able to ballance and define good and evil, right and wrong throughout every state of life; able to shew us the waies of the Lord, strait and faithfull as they are, not full of cranks and contradictions, and pit falling dispenses, but with divine insight and benignity measur'd out to the proportion of each mind and spirit, each temper and disposition, created so different each from other, and yet by the skill of wise conducting, all to become uniform in vertue. (38)

Many truths now of reverend esteem and credit, had their birth and beginning once from singular and private thoughts. (39)

Truth in some age or other will find her witnes, and shall be justify'd at last by her own children. (40)

The end then of Learning is . . . to know God aright, and out of

480

that knowledge to love him, to imitate him, to be like him, as we may the neerest by possessing our souls of true vertue, which being united to the heavenly grace of faith makes up the highest perfection. But because our understanding cannot in this body found itself but on sensible things, nor arrive so clearly to the knowledge of God and things invisible, as by orderly conning over the visible and inferior creature, the same method is necessarily to be follow'd in all discreet teaching. (41)

For this is not the liberty which wee can hope, that no grievance ever should arise in the Commonwealth, that let no man in this World expect; but that when complaints are freely heard, deeply consider'd, and speedily reform'd, then is the utmost bound of civill liberty attain'd, that wise men looke for. (42)

Books are not absolutely dead things, but doe contain a potencie of life in them to be as active as that soule was whose progeny they are; nay they do preserve, as in a violl the purest efficacie and extraction of that living intellect that bred them.(43)

A good Booke is the pretious life-blood of a master spirit, imbalm'd and treasur'd up on purpose to a life beyond life. (44)

Truth and understanding are not such wares as to be monopoliz'd and traded in by tickets and statutes, and standards. (45)

Well knows he who uses to consider, that our faith and knowledge thrives by exercise, as well as our limbs and complexion. Truth is compar'd in Scripture to a streaming fountain; if her waters flow not in a perpetuall progression, they sick'n into a muddy pool of conformity and tradition. A man may be a heretick in the truth; and if he beleeve things only because his Paster sayes so, or the Assembly so determine, without knowing other reason, though his belief be true, yet the very truth he holds, becomes his heresie. (46)

He who thinks we are to pitch our tent here, and have attain'd the utmost prospect of reformation, that the mortall glasse wherein we contemplate, can shew us, till we come to *beatific* vision, that man by this very opinion declares, that he is yet farre short of truth. (47)

We boast our light; but if we look not wisely on the Sun it self, it smites us into darkness. Who can discern those planets that are oft *Combust,* and those stars of brightest magnitude that rise and set with the Sun, untill the opposite motion of their orbs bring them to such a place in the firmament, where they may be seen evning or morning. The light that we have gain'd, was given us, not to be ever staring on, but by it to discover onward things more remote from our knowledge. (48)

They are the troublers, they are the dividers of unity, who neglect and permit not others to unite those dissever'd peeces which are yet wanting to the body of Truth. To be still searching what we know not, by what we know, still closing up truth to truth as we find it (for all her body is *homogeneal,* and proportionall) this is the golden rule in *Theology* as well as in *Arithmetick,* and makes up the best harmony in a Church; not the forc't and outward union of cold, and neutrall, and inwardly divided minds. (49)

Where there is much desire to learn, there of necessity will be much arguing, much writing, many opinions; for opinion in good men is but knowledge in the making. (50)

From thence derives it self to a gallant bravery and well grounded contempt of their enemies, as if there were no small number of as great spirits among us, as his was, who when Rome was nigh besieg'd by *Hannibal,* being in the City, bought that peece of ground at no cheap rate, whereon *Hannibal* himself encampt his own regiment. (51)

Methinks I see in my mind a noble and puissant Nation rousing herself like a strong man after sleep, and shaking her invincible locks: Methinks I see her as an Eagle muing her mighty youth, and kindling her undazl'd eyes at the full midday beam; purging and unscaling her long abused sight at the fountain it self of heav'nly radiance. (52)

Give me the liberty to know, to utter, and to argue freely according to conscience, above all liberties. (53)

Though all the windes of doctrin were let loose to play upon

482

the earth, so Truth be in the field, we do injuriously by licencing and prohibiting to misdoubt her strength. Let her and Falshood grapple; who ever knew Truth put to the wors, in a free and open encounter. (54)

For who knows not that Truth is strong next to the Almighty; she needs no policies, nor stratagems, nor licencings to make her victorious, those are the shifts and the defences that error uses against her power. (55)

What great purchase is this Christian liberty which *Paul* so often boasts of. His doctrine is, that he who eats or eats not, regards a day, or regards it not, may doe either to the Lord. How many other things might be tolerated in peace, and left to conscience, had we but charity, and were it not the chief strong hold of our hypocrisie to be ever judging one another. (56)

CHAPTER VII

RALPH WALDO EMERSON

Ralph Waldo Emerson was born in 1803 and died in 1882. A direct ancestor had settled at Concord, Mass. in 1635. His father, who was a liberal clergyman in Boston, died when Ralph was eight years old. His mother held her family together and was glad to have him follow an Emerson tradition and prepare for the ministry, entering Harvard in 1817. He had earlier become a devoted student of Plato and of Pascal. Now he added Shakespeare, Spinoza and Montaigne.

There was a considerable period between university and a settled pastorate. In 1829 Emerson was installed as minister of the Second (Unitarian) Church in Boston. But it was not long before Emerson's indifference to the sacrament of the Lord's Supper caused him to resign in 1832. He settled in Concord, after a brief sojourn in Europe, and thereafter devoted himself to writing and lecturing.

Emerson's first book Nature *(1836) contained the essence of his ideas, which were given further development in* The American Scholar *(1837), the so-called* Divinity School Address *(1838), two famous series of* Essays *(1841, 1844), and numerous other publications, including two collections of poems.*

William James pointed out that there were two Emersons—the instinctive New Englander, and the Emerson who exalted the Over-Soul, and before whom revelations of time, space, and nature shrank away. Emerson emphasized the oneness of man as "part and parcel of God." He regarded every man as the entrance to the universal mind, capable of feeling and comprehending that which at any time befell any man.

There is one mind common to all individual men. Every man is an inlet to the same and to all of the same. He that is once admitted to the right of reason is made a freeman of the whole estate. What Plato has thought, he may think; what a saint has felt, he may feel; what at any time has befallen any man, he can understand. Who hath access to this universal mind is a party to all that is or can be done, for this is the only and sovereign agent. (1)

I have no expectation that any man will read history aright, who thinks that what was done in a remote age, by men whose names have resounded far, has any deeper sense than what he is doing to-day. (2)

To the poet, to the philosopher, to the saint, all things are friendly and sacred, all events profitable, all days holy, all men divine. For the eye is fastened on the life, and slights the circumstance. (3)

I see that men of God have, from time to time, walked among men and made their commission felt in the heart and soul of the commonest hearer. (4)

In old Rome the public roads beginning at the Forum proceeded north, south, east, west, to the centre of every province of the empire, making each market-town of Persia, Spain, and Britain pervious to the soldiers of the capital: so out of the human heart go, as it were, highways to the heart of every object in nature, to reduce it under the dominion of man. A man is a bundle of relations, a knot of roots, whose flower and fruitage is the world. (5)

In the light of these two facts, namely, that the mind is One, and that nature is its correlative, history is to be read and written. (6)

A man shall be the Temple of Fame. He shall walk, as the poets have described that goddess, in a robe painted all over with wonderful events and experiences;—his own form and features by their exalted intelligence shall be that variegated vest. I shall find in him the Foreworld; in his childhood the Age of Gold; the Apples of Knowledge; the Argonautic Expedition; the calling of Abraham; the building of the Temple; the Advent of

Christ; Dark Ages; the Revival of Letters; the Reformation; the discovery of new lands; the opening of new sciences, and new regions in man. He shall be the priest of Pan, and bring with him into humble cottages the blessings of the morning stars and all the recorded benefits of heaven and earth. (7)

To believe your own thought, to believe that what is true for you in your private heart is true for all men,—that is genius. Speak your latent conviction, and it shall be the universal sense; for the inmost in due time becomes the outmost,—and our first thought is rendered back to us by the trumpets of the Last Judgment. Familiar as the voice of the mind is to each, the highest merit we ascribe to Moses, Plato, and Milton is, that they set at naught books and traditions, and spoke not what men but what they thought. (8)

Whoso would be a man must be a non-conformist. He who would gather immortal palms must not be hindered by the name of goodness, but must explore if it be goodness. Nothing is at last sacred but the integrity of your own mind. Absolve you to yourself, and you shall have the suffrage of the world. (9)

Pythagoras was misunderstood, and Socrates, and Jesus, and Luther, and Copernicus, and Galileo, and Newton, and every pure and wise spirit that ever took flesh. To be great is to be misunderstood. (10)

Everywhere I am hindered of meeting God in my brother, because he has shut his own temple doors, and recites fables merely of his brother's or his brother's brother's God. (11)

That country is the fairest which is inhabited by the noblest minds. (12)

We live in succession, in division, in parts, in particles. Meantime within man is the soul of the whole; the wise silence; the universal beauty, to which every part and particle is equally related; the eternal ONE. And this deep power in which we exist, and whose beatitude is all accessible to us, is not only self-sufficing and perfect in every hour, but the act of seeing and the thing seen, the seer and the spectacle, the subject and the

486

object, are one. We see the world piece by piece, as the sun, the moon, the animal, the tree; but the whole, of which these are the shining parts, is the soul. (13)

From within or from behind, a light shines through us upon things, and makes us aware that we are nothing, but the light is all. (14)

We know that all spiritual being is in man. A wise old proverb says, "God comes to see us without bell;" that is, as there is no screen or ceiling between our heads and the infinite heavens, so there is no bar or wall in the soul where man, the effect, ceases, and God, the cause begins. The walls are taken away. We lie open on one side to the deeps of spiritual nature, to the attributes of God. Justice we see and know, Love, Freedom, Power. These natures no man ever got above, but they tower over us, and most in the moment when our interests tempt us to wound them. (15)

Some thoughts always find us young, and keep us so. Such a thought is the love of the universal and eternal beauty. Every man parts from that contemplation with the feeling that it rather belongs to ages than to mortal life. (16)

Those who are capable of humility, of justice, of love, of aspiration, stand already on a platform that commands the sciences and arts, speech and poetry, action and grace. For whoso dwells in this moral beatitude already anticipates those special powers which men prize so highly. (17)

In all conversations between two persons, tacit reference is made, as to a third party, to a common nature. (18)

There is a certain wisdom of humanity which is common to the greatest men with the lowest, and which our ordinary education often labors to silence and obstruct. The mind is one; and the best minds, who love truth for its own sake, think much less of property in truth. They accept it thankfully everywhere, and do not label or stamp it with any man's name, for it is theirs long beforehand, and from eternity. The learned and the studious of thought have no monopoly of wisdom. (19)

The soul is the perceiver and revealer of truth. We know truth

487

when we see it, let sceptic and scoffer say what they choose. Foolish people ask you, when you have spoken what they do not wish to hear, "How do you know it is truth, and not an error of your own?" We know truth when we see it, from opinion, as we know when we are awake that we are awake. It was a grand sentence of Emanuel Swedenborg, which would alone indicate the greatness of that man's perception,—"It is no proof of a man's understanding to be able to confirm whatever he pleases; but to be able to discern that what is true is true, and that what is false is false, this is the mark and character of intelligence." (20)

We are wiser than we know. If we will not interfere with our thought, but will act entirely, or see how the thing stands in God, we know the particular thing, and every thing, and every man. For the Maker of all things and all persons stands behind us, and casts his dread omniscience through us over things. (21)

Christianity is rightly dear to the best of mankind; yet was there never a young philosopher whose breeding had fallen into the Christian Church, by whom that brave text of Paul's was not specially prized:—"Then shall also the Son be subject unto Him who put all things under him, that God may be all in all." Let the claims and virtues of persons be never so great and welcome, the instinct of man presses eagerly onward to the impersonal and il-limitable, and gladly arms itself against the dogmatism of bigots with this generous word out of the book itself. (22)

No truth so sublime but it may be trivial tomorrow in the light of new thoughts. People wish to be settled; only as far as they are unsettled is there any hope for them. (23)

The truth was in us before it was reflected to us from natural objects; and the profound genius will cast the likeness of all creatures into every product of his wit. (24)

God offers to every mind its choice between truth and repose. Take which you please—you can never have both. Between these, as a pendulum, man oscillates. He in whom the love of repose predominates will accept the first creed, the first philosophy, the first political party he meets,—most likely his father's. He gets rest, commodity, and reputation; but he shuts the door of truth. He in whom the love of truth predominates will keep himself aloof from all moorings, and afloat. He will abstain from dogmatism, and recognize all the opposite negations, between which, as walls, his being is swung. He submits to the inconvenience of suspense and imperfect opinion, but he is a candidate for truth, as the other is not, and respects the highest law of his being. (25)

Each new mind we approach seems to require an abdication of all our past and present possessions. A new doctrine seems, at first, a subversion of all our opinions, tastes, and manner of living. Such has Swedenborg, such has Kant, such has Coleridge, such has Hegel or his interpreter Cousin, seemed to many young men in this country. Take thankfully and heartily all they can give. Exhaust them, wrestle with them, let them not go until their blessing be won, and, after a short season, the dismay will be overpast, the excess of influence withdrawn, and they will be no longer an alarming meteor, but one more bright star shining serenely in your heaven, and blending its light with all your day. (26)

The angels are so enamored of the language that is spoken in heaven, that they will not distort their lips with the hissing and unmusical dialects of men, but speak their own, whether there be any who understand it or not. (27)

The Universe has three children, born at one time, which reappear, under different names, in every system of thought, whether they be called cause, operation, and effect; or more poetically, Jove, Pluto, Neptune; or, theologically, the Father, the Spirit, and the Son; but which we will call here, the Knower, the Doer, and the Sayer. These stand respectively for the love of truth, for the love of good, and for the love of beauty. These three are equal. Each is that which he is essentially, so that he cannot be surmounted or analyzed, and each of these three has

489

the power of the others latent in him, and has his own patent. (28)

God has not made some beautiful things, but Beauty is the creator of the universe. (29)

The experience of each new age requires a new confession, and the world seems always waiting for its poet. (30)

The fate of the poor shepherd, who, blinded and lost in the snowstorm, perishes in a drift within a few feet of his cottage door, is an emblem of the state of man. On the brink of the waters of life and truth, we are miserably dying. The inaccessibleness of every thought but that we are in, is wonderful. What if you come near to it,—you are as remote, when you are nearest, as when you are farthest. Every thought is also a prison; every heaven is also a prison. Therefore we love the poet, the inventor, who in any form, whether in an ode, or in an action, or in looks and behavior, has yielded us a new thought. He unlocks our chains, and admits us to a new scene. (31)

Wherever snow falls, or water flows, or birds fly, wherever day and night meet in twilight, wherever the blue heaven is hung by clouds, or sown with stars, wherever are forms with transparent boundaries, wherever are outlets into celestial space, wherever is danger, and awe, and love, there is Beauty, plenteous as rain, shed for thee, and though thou shouldest walk the world over, thou shalt not be able to find a condition inopportune or ignoble. (32)

The possibility of interpretation lies in the identity of the observer with the observed. Each material thing has its celestial side, has its translation, through humanity, into the spiritual and necessary sphere, where it plays a part as indestructible as any other. (33)

Life is girt all round with a zodiac of sciences, the contributions of men who have perished to add their point of light to our sky. Engineer, broker, jurist, physician, moralist, theologian, and every man, inasmuch as he has any science, is a definer and mapmaker of the latitudes and longitudes of our condition. These road-makers on every hand enrich us. We must extend the area of

490

life, and multiply our relations. We are as much gainers by finding a new property in the old earth, as by acquiring a new planet. (34)

Men are helpful through the intellect and the affections. Other help, I find a false appearance. If you affect to give me bread and fire, I perceive that I pay for it the full price, and at last it leaves me as it found me, neither better nor worse: but all mental and moral force is a positive good. (35)

With each new mind, a new secret of nature transpires; nor can the Bible be closed, until the last great man is born. (36)

It is as real a loss that others should be low, as that we should be low; for we must have society. (37)

Philosophy is the account which the human mind gives to itself of the constitution of the world. Two cardinal facts lie forever at the base; the one, and the two,—1. Unity, or Identity; and, 2. Variety. We unite all things, by perceiving the law which pervades them; by perceiving the superficial differences, and the profound resemblances. But every mental act,—this very perception of identity or oneness, recognizes the difference of things. Oneness and otherness. It is impossible to speak, or to think, without embracing both. (38)

CHAPTER VIII

JOHN DONNE

John Donne, English poet and churchman, was born in 1572 and died in 1631. His mother was a direct descendant of Sir Thomas More's sister.

In early life a Roman Catholic, Donne took Anglican orders in 1615, having long before that date essayed the roles of soldier, minor diplomat, and man of the world, as well as having explored the learning of Oxford, Cambridge, and Lincoln's Inn.

From 1621 until his death, John Donne was Dean of St. Paul's, London. By many he was considered the most eloquent preacher of the 17th century. The extraordinary range of his experience, both secular and religious, found full expression in his poetry, the first collection of which appeared in 1633. His Divine Poems, *although not numerous, are among the most important, setting the pattern for the so-called metaphysical school. As a prose writer he is at his best in his* Sermons, *of which three folios were published between 1640 and 1669.* Devotions upon Emergent Occasions (1624) *is also memorable.*

A Hymne To God The Father.

I.

Wilt thou forgive that sinne where I begunne,
    Which is my sin, though it were done before?
Wilt thou forgive those sinnes, through which I runne,
    And do run still: though still I do deplore?
When thou hast done, thou hast not done,
        For, I have more.

II.

Wilt thou forgive that sinne by which I have wonne
    Others to sinne? and, made my sinne their doore?
Wilt thou forgive that sinne which I did shunne
    A year or two: but wallowed in, a score?
When thou hast done, thou hast not done,
       For I have more.

III.

I have a sinne of feare, that when I have spunne
    My last thread, I shall perish on the shore;
Sweare by thy selfe, that at my death thy sonne
    Shall shine as he shines now, and heretofore;
And having done that, Thou hast done,
       I feare no more. (1)

We have a *Convenient Author*, who writ a *Discourse of Bells*, when he was prisoner in *Turkey*. How would hee have enlarged himselfe if he had beene my *fellow-prisoner* in this *sicke bed*, so neere to that *Steeple*, which never ceases, no more than the *harmony of the spheres*, but is more heard. When the *Turkes* took Constantinople, they melted the *Bells* into *Ordnance:* I have heard both *Bells* and *Ordnance*, but never been so much affected with those, as with these *Bells*. I have *lien* near a *Steeple*, in which there are said to be more than *thirty Bells;* And neere another, where there is one so bigge, as that the *Clapper* is said to weigh more than *six hundred pound*, yet never so affected as here. Here the *Bells* can scarce solemnise the funerall of any person, but that I knew him, or knew that he was my *Neighbour:* we dwelt in houses neere to one another before, but now hee has gone into that house, into which I must follow him. There is a way of correcting the *Children* of great persons; that other *Children* are corrected in their *behalfe*,—and in their *names*, and this works upon them, who indeed had more deserved it. And when

493

those *Bells* tell me, that now one, and now another is buried, must not I acknowledge, that they have the *correction* due to me, and paid the *debt* that I owe? There is a story of a *Bell* in a *Monastery* which, when any of the house was sicke to death, rung alwaies *voluntarily*, and they knew the inevitableness of the danger by that. It rung once, when no man was sick; but the next day one of the house, fell from the *steeple*, and died, and the *Bell* held the reputation of a *Prophet* still. If these *Bells* that warne to a *Funerall* now, were appropriated to none, may not I, by the houre of the *Funerall*, supply? How many men that stand at an *execution*, if they would aske, for what dies that man, should heare their own faults condemned, and see themselves executed, by *Atturney?* We scarce heare of any man *preferred*, but wee thinke of our selves, that we might very well have beene that *Man;* Why might not I have beene that *Man*, that is carried to his *grave* now? Could I fit my selfe, to *stand* or *sit* in any mans *place*, and not to lie in any mans *grave?* I may lacke much of the *good parts* of the meanest, but I lacke nothing of the *mortality* of the weakest; They may have acquired better *abilities* than I, but I was borne to as many *infirmities* as they. To be an *Incumbent* by lying down in a *grave*, to be a *Doctor* by teaching *Mortification* by *Example*, by *dying*, though I may have *seniors*, others may be *older* than I, yet I have proceeded apace in a good *University*, and gone a great way in a little time, by the furtherance of a vehement *Fever;* and whomsoever these *Bells* bring to the ground to day, if hee and I had been compared yesterday, perchance I should have been thought likelier to come to this preferment, then, than he. *God* hath kept the power of *death* in his owne hands, lest any man should *bribe death*. If man knew the *gaine of death*, the *ease of death*, he would solicite, he would provoke *death* to assist him, by any hand, which he might use. But as when men see many of their owne professions preferd, it ministers a hope that that may light upon them; so when these hourely *Bells* tell me of so many *funerals* of men like me, it presents, if

494

not a desire that it may, yet a *comfort* whensoever mine shall come. (2)

Perchance hee for whom this *Bell* tolls, may be so ill, as that he knowes not it tolls for him; And perchance I may thinke my selfe so much better than I am, as that they who are about mee, and see my state, may have caused it to toll for mee, and I know not that. The *Church* is *Catholike, universall,* so are all her *Actions;* All that she does, belongs to *all.* When she *baptizes a child,* that action concernes mee; for that child is thereby connected to that *Head* which is my *Head* too, and engraffed into that *body,* whereof I am a *member.* And when she *buries a Man,* that action concernes me: All *mankinde* is of one *Author,* and is one *volume;* when one Man dies, one *Chapter* is not *torne* out of the *booke,* but *translated* into a better *language;* and every *Chapter* must be so *translated;* God emploies several *translators;* some pieces are translated by age, some by *sicknesse,* some by *warre,* some by *justice;* but God's hand is in every *translation;* and his hand shall binde up all our scattered leaves againe, for that *Librarie* where every *booke* shall lie open to one another: As therefore the *Bell* that rings to a *sermon,* calls not upon the *Preacher* onely, but upon the *Congregation* to come; so this *Bell* calls us all: but how much more mee, who am brought so neere the *doore* by this *sicknesse.* There was a *contention* as far as a *suite,* (in which both *pietie* and *dignitie, religion, and estimation,* were mingled) which of the religious *Orders* should ring to *praiers* first in the *Morning;* and it was *determined,* that *they should ring first that rose earliest.* If we understand aright the *dignitie* of this *Belle* that tolls for our *evening prayer,* wee would bee glad to make it ours, by rising early, in that *application,* that it might bee ours, as wel as his, whose indeed it is. The *Bell* doth toll for him that *thinkes* it doth; and though it *intermit* againe, yet from that *minute,* that that occasion wrought upon him, hee is united to *God.* Who casts not up his *Eye* to the *Sunne* when it rises? but who takes off his *Eye* from a *Comet* when that breakes out? Who bends not his *eare* to any *bell*, which upon any occasion rings? but who can remove it from that *bell*, which is passing a *peece of himselfe* out of this *world?* No man is an *Iland*, intire of it selfe; every man is a peece of the *Continent*, a part of the *maine*; if a *Clod* bee washed away by the *Sea*, *Europe* is the lesse, as well as if a Promontorie were, as well as if a *Mannor* of thy *friends* or of *thine owne* were; any mans *death* diminishes *me*, because I am involved in *Mankinde*; And therefore never send to know for whom the *bell* tolls; It tolls for *thee*. Neither can we call this a *begging* of *Miserie* or a *borrowing* of *Miserie*, as though we were not miserable enough of our selves, but must fetch in more from the next house, in taking upon us the *Miserie* of our *Neighbours*. Truly it were an excusable *covetousnesse* if wee did; for *affliction* is a *treasure*, and scarce any man hath *enough* of it. No man hath *affliction* enough that is not matured, and ripened by it, and made fit for God by that *affliction*. If a man carry *treasure* in *bullion*, or in a *wedge* of *gold*, and have none coined into *currant Monies*, his *treasure* will not defray him as he travells. *Tribulation* is *Treasure* in the *nature* of it, but it is not *currant money* in the *use* of it, except wee get nearer and nearer our *home*, *Heaven*, by it. Another man may be sicke too, and sick to *death*, and this *affliction* may lie in his *bowels*, as *gold* in a *Mine*, and be of no use to him; but this *bell*, that tells me of his *affliction*, digs out, and applies that *gold* to *mee*: if by this consideration of anothers danger, I take mine owne into contemplation, and so secure my selfe, by making my recourse to my *God*, who is our onely securitie. (3)

The *Bell* rings out; the *pulse* thereof is changed; the *tolling* was a *faint*, and *intermitting pulse*, upon one side; this *stronger*, and argues *more* and *better* life. His *soule* is gone out; and as a Man, who had a lease of 1000 yeeres after the expiration of a short one, or an inheritance after the *life* of a man in a *consumption*, he is now enterd into the possession of his *better estate*. His *soule* is gone; *whither?* Who saw it *come in*, or who saw it *go out? No body:* yet every body is sure, he *had one*, and *hath none*. If I

496

will aske meere *Philosophers*, what the *soule* is, I shall finde amongst them, that will tell me, it is nothing, but the *temperament* and *harmony*, and *just and equall composition of the Elements in the body*, which produces all those *faculties* which we ascribe to the *soule;* and so, in it selfe is *nothing*, no *separable substance*, that overlives the *body*. They see the *soule* is nothing else in other *Creatures*, and they affect an *impious humilitie,* **to** think *as low* of *Man*. But if my *soule* were no more than the soul of a *beast*, I could not thinke so; that *soule* that can *reflect* upon it selfe, *consider* it selfe, is *more* than so. If I will aske, not meere *Philosophers*, but *mixt men, Philosophicall Divines, how* the *soule*, being a *separate substance*, enters into *Man*, I shall finde some that will tell me, that it is by *generation*, and *procreation* from *parents*, because they thinke it hard, to charge the *soule* with the guiltiness of *originall sinne*, if the *soule* were infused into a *body*, in which it must necessarily grow *foule*, and contract *originall sinne*, whether it *will* or *not:* and I shall finde some that will tell mee, that it is by *immediate infusion from God*, because they think it hard, to *maintaine* an *immortality* in such a *soule*, as should be begotten, and derived with the *body* from *mortall parents*. If I will aske, not a *few men*, but almost *whole bodies, whole Churches*, what becomes of the *soules* of the *righteous* at the *departing* thereof from the *body*, I shall be told by some, *That they attend an expiation, a purification, in a place of torment;* By some, *that they passe to an immediate possession of the presence of God. S.Augustine* studied the *nature* of the *soule*, as much as anything, but the *salvation of the soule;* and he sent an expresse *Messenger* to Saint *Hierome,* to consult of some things concerning the *soule:* But he satisfies himselfe with this: *Let the departure of my soule to salvation be evident to my faith, and I care the lesse, how darke the entrance of my soule, into my body, bee to my reason.* It is the *going out*, more than the *comming in*, that concernes us. This *soule*, this Bell tells me, is *gone out; Whither?* Who shall tell mee that? I know not *who it is:* much less *what he was;* The condition of the man, and the

497

course of his life, which should tell mee *whither* hee is gone, I
know not. I was not there in his *sicknesse,* nor at his *death;* I saw
not his *way,* nor his *end,* nor can aske them, who did, thereby to
conclude, or *argue,* whither he is gone. But yet I have one neerer
mee than all these; mine owne *Charity;* I aske that; and that tels
me, *He* is *gone to everlasting rest,* and *joy,* and *glory:* I owe him
a good *opinion;* it is but *thankfull charity* in mee, because I received *benefit* and *instruction* from him when his *Bell* told: and
I, being made the fitter to *pray,* by that disposition, wherein I
was assisted by his occasion, did *pray* for him; and I *pray* not
without *faith;* so I doe *charitably,* so I do *faithfully* believe, that
that *soule* is gone to everlasting *rest,* and *joy,* and *glory.* But for
the *body,* how poore a wretched thing is *that?* wee cannot expresse it *so fast,* as it grows *worse* and *worse.* That *body* which
scarce three minutes since was such a *house,* as that that *soule,*
which made but one step from thence to *Heaven,* was scarce
thorowly content, to leave that for *Heaven:* that *body* hath lost
the *name* of a *dwelling house,* because none dwells in it, and is
making haste to lose the name of a *body,* and dissolve to *putrefaction.* Who would not be affected, to see a cleere and sweet *River*
in the *Morning,* grow a *kennell* of muddy land water by *noone,*
and condemned to the saltnesse of the *Sea* by *night?* And how
lame a *picture,* how faint a *representation* is that, of the precipitation of mans body to *dissolution! Now* all the parts built up, and
knit by a lovely *soule, now* but a *statue* of *clay,* and *now,* these
limbs melted off, as if that *clay* were but *snow,* and now, the
whole *house* is but a *handfull* of *sand,* so much *dust,* and but a
pecke of *rubbidge,* so much *bone.* If *he,* who, as this *Bell* tells
me, is gone now, were some *excellent Artificer,* who comes to him
for a *clocke,* or for a *garment* now? or for *counsaile,* if hee were
a *Lawyer?* If a *Magistrate,* for *Justice? Man,* before hee hath his
immortall soule, hath a *soule* of *sense,* and a *soule* of *vegitation*
before that: This *immortall soule* did not forbid other *soules,* to
be in us before, but when this *soule* departs, it carries all with it;
no more *vegetation,* no more *sense:* such a *Mother in law* is the

498

Earth, in respect of our *naturall mother:* in her *wombe* we *grew:* and when she was delivered of us, wee were planted in some *place,* in some *calling* in the *world:* In the wombe of the *earth,* wee *diminish,* and when shee is *delivered* of us, our *grave opened* for another, wee were not *transplanted,* but *transported,* our *dust* blowne away with *prophane dust,* with every wind. (4)

Death be not proud, though some have called thee
Mighty and dreadfull, for, thou art not soe,
For, those, whom thou think'st, thou dost overthrow,
Die not, poore death, nor yet canst thou kill mee.
From rest and sleepe, which but thy pictures bee,
Much pleasure, then from thee, much more must flow,
And soonest our best men with thee doe goe,
Rest of their bones, and soules deliverie.
Thou art slave to Fate, Chance, kings and desperate men,
And dost with poyson, warre, and sicknesse dwell,
And poppie, or charmes can make us sleepe as well,
And better than thy stroake; why swell'st thou then?
One short sleepe past, wee wake eternally,
And death shall be no more; death thou shalt die. (5)

When senses, which thy souldiers are,
Wee arme against thee, and they fight for sinne,
    When want, sent but to tame, doth warre
And worke despaire a breach to enter in,
    When plenty, Gods image, and scale
    Makes us Idolatrous,
And love it, not him, whome it should reveale,
When wee are mov'd to seeme religious
Only to vent wit, Lord deliver us.

In Churches, when th' infirmitie
Of him which speakes, diminishes the Word,
    When Magistrates doe mis-apply
To us, as we judge, lay or ghostly sword,

When plague, which is thine Angell, raignes,
  Or wars, thy Champions, swaie,
When Heresie, thy second deluge, gaines;
In th' houre of death, th' Eve of last judgement day,
Deliver us from the sinister way.

  Heare us, O heare us Lord; to thee
A sinner is more musique, when he prayes,
  Than spheares, or Angells praises bee,
In Panegyrique Allelujaes;
  Heare us, for till thou heare us, Lord,
  We know not what to say;
Thine eare to our sighes, teares, thoughts give voice and word,
O Thou who Satan heard'st in Jobs sicke day,
Heare thy selfe now, for thou in us dost pray. (6)

CHAPTER IX

JOHANN GOTTLIEB FICHTE

Johann Gottlieb Fichte was born in 1762 at a village in Saxon Lusatia. His father, a descendant of one of Gustavus Adolphus's soldiers, made a poor living making and selling ribbons. A precocious boy, Johann was helped to an education by a neighboring landowner. He studied at Meissen, Pforta, Jena and Leipzig. As a means of livelihood he filled tutoring positions in Switzerland. In Zurich he met Johanna Rahn who subsequently became his wife.

En route from Switzerland Fichte met Kant whose moral and religious doctrines attracted him and caused him to change all his plans. Forthwith he wrote An Essay Towards A Critique of All Revelation. *For some unknown reason the publisher failed to put Fichte's name on the title page. The work was consequently hailed as a new work of Kant. When the real author became known, Fichte, overnight, was recognized as a first-rate philosopher and was called to Jena.*

Fichte lost his position at Jena because he regarded God as the moral order of the universe. He became professor at Erlangen, then at Berlin. When the French occupied Berlin (1806), Fichte left but returned the following year and devoted himself wholeheartedly to freeing Prussia of foreign domination. No philosopher has ever made a patriotic appeal upon a higher moral plane. His addresses to the German nation are still famous.

As a philosopher intent upon upholding the reality of religious and spiritual aspects of human life, Fichte asserts the independence, inwardness and vitality of spiritual life. In the consciousness of our empirical ego resides the more comprehensive infinite principle, the pure ego, the higher moral world order. Not being finished and in continuous development, the realization of the moral world is the

501

true goal of man. The vocation of individuals and nations is union with God in perfect love.

In the words of Fichte, "Whatever is great and good in our own age is wholly due to this, that noble and strong men in the past have for the sake of ideas made sacrifice of all the enjoyments of life."

In 1814 when Berlin hospital was filled with sick and wounded, Fichte's wife caught a fever through her attendance there. Fichte nursed her back to health but he himself caught the fever from which he died at about 52 years of age. On his tomb was placed the text: "Thy teachers shall shine as the brightness of the firmament, and they that turn many to righteousness as the stars that shine for ever and ever."

Whatever is great and good in our own age is wholly due to this, that noble and strong men in the past have for the sake of ideas made sacrifice of all the enjoyments of life. (1)

On his tomb was written the appropriate and beautiful text: "Thy teachers shall shine as the brightness of the firmament, and they that turn many to righteousness as the stars that shine for ever and ever." (2)

Every part contains the whole, for *only* through the whole is each part what it is, but through the whole it is *necessarily* what it is. (3)

The ground upon which I assume the existence of something beyond myself, does not lie out of myself, but within me, in the limitation of my own personality. (4)

In each individual, Nature beholds herself from a particular point of view. I call myself—*I* and thee—*thou;* thou callest thyself—*I,* and me—*thou;* I lie beyond thee, as thou beyond me. Of what is without me, I comprehend first those things which touch me most nearly; thou, those which touch thee most nearly;—from these points we each proceed onwards to the next proximate; but we describe very different paths, which may here and there intersect each other, but never run parallel. There is an infinite variety of possible individuals, and hence also an infinite variety of possible starting points of consciousness. This consciousness of

502

all individuals taken together, constitutes the complete consciousness of the universe; and there is no other, for only in the individual is there definite completeness and reality. (5)

The system of freedom satisfies my heart; the opposite system destroys and annihilates it. To stand, cold and unmoved, amid the current of events, a passive mirror of fugitive and passing phenomena,—this existence is insupportable to me; I scorn and detest it. I will love:—I will lose myself in sympathy;—I will know the joy and the grief of life. I myself am the highest object of this sympathy; and the only mode in which I can satisfy its requirements is by my actions. I will do all for the best;—I will rejoice when I have done right, I will grieve when I have done wrong; and even this sorrow shall be sweet to me, for it is a chord of sympathy,—a pledge of future amendment. In love only there is life;—without it is death and annihilation. (6)

The immediate consciousness of thyself, and of thy own determinations, is therefore the imperative condition of all other consciousness; and thou knowest a thing, only in so far as thou knowest that thou knowest it: no element can enter into the latter cognition which is not contained in the former. (7)

Always confess whatever thou perceivest to be true. The present obscurities will gradually become clear, and the unknown will be made known. (8)

The light is not out of, but in me, and I myself am the light. (9)

"Not merely TO KNOW, but according to thy knowledge TO DO, is thy vocation:" thus it is loudly proclaimed in the innermost depths of my soul, as soon as I recollect myself for a moment, and turn my observation upon myself. "Not for idle contemplation of thyself, not for brooding over devout sensations; —no, for action art thou here; thine action, and thine action alone, determines thy worth." (10)

Let me seek only that which I ought to seek, and I shall find; let me ask only that which I ought to ask, and I shall receive an answer. (11)

503

We do not act because we know, but we know because we are called upon to act:—the practical reason is the root of all reason. The laws of action for rational beings are *immediately certain;* their world is certain only through that previous certainty. We cannot deny these laws without plunging the world, and ourselves with it, into absolute annihilation;—we raise ourselves from this abyss, and maintain ourselves above it, solely by our moral activity. (12)

I cast a glance on the present relations of men towards each other and towards Nature; on the feebleness of their powers, the strength of their desires and passions. A voice within me proclaims with irresistible conviction—"It is impossible that it can remain thus; it must become different and better."

I cannot think of the present state of humanity as that in which it is destined to remain; I am absolutely unable to conceive of this as its complete and final vocation. Then, indeed, were all a dream and a delusion; and it would not be worth the trouble to have lived, and played out this ever-repeated game, which tends to nothing and signifies nothing. Only in so far as I can regard this state as the means toward a better, as the transition point to a higher and more perfect state, has it any value in my eyes; not for its own sake, but for the sake of that better world for which it prepares the way, can I support it, esteem it, and joyfully perform my part in it. My mind can accept no place in the present, nor rest in it even for a moment; my whole being flows onward, incessantly and irresistibly, towards that future and better state of things. (13)

It is not Nature, it is Freedom itself, by which the greatest and most terrible disorders incident to our race are produced; man is the cruelest enemy of man. Lawless hordes of savages still wander over vast wildernesses;—they meet, and the victor devours his foe at the triumphal feast:—or where culture has at length united these wild hordes under some social bond, they attack each other, as nations, with the power which law and union have given them. Defying toil and privation, their armies traverse peaceful plains and forests;—they meet each other, and the sight of their brethren is the signal for slaughter. Equipt with the mightiest inventions of the human intellect, hostile fleets plough their way through the ocean; through storm and tempest man rushes to meet his fellow men upon the lonely inhospitable sea;—they meet, and defy the fury of the elements that they may destroy each other with their own hands. Even in the interior of states, where men seem to be united in equality under the law, it is still for the most part only force and fraud that rule under that venerable name; and here the warfare is so much the more shameful that it is not openly declared to be war, and the party attacked is even deprived of the privilege of defending himself against unjust oppression. Combinations of the few rejoice in the ignorance, the folly, the vice, and the misery in which the greater number of their fellow-men are sunk, avowedly seek to retain them in this state of degradation, and even to plunge them deeper in it in order to perpetuate their slavery;—nay, would destroy any man who should venture to enlighten or improve them. No attempt at amelioration can anywhere be made without rousing up from slumber a host of selfish interests to war against it, and uniting even the most varied and opposite in a common hostility. The good cause is ever the weaker, for it is simple, and can be loved only for itself; the bad attracts each individual by the promise which is most seductive to him; and its adherents, always at war among themselves, so soon as the good makes its appearance, conclude a truce that they may unite the whole powers of their wickedness against it. Scarcely, indeed, is such an opposition needed, for even the good themselves are but too often divided by misunderstanding, error, distrust, and secret self-love, and that so much the more violently, the more earnestly each strives to propagate that which he recognizes as best; and thus internal discord dissipates a power, which, even when united, could scarcely hold the balance with evil. One blames the other for rushing onwards with stormy impetuosity to his object, without waiting until the good result shall have been prepared; whilst

505

he in turn is blamed that, through hesitation and cowardice, he accomplishes nothing, but allows all things to remain as they are, contrary to his better conviction, because for him the hour of action never arrives:—and only the Omniscient can determine whether either of the parties in the dispute is in the right. Every one regards the undertaking the necessity of which is most apparent to him, and in the prosecution of which he has acquired the greatest skill, as most important and needful,—as the point from which all improvement must proceed; he requires all good men to unite their efforts with his, and to subject themselves to him for the accomplishment of his particular purpose, holding it to be treason to the good cause if they hold back:—while they on the other hand make the same demands upon him, and accuse him of similar treason for a similar refusal. Thus do all good intentions among men appear to be lost in vain disputations, which leave behind them no trace of their existence; while in the meantime the world goes on as well, or as ill, as it can without human effort, by the blind mechanism of Nature. (14)

When men shall no longer be divided by selfish purposes, nor their powers exhausted in struggles with each other, nothing will remain for them but to direct their united strength against the one common enemy which still remains unsubdued,—resisting, uncultivated nature. No longer estranged from each other by private ends, they will necessarily combine for this common object; and thus there arises a body, everywhere animated by the same spirit and the same love. Every misfortune to the individual, is a misfortune to the whole, and to each individual member of the whole; and is felt with the same pain, and remedied with the same activity, by every member;—every step in advance made by one man is a step in advance made by the whole race. Here, where the petty, narrow self of mere individual personality is merged in the more comprehensive unity of the social constitution, each man truly loves every other as himself,—as a member of this greater *self* which now claims all his love, and of which he

506

himself is no more than a member, capable of participating only in a common gain or in a common loss. The strife of evil against good is here abolished, for here no evil can intrude. The strife of the good among themselves for the sake of good, disappears, now that they find it easy to love good for its own sake alone and not because they are its authors; now that it has become of all-importance to them that the truth should really be discovered, that the useful action should be done,—but not at all by whom this may be accomplished. Here each individual is at all times ready to join his strength to that of others; and whoever, according to the judgment of all, is most capable of accomplishing the greatest amount of good, will be supported by all, and his success rejoiced in by all with an equal joy. (15)

Reason is not for the sake of existence, but existence for the sake of reason. An existence which does not of itself satisfy reason and solve all her questions, cannot possibly be the true being. (16)

I will not refuse obedience to the law of duty; as surely as I live and am, I will obey, absolutely because it commands. This resolution shall be first and highest in my mind; that by which everything else is determined, but which is itself determined by nothing else;—this shall be the innermost principle of my spiritual life. (17)

And now the Eternal World rises before me more brightly, and the fundamental law of its order stands clearly and distinctly apparent to my mental vision. In this world, *will* alone, as it lies concealed from mortal eye in the secret obscurities of the soul, is the first link in a chain of consequences that stretches through the whole invisible realms of spirit; as, in the physical world, *action*—a certain movement of matter—is the first link in a material chain that runs through the whole system of nature. The will is the efficient, living principle of the world of reason, as motion is the efficient, living principle of the world of sense. I stand in the centre of two entirely opposite worlds:—a visible world, in which action is the only moving power; and an invisible and absolutely incomprehensible world, in which will is the moving principle. (18)

It is not necessary that I should first be severed from the terrestrial world before I can obtain admission into the celestial one; I am and live in it even now, far more truly than in the terrestrial; even now it is my only sure foundation, and the eternal life on the possession of which I have already entered is the only ground why I should still prolong this earthly one. That which we call heaven does not lie beyond the grave; it is even here diffused around us, and its light arises in every pure heart. My will is mine, and it is the only thing that is wholly mine and entirely dependent on myself; and through it I have already become a citizen of the realm of freedom and of pure spiritual activity. (19)

Should it still appear that, during my whole earthly life, I have not advanced the good cause a single hair's-breadth in this world, yet I dare not cease my efforts: after every unsuccessful attempt, I must still believe that the next will be successful. But in the spiritual world no step is ever lost. In short, I do not pursue the earthly purpose for its own sake alone, or as a final aim; but only because my true final aim, obedience to the law of conscience, does not present itself to me in the world in any other shape than as the advancement of this end. I may not cease to pursue it, unless I were to deny the law of duty, or unless that law were to manifest itself to me, in this life, in some other shape than as a commandment to promote this purpose in my own place;—I shall actually cease to pursue it in another life in which that commandment shall have set before me some other purpose wholly incomprehensible to me here. In this life I must *will* to promote it, because I must obey; whether it be *actually* promoted by the deed that follows my will thus fittingly directed is not my care; I am responsible only for the will, but not for the result. Previous to the actual deed, I can never resign this purpose; the deed, when it is completed, I may resign, and repeat it, or improve it. Thus

508

do I live and labour, even here, in my most essential nature and in my nearest purposes, only for the other world, and my activity for it is the only thing of which I am completely certain;—in the world of sense I labour only for the sake of the other, and only because I cannot work for the other without at least *willing* to work for it. (20)

That our virtuous will in, and for and through itself, must have consequences, we know already in this life, for reason cannot command anything which is without a purpose; but what these consequences may be,—nay, how it is even possible for a mere will to produce any effect at all,—as to this we can form no conception whatever, so long as we are still confined to this material world; and it is true wisdom not to undertake an inquiry in which we know beforehand that we shall be unsuccessful. With respect to the nature of these consequences, the present life is therefore, in relation to the future, *a life in faith*. In the future life, we shall possess these consequences, for we shall then proceed from them as our starting-point, and build upon them as our foundation; and this other life will thus be, in relation to the consequences of our virtuous will in the present, *a life in sight*. (21)

The present world exists for us only through the law of duty; the other will be revealed to us, in a similar manner, through another command of duty; for in no other manner can a world exist for any reasonable being. (22)

This, then, is my whole sublime vocation, my true nature. I am a member of two orders:—the one purely spiritual, in which I rule by my will alone; the other sensuous, in which I operate by my deed. The whole end of reason is pure activity, absolutely by itself alone, having no need of any instrument out of itself,—independence of everything which is not reason, absolute freedom. The will is the living principle of reason,—is itself reason, when purely and simply apprehended; that reason is active by itself alone, means, that pure will, merely as such, lives and rules. It is only the Infinite Reason that lives immediately and wholly in this purely spiritual order. The finite reason,—which

509

does not of itself constitute the world of reason, but is only one of its many members,—lives necessarily at the same time in a sensuous order; that is to say, in one which presents to it another object, beyond a purely spiritual activity:—a material object, to be promoted by instruments and powers which indeed stand under the immediate dominion of the will, but whose activity is also conditioned by their own natural laws. Yet as surely as reason is reason, must the will operate absolutely by itself, and independently of the natural laws by which the material action is determined;—and hence the sensuous life of every finite being points towards a higher, into which the will, by itself alone, may open the way, and of which it may acquire possession,—a possession which indeed we must again sensuously conceive of as a state, and not as a mere will. (23)

I *am* immortal, imperishable, eternal, as soon as I form the resolution to obey the laws of reason; I do not need to *become* so. The super-sensual world is no future world; it is now present; it can at no point of finite existence be more present than at another; not more present after an existence of myriads of lives than at this moment. My sensuous existence may, in future, assume other forms, but these are just as little the true life, as its present form. By that resolution I lay hold on eternity, and cast off this earthly life and all other forms of sensuous life which may yet lie before me in futurity, and place myself far above them. I become the sole source of my own being and its phenomena, and henceforth, unconditioned by anything without me, I have life in myself. My will, which is directed by no foreign agency in the order of the super-sensual world, but by myself alone, is this source of true life, and of eternity.

It is my will alone which is this source of true life, and of eternity;—only by recognising this will as the peculiar seat of moral goodness, and by actually raising it thereto, do I obtain the assurance and the possession of that super-sensual world. (24)

I am indeed compelled to believe, and consequently to act as

510

if I thought, that by my mere volition, my tongue, my hand, or my foot, might be set in motion. (25)

The faculty by which we lay hold on Eternal Life is to be attained only by actually renouncing the sensuous and its objects, and sacrificing them to that law which takes cognizance of our will only and not of our actions;—renouncing them with the firmest conviction that it is reasonable for us to do so,—nay, that it is the only thing reasonable for us. By this renunciation of the Earthly, does faith in the Eternal first arise in our soul, and is there enshrined apart, as the only support to which we can cling after we have given up all else,—as the only animating principle that can elevate our minds and inspire our lives. We must indeed, according to the figure of a sacred doctrine, first "die unto the world and be born again, before we can enter the Kingdom of God." (26)

Our philosophy becomes the history of our own heart and life; and according to what we ourselves are, do we conceive of man and his vocation. (27)

Only by the fundamental improvement of my will does a new light arise within me concerning my existence and vocation; without this, however much I may speculate, and with what rare intellectual gifts soever I may be endowed, darkness remains within me and around me. The improvement of the heart alone leads to true wisdom. Let then my whole life be unceasingly devoted to this one purpose. (28)

The conception of a *Law* expresses nothing more than the firm, immovable confidence of reason in a principle, and the absolute impossibility of admitting its opposite.

I assume such a law of a spiritual world,—not given by my will nor by the will of any finite being, nor by the will of all finite beings taken together, but to which my will, and the will of all finite beings, is subject. (29)

There is a spiritual bond between Him and all finite rational beings; and He himself is this spiritual bond of the rational universe. Let me will, purely and decidedly, my duty; and He wills that, in the spiritual world at least, my will shall prosper. Every moral resolution of a finite being goes up before Him, and—to speak after the manner of mortals—moves and determines Him, not in consequence of a momentary satisfaction, but in accordance with the eternal law of His being. With surprising clearness does this thought, which hitherto was surrounded with darkness, now reveal itself to my soul; the thought that my will, merely as such, and through itself, shall have results. It has results, because it is immediately and infallibly perceived by another Will to which it is related, which is its own accomplishment and the only living principle of the spiritual world; *in Him* it has its first results, and *through Him* it acquires an influence on the whole spiritual world, which throughout is but a product of that Infinite Will. (30)

Thus do I approach—the mortal must speak in his own language—thus do I approach that Infinite Will; and the voice of conscience in my soul, which teaches me in every situation of life what I have to do, is the channel through which again His influence descends upon me. That voice, sensualized by my environment, and translated into my language, is the oracle of the Eternal World which announces to me how I am to perform my part in the order of the spiritual universe, or in the Infinite Will who is Himself that order. I cannot, indeed, survey or comprehend that spiritual order, and I need not to do so;—I am but a link in its chain, and can no more judge of the whole, than a single tone of music can judge of the entire harmony of which it forms a part. But what I myself ought to be in this harmony of spirits I must know, for it is only I myself who can make me so,—and this immediately revealed to me by a voice whose tones descend upon me from that other world. Thus do I stand connected with the *One* who alone has existence, and thus do I participate in His being. There is nothing real, lasting, imperishable in me, but these two elements:—the voice of conscience, and my free obedience. By the first, the spiritual world bows down to me,

512

and embraces me as one of its members; by the second I raise myself into this world, apprehend it, and re-act upon it. That Infinite Will is the mediator between it and me; for He himself is the original source both of it and me. This is the one True and Imperishable for which my soul yearns even from its inmost depths; all else is mere appearance, ever vanishing, and ever returning in a new semblance. (31)

This Will unites me with himself; He also unites me with all finite beings like myself, and is the common mediator between us all. This is the great mystery of the invisible world, and its fundamental law, in so far as it is a world or system of many individual wills:—*the union, and direct reciprocal action, of many separate and independent wills;* a mystery which already lies clearly before every eye in the present life, without attracting the notice of any one, or being regarded as in any way wonderful. The voice of conscience, which imposes on each his particular duty, is the light-beam on which we come forth from the bosom of the Infinite, and assume our place as particular individual beings; it fixes the limits of our personality; it is thus the true original element of our nature, the foundation and material of all our life. The absolute freedom of the will, which we bring down with us from the Infinite into the world of Time, is the principle of this our life. (32)

Where then is the law within thyself, according to which thou canst realize the determinations of other wills absolutely independent of thee? In short, this mutual recognition and reciprocal action of free beings in this world, is perfectly inexplicable by the laws of nature or of thought, and can be explained only through the One in whom they are united, although to each other they are separate; through the Infinite Will who sustains and embraces them all in His own sphere. Not immediately from thee to me, nor from me to thee, flows forth the knowledge which we have of each other:—we are separated by an insurmountable barrier. Only through the common fountain of our spiritual being do we know of each other; only in Him do we recognise each

513

other, and influence each other. "Here reverence the image of freedom upon the earth;—here, a work which bears its impress:" thus is it proclaimed within me by the voice of that Will, which speaks to me only in so far as it imposes duties upon me:—and the only principle through which I recognise thee and thy work, is the command of conscience to respect them. (33)

This universal agreement concerning a sensible world,—assumed and accepted by us as the foundation of all our other life, and as the sphere of our duty—which, strictly considered, is just as incomprehensible as our unanimity concerning the products of our reciprocal freedom,—this agreement is the result of the One Eternal Infinite Will. Our faith, of which we have spoken as faith in duty, is only faith in Him, in His reason, in His truth. What, then, is the peculiar and essential truth which we accept in the world of sense, and in which we believe? Nothing less than that from our free and faithful performance of our duty in this world, there will arise to us throughout eternity a life in which our freedom and morality may still continue their development. If this be true, then indeed is there truth in our world, and the only truth possible for finite beings; and it must be true, for this world is the result of the Eternal Will in us,—and that Will, by the law of His own being, can have no other purpose with respect to finite beings, than that which we have set forth. (34)

That Eternal Will is thus assuredly the creator of the World, in the only way in which He can be so, and in the only way in which it needs creation:—in the finite reason. Those who regard Him as building up a world from an everlasting inert matter, which must still remain inert and lifeless,—like a vessel made by human hands, not an eternal procession of His self-development, —or who ascribe to Him the production of a material universe out of nothing, know neither the world nor Him. If matter only can be reality, then were the world indeed nothing, and throughout all eternity would remain nothing. Reason alone exists:—the Infinite in Himself,—the finite in Him and through Him. Only in our minds has He created a world; at least that *from which* we

514

unfold it, and that *by which* we unfold it;—the voice of duty and harmonious feelings, intuitions, and laws of thought. It is His light through which we behold the light, and all that it reveals to us. In our minds He still creates this world, and acts upon it by acting upon our minds through the call of duty, as soon as another free being changes aught therein. In our minds He upholds this world, and thereby the finite existence of which alone we are capable, by continually evolving from state of our existence other states in succession. When He shall have sufficiently proved us according to His supreme designs, for our next succeeding vocation, and we shall have sufficiently cultivated ourselves for entering upon it, then, by that which we call death, will He annihilate for us this life, and introduce us to a new life, the product of our virtuous actions. All our life is His life. We are in His hand, and abide therein, and no one can pluck us out of His hand. We are eternal, because He is eternal. (35)

In the contemplations of these Thy relations to me, the finite being, will I rest in calm blessedness. I know immediately only what I ought to do. This will I do, freely, joyfully, and without cavilling or sophistry, for it is Thy voice which commands me to do it; it is the part assigned to me in the spiritual World-plan; and the power with which I shall perform it is Thy power. Whatever may be commanded by that voice, whatever executed by that power, is, in that plan, assuredly and truly good. I remain tranquil amid all the events of this world, for they are in Thy world. Nothing can perplex or surprise or dishearten me, as surely as Thou livest, and I can look upon Thy life. For in Thee, and through Thee, O Infinite One! do I behold even my present world in another light. Nature, and natural consequences, in the destinies and conduct of free beings, as opposed to Thee, become empty, unmeaning words. Nature is no longer; Thou, only Thou, art. It no longer appears to me to be the end and purpose of the present world to produce that state of universal peace among men, and of unlimited dominion over the mechanism of nature, for its own sake alone,—but that this should be produced by man

515

himself,—and, since it is expected from *all*, that it should be produced by *all*, as one great, free, moral, community. Nothing new and better for an individual shall be attainable, except through his own virtuous will; nothing new and better for a community, except through the common will being in accordance with duty;—this is a fundamental law of the great moral empire, of which the present life is a part. The good will of the individual, and the will of the majority is not in harmony with his,—and then its results are to be found solely in a future world; while even the passions and vices of men cooperate in the attainment of good,—not in and for themselves, for in this sense good can never come out of evil,—but by holding the balance against the opposite vices, and, at last, by their excess, annihilating these antagonists and themselves with them. Oppression could never have gained the upper hand in human affairs, unless the cowardice, baseness, and mutual mistrust of men had smoothed the way to it. It will continue to increase, until it extirpate cowardice and slavishness; and despair at last reawaken courage. Then shall the two opposite vices have annihilated each other, and the noblest of all human relations, lasting freedom, come forth from their antagonism. (36)

There is but one world possible,—a thoroughly good world. All that happens in this world is subservient to the improvement and culture of man, and by means of this, to the promotion of the purpose of his earthly existence. It is this higher World-plan which we call Nature, when we say,—Nature leads men through want to industry; through the evils of general disorder to a just constitution; through the miseries of continual wars to endless peace on earth. Thy will, O Infinite One! Thy Providence alone, is this higher Nature. This, too, is best understood by artless simplicity, when it regards this life as a place of trial and culture, as a school for eternity; when, in all the events of life, the most trivial as well as the most important, it beholds Thy guiding Providence disposing all for the best; when it firmly believes that all things must work together for the good of those who love their duty, and who know Thee. (37)

Blessed be the hour in which I first resolved to inquire into myself and my vocation! All my doubts are solved; I know what I can know, and have no apprehensions regarding that which I cannot know. I am satisfied; perfect harmony and clearness reign in my soul, and a new and more glorious spiritual existence begins for me.

My entire complete vocation I cannot comprehend; what I shall be hereafter transcends all my thoughts. A part of that vocation is concealed from me; it is visible only to One, to the Father of Spirits, to whose care it is committed. I know only that it is sure, and that it is eternal and glorious like Himself. But that part of it which is confided to myself, I know, and know it thoroughly, for it is the root of all my other knowledge. I know assuredly, in every moment of my life, what I ought to do; and this is my whole vocation in so far as it depends on me. From this point, since my knowledge does not reach beyond it, I shall not depart; I shall not desire to know aught beyond this; I shall take my stand upon this central point, and firmly root myself here. To this shall all my thoughts and endeavours, my whole powers, be directed; my whole existence shall be interwoven with it. (38)

As with calmness and devotion I reverence this higher Providence, so in my actions ought I to reverence the freedom of other beings around me. The question for me is not what they, according to my conceptions, ought to do, but what I may venture to do in order to induce them to do it. I can only desire to act on their conviction and their will as far as the order of society and their own consent will permit; but by no means, without their conviction and consent, to influence their powers and relations. They do what they do on their own responsibility; with this I neither can nor dare intermeddle, and the Eternal Will will dispose all for the best. It concerns me more to respect their freedom, than to hinder or prevent what to me seems evil in its use. (39)

In this point of view I become a new creature, and my whole relations to the existing world are changed. The ties by which my mind was formerly united to this world, and by whose secret guidance I followed all its movements, are for ever sundered, and I stand free, calm and immovable, a universe to myself. No longer through my affections, but by my eye alone, do I apprehend outward objects and am connected with them; and this eye itself is purified by freedom, and looks through error and deformity to the True and Beautiful, as upon the unruffled surface of water shapes are more purely mirrored in a milder light.

My mind is forever closed against embarrassment and perplexity, against uncertainty, doubt, and anxiety;—my heart, against grief, repentance and desire. There is but one thing that I may know,—namely, what I ought to do; and this I always know infallibly. Concerning all else I know nothing, and know that I know nothing. I firmly root myself in this my ignorance, and refrain from harassing myself with conjectures concerning that of which I know nothing. No occurrence in this world can affect me either with joy or sorrow; calm and unmoved I look down upon all things, for I know that I cannot explain a single event, nor comprehend its connexion with that which alone concerns me. (40)

In His world all things prosper;—this satisfies me, and in this belief I stand fast as a rock;—but what in His world is merely the germ, what the blossom, and what the fruit itself, I know not. (41)

I rest in the most perfect tranquillity, for I know nothing whatever about any other thing. Those, to me, so sorrowful events may, in the plan of the Eternal One, be the direct means for the attainment of a good result;—that strife of evil against good may be their last decisive struggle, and it may be permitted to the former to assemble all its powers for this encounter only to lose them, and thereby to exhibit itself in all its impotence. These, to me, joyful appearances may rest on very uncertain foundations;—what I had taken for enlightenment may perhaps be but hollow superficiality, and aversion to all true ideas; what I had taken

518

for independence but unbridled passion; what I had taken for gentleness and moderation but weakness and indolence. I do not indeed know this, but it might be so; and then I should have as little cause to mourn over the one as to rejoice over the other. But I do know, that I live in a world which belongs to the Supreme Wisdom and Goodness, who thoroughly comprehends its plan, and will infallibly accomplish it; and in this conviction I rest, and am blessed. (42)

Now that my heart is closed against all desire for earthly things, now that I have no longer any sense for the transitory and perishable, the universe appears before my eyes clothed in a more glorious form. The dead heavy mass, which only filled up space, has vanished; and in its place there flows onward, with the rushing music of mighty waves, an eternal stream of life and power and action, which issues from the original Source of all life— from Thy Life, O Infinite One; for all life is Thy Life, and only the religious eye penetrates to the realm of True Beauty. (43)

I am related to Thee, and what I behold around me is related to me; all is life and blessedness, and regards me with bright spirit-eyes, and speaks with spirit-voices to my heart. In all the forms that surround me, I behold the reflection of my own being, broken up into countless diversified shapes, as the morning sun, broken in a thousand dew drops, sparkles towards itself. (44)

But pure and holy, and as near to Thine own nature as aught can be to mortal eye, does this Thy life flow forth as the bond which unites spirit with spirit, as the breath and atmosphere of a rational world, unimaginable, and incomprehensible, and yet there, clearly visible to the spiritual eye. Borne onwards in this stream of light, thought floats from soul to soul, without pause or variation, and returns purer and brighter from each kindred mind. Through this mysterious union does each individual perceive, understand, and love himself only in another; every soul develops itself only by means of other souls, and there are no longer individual men, but only one humanity; no individual thought, or love, or hate, but only thought, love, and hate, in and

519

through each other. Through this wondrous influence the affinity of spirits in the invisible world permeates even their physical nature;—manifests itself in two sexes, which, even if that spiritual bond could be torn asunder, would, simply as creatures of nature, be compelled to love each other;—flows forth in the tenderness of parents and children, brothers and sisters, as if the souls were of one blood like the bodies, and their minds were branches and blossoms of the same stem;—and from these, embraces in narrower or wider circles, the whole sentient world. Even at the root of their hate, there lies a secret thirst after love, and no enmity springs up but from friendship denied. (45)

All Death in Nature is Birth, and in Death itself appears visibly the exaltation of Life. There is no destructive principle in Nature, for Nature throughout is pure, unclouded Life; it is not Death which kills, but the more living Life, which, concealed behind the former, bursts forth into new development. Death and Birth are but the struggle of Life with itself to assume a more glorious and congenial form. And *my* death,—how can it be aught else, since I am not a mere show and semblance of life, but bear within me the one original, true and essential Life? It is impossible to conceive that Nature should annihilate a life which does not proceed from her:—the Nature which exists for me, and not I for her. (46)

Every one of my fellow-creatures who leaves this earthly brotherhood and whom my spirit cannot regard as annihilated because he is my brother, draws my thoughts after him beyond the grave;—he is still, and to him belongs a place. While we mourn for him here below, as in the dim realms of unconsciousness there might be mourning when a man bursts from them into the light of this world's own,—above there is rejoicing that a man is born into that world, as we citizens of the earth receive with joy those who are born unto us. When I shall one day follow, it will be but joy for me; sorrow shall remain behind in the sphere I shall have left.

The world on which but now I gazed with wonder passes away

from before me and sinks from my sight. With all the fulness of life, order, and increase which I beheld in it, it is yet but the curtain by which a world infinitely more perfect is concealed from me, and the germ from which that other shall develop itself. My FAITH looks behind this veil, and cherishes and animates this germ. It sees nothing definite, but it expects more than it can conceive here below, more than it will ever be able to conceive in all time. (47)

Thus do I live, thus am I, and thus am I unchangeable, firm, and completed for all Eternity:—for this is no existence assumed from without,—it is my own, true, essential Life and Being. (48)

CHAPTER X

SIR THOMAS BROWNE

Sir Thomas Browne was born in 1605. He died in 1682. He is an English prose writer who was by profession a physician. He lived in Norwich, England, practising medicine there. Throughout the Civil War he kept clear of active participation therein. It is believed that his sentiments and sympathies were on the Royalist side, but that he refrained from expressing them in such a way as to be drawn into the conflict.

Browne brought to his meditations on religion an innate mysticism qualified by the eclecticism of studies at Oxford, Montpellier, Padua and Leyden. His most notable work is Religio Medici, *published in 1643, but written in the main seven years earlier. It is at once a confession of faith and a collection of curiously compounded opinions.*

Among Browne's other works are Pseudodoxia Epidemica *(1646), better known as* Vulgar Errors, Garden of Cyrus, *and* Burial Urn *(1658).*

With respect to his own religious position, Sir Thomas Browne wrote in Religio Medici, *"But (to difference myself nearer, and draw into a lesser Circle), there is no church whose every part so squares unto my Conscience; whose Articles, Constitutions, and Customs seems so consonant unto reason, and as it were framed to my particular Devotion, as this whereof I hold my Belief, the Church of England; to whose Faith I am a sworn Subject, and therefore in a double Obligation subscribe unto her Articles and endeavour to observe her Constitution. Whatsoever is beyond, as points indifferent, I observe according to the rules of my private reason, or the humour and fashion of my Devotion. . . . In brief, where the Scripture is silent, the Church is my Text; where that speaks, 'tis but my Comment: where*

there is a joynt silence of both, I borrow not the rules of my re-
ligion from Rome or Geneva, but the dictates of my own reason."

It is the method of Charity to suffer without reaction: those
usual Satyrs and invectives of the Pulpit may perchance produce
a good effect on the vulgar, whose ears are opener to Rhetorick
than Logick; yet do they in no wise confirm the faith of wiser
Believers, who know that a good cause needs not to be patron'd
by passion, but can sustain it self upon a temperate dispute. (1)

I could never divide my self from any man upon the difference
of an opinion, or be angry with his judgment for not agreeing
with me in that from which perhaps within a few days I should
dissent my self. (2)

A man may be in as just possession of Truth as of a City, and
yet be forced to surrender. (3)

One General Council is not able to extirpate one single
Heresie: it may be cancell'd for the present; but revolution of
time, and the like aspects from Heaven, will restore it, when it
will flourish till it be condemned again. For as though there were
a Metempsuchosis, and the soul of one man passed into another,
Opinions do find, after certain Revolutions, men and minds like
those that first begat them. To see our selves again, we need not
look for Plato's year: every man is not only himself; there have
been many Diogenes, and as many Timons, though but few of that
name: men are liv'd over again, the world is now as it was in
Ages past; there was none then, but there hath been some one
since that parallels him, and is, as it were, his revived self. (4)

I remember I am not alone, and therefore forget not to contemplate Him and His Attributes Who is ever with me, especially
those two mighty ones, His Wisdom and Eternity. With the one
I recreate, with the other I confound, my understanding. (5)

In this Mass of Nature there is a set of things that carry in
their Front (though not in Capital Letters, yet in Stenography
and short Characters), something of Divinity, which to wiser
Reasons serve as Luminaries in the Abyss of Knowledge, and to

523

judicious beliefs as Scales and Roundles to mount the Pinacles and highest pieces of Divinity. The severe Schools shall never laugh me out of the Philosophy of Hermes, that this visible world is but a Picture of the invisible, wherein, as in a Pourtraiet, things are not truly, but in equivocal shapes, and as they counterfeit some more real substance in that invisible fabrick. (6)

Wisdom is His most beauteous Attribute; no man can attain unto it, yet Solomon pleased God when he desired it. He is wise, because He knows all things; and He knoweth all things, because He made them all: but His greatest knowledge is in comprehending *that* He made not, that is, Himself. And this is also the greatest knowledge in man. (7)

I know He is wise in all, wonderful in what we conceive, but far more in what we comprehend not. (8)

Search while thou wilt, and let thy Reason go,
To ransome Truth, even to th' Abyss below.
Rally the scattered Causes; and that line,
Which Nature twists, be able to entwine.
It is thy Maker's will, for unto none
But unto Reason can He e'er be known.
The Devils do know Thee, but those damnèd Meteors
Build not Thy Glory, but confound Thy Creatures.
Teach my indeavours so Thy works to read,
That learning them in Thee, I may proceed.
Give Thou my reason that instructive flight,
Whose weary wings may on Thy hands still light.
Teach me to soar aloft, yet ever so
When neer the Sun, to stoop again below.
Thus shall my humble Feathers safely hover,
And, though near Earth, more than the Heavens discover. (9)

We carry with us the wonders we seek without us: there is all Africa and her prodigies in us; we are that bold and adventurous piece of Nature, which he that studies wisely learns in a compendium what others labour at in a divided piece and endless volume. (10)

524

There are two Books from whence I collect my Divinity; besides that written one of God, another of His servant Nature, that universal and publick Manuscript, that lies expans'd unto the eyes of all: those that never saw him in the one, have discover'd Him in the other. (11)

I call the effects of Nature the works of God, Whose hand and instrument she only is; and therefore to ascribe His actions unto her, is to devolve the honour of the principal agent upon the instrument; which if with reason we may do, then let our hammers rise up and boast they have built our houses, and our pens receive the honour of our writings. (12)

There are in every man's Life certain rubs, doublings, and wrenches, which pass awhile under the effects of chance, but at the last, well examined, prove the meer hand of God. (13)

I like the Victory of '88 better for that occurrence, which our enemies imputed to our dishonour and the partiality of Fortune, to wit, the tempests and contrariety of Winds. King Philip did not detract from the Nation, when he said, *he sent his Armado to fight with men, and not to combate with the Winds.* (14)

Persecution is a bad and indirect way to plant Religion. (15)

One reason I tender so little Devotion unto Reliques, is, I think, the slender and doubtful respect I have always held unto Antiquities. For that indeed which I admire, is far before Antiquity, that is, Eternity; and that is, God Himself; Who, though He be styled *the Ancient of Days*, cannot receive the adjunct of Antiquity; Who was before the World, and shall be after it, yet is not older than it; for in His years there is no Climacter; His duration is Eternity, and far more venerable than Antiquity. (16)

I hold not so narrow a conceit of this virtue, as to conceive that to give Alms is onely to be Charitable, or think a piece of Liberality can comprehend the Total of Charity. Divinity hath wisely divided the act thereof into many branches, and hath taught us in this narrow way many paths unto goodness; as many ways as we may do good, so many ways we may be charitable. There are infirmities not onely of Body, but of Soul, and Fortunes, which do require the merciful hand of our abilities. I cannot contemn a man for ignorance, but behold him with as much pity as I do Lazarus. It is no greater Charity to cloath his body, than apparel the nakedness of his Soul. It is an honourable object to see the reasons of other men wear our Liveries, and their borrowed understandings do homage to the bounty of ours: it is the cheapest way of beneficence, and, like the natural charity of the Sun, illuminates another without obscuring itself. To be reserved and caitiff in this part of goodness, is the sordidest piece of covetousness, and more contemptible than pecuniary Avarice. To this (as calling my self a Scholar), I am obliged by the duty of my condition: I make not therefore my head a grave, but a treasure, of knowledge; I intend no Monopoly, but a community, in learning; I study not for my own sake only, but for theirs that study not for themselves. I envy no man that knows more than my self, but pity them that know less. I instruct no man as an exercise of my knowledge, or with an intent rather to nourish and keep it alive in mine own head then beget and propagate it in his: and in the midst of all my endeavours there is but one thought that dejects me, that my acquired parts must perish with my self, nor can be Legacied among my honoured Friends. (17)

I cannot fall out or contemn a man for an errour, or conceive why a difference in Opinion should divide an affection; for Controversies, Disputes, and Argumentations, both in Philosophy and in Divinity, if they meet with discreet and peaceable natures, do not infringe the Laws of Charity. In all disputes, so much as there is of passion, so much there is of nothing to the purpose. (18)

No man can justify censure or condemn another, because indeed no man truly knows another. This I perceive in my self; for I am in the dark to all the world, and my nearest friends behold me but in a cloud. Those that know me but superficially, think less of me than I do myself; those of my neer acquaintance think more; God, Who truly knows me, knows that I am nothing; for He only beholds me and all the world, Who looks not on us through a divided ray, or a trajection of a sensible species, but

526

beholds the substance without the help of accidents, and the forms of things as we their operations. Further, no man can judge another, because no man knows himself: for we censure others but as they disagree from that humour which we fancy laudable in our selves, and commend others but for that wherein they seem to be quadrate and consent with us. (19)

There is a musick where ever there is a harmony, order, or proportion: and thus far we may maintain the music of the Sphears; for those well-ordered motions and regular paces, though they give no sound unto the ear, yet to the understanding they strike a note most full of harmony. (20)

This I think charity, to love God for Himself, and our neighbour for God. (21)

Bless me in this life with but peace of my Conscience, command of my affections, the love of Thy self and my dearest friends, and I shall be happy enough to pity Caesar. These are, O Lord, the humble desires of my most reasonable ambition, and all I dare call happiness on earth; wherein I set no rule or limit to Thy Hand of Providence. Dispose of me according to the wisdom of Thy pleasure: Thy will be done, though in my own undoing. (22)

CHAPTER XI

EURIPIDES

Euripides was born between 485 and 480 B.C. He does not appear to have been of aristocratic birth, although he seems to have had a good education. In fact he first took up painting and abandoned that for literature. We do not hear of much activity in public affairs.

During his life time Euripides presented eighty-eight plays out of about ninety-two which he wrote. He won the prize only four times, the first time being with Hippolytus. *Some say that this is because of what seemed to be new, sceptical, and unorthodox elements in his plays, which the public up to then had not generally adopted. It is pointed out that later, in the fourth century and subsequently, Euripides became much more popular, and that there were more revivals of his plays than of those of Aeschylus and Sophocles.*

Euripides left Athens for exile, voluntary or otherwise, at the court of King Archelaus of Macedonia in 408 B.C. His death two years later was both strange and tragic. In some manner, whether by intent or by accident is not known, the hounds of Archelaus were set on him. He was terribly injured, and died from his wounds.

Eighteen plays survive. The quotations which follow in this chapter are from Hecuba, Helen, Andromache, Iphigenia in Aulis, Iphigenia in Tauris, Media, Hippolytus, The Phoenician Damsels, The Suppliants, *and* The Children of Hercules.

There is wisdom, e'en when we are wretched,
In following reason's dictates. (1)

To live
Ignobly were the utmost pitch of shame. (2)

Alas! there's no man free: for some are slaves
To gold, to fortune others, and the rest,
The multitude or written laws restrain
From acting as their better judgment dictates. (3)

The best of seers are Prudence and Discernment. (4)

A thousand shapes our varying fates assume.
The gods perform what least we could expect,
And oft the things for which we fondly hoped
Come not to pass; but Heaven still finds a clue
To guide our steps through life's perplexing maze,
And thus doth this important business end. (5)

From experience, best of tutors,
Men gather all the knowledge they possess. (6)

    Better is conquest, when we gain our right
By no reproachful means, no deeds of shame,
Than if to envy we expose our fame,
    And trample on the laws with impious might.
Such laurels which at first too sweetly bloom,
    Ere long are withered by the frost of time,
And scorn pursues their wearers to the tomb.
I in my household or the state presume
To seek that power alone which rules without a crime. (7)

    The dignity of life in greatness lies. (8)

It must be thine
To joy, it likewise must be thine to grieve,
For thou art mortal born. (9)

Of mortals none
Knows a pure course of unmixed happiness;
None yet was born without a share of grief. (10)

Ill it becomes
An honest man, when raised to power, to change
His manners. (11)

In evil hour
Impiety hath seized the power;
A slighted outcast Virtue fails,
Injustice o'er the laws prevails:
The common danger none descries,
Th' impending vengeance of the skies. (12)

O Victory, I revere thy awful power:
Guard thou my life, nor ever cease to crown me! (13)

I was born
Indeed a slave, yet I with generous slaves
Would still be numbered, for although the name
I bear is abject, yet my soul is free.
Far better this, than if I had at once
Suffered two evils, a corrupted heart,
And vile subjection to another's will. (14)

In my judgment, he
Who tramples on the laws, but can express
His thoughts with plausibility, deserves
Severest punishment: for that injustice
On which he glories, with his artful tongue,
That he a fair appearance can bestow,
He dares to practise, nor is truly wise. (15)

From your soul
Banish resentment, and no trifling gain
Will hence ensue. (16)

Most glorious are the lives
Of those who act with such determined zeal. (17)

My life as it began
May I with spotless purity conclude! (18)

Through many a wakeful night
Have I considered whence mankind became
Thus universally corrupt, and deem
That to the nature of the human soul
Our failures are not owing, for to form
Sound judgments is a privilege enjoyed
By many. But the matter in this light
Ought to be viewed; well knowing what is good,
We practise not. (19)

One only good,
A just and virtuous soul, the wise affirm,
Strives for pre-eminence with life: for time,
At length, when like some blooming nymph her charms
Contemplating, he to our eyes holds up
His mirror, every guilty wretch displays.
Among that number may I ne'er be found! (20)

O mortals, why unprofitably lost
In many errors, strive ye to attain
A thousand specious arts, some new device
Still meditating, yet ye neither know
One rare attainment, nor by your inquiries
Could ever reach the gift of teaching those
Who lack discretion how to think aright? (21)

He's subject
To one severe calamity—he wants
Freedom of speech.
The wretch of whom you talk,
Who utters not his thoughts, is but a slave. (22)

No ornaments of speech to evil deeds
Are due, for justice hates such borrowed charms. (23)

Would every man exert
To their full stretch his talents to promote

The public interest, every state, exposed
To fewer ills, hereafter might be blessed. (24)

Doth not justice
Behold the sinner, and with penal strictness
Each foolish action of mankind repay? (25)

'Tis wisdom in the opulent to look
With pity on the sorrows of the poor,
And in the poor man to look up to those
Who have abundant riches, as examples
For him to imitate, and thence acquire
A wish his own possessions to improve.
They too who are with prosperous fortunes blest
Should feel a prudent dread of future woes. (26)

That god, who'er he was,
I praise, who severed mortals from a life
Of wild confusion and of brutal force,
Implanting reason first, and then a tongue
That might by sounds articulate proclaim
Our thoughts, bestowing fruit for food, and drops
Of rain descending from the skies, to nourish
Earth's products and refresh the thirst of man,
Yet more, fit coverings, from the wintry cold
To guard us, and Hyperion's scorching rays;
The art of sailing o'er the briny deep,
That we by commerce may supply the wants
Of distant regions, to these gifts by Heaven
Is added;

— — — — — — — —

Are we not then puffed up
With vanity, if, when the gods bestow
Conveniences like these on life, we deem

532

Their bounty insufficient? Our conceit
Is such, we aim to be more strong than Jove:
Though pride of soul be all that we possess,
We in our own opinion are more wise
Than th' immortal powers. (27)

In him who leads
A host, or pilot stationed at the helm,
Rashness is dangerous: he who by discretion
His conduct regulates desists in time,
And caution I esteem the truest valour. (28)

Human life
Is but a conflict: some there are whose bliss
Approaches them, while that of others waits
Till a long future season, others taste
Of present joys: capricious Fortune sports
With all her anxious votaries; through a hope
Of better times to her the wretched pay
Their homage; he who is already blest
Extols her matchless beauty to the skies,
And trembles lest the veering gale forsake him.
But we, who know by what precarious tenure
We hold her gifts, should bear a trifling wrong
With patience, and, if we the narrow bounds
Of justice overleap, abstain from crimes
Which harm our country. (29)

Why was this privilege, alas! denied
To mortals, twice to flourish in the bloom
Of youth, and for a second time grow old?
For in our houses, we, if aught is found
To have been ill contrived, amend the fault
Which our maturer judgment hath descried;
While each important error in our life

Admits of no reform: but if with youth
And ripe old age we twice had been indulged,
Each devious step that marked our first career
We in our second might set right. (30)

Long have I held this sentiment: the just
Are born the streams of beauty to diffuse
On all around them; while the man whose soul
Is warped by interest, useless in the State,
Untractable and harsh to every friend,
Lives only for himself; in words alone
This doctrine I imbibed not. (31)

Follow the plain and beaten way,
From Justice, O my country, never stray,
Nor cease the powers immortal to revere. (32)

CHAPTER XII

SCHLEIERMACHER

Friedrich Daniel Ernst Schleiermacher was a German Protestant theologian and philosopher. His father was a clergyman of the Reformed Church. He was born at Breslau November 21, 1768 and died at Berlin February 12, 1834.

In his youth Schleiermacher was educated mainly in Moravian schools. He subsequently studied at Halle. Ordained in 1794, he became pastor of Christ's Hospital at Berlin where he remained 1796-1802. In the latter year he went as pastor to the little town of Stolpe in Pomerania. In 1804 he went to Halle where until 1807 he was university preacher and professor. From Halle Schleiermacher went to Berlin as pastor of Trinity Church. In 1810 he also became professor of theology at the University of Berlin. He remained in both of these positions in Berlin until his death.

Schleiermacher wrote and lectured on a wide variety of subjects including logic, epistemology, metaphysics, ethics, aesthetics, the history of philosophy, theology, church history, the New Testament, and psychology. He also translated the works of Plato. He made substantial contributions in the theory of knowledge, through his influence upon German philosophers in the direction of a critical empirical realism, and in systematic theology, where his idea of an "empirical theology" has exercised a very wide influence.

Religion Schleiermacher regarded as a natural, even necessary, aspect of the developed human personality, essentially feeling (probably better attitude*) which is sympathy or love for the universe, often called a feeling of absolute dependence on God. Sometimes he seems to regard this feeling as partially cognitive awareness of*

535

divine reality. Theological doctrines are expressions of this experi-
ence, or descriptive of its relations. The doctrine is dependent on
religious experience, not experience on belief in dogma.

In the history of the Church, Schleiermacher achieved a notable
success by effecting the union between Lutheran and Reformed
churches in Prussia.

The common element in all howsoever diverse expressions of
piety, by which these are conjointly distinguished from all other
feelings, or, in other words, the self-identical essence of piety,
is this: the consciousness of being absolutely dependent, or,
which is the same thing, of being in relation with God. (1)

The religious self-consciousness, like every essential element
in human nature, leads necessarily in its development to fellowship or communion; a communion which, on the one hand, is
variable and fluid, and, on the other hand, has definite limits, i.e.
is a Church. (2)

The various religious communions which have appeared in
history with clearly defined limits are related to each other in
two ways: as different stages of development, and as different
kinds. (3)

Those forms of piety in which all religious affections express
the dependence of everything finite upon one Supreme and
Infinite Being, i.e., the monotheistic forms, occupy the highest
level; and all others are related to them as subordinate forms,
from which men are destined to pass to those higher ones. (4)

This feeling of absolute dependence, in which our self-
consciousness in general represents the finitude of our being is
therefore not an accidental element, or a thing which varies from
person to person, but is a universal element of life; and the
recognition of this fact entirely takes the place, for the system
of doctrine, of all the so-called proofs of the existence of God.(5)

The original expression of this relation, i.e. that the world
exists only in absolute dependence upon God, is divided in

Church doctrine into the two propositions—that the world was created by God, and that God sustains the world. (6)

The religious self-consciousness, by means of which we place all that affects or influences us in absolute dependence on God, coincides entirely with the view that all such things are conditioned and determined by the interdependence of Nature. (7)

It can never be necessary in the interest of religion so to interpret a fact that its dependence on God absolutely excludes its being conditioned by the system of Nature. (8)

Whether or not that which arouses our self-consciousness and consequently influences us, is to be traced back to any part of the so-called nature-mechanism or to the activity of free causes—the one is as completely ordained by God as the other. (9)

All attributes which we ascribe to God are to be taken as denoting not something special in God, but only something special in the manner in which the feeling of absolute dependence is to be related to Him. (10)

The Absolute Causality to which the feeling of absolute dependence points back can only be described in such a way that, on the one hand, it is distinguished from the content of the natural order and thus contrasted with it, and, on the other hand, equated with it in comprehension. (11)

By the Eternity of God we understand the absolutely timeless causality of God, which conditions not only all that is temporal, but time itself as well. (12)

By the Omnipresence of God we understand the absolutely spaceless causality of God, which conditions not only all that is spatial, but space itself as well. (13)

In the conception of the divine Omnipotence two ideas are contained: first, that the entire system of Nature, comprehending all times and spaces, is founded upon divine causality, which as eternal and omnipresent is in contrast to all finite causality; and second, that the divine causality, as affirmed in our feeling of absolute dependence, is completely presented in the totality of

537

finite being, and consequently everything for which there is a causality in God happens and becomes real. (14)

By the divine Omniscience is to be understood the absolute spirituality of the divine Omnipotence. (15)

God is thought to be outside the world of time, and after death man is to be freed forever from temporal limitations in order to behold and praise the Deity. But even now the spirit spans the world of time. Eternity is in the sight thereof, and the celestial rapture of immortal choirs. Wherefore begin at once your life eternal in the constant contemplation of your own true being. Be not troubled for the future, nor weep for things which pass, but take heed lest you lose yourself, and weep if you are swept along in the stream of time, without carrying heaven with you. (16)

To behold humanity within oneself, and never to lose sight of the vision when once found, is the only certain means of never straying from its sacred precincts. This vision is the intimate and necessary tie between conduct and the perception of truth. (17)

It is sheer folly and vain trifling to make experiments or to lay down rules in the realm of freedom. To be a man calls for a single free resolve; he who has taken that resolve will always remain one; he who ceases to be one has never taken it. (18)

The piteous fate of the negro, torn from his loved ones and his native land, for base servitude in a strange and distant country, is daily meted out in the routine of the world to better men also, who, prevented from reaching the distant homeland where dwell their unfound friends, must waste away their inner lives ineffectually in surroundings that ever remain alien and barren to them. (19)

What grievous doubts would assail me of man's ability to draw nearer his goal, if by weakness of imagination I were riveted to the actual and its immediate consequences. (20)

When friends extend to each other the hand of fellowship, the bond should issue in something greater than each could achieve independently; each ought to grant the other full play to follow

538

the promptings of his spirit, offering assistance only where the other feels a lack, and not insinuating his own ideas in place of his friend's. In this wise each would find life and strength in the other, and the potentialities within him would be fully realized. (21)

Culture will develop out of barbarism, and life will spring even from the sleep of death! The elements of a better life are already present. Their superior potency will not remain forever in dormant hiding; sooner or later the spirit dwelling in man will arouse them into activity. As the cultivation of the earth for man's benefit is now superior to that crude dominion over nature, wherein men fled timidly before every manifestation of her powers, so the blessed time when a true and spiritual society shall arise cannot be remote from this present childhood of humanity. (22)

Yet if our present, much vaunted enlightenment developed out of a wretched barbarism, in which the germs of progress are scarcely discernible even now to a vision trained by the subsequent course of events, why should not our chaotic philistinism, amid which the eye already discerns through sinking mists the rudiments of a better world, give place at last to the sublime rule of moral and spiritual cultivation? It is coming! Why should I with faint heart count the hours which must still transpire or the generations that must pass away ere then? Why let the time of its coming trouble me, since time does not comprehend my inner life? (23)

Wherever I do see a spark of the hidden fire that must sooner or later consume the outworn and recreate the world, I am drawn toward it with love and true hope as to a welcome sign of my distant home. And close at hand the sacred flame has appeared shedding its unearthly light, a sign, to the knowing, that the spirit is there. All who like myself belong to the future are drawing toward each other in love and hope, and each in his every word and act cements and extends a spiritual bond by which we are pledged to better times. (24)

No one can live simply and in the way of beauty save he who

hates lifeless formulas, seeks after genuine self-cultivation, and so belongs to a world that is yet to be. (25)

Amid all the diversities of the world's motley spectacle I learned to discount appearances and to recognize the same reality whatever its garb, and I also learned to translate the many tongues that it acquires in various circles. (26)

What a galaxy of individuals I see close at hand, men so different from myself yet all of them engaged in perfecting the humanity that is in them! What an amazing number of learned men are about me, who out of pride or hospitality offer me the golden fruit of their lives in handsome jars, and the plants of distant times and places too, transplanted to the fatherland by their faithful toil! (27)

In beholding himself, man triumphs over discouragement and weakness, for from the consciousness of inner freedom there blossoms eternal youth and joy. On these have I laid hold, nor shall I ever give them up, and so I can see with a smile my eyes growing dim, and my blond locks turning white. Nought can happen to affright my heart, and the pulse of my inner life will beat with vigor until death. (28)

CHAPTER XIII

CHARLES EDWARD GARMAN

Charles E. Garman (1850-1907) was born in Limington, Maine, the son of a Congregational minister. He graduated from Amherst College in 1872, and became principal of the Ware (Massachusetts) High School. Entering Yale Divinity School in 1876 and graduating in 1879, he was awarded the Hooker Fellowship for two years of further study but held it for only one year because of his appointment as Walker instructor in mathematics at Amherst. Garman became instructor in Philosophy in 1881, associate professor of Mental and Moral Philosophy in 1882, professor of Mental Philosophy in 1889, and in 1892 professor of Mental and Moral Philosophy, which position he continued to hold until his death in 1907. He was a trustee of Mount Holyoke College. Garman concentrated on teaching; he seldom preached or lectured outside of his classroom, published no books and left but scanty record of his work other than in its potent influence on the minds of his pupils.*

So intense was Garman's interest and that of his students that his home became more of an extension of the classroom than a social centre. He declined several calls to larger institutions because of his devotion to his work at Amherst. While at Yale, he had become a victim of severe bronchitis and, during the last decade of his life, students remember him as a semi-invalid.

His students say that his course was not the presentation of a system of philosophy, but essentially one of emphasis upon method, holding that if methods were correct the right conclusions were bound ultimately to be reached. The method was the weighing of evidence. He first showed that many writers had given better reasons for doubt or agnosticism than the students could possibly present. Then he aroused in them the urge to learn how science and art, government, justice, charity, business and history could be brought together in a rational system. He turned his students from unthinking youths into thoughtful men trying to find unity in their everenlarging experience. No teacher was held in greater reverence by the majority of the class or exerted a more profound and immediate influence on their processes of thought. William James characterized him as "the greatest teacher in the United States."

"The educational process has not yet begun and it never will begin for most men, without guidance and methods of instruction which excite the student's intellectual curiosity, develop his intellectual self-reliance, and inspire in him faith in the truth and his ability to find it. It is the introduction of these spiritual and intellectual ferments into the educational process which marks the difference between intellectual sterility and the beginning of that moral and intellectual growth which is the first essential of all true education. And whenever that has occurred, from the time of Socrates to the days of Garman or of some of the teachers you and I knew in professional school, there you will find more than books and courses and curricula. You will find a man whose students rise to call him blessed because his was the God-given gift of the teacher." (Chief Justice Harlan Fiske Stone at the Fiftieth Reunion of his class in 1944—see Amherst Alumni Council News, July, 1944.)

*See Letters, Lectures and Addresses of Charles Edward Garman. Eliza Miner Garman, Houghton, Mifflin Company, 1911. Also, *Great Teachers*. Edited by Houston Peterson. Rutgers University Press, 1946.

One can copy the superficial but not the genuine qualities. (1)

We must do with the lower passions, by aid of discipline, just what science has accomplished with steam and electricity, the agencies that work destruction in the earthquake and the thunderbolt: viz, not annihilate them, but convert them to higher forms of activity, and so make them bless our age. (2)

I think it is Ruskin who says that when we witness the wonderful phenomena of nature—the earthquake, the lightning, the tornado, or those other great miracles of which the transfiguration of nature in the month of May is a type—we never say,

"There has been a great effort here," but, instead, "What a mighty power has wrought this!" Nature accomplishes her work with ease. She has a reserve force that we cannot measure, and we stand in her presence dumb with wonder or admiration. (3)

Sentiments spring from an act of will. They are the feelings of ownership that arises from an investment. When one has identified himself with a cause so that he stands or falls with it, there occurs a transfer of all interests in self to the cause. The clear realization that henceforth one can prosper only as his cause is successful, that "A" can determine himself only through "B", secures that "A" shall forget himself and think only of "B". This is ownership; not that "A" owns "B", but the reverse. The patriot is owned by his country; the soldier by his cause; the lawyer by his case; the man of business by his investments. (4)

When a teacher depends on interesting a pupil by appealing to native interests, at best he can only give him information, but not discipline. He is simply trying to lead him to the tree of knowledge, which is also the tree of happiness. But when he inspires sentiment, he takes him by the hand and leads him to the tree of life, of which if he eat he shall live forever. (5)

Those religious workers who spend all their efforts in converting men, and getting them to unite with the church, and then leave them to shift for themselves in the religious life, make a very near approach to adopting the methods which Spain has followed in dealing with the non-combatants in Cuba. Such converts are little better than spiritual reconcentrados, and they excite our pity in the extreme. (6)

To be guided by the holy spirit of truth is to come into a larger apprehension of the divine character, and of the divine plan, and to be able to fit one's own life into that plan so that God may work through the individual both to will and to do His good pleasure. (7)

It is sometimes claimed that mystery is essential to religion, and that if the mysteries could be removed it would be taking away our reverence; that a God understood would be no God at all. But I beg leave to ask you to what are you looking forward in your future life? To a period of greater mystery, or, with the Apostle Paul, do you say, "Then shall I know even as I am known?" Will the sanctity, the love, and the adoration of worshipers in the New Jerusalem be diminished by this increase of knowledge? Must not the law of life which holds in heaven hold on earth? Therefore in proportion as we can reach out towards that larger knowledge of God, is not the light of that other world breaking upon the hilltops of this life with its morning splendor? This is the aim of philosophy, and I feel that to this end the preacher must strive if the Spirit speaks through him to the church. (8)

The public at large are beginning to feel that there is no dividing line between time and eternity, the here and the hereafter; that a man's character will be governed by exactly the same laws, no matter how changed his environment may be. From a scientific point of view, then, men determine the value of religion by its influence upon the present life. If not essential for the life that now is, they ask what evidence do we have that it will be of any avail hereafter? On the other hand, if you can show us that it is the mainspring of existence here, we will trust it now, and we will trust it for the future also. (9)

Whatever may be true of men's creed, nothing is clearer than the fact that the personality and the sovereignty of God are not a large factor in the practical life and thought of our age. (10)

The church must not merely affirm the personality of God— for to many this would be a mere formula—the church must help men realize the divine personality; it must force men to see that personality and sovereignty are the supreme facts of the universe. But this cannot be done unless you philosophize. (11)

Some time ago a student expressed his estimate of German philosophy in these words: "Bricks without straw, but plenty of mud, though," and this is about the estimate that any one will have who gives to philosophical writers only a superficial attention.

But if one were not making a campaign of criticism, if one were really in earnest in his search for truth, he would find this so-called mud very different stuff from what it first appeared to be. He would find it composed of ingredients quite as marvelous as those Ruskin found in the mud of a manufacturing village. You remember Ruskin's description of these chemical elements, which at first had so repelled him. He says: "Beginning with the clay. Leave it still quiet to follow its own instinct of unity, and it becomes not only white, but clear, not only clear, but hard, not only clear and hard, but so set that it can deal with the light in a wonderful way and gather out of it the loveliest blue rays, refusing the rest. We call it then a sapphire."

Then he takes the sand and, under similar conditions, finds it arranging itself in such a form that it has the power to reflect not merely the blue rays, but blue, green, purple, and red in the greatest beauty in which they can be seen through any hard material whatsoever. We call it then an opal.

Encouraged by these discoveries, Ruskin sets himself to examine what appears to be the filthy soot. It cannot make itself white at first, but, instead of being discouraged, tries harder and harder and comes out at last the hardest thing in the world; in exchange for the blackness that it had, it obtains the power of reflecting all the rays of the sun at once, in the vividest blaze that any solid thing can shoot. We call it then a diamond. The ounce of slime which we despised has, under favorable conditions, become three of the most precious jewels—a sapphire, an opal, and a diamond. (12)

In a similar manner those difficult and confusing philosophical treatises, with their repulsive terminology, that seemed so absurd on their first reading, will, if time and thought are given to them by a candid mind, crystallize into the most precious truths that have ever rewarded the search of a finite human being. It is just these truths, in their crystallized form, that preachers need to make accessible to their congregation in this age of criticism and reconstruction. (13)

545

Among the great truths thus brought within our reach are these three:

First, Idealism; or the conception of the universe, material as truly as moral, as dependent on God for its continued existence from moment to moment, as truly as the rainbow on the continued shining of the sun. Philosophy takes literally Christ's words, that not a sparrow falls to the ground "without your Father." So also the words of the Apostle Paul: "For in Him we live, and move, and have our being."

Secondly, the conception of Personality is the ultimate fact of the universe. From which it follows that all nature as truly as all human history has not merely a scientific, but also an ethical and a religious, import, and is progressing towards the realization of divine ideals. This is the foundation for all true optimism. (14)

The great doctrine of Sovereignty is the third of the jewels that crystallize out of philosophical discussions. This is something infinitely more than mere cause and effect. It is the ultimate principle of all personal relationship, not merely between God and man, but quite as much between man and his fellows. Philosophy shows that human government and divine government stand or fall together. We cannot hold to the former and deny the latter. (15)

Either human beings cannot think at all, or the conceptions they apply to men must be the standards by which they judge of God. Our mental processes are exactly the same whether we think about divine things or about human affairs. It follows that if personality, intelligence, consciousness is a transitional stage with men, it cannot be attributed to God. He must be perfect, therefore He must have advanced beyond this stage of existence. (16)

A true philosophy lays the axe at the root of this tree. It recognizes clearly that spiritual impulses are not blind, but can act only through intelligence. Then perfection of life will consist in perfection of knowledge and personality; then it will be impossible to think of the Divine Being as other than omniscient, the tender, loving Father. Impersonal law will give place to the liberty

546

of the sons of God. This is the only true view. Take Longfellow's Evangeline. The impulse to follow her lover through all these years of wandering is indeed the mainspring of her action, but can this impulse, acting blindly, find him? Is there a more pathetic scene in literature than when, floating down the Ohio River, her party lands on an island for rest, in the middle of the day, at the very time when her lover is rowing by on the other side? The animal impulse to rest can execute itself without intelligence. When Evangeline was tired she could drop to sleep without understanding the processes involved in slumber; she could take a reclining position without knowing the physiological principles which required it, for these animal impulses are as blind and automatic as magnetism which turns the needle to the pole. Had her spiritual impulse of devotion to her lover been of this type she would have moved towards him as unconsciously as a stone falls towards the earth. But because the spiritual impulses could only be guided by intelligence, and she knew not what was going on about her, she embarks again, and every hour carries her farther and farther in the direction opposite to that taken by her lover.

What is true here is true in the religious life, if we do not add to our faith knowledge in the services of God. We need a philosophy of the divine life to fit our own actions into the course of events and make our lives count in our generation. (17)

The first record of a vacation was that of the Sabbath when God rested from all His works, "wherefore the Lord blessed the Sabbath day and hallowed it." There is something worshipful among these grand old hills in northern New Hampshire which makes one feel that it is godlike to rest from his labors of the year, and he wonders why, in the solemn quiet of the eternal calm which rests upon the mountains, he too should not call his vacation a Sabbath. . . . The solemn silence of these old hills is as undisturbed as on Creation's morn. Men may come and men may go, but these hills rest forever. (18)

If one has a scientific turn of mind, his thought wanders back to that period of grand upheaval and convulsion when they were reared by the folding of the earth's crust; that was the period of their activity, their Wall Street panic; but they have now retired from active labor, and every line of their wrinkled brows speaks of the work that has been done and of the rest that has followed. . . . Truly, the mountains are the place for rest. And yet it is not the rest of the grave, for that which overcomes one at every turn is the consciousness of life, of strength, of reserve power, not death, but immortality. Eternity, not time, is before him, and in him, and the Eternal speaks through Him and the hills echo His voice, and I said, "O, my God, take me not away in the midst of my days; thy years are throughout all generations. Of old hast thou established the mountains, and the hills are the work of thy hands. They shall perish, but thou shalt endure. Yea, all of them shall wax old like a garment, and as a vesture shalt thou change them, and they shall be changed; but thou art the same and thy years shall have no end." * The thought which has impressed me over and over during the few days of my stay here is this: The strength of the hills is His also; that nature is not something apart from God, but simply the hem of His garment, or rather the veil over His face like that which Moses wore when he came down from the mount where he talked with God face to face. (19) * It will be noted that the language is in part quoted and in part adapted from Psalm 102:24-26.

The other thought, the companion of this, is the names which have been given to these hills, names which figure prominently in our country's history: Mounts Washington, Jefferson, Adams, Lafayette. What is the sense of this nomenclature? Is a mountain simply a monument to a great man's name, a monument reared by nature instead of by man? This is ridiculous. I feel like apologizing even for the suggestion, and yet there is a fitness in the names. Wherein lies the symbolism; is it not this? These mountains were made of common clay, they were once the bed of the ocean; but the great geological forces which shaped our earth and transformed chaos into cosmos lifted them high in air, and gave them a formative influence in determining the climate and fertility of the country at their feet. So our great men in history—men like Washington and Lincoln—were men of the common people, but they were not self-made men. Those great historic forces which have been shaping the destiny of the race brought about the convulsions in our national life that forced them to the front, lifted them high above their fellows, gave them a formative influence in determining the conditions of our national career; and as the mountains drop down the dew, condense the clouds, cool the heated air and send it back laden with balsam odors, and give birth to those streams which have created our mill towns and brought wealth and prosperity where there was only desolation, so have these great men blessed all who came after them, and lived immortal lives. Catching the first beams of the morning sun of reform, and reflecting the last rays of the day whose work is done, their biographies become mountains of our historic life, whither we turn in our partisan troubles and bigoted strifes for that mental vacation, those grand thoughts, that champagne atmosphere of truth, which is the only tonic for a weak mind. And now whence these forces of history, whence these forces of geology, if the strength of the hills is His also? Is not the spirit of the prophet the inspiration of the age? are not the instincts of human society a power through which God is working to will and to do of His good pleasure in human affairs? Is not this the difference between the old dispensation and the new? Moses received his revelation on tables of stone from the top of Mount Sinai shrouded with clouds and thick darkness. We find God revealed in the lives of our great men; they are our Sinais, and their summits, instead of being shrouded with clouds and thick darkness, are lighted up with the light of coming day, and we learn that the strength of the hills is His also. (20)

If you notice, all the beneficent institutions of humanity when they first appeared on earth were disguised by what is now most repulsive to us. Religion in its earlier forms was a cruel superstition, offering human sacrifices. Government was a despotism such as you can at present hardly realize. Civilization itself took its first steps in progress in the form of war and slavery. Chemistry was alchemy, astronomy was astrology. Even so beneficent a science as medicine was disguised as magic. (21)

Students think of intellect and forms and leave out of account will power; but just as the most powerful engine is helpless without fuel, so the most brilliantly equipped mind is weakness itself without a strong will. But will is not an accident; it depends on inspiration, and inspiration is impossible without motive.

All history teaches that the deepest, truest, most efficient motives come only from ethical and religious convictions. (22)

As X-rays pass readily through opaque substances, as the waves of electricity used in wireless telegraphy are not hindered by even mountain walls, so evidence will penetrate all sophistry and all pretences. (23)

CHAPTER XIV

WALTER BAGEHOT

Walter Bagehot was born at Langport, Somersetshire, February 3, 1826. He died at the age of fifty-one, March 24, 1877. His father was managing director of Stuckey's Banking Company, and his mother was of the Stuckey family.

Bagehot attended University College, London, where he received the bachelor's degree in 1846, and the Master's degree two years later, with the gold medal in Moral Philosophy. He then studied law, but before the coup d'etat *in 1851 went to France from where he wrote letters to the* Inquirer *which drew much attention.*

In 1858 Bagehot married the daughter of Mr. James Wilson then editor of the Economist, *the most important financial journal of the world. Two years later upon the decease of Mr. Wilson, Walter Bagehot became editor, a position which he filled until his untimely death nineteen years later.*

Among the numerous writings of Bagehot are:
The English Constitution, *1867*
Physics and Politics, *1872*
Lombard Street, a Description of the Money Market, *1873*
Postulates of Political Economy, *1876*
Literary Studies, Economic Studies, *and* Biographical Studies *were edited and published after his death.*

The sub-title of Physics and Politics *explains the scope of the work, namely,* Or, Thoughts on the Application of the Principles of "Natural Selection" and "Inheritance" to Political Society.

Those kinds of morals and that kind of religion which tend to make the firmest and most effectual character are sure to prevail, all else being the same; and creeds or systems that conduce to a soft, limp mind tend to perish, except some hard extrinsic force kept them alive. Thus Epicureanism never prospered at Rome, but Stoicism did; the stiff, serious character of the great prevailing nation was attracted by what seemed a confirming creed, and deterred by what looked like a relaxing creed. The inspiring doctrines fell upon the ardent character, and so confirmed its energy. Strong beliefs win strong men, and then make them stronger. Such is no doubt one cause why monotheism tends to prevail over polytheism; it produces a higher, steadier character, calmed and concentrated by a great single object; it is not confused by competing rites, or distracted by miscellaneous deities. (1)

It is very dubious whether the spirit of war does not still color our morality far too much. Metaphors from law and metaphors from war make most of our current moral phrases, and a nice examination would easily explain that both rather vitiate what both often illustrate. The military habit makes man think far too much of definite action, and far too little of brooding meditation. Life is not a set campaign, but an irregular work, and the main forces in it are not overt resolutions, but latent and half-involuntary promptings. The mistake of military ethics is to exaggerate the conception of discipline, and so to present the moral force of the will in a barer form than it ever ought to take. Military morals can direct the axe to cut down the tree, but it knows nothing of the quiet force by which the forest grows. (2)

Tolerance too is learned in discussion, and, as history shows, is only so learned. In all customary societies bigotry is the ruling principle. In rude places to this day any one who says anything new is looked on with suspicion, and is persecuted by opinion if not injured by penalty. One of the greatest pains to human nature is the pain of a new idea. It is, as common people say, so "upsetting"; it makes you think that, after all, your favorite notions may be wrong, your firmest beliefs illfounded; it is certain that till now there was no place allotted in your mind to the new and startling inhabitant, and now that it has conquered

552

an entrance, you do not at once see which of your old ideas it will or will not turn out, with which of them it can be reconciled, and with which it is at essential enmity. Naturally, therefore, common men hate a new idea, and are disposed more or less to ill-treat the original man who brings it. Even nations with long habits of discussion are intolerant enough. (3)

If we know that a nation is capable of enduring discussion, we know that it is capable of practising with equanimity continuous tolerance. (4)

The power of a government by discussion as an instrument of elevation plainly depends—other things being equal—on the greatness or littleness of the things to be discussed. There are periods when great ideas are "in the air," and when, from some cause or other, even common persons seem to partake of an unusual elevation. The age of Elizabeth in England was conspicuously such a time. The new idea of the Reformation in religion, and the enlargement of the *moenia mundi* by the discovery of new and singular lands, taken together, gave an impulse to thought which few, if any, ages can equal. The discussion, though not wholly free, was yet far freer than in the average of ages and countries. Accordingly, every pursuit seemed to start forward. Poetry, science, and architecture, different as they are, and removed as they all are at first sight from such an influence as discussion, were suddenly started onward. Macaulay would have said you might rightly read the power of discussion "in the poetry of Shakespeare, in the prose of Bacon, in the oriels of Longleat, and the stately pinnacles of Burleigh." This is, in truth, but another case of the principle of which I have had occasion to say so much as to the character of ages and countries. If any particular power is much prized in an age, those possessed of that power will be imitated; those deficient in that power will be despised. In consequence an unusual quantity of that power will be developed, and be conspicuous. Within certain limits vigorous and elevated thought was respected in Elizabeth's time, and, therefore, vigorous and elevated thinkers were many; and the effect went far beyond the cause: It penetrated into physical science, for which very few men cared; and it began a reform in philosophy to which almost all were then opposed. In a word, the temper of the age encouraged originality, and in consequence original men started into prominence, went hither and thither where they liked, arrived at goals which the age never expected, and so made it ever memorable. (5)

All the great movements of thought in ancient and modern times have been nearly connected in time with government by discussion. Athens, Rome, the Italian republics of the Middle Ages, the communes and states-general of feudal Europe, have all had a special and peculiar quickening influence, which they owed to their freedom, and which states without that freedom have never communicated. And it has been at the time of great epochs of thought—at the Peloponnesian war, at the fall of the Roman Republic, at the Reformation, at the French Revolution,—that such liberty of speaking and thinking have produced their full effect. (6)

Every page of Aristotle and Plato bears ample and indelible trace of the age of discussion in which they lived; and thought cannot possibly be freer. The deliverance of the speculative intellect from traditional and customary authority was altogether complete. (7)

The minds of the highest philosophers were then as ready to obey evidence and reason as they have ever been since; probably they were more ready. The rule of custom over them at least had been wholly broken, and the primary conditions of intellectual progress were in that respect satisfied. (8)

Civilized ages inherit the human nature which was victorious in barbarous ages, and that nature is, in many respects, not at all suited to civilized circumstances. . . . All the inducements of early society tend to foster immediate action; all its penalties fall on the man who pauses; the traditional wisdom of those times was never weary of inculcating that "delays are dangerous," and that the sluggish man—the man "who roasteth not that which he took

554

in hunting"—will not prosper on the earth, and, indeed will very soon perish out of it. And in consequence an inability to stay quiet, an irritable desire to act directly, is one of the most conspicuous failings of mankind.

Pascal said that most of the evils of life arose from "man's being unable to sit still in a room"; and though I do not go that length, it is certain that we should have been a far wiser race than we are if we had been readier to sit quiet—we should have known much better the way in which it was best to act when we came to act. The rise of physical science, the first great body of practical truth provable to all men, exemplifies this in the plainest way. If it had not been for quiet people, who sat still and studied the sections of the cone, if other quiet people had not sat still and studied the theory of infinitesimals, or other quiet people had not sat still and worked out the doctrine of chances, the most "dreamy moonshine," as the purely practical mind would consider, of all human pursuits; if "idle star-gazers" had not watched long and carefully the motions of the heavenly bodies—our modern astronomy would have been impossible, and without our astronomy "our ships, our colonies, our seamen," all that makes modern life, modern life could not have existed. Ages of sedentary, quiet, thinking people were required before that noisy existence began, and without those pale preliminary students it could not have been brought into being. (9)

Most men inherited a nature too eager and too restless to be quiet and find out things; and even worse—with their idle clamor they "disturbed the brooding hen," they would not let those be quiet who wished to be so, and out of whose calm thought much good might have come forth. (10)

The issues of life are plain no longer. To act rightly in modern society requires a great deal of previous study, a great deal of assimilated information, a great deal of sharpened imagination; and these pre-requisites of sound action require much time, and, I was going to say, much "lying in the sun," a long period of "mere passiveness." (11)

555

I wish the art of benefiting men had kept pace with the art of destroying them. . . . One may incline to hope that the balance of good over evil is in favor of benevolence; one can hardly bear to think that it is not so; but anyhow it is certain that there is a most heavy debt of evil, and that this burden might almost all have been spared us if philanthropists as well as others had not inherited from their barbarous forefathers a wild passion for instant action. (12)

Every sort of philosophy has been systematized, and yet as these philosophies utterly contradict one another, most of them cannot be true. Unproved abstract principles without number have been eagerly caught up by sanguine men, and then carefully spun out into books and theories, which were to explain the whole world. But the world goes clear against these abstractions, and it must do so, as they require it to go in antagonistic directions. The mass of a system attracts the young and impresses the unwary; but cultivated people are very dubious about it. They are ready to receive hints and suggestions, and the smallest real truth is ever welcome. But a large book of deductive philosophy is much to be suspected. No doubt the deductions may be right; in most writers they are so; but where did the premises come from? Who is sure that they are the whole truth, and nothing but the truth, of the matter in hand? Who is not almost sure beforehand that they will contain a strange mixture of truth and error, and, therefore, that it will not be worth while to spend life in reasoning over their consequences? In a word, the superfluous energy of mankind has flowed over into philosophy, and has worked into big systems what should have been left as little suggestions.

And if the old systems of thought are not true as systems, neither is the new revolt from them to be trusted in its whole vigor. There is the same original vice in that also. There is an excessive energy in revolutions if there is such energy anywhere. The passion for action is quite as ready to pull down as to build up; probably it is more ready, for the task is easier:

556

"Old things need not be therefore true,
   O brother men, not yet the new;
   Ah, still awhile the old thought retain,
   And yet consider it again." (13)

In old times a few ideas got possession of men, and communities, but this is happily now possible no longer. We see how incomplete these old ideas were; how almost by chance one seized on one nation, and another on another; how often one set of men have persecuted another set for opinions on subjects of which neither, we now perceive, knew anything. It might be well if a greater number of effectual demonstrations existed among mankind; but while no such demonstrations exist, and while the evidence which completely convinces one man seems to another trifling and insufficient, let us recognize the plain position of inevitable doubt. Let us not be bigots with a doubt, and persecutors without a creed. We are beginning to see this, and we are railed at for so beginning. But it is a great benefit, and it is to the incessant prevalence of detective discussion that our doubts are due. (14)

If anyone were asked to describe what it is which distinguishes the writings of a man of genius who is also a great man of the world from all other writings, I think he would use these same words, "animated moderation." He would say that such writings are never slow, are never excessive, are never exaggerated; that they are always instinct with judgment, and yet that judgment is never a dull judgment; that they have as much spirit in them as would go to make a wild writer, and yet that every line of them is the product of a sane and sound writer. (15)

Upon plausible grounds—looking, for example, to the position of Locke and Newton in the science of the last century, and to that of Darwin in our own—it may be argued that there is some quality in English thought which makes them strike out as many, if not more, first-rate and original suggestions than nations of greater scientific culture and more diffused scientific interest. In both cases I believe the reason of the English originality to be

557

that government by discussion quickens and enlivens thought all through society; that it makes people think no harm may come of thinking; that in England this force has long been operating, and so it has developed more of all kinds of people ready to use their mental energy in their own way, and not ready to use it in any other way, than a despotic government. And so rare is great originality among mankind, and so great are its fruits, that this one benefit of free government probably outweighs what are in many cases its accessory evils. Of itself it justifies or goes far to justify our saying with Montesquieu, "Whatever be the cost of this glorious liberty, we must be content to pay it to heaven."(16)

CHAPTER XV

AESCHYLUS

Of the three great Athenian tragic poets, Aeschylus was the earliest, followed in chronological order by Sophocles and Euripides. Aeschylus was born, as a member of a rather prominent Athenian family, at Eleusis, the home of the Mysteries, near Athens, in 529 B.C.

Aeschylus fought for Athens in the war against the Persians. Among other battles, he is believed to have fought at Marathon and Salamis, and to have been wounded at the first named.

In his career as playwright Aeschylus entered the annual Athenian tragic drama competition more than twenty times in the period 499-458 B.C. He won first prize thirteen times. He was defeated in 468 by Sophocles. After that he visited Sicily. The last great victory of Aeschylus was in the year 458 B.C. with the Orestean trilogy which we still possess. He died in Gela, Sicily, in 456. The plays of Aeschylus are marked by deep religious and theological concepts.

Of approximately ninety plays, seven survive:

The Suppliants

The Persians

The Seven Against Thebes

Prometheus Bound *(only surviving drama of his Promethean trilogy)*

and the Orestean trilogy:

Agamemnon

Eumenides

Choephorae

Jove, or what other name
The god that reigns supreme delights to claim,

Him I invoke; him of all powers that be,
Alone I find,
Who from this bootless load of doubt can free
My labouring mind. (1)

Justice doth wait to teach
Wisdom by suffering. (2)

For Jove doth teach men wisdom, sternly wins
To virtue by the tutoring of their sins;
Yea! drops of torturing recollection chill
The sleeper's heart; 'gainst man's rebellious will
Jove works the wise remorse. (3)

The gods are blind, and little caring,
So one hath said, to mark the daring
Of men, whose graceless foot hath ridden
O'er things to human touch forbidden.
Godless who said so; sons shall rue
Their parents' folly,
Who flushed with wealth, with insolence flown,
The sober bliss of man outgrown,
The trump of Mars unchastened blew,
And stirred red strife without the hue
Of justice wholly.
Live wiselier thou; not waxing gross
With gain, thou shalt be free from loss. (4)

'Twas said of old, and 'tis said to-day,
That wealth to prosperous stature grown
Begets a birth of its own:
That a surfeit of evil by good is prepared,
And sons must bear what allotment of woe
Their sires were spared.
But this I rebel to believe: I know

That impious deeds conspire
To beget an offspring of impious deeds
Too like their ugly sire.
But whoso is just, though his wealth like a river
Flow down, shall be scatheless; his house shall rejoice
In an offspring of beauty for ever. (5)

A sober heart
Is the best gift of God; call no man happy
Till death hath found him prosperous to the close. (6)

'Tis robber robbed, and slayer slain, for, though
Oft-times it lag, with measured blow for blow
Vengeance prevaileth
While great Jove lives. Who breaks the close-linked woe
Which heaven entaileth? (7)

Blood for blood and blow for blow,
Thou shalt reap as thou didst sow:
Age to age with hoary wisdom
Speaketh thus to men. (8)

O thou, o'er all Olympian gods that be,
      Supremely swaying,
With words of wisdom, when I pray to thee,
      Inspire my praying.
We can but pray; to do, O Jove, is thine,
      Thou great director;
Of him within, who works thy will divine,
      Be thou protector!
Him raise, the orphaned son whom thou dost see
      In sheer prostration;
Twofold and threefold he shall find from thee
      Just compensation. (9)

Ye rulers on Earth, fear the rulers in Heaven,
No aid by the gods to the forward is given;
For the bonds of our thraldom asunder are riven,
     And the day dawns clear. (10)

     Men
Oft-times have slain their best friends unawares. (11)

He is strong whom God defends. (12)

When men are proud beyond the mark of right,
They do proclaim with forward tongue their folly,
Themselves their own accuser. (13)

Of substance studious, careless of the show,
The wise man is what fools but seem to be,
Reaping rich harvest from the mellow soil
Of quiet thought, the mother of great deeds. (14)

Without men much riches profit little; without wealth the state,
Though in numbers much abounding, may not look on joyous
                              light. (15)

Proud thoughts were never made for mortal man. (16)

Suspicion's a disease that cleaves to tyrants. (17)

'Tis a light thing for him whose foot's unwarped
By misadventure's meshes to advise
And counsel the unfortunate. (18)

Do good to men, but do it with discretion. (19)

Though Art be strong, Necessity is stronger. (20)

I both speak truth and wish the truth to be. (21)

As Time grows old he teaches many things. (22)

If thou art not the bought and sold of folly,
Dare to learn wisdom from thy present ills. (23)

562

Ponder and weigh,
Close not thy stubborn ears to good advice. (24)

Urge no reasons to convince me
That an honest heart must hate. (25)

      From anarchy
And slavish masterdom alike my ordinance
Preserve my people! Cast not from your walls
All high authority; for where no fear
Awful remains, what mortal will be just?
This holy reverence use, and ye possess
A bulwark, and a safeguard of the land. (26)

      One moment blinds me quite,
Or to a blaze of glory opens my eyes.
We sink to shame, or to more honor rise. (27)

Blest the man in whose heart reigneth
    Holy Fear;
Fear his heart severely traineth;
Blest, from troublous woe who gaineth
Ripest fruits of wisdom clear;
But who sports, a careless liver,
In the sunshine's flaunting show,
Holy Justice, he shall never
Thy severest virtue know.

Lordless life, or despot-ridden,
Be they both from me forbidden.
To the wise mean strength is given,
Thus the gods have ruled in heaven;
Gods, that gently or severely
Judge, discerning all things clearly.
Mark my word, I tell thee truly,

563

Pride, that lifts itself unduly,
    Had a godless heart for sire.
Healthy-minded moderation
Wins the wealthy consummation,
    Every heart's desire.

Yet, again, I tell thee truly,
At Justice' altar bend thee duly.
Wean thine eyes from lawless yearning
After gain; with godless spurning
Smite not thou that shrine most holy.
Punishment, that travels slowly,
Comes at last, when least thou fearest.
Yet, once more, with truth sincerest,
Love thy parents and revere,
And the guest, that to protect him,
Claims thy guardian roof, respect him,
      With an holy fear.

Whoso, with no forced endeavour,
    Sin-eschewing liveth,
Him to hopeless ruin never
    Jove the Saviour giveth.
But whose hand, with greed rapacious,
    Draggeth all things for his prey,
He shall strike his flag audacious,
    When the god-sent storm shall bray,
      Winged with fate at last;
When the stayless sail is flapping,
When the sail-yard swings, and, snapping,
    Crashes to the blast.

He shall call, but none shall hear him,
    When dark ocean surges;
None with saving hand shall near him,
    When his prayer he urges. (28)

CHAPTER XVI

FREDERICK SCHILLER

Johann Christoph Friedrich von Schiller was born at Marbach, Germany, November 10, 1759 and died at Weimar May 9, 1805, at the age of forty-five years. Schiller was a notable German poet, dramatist, and historian.

His father, who had been a surgeon, at the outbreak of the Seven Year War entered Würtemburg service. At the birth of his son he was lieutenant. He rose to captain. After the war he (the father) became park-keeper at Ludwigsburg, the Duke's country seat. It appears that Friedrich was precocious and that the Duke helped in his education, at the same time trying to control his courses of studies more than Schiller wished. Originally Schiller had intended to study theology. He did study jurisprudence, and at Stuttgart medicine.

Schiller's literary career began in 1781 with Die Räuber. *He felt it necessary to flee to avoid interference with his chosen work. His life may be divided into three periods:*

1. Youth, 1759-1785. About the latter date Schiller went to Leipzig. To this first period belong several plays including Don Carlos.

2. A second period is that of about 1785-1795. This period includes his historical writings, and Die Aesthetische Erziehung des Mensches, *dealing with art as supreme educational factor. In 1788 he was named to a professorship at Jena. He became intimate with Fichte and Wilhelm von Humboldt. He married in 1790.*

3. A third period is from 1794 or 1795 to his death in 1805. This is the period of close intimacy with Goethe and includes his most productive years, for it is as a dramatist that he excelled. This is the period when he produced the Wallenstein *trilogy (1799 and 1800),* Maria Stuart *(1801),* Die Jungfrau von Orleans *(1802),* Die Braut von Messina *(1803), and* Wilhelm Tell *(1804). Schiller was ennobled in 1802.*

All his life Schiller had to struggle against pecuniary difficulties, but he always lived honorably. He died in 1805 from a lung disease of long duration.

Of Schiller, Carlyle wrote:

> It is true he died early; but the student will exclaim with Charles XII in another case, "Was it not enough of life when he had conquered kingdoms?" These kingdoms which Schiller conquered were not for one nation at the expense of suffering to another; they were soiled by no patriot's blood, no widow's, no orphan's tear: they were kingdoms conquered from the barren realms of Darkness, to increase the happiness, and dignity, and power, of all men; new forms of Truth, new maxims of Wisdom, new images and scales of Beauty, won from the "void and formless Infinite"; "a possession forever," to all the generations of the Earth.

The will of a man is his fortune alone. (1)

The earth-ball is open before you—yet there
Nought's to be gained, but by those who dare. (2)

Why, brother, the blessed God above
Can't have from us all an equal love.
One prays for the sun, at which t'other will fret:
One is for dry weather—t'other for wet.
What you, now, regard as with misery rife,
Is to me the unclouded sun of life. (3)

Who life would win, he must dare to die! (4)

If we should wait till you, in solemn council,
With due deliberation had selected
The smallest out of four-and-twenty evils,
I' faith we should wait long—

566

"Dash! and through with it!" That's the better watchword.
Then after come what may come. 'Tis man's nature
To make the best of a bad thing once past.
A bitter and perplex'd "what shall I do?"
Is worse to man than worst necessity. (5)

      There exist
Few fit to rule themselves, but few that use
Their intellects intelligently. Then
Well for the whole, if there be found a man,
Who makes himself what nature destined him,
The pause, the central point, to thousand thousands—
Stands fixed and stately, like a form-built column,
Where all may press with joy and confidence. (6)

      Every power
Seems as it were redoubled by his presence:
He draws forth every latent energy,
Showing to each his own peculiar talent,
Yet leaving all to be what nature made them. (7)

The oracle within him, that which *lives,*
He must invoke and question—not dead books,
Not ordinances, not mould-rotted papers. (8)

The way of ancient ordinance, though it winds,
Is yet no devious path. Straight forward goes
The lightning's path, and straight the fearful path
Of the cannon ball. Direct it flies, and rapid;
Shattering what it *may* reach, and shattering what it reaches.
My son! the road the human being travels,
That, on which BLESSING comes and goes, doth follow
The river's course, the valley's playful windings,
Curves round the corn-field and the hill of vines,
Honouring the holy bounds of property!
And thus secure, though late, leads to its end. (9)

My son, there's *nothing* insignificant,
Nothing! But yet in every earthly thing
First and most principal is place and time. (10)

But how can it be *known* that you are in earnest,
If the act follows not upon the word? (11)

       'Tis not merely
The human being's Pride that peoples space
With life and mystical predominance;
Since likewise for the stricken heart of Love
This visible nature, and this common world,
Is all too narrow; yea, a deeper import
Lurks in the legend told my infant years
Than lies upon that truth, we live to learn.
For fable is Love's world, his home, his birth-place;
Delightedly dwells he 'mong fays and talismans,
And spirits; and delightedly believes
Divinities, being himself divine.
The intelligible forms of ancient poets,
The fair humanities of old religion,
The Power, the Beauty, and the Majesty,
That had her haunts in dale, or piny mountain,
Or forest by slow stream, or pebbly spring,
Or chasms, and wat'ry depths; all these have vanish'd.
They live no longer in the faith of reason!
But still the heart doth need a language, still
Doth the old instinct bring back the old names,
And to yon starry world they now are gone,
Spirits or gods, that used to share this earth
With man as with their friend; and to the lover
Yonder they move, from yonder visible sky
Shoot influence down: and even at this day
'Tis Jupiter who brings whate'er is great,
And Venus who brings everything that's fair. (12)

568

And if this be the science of the stars,
I too, with glad and zealous industry,
Will learn acquaintance with this cheerful faith.
It is a gentle and affectionate thought,
That in immeasurable heights above us,
At our first birth, the wealth of love was woven,
With sparkling stars for flowers. (13)

Dear son, it is not always possible
Still to preserve that infant purity
Which the voice teaches in our inmost heart,
Still in alarm, for ever on the watch
Against the wiles of wicked men: e'en Virtue
Will sometimes bear away her outward robes
Soiled in the wrestle with Iniquity.
This is the curse of every evil deed,
That propagating still, it brings forth evil. (14)

For of the wholly common is man made,
And custom is his nurse! Woe then to them,
Who lay irreverent hands upon his old
House furniture, the dear inheritance
From his forefathers! For time consecrates;
And what is grey with age becomes religion. (15)

The doing evil to avoid an evil·
Cannot be good! (16)

Virtue hath her heroes too,
As well as fame and fortune. (17)

With an unpolluted heart
Thou canst make conquest of whate'er seems highest!
But he, who once hath acted infamy,
Does nothing more in this world. (18)

To him
Nothing on earth remains unwrench'd and firm,
Who has no faith. (19)

A brave man hazards life, but not his conscience. (20)

O think not of his errors now! remember
His greatness, his magnificence; think on all
The lovely features of his character,
On all the noble exploits of his life,
And let them, like an angel's arm, unseen,
Arrest the lifted sword. (21)

The pilgrim, travelling to a distant shrine
Of hope and healing, doth not count the leagues. (22)

Yet I feel what I have lost
In him. The bloom is vanish'd from my life.
For O! he stood beside me, like my youth,
Transform'd for me the real to a dream,
Clothing the palpable and the familiar
With golden exhalations of the dawn.
Whatever fortunes wait my future toils,
The *beautiful* is vanish'd—and returns not. (23)

What! dost thou not believe that oft in dreams
A voice of warning speaks prophetic to us?
There is no doubt that there exist such voices
Yet I would not call *them*
Voices of warning that announce to us
Only the inevitable. As the sun,
Ere it is risen, sometimes paints its image
In the atmosphere, so often do the spirits
Of great events stride on before the events,
And in to-day already walks to-morrow.

That which we read of the fourth Henry's death
Did ever vex and haunt me like a tale
Of my own future destiny. The king
Felt in his breast the phantom of the knife,

Long ere Ravaillac arm'd himself therewith.
His quiet mind forsook him; the phantasma
Started him in his Louvre, chased him forth
Into the open air: like funeral knells
Sounded that coronation festival;
And still with boding sense he heard the tread
Of those feet that even then were seeking him
Throughout the streets of Paris. (24)

      O—Time
Works miracles. In one hour many thousands
Of grains of sand run out; and quick as they,
Thought follows thought within the human soul.
Only one hour! *Your* heart may change its purpose,
His heart may change its purpose—some new tidings
May come; some fortunate event, decisive,
May fall from Heaven and rescue him. O what
May not one hour achieve. (25)

    God ne'er deserts the brave. (26)

Despise the land that gave thee birth! Ashamed
Of the good ancient customs of thy sires!

The day will come, when thou, with burning tears,
Wilt long for home, and for thy native hills,
And that dear melody of tuneful herds,
Which now, in proud disgust, thou dost despise!
A day when thou wilt drink its tones in sadness,
Hearing their music in a foreign land.
Oh! potent is the spell that binds to home! (27)

We purchase liberty
More cheaply far than bondage. (28)

Force is at best
A fearful thing e'en in a righteous cause. (29)

For every road conducts to the world's end. (30)

Revenge is barren. Of itself it makes
The dreadful food it feeds on; its delight
Is murder—its satiety despair. (31)

'Tis through Love that atom pairs with atom,
    In a harmony eternal, sure;
And 'tis Love that links the spheres together—
    Through her only, systems can endure.

Were she but effaced from Nature's clockwork,
    Into dust would fly the mighty world;
O'er thy systems thou wouldst weep, great Newton,
    When with giant forces to Chaos hurl'd!

Blot the goddess from the Spirit order,
    It would sink in death, and ne'er arise.
Were Love absent, spring would glad us never;
    Were Love absent, none their God would prize! (32)
Stay, thou sailest in vain! 'Tis INFINITY yonder!—
'Tis INFINITY, too, where *thou*, Pilgrim, wouldst wander!
        Eagle thoughts that aspire,
        Let your proud pinions tire!
For 'tis here that sweet Phantasy, bold to the last,
Her anchor in hopeless dejection must cast! (33)

Where's the Man who God to tempt presumes?
    Where the eye that thro' the Gulf can see?
Holy, holy, holy, art Thou, God of Tombs!
    We, with awful trembling, worship Thee!

572

Dust may back to native dust be ground,
   From its crumbling house the Spirit fly,
And the storm its ashes strew around,—
   But its Love, its Love shall never die! (34)

If Love had beckon'd not from high,
Had we gain'd Immortality?
If Love had not inflam'd each thought,
Had we the Master Spirit sought?
'Tis Love that guides the Soul alone
To Nature's Father's heavenly throne!

By Love are blest the Gods on high,
Frail man becomes a Deity
When Love to him is given;
'Tis Love that makes the Heavens shine
With hues more radiant, more divine,
And turns dull Earth to Heaven! (35)

I am a man!—Let ev'ry one
   Who is a man too, spring
With joy beneath God's shining sun,
   And leap on high, and sing!

To God's own image fair on earth
   Its stamp I've power to show;
Down to the font, where heaven has birth
With boldness I dare go. (36)

Though in vain is my sorrow,
   Though in vain my tears fall,
Though the Dead from their slumbers
   They ne'er can recall,
Yet no balm is so sweet to the desolate heart,
When love its soft pleasures no more can impart,
As the torments that love leaves behind it! (37)

"Take the world!" Zeus exclaim'd from his throne in the skies
    To the children of man—"take the world I now give;
It shall ever remain as your heirloom and prize,
    So divide it as brothers, and happily live."

Then all who had hands sought their share to obtain,
    The young and the aged made haste to appear;
The husbandman seiz'd on the fruits of the plain,
    The youth thro' the forest pursu'd the fleet deer.

The merchant took all that his warehouse could hold,
    The abbot selected the last year's best wine,
The king barr'd the bridges,—the highways control'd,
    And said, "Now remember, the tithes shall be mine!"

But when the division long settled had been,
    The poet drew nigh from a far distant land;
But alas! not a remnant was now to be seen,
    Each thing on the earth own'd a master's command.

"Alas! shall then I, of thy sons the most true,
    Shall I, 'mongst them all, be forgotten alone?"
Thus loudly he cried in his anguish, and threw
    Himself in despair before Jupiter's throne.

"If thou in the region of dreams didst delay,
    Complain not of me," the Immortal replied;
"When the world was apportion'd, where then wert thou, pray?"
    "I was," said the poet, "I was—by thy side!

"Mine eye was then fix'd on thy features so bright,
    Mine ear was entranc'd by thy harmony's power;
Oh, pardon the spirit that, aw'd by thy light,
    All things of the earth could forget in that hour!"

574

"What to do?" Zeus exclaimed—"for the world has been given;
  The harvest, the market, the chase, are not free;
But if thou with me wilt abide in my heaven,
  Whenever thou com'st, 'twill be open to thee!" (38)

Trust to the guiding God, and follow the world's silent ocean!
And though as yet never seen, lo! it ascends from the flood!
With the intellect Nature standeth in union eternal:
And what is promised by one, that will the other fulfil. (39)

Love divine, 'tis thou that joinest mortality's flowers!
Parted forever, by thee are they forevermore link'd! (40)

Three words of mighty moment I'll name,
  From mouth unto mouth they fly ever,
Yet the heart can alone their great value proclaim,
  For their source from without rises never.
No virtue, no merit, man's footsteps e'er guides,
When in those three words he no longer confides.

For *Liberty*, man is created,—*is* free,
  Though fetters around him chinking;
Let the cry of the mob never terrify thee,
  Not the scorn of the doltard unthinking!
Fear not the bold slave when he breaks from his chains,
Nor the man who in freedom enduring remains!

And *Virtue* is more than an empty sound,
  His practice thro' life man may make it;
And tho' oft, ere he yet the divine one has found,
  He may stumble, he still may o'ertake it.
And that which the wise in his wisdom ne'er knew,
Can be done by the mind that is childlike and true.

And a *God*, too, there is, with a purpose sublime,
  Tho' frail may be reason's dominion,
High over the regions of space and of time

575

The noblest of thoughts waves its pinion;
And tho' all things in ceaseless succession may roll,
Yet constant forever remains a calm soul.

Preserve, then, the three mighty words I have nam'd,
    From mouth unto mouth spread them ever,
By thy heart will their infinite worth be proclaim'd,
    Tho' their source from without rises never.
Forget not that virtue man's footsteps still guides,
While in those three words he with firmness confides. (41)

What no ear could e'er hear, what no eye could e'er see,
Remains still the truthful, the glorious!
It is not without, for the fool seeks it there;
Within thee it flourishes, constant and fair. (42)

What thou thinkest, belongs to all; what
Thou feel'st is thine only.
Would'st thou make him thine own, feel
Thou the God whom thou think'st! (43)

Would'st thou know thyself, observe the actions of others,
Would'st thou other men know, look thou within thine own heart.
                                                            (44)

Thou canst not sufficiently prize Humanity's value;
Let it be coin'd in deed as it exists in thy breast.
E'en to the man whom thou chancest to meet in life's
                                    narrow pathway,
If he should ask it of thee, hold forth a succoring hand.
But for rain and for dew, for the general welfare of mortals,
Leave thou Heaven to care, friend, as before, so e'en now. (45)

    Buried deep, truth ever lies! (46)

Which religion do I acknowledge? None that thou namest.
"None that I name? And why so?"—
Why, for religion's own sake! (47)

See how we hate, how we quarrel, how thought and how
      feeling divide us!
But thy locks, friend, like mine, meanwhile
      are bleachening fast. (48)

Knowledge to one is a goddess both heav'nly and high,—
      to another
Only an excellent cow, yielding the butter he wants. (49)

Time and Eternity!—linked together by a single instant!—
      Fearful key, which locks
behind me the prison-house of life, and opens
before me the habitations of eternal night—tell me—
oh, tell me—*Whither—Whither* wilt thou lead me!—
Strange, unexplored land!—Humanity is unnerved
at the *Fearful Thought,* the elasticity of our finite
nature is paralyzed, and fancy, that wanton ape
of the senses, juggles our credulity with appalling
phantoms.—No! no! a man must be firm.—
Be what thou wilt, thou *Undefined Futurity,* so
I remain but true to *Myself.*—Be what thou
wilt, so I but take this inward *Self* hence with
me,—External forms are but the trappings of the
man.—My heaven or my hell is within. (50)

    How lovely a thing it is when brethren dwell together in unity;
as the dew drops of heaven that fall upon the mountains of Zion.
—Learn to deserve that happiness, young man, and the angels of
heaven will sun themselves in thy glory. Let thy wisdom be the
wisdom of gray hairs, but let thy heart be the heart of innocent
childhood. (51)

Yet have I ever heard it said, that those
Who watch men's looks, and carry tales about,
Have done more mischief in this world of ours,
Than the assassin's knife, or poison'd bowl. (52)

O! how sweet,
Divinely sweet it is, to feel our being
Reflected in another's beauteous soul;
To see our joys gladden another's cheek,
Our pains bring anguish to another's bosom,
Our sorrows fill another's eye with tears!
How sweet, how glorious it is, hand in hand,
With a dear child, in inmost soul beloved,
To tread once more the rosy paths of youth,
And dream life's fond illusions o'er again!
How proud to live through endless centuries,
Immortal in the virtues of a son;
How sweet to plant what his dear hand shall reap;
To gather what will yield him rich return,
And guess how high his thanks will one day rise! (53)

Love is the only treasure on the face
Of this wide earth, that knows no purchaser
Besides itself—love has no price but love,
It is the costly gem, beyond all price,
Which I must freely give away, or—bury
For ever unenjoyed—like that proud merchant
Whom not the wealth of all the rich Rialto
Could tempt—a great rebuke to kings!—to save
From the deep ocean waves his matchless pearl,
Too proud to barter it beneath its worth! (54)

Give me the man,
So rarely found, of pure and open heart,
Of judgment clear, and eyes unprejudiced. (55)

I live
A citizen of ages yet to come. (56)

Once degrade mankind,
And make him but a thing to play upon.
Who then can share the harmony with you! (57)

You would plant
For all eternity—and yet the seeds
You sow around you are the seeds of death!
This hopeless task, with nature's laws at strife,
Will ne'er survive the spirit of its founder.
You labor for ingratitude:—in vain,
With nature you engage in desperate struggle—
In vain you waste your high and royal life,
In projects of destruction. Man is greater
Than you esteem him. He will burst the chains
Of a long slumber, and reclaim once more
His just and hallow'd rights. (58)

Grant us liberty of thought. (59)

The great Creator,
We see not—he conceals himself within
His own eternal laws. The sceptic sees
Their operation, but beholds not Him.
"Wherefore a god!" he cries, "the world itself
Suffices for itself." And Christian prayer
Ne'er praised him more, than doth this blasphemy. (60)

O bid him realize the dream,
The glowing vision which our friendship painted,
Of a new-perfect realm! And let him lay
The first hand on the rude unshapen'd stone.
Whether he fail or prosper—all alike—
Let him commence the work. When centuries
Have roll'd away, shall Providence again
Raise to the throne, a princely youth like him,
And animate again a favorite son,
Whose breast shall burn with like enthusiasm.
Tell him, in manhood, he must still revere
The dreams of early youth, nor ope the heart

579

Of Heaven's all-tender flower, to canker-worms
Of boasted reason,—nor be led astray
When, by the wisdom of the dust, he hears
Enthusiasm, heavenly-born, blasphemed. (61)

A gracious sovereign throws his portals wide,
Admitting every guest, excluding none;
As freely as the firmament the world,
So mercy must encircle friend and foe.
Impartially the sun pours forth his beams
Through all the regions of infinity;
The heaven's reviving dew falls everywhere,
And brings refreshment to each thirsty plant;
Whate'er is good, and cometh from on high,
Is universal, and without reserve;
But in the heart's recesses darkness dwells! (62)

CHAPTER XVII

SAMUEL TAYLOR COLERIDGE

Samuel Taylor Coleridge was an English poet, literary critic, lecturer, political journalist, philosopher and theologian. He was born, youngest of a numerous family at Ottery St. Mary, Devonshire, October 21, 1772. His father was a clergyman of very small financial means. After his father's death, Samuel received a presentation (1782) to the school called Christ's Hospital, where Charles Lamb was a school-fellow. From there he passed to Jesus College, Cambridge (1791-93, 1794) by means of scholarships. He did not take a degree but with Southey planned to establish a small communistic society in America. The plan fell through for lack of money.

Coleridge married in 1795. The following year his first book of poems was published. Coleridge was considering entrance to the Unitarian ministry, when he received an annuity of 150 pounds from the brothers Josiah and Thomas Wedgwood which permitted him to continue his literary life. Coleridge was stimulated by companionship with Wordsworth, to his greatest achievements in poetry, including The Ancient Mariner *and part of* Christabel. *After the joint publication by Wordsworth and Coleridge of* Lyrical Ballads, *both went to Germany. Coleridge learned the language and studied at the University of Göttingen. In 1799 he translated Schiller's* Wallenstein. *On his return to England Coleridge settled in the Lake District where his health suffered, and, worse yet, he became in a period a slave to opium, first taken as a remedy.*

From 1816, until his death in 1834, Coleridge lived with Mr. Gillman, his physician, who finally cured him, at Highgate, London.

Among the more important of Coleridge's critical and philosophical works are Biographia Literaria *(1817), which developed a theory of literary criticism and influenced British and American aesthetics and philosophy;* Aids to Reflection *(1825)* ; Table Talk *(1835)* ; Confessions of an Enquiring Spirit *(posthumously in 1840). Perhaps the greatest of his contributions to English thought was the currency which he gave to German idealism.*

For of all we see, hear, feel, and touch the substance is and must be in ourselves; and therefore there is no alternative in reason between the dreary (and thank heaven! almost impossible) belief that everything around us is but a phantom, or that the life which is in us is in them likewise; and that to know is to resemble, when we speak of objects out of ourselves, even as within ourselves to learn is, according to Plato, only to recollect. (1)

From hope and former faith to perfect love
Attracted and absorbed: and centred there
God only to behold, and know, and feel,
Till by exclusive consciousness of God
All self-annihilated it shall make
God its identity: God all in all! (2)

And blest are they,
Who in this fleshly world, the elect of heaven,
Their strong eye darting thro' the deeds of men,
Adore with stedfast unpresuming gaze
Him, nature's essence, mind, and energy!
And gazing, trembling, patiently ascend,
Treading beneath their feet all visible things
As steps, that upward to their Father's throne
Lead gradual—else nor glorified nor loved. (3)

They cannot dread created might, who love
God, the Creator! fair and lofty thought!
It lifts and swells my heart! (4)

There is one Mind, one omnipresent Mind,
Omnific. His most holy name is Love.

Truth of subliming import! with the which
Who feeds and saturates his constant soul,
He from his small particular orbit flies
With blest outstarting! from himself he flies,
Stands in the sun, and with no partial gaze
Views all creation; and he loves it all,
And blesses it, and calls it very good!
This is indeed to dwell with the Most High! (5)

      'Tis the sublime of man,
Our noonday majesty, to know ourselves.
Parts and proportions of one wondrous whole!
This fraternizes man, this constitutes
Our charities and bearings. But 'tis God
Diffused through all, that doth make us all one whole. (6)

      Believe thou, O my soul,
Life is a vision shadowy of truth;
And vice, and anguish, and the wormy grave,
Shapes of a dream! The veiling clouds retire,
And lo! the throne of the redeeming God
Wraps in one light earth, heaven, and deepest hell. (7)

Auspicious Reverence! Hush all meaner song,
Ere the deep preluding strain have poured
To the Great Father, only Rightful King,
Eternal Father! King Omnipotent!
To the Will Absolute, the One, the Good!
The I AM, the Word, the Life, the Living God! (8)

For what is freedom, but the unfettered use
Of all the powers which God for use had given?
But chiefly this, him first, him last, to view
Through meaner powers and secondary things
Effulgent, as through clouds that veil his blaze.

For all that meets the bodily sense I deem
Symbolical, one mighty alphabet
For infant minds; and we in this low world
Placed with our backs to bright reality,
That we may learn with young unwounded ken
The substance from its shadow. Infinite Love,
Whose latence is the plenitude of all,
Thou with retracted beams, and self-eclipse
Veiling revealest thine eternal Sun. (9)

Glory to Thee, Father of Earth and Heaven!
All-conscious presence of the Universe!
Nature's vast ever-acting Energy!
In will, in deed, impulse of All to All!
Whether thy Love with unrefracted ray
Beam on the Prophet's purged eye, or if
Diseasing realms the enthusiast, wild of thought,
Scatter new frenzies on the infected throng,
Thou both inspiring and predooming both,
Fit instruments and best, and perfect end:
Glory to Thee, Father of Earth and Heaven! (10)

To meet, to know, to love—and then to part,
Is the sad tale of many a human heart. (11)

He prayeth well, who loveth well
Both man and bird and beast.
He prayeth best, who loveth best
All things both great and small;
For the dear God who loveth us,
He made and loveth all. (12)

   The sweet words
Of Christian promise, words that even yet
Might stem destruction, were they wisely preached,
Are muttered o'er by men, whose tones proclaim

How flat and wearisome they feel their trade:
Rank scoffers some, but most too indolent
To deem them falsehoods or to know their truth.
Oh! blasphemous! the book of life is made
A superstitious instrument, on which
We gabble o'er the oaths we mean to break;
For all must swear—all and in every place,
College and wharf, council and justice-court;
All, all must swear, the briber and the bribed,
Merchant and lawyer, senator and priest,
The rich, the poor, the old man and the young;
All, all make up one scheme of perjury,
That faith doth reel; the very name of God
Sounds like a juggler's charm; and, bold with joy,
Forth from his dark and lonely hiding-place,
(Portentous sight!) the owlet Atheism,
Sailing on obscene wings athwart the noon,
Drops his blue fringed lids, and holds them close,
And hooting at the glorious Sun in Heaven,
Cries out, 'Where is it?' (13)

Never can true courage dwell with them,
Who, playing tricks with conscience, dare not look
At their own vices. (14)

How shouldst thou prove aught else but dear and holy
To me, who from thy lakes and mountain-hills,
Thy clouds, thy quiet dales, thy rocks and seas,
Have drunk in all my intellectual life,
All sweet sensations, all ennobling thoughts,
All adoration of the God in nature,
All lovely and all honorable things,
Whatever makes this mortal spirit feel
The joy and greatness of its future being?
There lives nor form nor feeling in my soul
Unborrowed from my country. (15)

My native Land!
Filled with thought of thee this heart was proud,
Yea, mine eye swam with tears: that all the new
From sovran Brocken, woods and woody hills,
Floated away, like a departing dream,
Feeble and dim! Stranger, these impulses
Blame thou not lightly; nor will I profane,
With hasty judgment or injurious doubt,
That man's sublimer spirit, who can feel
That God is everywhere! the God who framed
Mankind to be one mighty family,
Himself our Father, and the World our Home. (16)

We receive but what we give,
And in our life alone does nature live:
Ours is her wedding garment, ours her shroud!
   And would we aught behold, of higher worth,
Than that inanimate cold world allowed
To the poor loveless ever-anxious crowd,
   Ah! from the soul itself must issue forth,
A light, a glory, a fair luminous cloud
   Enveloping the Earth—
And from the soul itself must there be sent
   A sweet and potent voice, of its own birth,
Of all sweet sounds the life and element! (17)

O pure of heart! thou need'st not ask of me
What this strong music in the soul may be!
What, and wherein it doth exist,
This light, this glory, this fair luminous mist,
This beautiful and beauty-making power.
      Joy, virtuous Lady! Joy that ne'er was given,
Save to the pure, and in their purest hour,
Life, and Life's effluence, cloud at once and shower,
Joy, Lady! is the spirit and the power,

586

Which wedding Nature to us gives in dower,
    A new Earth and new Heaven,
Undreamt of by the sensual and the proud—
Joy is the sweet voice, Joy the luminous cloud—
    We in ourselves rejoice!
And thence flows all that charms or ear or sight,
    All melodies the echoes of that voice,
All colours a suffusion from that light. (18)

The feeling heart, the searching soul,
To thee I dedicate the whole!
And while within myself I trace
The greatness of some future race,
Aloof with hermit-eye I scan
The present works of present man—
A wild and dream-like trade of blood and guile,
Too foolish for a tear, too wicked for a smile! (19)

In philosophy equally as in poetry, it is
the highest and most useful prerogative of
genius to produce the strongest impressions
of novelty, while it rescues admitted truths from
the neglect caused by the very circumstance of
their universal admission. Extremes meet.
Truths, of all others the most awful and interesting,
are too often considered as so true, that they
lose all the power of truth, and lie bed-ridden
in the dormitory of the soul, side by side with
the most despised and exploded errors. (20)

It is the advice of the wise man, "Dwell at home," or, with
yourself; and though there are very few that do this, yet it is
surprising that the greatest part of mankind cannot be prevailed
upon, at least to visit themselves sometimes; but, according to
the saying of the wise Solomon, *The eyes of the fool are in the
ends of the earth.* (21)

587

The largest part of mankind are nowhere greater strangers than at home. (22)

An hour of solitude passed in sincere and earnest prayer, or the conflict with, and conquest over, a single passion or "subtle bosom sin," will teach us more of thought, will more effectually awaken the faculty, and form the habit, of reflection, than a year's study in the Schools without them. (23)

Never yet did there exist a full faith in the Divine Word (by whom light, as well as immortality, was brought into the world), which did not expand the intellect, while it purified the heart;—which did not multiply the aims and objects of the understanding, while it fixed and simplified those of the desires and passions.
(24)

Among the various undertakings of men, can there be mentioned any more important, can there be conceived any more sublime, than an intention to form the human mind anew after the Divine Image? The very intention, if it be sincere, is a ray of its dawning. (25)

In general, morality may be compared to the consonant; prudence to the vowel. The former cannot be uttered (reduced to practice) but by means of the latter. (26)

With respect to any final aim or end, the greater part of mankind live at hazard. They have no certain harbour in view, nor direct their course by any fixed star. But to him that knoweth not the port to which he is bound, no wind can be favorable; neither can he, who has not yet determined at what mark he is to shoot, direct his arrow right. (27)

Without kind offices and useful services, wherever the power and opportunity occurs, love would be a hollow pretense. Yet what noble mind would not be offended, if he were thought to value the love for the sake of the services, and not rather the services for the sake of the love. (28)

Though prudence in itself is neither virtue nor spiritual holiness, yet without prudence, or in opposition to it, neither virtue nor holiness can exist. (29)

588

What the Apostles were in an extraordinary way, befitting the first annunciation of a religion for all mankind, this all teachers of moral truth, who aim to prepare for its reception by calling the attention of men to the law in their own hearts, may, without presumption, consider themselves to be under ordinary gifts and circumstances: namely, ambassadors for the greatest of kings, and upon no mean employment, the great treaty of peace and reconcilement betwixt him and mankind. (30)

Whatever must be misrepresented in order to be ridiculed, is in fact not ridiculed; but the thing substituted for it. It is a satire on something else, coupled with a lie on the part of the satirist, who knowing, or having the means of knowing the truth, chose to call one thing by the name of another. (31)

We are in the silent school of reflection, in the secret confessional of thought. Should we *lie for God*, and that to our own thoughts? . . . They, indeed, who dare do the one, will soon be able to do the other. (32)

A grief of recent birth is a sick infant that must have its medicine administered in its milk, and sad thoughts are the sorrowful heart's natural food. This is a complaint that is not to be cured by opposites, which for the most part only reverse the symptoms while they exasperate the disease—or like a rock in the mid channel of a river swoln by a sudden rain-flush from the mountain, which only detains the excess of waters from their proper outlet, and makes them foam, roar, and eddy. The soul in her desolation hugs the sorrows close to her, as her sole remaining garment: and this must be drawn off so gradually, and the garment to be put in its stead so gradually slipt on and feel so like the former, that the sufferer shall be sensible of the change only by the refreshment. The true spirit of consolation is well content to detain the tear in the eye, and finds a surer pledge of its success in the smile of resignation that dawns through that, than in the liveliest shows of a forced and alien exhilaration. (33)

Plotinus thanked God, that his soul was not tied to an immortal body. (34)

There have been too many commentators who are content not to understand a text themselves, if only they can make the reader believe they do. (35)

As the flowers from an orange tree in its time of blossoming, that burgeon forth, expand, fall, and are momently replaced, such is the sequence of hourly and momently charities in a pure and gracious soul. (36)

When courtiers come down into the country, the common home-bred people possibly think their habit strange; but they care not for that, it is the fashion at court. What need, then, that Christians should be so tender-foreheaded, as to be put out of countenance because the world looks on holiness as a singularity; it is the only fashion in the highest court, yea, of the king of kings himself. (37)

When, after variances, men are brought to an agreement, they are much subject to this, rather to cover their remaining malices with superficial verbal forgiveness than to dislodge them and free the heart of them. This is a poor self-deceit. As the philosopher said to him, who being ashamed that he was espied by him in a tavern in the outer room, withdrew himself to the inner, "That is not the way out: the more you go that way, you will be the farther in:"—so when hatreds are upon admonition not thrown out, but retire inward to hide themselves, they grow deeper and stronger than before; and those constrained semblances of reconcilement are but a false healing, do but skin the wound over, and therefore it usually breaks forth worse again. (38)

The most approved teachers of wisdom, in a human way, have required of their scholars, that to the end their minds might be capable of it, they should be purified from vice and wickedness. And it was Socrates' custom, when anyone asked him a question, seeking to be informed by him, before he would answer them, he asked them concerning their own qualities and course of life. (39)

In times of peace, the Church may dilate more, and build as it were into breadth, but in times of trouble, it arises more in height; it is then built upwards: as in cities where men are straitened, they build usually higher than in the country. (40)

Where there is a great deal of smoke and no clear flame, it argues much moisture in the matter, yet it witnesseth certainly that there is fire there; and therefore dubious questioning is a much better evidence, than that senseless deadness which most take for believing. Men that know nothing in science, have no doubts. He never truly believed, who was not made first sensible and convinced of unbelief.

Never be afraid to doubt, if only you have the disposition to believe, and doubt in order that you may end in believing the truth. (41)

He, who begins by loving Christianity better than truth, will proceed by loving his own sect or church better than Christianity, and end in loving himself better than all. (42)

The boasted peaceableness about questions of faith too often proceeds from a superficial temper, and not seldom from a supercilious disdain of whatever has no marketable use or value, and from indifference to religion itself. Toleration is a herb of spontaneous growth in the soil of indifference; but the weed has none of the virtue of the medicinal plant, reared by humility in the garden of zeal. Those, who regard religions as matters of taste, may consistently include all religious differences in the old adage, *De Gustibus non est disputandum.* And many there be among those of Gallio's temper, who *care for none of these things,* and who account all questions in religion, as he did, but matters of words and names. And by this all religions may agree together. But that were not a natural union produced by the active heat of the spirit, but a confusion rather, arising from the want of it; not a knitting together, but a freezing together, as cold congregates all bodies how heterogeneous soever, sticks, stones, and water,— but heat makes first a separation of different things, and then unites those that are of the same nature.

Much of our common union of minds, I fear, proceeds from no

other than the aforementioned causes, want of knowledge, and want of affection in religion. You that boast you live comformably to the appointments of the Church, and that no one hears of your noise, we may thank the ignorance of your minds for that kind of quietness. (43)

The Jews would not willingly tread upon the smallest piece of paper in their way, but took it up: for possibly, said they, the name of God may be on it. Though there was a little superstition in this, yet truly there is nothing but good religion in it, if we apply it to men. Trample not on any; there may be some work of grace there, that thou knowest not of. The name of God may be written upon that soul thou treadest on. (44)

Great is he who enjoys his earthenware as if it were plate, and not less great is the man to whom all his plate is no more than earthenware. (45)

It is not expressible how deep a wound a tongue sharpened to this work will give, with no noise and a very little word. This is the true white gunpowder, which the dreaming projectors of silent mischiefs and insensible poisons sought for in the laboratories of art and nature, in a world of good; but that which was to be found in its most destructive form, in *the world of evil, the tongue.* (46)

Seek much after this, to speak nothing with God, nor men, but what is the sense of a single unfeigned heart. O sweet truth! excellent but rare sincerity! He that *loves that truth within,* and who is Himself at once *The Truth* and *The Life,* He alone can work it there! Seek it of him. (47)

In conversation seek not so much either to vent thy knowledge, or to increase it, as to know more spiritually and effectually what thou dost know. And in this way those mean despised truths, that every one thinks he is sufficiently seen in, will have a new sweetness and use in them, which thou didst not so well perceive before —(for these flowers cannot be sucked dry); and in this humble sincere way thou shalt *grow in grace and in knowledge too.* (48)

Truth needs not the service of passion; yea, nothing so disserves it, as passion when set to serve it. The *Spirit of Truth* is withal the *Spirit of Meekness*. (49)

Imprudence makes some kind of Christians lose much of their labour in speaking for religion, and drive those further off, whom they would draw into it.

The confidence that attends a Christian's belief makes the believer not fear men, to whom he answers, but still he fears his God, for whom he answers, and whose interest is chief in those things he speaks of. The soul that hath the deepest sense of spiritual things, and the truest knowledge of God, is most afraid to miscarry in speaking of Him, most tender and wary how to acquit itself when engaged to speak of and for God. (50)

If you would have a good conscience, you must by all means have so much light, so much knowledge of the will of God, as may regulate you, and show you your way, may teach you how to do, and speak, and think, as in His presence. (51)

It is the glory of the Gospel charter and the Christian constitution, that its author and head is the Spirit of truth, essential reason as well as absolute and incomprehensible Will. Like a just monarch, he refers even his own causes to the judgment of his high courts.—He has his King's bench in the reason, his Court of Equity in the conscience; that the representative of his majesty and universal justice, this the nearest to the king's heart, and the dispenser of his particular decrees. He has likewise his Court of Common Pleas in the understanding, his Court of Exchequer in the prudence. The laws are his laws. And though by signs and miracles he has mercifully condescended to interline here and there with his own hand the great statute-book, which he has dictated to his *amanuensis*, Nature, yet has he been graciously pleased to forbid our receiving as the king's mandates aught that is not stamped with the Great Seal of the Conscience, and countersigned by the Reason. (52)

What you have acquired by patient thought and cautious discrimination, demands a portion of the same effort in those who are to receive it from you. (53)

I can never believe that a man may not be saved by that religion, which doth but bring him to the true love of God and to a heavenly mind and life: nor that God will ever cast a soul into hell that truly loveth him. (54)

In wonder all philosophy began; in wonder it ends: and admiration fills up the interspace. But the first wonder is the offspring of ignorance: the last is the parent of adoration . . . The first is the birth-throe of our knowledge: the last is its euthanasy and *apotheosis*. (55)

The origin of Evil, meanwhile, is a question interesting only to the metaphysician, and in a system of moral and religious philosophy. The man of sober mind who seeks for truths that possess a moral and practical interest, is content to be certain, first, that evil must have had a beginning, since otherwise it must either be God, or a co-eternal and co-equal rival of God; both impious notions, and the latter foolish to boot:—secondly that it could not originate in God; for if so, it would be at once evil and not evil, or God would be at once God, that is, infinite goodness, and not God—both alike impossible positions. Instead, therefore, of troubling himself with this barren controversy, he more profitably turns his inquiries to the evil which most concerns himself, and of which he may find the origin. (56)

Whatever is against right reason, that no faith can oblige us to believe. For though reason is not the positive and affirmative measure of our faith, and our faith ought to be larger than (speculative) reason, and take something into her heart, that reason can never take into her eye; yet in all our creed there can be nothing against reason. If reason justly contradicts an article, it is not of the household of faith. (57)

He that speaks against his own reason, speaks against his own conscience: and therefore it is certain, no man serves God with a good conscience, who serves him against his reason. (58)

CHAPTER XVIII

BOETHIUS

Anicius Manlius Severinus Boethius was born of patrician family around the year 475 A.D. He received the best education possible in the Rome of his day. He early rose to political eminence, and in 510 he became consul. Twelve years later his two sons were raised to the consular dignity, and on him was conferred the title, Magister Officiorum. *But his fortune was soon to change. Charged with treasonable relations with the Byzantine Court, he lost the friendship of Theodoric and was exiled to Pavia. After lingering some months there in prison he was cruelly put to death in 524/25.*

Boethius knew Greek, and his early ambition was to make the works of Plato and Aristotle accessible to his Latin contemporaries. In this he was little successful, but in compensation he wrote several original works in the arts, in philosophy, and in theology. He was especially influential in mediaeval music, while his translations of On Interpretation *and the* Categories *were the only logical works of Aristotle known to the West until the twelfth century. Boethius was a Christian and the theological works attributed to him are now known to be authentic.*

His great philosophical work is On the Consolations of Philosophy *which contains his thoughts while in prison awaiting execution. This book has been translated into almost every European language. It asserts that man is superior to the blind forces of nature; that the power of fortune affecting the practical affairs of mankind is irrelevant; and that Providence is infinite. Many persons of considerable achievement, such as Dante, Chaucer, and Queen Elizabeth, have found that the writings of Boethius enabled them to face life with courage and renewed confidence whenever they were beset by doubts or alarmed by the mystery of the future.*

Should I (Philosophy) not share and bear my part of the burden which has been laid upon my name? Surely Philosophy never allowed herself to let the innocent go upon their journey unbefriended. Think you I would fear calumnies? That I would be terrified as though they were a new misfortune? Think you that this is the first time that wisdom has been harassed by dangers among men of shameless ways? In ancient days before the time of my child, Plato, have we not as well as nowadays fought many a mighty battle against the recklessness of folly? And though Plato did survive, did not his master, Socrates, win his victory of an unjust death, with me present at his side? When after him the followers of Epicurus, and in turn the Stoics, and then others did all try their utmost to seize his legacy, they dragged me, for all my cries and struggles, as though to share me as plunder; they tore my robe which I had woven with mine own hands, and snatched away the fragments thereof: and when they thought that I had altogether yielded myself to them, they departed. And since among them were to be seen certain signs of my outward bearing, others ill-advised did think they wore my livery: thus were many of them undone by the errors of the herd of uninitiated. But if you have not heard of the exile of Anaxagoras, nor the poison drunk by Socrates, nor the torture of Zeno, which all were of foreign lands, yet you may know of Canius, Seneca, and Soranus, whose fame is neither small nor passing old. Naught else brought them to ruin but that, being built up in my ways, they appeared at variance with the desires of unscrupulous men. So it is no matter for your wonder if, in this sea of life, we are tossed about by storms from all sides; for to oppose evil men is the chief aim we set before ourselves. Though the band of such men is great in numbers, yet it is to be contemned: for it is guided by no leader, but is hurried along at random only by error running riot everywhere. If this band when warring against us presses too closely upon us, our leader, Reason, gathers her forces into her citadel, while the enemy are busied in plundering useless baggage. As they seize the most worthless things, we laugh

at them from above, untroubled by the whole band of mad ma-
rauders, and we are defended by that rampart to which riotous
folly may not hope to attain. (1)

Fear naught, and hope naught: thus shall you have a weak
man's rage disarmed. But whoso fears with trembling, or aught
desires from them, he stands not firmly rooted, but dependent:
thus has he thrown away his shield; he can be rooted up, and he
links for himself the very chain whereby he may be dragged. (2)

Founder of the star-studded universe, resting on Thine eternal
throne whence Thou turnest the swiftly rolling sky, and bindest
the stars to keep Thy law; at Thy word the moon now shines
brightly with full face, ever turned to her brother's light, and so
she dims the lesser lights; or now she is herself obscured, for
nearer to the sun her beams shew her pale horns alone. Cool rises
the evening star at night's first drawing nigh: the same is the
morning star who casts off the harness that she bore before, and
paling meets the rising sun. When winter's cold doth strip the
trees, Thou settest a shorter span to day. And Thou, when summer comes to warm, dost change the short divisions of the night.
Thy power doth order the seasons of the year, so that the western
breeze of spring brings back the leaves which winter's north wind
tore away; so that the dog-star's heat makes ripe the ears of corn
whose seed Arcturus watched. Naught breaks that ancient law:
naught leaves undone the work appointed to its place. Thus all
things Thou dost rule with limits fixed: the lives of men alone
dost Thou scorn to restrain, as a guardian, within bounds. For
why does Fortune with her fickle hand deal out such changing
lots? The hurtful penalty is due to crime, but falls upon the
sinless head: depraved men rest at ease on thrones aloft, and by
their unjust lot can spurn beneath their hurtful heel the necks of
virtuous men. Beneath obscuring shadows lies bright virtue hid:
the just man bears the unjust's infamy. They suffer not for for-
sworn oaths, they suffer not for crimes glazed over with their lies.
But when their will is to put forth their strength, with triumph
they subdue the mightiest kings whom people in their thousands

fear. O Thou who dost weave the bonds of Nature's self, look down upon this pitiable earth! Mankind is no base part of this great work, and we are tossed on Fortune's wave. Restrain, our Guardian, the engulfing surge, and as Thou dost the unbounded heaven rule, with a like bond make true and firm these lands. (3)

It is not the walls of your library, decked with ivory and glass, that I need, but rather the resting-place in your heart, wherein I have not stored books, but I have of old put that which gives value to books, a store of thoughts from books of mine. (4)

When the stars are hidden by black clouds, no light can they afford. When the boisterous south wind rolls along the sea and stirs the surge, the water, but now clear as glass, bright as the fair sun's light, is dark, impenetrable to sight, with stirred and scattered sand. The stream, that wanders down the mountain's side, must often find a stumbling-block, a stone within its path torn from the hill's own rock. So too shalt thou: if thou wouldst see the truth in undimmed light, choose the straight road, the beaten path; away with passing joys! away with fear! put vain hopes to flight! and grant no place to grief! Where these distractions reign, the mind is clouded o'er, the soul is bound in chains.

(5)

Whose happiness is so firmly established that he has no quarrel from any side with his estate of life? For the condition of our welfare is a matter fraught with care: either its completeness never appears, or it never remains. One man's wealth is abundant, but his birth and breeding put him to shame. Another is famous for his noble birth, but would rather be unknown because he is hampered by his narrow means. A third is blessed with wealth and breeding, but bewails his life because he has no wife. Another is happy in his marriage, but has no children, and saves his wealth only for an heir that is no son of his. Another is blessed with children, but weeps tears of sorrow for the misdeeds of son or daughter. So none is readily at peace with the lot his fortune sends him. For in each case there is that which is un-

598

known to him who has not experienced it, and which brings horror to him who has experienced it. (6)

Through Love the universe with constancy makes changes all without discord: earth's elements, though contrary, abide in treaty bound: Phoebus in his golden car leads up the glowing day; his sister rules the night that Hesperus brought: the greedy sea confines its waves in bounds, lest the earth's borders be changed by its beating on them: all these are firmly bound by Love, which rules both earth and sea, and has its empire in the heavens too. If Love should slacken this its hold, all mutual love would change to war; and these would strive to undo the scheme which now their glorious movements carry out with trust and with accord. By Love are peoples too kept bound together by a treaty which they may not break. Love binds with pure affection the sacred tie of wedlock, and speaks its bidding to all trusty friends. O happy race of mortals, if your hearts are ruled as is the universe, by Love! (7)

Though the rich man with greed heap up from everflowing streams the wealth that cannot satisfy, though he deck himself with pearls from the Red Sea's shore, and plough his fertile field with oxen by the score, yet gnawing care will never in his lifetime leave him, and at his death his wealth will not go with him, but leave him faithlessly. (8)

The man who would true power gain, must needs subdue his own wild thoughts: never must he let his passions triumph and yoke his neck by their foul bonds. For though the earth, as far as India's shore, tremble before the laws you give, though Thule bow to your service on earth's farthest bounds, yet if thou canst not drive away black cares, if thou canst not put to flight complaints, then is no true power thine. (9)

From like beginning rise all men on earth, for there is one Father of all things; one is the guide of everything. 'Tis He who gave the sun his rays, and horns unto the moon. 'Tis He who set mankind on earth, and in the heavens the stars. He put within our bodies spirits which were born in heaven. And thus a high-born race has He set forth in man. Why do you men rail on your forefathers? If you look to your beginning and your author, which is God, is any man degenerate or base but he who by his own vices cherishes base things and leaves that beginning which was his? (10)

Thou who dost rule the universe with everlasting law, founder of earth and heaven alike, who hast bidden time stand forth from our Eternity, for ever firm Thyself, yet giving movement unto all. No causes were without Thee which could thence impel Thee to create this mass of changing matter, but within Thyself exists the very idea of perfect good, which grudges naught, for of what can it have envy? Thou makest all things follow that high pattern. In perfect beauty Thou movest in Thy mind a world of beauty, making all in a like image, and bidding the perfect whole to complete its perfect functions. (11)

Grant them, O Father, that this mind of ours may rise to Thy throne of majesty; grant us to reach that fount of good. Grant that we may so find light that we may set on Thee unblinded eyes; cast Thou therefrom the heavy clouds of this material world. Shine forth upon us in Thine own true glory. Thou art the bright and peaceful rest of all Thy children that worship Thee. To see Thee clearly is the limit of our aim. Thou art our beginning, our progress, our guide, our way, our end. (12)

You must not think of God, the Father of all, whom we hold to be filled with the highest good, as having received this good into Himself from without, nor that He has it by nature in such a manner that you might consider Him, its possessor, and the happiness possessed, as having different essential existence. For if you think that good has been received from without, that which gave it must be more excellent than that which received it; but we have most rightly stated that He is the most excellent of all things. And if you think that it is in Him by His nature, but different in kind, then, while we speak of God as the fountain-head of all things, who could imagine by whom these different kinds can have been united? Lastly, that which is different from anything cannot be the thing from which it differs. So anything which is by its nature different from the highest good, cannot be the highest good. And this we must not think of God, than whom there is nothing more excellent, as we have agreed. Nothing in this world can have a nature which is better than its origin, wherefore, I would conclude that that which is the origin of all things, according to the truest reasoning, is by its essence the highest good. (13)

We may safely conclude that the essence of God also lies in the absolute good and nowhere else.

Come hither all who are the prey of passions, bound by their ruthless chains; those deceiving passions which blunt the minds of men. Here shall you find rest from your labours; here a haven lying in tranquil peace; this shall be a resting-place open to receive within itself all the miserable on earth. Not all the wealth of Tagus's golden sands, nor Hermus's gleaming strand, nor Indus, nigh earth's hottest zone, mingling its emeralds and pearls, can bring light to the eyes of any soul, but rather plunge the soul more blindly in their shade. In her deepest caverns does earth rear all that pleases the eye and excites the mind. The glory by which the heavens move and have their being, has naught to do with the darknesses which bring ruin to the soul. Whosoever can look on this true light will scarce allow the sun's rays to be clear.

(14)

If any man makes search for truth with all his penetration, and would be led astray by no deceiving paths, let him turn upon himself the light of an inward gaze, let him bend by force the long-drawn wanderings of his thoughts into one circle; let him tell surely to his soul, that he has, thrust away within the treasures of his mind, all that he labors to acquire without. Then shall the truth, which now was hid in error's darkening cloud, shine forth more clear than Phoebus's self. For the body, though it brings material mass which breeds forgetfulness, has never driven forth all light from the mind. The seed of truth does surely cling with-

601

in, and can be roused as a spark by the fanning of philosophy. For if it is not so, how do ye men make answers true of your own instinct when teachers question you? Is it not that the quick spark of truth lies buried in the heart's low depths? And if the Muse of Plato sends through those depths the voice of truth, each man has not forgotten and is but reminding himself of what he learns. (15)

Kings you may see sitting aloft upon their thrones, gleaming with purple, hedged about with grim guarding weapons, threatening with fierce glances, and their hearts heaving with passion. If any man take from these proud ones their outward covering of empty honour, he will see within, will see that these great ones bear secret chains. For the heart of one is thus filled by lust with the poisons of greed, or seething rage lifts up its waves and lashes his mind therewith: or gloomy grief holds them weary captives, or by slippery hopes they are tortured. So when you see one head thus labouring beneath so many tyrants, you know he cannot do as he would, for by hard task-masters is the master himself oppressed. (16)

Since every reward is sought for the reason that it is held to be good, who shall say that the man, that possesses goodness, does not receive his reward? And what reward is this? Surely the fairest and greatest of all. Remember that corollary which I emphasised when speaking to you a little while ago; and reason thus therefrom. While happiness is the absolute good, it is plain that all good men become good by virtue of the very fact that they are good. But we agreed that happy men are as gods. Therefore this is the reward of the good, which no time can wear out, no power can lessen, no wickedness can darken; they become divine. In this case, then, no wise man can doubt of the inevitable punishment of the wicked as well. For good and evil are so set, differing from each other just as reward and punishment are in opposition to each other: hence the rewards, which we see fall to the good, must correspond precisely to the punishments of the evil on the other side. As, therefore, honesty is itself the reward

602

of the honest, so wickedness is itself the punishment of the wicked. Now whosoever suffers punishment, doubts not that he is suffering an evil: if, then, they are ready so to judge of themselves, can they think that they do not receive punishment, considering that they are not only affected but thoroughly permeated by wickedness, the worst of all evils? (17)

There would be no place left for hatred among wise men. For who but the most foolish would hate good men? And there is no cause to hate bad men. Vice is as a disease of the mind, just as feebleness shews ill-health in the body. As, then, we should never think that those, who are sick in the body, deserve hatred, so are those, whose minds are oppressed by a fiercer disease than feebleness, namely wickedness, much more worthy of pity than of persecution. (18)

Wouldst thou apportion merit to merit fitly? Then love good men as is their due, and for the evil shew your pity. (19)

Nor is it right for a man to try to comprehend with his mind all the means of divine working, or to explain them in words. Let it be enough that we have seen that God, the Creator of all nature, directs and disposes all things for good. And while He urges all, that He has made manifest, to keep His own likeness, He drives out by the course of Fate all evil from the bounds of His state. Wherefore if you look to the disposition of Providence, you will reckon naught as bad of all the evils which are held to abound upon earth. (20)

The Creator sits on high, rules all and guides, King and Lord, fount and source of all, Law itself and wise judge of justice. He restrains all that stirs nature to motion, holds it back, and makes firm all that would stray. If He were not to recall them to their true paths, and set them again upon the circles of their courses, they would be torn from their source and so would perish. This is the common bond of love; all seek thus to be restrained by the limit of the good. In no other manner can they endure if this bond of love be not turned round again, and if the causes, which He has set, return not again. (21)

Go forth then bravely whither leads the lofty path of high example. Why do ye sluggards turn your backs? When the earth is overcome, the stars are yours. (22)

Homer with his honeyed lips sang of the bright sun's clear light; yet the sun cannot burst with his feeble rays the bowels of the earth or the depths of the sea. Not so with the Creator of this great sphere. No masses of earth can block His vision as He looks over all. Night's cloudy darkness cannot resist Him. With one glance of His intelligence He sees all that has been, that is, and that is to come. He alone can see all things, so truly He may be called the Sun. (23)

The common opinion, according to all men living, is that God is eternal. Let us therefore consider what is eternity. For eternity will, I think, make clear to us at the same time the divine nature and knowledge.

Eternity is the simultaneous and complete possession of infinite life. This will appear more clearly if we compare it with temporal things. All that lives under the conditions of time moves through the present from the past to the future; there is nothing set in time which can at one moment grasp the whole space of its lifetime. It cannot yet comprehend tomorrow; yesterday it has already lost. And in this life of to-day your life is no more than a changing, passing moment. And as Aristotle said of the universe, so it is of all that subject is to time; though it never began to be, nor will ever cease, and its life is co-extensive with the infinity of time, yet it is not such as can be held to be eternal. For though it apprehends and grasps a space of infinite lifetime, it does not embrace the whole simultaneously; it has not yet experienced the future. What we should rightly call eternal is that which grasps and possesses wholly and simultaneously the fulness of unending life, which lacks naught of the future, and has lost naught of the fleeting past; and such an existence must be ever present in itself to control and aid itself, and also must keep present with itself the infinity of changing time. Therefore, people who hear that Plato thought that this universe had no beginning of time and

604

will have no end, are not right in thinking that in this way the created world is co-eternal with its creator. For to pass through unending life, the attribute which Plato ascribes to the universe is one thing; but it is another thing to grasp simultaneously the whole of unending life in the present; this is plainly a peculiar property of the mind of God. (24)

Hopes are not vainly put in God, nor prayers in vain offered: if these are right, they cannot but be answered. Turn therefore from vice: ensue virtue: raise your soul to upright hopes: send up on high your prayers from this earth. If you would be honest, great is the necessity enjoined upon your goodness, since all you do is done before the eyes of an all-seeing Judge. (25)

CHAPTER XIX

JOHANN GOTTLIEB FICHTE*

The surest means of acquiring a conviction of a life after death, is so to act in this life that we can venture to wish for another. He who feels that if there is a God He must look down graciously upon him, will not be disturbed by arguments *against* his being, and he needs none *for* it. He who has sacrificed so much for virtue that he looks for recompense in a future life, needs no proof of the reality of such a life,—he does not *believe* in it—he *feels* it. And so, thou dear companion for this short life and for eternity, we shall strengthen each other in this conviction, not by arguments but by deeds. (1)

The ONE remains, the many change and pass;
Heaven's light forever shines; Earth's shadows fly;
Life, like a dome of many-colored glass,
Stains the white radiance of Eternity,
Until Death tramples it to fragments. (2)

Sublime and living Will, named by no name, compassed by no thought, I may raise my soul to Thee, for Thou and I are not divided. Thy voice is heard within me, mine is heard by Thee, and all my thoughts, if they are good and true, live in Thee alone. In Thee, the Incomprehensible, I myself, and the world in which I live, stand clear before me; all the secrets of my existence are laid open, and perfect harmony arises in my soul.

Thou art best known to the childlike, devoted, simple heart. To it Thou art the searcher of all hearts, who seest the minds of

* See Chapter IX.

606

men; the ever-present true witness of their thoughts, who knowest if they are good, who knowest them though all the world know them not. Thou art the Father who ever desirest their good, who rulest all things for the best. To Thy will they resign themselves: 'Do with me', they say, 'what Thou wilt; I know that it is good, for it is Thou who doest it.' The inquisitive understanding, which has heard of Thee, but seen Thee not, would teach us Thy nature, and, as Thy image, shows us a monstrous and incongruous shape, which the sagacious laugh at, and the wise and good abhor.

I hide my face before Thee, and lay my hand upon my mouth. How Thou art, and seemest to Thine own being, I can never know, any more than I can assume Thy nature. After thousands upon thousands of spirit-lives, I shall comprehend Thee as little as I do now in this earthly house. That which I conceive, becomes finite through my very conception of it, and this can never, even by endless exaltation, rise into the infinite. Thou differest from men, not in degree but in nature. In every stage of their advancement they think of Thee as a greater *man*, and still a greater, but never as God—the Infinite,—whom no measure can mete. I have only this discursive, progressive thought, and I can conceive of no other. How can I venture to ascribe it to Thee? In the idea of *person* there are imperfections, limitations. How can I clothe Thee with it without these?

I will not attempt that which imperfection of my nature forbids, and which would be useless to me:—*how* Thou art, I may not know. But thy relations to me—the mortal—and to all mortals, lie open before my eyes, were I only what I should be—they surround me as clearly as the consciousness of my own existence. *Thou workest* in me the knowledge of my duty, of my vocation in the world of reasonable beings:—*how*, I know not, nor need I to know. *Thou knowest* what I think and what I will:—*how* Thou canst know, through what act Thou bringest about that consciousness, I cannot understand,—nay, I know that the idea of an act, of a particular act of consciousness, belongs to me alone, and not to Thee. *Thou willest* that my free obedience shall bring with it eternal consequences:—the act of Thy will I cannot comprehend —I only know that it is not like mine. *Thou doest,* and Thy will itself is the deed; but the way of Thy working is not as my ways —I cannot trace it. *Thou livest and art,* for Thou knowest and willest and workest, omnipresent to finite reason; but Thou *art not* as *I* now and always must conceive of being. (3)

Hence it is an error to say that it is doubtful whether or not there is a God. It is not doubtful, but the most certain of all certainties,—nay, the foundation of all other certainties—the one absolutely valid objective truth,—that there is a moral order in the world; that to every rational being is assigned his particular place in that order, and the work which he has to do; that his destiny, in so far as it is not occasioned by his own conduct, is the result of this plan; that in no other way can even a hair fall from his head, nor a sparrow fall to the ground around him; that every true and good action prospers, and every bad action fails; and that all things must work together for good to those who truly love goodness. On the other hand, no one who reflects a moment, and honestly avows the result of his reflection, can remain in doubt that the conception of God as *a particular substance* is impossible and contradictory: and it is right candidly to say this, and to silence the babbling of the schools, in order that the true religion of cheerful virtue may be established in its room.

Two great poets have expressed this faith of good and thinking men with inimitable beauty. Such an one may adopt their language:—

'Who dares to say,
"I believe in God"?
Who dares to name him
And to profess,
"I believe in him"?
Who can feel,
And yet affirm,
"I believe him not"?

608

Does he not embrace, support,
  The All-Embracer,
  The All-Sustainer,
  Thee, me, himself?
Does not the vault of heaven arch o'er us there?
  Does not the earth lie firmly here below?
  And do not the eternal stars
  Rise on us with their friendly beams?
Do I not see my image in thine eyes?
  And does not the All
  Press on thy head and heart,
  And weave itself around thee, visibly and invisibly,
  In eternal mystery?
Fill thy heart with it till it overflow;
  And in the feeling, when thou'rt wholly blest,
  Then call it what thou wilt,—
  Happiness! Heart! Love! God!
  I have no name for it:
  Feeling is all; name is but sound and smoke,
  Veiling the glow of heaven.' *

And the second sings—
'And God is!—a holy Will that abides,
  Though this human will may falter;
High over both Space and Time it rides,
  The high thought that will never alter:
And while all things in change eternal roll,
It endures, through change, a motionless soul.' ‡ (4)

    I perceive that organic unity in which no member regards the
fate of another as the fate of a stranger. (5)
    Strict proof can, and in due course will, be given that no man

*Goethe's Faust
‡The above stanza of Schiller's "Worte des Glaubens" is taken
from Mr. Merivale's excellent translation.

609

and no god and not one of all the events that are within the bounds of possibility can help us, but that we alone must help ourselves if help is to come to us. (6)

It is manly courage to look evil full in the face, to compel it to make a stand, to scrutinize it calmly, coolly, and freely, and to resolve it into its component parts. Moreover, by this clear perception alone is it possible to master evil and to proceed with sure step in the fight against it. For the man who sees the whole in each part always knows where he stands, and is sure of his ground by reason of the insight he has once gained; whereas another man, lacking sure clue or definite certainty, gropes blindly in a dream. (7)

This proves beyond dispute that the system may, indeed, have been able to fill the memory with some words and phrases and the cold and indifferent imagination with some faint and feeble pictures; but that it has never succeeded in making its picture of a moral world-order so vivid that the pupil was filled with passionate love and yearning for that order, and with such glowing emotion as to invite him to realize it in his life—emotion before which self-seeking falls to the ground like withered leaves. (8)

Finally, it is the general aim of these addresses to bring courage and hope to the suffering, to proclaim joy in the midst of deep sorrow, to lead us gently and softly through the hour of deep affliction. This age is to me as a shade that stands weeping over its own corpse, from which it has been driven forth by a host of diseases, unable to tear its gaze from the form so beloved of old, and trying in despair every means to enter again the home of pestilence. Already, it is true, the quickening breezes of that other world, which the departed soul has entered, have taken it unto themselves and are surrounding it with the warm breath of love; the whispering voices of its sisters greet it with joy and bid it welcome; and already in its depths it stirs and grows in all directions towards the more glorious form into which it shall develop. But as yet the soul has no feeling for these breezes, no ear for these voices—or if it had them, they have disappeared in sorrow for the loss of mortal form; for with its form the soul thinks it has lost itself too. What is to be done with it? The dawn of the new world is already past its breaking; already it gilds the mountain tops, and shadows forth the coming day. I wish, so far as in me lies, to catch the rays of this dawn and weave them into a mirror, in which our grief-stricken age may see itself; so that it may believe in its own existence, may perceive its real self, and, as in prophetic vision, may see pass by its own development, its coming forms. In the contemplation of this, the picture of its former life will doubtless sink and vanish; and the dead body may be bourne to its resting-place without undue lamenting. (9)

Man can will only what he loves; His love is the sole and at the same time the infallible motive of his will and of all his vital impulses and actions. (10)

Further, he will perceive that, amid the various forms which it received, not by chance, but according to a law founded in God Himself, the spiritual life which alone really exists is one, the divine life itself, which exists and manifests itself only in living thought. He will thus learn to know and keep holy his own and every other spiritual life as an eternal link in the chain of the manifestations of the divine life. Only in immediate contact with God and in the direct emanation of his life from Him will he find life, light, and happiness, but in any separation from that immediate contact, death, darkness, and misery. In a word, this development will train him to religion; and this religion of the indwelling of our life in God shall indeed prevail and be carefully fostered in the new era. On the other hand, the religion of the past separated the spiritual life from the divine, and only by apostasy against the divine life could it procure for the spiritual life the absolute existence which it had ascribed to it. It used God as a means to introduce self-seeking into other worlds after the death of the mortal body, and through fear and hope of these other worlds to reinforce for the present world the self-seeking which would otherwise have remained weak. Such a religion, which was obviously a servant of selfishness, shall indeed be

611

borne to the grave along with the past age. In the new era eternity does not dawn first on yon side of the grave, but comes into the midst of the present life; while self-seeking is dismissed from serving and from ruling, and departs, taking its servants with it. (11)

When good is done even to the ungrateful, and those who curse are blessed with deeds and gifts, although it is clearly foreseen that they will curse again; when after a hundred failures man persists in faith and love; then, it is not mere morality which is the motive, for that requires a purpose, but it is religion, the submission to a higher and unknown law, the humble silence before God, the sincere love of His life that is manifested in us, which alone and for its own sake shall be saved, where the eye sees nothing else to save. (12)

First of all and before all things: man does not form his scientific view in a particular way voluntarily and arbitrarily, but it is formed for him by his life, and is in reality the inner, and to him unknown, root of his own life, which has become his way of looking at things. It is what you really are in your inmost soul that stands forth to your outward eye and you would never be able to see anything else. (13)

Freedom, taken in the sense of indecisive hesitation between several courses equally possible, is not life, but only the forecourt and portal to real life. At some time or other there must be an end of this hesitation and an advance to decision and action; and only then does life begin. (14)

Do you believe in something absolutely primary and original in man himself, in freedom, in endless improvement, in the eternal progress of our race, or do you not believe in all this, but rather imagine that you clearly perceive and comprehend that the opposite of all this takes place? (15)

Whoever believes in spirituality and in the freedom of this spirituality, and who wills the eternal development of this spirituality by freedom, wherever he may have been born, and whatever

612

language he speaks, is of our blood; he is one of us, and will come over to our side. (16)

Although it is true that religion is, for one thing, the consolation of the unjustly oppressed slave, yet this above all is the mark of a religious disposition, viz:—to fight against slavery and, as far as possible, to prevent religion from sinking into a mere consolation for captives. No doubt it suits the tyrant well to preach religious resignation and to bid those look to heaven to whom he allows not the smallest place on earth. But we for our part must be in less haste to adopt this view of religion that he recommends; and we must, if we can, prevent earth from being made into a hell in order to rouse a greater longing for heaven. (17)

The natural impulse of man, which should be abandoned only in case of real necessity, is to find heaven on this earth, and to endow his daily work on earth with permanence and eternity. (18)

Love that is truly love, and not a mere transitory lust, never clings to what is transient; only in the Eternal does it awaken and become kindled, and there alone does it rest. Man is not able to love even himself unless he conceives himself as eternal; apart from that he cannot even respect, much less approve of, himself. (19)

The aim of the State is positive law, internal peace, and a condition of affairs in which everyone may by diligence earn his daily bread and satisfy the needs of his material existence, so long as God permits him to live. All this is only a means, a condition, a framework for what love of fatherland really wants, viz., that the eternal and the divine may blossom in the world and never cease to become more and more pure, perfect and excellent. (20)

Freedom, including freedom in the activities of external life, is the soil in which higher culture germinates; a legislation which keeps the higher culture in view will allow to freedom as wide a field as possible, even at the risk of securing a smaller degree of

uniform peace and quietness, and of making the work of government a little harder and more troublesome. (21)

These men, and all others of like mind in the history of the
world, won the victory because eternity inspired them, and this
inspiration always does, and always must, defeat him who is not
so inspired. It is neither the strong right arm nor the efficient
weapon that wins victories, but only the power of the soul. (22)

Let us be on our guard against being taken unawares by this
sweetness of servitude, for it robs even our posterity of the hope
of future emancipation. If our external activity is restricted and
fettered, let us elevate our spirit all the more boldly to the thought
of freedom; let us rise to live in this thought and make it the sole
object of our wish and longing. What if freedom disappear for
a time from the visible world? Let us give it a place of refuge in
our innermost thoughts, until there shall grow up round about us
the new world which has the power of manifesting our thoughts
outwardly. In the sphere where no one can deprive us of the
freedom to do as we think best—in our own minds let us make
ourselves a pattern, a prophecy, and a guarantee of that which
will become a reality when we are gone. Let us not allow our
spirit, as well as our body, to be bent and subjected and brought
into captivity. (23)

On what is all human greatness based, if not on the independence and originality of the person and on the fact that the person
is not an artificial product of his age, but a growth out of the
eternal and spontaneous spirit-world which has grown up just as
it is? Is not greatness based on the fact that to one person a new
and individual view of the universe has dawned, and that this
person has the firm will and the iron strength to impose his view
on the actual world? But it is quite impossible for such a soul not
to honour in peoples and individuals external to himself that in
which his own eternal greatness consists, viz., independence, constancy, and individuality of existence. In proportion as the great
soul feels sure of his own greatness and trusts thereto, he disdains
to rule over a people with a wretched servile spirit or to be a

614

giant among dwarfs; he disdains the thought that he must first degrade men in order to rule over them; he is oppressed by the sight of degeneration round about him. Not to be able to respect men causes him pain; but everything that elevates and ennobles his brother men and places them in a worthier light is a cause of satisfaction to his own noble spirit and is his greatest delight. (24)

In all ages and among all peoples true greatness has remained the same in this respect, that it was not vain; just as, on the other hand, whatever displayed vanity has always been beyond a doubt base and petty. True greatness, resting on itself, finds no pleasure in monuments erected by contemporaries, or in being called "The Great," or in the shrieking applauses and praises of the mob; rather it rejects these things with fitting contempt, and awaits first the verdict on itself from its own indwelling judge, and then the public verdict from the judgment of posterity. True greatness has always had this further characteristic: it is filled with awe and reverence in the face of dark and mysterious fate, it is mindful of the ever-rolling wheel of destiny, and never allows itself to be counted great or happy before its end. (25)

Let our standard be the old one: that alone is great which is capable of receiving the ideas which always bring nothing but salvation upon the peoples, and which is inspired by those ideas. (26)

CHAPTER XX

CHARLES EDWARD GARMAN*

The determining note in Professor Garman's teaching of philosophy was his conception of philosophy. It was not for him primarily a subject to be studied for its own sake. One might say it was not studied as a subject at all. He believed that every man who thinks at all must sooner or later face the alternatives which are represented in general by a spiritual or a materialistic view of the world and of human action. He conceived it his task to aid young men in facing the problem squarely, and with a method for its solution. For this purpose he selected his material, planned the order of subjects, and developed the technique of his instruction. (1)

Theism was for him the solution of the problem of knowledge; the biblical history was a revelation of an unfolding divine plan; the New Testament doctrine "not to be ministered unto but to minister" was his central ethical principle; the conception of a change of heart was primary in his theory of social reform; the principles of divine sovereignty and atonement afforded in his judgment the true basis of human political society; the teaching of philosophy was an opportunity to show men the eternal and to aid in shaping their lives. (2)

Nothing in his course was more difficult for some of the students to adjust themselves to than this interpenetration of philosophy, religion, and practical life. Those to whom religion had been cut off by watertight bulkheads, whether they cherished it as too sacred for scrutiny, or treated it with indifference as senti-

* See Chapter XIII.

616

mental and "not for them," found Garman's attitude disturbing to old habits. By the end of the course few of the latter class failed to gain a respect for religion as Garman interpreted it, and many in the former class found religion transformed from a treasure timidly guarded and carefully concealed to a vital power which itself should guard the values of daily life. To adopt in slightly different form one of his own metaphors, they were no longer the anxious disciples concerned for a dead body taken away, but bold apostles who had seen the vision of a risen Master, and believed him not a body to be protected, but a power that would itself protect and inspire. (3)

Garman became more and more convinced that the light of reason was not and could not be appreciated by the students of his day unless they were first awakened to feel their need of it. It was necessary, Garman believed, to show that darkness was dangerous, and that life might be shipwrecked if its master did not learn to take observations of the fixed stars. The logical results of typical attitudes were shown, and the futility of blinking or evading the issues was forced home, until a large proportion of the class were anxious to investigate and willing to work hard for their results. This preliminary process was naturally to a considerable degree negative. The old complaints made against Socrates were occasionally heard. Partly for this reason, Professor Garman was at one time accustomed to ask his students not to discuss their work with others until they had reached the constructive portions— a caution which to those who did not understand the whole situation seemed to give a sort of esoteric character to the course. (4)

He did not consider the course a success unless every member of the class reached, not indeed an identical result, but a method, an ability to weigh evidence, a spirit of intellectual honesty, patience, and thoroughness that would neither jump at conclusions, balk at difficulties, or shy at novel and unwelcome truths. (5)

No notice of Professor Garman would be at all adequate which

617

did not speak of his extraordinary charm of illustration. The expulsive power of a new affection is an obvious psychological truth, but the student who saw this through the symbol of the oaks which kept their leaves through all the winter's storms but shed them at the first start of the new life of spring found it a more vital fact than if stated in general form only. (6)

It was because there was first of all this great personality, with a genuine interest in every student, that Professor Garman has achieved the immortality which Plato tells us every great soul craves, the living on in ideals, aspirations, and enthusiasms that it has begotten in other souls. (7)

Everybody philosophizes; this is only saying that everybody has some idea of the world in which he lives. Even the child or the savage has his ultimate premises from which he reasons to the particular facts about him. Aristotle used to say that we must philosophize, and if one saith that he may not philosophize (of course the statement would mean nothing unless he gave some reason to support it, and a reason would imply certain premises in the light of which his statement was a conclusion), therefore in that very statement he doth philosophize and must. (8)

Scientific philosophizing is solely a matter of evidence. The investigator does not ask what is the universe, or what may it be, or why could it not be so; his whole inquiry is, What does evidence reveal concerning the actual world in which we live? Having found that appearances are deceitful and having discovered that the senses give us simply effects, he considers that any attempt to appeal ultimately to sense perception as the basis for knowledge of things as they really are is so ridiculous that every honest man can have no respect for those who deliberately make the attempt. He can see no difference between these people and the heathen who set up graven images made by their own hands for their gods, and then fall down and worship them as their creators.

Here, then, is the line of cleavage which runs through humanity. All start in ignorance in childhood and all attempt to get

618

some conception of the world they live in, and all make blunders. But some fall back simply on the imagination, and postulate a world dogmatically which is gained through abstraction from their own experience. Others attempt a scientific analysis of their experience and insist on weighing evidence, and then they take this great step, namely, they affirm that concerning the things for which we have not a vestige of evidence we must speak and act in exactly the same way as we do concerning the things that do exist. (9)

If this world is governed by law, law is by its very nature universal. There can be no exceptions, given the conditions. Therefore whenever a man claims the privilege of being an exception, and adopts modes of thought and of life that he would not approve if every one else did exactly the same under the same conditions, he confesses himself to be unscientific, lawless, criminal. He stands self-condemned, and when he condemns himself he cannot wonder that others join in the condemnation. (10)

The choice is between living up to the light you have or doing something infinitely worse. It is not between living up to the light you have or being guided by an infallible instinct that acts blindly and always turns you in the right direction, just as the needle points to the pole. Matter can act that way, but mind cannot. Matter never errs; it always obeys the laws of nature without varying a hair's-breadth. But the mind cannot do right without intelligence to guide it. . . . That is the penalty man pays for his exaltation. He has got to be something better than matter or he will be infinitely worse. The scientist realizes it, accepts the issue, and determines to work out his own salvation. But the dogmatist shuts his eyes to this fact and does what he can for his own destruction. The fact that he sometimes does not get destroyed is due not to himself but to the influence of the environment upon him, provided he is so fortunate as to live in an age when the traditions that he imitates have been produced by a prior science and therefore not wholly in the wrong direction. (11)

Philosophy means literally love of the truth; not love in the sense of like, as a child likes molasses, for everybody must like the truth provided it is favorable to himself. But love in the sense of service, allegiance in the pursuit of truth, is the real meaning of the term philosophy. It does not mean that a man is wise, but simply that he is striving to know what is true in order that he may do what is right. (12)

There are any number of people who have absolutely no faith at all in the ability of the human mind to come out anywhere if it once begins to think about serious things. It seems to me worth everything to young men if they can see once for themselves that there is something more to truth than the superficial glimpses and side issues with which ordinary thought is occupied. It creates a spirit of candor and inquiry and faith in human effort, and at the same time a depth of humility and carefulness as they realize how often mistakes are made. (13)

Man as a thinking being is largely a spectator in the universe, discovering and formulating knowledge of what already exists. But man as an ethical being is a creator of social and political relations and institutions whose perfection cannot be attained save through a long struggle on the part of the individual and the race towards an ideal. Correct ideals are shown to be as essential to the ethical life of the individual and the community as are correct architectural drawings and calculations in architecture and civil engineering. (14)

A mother can do more for a child than any other being in the universe, therefore, if the mother refuse and fail, the defect may be one that cannot be made up. Possibly much of the want of influence for good to-day is due to the failure of previous generations to be co-workers together with God. (15)

If we sustain an immediate relation to God, if all our springs are in Him, if without Him we cannot so much as think a good thought, none of us have exhausted the supply of strength and help received from Him. (16)

If all knowledge is relative, if the human mind can know only

620

effects, then the highest ethical consideration possible for a human being would be, as stated by the Sophist, nothing more than individual utilitarianism; the individual man becomes the measure of all things. (17)

It is our conviction that in the churches at the present day there is a subtle agnosticism that is sapping the very vitals of life, and that men cannot experience the inspiration of apostolic days without the deep convictions and realizations of the divine presence and of man's responsibility to God which the Apostles had. (18)

Analyze external nature as you will and not a single attribute can you find there that is not mental so far as it goes. You have projected it out there or you could never have found it there. You remember the words of Coleridge:

"we receive but what we give,
And in our life alone does nature live;
Ours is her wedding-garment, ours her shroud." (19)

It is common to look at life in an economic way and to consider each deed on its own merits. From that point of view it is affirmed that a man can reform from evil practices as easily as he can turn his hand over. But if we clearly realize what a decision means we shall see that the change of a very simple act may be possible only on condition that a very profound governing purpose can be removed, which would be harder to accomplish than to move a mountain into the sea. (20)

It is this act of sovereignty of the supreme choice which gives unity to our life. This is only another form of saying that all intelligence works backward; that a man must have an end in view in every intelligent action, and the end must sooner or later imply an ultimate end. The doctrine of the Scripture is that "Ye must be born again." That is, if the man's supreme choice is bad he cannot be changed by halves. There is no change that is radical that does not change the supreme choice. (21)

We understand now the meaning of Scripture when it says, "Lay not up for yourselves treasures upon earth, where moth and rust doth corrupt, and where thieves break through and steal." This is the ordinary way of quoting this passage, and we are led to infer that the reason for avoiding earthly treasures is because they are liable to take wing and fly away. Therefore, for prudence' sake we should not risk too much. But such was not the meaning of Christ. He adds, "For where your treasure is, there your heart (your sentiment, your thought) will be also." The treasure is the end or object of our choice. If we live for earthly things, then these thoughts drive out all others and ideo-motor action makes us of the earth, earthy. But if we choose heavenly things, the divine ideal of manliness and honor, we become conscious of ownership by such a master, our endeavors are identified with such a cause, and thoughts on such subjects so fill our minds as to drive out everything base and mean and earthy; ideo-motor action stamps such a likeness upon our countenance. Therefore wherever and whatever your treasure (end) is, you yourself will be, and it is simply a choice of which world you will live in now. (22)

When you criticise a person who lived so long ago that you can eliminate the personal equation, is not your one question simply this: Was he true to his truest self, to the divine nature of which he was a partaker, or did he prostitute this gift to action along the lines of least resistance? If this is the standard by which you judge others, it is surely the ideal of your own life, for you know nothing about others save in terms of yourself. No man can have two sets of values, one for self, the other for historic characters, if he is thinking of processes instead of products. Does the world in its sober moments ever admire anything that will not stand the test of truth? Men are dazzled by success. But take the cases of honor bestowed on the boss, on the tyrant like Napoleon, on the train robber like Jesse James: Is it the evil deed that is worshiped, or is it the courage, persistence, self-control, patience, endurance, will power, independence, or brilliant intellectual ability revealed in the deed under such dangerous conditions, that inspires enthusiasm? Are not these in

622

themselves all noble qualities, just what every man ought to aspire to? Men worship power because it is divine. Even when wrongly used it is still a divine gift that has been debased. (23)

To be personal is to be sovereign. When circumstances conspire to bring a matter in the sphere of our knowledge, then we have to interfere, either in the line of aiding and abetting or in that of resisting. This is the only sovereignty that can exist consistently with personality. The question of how we shall aid or how we shall resist is wholly a question of means. We may do it in an organized form and then we have government, or we do so without a form of organization and we have simply society, but in both cases we have sovereignty. (24)

Sovereignty, we may say, then, is the interference of one individual with the affairs of another individual, either in the line of resisting or in that of assisting. You will see that it does not depend upon any compact any more than the attraction of the earth by the sun depends upon compact. You see that it is only a form of that relationship of cause and effect by virtue of which personal life is possible. Sovereignty simply postulates that the mind is a cause in the universe as truly as matter, the only difference being, matter can work automatically without intelligence, mind can work only when it is intelligent. Matter can work only one way, that is, it is fated. Mind can work either rightly or wrongly if you have free will. But when man does wrong he interferes with his fellow-man and exercises sovereignty as truly as when he does right, unless you please to define sovereignty as right interference, and tyranny as wrong interference. It seems to be better, however, to speak of sovereignty as interference. Human sovereignty has limits, but they are simply limits of knowledge and ability. Our ability is much more limited than our knowledge. Many things which we know about we have not strength enough to remedy; hence we aid and abet them unwillingly. Other things we are not skillful enough to remedy, but should do greater evil if we attempted it. The ordinary man is not skillful enough to perform an operation upon appendicitis, and if, on a hunting tour, he is with his friend who is taken ill in this way, he would have to allow him to die a natural death rather than to torture him to death by a bungling operation. These are simply the limitations of finiteness. They do not exist with God, who is the ideal sovereign, and who cannot know human deeds without interfering either in the line of aiding or in that of resisting them. (25)

Every man must make a success of what he undertakes or the result is disastrous to his own manhood. (26)

Business is the action and reaction in the state under conditions of equality. The law is that each person engaged in the transaction must be both means and end. This occurs only when the service rendered is an equivalent for the service received. This is justice, and only this can be allowed by the organism. Observe that such a transaction under the conditions is as truly a *"labor of love,"* that is, as truly conforms to the requirements of the organic unity, as charity and martyrdom under different conditions. (27)

Charity is the action and reaction that takes place in the state under conditions of relative inequality on the part of those engaged. It is a condition of a diseased organism. The law of charity is that, for the time being, the strong shall help the weak without recompense, i.e., shall be means, not end, until the condition of health is restored. If the hand is diseased the body must heal it, and, in the meantime, give it rest. This may be a severer test, but is no more a labor of love than is business. Charity under conditions of relative equality is as truly a crime as dishonesty. (28)

It is freely granted that the truths of scientific sociology will not regenerate humanity in a day, that forces of evil in human nature are deep-seated; but the more you say about their strength and persistence, the more you emphasize the need of ideals for society. For there are no other human agencies to antagonize these powers of evil except the spiritual impulses that can be awakened only by a knowledge of ideals, and whose strength and

624

efficiency are proportioned to the clearness with which those ideals are realized. (29)

In all the schemes that are proposed by politicians, labor agitators, statesmen, and scholars, we are able by careful study to discover that there are only two distinct trends. Antagonistic as these writers are to each other in details, there is only one comprehensive antagonism. We can overlook particular differences and give our attention to the fundamental distinction that sharply outlines the position of all writers as belonging to either one party or the other. The first party, including by far the larger number, is devoted to the great effort of bringing about the millennium through a variety of contrivances, all of which reduce to attempts of a purely quantitative character. Just as in music you get harmony or discord, treble or bass, by a quantitative increase or decrease in the number of vibrations, so that the whole scheme of music can be worked out in terms of mathematics; so there are writers and critics who aim by simply quantitative devices for distributing wealth, or suffrage, or wages, to change the great national discord to be found in each country to a grand anthem of contentment and prosperity.

The other great party, while not undervaluing the efforts for quantitative justice, yet feel that the labor problems, the political evils, the corruption of municipal politics, are but symptoms of deep-seated disease in human nature for which there is no remedy of a superficial character that is seriously worth experimenting with. We must go to the very source of the whole trouble and seek a change in the quality of human life. There must be truer conceptions of human nature and less selfishness. These thinkers are never tired of reechoing the words of Christ to Nicodemus as the great hope for the evils of our time, *"Ye Must Be Born Again."* This is true not merely of individuals, but of institutions and of society itself. (30)

As the twelve disciples were given the privilege of laying the foundations of the early church, young men of this age are given the opportunity of instructing the people in the true foundations of a Christian civilization. It is your opportunity to do something.

This is a new way of looking at things, and it requires something besides thinking to take this view. No one can follow truth without being an actual hero, for the multitude do not go that way; they follow custom. Remember the experience of Columbus when he dared to live up to the evidence which proved to him that the world was round. Derided by his contemporaries, he steered his ships towards the west with nothing to guide him except the great truths which science had revealed. Was the courage of that man a small achievement? To be a hero in battle is merely to follow the footsteps of a great company of patriots who fairly blaze with glory. But to be alone on an unknown sea, where the very laws of nature seem to be changing and the most trusted friends call you crazy, and then to dare every peril, inspired by the faith in the unseen country, is sublime. Let this be a prophecy for your life. The old country from which you set sail on your voyage of life is the material shore. It is the kingdom of brain paths, where selfishness is not sovereign, but tyrant. It is the prevailing view of the citizens of this country that there is no other land. We have given evidence to show that there is a Western hemisphere, a spiritual America, the home of freedom, a commonwealth whose inhabitants are citizens of the kingdom of Truth, whose achievements constitute all that is grand and heroic in human life. I beg you to follow Columbus. You will be ridiculed for your faith as he was for his. But refuse to deal with men simply as selfish beings. If your efforts seem to come to naught, and even those who are your helpers beg you to give up the voyage and turn back, push boldly on towards the other shore. If your heart does not fail, there will come a time when you shall have passed the fogs of doubt, weathered the storms of ridicule, and at last made a harbor in the spiritual life of humanity. (31)

CHAPTER XXI

JOHN WESLEY

John Wesley, the fifteenth child of Samuel and Susannah Wesley, was born in 1703, at Epworth Rectory, Lincolnshire. He lived to advanced age, his death taking place in 1791. Both parents were children of distinguished non-conformists, who themselves by deliberate choice entered the Church of England. The story of their life for 38 years at Epworth Rectory is an epic. It was above all a story of "plain living and high thinking." This influence of Susannah upon her sons, whose education and spiritual nurture from the cradle was her especial care, is particularly notable.

It was at Oxford in 1727 or 1728 that Charles Wesley, a brother, about four years younger than John, began going to the weekly Sacrament and persuading two or three fellow-students to do the same. This was the beginning of the "Holy Club," also called "a new set of Methodists," of which John, on his return to Oxford in 1729, assumed the leadership.

In October 1735 the two brothers set sail for Georgia. On shipboard and later they saw much of the Moravians. Through them John, after disillusionment in Georgia, discovered Luther and was led to a personal experience of salvation through faith alone. Charles had a similar experience and both began to preach a Gospel of power. They began in 1739, with Whitfield for a time, the powerful movement known as the Evangelical Revival. Henceforth their lives were bound up with its progress, John taking the more active and executive role and hardly living save for his preaching, direction of societies, and literary and educational projects. He was accustomed to travel five thousand miles a year on horseback and to preach an average of fifteen sermons a week.

Separation from the English Church was inevitable, though John

627

Wesley counseled against it with strong words until his death, three years after that of his brother.

When I was about twenty-two, my father pressed me to enter into holy orders. At the same time, the providence of God directing me to Kempis's *Christian's Pattern*, I began to see, that true religion was seated in the heart, and that God's law extended to all our thoughts as well as words and actions. (1)

Meeting now with Mr. Law's *Christian Perfection* and *Serious Call*, although I was much offended at many parts of both, yet they convinced me more than ever of the exceeding height and breadth and depth of the law of God. (2)

He deigns His influence to infuse,
Secret, refreshing as the silent dews. (3)

The Scripture that came in course was, "After the way which they call heresy, so worship I the God of my fathers," (4)

I read to-day part of the *Meditations of Marcus Antoninus*. What a strange Emperor! And what a strange heathen! Giving thanks to God for all the good things he enjoyed! . . . I make no doubt, but this is one of those "many" who "shall come from the east and the west, and sit down with Abraham, Isaac, and Jacob," while "the children of the kingdom," nominal Christians, are "shut out." (5)

In riding to Newcastle I finished the tenth *Iliad* of Homer. What an amazing genius had this man! To write with such strength of thought, and beauty of expression, when he had none to go before him! And what a vein of piety runs through his whole work, in spite of his pagan prejudices! (6)

I seek another country, and therefore am content to be a wanderer upon earth. (7)

The work of God does not, cannot need the work of the devil to forward it. And a calm, even spirit goes through rough work far better than a furious one. Although, therefore, God did use, at the time of the Reformation, some sour, overbearing, passionate men, yet He did not use them because they were such, but

628

notwithstanding they were so. And there is no doubt, He would have used them much more, had they been of an humbler and milder spirit. (8)

How delicate a thing it is to reprove! To do it well requires more than human wisdom. (9)

Writer	Book	Publisher Whose Courtesy Is Acknowledged
Sophocles	Seven Greek Plays	Random House, Inc.
Montesquieu	The Spirit of Laws	P. F. Collier & Son
Longfellow	The Complete Poetical Works of Longfellow	Houghton Mifflin Company
Epictetus	The Golden Sayings of Epictetus (translated by Hastings Crossley)	P. F. Collier & Son
Marcus Aurelius	The Meditations of Marcus Aurelius (translated by George Levy)	P. F. Collier & Son
Elizabeth Barrett Browning	A Library of Poetic Literature	P. F. Collier & Son
Schleiermacher	The Christian Faith	T. & T. Clark (Edinburgh)
Marcus Aurelius	The Golden Book of Marcus Aurelius	E. P. Dutton & Co.
Lessing	Everyman's Library No. 843	E. P. Dutton & Co.
Euripides	Everyman's Library (2 vols)	E. P. Dutton & Co.
Aeschylus	The Dramas of Aeschylus	E. P. Dutton & Co.
John Milton	Complete Poetry and Selected Prose of John Milton	Random House, Inc.
John Donne	The Complete Poetry and Selected Prose of John Donne	Random House, Inc.
Boethius	The Consolation of Philosophy	Random House, Inc.
Sir Thomas Browne	Religio Medici	Random House, Inc.
Emerson	The Works of Ralph Waldo Emerson	Tudor Publishing Company
John Wesley	Selections from John Wesley's Journal	Philosophical Library, Inc.

BIBLIOGRAPHIC ACKNOWLEDGMENTS

Chapter I

Selections from the *Dialogues* of Plato, from the Third Jowett Translation, edited by Professor William Chase Greene, Harvard University, Liveright Publishing Corp.; copyright 1893, by the Oxford University Press, American Branch; copyright, 1927, by Horace Liveright, Inc.; Liveright Publishing Corp. All rights of reprinting are reserved.

From *Apology*
1. See p. 3.
2. See p. 15.
3. See p. 15.
4. See pp. 15-16.
5. See p. 16.
6. See p. 16.
7. See pp. 16-17.
8. See pp. 17-18.
9. See p. 26.
10. See p. 27.
11. See pp. 27-28.
12. See p. 28.
13. See p. 29.

From *Crito*
14. See p. 36.

15. See p. 36.
16. See p. 39.
17. See p. 40.
18. See p. 46.

From *Phaedo*
19. See p. 50.
20. See p. 109.
21. See p. 116.

From *Protagorus*
22. See p. 148.

From *Meno*
23. See p. 163.

From *Gorgias*
24. See pp. 179-180.
25. See p. 180.

From *The Republic*
26. See p. 360.
27. See p. 365.
28. See p. 377.
29. See pp. 378-379.
30. See p. 379.
31. See p. 379.
32. See p. 379.
33. See p. 383.
34. See p. 388.
35. See p. 393.
36. See p. 430.

From *Timaeus*
37. See pp. 511-512.

Chapter II

Sophocles, *Seven Famous Greek Plays*, Modern Library No. 158, Random House, New York, copyright 1938, 1950.

From *Oedipus the King*
1. See p. 131.
2. See p. 131.
3. See p. 143.
4. See p. 171.
5. See p. 172.
6. See p. 177.
7. See p. 182.

From *Antigone*
8. See p. 193.
9. See p. 195.
10. See p. 197.
11. See p. 199.
12. See p. 202.
13. See p. 203.
14. See p. 205.

15. See p. 207.
16. See p. 211.
17. See pp. 211-212.
18. See p. 222.
19. See p. 228.
20. See p. 230.
21. See p. 230.
22. See p. 234.

Chapter III

Montesquieu, *The Spirit of Laws*, P. F. Collier & Son, New York; copyright 1900 and 1901, by the Colonial Press (The World's Greatest Literature).

1. From Book I, see p. 1.   6. From Book XXIV, see p. 32,
2. From Book I, see p. 2.   Vol. 2.
3. From Book I, see p. 6.   7. From Book XXV, see p. 45,
4. From Book V, see p. 62.   Vol. 2.
5. From Book XI, see p. 150.

Chapter IV

Lessing, Everyman's Library No. 843, J. M. Dent & Sons Ltd., London; E. P. Dutton & Co., Inc., New York, New York.

From *Laocoon*
1. See p. 11
From *Nathan the Wise*
2. See pp. 118-119.
3. See p. 122.
4. See pp. 127-128.
5. See p. 187.

6. See pp. 188-189.
7. See p. 205.
8. See p. 212.
9. See p. 212.
10. See p. 216.
From *Minna von Barnhelm*
11. See p. 236.

12. See p. 236.
13. See p. 236.
14. See p. 270.
From *Nathan the Wise*
15. See pp. 164-169.

Chapter V

Alexander Pope, *The Poetical Works of Alexander Pope*, American Publishers Corporation, New York.

From *Essay on Criticism*
1. See p. 46.
2. See p. 48.
3. See p. 48.
4. See p. 49.
5. See p. 51.
6. See p. 53.

7. See p. 54.
8. See p. 56.

From *An Essay on Man*
9. See p. 189.
10. See p. 194.
11. See pp. 194-195.

12. See p. 209.
13. See p. 215.
14. See p. 216.
15. See p. 217.
16. See p. 219.
From *The Universal Prayer*
17. See pp. 221-222.

Chapter VI

John Milton, *Complete Poetry and Selected Prose of John Milton*, The Modern Library, Random House, New York.

1. See p. 86.
2. See p. 85.

From *Paradise Lost*
3. See p. 92.
4. See pp. 98-99.
5. See p. 109.

6. See p. 128.
7. See p. 146.
8. See p. 164.
9. See p. 167.
10. See p. 168.
11. See p. 250.
12. See pp. 251-252.

13. See p. 252.
14. See p. 264.
15. See p. 264.
16. See p. 271.
17. See p. 276.
18. See p. 277.
19. See p. 344.

20. See p. 345.
21. See p. 350.
22. See p. 359.
23. See pp. 359-360.
24. See p. 365.
25. See p. 367.

From *Samson Agonistes*
26. See p. 464.

From *Animadversions*
27. See pp. 523-524.

From *The Reason of Church-Government*
28. See pp. 540-541.
29. See pp. 541-542.
30. See pp. 542-543.

From *An Apology Against a Pamphlet*
31. See p. 601.

From *Doctrine and Discipline of Divorce*
32. See p. 617.
33. See pp. 617-618.
34. See pp. 618-619.
35. See pp. 619-620.
36. See p. 620.
37. See p. 620.
38. See p. 621.
39. See p. 628.
40. See p. 628.

From *Of Education*
41. See p. 664.

From *Areopagitica*
42. See p. 678.
43. See p. 681.
44. See p. 681.
45. See p. 704.
46. See p. 708.
47. See pp. 711-712.
48. See p. 712.
49. See p. 713.
50. See p. 714.
51. See p. 716.
52. See p. 716.
53. See p. 718.
54. See p. 719.
55. See p. 720.
56. See p. 720.

Chapter VII

Emerson, *The Works of Ralph Waldo Emerson,* Tudor Publishing Company, New York.

From *Essays: History*
1. See p. 3.
2. See p. 6.
3. See p. 9.
4. See p. 20.
5. See pp. 25-26.
6. See p. 27.
7. See pp. 27-28.

From *Essays: Self-Reliance*
8. See p. 30.
9. See pp. 33-34.
10. See p. 39.
11. See p. 53.

From *Essays: Heroism*
12. See p. 166.

From *Essays: The Over-Soul*
13. See pp. 172-173.
14. See p. 174.
15. See pp. 174-175.
16. See p. 175.
17. See p. 177.
18. See p. 178.
19. See pp. 178-179.

20. See p. 180.
21. See p. 180.

From *Essays: Circles*
22. See p. 201.
23. See p. 206.

From *Essays: Intellect*
24. See p. 219.
25. See p. 219.
26. See pp. 220-221.
27. See p. 223.

From *Essays: The Poet*
28. See pp. 241-242.
29. See p. 242.
30. See p. 244.
31. See p. 260.
32. See p. 266.

From *Representative Men*
33. See p. 230.
34. See pp. 231-232.
35. See p. 232.
36. See p. 237.
37. See p. 244.
38. See p. 254.

Chapter VIII

John Donne, *The Complete Poetry and Selected Prose of John Donne,* The Modern Library, Random House, Inc., New York; copyright 1941, by Random House, Inc.

1. From *A Hymne to God The Father,* see p. 272.
2. From *Devotions, XVI,* see pp. 330-331.
3. From *Devotions, XVII,* see pp. 331-332.
4. From *Devotions, XVIII,* see pp. 332-334.
5. From *Holy Sonnets,* see pp. 239-240.
6. From *Holy Sonnets,* see pp. 253-254.

Chapter IX

Fichte, *The Vocation of Man,* translated by William Smith, L.L.D., with Biographical Introduction by E. Ritchie, Ph.D., reprint edition published by the Open Court Publishing Company, 1946.

1. See p. iii.
2. See p. vi.
3. See p. 7.
4. See p. 20.
5. See pp. 21-22.
6. See p. 32-33.
7. See pp. 38-39.
8. See p. 50.
9. See p. 71.
10. See p. 94.
11. See p. 105.
12. See p. 111.
13. See pp. 113-114.
14. See pp. 117-119.
15. See pp. 127-128.
16. See pp. 129-130.
17. See p. 131.
18. See pp. 133-134.
19. See pp. 134-135.
20. See pp. 136-137.
21. See p. 138.
22. See p. 140.
23. See pp. 140-141.
24. See pp. 141-142.
25. See p. 143.
26. See p. 145.
27. See p. 146.
28. See p. 147.
29. See p. 149.
30. See p. 152.
31. See pp. 152-153.
32. See pp. 153-154.
33. See pp. 155-156.
34. See p. 157.
35. See pp. 157-158.
36. See pp. 160-162.
37. See pp. 162-163.
38. See p. 165.
39. See pp. 166-167.
40. See pp. 167-168.
41. See p. 168.
42. See pp. 169-170.
43. See p. 172.
44. See p. 172.
45. See pp. 173-174.
46. See pp. 174-175.
47. See pp. 175-176.
48. See p. 176.

Chapter X

Sir Thomas Browne, *Religio Medici,* The Modern Library, Random House, New York; copyright 1943, by Random House, Inc.

1. See pp. 326-327.
2. See p. 327.
3. See p. 327.
4. See p. 328.
5. See p. 332.
6. See p. 333.
7. See p. 334.
8. See p. 334.
9. See p. 335.
10. See p. 337.
11. See p. 337.
12. See p. 338.
13. See p. 339.
14. See p. 339.
15. See p. 349.
16. See p. 352.
17. See pp. 386-387.
18. See p. 387.
19. See pp. 389-390.
20. See p. 397.
21. See p. 405.
22. See p. 406.

Chapter XI

Euripides, *The Plays of Euripides*, Everyman's Library, 2 Vols., J. M. Dent
& Co., London; E. P. Dutton & Co., New York

Volume I

From *Hecuba*
1. See p. 28.
2. See p. 32.
3. See p. 47.

From *Helen*
4. See p. 126.
5. See p. 158.

From *Andromache*
6. See p. 266.
7. See p. 269.

From *Iphigenia in Aulis*
8. See p. 286.
9. See p. 287.
10. See p. 290.
11. See p. 295.
12. See p. 317.

From *Iphigenia in Tauris*
13. See p. 375.

From *Helen*
14. See p. 125.

Volume II

From *Medea*
15. See p. 88.
16. See p. 89.
17. See p. 96.

From *Hippolytus*
18. See p. 118.
19. See p. 128.
20. See p. 129.
21. See p. 146.

From *The Phoenician Damsels*
22. See p. 233.
23. See p. 238.
24. See p. 257.
25. See p. 280.

From *The Suppliants*
26. See p. 288.
27. See p. 289.
28. See p. 299.
29. See pp. 300-301.
30. See p. 318.

From *The Children of Hercules*
31. See p. 371.
32. See p. 401.

Chapter XII

Schleiermacher, *The Christian Faith*, T. & T. Clark, Edinburgh; Charles
Scribner's Sons, New York.

1. See p. 12.
2. See p. 26.
3. See p. 31.
4. See p. 34.
5. See pp. 133-134.
6. See p. 142.
7. See p. 170.
8. See p. 178.
9. See p. 189.
10. See p. 194.
11. See p. 200.
12. See p. 203.
13. See p. 206.
14. See p. 211.
15. See p. 219.

Schleiermacher's Soliloquies, an English translation of *The Monologen*, with
Critical Introduction and Appendix by Horace Leland Fries, Asst. Professor
of Philosophy, Col. Univ., The Open Court Publishing Company, Chicago, 1926.

From *Reflection*
16. See p. 25.

From *Soundings*
17. See p. 28.
18. See p. 28.

From *The World*

19. See p. 54.
20. See p. 56.
21. See p. 56.
22. See p. 61.
23. See pp. 61-62.
24. See p. 63.

25. See p. 67.

From *Prospect*

26. See p. 74.
27. See pp. 76-77.

From *Youth and Age*

28. See pp. 102-103.

Chapter XIII

Charles Edward Garman, *Letters, Lectures and Addresses of Charles Edward Garman, A Memorial Volume,* Houghton Mifflin Company; copyright 1909, by Eliza Miner Garman.

From *The Training of a Boy*

1. See p. 390.
2. See pp. 391-392.
3. See p. 398.
4. See pp. 402-403.
5. See p. 404.

From *Philosophy in the Pulpit*

6. See p. 411.
7. See p. 412.
8. See p. 413.
9. See p. 414.
10. See p. 417.
11. See p. 417.
12. See pp. 418-419.

13. See pp. 419-420.
14. See p. 420.
15. See p. 423.
16. See p. 421.
17. See pp. 421-422.

From *Sunday in the Mountains*

18. See p. 434.
19. See pp. 434-435.
20. See pp. 435-437.

From *The Changes of Twenty Years*

21. See p. 458.

From *Off to the Front*

22. See p. 462.
23. See p. 463.

Chapter XIV

Walter Bagehot, *Physics and Politics,* copyright 1900, by The Colonial Press; from a volume of The World's Greatest Literature, P. F. Collier & Son, New York.

1. See pp. 47-48.
2. See pp. 49-50.
3. See pp. 100-101.
4. See p. 101.
5. See pp. 101-102.
6. See p. 102.

7. See p. 105.
8. See p. 105.
9. See pp. 114-115.
10. See p. 115.
11. See pp. 115-116.
12. See p. 116.

13. See pp. 117-118.
14. See pp. 119-120.
15. See p. 123.
16. See pp. 125-126.

Chapter XV

Aeschylus, *The Lyrical Dramas of Aeschylus,* Everyman's Library, No. 2, translated by John Stuart Blackie, J. M. Dent & Sons, Ltd., London; E. P. Dutton & Co., New York.

Chapter XVI

Schiller, *The Works of Frederick Schiller,* Vol. 2, *Historical Dramas,* Bohn's Standard Library, H. G. Bohn, London, 1847.

Schiller's Works, George Barrie, Philadelphia; copyright 1883, by George Barrie.

Volume I

32. From *Phantasy*, see p. 8.
33. From *The Greatness of the World*, see p. 15.
34. From *Elegy on the Death of a Young Man*, see p. 17.
35. From *The Triumph of Love*, see p. 27.
36. From *Man's Dignity*, see p. 27.
37. From *The Maiden's Lament*, see p. 52.
38. From *The Division of the Earth*, see p. 95.
39. From *Columbus*, see p. 119.
40. From *The Sexes*, see p. 124.
41. From *The Words of Faith*, see p. 130.
42. From *The Words of Error*, see p. 130.
43. From *The Peculiar Ideal*, see p. 136.
44. From *The Key*, see p. 136.
45. From *To a World-Reformer*, see p. 137.

46. From *Proverbs of Confucius*, see p. 131.
47. From *My Faith*, see p. 137.
48. From *The Common Fate*, see p. 140.
49. From *Knowledge*, see p. 145.
50. From *The Robbers*, see p. 229.
51. From *The Robbers*, see pp. 240-241.

Volume II
From *Don Carlos*

52. See p. 6.
53. See p. 25.
54. See p. 34.
55. See p. 51.
56. See p. 55.
57. See p. 56.
58. See p. 56.
59. See p. 57.
60. See p. 57.
61. See p. 75.
62. From *The Maid of Orleans*, see p. 356.

Chapter XVII

Samuel Taylor Coleridge, *On Poesy or Art*, The World's Great Classics, The Colonial Press, New York, 1899; copyright 1900, by The Colonial Press.

1. From *Essays of British Essayists*, Vol. 1, see p. 492.

Samuel Taylor Coleridge, *The Poetical Works of S. T. Coleridge, Reprinted from the Early Editions*, Frederick Warne & Co., London; Scribner, Welford, and Armstrong, New York.

From *Religious Musings*

2. See p. 49.
3. See pp. 49-50.
4. See p. 50.
5. See pp. 51-52.
6. See p. 52.
7. See p. 59.

From *The Destiny of Nations*

8. See p. 60.

9. See pp. 60-61.
10. See p. 73.

From *A Couplet*

11. See p. 91.

From *The Ancient Mariner*

12. See p. 110.

From *Fears in Solitude*

13. See p. 140.

638

14. See p. 142.
15. See p. 143.

From *Sibylline Leaves*

16. See pp. 176-177.

17. See p. 203.
18. See p. 203.

From *Ode to Tranquillity*

19. See p. 209.

Samuel Taylor Coleridge, *Aids to Reflection,* Eighth Edition, Edward Maxon & Co., London, 1859.

20. See p. 1.	33. See pp. 60-61.	46. See p. 80.
21. See p. 2.	34. See p. 61.	47. See p. 81.
22. See p. 4.	35. See p. 64.	48. See pp. 81-82.
23. See p. 6.	36. See p. 65.	49. See p. 90.
24. See p. 7.	37. See pp. 68-69.	50. See p. 90.
25. See p. 12.	38. See p. 69.	51. See p. 92.
26. See p. 23.	39. See p. 73.	52. See p. 109.
27. See p. 30.	40. See p. 75.	53. See p. 148.
28. See pp. 37-38.	41. See p. 75.	54. See p. 166.*
29. See p. 38.	42. See p. 75.	55. See p. 185.
30. See p. 39.	43. See p. 76.	56. See p. 203.
31. See p. 53.	44. See p. 78.	57. See pp. 280-281.
32. See p. 54.	45. See p. 79.	58. See p. 281.

*quoted from Richard Baxter.

Chapter XVIII

Boethius, *The Consolation of Philosophy,* Translated by W. V. Cooper, The Modern Library, Random House, Inc., New York; copyright 1943, by Random House, Inc.

1. See pp. 7-8.	10. See p. 53.	19. See p. 88.
2. See p. 8.	11. See p. 59.	20. See p. 96.
3. See pp. 14-15.	12. See p. 60.	21. See p. 97.
4. See p. 16.	13. See p. 61.	22. See p. 100.
5. See p. 19.	14. See p. 64.	23. See p. 104.
6. See pp. 27-28.	15. See pp. 68-69.	24. See pp. 115-116.
7. See pp. 40-41.	16. See p. 80.	25. See p. 120.
8. See p. 48.	17. See pp. 81-82.	
9. See p. 52.	18. See p. 88.	

Chapter XIX

Fichte, *Memoir of Johann Gottlieb Fichte,* by William Smith, James Munroe and Company, Boston, 1846.

1. From a letter from Fichte to Johanna Rahn, who became his wife. See pp. 50-51.

2. See p. 88.

3. From *Bestimmung des Menschen,* Book III, see pp. 88-90.

4. From *On The Grounds of Our Faith in a Divine Government of the World,* see pp. 121-123.

Fichte, *Addresses to the German Nation*, Translated by R. F. Jones and G. H. Turnbull, The Open Court Publishing Company, Chicago and New York; copyright 1922.

5. See p. 4.	13. See pp. 109-110.	21. See pp. 138-139.
6. See p. 5.	14. See p. 120.	22. See p. 145.
7. See pp. 6-7.	15. See p. 125.	23. See p. 207.
8. See p. 14.	16. See pp. 126-127.	24. See pp. 218-219.
9. See pp. 17-18.	17. See p. 132.	25. See pp. 245-246.
10. See p. 22.	18. See p. 132.	26. See p. 247.
11. See p. 38.	19. See pp. 136-137.	
12. See p. 40.	20. See p. 138.	

Chapter XX

Charles Edward Garman, *Letters, Lectures, and Addresses of Charles Edward Garman, A Memorial Volume*, Houghton Mifflin Company, copyright 1909, by Eliza Miner Garman.

From *Introduction*

1. See p. 31.
2. See pp. 37-38.
3. See p. 38.
4. See pp. 39-40.
5. See p. 42.
6. See pp. 45-46.
7. See p. 47.

From *The Line of Cleavage*

8. See pp. 79-80.
9. See pp. 81-82.
10. See p. 83.
11. See pp. 84-85.
12. See pp. 87-88.

From *The Aims and Divisions of the Course*

13. See pp. 91-92.
14. See p. 98.

From *Ultimate Problems*

15. See p. 117.
16. See p. 126.

From *A General Survey of the Course*

17. See p. 139.
18. See p. 143.

From *Communicating with Friends*

19. See p. 220.

From *The Will and the Sentiments*

20. See p. 262.
21. See p. 264.
22. See p. 267.

That part of the Introduction from which items 1 to 7 are taken is reproduced, with additions from a paper printed in *The Journal of Philosophy, Psychology, and Scientific Methods*, May 9, 1907.

From *Pleasure or Righteousness*

23. See pp. 291-292.

From *Sovereignty from the Standpoint of Theism*

24. See p. 330.
25. See pp. 330-331.

From *The Members of the State*

26. See p. 335.
27. See p. 336.
28. See pp. 336-337.

From *Scientific Ideals and Social Practice*

29. See p. 350.

From *The Coming Reform*
30. See pp. 353-354.

From *The Twentieth Century*
31. See pp. 384-385.

Chapter XXI

Selections from John Wesley's Journal (as abridged by Nehemiah Curnock),
The Philosophical Library, Inc., New York, 1951.

1. See p. 47.
2. See p. 47.
3. See p. 95.

4. See p. 96.
5. See p. 187.
6. See p. 225.

7. See p. 283.
8. See pp. 322-323.
9. See p. 336.

REFERENCES, *Sections I to IV*

(Chapter numbers followed by an asterisk denote reference to RELIGION THROUGH THE AGES; those chapter numbers not followed by an asterisk denote CURRENT PROBLEMS IN RELIGION.)

Page	Author Quoted	Chapter	Item	Page	Author Quoted	Chapter	Item
13-14	Maurice	XXII*	7	28	G. Eliot	XXXI*	18
14	Garman	XIII	7	28	G. Eliot	VIII*	46
14	Garman	XIII	10	28	Amiel	XII*	11
14	Garman	XIII	11	28	Tennyson	XXX*	4
14-15	Garman	XXXI*	65	29	Tennyson	XXX*	18
15	Bagehot	XIV	6	29	Browning	XXIII*	34
15	Milton	VI	39	29	Browning	XXIII*	33
15	Milton	VI	46	29	Whittier	XIV*	4
15	Milton	VI	53	31	Garman	XXXI*	56
16	Milton	VI	27	45	Plato	I	3
16-17	Milton	VI	28	45-47	Plato	I	11
17	Carlyle	VI*	2	47	Plato	I	12
17	Carlyle	VI*	2	47	Plato	I	6
17	Carlyle	VI*	2	47	Plato	I	19
17	Carlyle	VI*	9	47	Plato	I	20
18	Carlyle	VI*	31	47-48	Plato	I	21
18	Carlyle	XXIX*	15	48	Browne	X	5
19	Emerson	VII	8	48	Browne	X	8
19	Emerson	VII	9	48	Browne	X	16
19	Emerson	VII	10	48	Browne	X	21
19	Emerson	VII	22	48	Browne	X	22
19-20	Emerson	VII	25	49	Donne	VIII	1
20	Coleridge	XVII	57	49-50	Donne	VIII	2
20	Coleridge	XVII	41	50-52	Donne	VIII	3
20	Coleridge	XVII	42	52-55	Donne	VIII	4
21-22	Fichte	IX	38	55-56	Donne	VIII	6
24-27	Hugo	XXVI*	3	56-57	Boethius	XVIII	24
27	Garman	XIII	21	57	Fichte	IX	4
				57	Fichte	IX	47

643

646